THE NAPOLEONIC SOURCE BOOK

THE
NAPOLEONIC
SOURCE BOOK
PHILIP J. HAYTHORNTHWAITE

'As usual on such occasions, the town was plundered as a matter of course; though, I dare say, if the truth were known, the French had left us little to do in that way. Such is war, even among the most civilized people! O, my countrymen! may its horrors never be brought home to you! and, while you sit snugly by your fire-sides, grumble not, I beseech you, at your taxes, so long as they keep the enemy from your gates!'

(Blakiston on St. Sebastian: II, p. 271)

ARMS AND
ARMOUR

Dedication: To my Mother

First published in Great Britain in 1990
by Arms and Armour Press, Wellington
House, 125 Strand, London WC2R 0BB
An imprint of the Cassell Group

Reprinted 1991
Reprinted 1993

This paperback edition 1995
Reprinted 1996

Distributed in Australia by Capricorn
Link (Australia) Pty. Ltd.
2/13 Carrington Road,
Castle Hill, NSW 2154.

© Philip J. Haythornthwaite 1990

Cover illustration: square of the 73rd
Foot under attack from the French
Cuirassiers at Waterloo.
(Print after P. Jazet)

British Library Cataloguing-in-
Publication Data:
A catalogue entry for this title is
available from the British Library

ISBN 1-85409-287-1

Cartography by Richard Natkiel.

Designed and edited by DAG
Publications Ltd. Designed by David
Gibbons; edited by Michael Boxall;
layout by David Gibbons and Anthony
A. Evans; typeset by Ronset Typesetters,
Darwen, and Typesetters (Birmingham)
Ltd, Warley; camerawork by M&E
Reproductions, North Fambridge, Essex;
printed and bound in Great Britain by
The Bath Press, Bath.

◀ *Overleaf:*
General Bonaparte. (Engraving
by T. W. Harland after Appiani)

CONTENTS

6 CONTENTS

LIST OF MAPS

INTRODUCTION

'A man must appear somewhat vain, who declares that he has been obliged to reject much useful information, for fear of increasing too much the size of his work: and yet manages to find room for a few pages of his own, by way of Preface: but lest the objects which the compiler of this little work has had in view should be mistaken, he finds it absolutely necessary to say a few words in explanation of them.'

(*Ralph Willett Adye*, Bombardier & Pocket Gunner, *1802*)

Concerning the compilation of this *Napoleonic Source Book*, a quotation from Gowing may be apposite: 'My object has been to compress the largest amount of information into the smallest possible space, and to insert in one volume some of the most surprising and interesting events that have ever taken place . . .'[1] The process involved has been something akin to that described by the ancient chronicler Nennius: 'I have therefore made a heap of all that I have found',[2] to result in what Surgeon-General Munro described as 'a Bundle of Fagots',[3] and, it is to be hoped, to avoid the criticism levelled at *The Aide de Camp, or Staff Officer's Assistant* ('. . . we must think that the author might have retrenched much of the repetitions . . . and thus have diminished the expence [sic] of the work'),[4] so that 'Some may regard the work as of a very mixed character, nevertheless I am in hopes that it will both interest and entertain.'[5]

Section I presents a brief chronological account of the Revolutionary and Napoleonic Wars, with list of battles and treaties, to act as an *aide-mémoire* or quick reference. Section II comprises a survey of the basic capabilities and use of the weaponry of the era, and a brief review of the 'art of war' on sea and land, not so much the tenets of 'grand strategy' as the basics of what might be termed 'minor tactics', which would be familiar to every capable company officer of the period, but which have tended in some cases to be overlooked in studies which concentrate upon the methods of the great commanders. Section III presents a review of each state's participation in the conflicts of the era, and a brief account of their military and (where applicable) naval forces, a coverage which for reasons of space must be somewhat superficial, especially in the minutiae of uniforms and equipment. Section IV comprises brief biographical notices of some of the leading *military* characters of the Napoleonic Wars, concentrating not upon a list of appointments and battles but endeavouring to illuminate the personalities with contemporary comments and anecdotes.[6] Section V is a brief review of the development of Napoleonic literature and a list of references for further reading; Section VI what Kincaid might have termed 'Random Shots'; and Section VII a glossary of military terms in use at the time of the Napoleonic Wars, but which are generally not completely understandable by reference to a modern dictionary.

Each section and most entries are accompanied by a reference list intended to facilitate further reading; though it must be emphasized that the works cited are by no means the exclusive sources of the text which precedes them, but simply that they include some of the most convenient sources for additional reading. For reasons of space, none of these reference-lists are at all comprehensive, but are simply a representative selection of the works most easily accessible.[7] Accessibility has been a major criterion in the selection of these, and the whole is compiled deliberately for basically an English-speaking readership, so that preference is given to works in the English language and which are thus the most easily obtainable. In many cases, however, foreign-language editions are cited, principally where these are of great significance to the topic in question, or modern works which are commonly available in English-speaking countries. For reasons of space, footnotes have been limited to the identification of the source of quotations (itself a further pointer towards supplementary sources), and for the same reasons English-language editions have been identified wherever possible, to facilitate the reader's tracing of the passages in question (for many of the works that appear as sources of quotation are not listed elsewhere). Original editions have generally been identified, even though in some cases subsquent reprints have appeared, many of which are themselves identified in the reference-lists. References have been limited largely to books rather than to periodicals, except in those cases where the most accessible material appears in the latter.

Some apparent inconsistency in the spelling of personal names may be discerned, in that some are rendered in the original foreign-language spelling, while others have English spelling. It would seem unduly pedantic if the 'correct' versions, e.g. 'Kaiser Franz', 'Friedrich Wilhelm', 'Napoléon', etc., were employed instead of the almost universal use in English-language works of 'Emperor Francis', 'Frederick William', 'Napoleon', etc., so in general where an accepted English version is in common use, this has been adopted; otherwise, the foreign-language spelling is used. The choice has to a degree been somewhat arbitrary, but the question perhaps serves to demonstrate Ben Jonson's remark that it is a dull fellow who can spell a word only one way.

Despite Disraeli's remark that 'When a man fell into his anecdotage it was a sign for him to retire from the world,'[8] throughout the book are scattered a number of anecdotes. The selection of these has been a purely personal exercise, and they are included not simply to improve the readability of what might otherwise be a Gradgrindesque collection of facts, but to illuminate the various aspects of the Napoleonic Wars, encompassing the realities of war, the bizarre and the humorous, with the main criterion of selection being an avoidance of the oft-repeated stories of the 'I have lost my leg, by God', and 'The Guard dies but does not surrender' variety.

Notes

1. *A Soldier's Experience, or, A Voice from the Ranks*, T. Gowing, Nottingham, 1907, p. v.

2. *Nennius: British History and Welsh Annals*, trans. J. Morris, Chichester, 1980, p. 9.

3. *Reminiscences of Military Service with the 93rd Sutherland Highlanders*, London, 1883, p. 4.

4. *The Monthly Review, or Literary Journal*, London, December 1804, p. 331.

5. Gowing, op. cit., p. v.

6. For a more conventional and comprehensive work of biography, as mentioned elsewhere, *A Dictionary of the Napoleonic Wars*, D. G. Chandler, London 1979, is recommended.

7. For a more exhaustive list of pertinent titles, *Napoleonic Military History: A Bibliography* (ed. D. D. Horward), London 1986 is recommended.

8. *Lothair*, 1870.

British infantry advancing with skirmishers thrown forward, at the Battle of Toulouse. (Print after A. Dupray)

I
THE CAMPAIGNS

THE CAMPAIGNS

The French Revolution

The entire Napoleonic conflict arose from the embers of the French Revolution, a term which does not describe any cataclysmic incident but rather a political and social upheaval of which the roots extended back into the eighteenth century. The causes and events of the Revolution are outside the scope of the present work, though the changes in French internal administration are summarized in the 'national' section on France (pp. 157–193).

The Revolution was regarded initially in the more liberal European circles as not necessarily a bad thing, though the bloodshed it unleashed and the implications which arose from it soon turned the other European states into violent opposition. As with many revolutionary movements, that in France began as a moderate, rational attempt to correct many of the ills which afflicted French society; it swung to the radical and then to the almost manic, involving a complete dismantling of the social order, and amidst the blood-soaked purging of the nation's internal ills, the philosophy of 'liberty, equality, fraternity' led the revolutionary regime to attempt to export their new ideology.

Thus, the wars which arose initially were unlike earlier campaigns of the eighteenth century which were fought in a more (ostensibly) 'civilized' manner between sovereigns who respected their mutual position at the head of creation; now, under threat was the very fabric of society, by which nations were controlled by an annointed sovereign, at the head of a carefully constructed and monolithic social structure in which all classes and occupations had an ordained place. Once the wall of royal and aristocratic privilege had been breached in France, the other European monarchs feared the same (even in Britain, a uniquely constitutional monarchy), which forced them to co-operate against the common threat; and conversely, France was gripped by an almost messianic fervour to 'liberate' the subject peoples of Europe from their aristocratic 'oppressors'. Although this is a simplistic assessment, such attitudes prevailed in the early part of the Revolutionary Wars, and only later did the conflict assume the characteristics of a more traditional clash between nation-states; but despite the establishment in France of a regime no less absolute and scarcely less autocratic than that of the monarchy, the French Revolution had changed irrevocably the course of European history and warfare.

The War to 1793

The trigger for the Revolutionary Wars was the Declaration of Pillnitz (2 August 1791) which announced the willingness of King Frederick William II of Prussia and the Holy Roman Emperor Leopold II to co-operate with other European monarchs to restore the king to power in France. On 7 February 1792 an Austro-Prussian alliance was concluded, preparatory to an attempt to take advantage of the internal chaos in France, which had caused as much upheaval in the military forces as in the social order. On 20 April 1792 the French National Assembly declared war on 'the King of Hungary and Bohemia' (a subsidiary title of the Emperor) as

the first step in exporting revolution; Prussia and Austria responded by forming the First Coalition on 26 June, joined by Britain in January 1793 (after the shock of the execution of Louis XVI) and Spain in March; Russia, the Netherlands, Naples and Tuscany were also affiliated loosely but contributed little in military terms.

The French army had been beset by emigration and the upheaval of the Revolution, but the ex-Royal regiments retained sufficient discipline to give a good account of themselves; the vast numbers of new troops included the basically middle-class National Guard (disciplined but totally inexperienced) and immense numbers of volunteer and conscript units whose only saving grace was patriotic fervour. In the early skirmishes these troops were brushed aside by the Austrians around Lille, and Marshal Rochambeau resigned his post as commander of the Army of the North in disgust, to be replaced by the Marquis de Lafayette, a supporter of the Revolution (but not of the anarchic chaos which was to follow). On 10 August the Tuileries palace was stormed by the Paris mob, and the king deprived of what powers he still retained; Lafayette considered marching on Paris to restore order, but fled from his command and surrendered to the Austrians on 20 August.

On 19 August France was invaded by the Allied army which had assembled at Coblenz under the Prussian commander the Duke of Brunswick, some 80,000 strong (more than 40,000 Prussians, 30,000 Austrians and smaller contingents of Hessians and French royalist émigrés). Capturing the fortresses of Longwy and Verdun, the army moved slowly towards Paris, driving before them General François Kellermann's French Army of the Centre. Lafayette's replacement, General Charles Dumouriez, marched with part of his Army of the North to aid Kellermann, and on 20 September 1792 they assembled some 36,000 men to oppose Brunswick at Valmy. The battle was settled by a French cannonade (mounted by the ex-royal gunners) which mauled the Prussian infantry, so that Brunswick (who was unenthusiastic about the whole plan) withdrew to Germany; Paris and the infant French republic was saved. The monarchy was abolished by the National Convention on the day after Valmy.

Elsewhere, French forces enjoyed success: General Adam Custine invaded Germany from Alsace and reached Frankfurt; Dumouriez returned north after Valmy and marched into the Austrian Netherlands. The Austrians retired before him; greatly out-numbering them, Dumouriez followed and defeated them at Jemappes on 6 November, capturing Brussels ten days later. These Allied defeats were partly offset by Brunswick's counter-attack against Custine, who was driven back upon the Rhine and Frankfurt was recovered.

The War in 1793

In 1793 the French republic was brought to the brink of extinction. At the beginning of the year the execution of Louis XVI (21 January) was followed by France's declaration of war upon Britain, Spain and the United

Provinces (Holland), and by the annexation of the Austrian Netherlands. Allied armies almost immediately began their offensive, Brunswick besieging Custine in Mainz while Prince Frederick of Saxe-Coburg with his Austrian army attempted to recover the Austrian Netherlands. Dumouriez attacked him at Neerwinden on 18 March, but was soundly beaten; the Austrians recovered Brussels and Dumouriez, falsely accused of treachery, defected to the Allies, having first handed over to them the political commissars who accompanied his army. His replacement, General Dampierre, was killed trying to halt Saxe-Coburg's advance near Condé on 8 May, and Custine was appointed to the shattered Army of the North. Defeated near Valenciennes (21–23 May), Custine was guillotined by the Committee of Public Safety as a punishment for his failure, and Jean Houchard was appointed in his place. Condé fell on 10 July

▶

Battle off Ushant, or 'the Glorious 1st of June', 1794; the French ship-of-the-line Vengeur *sinks in the foreground, the crew shouting* Vive la liberté! *as she was bombarded by HMS* Brunswick. *(Print by Ozanne)*

Richard, 1st Earl Howe (1726–99). Victor of the 'Glorious First of June', 'Black Dick' Howe's final services to his country was in helping to negotiate the end of the 'great mutiny' of 1797. (Engraving by W.T. Fry after C. Dupoint)

and Valenciennes 19 days later; Mainz was captured in the following month. With France torn asunder internally by 'the Terror', royalist counter-revolutions in the Vendée and Toulon threatened to extinguish the republican government, and an Anglo-Spanish force occupied Toulon and destroyed virtually the entire French naval strength in the Mediterranean.

On 23 August the Committee of Public Safety took the most desperate measure of proclaiming a *Levée en Masse*, which allowed for the conscription of the entire male population. The first glimmer of success came on 6 September when Houchard attacked the Duke of York's Anglo-Hanoverian force (which was besieging Dunkirk, collaborating with the Austrians in the Austrian Netherlands) at Hondschoote, and forced back York by sheer weight of numbers of the untrained but patriotically inspired French levies. A week later Houchard defeated the Prince of Orange's Dutch at Menin, but was accused of not trying hard enough and was guillotined like his predecessor; Jean-Baptiste Jourdan took his place, doubtless with some trepidation. War Minister Lazare Carnot joined the army

and ordered him to relieve Maubeuge, besieged by Saxe-Coburg; this was accom-plished by the battle of Wattignies (15–16 October) and suddenly the pendulum began to swing in France's favour. The Anglo-Spanish force in Toulon was evicted, partly by a plan devised by the young artillery colonel Napoleon Bonaparte; the uprising in the Vendée was crushed with extreme brutality, and in the Alsace/Rhine theatre General Lazare Hoche recovered from a check by Brunswick at Kaiserslautern (28–30 November) to defeat both the Prussians at Fröschwiller (22 December) and the Austrian general Dagobert Wurmser at Geisberg four days later. By the beginning of 1795 the Rhine frontier had been stabilized and Mainz recaptured.

The War in 1794

French success continued in 1794, especially in the Netherlands, as Saxe-Coburg was defeated at Tourcoing on 18 May by General Souham, temporarily commanding General Pichegru's Army of the North; this was seconded by a drawn battle at Tournai (23 May) and a victory at Hooglede (17 June), and in that month a new army 'of the

Henri de La Rochejaquelin (1773–94), one of the most outstanding of the Royalist leaders in the counter-revolution in the Vendée. Displayed here is the Sacre-Coeur *badge which, sewn on to civilian clothes, comprised the only real 'uniform' of the Vendéan rebels. (Engraving by W. Greatbatch)*

Victims of 'The Terror':

'Jean Julien, waggoner . . . took it into his head to cry "*Vive le Roi!*" . . . condemned to death . . .

'Jean Baptiste Henry, aged eighteen, journeyman tailor, convicted of having sawed a tree of liberty; executed the 6th September 1793 . . .

'Henriette Françoise de Marboeuf, aged fifty-five, widow of the *ci-devant* Marquis de Marboeuf . . . convicted of having hoped for the arrival of the Austrians and Prussians . . . Condemned to death the 5th February 1794, and executed the same day . . .

'François Bertrand, aged thirty-seven . . . convicted of having furnished to the defenders of the country sour wine injurious to the health of citizens, was condemned to death at Paris, 15th May 1793, and executed the same day . . .

'Marie Angelique Plaisant, sempstress at Douai, convicted of having exclaimed that she was an aristocrat, and "A fig for the nation" . . . executed the same day . . .'

(*History of the French Revolution*, L. A. Thiers, London 1895, III, pp. 532–3.)

Sambre and Meuse' was formed by the incorporation of the Army of the Moselle, whose commander Jourdan took over the northern theatre. He invested Charleroi (12 June) and defeated Saxe-Coburg's attempt at relief, at Fleurus on 26 June; Brussels was taken on 10 July and Antwerp on the 27th, and the Austrians forever driven from the Netherlands which bore their name. Another new army, 'of the Rhine and Moselle', was formed under General Jean Moreau who pushed the Allies back and again invested Mainz. In the minor theatres, the French drove the Allies from Savoy and held off Spanish advances in the Pyrenees; their only setbacks of the year occurred against the British, who occupied the French West Indian colonies, captured Corsica (10 August) and defeated the French Atlantic fleet at the battle of the First of June. But though Admiral Villaret de Joyeuse's fleet was defeated comprehensively in this action, the grain-convoy it had been sent to escort reached port safely, bringing food from the United States to alleviate the widespread starvation in France.

The War in 1795

The situation for France had stabilized to the extent that the existence of the republic was no longer under threat. In the early part of 1795 Pichegru pushed on into the United Provinces, capturing the icebound Dutch fleet with cavalry, and Holland was transformed into a satellite state, the Batavian Republic. By mid-year the exhausted Prussians had made peace by the Treaty of Basel, followed by Spain, Saxony, Hesse-Cassel and Hanover; only Austria and Britain remained in opposition, though the operations of the latter in this year were largely restricted to an abortive landing of French emigrant corps at Quiberon in June/July, intended to instigate a royalist counter-revolution in Brittany; it was defeated comprehensively by Hoche's Army of the West. A similar attempt to rekindle the royalist insurrection in the Vendée failed, and again the royalist adherents were brutally repressed by Hoche. Only a little progress was made in Italy, where General André Massena won a smallish action at Loano (23–25 November). Most of the military operations occurred on the Rhine, where Jourdan's Army of the Sambre and Meuse faced the Austrian armies of Marshal Charles von Clerfayt and Wurmser. Jourdan's attempt to invade Germany in September/October was outmanoeuvred by Cleryfayt, who then defeated Pichegru at Mainz (29 October). At this stage, when the French position was difficult, Clerfayt proclaimed an armistice; Pichegru defected to the Allies, having betrayed the French plans, which accounts for Jourdan's defeat.

The War in 1796

From 1796 the war (now basically between France and Austria) split into two 'fronts', Germany and Italy, though neither was independent of the consequences of the other. In

François-Athanase Charette de la Contrie (1763–96), one of the leaders of the Royalist counter-revolution, commander of the 'Army of the Marais'; he *survived longer than the majority of his fellow-royalist leaders, being captured and executed at Nantes on 24 May 1796. (Engraving by W. Greatbatch)*

'The Grand Old Duke of York': Frederick Augustus, Duke of York and Albany (1763–1827), commander-in-chief of the British army from 1795 (less a break of 1809–11 after a scandal concerning the disposal of commissions *involving his mistress). The Duke was not a talented general but a most capable administrator whose efforts benefited the army. (Engraving by W. Skelton after Sir William Beechey)*

the German theatre, the French generals Jourdan and Moreau acted in concert against the new Austrian commander, the young Archduke Charles, Jourdan intending to divert Austrian attention to allow Moreau to invade Bavaria. Jourdan crossed the Rhine on 10 June, and though defeated by Charles at Wetzlar six days later (resulting in Jourdan's withdrawal back across the Rhine), his offensive permitted Moreau to cross the Rhine at Strasbourg. Leaving a detachment to cover Jourdan, Charles moved against Moreau, whereupon Jourdan re-crossed the Rhine. Charles fought a drawn battle at Malsch (9 July) but was compelled to retire across the Danube, but when reinforced left a detachment under General Latour to cover Moreau while he again switched his attention to Jourdan, whom he defeated decisively at Amberg on 24 August. Pressing after the retiring French, Charles defeated Jourdan again at Würzburg on 3 September; the French fell back on to the Rhine and an armistice was concluded. Meanwhile, Moreau had beaten Latour at Friedberg on the day of the battle of

Amberg, but when he learned of Jourdan's discomfiture Moreau also retraced his steps and crossed the Rhine to safety on 26 October.

On the Italian front, the young General Bonaparte took command of the ragged and ill-equipped French forces in March; he was positioned along the Riviera and opposed by an Austrian army under General Jean Beaulieu and a Piedmontese army under Baron Colli. Bonaparte immediately struck between the two and widened their separation at Montenotte on 12 April, and seconded this attack on Beaulieu with another at Dego (14–15 April). Bonaparte then turned on Colli and smashed his army at Mondovi (21 April); two days later Colli sued for an armistice and Piedmont withdrew from the war on 28 April. Bonaparte continued to outmanoeuvre Beaulieu, his retiring rearguard being defeated at Lodi on 10 May. Having conquered Lom-

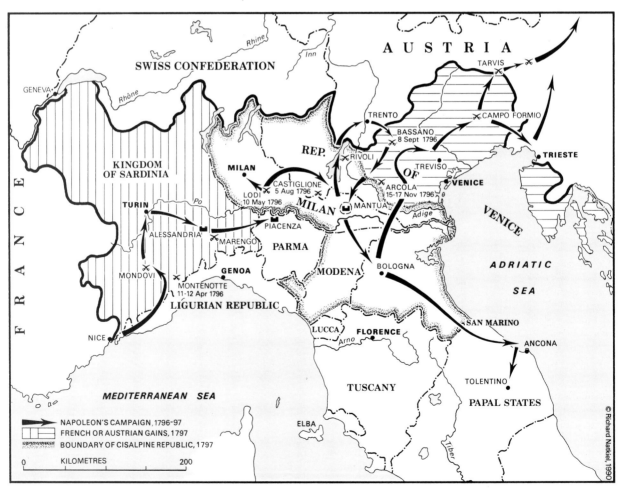

© Richard Natkiel, 1990

SWISS CONFEDERATION

Rhine

Inn

AUSTRIA

GENEVA

Rhône

TARVIS

TRENTO

CAMPO FORMIO

KINGDOM
OF SARDINIA

Po

MILAN

REP.

BASSANO
8 Sept 1796

TRIESTE

RIVOLI

TREVISO

TURIN

LODI
10 May 1796

CASTIGLIONE
5 Aug 1796

OF

ALESSANDRIA

MILAN

ARCOLA
15-17 Nov 1796

VENICE

MARENGO

PIACENZA

MANTUA

VENICE

MONDOVI

PARMA

Adige

NICE

MONTENOTTE
11-12 Apr 1796

GENOA

MODENA

BOLOGNA

ADRIATIC

LIGURIAN REPUBLIC

SEA

SAN MARINO

LUCCA

FLORENCE

Arno

ANCONA

MEDITERRANEAN SEA

TUSCANY

TOLENTINO

ELBA

PAPAL STATES

Tiber

F R A N C E

NAPOLEON'S CAMPAIGN, 1796-97
FRENCH OR AUSTRIAN GAINS, 1797
BOUNDARY OF CISALPINE REPUBLIC, 1797

0   KILOMETRES   200

The bridge at Lodi, 10 May 1796: the French army attempts to fight its way across, under cover of the fire of light artillery (foreground). (Print after Baron Lejeune)

The Battle of Rivoli (14 January 1797) and (inset) the manoeuvres leading to the action, as the Austrian general Alvintzy (or Alvinci) made the fourth and final attempt to relieve Mantua.

A U S T R I A

Alvinci

LA CORONA

Joubert

RIVOLI

Lake Garda

12 Jan 1797
Alvinci attacks
La Corona, pushing
Joubert back to
Rivoli

VERONA   Bayalitsch

Massena

Rey

Augereau

Adige

Mincio

Provera

LEGNAGO

Sérurier

MANTUA
(under siege)

Po

0   MILES   10
0   KM   16

© Richard Natkiel, 1988

LUMINI

Lusignan

Monte Baldo

Austrian Army
(Alvinci)
28,000 men

Quasdanowitch

LA CORONA

Liptay   Koblos   Ockzay

Monte Magnone

Adige

Wukassowitch

CAPRINO

Massena

Joubert
SAN MARCO

DOLCE

Trombalore Heights

Osteria Gorge

OSTERIA

Tasso

GARDA

RIVOLI

Monnier

**Monte
Pipolo**

French Army
(Bonaparte)
10,000 men (0500 hrs)
17,000 men (0800 hrs)
20,000 men (1500 hrs)

AFFI

Lake Garda

Rey & Victor

Adige

To Verona

INITIAL
POSITIONS
DAWN,
14 JAN

FINAL
BATTLE
POSITIONS
EVENING

FRENCH

AUSTRIAN

0   MILES   2
0   KILOMETRES   3

◀ *The manoeuvres of the 1796–97 Italian campaign, plus the location of the Battle of Marengo (1800). The strategic importance of Mantua, the main Austrian garrison in northern Italy, is apparent from its geographical location.*

bardy in less than three weeks, Bonaparte continued to pursue Beaulieu who retired into the Tyrol, leaving the whole of north Italy in French hands save the Austrian garrison of Mantua, which Bonaparte invested (4 June). Seeking its relief, a new Austrian army poured from the Tyrol under Wurmser, who unwisely split his forces, heading for Mantua himself and sending General Quasdanovich to sever French communications. Again faced with converging enemy forces, Bonaparte again interposed himself between the two, holding Wurmser while he defeated Quasdanovich at Lonato on 3 August. Having wrecked one Austrian advance, Bonaparte then concentrated his forces and fell upon Wurmser at Castiglione on 5 August, throwing him back upon the Tyrol.

Despite the Austrians having twice divided their forces and being defeated in detail, when Wurmser regrouped and made a second attempt to relieve Mantua he made the same mistake, leaving General Paul Davidovich to defend the Tyrol while he led his main body down the Brenta Valley towards Mantua. Bonaparte defeated Davidovich at Caliano (5 September), but learning of Wurmser's progress made a forced march which caught the Austrians at Bassano (8 September); part of Wurmser's force was routed but the general himself fought his way through to Mantua, swelling its garrison to 28,000, and an attempt to break out was repelled by Massena on 15 September. With Wurmser now besieged in Mantua, the next attempt at its relief was made by General Joseph Alvintzy, who also divided his forces. Again Bonaparte sent a small detachment to hold off Davidovich's column, while he attacked Alvintzy at Caldiero (12 November). The Austrians had slightly the better of the encounter, but in a hard-fought battle at Arcola (15–17 November) – which Bonaparte came near to losing – he finally succeeded in routing Alvintzy, and was free to turn on Davidovich and repel him as well.

The Allied position in the Mediterranean worsened dramatically in 1796, as the Treaty of San Ildefonso between Spain and France compelled the British navy to evacuate the Mediterranean (relinquishing Corsica in the process), the Mediterrancean fleet moving to Gibraltar in the face of the now combined Spanish and French navies.

The War in 1797

At the beginning of the year, Alvintzy launched the fourth and final attempt to relieve Mantua, and again divided his forces so that only a portion of the Austrian resources were available when he attacked Bonaparte at Rivoli on 14 January. Initially he had some success, but the arrival of Massena with French reinforcements turned the battle against Alvintzy. Bonaparte was thus free to return to Mantua where General Jean Sérurier was struggling to maintain the siege against the second Austrian column of General Provera, and a sortie from Mantua by Wurmser. While Sérurier chased Wurmser back into Mantua, Bonaparte surrounded Provera and forced him to surrender; and on 2 February Mantua at last capitulated, the Austrian defenders having been ravaged by disease which had cost them 18,000 men. With northern Italy finally cleared of Austrians, Bonaparte was free to invade Austria; he was now opposed by Alvintzy's replacement, the Archduke Charles.

Again Bonaparte thrust between two enemy forces, sending Joubert to contain the Austrians in the Tyrol while he manoeuvred in front of Charles, Massena winning a minor victory at Malborghetto on 23 March. In three columns Bonaparte crossed the Alps and Joubert advanced to join him; and with the French forces only 95 miles from Vienna at Leoben, the Emperor sued for an armistice. Bonaparte dictated peace terms without reference to his political masters, the Directory, and hostilities ended by the Peace of Leoben (18 April), confirmed by the Treaty of Campo Formio (17 October) by which the Austrian Netherlands were formally taken into metropolitan France and the French satellite state of the Cisalpine Republic in

northern Italy was recognized by Austria, whose only consolation was her receipt of the ex-Republic of Venice. The War of the First Coalition had ended with humiliation for Austria, and the rising star of the French army, Napoleon Bonaparte, had established himself as the foremost soldier of the age.

In Germany the Austrian military situation deteriorated similarly. Jourdan had been replaced by Hoche as commander of the Army of the Sambre and Meuse, who now proceeded to collaborate with Moreau's Army of the Rhine and Moselle in a renewed crossing of the Rhine; deprived of the skill of Archduke Charles (sent to oppose the greater threat of Bonaparte) the Austrians were driven from the Rhine, Hoche defeating the Austrian general Werneck at the battle of the Lahn (18 April). The Austrians were continuing to retire when Leoben ended hostilities.

Only in the war at sea were the French checked. An attempt to invade Britain depended upon the collaboration of the French and Spanish fleets, and in February Admiral José de Cordova with 27 Spanish ships left the Mediterranean for the French naval base at Brest. He was intercepted at Cape St. Vincent (14 February) by Admiral Sir John Jervis with fifteen British ships, which had been cruising off Portugal in anticipation. When Captain Horatio Nelson left the line-of-battle and halted the Spanish progress, a mêlée battle developed in which four Spaniards were captured and the rest mauled, marking the end of the invasion threat. Later in the year the Royal Navy in the home station was shaken by mutinies at Spithead and the Nore (in pursuit of better conditions rather than politically motivated), but the French navy was in so low a state that no advantage could be taken. In October the fleet of the Batavian Republic under Admiral Jan de Winter was engaged by Admiral Adam Duncan as it emerged from the Texel; again a mêlée developed in which the Royal Navy captured nine of the fifteen Dutch ships-of-the-line.

The War in 1798: Europe

There were only minor operations in Europe in 1798, principally the French occupations of Rome (February) and Switzerland (April), resulting in the establishment of the French satellite states of the Roman and Helvetian Republics respectively. France sent a small expedition under General Jean Humbert in support of the rebellion of the 'United Irish' society in Ireland; but by the time Humbert arrived, the rebellion had been crushed with some brutality, the most decisive British victory being at Vinegar Hill in Wexford on 12 June. Landing at Killala Bay on 22 August, Humbert had some minor success but was surrounded and forced to surrender by Lord Cornwallis at Ballinamuck (8 September). Humbert's reinforcing squadron was intercepted on 12 October by Sir John Borlase Warren's British fleet.

The Egyptian Campaign

With the cessation of war in Europe, and realizing that an invasion of England was not a realistic proposition given the domination of the sea by the Royal Navy, Bonaparte convinced the Directory of the value of an expedition to Egypt, possession of which would confirm the French hold on the Mediterranean and possibly open a channel of attack upon British possessions in India. Probably wishing the growing influence of Bonaparte to be put at a safe distance, the Directory sanctioned an expedition, which sailed from Toulon on 19 May accompanied by thirteen ships-of-the-line, capturing Malta en route (12 June). Forty thousand French troops landed in Egypt on 1 July, and on the following day stormed Alexandria, before advancing on Cairo. The Mameluke rulers of Egypt (nominally an Ottoman province) resisted the French with vigour. On 21 July a vast Mameluke/Egyptian army fell upon Bonaparte at the Battle of the Pyramids, but was utterly routed by the steady French troops, a triumph of modern European tactics over a basically medieval army, and Cairo was occupied on the following day. The vital action of the campaign, however, was fought in Aboukir Bay on 1 August. In reaction to the French expedition, Britain re-entered the Mediterranean by

sending a small fleet under Horatio Nelson to intercept Bonaparte at sea; in this he failed, but attacked the French fleet at anchor and utterly destroyed it, killing the French Admiral François Brueys; only two French ships escaped.

Bonaparte was thus completely isolated, bereft of reinforcement and unable even to evacuate Egypt. Ottoman armies gathered in Syria and at Rhodes, but rather than await their arrival Bonaparte took the offensive, marching into Syria with 8,000 men. He captured El Arish (14–15 February 1799) and Jaffa (3–7 March) and invested Acre, the defence of which was inspired by the British naval captain Sir Sydney Smith. An Ottoman attempt to relieve the city was defeated by Bonaparte at Mount Tabor, but after plague decimated the French army he withdrew from Acre and retired on Egypt. On 15 July the Ottoman force from Rhodes landed from British transports and entrenched at Aboukir; on 25 July Bonaparte smashed through their lines and Aboukir surrendered on 2 August. With the French position stabilized, Bonaparte decided to return home, slipping past the British fleet in a frigate and reaching France by 9 October. General Jean-Baptiste Kléber was left in command of the French army, and concluded the Convention of El Arish (21 January 1800) with the Ottoman

The Battle of Aboukir Bay (or 'the Battle of the Nile'), 1 August 1798, showing Nelson's attack upon the anchored French fleet.

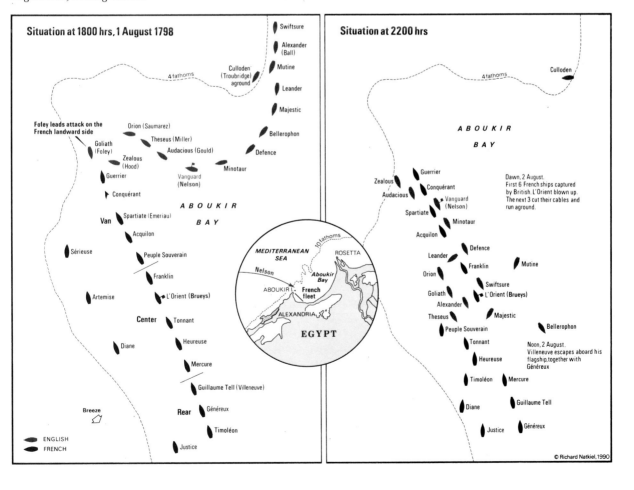

© Richard Natkiel, 1990

The battle of Aboukir Bay, or 'the Nile': the French flagship l'Orient explodes at the height of the battle. Benjamin Hallowell, captain of the British HMS Swiftsure (centre) kept his ship close-in to the blazing Frenchman, knowing that when l'Orient blew up the explosion would arch over the top of the British warship. (Engraving by J. Le Petit after G. Arnold)

General Jean-Baptiste Kléber (1753–1800), an extremely brave general who took command of the French forces in Egypt after Bonaparte's return to France, but who was assassinated by a knife-wielding fanatic on 14 June 1800. (Engraving by T. Johnson after J. B. P. Guérin)

representatives (largely the unauthorized work of Sydney Smith), by which the French were to be allowed to evacuate Egypt unhindered; but when Britain refused to recognize the Convention, Kléber attacked the Ottoman forces at Heliopolis (20 March) and recovered Cairo. On 14 June he was assassinated by a fanatic, and command passed to General Jacques Menou. British fears that the growing hostility of Russia might compel them to divert forces from the Mediterranean to the Baltic led to the dispatch of an expedition to Egypt under General Sir Ralph Abercromby, which landed in the face of heavy opposition at Aboukir (8 March 1801). Menou was heavily defeated at Alexandria on 20 March, where Abercromby was mortally wounded; Cairo was captured in July, and with his situation hopeless Menou capitulated on 31 August. His troops were given unhindered passage home; and French aspirations of an oriental empire were ended forever.

The War of the Second Coalition: 1799

The Second Coalition against France was completed by the signature of an Austro-British alliance on 22 June 1799, though a number of treaties had been concluded in the previous year, most notably the Russo-British alliance of December 1798; Naples, the Ottoman Empire and the Vatican were already united against France, to which Portugal and Austria joined. A Neapolitan army under the Austrian General Karl Mack von Leiberich captured Rome (29 November 1798), but sixteen days later was expelled by the French. Despite being outnumbered by the Allies, and with no great general to inspire them (Bonaparte being still in Egypt), Carnot determined to attack on all fronts. There were three main areas of conflict: the Netherlands, where an Anglo-Russian army under the Duke of York was intended to land and expel the French; Italy, where the Austro-Russian army was to be led by the famous old veteran Alexander Suvarov; and Germany, where the Archduke Charles was to lead an Austrian army.

In Germany, Jourdan's 'Army of Mayence' advanced against the Archduke; checked at Ostrach (21 March) he advanced again and met Charles at Stockach four days later, initially driving back the Austrians, but was overthrown by Charles's counter-attack. Jourdan extricated his forces and retired to the Rhine, where he resigned his command. Against the Austrians in Switzerland, Massena's French army made some progress but halted operations to await the outcome of Jourdan's campaign; upon his resignation Massena took over Jourdan's forces as well as his own in a new 'Army of the Danube'. Massena entrenched at Zurich but an Austrian attack on 4–7 June caused him to retire westward, but Charles prudently declined to follow. Massena advanced again but was again beaten at Zurich (14 August), though successfully repelled an Austrian push against his left at Dottingen (16 August).

In Italy, Mack fled to the French to escape his mutinous Neapolitan rabble, and the French General Etienne Championnet stormed into Naples and established another French satellite, the Parthenopean Republic. Farther north, however, the situation deteriorated for the French; General Barthélemy Schérer tried to defeat the Austrian army of General Paul Kray before Suvarov's Russians could arrive, but on 5 April 1799 was himself defeated at Magnano, south of Verona. The French retired before the Allied forces (Suvarov now in command), Moreau taking over the French army; but at Cassano (27 April) Suvarov routed them, seizing Milan and Turin shortly afterwards. General Jacques Macdonald hurried north with a French army from southern Italy to assist Moreau, but was defeated by Suvarov in the battle of the Trebbia (17–19 June), whereupon Macdonald managed to join Moreau, their combined forces retiring upon the Riviera with Suvarov in pursuit. Moreau was relieved of his command and replaced by Joubert, who was killed and his army routed when he attacked Suvarov at Novi (15 August); but before he could exploit the victory Suvarov was ordered to march to Switzerland. Allied forces in Italy were left under the command of the Austrian general Michael Melas, who defeated Championnet's 'Army of the Alps' at Genoa on 4 November. Under Suvarov's skilled direction, virtually all Bonaparte's gains of the 1796–7 Italian campaign had been recovered.

It was decided that the Archduke Charles should leave Switzerland and join the Duke of York in the Netherlands, with Suvarov replacing him; but in the period between Charles's departure and Suvarov's arrival, Massena attacked the remaining Allied forces of the Russian General Alexander Korsakov, whom he routed at Zurich on 25 September. Suvarov fought his way through the St. Gotthard Pass, but the war in Switzerland was irretrievable, and the mad Tsar Paul dismissed Suvarov from command, a tragic end to the career of the splendid old warrior.

Ironically, the war in the Netherlands was lost before the Archduke Charles arrived. The Duke of York's British army had landed in August and, reinforced by the Russian contingent, advanced against General Brune's Franco-Batavians, who checked them at Bergen on 19 September. On 2 October the Duke tried again, and won the second battle of Bergen, only to be checked again at Castricum four days later. With Anglo-Russian co-operation wretched and with insufficient resources to defeat the French, and having captured the Batavian fleet (one of the prime objectives of the expedition), York withdrew, and the Convention of Alkmaar (18 October 1799) ended the war in the Netherlands. Although the year had seen the loss of virtually all the French conquests in Italy, Allied lack of co-ordination had failed elsewhere, and disgusted with the state of the war the Tsar withdrew from the Coalition. In November, Bonaparte's *coup d'état* made him virtual dictator of France as First Consul, and he prepared to smash his enemies.

The War of the Second Coalition: 1800–1

Bonaparte assembled a new 'Army of the Reserve' at Dijon, and decided not to reinforce Moreau in Switzerland and Alsace but invade Italy through Switzerland. In early 1800, however, the French toehold in Italy was virtually extinguished as Massena was besieged in Genoa and Melas chased the remaining French forces beyond Nice. In May Bonaparte crossed the Alps from Switzerland into the plain of Lombardy, a most difficult and audacious march over appalling, icy terrain. Melas retraced his steps from Nice as soon as he learned of Bonaparte's return to Italy, but on 4 June Massena was starved into surrender at Genoa. Shortly afterwards Melas learned that Bonaparte had cut his communications with Austria, and concentrated his forces around Alessandria on 13 June. Four days earlier the Austrians of General Karl Ott, which had been the force besieging Genoa, had been defeated at Montebello by General Jean Lannes's French corps, Ott's shattered command falling back on Alessandria. On 14 June, believing Melas to be at Turin, Bonaparte's army was advancing widely separated when at Marengo, a mile east of Alessandria, he ran into the entire Austrian army. Bonaparte had barely 18,000 men against double that number, and tried to hang on until the scattered French corps could come to his assistance. Melas attacked immediately and by mid-afternoon was so confident of victory that he handed over command to a subordinate. At this moment, with the French virtually defeated, General Louis Desaix arrived with two divisions and, remarking that though the battle was lost there was still time to win another, counter-attacked and drove the Austrians from the field in confusion. Bonaparte was generous in his praise of the man who had saved his battle; he could afford to be, for Desaix had been killed at the head of his attack. The Austrian army in Italy was virtually annihilated; on 15 June Melas surrendered, and Bonaparte returned to Paris.

The only minor reverse for the French was the loss of Malta, its garrison being starved into submission in September, after a two-year Maltese insurrection with British assistance. In Germany, Moreau drove the Austrian Kray before him, winning victories at Stockach (3 May), Möskirch (5 May), Ulm (16 May) and Hochstadt (19 June). From July to November an armistice was agreed, young Archduke John replacing the luckless Kray; when operations renewed Moreau defeated him comprehensively at Hohenlinden (3 December). With Moreau advancing on Vienna, General Guillaume Brune coming over the Julian Alps with the French forces from Italy and Macdonald invading the Tyrol from Switzerland, the Austrian position was clearly hopeless and on Christmas Day they sued for peace, which was concluded at Lunéville on 9 February 1801, confirming Campo Formio. The War of the Second Coalition was thus ended with complete French victory.

The Peace of Amiens and the Resumption of War

Austria's exit left Britain virtually alone in opposition to France, and apart from the operations in Egypt the effort was sustained almost entirely at sea, with the continuing blockade and 'war of commerce' against France. A new challenge was presented by the 'League of Armed Neutrality' between Russia, Denmark, Sweden and Prussia, instigated by the mad and now anti-British Tsar, to protect Baltic shipping against the British attempts to strangle

French commerce. As the threat could not be ignored (the Baltic providing much of Britain's strategic imports such as timber and pitch), a British fleet was dispatched under Admiral Sir Hyde Parker with Horatio Nelson as second in command. On 2 April 1801 Nelson (in defiance of Parker's orders) took a squadron into Copenhagen harbour and in a very hard-fought battle destroyed the Danish fleet; he intended to second it by attacking the Russian fleet at Revel, but the assassination of the Tsar by a court conspiracy and the crowning of his pro-British son as Tsar Alexander I (who had been implicated in his father's murder) obviated the need for further action; the new Tsar terminated hostilities and the League dissolved.

The only other major naval activity was in the two battles of Algeciras: the first (6 July 1801) an indecisive battle when Admiral Sir James Saumarez engaged a French fleet, and the second six days later when he convincingly defeated a much larger Franco-Spanish force.

With a change of administration in Britain and the temporary exhaustion of France, peace was signed at Amiens on 27 March 1802, which resulted in the only year of peace in Europe from the French Revolution until the Battle of Waterloo. It lasted less than fourteen months, during which time Bonaparte had himself proclaimed Consul for Life, a brief step from crowning himself Emperor of the French as Napoleon I on 2 December 1804. On 16 May 1803 hostilities were resumed, Britain re-establishing the naval blockade and Napoleon planning an invasion of England, assembling a large fleet of invasion-craft to transport his army across the Channel.

The War of the Third Coalition

In order to achieve the temporary mastery of the sea necessary to invade England, Napoleon planned to decoy away the Royal Navy long enough for him to cross the Channel. The scheme was mismanaged from the beginning, Napoleon interfering with his admirals' strategy despite knowing little of sea warfare; yet Admiral Pierre Villeneuve's fleet did evade the British blockade of Toulon in April 1805, sailed for the West Indies and drew Horatio Nelson after him. Joined by a strong Spanish contingent, Villeneuve returned to European waters to be engaged by Sir Robert Calder off Cape Finisterre on 22 July 1805, and put in to Cadiz. The plan of invasion was wrecked, but goaded by Napoleon's taunts of cowardice, Villeneuve put to sea again to challenge the British in the Mediterranean. Nelson barred his path; Villeneuve attempted to return to the safety of Cadiz but was intercepted on 21 October off Cape Trafalgar. Though outnumbered, Nelson's 27 ships smashed the Franco-Spanish force, of which only eleven escaped; French naval resources were virtually annihilated in one of the most decisive sea battles in history, for the loss of not one British ship, but at the cost of Nelson's life. Trafalgar assured British naval supremacy for the remainder of the Napoleonic Wars; but contrary to some opinions, it did not directly prevent the invasion of England, for Napoleon had already abandoned the scheme despite his extensive planning. What it did

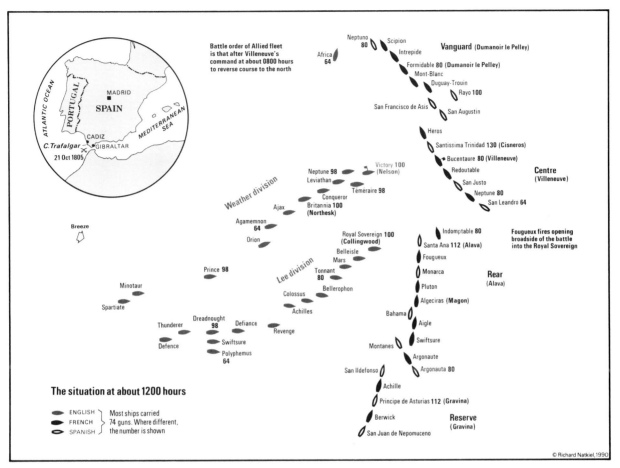

Battle order of Allied fleet is that after Villeneuve's command at about 0800 hours to reverse course to the north

Vanguard (Dumanoir le Pelley)

Neptuno 80
Scipion
Intrepide
Africa 64
Formidable 80 (Dumanoir le Pelley)
Mont-Blanc
Duguay-Trouin
Rayo 100
San Francisco de Asis
San Augustin
Heros
Santissima Trinidad 130 (Cisneros)
Bucentaure 80 (Villeneuve)
Redoutable
Centre (Villeneuve)
San Justo
Neptune 80
San Leandro 64

Weather division

Neptune 98
Leviathan
Victory 100 (Nelson)
Conqueror
Téméraire 98
Ajax
Britannia 100 (Northesk)
Agamemnon 64
Orion

Breeze

Royal Sovereign 100 (Collingwood)
Belleisle
Mars
Tonnant 80
Lee division
Colossus
Bellerophon
Achilles

Indomptable 80
Santa Ana 112 (Alava)
Fougueux
Monarca
Pluton
Algeciras (Magon)
Bahama
Aigle
Swiftsure
Montanes
Argonaute
Argonauta 80
San Ildefonso
Achille
Principe de Asturias 112 (Gravina)
Berwick
San Juan de Nepomuceno

Rear (Alava)

Fougueux fires opening broadside of the battle into the Royal Sovereign

Prince 98
Minotaur
Spartiate
Thunderer
Dreadnought 98
Defiance
Revenge
Defence
Swiftsure
Polyphemus 64

Reserve (Gravina)

The situation at about 1200 hours

ENGLISH
FRENCH
SPANISH

Most ships carried 74 guns. Where different, the number is shown

© Richard Natkiel, 1990

The battle of Trafalgar, 21 October 1805. The formation adopted by Nelson probably represented the ultimate development of the tactic of 'breaking the line': an attack in two columns to cut the enemy fleet in two places, and bring about the 'pell-mell battle' which was Nelson's stated objective.

Pierre Charles Jean Baptiste Sylvestre de Villeneuve (1763–1806), the most capable French admiral of the period and yet one who was persistently harassed by Napoleon into giving battle under disadvantageous circumstances at Trafalgar. He committed suicide from the disgrace of defeat.

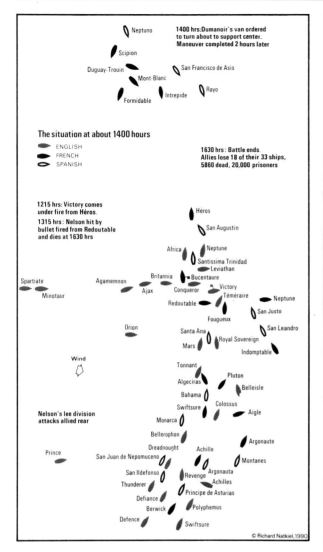

Neptuno

1400 hrs:Dumanoir's van ordered
to turn about to support center.
Maneuver completed 2 hours later

Scipion

Duguay-Trouin

San Francisco de Asis

Mont-Blanc

Formidable   Intrepide   Rayo

The situation at about 1400 hours

◀ ENGLISH
◀ FRENCH
◁ SPANISH

1630 hrs: Battle ends.
Allies lose 18 of their 33 ships,
5860 dead, 20,000 prisoners

1215 hrs: Victory comes
under fire from Héros.
1315 hrs: Nelson hit by
bullet fired from Redoutable
and dies at 1630 hrs

Héros
San Augustin

Africa   Neptune
Santissima Trinidad
Britannia   Leviathan
Agamemnon   Bucentaure
Spartiate   Conqueror   Victory
Minotaur   Ajax   Redoutable   Téméraire   Neptune
Fougueux   San Justo
Orion   San Leandro
Santa Ana   Royal Sovereign
Mars   Indomptable
Wind
⬇
Tonnant
Algeciras   Pluton
Bahama   Belleisle
Swiftsure   Colossus
Nelson's lee division   Monarca   Aigle
attacks allied rear   Bellerophon   Argonaute
Dreadnought   Achille
Prince   San Juan de Nepomuceno   Montanes
San Ildefonso   Argonauta
Thunderer   Revenge   Achilles
Defiance   Principe de Asturias
Berwick   Polyphemus
Defence   Swiftsure

© Richard Natkiel, 1990

Nelson's attack at Trafalgar overwhelmed Villeneuve's centre and rear before Admiral Dumanoir's van could change its course and return to assist; in such close-quarter ship-to-ship actions, the excellence of British gunnery and ship-handling was paramount.

The realities of naval warfare: the almost-dismasted Redoutable *(centre) is entangled with HMS* Temeraire *(left). The wreckage in the sea is from the shattered Spanish leviathan* Santissima Trinidad *(right): Trafalgar, 21 October 1805. (Print after W. L. Wyllie)*

ensure, however, was that no invasion could be contemplated seriously in the future.

The Third Coalition was organized against Napoleon on 11 April 1805 (effective from 9 August), between Britain, Austria, Russia, Sweden and some minor German princes. With the bulk of the French army concentrated in the invasion-camps around Boulogne, Allied strategy was to destroy Massena's French army in Italy and then advance westward upon France. Napoleon, however, moved first, secretly beginning to march his troops eastwards from Boulogne on 31 August. Unaware of this, the Austrian general Mack invaded Bavaria on 2 September; Archduke Charles prepared to move against Massena, while old General Mikhail Kutuzov began to advance in support with a large Russian reinforcement. Before the Austrians knew what was happening, Napoleon's rapid advance crossed the Rhine (26 September) and reached the Danube on 6 October, making a wide sweep around Mack's forces at Ulm, severing him from his support. After a half-hearted attempt to break out at Elchingen (14 October), the inept Mack surrendered his entire army on 17 October. It was one of the greatest triumphs of manoeuvre in history; without the cost of a major battle, Napoleon had out-manoeuvred his opponent and achieved a strategic victory of stunning proportions. With a vast part of the Austrian field army thus negated, Napoleon advanced towards Vienna, occupying the

The surrender of Mack at Ulm, to Napoleon and his entourage (right). (Print after E. Boutigny)

▶ *The Battle of Austerlitz, 2 December 1805. Napoleon's master-stroke: having manoeuvred the enemy into a disadvantageous position, his counter-attack along the Pratzen Heights destroyed the Allied army.*

capital and driving Kutuzov before him, despite the Russians' fighting of delaying actions at Dürrenstein (11 November) and Hollabrünn (15–16 November). On the Italian front, Massena defeated Charles at Caldiero, the Austrians falling back across the Julian Alps, though they were blocked from uniting with the main Austro-Russian army by detachments from Napoleon's force.

Napoleon advanced some 70 miles north from Vienna, a position of apparent vulnerability which might tempt his enemies to attack injudiciously. The Allied army under Kutuzov (with the Tsar and the Emperor both present to interfere) fell into the trap and began to move to sever Napoleon's communications. On 2 December 1805, near the village of Austerlitz, they began to swing around the French flank; as they advanced, Napoleon lunged forward, split their centre and overwhelmed the Allied left in another stunning display of tactical brilliance. The Austro-Russian

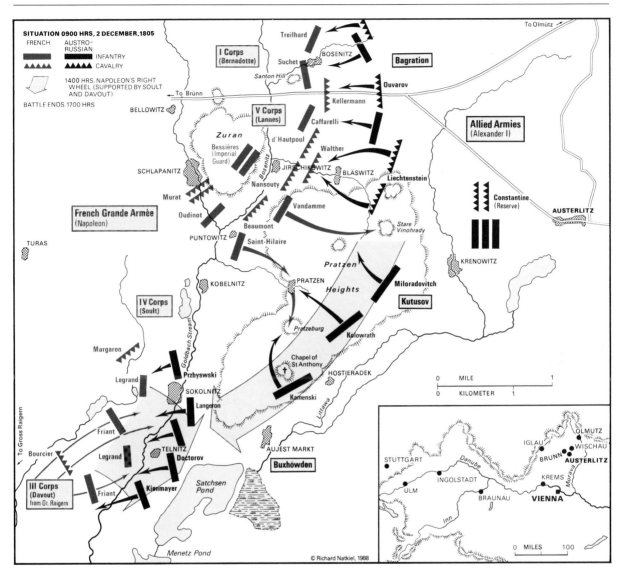

SITUATION 0900 HRS, 2 DECEMBER, 1805

FRENCH   AUSTRO-RUSSIAN

INFANTRY

CAVALRY

1400 HRS, NAPOLEON'S RIGHT WHEEL (SUPPORTED BY SOULT AND DAVOUT)

BATTLE ENDS.1700 HRS

© Richard Natkiel, 1988

army was overthrown totally, and on 4 December the Emperor Francis surrendered unconditionally; the Tsar withdrew his mauled contingent to Russia. By the Treaty of Pressburg (26 December) Austria surrendered territory to France in Germany and Italy; Napoleon was half-way towards his goal of achieving domination in Germany. The victory of Austerlitz was not entirely dependent upon Napoleon's strategic genius, however; much of it was due to the quality of his army, which had reached its peak of quality and efficiency. With the attritional warfare of the succeeding years, that quality was to decline inexorably.

The War of the Fourth Coalition

The Third Coalition collapsed with the defeat at Austerlitz and the death of the British prime minister, William Pitt, in January 1806. Britain and Russia remained at war, however, and the Fourth Coalition (which came into effect in October

1806) at last included Prussia, which had stood by to no great credit while Britain and Austria maintained the war against France. Now, alarmed by French progress in Germany, and especially by the formation of the satellite organization of German states in the Confederation of the Rhine, which threatened to tilt irrevocably the balance of power, with British encouragement King Frederick William III of Prussia prepared for war, in which he was joined by Saxony.

Napoleon concentrated his *Grande Armée* in north-east Bavaria, intent on a rapid invasion of Prussia. The Prussian army was commanded by the old Duke of Brunswick, with an even more ancient Frederickian warrior, Field Marshal Richard Mollendorf, in nominal senior command, though the King was also present with the army. Napoleon's invasion was incredibly rapid, taking the Prussians completely by surprise; beginning on 8 October 1806, in four

days Napoleon had turned their left flank and was threatening Berlin, Marshal Lannes having defeated and killed Prince Louis Ferdinard of Prussia at Saalfeld on 10 October. Napoleon ordered Marshals Davoût and Bernadotte to cut the Prussian communications while he advanced on the main body; but Bernadotte, perhaps deliberately (being unwilling to serve under a fellow-marshal!) moved in the wrong direction. On 14 October Napoleon engaged a Prussian force at Jena, believing it to be Brunswick's main army; in fact it was only the smaller detachment under Prince Friedrich Hohenlohe, protecting Brunswick's rear. Thus greatly outnumbered, Hohenlohe's force was routed. Fifteen miles north, Davoût's attempt to cut Prussian communications brought him into contact with the main body under Brunswick, at Auerstädt. Outnumbered more than two to one, Davoût fought a classic defensive action, and when Bernadotte finally arrived the French counter-attack swept the Prussians from the field, both Brunswick and Mollendorf being mortally wounded. Jena–Auerstädt destroyed the Prussian field army and to all intents knocked the country out of the war, a triumph for Napoleon's *Blitzkrieg*-style of advance and his strategic ability, though much of the credit goes to Davoût for holding Brunswick so long. What followed was basically a mopping-up operation; Berlin was captured on 24 October and the remaining Prussian forces were mostly harried out of existence, the final contingent (that of General Gebhard von Blücher) surrendering near Lübeck on 24 November.

Frederick William III fled to Russia, his surviving continental ally; Napoleon immediately marched into

Russian artillery crashes through the ice in an attempt to escape after the battle of Austerlitz. (Print after F. de Myrbach)

▶ *The Battles of Jena and Auerstädt, 14 October 1806. Napoleon believed himself to be attacking the main Prussian army, whereas this was actually engaged by Davoût, who defeated Brunswick at Auerstädt despite being heavily outnumbered.*

On the colonel of the 20th Chasseurs à Cheval:
'This M. de Marigny came from Dauphiné; he was rather over thirty years old, of handsome person, had not a penny of private fortune, and spent a thousand a year; so his poor regiment was his farm, and he squeezed it in every possible way, without regard for justice. Afterwards an inquiry took place, orders were given for his arrest and trial, but he made his escape, and no news was ever heard of him till the very day of the battle of Jena, when he joined his regiment with a perfectly regular order to resume the command. A few minutes afterwards a shot carried off his head.'
(*Recollections of Colonel de Gonneville*, ed. C. M. Yonge, London 1875, I, p. 33.)

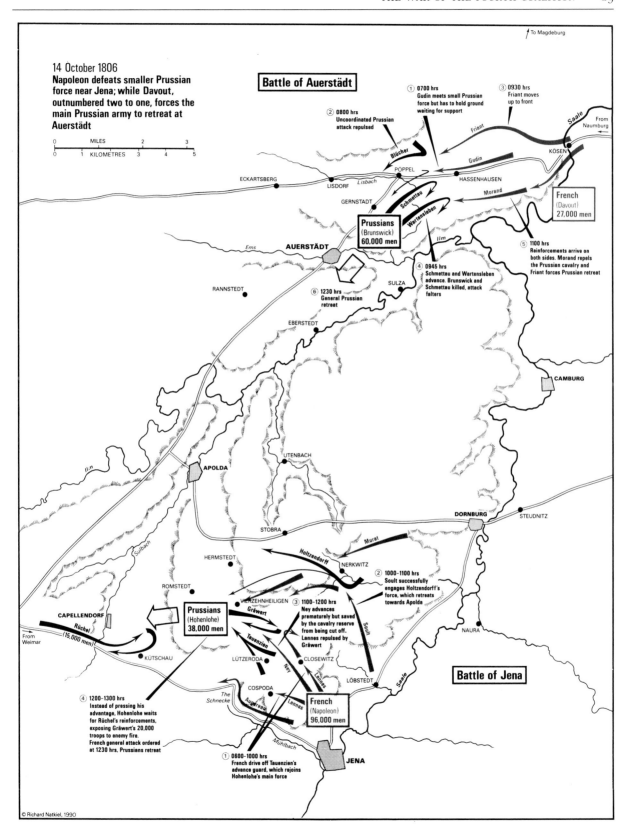

To Magdeburg

14 October 1806
Napoleon defeats smaller Prussian force near Jena; while Davout, outnumbered two to one, forces the main Prussian army to retreat at Auerstädt

MILES
0   1   2   3
KILOMETRES
0 1 2 3 4 5

Battle of Auerstädt

① 0700 hrs
Gudin meets small Prussian force but has to hold ground waiting for support

③ 0930 hrs
Friant moves up to front

② 0800 hrs
Uncoordinated Prussian attack repulsed

Saale
From Naumburg

Friant

Blücher

Gudin

KÖSEN

ECKARTSBERG

POPPEL

HASSENHAUSEN

Morand

French
(Davout)
27,000 men

LISDORF
Lisbach

GERNSTEDT

Schmettau

Wartensleben

Prussians
(Brunswick)
60,000 men

Ilm

⑤ 1100 hrs
Reinforcements arrive on both sides. Morand repels the Prussian cavalry and Friant forces Prussian retreat

Ems

AUERSTÄDT

SULZA

④ 0945 hrs
Schmettau and Wartensleben advance. Brunswick and Schmettau killed, attack falters

RANNSTEDT

⑥ 1230 hrs
General Prussian retreat

EBERSTEDT

CAMBURG

Ilm

APOLDA

UTENBACH

DORNBURG

STEUDNITZ

STOBRA

Murat

Holtzendorff

Sulbach

HERMSTEDT

NERKWITZ

② 1000–1100 hrs
Soult successfully engages Holtzendorff's force, which retreats towards Apolda

ROMSTEDT

VIERZEHNHEILIGEN

③ 1100–1200 hrs
Ney advances prematurely but saved by the cavalry reserve from being cut off. Lannes repulsed by Gräwert

Soult

CAPELLENDORF

Prussians
(Hohenlohe)
38,000 men

Gräwert

NAURA

Rüchel
(15,000 men)

From
Weimar

Tauenzien

KÜTSCHAU

LÜTZERODA

CLOSEWITZ

Ney

Lannes

LÖBSTEDT

Saale

Battle of Jena

④ 1200–1300 hrs
Instead of pressing his advantage, Hohenlohe waits for Rüchel's reinforcements, exposing Gräwert's 20,000 troops to enemy fire. French general attack ordered at 1230 hrs, Prussians retreat

COSPODA

The
Schnecke

Augereau

Lannes

French
(Napoleon)
96,000 men

Mühlbach

JENA

① 0600–1000 hrs
French drive off Tauenzien's advance guard, which rejoins Hohenlohe's main force

© Richard Natkiel, 1990

▲ Prelude to the 1806 campaign: Prussian Noble Guardsmen (Garde du Corps) sharpen their sabres on the steps of the French embassy, a gesture of defiance but one which went terribly awry in the actions of the brief Jena-Auerstädt campaign. (Print after F. de Myrbach)

▶ Above right: The death of Prince Louis Ferdinand of Prussia ('the Alcibiades of Prussia') at the hands of quartermaster Guindet of the French 10th Hussars at Saalfeld, 10 October 1806. (Print from Die Königin Luise, 1896, typical of the excellent draughtsmanship and accurate uniform-portrayal of the great Richard Knötel)

◀The beautiful Louise of Mecklenburg-Strelitz, Queen of Prussia (1776–1810), wife of Frederick William III, whose anti-French determination led to her being styled 'the only man in Prussia'. Coignet gave the general impression of her bearing: 'Lord, how beautiful she looked. . . . I would have given one of my ears to stay with her as long as the Emperor did'. (1929 edn., p. 157)

▶ Murat leads the charge of French dragoons at Jena, armed only with his riding-whip, a typical gesture by this flamboyant character. (Print after H. Chartier)

Poland, occupying Warsaw, to prevent any Russian attempt to relieve Prussia. He aimed to destroy the Russian field army of General Levin Bennigsen (a German in Russian service), but in a ferocious rearguard action at Pultusk (26 December) Bennigsen avoided Napoleon's attempt to trap him. In January 1807, with Napoleon's army in winter quarters recovering from its exertions and from the severe cold, Bennigsen made a lightning strike, and then withdrew as Napoleon concentrated and pursued him. On 8 February Napoleon (with considerably inferior forces) caught him at Preussiches–Eylau and attacked in a blizzard; after a most bloody, indecisive action which decimated both armies, Bennigsen withdrew leaving Napoleon in control of the field, but the weather was so impossible that both sides went into winter quarters to await the spring.

Both sides planned an offensive; Bennigsen moved first, but his advance was stopped on 10 June at Heilsberg, and four days later he unwisely crossed the River Alle at Friedland in a thrust towards Napoleon. With the river at their back, as Napoleon's forces progressively came into action, the Russians had no means of escape, and despite sterling resistance the Russian army disintegrated with enormous loss. On 19 June Napoleon reached Tilsit; Russia, with her field army wrecked at Friedland, sued for peace. Napoleon met the Tsar and Frederick William III on a raft moored in the middle of the River Niemen, to conclude the Treaty of Tilsit (7–9 July), which confirmed Napoleon's complete mastery of north-west Europe, humiliating terms being forced upon both Allied sovereigns. Prussia relinquished all the Polish territory acquired under the several Partitions of Poland to the new French satellite state of the Duchy of Warsaw, and to the Confederation of the Rhine all her territory between the Rhine and the Elbe. Prussia was to be occupied by a French army until a massive indemnity was paid (140,000,000 francs); Russia was compelled to accede to an alliance with Napoleon against Britain and the recognition of the Duchy of Warsaw. Once again, only Britain was left to oppose Napoleon.

The War of the Fifth Coalition
On 9 April 1809 yet another Coalition against France came into being, when Austria took the field once more,

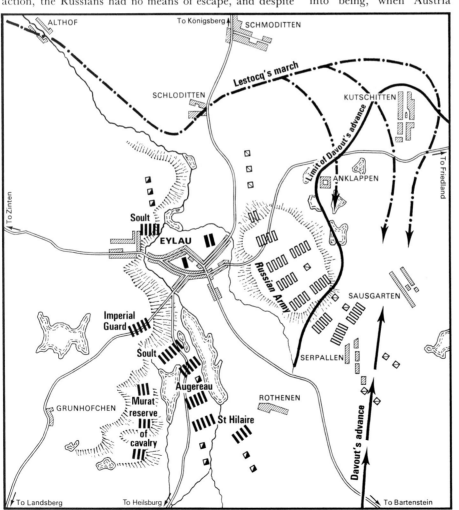

The Battle of Eylau, 7/8 February 1807. Fighting on 7 February was inconclusive. Napoleon planned a double envelopment of Bennigsen's position by Ney on the French left and Davoût on the right; in the event, although Davoût drove in the Russian left, Ney's non-arrival and Bennigsen's reinforcement by Lestocq enabled the Russians to withdraw without suffering an overwhelming defeat.

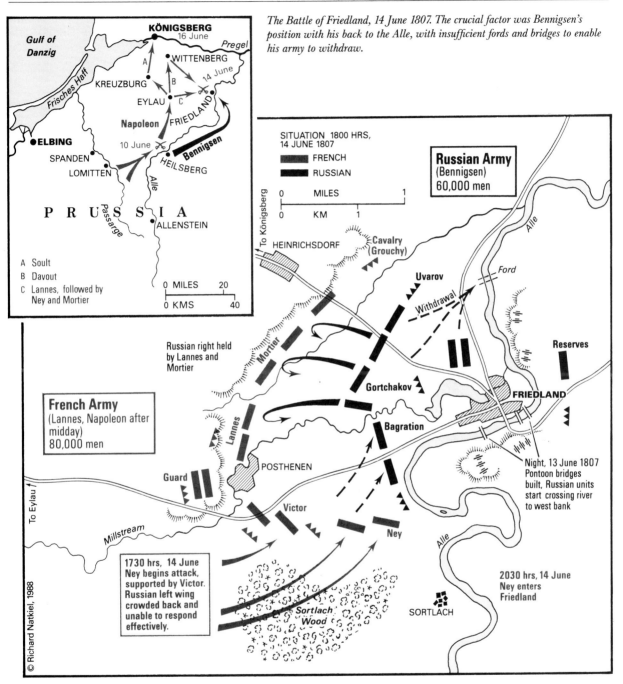

The Battle of Friedland, 14 June 1807. The crucial factor was Bennigsen's position with his back to the Alle, with insufficient fords and bridges to enable his army to withdraw.

encouraged by Britain and by the transfer of French troops from central Europe to the war in Spain (see below). Austria was to supply the main military effort, though a British expedition was landed at Walcheren in July to divert some of Napoleon's resources, which proved a complete fiasco as the troops were ravaged with fever and the force was withdrawn in October.

In early April 1809 Austrian troops under the Archduke Charles invaded Bavaria, Napoleon's principal German ally; Austria encouraged a revolt in the Tyrol against the Bavarian occupiers, and the Archduke John invaded Italy via the Julian Alps, beating off an attack by the Viceroy of Italy (Eugène de Beauharnais) at Sacile on 16 April. Napoleon arrived in Germany from the war in Spain to find Marshal Berthier's unskilled dispositions under great threat from the Austrians; he reorganized the French troops and immediately took the offensive, swiftly crossing the Danube and dividing the Austrian forces in the battle of Abensberg

◄ *Napoleon oversees the construction of pontoons at Lobau, 1809: bridging the Danube was crucial in the eventual victory of Wagram. (Print after F. de Myrbach)*

◄ *Below left:*
The defence of the granary at Essling, one of the great epics of the 1809 campaign, French infantry repelling the Austrian attackers. Illustrated here are 'German' grenadiers wearing the distinctive Austrian grenadier-cap, nicknamed 'fauteuil' (armchair) by the French (from its shape); the officer (mid-ground, centre), wears the dark grey Oberrock *popular with Austrian officers on campaign, (Print after F. de Myrbach)*

▼ *The Battle of Wagram, 5/6 July 1809. Following the desperate fight at Aspern-Essling (21/22 May) in which the difficulties of crossing the Danube prevented Napoleon from adequately reinforcing his bridgehead, the Wagram operation was planned much more carefully, so that the Austrian attacks were unsuccessful.*

(19–20 April), the left wing of which he pursued with his main body, though these Austrian forces under General Johann Hiller managed to escape encirclement in the battle of Landeshut (21 April). Napoleon then switched his attention to the Austrian wing commanded by the Archduke Charles, which was being held temporarily by Marshal Davoût. On 22 April Charles attacked Davoût's greatly outnumbered command at Eckmühl, but Napoleon's arrival won the day for the French, though no attempt at pursuit was possible due to the exhaustion of the French forces after so much counter-marching and three battles in as many days. Charles covered his retreat by defending the city of Ratisbon, which fell to a French attack on 23 April. On 13 May Napoleon occupied Vienna without encountering any resistance.

Charles marshalled his forces on the far bank of the Danube, which Napoleon crossed at the island of Lobau, establishing a bridgehead in the villages of Aspern and Essling. In two days of the most severe fighting (21–22 May), though he succeeded in holding his ground, reinforcement over the narrow bridge was impossible and Napoleon was forced to evacuate his troops back to the south bank of the Danube; insufficient preparation and sterling work by the Austrian army had brought about Napoleon's first real

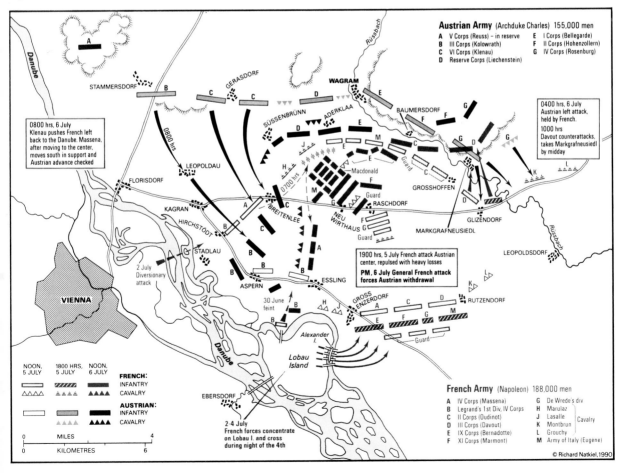

defeat. He now made more careful plans so as not to repeat his error; meanwhile, Archduke John had evacuated Italy, pursued by Eugène, who defeated the Austrians at Raab (16 June) and then moved to reinforce Napoleon. On the night of 4/5 July Napleon again crossed the Danube in force, this time without opposition, and determined to defeat Charles before Archduke John's contingent could arrive. In two days of heavy fighting at Wagram (5-6 July) Charles' attempt to cut off Napoleon from his bridgehead failed, and when the Austrian centre was split he quit the field, having suffered a heavy defeat. The situation was now hopeless; the capital was occupied, the field army mauled, and Russia had not joined the coalition, so Austria sued for peace (10 July), which was concluded by the Treaty of Schönbrunn (14 October). Austria ceded vast tracts of her territory to Napoleon and agreed to join his 'Continental System' aimed at strangling British commerce; in effect, Napoleon was now master of mainland Europe. The revolt in the Tyrol was finally suppressed by February 1810.

Britain against Napoleon

Although Britain's military efforts in continental Europe were limited until the outbreak of the Peninsular War, her efforts overseas were unceasing against French commerce and colonies. Cape Colony, first captured from the Dutch in 1795 but relinquished at the Peace of Amiens, was

The Archduke Charles criticized the Austrian troops for the defeat of 1809, whereas many of the failings were in the central command; in this order of the day he threatens dire and archaic consequences:

'Several regiments marched forward too soon, and began to fire without command. They were besides so crowded together that they galled each other with their fire. The officers were not able to rally the large bodies, which fled in disorder, and thus the ground was lost. The confused cry, which was heard among the troops, drowned the voice of the commanding officer . . . In every regiment which shall hereafter conduct itself in a similar manner, the tenth man shall be condemned to die, and the rest distributed among other regiments. The commanding officers shall be cashiered, and all other officers dismissed. Cries of alarm among the troops shall be punished with death.'

(Order of 7 July 1809; in *Relation of the Operations and Battles of the Austrian and French Armies in the Year 1809*, W. Müller, London 1810, p. 97.)

Among the most bitter combat of the period was the street-fighting at Saragossa; here, Spanish partisans defend a church against the French attackers. (Print after Jules Girardet)

recaptured in January 1806, after which the British forces, at the instigation of Admiral Sir Home Popham, went on an unauthorized foray to 'liberate' the Spanish colonies of south America. Faced with a *fait accompli* by the occupation of Buenos Ayres in June 1806, the British government supported the occupation and captured Montevideo in July 1807, but when General Whitelocke completely mishandled the expedition the Spanish colonists forced the British troops to surrender; they returned home and the whole, sorry South American venture ended.

Elsewhere, British efforts were more productive. Admiral Duckworth destroyed a French squadron off San Domingo (6 February 1806); Martinique and San Domingo were captured by an Anglo-Spanish expedition (June 1809), and Mauritius and Réunion were taken in December 1810. French attempts to occupy Sicily were repulsed with ease, and in mid-1806 Sir John Stuart raided Calabria, culminating with the defeat of General Reynier's French army at Maida (4 July). During a brief period of conflict with the Ottoman Empire, a second expedition to Egypt (1807) brought no tangible results, but the expedition to Copenhagen in the same year was a complete success. Instigated to prevent the powerful Danish fleet from falling into Napoleon's hands, the affair was ill-managed diplomatically (for until the British landed the Danes were more inclined to fight against Napoleon than on his side), but when hostilities commenced Copenhagen was bombarded, the Danes were beaten at Kjöge by Sir Arthur Wellesley (recently returned from his triumphs in India) and the Danish fleet was captured. Other operations were confined to naval raids against the French, most notably Thomas Cochrane's attack on the French anchorage at Basque Roads (11–12 April 1809), which was less than a total success due to the over-caution of Cochrane's superior, Admiral Gambier.

The Peninsular War

The Peninsular War (1807–14) provided the scene for Britain's major military contribution in the war against Napoleon, and exerted a continual drain upon French resources and morale, the 'Spanish ulcer' as Napoleon termed it, which eventually had the greatest effect upon the campaigns in central Europe. It originated from Napoleon's desire to extend the 'Continental System' (his embargo on British trade) throughout Europe; for after Tilsit, excepting the smuggling which was so rife as to wreck the entire scheme, only Portugal remained an open market for British imports. Napoleon determined to plug the gap by invading Portugal via Spain, and simultaneously to extend his grip to the whole of the Iberian Peninsula. (In the event, the Continental System was a total failure; whereas the British 'war of commerce' against France was a most spectacular success).

Sergeant Patrick Masterson of the 87th (Prince of Wales's Irish) Regiment capturing the 'Eagle' of the French 87th Line at Barossa, from its bearer Sous-Lieutenant *Edmé Guillemin. This first British capture of an 'Eagle' in combat was the subject of at least three popular prints; this was published four years after the event. Although it depicts the British uniform accurately (note the regimental number on the canteen) it shows the French incorrectly in the 1812 uniform, a common failing of prints of the era. (Print by Clark & Dubourg)*

Sir John Moore is borne away after receiving his mortal wound at Corunna; an illustration which while not inaccurate in setting, depicts the 1812 uniform of the British infantry and artillery, an example of the hazards of relying upon post-contemporary artwork. (Print after A. Dupray)

▼ Fuentes de Oñoro: a British square repels an attack by French hussars. (Print after A. Dupray)

▶ The Peninsular War, 1807–14, showing the main French offensives and Wellington's advances.

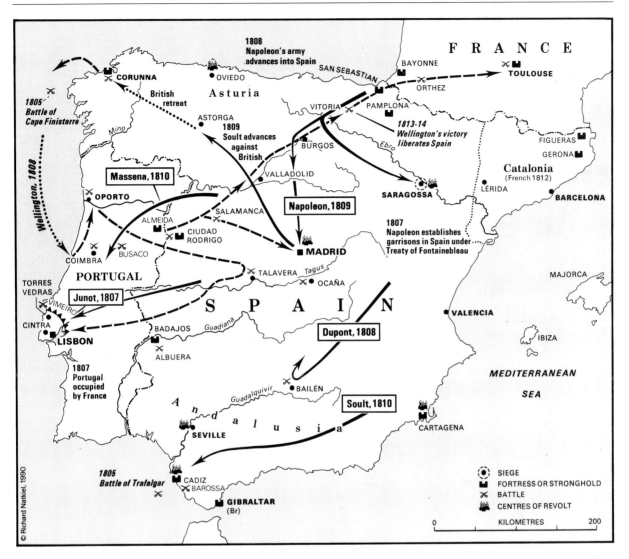

In November–December 1807 General Andoche Junot led a French army through Spain and into Portugal; Lisbon was occupied (1 December) and the Portuguese royal family fled to their Brazilian colony, leaving the government in the hands of a Council of Regency which appealed to Britain for assistance. In March 1808 Murat led a massive French army into Spain; the ineffectual King Charles IV and his equally inept son Ferdinard were compelled to renounce the throne and were taken as virtual prisoners to France, and Napoleon's brother Joseph was 'elected' as the new king of Spain by the Bonapartist faction. In May insurrections against the French occupation began, the genesis of the guerrilla war which was to be waged until 1814, characterized by the most hideous brutality on both sides but which restored the pride of the Spanish nation, their regular military forces being largely ineffective. In June–August 1808 the Spanish population of Saragossa successfully resisted a French attempt to capture the city, and on 19 July

the Spanish achieved their one real success of the war when General Pierre Dupont's French army surrendered at Baylen, the survivors of the resulting massacre being consigned to rot in prison-hulks. Junot was thus isolated in Portugal, where on 1 August 1808 a British expedition landed, temporarily commanded by Sir Arthur Wellesley. He defeated the French at Roliça (17 August) and Vimeiro (21 August) before his old and inept superiors arrived, Hew Dalrymple and Harry Burrard. These two foolishly arranged the Convention of Cintra by which Junot's troops were sent home in British ships; this was greeted with such outrage in Britain that all three generals were called to face a court of inquiry, by which only Wellesley was exonerated.

In the meantime, Sir John Moore had taken command of an increased British army in Portugal, and agreed to collaborate with the Spanish. He advanced into the interior of Spain but, misled by the untrustworthy Spaniards, found himself alone against vast French forces commanded by

Busaco: this illustration encapsulates the tactics adopted by the British as a counter to the French charge: a fusillade from the two-deep line, followed by a bayonet-charge to shatter both the formation and the morale of the advancing French columns. (Print after Major T. S. St. Clair, showing the precipitous nature of the terrain, taken from drawings made on the spot)

Spanish guerrilla officers (centre) conversing with Marshal Beresford (mounted, plain frock-coat, centre) at the Battle of Orthes. By this late stage of the Peninsular War some guerrillas had adopted conventional uniforms. (Print by T. Sutherland after William Heath)

Napoleon, who had arrived to take personal command of the operations. Madrid fell to the French on 4 December and Moore had to endure a retreat of terrible privation to Corunna and Vigo, which attracted the French attention and thus prevented them from crushing completely the Spanish forces. With the war apparently almost over, Napoleon left for Paris and the coming war against Austria on 1 January 1809, leaving Soult to finish the destruction of Moore. In the event, Moore's army turned at bay at Corunna and defeated Soult on 16 January (when Moore was killed), and was then evacuated by sea. On 20 February Saragossa finally fell, after a second, most harrowing siege.

Despite the withdrawal of Moore, British command of the sea gave a secure base of operations at Lisbon to which supplies could be landed from Britain, and Wellesley returned to command the British army in Portugal, eventually greatly assisted by the Portuguese army, reorganized under British command by Marshal William Beresford. In spring 1809 Soult invaded Portugal, but was driven away when Wellesley crossed the Douro and defeated the French at Oporto (12 May); Wellesley then advanced into Spain to collaborate with the Spanish. They, and particularly their old General Gregorio de la Cuesta, proved unreliable allies from the beginning; when the Allied armies were attacked by Marshal Victor and Joseph Bonaparte at Talavera (28 July 1809), the Spanish stood by and let Wellesley defeat the French unaided in a most desperate

fight. As co-operation with the Spanish was clearly impossible, Wellesley retired to Portugal; henceforth he was known by the title granted him as a reward, Wellington, which he carried through successive elevations in the peerage until he became Duke in 1814. Very soon Wellington's Anglo-Portuguese army was the only one capable of taking the field against the French; Cuesta's successor, General Areizago, was crushed at Ocaña by Soult and Joseph (19 November 1809), and what remained of the Spanish armies concentrated on the defence of the new capital of free Spain, Cadiz. Knowing that it was impossible to hold all Portugal, Wellington ordered the construction of a double line of impenetrable fortifications to cut off the Lisbon peninsula, the 'Lines of Torres Vedras'.

In early 1810 there were two main French armies on the frontier of Portugal, Marshal André Massena's Army of Portugal, and Soult's Army of Andalusia, though personal animosity throughout the French command prevented effective collaboration. In July 1810 Massena invaded Portugal; Wellington defeated him at Busaco (27 September) and withdrew behind the Lines of Torres Vedras. Massena sat outside and starved throughout the winter of 1810–11 before limping away with his ravaged army. No more success was enjoyed by the French attempt to capture Cadiz, Sir Thomas Graham's small British army winning a notable victory at Barrosa (5 March 1811). The strategic situation changed little in 1811; Massena fought an

▶ *The Battle of Salamanca, 22 July 1812.*

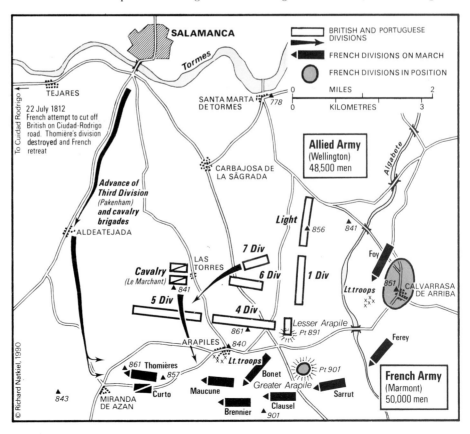

almost drawn battle at Fuentes de Oñoro (5 May), Wellington emerging just the victor; and in the south on 16 May 1811 Soult engaged Marshal Beresford's Allied–Spanish army at Albuera in an attempt to relieve the French garrison of the border fortress of Badajoz. The action was one of utter butchery, only the steadfast conduct of the British infantry saving the day, but the French still held the gateways to Spain at the end of the year. They enjoyed more success in southern Spain, where Marshal Louis Suchet captured Tarragona (28 July) and Valencia (9 January 1812), defeating a mixture of Spanish regulars and guerrilla/militia formations.

In January 1812 Wellington switched to the offensive, capturing the border fortresses of Ciudad Rodrigo (19 January) and Badajoz (19 April) in bloody assaults, the British troops embarking on an appalling orgy of ransack and rapine after the capture of the latter; advancing into Spain, Wellington defeated Marshal Auguste Marmont (who had replaced Massena) at Salamanca on 22 July. Madrid was occupied briefly in August 1812, but when

Wellington's attempt to take Burgos failed for lack of an adequate siege-train, he was forced to withdraw to Portugal. Despite this unfortunate end to a successful year, the Peninsular War was already turned irreversibly against the French; in 1813 Wellington again took the offensive and annihilated Joseph Bonaparte's combined French army at Vittoria (21 June). With Suchet harassed by a somewhat ineffectual British landing on the eastern Spanish seaboard, Soult took command of the remaining French forces in Spain (now unified into one army) and attempted to defend the southern French frontier; but Wellington forced the passes of the Pyrenees in a series of hard-fought actions, captured the border fortresses of San Sebastian (31 August) and Pampelona, and debouched on the French side of the border. Soult was forced back at Orthez (27 February 1814), Bordeaux was captured and the final defeat was inflicted on Soult at Toulouse (10 April 1814), ironically fought after Napoleon's abdication, news of which had not yet reached southern France. The Peninsular War not only proved an insupportable drain upon French resources, it also demonstrated the

◄ *Campo Mayor (25 March 1811): single combat between Corporal Logan of the British 13th Light Dragoons and the French Colonel Chamorin of the 26th Dragoons, the latter being slain in the encounter. In this print after Denis Dighton, Logan is shown erroneously in the 1812 light dragoon uniform instead of the braided dolman and Tarleton worn at the time.*

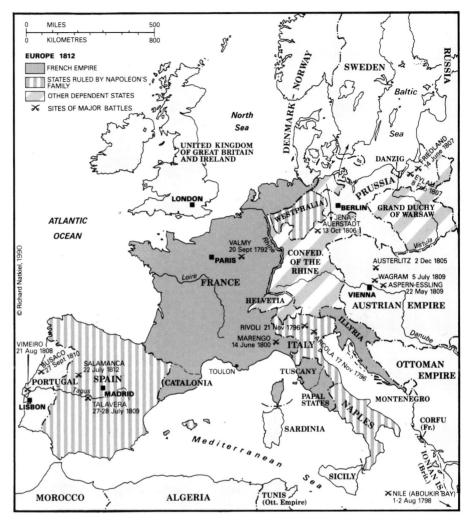

Europe in 1812, showing the sites of major battles up to the end of that year. The French Empire extends into the Netherlands and Italy, but note that although nominally under Joseph Bonaparte's control, Spain was never fully subjugated.

military genius of one of the greatest commanders in history, Wellington, who was personally responsible for the British success; no other commander of the era, save Napoleon himself, was so effective in moulding and commanding his army.

The Russian Campaign

The Franco-Russian alliance after Tilsit had always been uncomfortable, and the Tsar gradually turned away from Napoleon and towards Britain, finally renouncing the 'Continental System'. Napoleon responded by assembling a *Grande Armée* of mammoth proportions, probably half a million strong, drawn from every allied or satellite state of the Empire, and including an Austrian reserve corps unwillingly pressed into service. In response, Russia assembled two main armies under Generals Barclay de Tolly and Bagration along the border, but they were unable to prevent Napoleon crossing the River Niemen on 24 June 1812. The Russian armies fell back and united at Smolensk (3 August), Barclay assuming overall command. Napoleon

As the British army marched into Valenciennes, J. F. Neville spoke to the Abbé Parisis, who:

'... very politely requested me to point out to him the British Prince, to whose gallantry and perseverance, he, like many other emigrants, was indebted for the liberty of returning among his relatives. As His Royal Highness was passing under the grateful shade of his laurels, I informed the Priest, that the son of my King was at the head of the troops. He looked with astonishment at, perhaps, the most martial figure he ever saw, and, at last, turning round to one of his countrymen, exclaimed ... "Good Lord! what a fine man! what a pity that he is destined for hell fire!"' (Neville notes that this priest 'was afterwards a pensioner on the eleemosynary bounty of Englishmen'.)

(*Leisure Moments in the Camp and in the Guard-Room*, J. F. Neville, alias 'A Veteran British Officer', York 1812, pp. 24–5.)

attempted to outflank them, but despite engagements at Smolensk (17 August, when the French stormed the city) and Valutino (19 August) the Russians continued to withdraw. At this juncture the Tsar was compelled to appoint to overall command the old general Mikhail Kutuzov, a wily and experienced campaigner. He attempted to defend Moscow by engaging Napoleon at Borodino ('the battle of the Moskowa' to the French) on 7 September, 60 miles west of Moscow, an action in which Napoleon showed little imagination (the first symptom of lethargy which was to plague his later campaigns), mounting a simple frontal attack. In some of the most sustained carnage of the age, the armies battered each other to exhaustion; Bagration was mortally wounded. Kutuzov continued to withdraw, and Napoleon occupied Moscow on 14 September. Almost immediately Russian incendiaries burned down much of the city; yet though it was thus devastated and despite the approach of winter, Napoleon remained in Moscow for more than a month, expecting the Tsar to sue for peace. No such approach was made, and when Napoleon finally decided to retire on Smolensk (19 October) it was already too late.

The retreat from Moscow has become a byword for misery, privation and slaughter, as the *Grande Armée* was hounded into extinction by a combination of marauding

The 18th Bulletin of the *Grande Armée* (Mojaisk, 10 September 1812) records a typical example of Napoleonic rhetoric, on the morning of Borodino:

'On the 7th, at two in the morning, the emperor was surrounded by the marshals in the position taken the evening before. At half past five o'clock the sun rose without clouds; it had rained the preceding evening. "This is the sun of Austerlitz," said the emperor. Though but the month of September, it was as cold as a December in Moravia. The army received the omen; the drum beat, and the following order of the day was read: "Soldiers! behold the field of battle you have so much desired! henceforth victory depends on you; it is necessary to us; it will give us plenty, good quarters for the winter, and a speedy return to your country. Behave yourselves as you did at Austerlitz, at Friedland, at Witepsk, and at Smolensko; and that the latest posterity may speak of your conduct this day with pride, that it may say of you, 'He was at that great battle under the walls of Moscow'." The army answered with reiterated acclamations. The ground on which the army stood was spread with the dead bodies of the Russians killed the preceding day.'

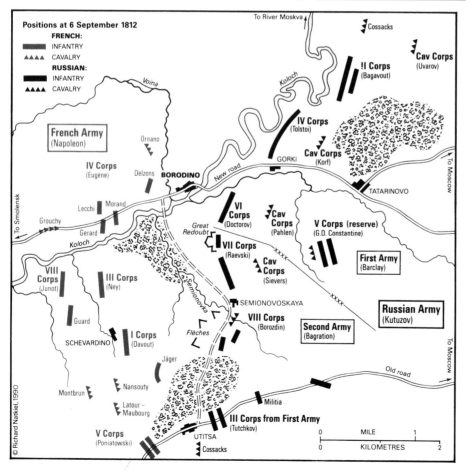

Disposition of the armies before the commencement of the Battle of Borodino, Napoleon having captured the Schevardino redoubt on 5 September 1812. The Russian position was anchored on the villages of Semionovskaya and Borodino, and strengthened by the Great or Raevski redoubt and the Flèches. Napoleon's refusal to commit his reserve was crucial in the battle of 7 September.

Retreat from Moscow: the mob of stragglers into which the Grande Armée *had degenerated attempts to cross the Berezina, the ramshackle bridges giving way under their weight. (Print after F. de Myrbach)*

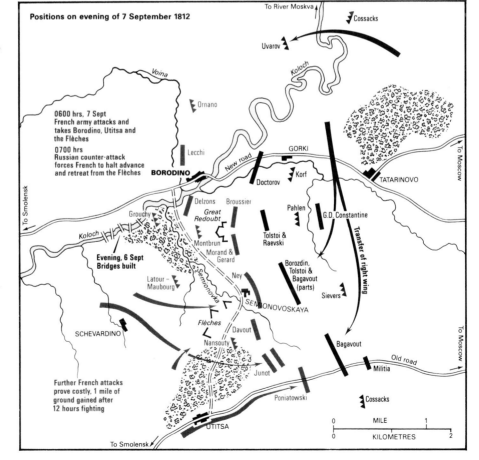

Positions on evening of 7 September 1812

To River Moskva

Cossacks

Uvarov

Voina

Koloch

Ornano

0600 hrs, 7 Sept
French army attacks and takes Borodino, Utitsa and the Flèches

0700 hrs
Russian counter-attack forces French to halt advance and retreat from the Flèches

Lecchi

New road

GORKI

To Moscow

Korf

TATARINOVO

BORODINO

Doctorov

To Smolensk

Delzons   Broussier

Pahlen

Koloch

Grouchy

Great Redoubt

G.D. Constantine

Montbrun

Tolstoi & Raevski

Evening, 6 Sept Bridges built

Morand & Gerard

Borozdin, Tolstoi & Bagavout (parts)

Transfer of right wing

Latour – Maubourg

Semionovka

Ney

Sievers

SEMIONOVOSKAYA

SCHEVARDINO

Flèches   Davout

Bagavout

To Moscow

Old road

Nansouty

Militia

Further French attacks prove costly, 1 mile of ground gained after 12 hours fighting

Junot

Cossacks

Poniatowski

| 0 | | MILE | | 1 |
| 0 | | KILOMETRES | | 2 |

UTITSA

To Smolensk

Positions of the armies at the end of the Battle of Borodino, 7 September 1812. Napoleon did little more than mount a sustained frontal assault throughout the day, and although the Russian strongpoints were captured in an action of unprecedented bloodshed, despite their huge losses the Russians were still able to conduct an orderly withdrawal.

Colonel Raymond de Montesquiou, Duc de Fezensac, took command of the French 4th Line after its colonel, Massy, had been killed at Borodino, and watched it desintegrate during the retreat from Moscow:

'Amongst these calamities, the annihilation of my regiment was a source of the greatest grief to me. It had become my most severe, and, I may be allowed to say, my only suffering; for I considered hunger, cold, and fatigue as very secondary evils. As long as the health is proof against these physical ills, courage will soon lead us to despise them, particularly when that courage is sustained by the idea of God, by the hope of eternal life. But I will admit that courage itself abandoned me, on seeing daily fall before my eyes those friends, and companions in arms, so justly designated as the Colonel's family, but which it seemed as if I was reserved only to command that I might preside at their destruction. Nothing attaches men more to each other than a community in misfortune, and I invariably found the warm feeling which I entertained for my men reciprocated by them. Neither officer nor soldier was ever in possession of a bit of bread without coming to share it with me. And this reciprocity was not peculiar to my own regiment. It existed throughout the army, an army in which the authority resembled that of a father's; a subordination which resulted from confidence and attachment towards those by whom it was commanded.'

(*Journal of the Russian Campaign*, Duc de Fezensac, with intro. by W. Knollys, London 1852, pp. 150–2.)

Matvei Ivanovich Platov (1751–1818), semi-legendary hero and Hetman of the Don Cossacks, a leading commander in the 1812 campaign and a man idolized in the other Allied states, to such an extent that the 'Platov cap' became a leading ladies' fashion in England in 1813!

The retreat from Moscow: Marshal Ney (centre) leads the rearguard of the Grande Armée. (Print after Yvon)

Cossacks, the collapse of the army's morale and the rigours of the oncoming winter, bringing snow and freezing temperatures. On 24 October Eugène's part of the *Grande Armée* was mauled at Maloyaroslavets, and by the time Smolensk was reached much of the army was a straggling mass of fugitives. At Krasnyi (16–17 November) Kutuzov cut off part of the army; Napoleon retraced his steps and dragged it free, but the retreat stumbled on, to the River Berezina. This was crossed on 26–28 November on two ramshackle bridges, with the few formed elements of the *Grande Armée* desperately holding off the constant Russian

attacks. Thousands were left on the Russian bank when the bridges collapsed, to be massacred by the Cossacks. The survivors staggered to the Niemen, where the Russian pursuit halted; to all practical purposes, the *Grande Armée* was totally annihilated. Napoleon left for Paris on 8 December, to raise a new army.

The War of Liberation

The destruction of Napoleon's army marked the beginning of the end of his Empire. The Sixth Coalition had been formed in June 1812, between Britain, Russia, Spain and Portugal,

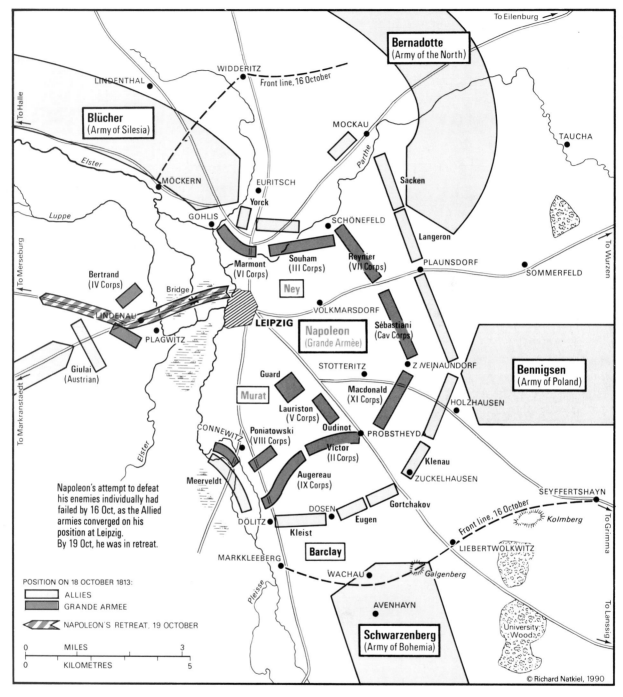

To Eilenburg

Bernadotte
(Army of the North)

WIDDERITZ

Front line, 16 October

LINDENTHAL

To Halle

Blücher
(Army of Silesia)

Elster

Luppe

MÖCKERN

EURITSCH

Yorck

GOHLIS

MOCKAU

Parthe

Sacken

SCHÖNEFELD

Langeron

TAUCHA

To Wurzen

Marmont
(VI Corps)

Souham
(III Corps)

Reynier
(VII Corps)

PLAUNSDORF

SOMMERFELD

Ney

To Merseburg

Bertrand
(IV Corps)

Bridge

LINDENAU

PLAGWITZ

LEIPZIG

VOLKMARSDORF

Napoleon
(Grande Armèe)

Sébastiani
(Cav Corps)

Z VEINAUNDORF

Bennigsen
(Army of Poland)

Giulai
(Austrian)

Elster

To Markranstaedt

Murat

STOTTERITZ

Guard

Macdonald
(XI Corps)

HOLZHAUSEN

Lauriston
(V Corps)

Poniatowski
(VIII Corps)

CONNEWITZ

Oudinot

Victor
(II Corps)

PROBSTHEYDA

Klenau

ZUCKELHAUSEN

SEYFFERTSHAYN

Meerveldt

Augereau
(IX Corps)

*Napoleon's attempt to defeat
his enemies individually had
failed by 16 Oct, as the Allied
armies converged on his
position at Leipzig.
By 19 Oct, he was in retreat.*

DOSEN

Gortchakov

Front line, 16 October

Kolmberg

To Grimma

DÖLITZ

Eugen

Kleist

Barclay

LIEBERTWOLKWITZ

POSITION ON 18 OCTOBER 1813:

☐ ALLIES

■ GRANDE ARMEE

◀◀◀ NAPOLEON'S RETREAT, 19 OCTOBER

MARKKLEEBERG

WACHAU

Galgenberg

To Lanssig

University
Wood

Pleisse

0   MILES   3

0   KILOMETRES   5

AVENHAYN

Schwarzenberg
(Army of Bohemia)

© Richard Natkiel, 1990

*The Battle of Leipzig, 16/18
October 1813, styled 'the Battle
of the Nations' from the multi-
national force attempting to*

*trap Napoleon in his defensive
perimeter around Leipzig, an
envelopment from which he
escaped with difficulty.*

▶ *Leipzig: French infantry (left)
attempt to hold a barricade to
enable the army to escape, while
Prussian* Landwehr *attempt to
break through (right); the latter*

wear the usual litewka *and soft
cloth cap bearing the
'Landwehr cross'. (Print after
F. de Myrbach)*

and now other states joined the fight. The Prussian contingent of the *Grande Armée* – unwilling allies at best – collaborated with the Russians in the Convention of Tauroggen (30 December 1812) by which they became neutral, only a short step from joining the Coalition, which Frederick William III was prevailed upon to do on 27 February 1813 by the Convention of Kalisch. The Austrian 'Reserve Corps' had carefully remained unengaged in the 1812 campaign, retreating into Bohemia, and Austria also joined the Coalition, followed by Sweden and an increasing number of German states as the Confederation of the Rhine fell apart.

By spring 1813 Napoleon had gathered a new army and returned to Germany, intending to defeat his enemies in detail, and at times in the next twelve months showed flashes of his old genius. He captured Dresden (7–8 May) and defeated the Russian general Wittgenstein at Lützen (2 May) and Bautzen (20–21 May), and from 4 June to 16 August Napoleon negotiated an armistice to allow him to train his young army; but in this period the Allies gathered in increasing strength. When Austria declared war officially on 12 August Napoleon faced three armies: that of Bohemia, commanded by the Austrian Karl Schwarzenberg; of Silesia, under Wittgenstein's replacement, the old Prussian Blücher; and of the North, under Bernadotte. The Allies planned to defeat Napoleon's subordinates in detail; Bernadotte beat Oudinot at Grossbeeren (23 August) and Blücher beat Macdonald at the Katzbach (26 August), but Napoleon succeeding in defeating Schwarzenberg at Dresden (26–27 August), then allowed the Austrians to escape by one of his bouts of lethargy. When General Vandamme tried to cut off Schwarzenberg's retreat he was unsupported and his corps was wiped out at Kulm (29–30 August).

French fortunes worsened rapidly; Napoleon was unable to bring the Army of Silesia to battle, but Bernadotte defeated Ney (Oudinot's successor) at Dennewitz (6 September), and on 8 October Bavaria changed sides by withdrawing from the Confederation of the Rhine, the defection of Napoleon's most important German ally. The Allied forces closed in around Napoleon, and for three days (16–19 October) the French attempted to hold a defensive perimeter around Leipzig, assailed by Blücher, Schwarzenberg and finally Bernadotte. This 'Battle of the Nations' was the decisive blow in the campaign; for though the French army managed to escape complete encirclement, Leipzig was a defeat of crushing proportions, and resulted in the loss of Napoleon's last allies: the Saxons changed sides during the battle. As Napoleon retired towards the Rhine, the Bavarian army of General von Wrede attempted to cut his path of

retreat at Hanau (30–31 October), but Napoleon defeated his recent ally and cut his way across the Rhine in early November. The 'war of liberation' of the 'occupied' German territory had succeeded in evicting the French; and now the territorial integrity of France was threatened for the first time in almost twenty years.

'The Campaign of 1814', a picture of Napoleon at the head of a weary staff, which is often mis-interpreted as representing the retreat from Moscow. It is perhaps the most famous of all Meissonier's splendid work.

The Invasion of France

Napoleon rejected an offer of peace which would have restricted France's boundaries to the Rhine and the Alps, but elected to fight on in circumstances which could only be described as hopeless, perhaps deluded into a belief in his own invincibility; yet the 1814 campaign demonstrated that his old skill and vigour had not entirely deserted him. Though Napoleon's forces were numerically impressive, a large proportion was employed in the vain attempt to hold the Pyrenees against Wellington, in Italy or besieged in German garrisons; those capable of defending France included a large proportion of young or newly raised units,

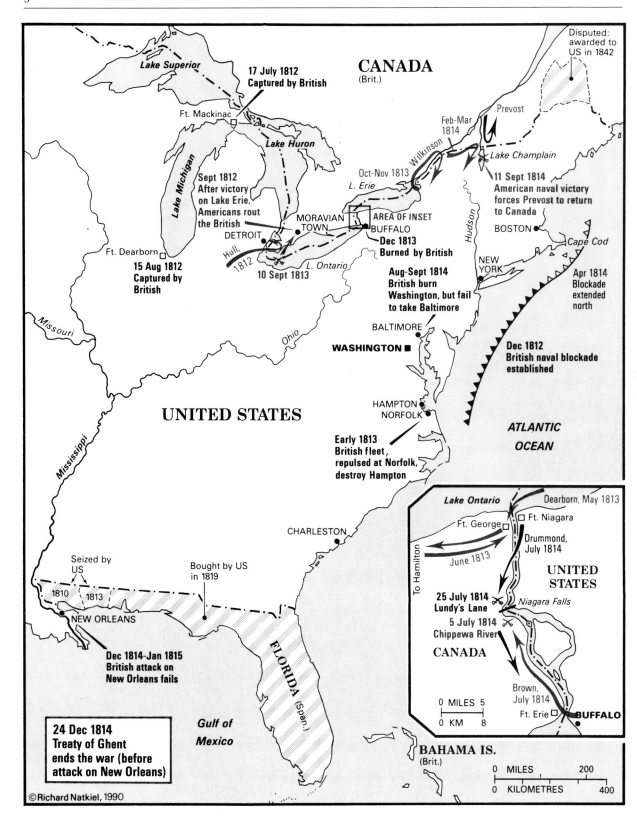

Disputed: awarded to US in 1842

CANADA
(Brit.)

Lake Superior

17 July 1812 Captured by British

Ft. Mackinac

Lake Huron

Feb-Mar 1814

Prevost

Lake Champlain

11 Sept 1814 American naval victory forces Prevost to return to Canada

Wilkinson

Oct-Nov 1813

L. Erie

AREA OF INSET

BOSTON

Cape Cod

Lake Michigan

Sept 1812 After victory on Lake Erie, Americans rout the British

MORAVIAN TOWN

BUFFALO

Dec 1813 Burned by British

Hudson

NEW YORK

DETROIT

Hull, 1812

Ft. Dearborn

15 Aug 1812 Captured by British

L. Ontario

10 Sept 1813

Aug-Sept 1814 British burn Washington, but fail to take Baltimore

Apr 1814 Blockade extended north

Missouri

Ohio

BALTIMORE

WASHINGTON ■

Dec 1812 British naval blockade established

UNITED STATES

HAMPTON
NORFOLK

Early 1813 British fleet, repulsed at Norfolk, destroy Hampton

ATLANTIC OCEAN

Mississippi

CHARLESTON

Seized by US

1810   1813

Bought by US in 1819

NEW ORLEANS

Dec 1814-Jan 1815 British attack on New Orleans fails

FLORIDA (Span.)

Gulf of Mexico

24 Dec 1814 Treaty of Ghent ends the war (before attack on New Orleans)

©Richard Natkiel, 1990

INSET:

Lake Ontario

Dearborn, May 1813

Ft. George

Ft. Niagara

Drummond, July 1814

June 1813

To Hamilton

UNITED STATES

25 July 1814 Lundy's Lane

Niagara Falls

5 July 1814 Chippewa River

CANADA

Brown, July 1814

0 MILES 5
0 KM 8

Ft. Erie

BUFFALO

BAHAMA IS.
(Brit.)

0 MILES 200
0 KILOMETRES 400

which had to resist three Allied armies intent on converging on Paris: Schwarzenberg from Switzerland, Bernadotte from the Netherlands and Blücher into Lorraine. Napoleon performed prodigies in his attempts to prevent the unification of the Allied armies, defeating isolated corps in detail in a number of impressive victories, inflicting defeats on Blücher at Brienne (29 January), La Rothière (30 January), Champaubert (10 February), Montmirail (11 February), Château-Thierry (12 February) and Vauchamps (14 February) which temporarily threw back the Army of Silesia. Napoleon then turned against the threat from Schwarzenberg and defeated him at Montereau (18 February) before switching back again against Blücher who had approached within 25 miles of Paris. Blücher was again repelled at Craonne (7 March), but in Napoleon's absence Schwarzenberg had defeated Macdonald at Bar-sur-Aube (27 February); no matter how skilfully Napoleon managed his own forces, his enemies were simply too numerous and his subordinates unable to sustain Napoleon's habit of victory. A desperate attack on Blücher (who had been reinforced by Bernadotte, vastly outnumbering Napoleon) failed at Laon (9–10 March), but Napoleon mauled one of Blücher's corps at Rheims (13 March) before desperately striking at Schwarzenberg, only to be repulsed at Arcis-sur-Aube (20–21 March). On 25 March Schwarzenberg defeated the corps of Mortier and Marmont at La Fère-Champenoise, and joined Blücher near Paris three days later. Before Napoleon could act in their support, a vain attempt to defend Paris failed; with fighting reaching Montmartre, Marmont surrendered his command and Paris was occupied (31

March). When his marshals finally turned against him, Napoleon abdicated in favour of his son on 6 April, but when this was rejected by the Allies his surrender was unconditional (11 April); he was assigned the tiny island of Elba as his new 'kingdom' and Louis XVIII was installed as King of France. The Treaty of Paris (30 May) restored France to her 1792 boundaries.

The War of 1812

Although the Anglo-American 'War of 1812' was not officially part of the Napoleonic conflict, it is often considered as such due to its origin as an American reaction to what was seen as British provocation in the interruption of American commerce in support of the 'Orders in Council' (British trade sanctions against Napoleon, replying to his 'Continental System') and other frictions such as the impressment of seamen from American ships into the Royal Navy. The American wish to protect the freedom of the high seas was also a convenient excuse for those in the US administration who wished to take the opportunity of Britain's preoccupation with the war against France to conquer Canada.

The United States declared war on 19 June 1812, and almost immediately planned an offensive against Canada, which was held by only the thinnest of British garrisons

◄ *Opposite page: North America during the War of 1812, showing the major offensives.*

Log-built blockhouses were a feature of campaigning in the War of 1812; this typical example was at La Colle Mill, scene of a sharp action.

Stephen Van Rensselaer, US commander at the Battle of Queenston.

(throughout the war, battles were fought with such small forces on either side that many would barely have rated as skirmishes in the European war). Britain struck first, capturing Fort Dearborn (now Chicago) on 15 August and Detroit on the following day. American attacks on Canada were repelled at Queenston (13 October), where the British commander Sir Isaac Brock was killed (having probably saved Canada by his prompt and skilled actions), and their expedition on Lake Champlain failed when the American militia insisted on their constitutional right not to be sent to Canada!

In September 1813 the Americans recaptured Detroit (29 September), following the defeat of the British naval squadron on Lake Erie (10 September), and won a further victory at the battle of the Thames (5 October). The year's other operations occurred to the north, where on 24 April US forces burned York (now Toronto), the capital of Upper Canada, and on 27 May captured Fort George, though the American forces were routed at Stony Creek (6 June). On 28–29 May the Americans repelled a British attack on Sacketts Harbor, but their planned attack on Montreal was defeated at the Chateauguay (25 October) and Chrysler's Farm (11 November), and the year ended with the British capture of Fort Niagara (18 December).

From 1814 large numbers of British reinforcements were dispatched from Europe, especially after the conclusion of the war against Napoleon. In the Niagara area, though the British suffered a check at the Chippewa (5 July), a successful battle at Lundy's Lane (25 June) and the siege of Fort Erie (where a sharp action occurred on 17 September) put an end to American plans for the invasion of Canada. In August–September, however, a British advance on Lake Champlain was checked at Plattsburg (11 September) and the British naval forces were beaten on the lake on the same day, and the proposed operations were carried no further. On the eastern seaboard of the United States a British force inflicted considerable damage, winning a victory at Bladensburg (24 August), after which Washington was captured and the public buildings burned (including the Capitol and the White House), though an attack on Baltimore was beaten off (12–14 September) in which the British commander, Major-General Robert Ross, was mortally wounded.

The remaining actions occurred in the south, where a British expedition was launched against New Orleans under the command of Wellington's brother-in-law and Peninsular divisional commander Sir Edward Pakenham. A force of American regulars and militia was assembled under General Andrew Jackson, the only American commander of any great skill to emerge during the war. Pakenham arrived on 13 December 1814 and on 8 January 1815 made a frontal attack on Jackson's fortified position in front of New Orleans; though the British troops displayed great courage, Jackson's entrenchment was of such strength that they were beaten off with severe casualties, and Pakenham was killed. A week later the British force withdrew; ironically, like Toulouse, New Orleans was an unnecessary battle, as peace had been signed at Ghent on 24 December, though news had not yet crossed the Atlantic.

Excluding the actions on the lakes (fought between squadrons of small ships, sloops and gunboats), the only naval combat in the War of 1812 were the single-ship 'frigate actions', in which the few American frigates (swifter and vastly better-armed than their British opponents) scored a number of remarkable victories over a navy which had until then enjoyed virtually unrelieved success. These defeats at the hands of the Americans caused much disquiet in Britain, but were redressed partly by the most famous single-ship action of the period, when on 1 June 1813 Captain Philip Broke of HMS *Shannon* defeated Captain James Lawrence of USS *Chesapeake* outside Boston, capturing the American frigate in a stunning display of disciplined gunnery; and partly by the British blockade of American ports, which virtually bankrupted that nation.

The Hundred Days

After brooding on Elba for almost a year, Napoleon made an audacious attempt to regain his throne in 1815, landing in southern France and advancing on Paris to ever-increasing acclaim as many of his marshals and virtually all the army rallied to him in preference to the vindictive and unpopular royalist regime. The Allied nations, then meeting at the

'The line remained steady': Sir
Charles Belson and his 28th
(North Gloucestershire)
Regiment at Quatre Bras. This
shows the usual formation of the
British two-deep line, the front
rank kneeling with bayonets at
the 'present' while the second
rank fires; it was unusual for
infantry to meet cavalry except
in a square, unless the
battalion's flanks were
completely secure. The 28th did
this at Quatre Bras, as they had
at Alexandria, when their rear-
rank faced-about to meet a
second charge, which led to the
regimental custom of wearing a
badge at the rear of the head-
dress as well as on the front.
This practice was established as
early as the incident depicted
(which portrays the unique
regimental 'stove-pipe' shako)
and is retained by the 28th's
successor, the Gloucestershire
Regiment. (Print after Captain
George Jones)

Congress of Vienna, declared him an outlaw (13 March) and
organized the Seventh Coalition to overthrow him a second
time. Their resources were immense, and Napoleon's only
realistic hope was to inflict upon them a sharp defeat to allow
him to negotiate from a position of strength; thus, he
determined to strike into the Netherlands at the only major
Allied forces within easy reach, before they could be
reinforced. Napoleon concentrated a powerful army near
Charleroi (14 June), entrusting to senior command the
Marshals Ney and Grouchy, neither of whom was particularly talented in the highest echelon of command; one of
Napoleon's greatest mistakes was to use Davoût and Soult in
basically administrative posts.

Two Allied armies were present in the Netherlands: a
Prussian force under Blücher and a hotchpotch Anglo-
Netherlands-German army under Wellington, the latter
relying to a great extent upon its nucleus of British troops. In
his usual way, Napoleon intended to interpose himself
between the two Allied armies and defeat them in detail; the
Allied commanders pledged mutual co-operation and it is
greatly to the credit of the Prussians that despite everything
they attempted to support Wellington as best they could.

On 16 June 1815, having taken the Allies by surprise by
the rapidity of his march, Napoleon sent Ney to capture the
crossroads of Quatre Bras (held by Wellington's forward
elements) while he fell upon Blücher at Ligny with the bulk
of his force. The operation was foiled by Ney's lack of success
in driving-in the Anglo-Allied detachment (which was
reinforced progressively throughout the day) and by the
corps of General d'Erlon which marched back and forth
between Ney and Napoleon and thus assisted neither; but
the Prussians were severely mauled at Ligny and limped off
the field in the direction of Wavre, to reorganize. Having
held Ney, Wellington made an orderly withdrawal from
Quatre Bras (17 June) to a previously reconnoitred defensive
position along the ridge of Mont St. Jean, a short distance
south of the village of Waterloo.

On 18 June, Napoleon prepared to attack Wellington with
the bulk of his army, having detached Grouchy to engage the
Prussians and prevent them from reinforcing Wellington;
but though Grouchy made some progress, the Prussians
hung on to their positions at Wavre, allowing considerable

The square in action: Lady
Butler's famous painting of the
28th Foot at Quatre Bras,
which portrays accurately the
corner of a 'square' (or oblong);
though she was incorrect in
showing the regiment wearing
the 1812 shako, whereas they
actually wore the earlier
'stovepipe' cap.

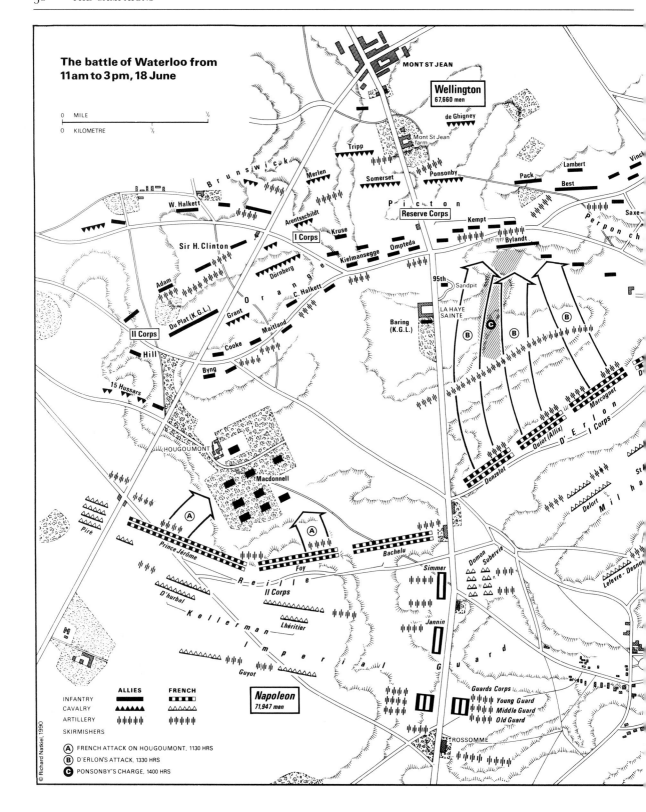

The battle of Waterloo from
11am to 3pm, 18 June

0   MILE   ½

0   KILOMETRE   ½

MONT ST JEAN

Wellington
67,660 men

de Ghigney

Mont St Jean
farm

Tripp

Merlen   Somerset   Ponsonby   Pack   Lambert   Vinc

Brunswick   P i c t o n   Saxe-

W. Halkett   Reserve Corps   Kempt   Per ponch

Arentsschildt   Best

I Corps   Kruse   Bylandt

Sir H. Clinton   Kielmansegge   Ompteda

Orange   Dornberg   95th   Sandpit

Adam   C. Halkett   LA HAYE   C

Du Plat (K.G.L.)   Grant   Baring   SAINTE   B   B

II Corps   Maitland   (K.G.L.)

Hill   Cooke   Donzelot

Byng   Ouiot (Allix)   Marcognet

15 Hussars   D _ E r l o n   I Corps

Piré   Delort   Mil

HOUGOUMONT   Donzelot

Macdonnell   A

A   Domon   Subervie

Prince Jérôme   Bachelu   Simmer

Foy   Jannin

R = e i l l e

II Corps   D'hurbal   Lhéritier   Guard

K e l l e r m a n

I m p e r i a l

Guyot   ROSSOMME

Guards Corps

Young Guard

Middle Guard

Old Guard

INFANTRY   ▼▼▼▼   ▬▬▬▬
                ALLIES   FRENCH
CAVALRY   ▲▲▲▲▲   △△△△△
ARTILLERY   ⅰⅰⅰⅰ   ⅰⅰⅰⅰ
SKIRMISHERS

Napoleon
71,947 men

Ⓐ FRENCH ATTACK ON HOUGOUMONT, 1130 HRS

Ⓑ D'ERLON'S ATTACK, 1330 HRS

Ⓒ PONSONBY'S CHARGE, 1400 HRS

© Richard Natkiel, 1990

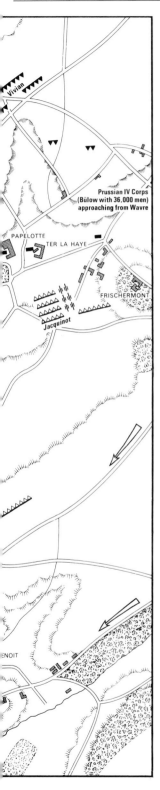

The Battle of Waterloo, 18 June 1815. As the day progressed and Napoleon's assaults failed to defeat Wellington, the arrival of the Prussians forced Napoleon to commit an increasing amount of resources into the defence of his right flank at Plancenoit.

forces to reinforce Wellington's left, though they were a long time in making their presence felt. In the meantime, Napoleon launched a succession of attacks upon Wellington's positions, to be repelled time and again by the stalwart Anglo-German troops; by mid-afternoon Prussian pressure was such that Napoleon had to form a defensive flank upon the village of Plancenoit at his right. After his forces exhausted themselves battering in vain against Wellington's line, and when the final attack of the Imperial Guard was repelled, the French army collapsed in disorder and was swept from the field by a united Allied advance. Although there were some minor skirmishes following the battle of Waterloo, it was the most decisive battle of the age, smashing Napoleon's power for ever. He abdicated on 21 June and, surrendering to the British, was exiled to the Atlantic island of St. Helena where he remained in isolation until his death on 5 May 1821. The Second Peace of Paris (20 November 1815) brought to a close almost a quarter of a century of conflict, restoring the *status quo* to what appeared to be superficially the situation of 1789; but the years of bloodshed and social upheaval had changed the face of Europe irrevocably.

The British Waterloo Medal, the first authorized for general distribution to all those present. Silver, with dark red ribbon with dark blue edges; this example named to John Clarke of the 3rd Battalion, 1st Foot Guards.

The Prussian campaign medal for 1815 (Waterloo and Ligny); bronze with yellow ribbon with black and white edges.

BATTLES OF THE REVOLUTIONARY AND NAPOLEONIC ERA

(In the following list, the names of commanders are sometimes those of the generals in overall command, rather than actual battlefield commanders)

Date	Action	Victors	Defeated
1792			
20 September	Valmy	French (Dumouriez/Kellermann)	Austro-Prussians (Brunswick)
6 November	Jemappes	French (Dumouriez)	Austrians (Albert of Saxe-Teschen)
1793			
18 March	Neerwinden	Austrians (Saxe-Coburg)	French (Dumouriez)
21–23 May	Valenciennes	Austrians (Saxe-Coburg)	French (Custine)
6 September	Hondschoote	French (Houchard)	Anglo-Hanoverians (York)
13 September	Menin	French (Houchard)	Netherlandish (Orange)
15–16 October	Wattignies	French (Jourdan)	Austrians (Saxe-Coburg)
28–30 November	Kaiserslautern	Prussians (Brunswick)	French (Hoche)
22 December	Fröschwiller	French (Hoche)	Prussians (Brunswick)
26 December	Geisberg	French (Hoche)	Austrians (Wurmser)
1794			
24 April	Villers-en-Cauchies (incorrectly, Villiers-en-Couche)	Anglo-Austrians (Ott)	French
18 May	Tourcoing	French (Souham)	Allies (Saxe-Coburg)
26 June	Fleurus	French (Jourdan)	Allies (Saxe-Coburg)
1795			
16–20 July	Quiberon	French (Hoche)	French royalists/British (Puisaye and d'Hervilly)
29 October	Mainz	Austrians (Clerfayt)	French (Pichegru)
24 November	Loano	French (Massena)	Austro-Piedmontese (Wallis)
1796			
Italian Front			
12 April	Montenotte	French (Bonaparte)	Austrians (Beaulieu)
14 April	Millesimo	French (Augereau)	Austro-Piedmontese (Provera)
14–15 April	Dego	French (Bonaparte)	Austrians (Beaulieu)
16–17 April	Ceva	Austro-Piedmontese (Colli)	French (Augereau)
21 April	Mondovi	French (Bonaparte)	Piedmontese (Colli)
8 May	Fombio	French (Bonaparte)	Austrians (Beaulieu)
10 May	Lodi	French (Bonaparte)	Austrians (Beaulieu)
30 May	Borghetto	French (Bonaparte)	Austrians (Beaulieu)
3 August	Lonato	French (Bonaparte)	Austrians (Quasdanovich)
5 August	Castiglione	French (Bonaparte)	Austrians (Wurmser)
4 September	Roveredo	French (Massena)	Austrians (Davidovich)
8 September	Bassano	French (Bonaparte)	Austrians (Wurmser)
12 November	Caldiero (1st battle)	Austrians (Alvintzy)	French (Bonaparte)
15–17 November	Arcola	French (Bonaparte)	Austrians (Alvintzy)
German Front			
16 June	Wetzlar	Austrians (Charles)	French (Jourdan)
9 July	Malsch	Inconclusive encounter between French (Moreau) and Austrians (Charles)	
24 August	Amberg	Austrians (Charles)	French (Jourdan)
24 August	Friedberg	French (Moreau)	Austrians (Latour)
3 September	Würzburg	Austrians (Charles)	French (Jourdan)

Date	Action	Victors	Defeated
1797			
Italian Front			
14 January	Rivoli	French (Bonaparte)	Austrians (Alvintzy)
23 March	Malborghetto	French (Massena)	Austrians (Charles)
German Front			
18 April	Neuweid (or Lahn)	French (Hoche)	Austrians (Werneck)
1798			
Ireland			
9 June	Arklow	British (Needham)	Irish insurgents
12 June	Vinegar Hill	British (Lake)	Irish insurgents
27 August	Castlebar	French (Humbert)	British (Lake)
5 September	Collooney	French (Humbert)	British (Vereker)
8 September	Ballinamuck	British (Cornwallis)	French (Humbert)
23 September	Killala	British (Trench)	Irish insurgents
Egyptian Campaign			
2 July	Alexandria	French (Bonaparte)	Egyptians (Coraim)
21 July	Pyramids	French (Bonaparte)	Egyptians (Murad & Ibrahim)
1799			
Egyptian Campaign			
19 February	El Arish	French (Bonaparte)	Ottoman (Ibrahim Aga)
7 March	Jaffa	French (Bonaparte)	Ottoman (Abou-Saad)
18 March–20 May	Acre (siege)	Ottoman (Djezzar)	French (Bonaparte)
17 April	Mount Tabor	French (Bonaparte)	Ottoman (Achmed)
25 July	Aboukir	French (Bonaparte)	Ottoman (Mustapha)
German Front			
21 March	Ostrach	Austrians (Charles)	French (Jourdan)
25 March	Stockach (1st battle)	Austrians (Charles)	French (Jourdan)
Italian Front			
5 April	Magnano	Austrian (Kray)	French (Schérer)
27 April	Cassano	Austro-Russians (Suvarov)	French (Moreau)
17–19 July	Trebbia	Austro-Russians (Suvarov)	French (Macdonald)
15 August	Novi	Austro-Russians (Suvarov)	French (Joubert)
4 November	Genoa	Austrians (Melas)	French (Championnet)
Switzerland			
4–7 June	Zürich (1st battle)	Austrians (Charles)	French (Massena)
14 August	Zürich (2nd battle)	Austrians (Charles)	French (Massena)
25 September	Zürich (3rd battle)	French (Massena)	Allies (Korsakov)
Netherlands Front			
19 September	Bergen-op-Zoom (1st battle)	French (Brune)	Anglo-Russians (York)
2 October	Bergen-op-Zoom (2nd battle)	Anglo-Russians (York)	French (Brune)
6 October	Castricum	French (Brune)	Anglo-Russians (York)
1800			
Egyptian Campaign			
20 March	Heliopolis	French (Kléber)	Ottoman (Vizier)
German Front			
3 May	Stockach (2nd battle)	French (Moreau)	Austrians (Kray)
5 May	Möskirch	French (Moreau)	Austrians (Kray)
16 May	Ulm	French (Moreau)	Austrians (Kray)
19 June	Höchstadt	French (Moreau)	Austrians (Kray
3 December	Hohenlinden	French (Moreau)	Austrians (Archduke John)

Date	Action	Victors	Defeated
Italian Front			
9 June	Montebello	French (Lannes)	Austrians (Ott)
14 June	Marengo	French (Bonaparte)	Austrians (Melas)
1801			
Egyptian Campaign			
20 March	Alexandria (or 2nd battle of Aboukir)	British (Abercromby)	French (Menou)
1805			
11 October	Haslach	French (Dupont)	Austrians (Mack)
14 October	Elchingen	French (Ney)	Austrians (Werneck/Riesch)
17 October	Ulm (capitulation)	French (Napoleon)	Austrians (Mack)
30 October	Caldiero (2nd battle)	French (Massena)	Austrians (Charles)
8 November	Zell	French (Davoût/Marmont)	Austrians (Merveldt)
11 November	Dürrenstein	French (Mortier)	Russians (Miloradovich/Dokhturov)
16 November	Oberhollabrünn (or Hollabrünn)	French (Napoleon)	Russians (Bagration)
2 December	Austerlitz	French (Napoleon)	Austro-Russians (Kutuzov)
1806			
8 January	Cape Town	British (Baird)	Franco-Dutch (Janssens)
6 July	Maida	British (Stuart)	French (Reynier)
9 October	Schleiz	French (Bernadotte)	Saxons (Tauenzein)
10 October	Saalfeld	French (Lannes)	Prussians (Louis)
14 October	Jena	French (Napoleon)	Prussians (Hohenlohe)
14 October	Auerstädt	French (Davoût)	Prussians (Brunswick)
6 November	Lübeck	French (Soult/Bernadotte)	Prussians (Blücher)
26 December	Pultusk	Indecisive encounter between French (Lannes) and Russians (Bennigsen)	
26 December	Golymin	Indecisive encounter between French (Murat) and Russians (Gallitzin)	
1807			
Polish Front			
25 January	Mohrungen	French (Bernadotte)	Russians (Markov)
7–8 February	Eylau	French (Napoleon)	Russians (Bennigsen)
10 June	Heilsberg	French (Napoleon)	Russians (Bennigsen)
14 June	Friedland	French (Napoleon)	Russians (Bennigsen)
Egypt			
20 April	Rosetta	Indecisive encounter between British (Fraser) and Ottomans	
South America			
5 July	Buenos Ayres	Argentinians (Liniers)	British (Whitelock)
Denmark			
29 August	Kjöge (or Roskilde)	British (Wellesley)	Danish (Castenskiold)
2–5 September	Copenhagen	British (Cathcart)	Danish (Peimann)
1808			
Peninsular War			
15 June–17 August	Saragossa (1st siege)	Spanish (Palafox)	French (Verdier)
14 July	Medina del Rio Seco	French (Bessières)	Spanish (Cuesta/Blake)
19 July	Baylen	Spanish (Castaños)	French (Dupont)
17 August	Roliça (or Roleia)	British (Wellesley)	French (Delaborde)

Date	Action	Victors	Defeated
21 August	Vimeiro	British (Wellesley)	French (Junot)
23 November	Tudela	French (Lannes)	Spanish (Castaños)
30 November	Somosierra	French (Napoleon)	Spanish (San Juan)
20 December–20 February 1809	Saragossa (2nd siege)	French (Lannes)	Spanish (Palafox)
21 December	Sahagun	British (Paget)	French (Debelle)
29 December	Benevente	British (Paget)	French (Lefebvre-Desnouëttes)

1809
Peninsular War

16 January	Corunna	British (Moore)	French (Soult)
20 February	Saragossa	French (Lannes)	Spanish (Palafox)
28 March	Medellin	French (Victor)	Spanish (Cuesta)
12 May	Oporto	British (Wellesley)	French (Soult)
28 July	Talavera	British (Wellesley)	French (Victor)
19 November	Oçana	French (Soult)	Spanish (Areizago)

Austrian Campaign

16 April	Sacile	Austrians (John)	French (Eugène)
19 April	Tengen	French (Davoût)	Austrians (Hohenzollern)
19–20 April	Abensberg	French (Napoleon)	Austrians (Charles)
21 April	Landeshut	French (Napoleon)	Austrians (Hiller)
22 April	Eckmühl (or Eggmühl)	French (Davoût/Lannes)	Austrians (Charles)
23 April	Ratisbon	French (Napoleon)	Austrians (Charles)
3 May	Ebersberg (or Ebelsberg)	French (Massena)	Austrians (Hiller)
21–22 May	Aspern-Essling	Austrians (Charles)	French (Napoleon)
14 June	Raab	French (Eugène)	Austrians (John)
5–6 July	Wagram	French (Napoleon)	Austrians (Charles)
10 July	Znaim	Inconclusive encounter between French (Napoleon) and Austrians (Charles)	

1810
Peninsular War

27 September	Busaco	Anglo-Portuguese (Wellington)	French (Massena)
15 October	Fuengirola	French (Sébastiani)	British (Blayney)

1811
Peninsular War

4 March	Barrosa (or Chiclana)	British (Graham)	French (Victor)
3 April	Sabugal	Anglo-Portuguese (Wellington)	French (Reynier)
5 May	Fuentes de Oñoro	Anglo-Portuguese (Wellington)	French (Massena)
16 May	Albuera	Anglo-Portuguese/Spanish (Beresford)	French (Soult)
25 May	Usagre	British (Lumley)	French (Latour-Maubourg)
25 September	El Bodon	Anglo-Portuguese (Picton)	French (Montbrun)
28 October	Arroyo dos Molinos	Anglo-Portuguese (Hill)	French (Girard)

1812
Peninsular War

9 January	Valencia	French (Suchet)	Spanish (Blake)
19 January	Ciudad Rodrigo	Anglo-Portuguese (Wellington)	French (Barrié)
6 April	Badajoz	Anglo-Portuguese (Wellington)	French (Phillipon)
22 July	Salamanca	Anglo-Portuguese (Wellington)	French (Marmont)
23 July	Garcia Hernandez	King's German Legion (Bock)	French (Foy)

Date	Action	Victors	Defeated
Russian Campaign			
28 July	Vitebsk	French (Napoleon)	Russians (Barclay de Tolly)
8 August	Inkovo	Inconclusive encounter between French (Sébastiani) and Russians (Platov)	
17 August	Smolensk	French (Napoleon)	Russians (Barclay de Tolly)
17–18 August	Polotsk	French (Oudinot/St. Cyr)	Russians (Wittgenstein)
19 August	Valutino	French (Napoleon)	Russians (Barclay de Tolly)
7 September	Borodino (or 'the Moskowa')	French (Napoleon)	Russians (Kutuzov)
18 October	Vinkovo	Russians (Bagration)	French (Murat)
24 October	Maloyaroslavets	French (Eugène)	Russians (Kutuzov)
3 November	Fiodoroivskoy	French (Davoût)	Russians (Miloradovich)
14 November	Polotsk (or Smoliani)	French (Victor)	Russians (Wittgenstein)
16–17 November	Krasnyi	French (Napoleon)	Russians (Kutuzov)
23 Novembr	Loshnitsa	French (Oudinot)	Russians (Chichagov)
26–28 November	Berezina	French (Napoleon)	Russians (Chichagov/Kutuzov)
War of 1812			
13 October	Queenston	British (Brock)	US (Van Renssalaer)

1813

Date	Action	Victors	Defeated
War of 1812			
22 January	Raisin River	British (Proctor)	US (Harrison)
28–29 May	Sacketts Harbor	US (Brown)	British (Prevost)
6 June	Stony Creek	British (Vincent)	US (Winder/Chandler)
5 October	The Thames (or Chatham)	US (Harrison)	British (Proctor)
25 October	Chateaugay	British (de Salaberry)	US (Hampton)
11 November	Chrysler's Farm	British (Morrison)	US (Wilkinson)
German Campaign ('War of Liberation')			
1 May	Poserna	French (Ney)	Allies (Winzingerode)
2 May	Lützen	French (Napoleon)	Allies (Wittgenstein)
20–21 May	Bautzen	French (Napoleon)	Allies (Wittgenstein)
23 August	Grossbeeren	Allies (Bernadotte)	French (Oudinot)
26 August	Katzbach	Allies (Blücher)	French (Macdonald)
26 August	Pirna	French (Vandamme)	Allies (Eugene of Württemberg)
26–27 August	Dresden	French (Napoleon)	Allies (Schwarzenberg)
30 August	Kulm-Priesten	Allies (Ostermann-Tolstoy/Kleist)	French (Vandamme)
6 September	Dennewitz	Allies (Bernadotte)	French (Ney)
12 October	Colditz	French (Murat)	Allies (Schwarzenberg)
14 October	Liebertwolkwitz	Inconclusive encounter between French (Murat) and Allies	
16–19 October	Leipzig	Allies (Schwarzenberg/Bernadotte/Blücher)	French (Napoleon)
16 October	Lindenau (actually part of the battle of Leipzig)	French (Bertrand)	Allies (Gyulai)
16 October	Mockern (actually part of the battle of Leipzig)	Allies (Blücher)	French (Marmont)
30–31 October	Hanau	French (Napoleon)	Bavarians (Wrede)
Peninsular War			
21 June	Vittoria	Anglo-Portuguese (Wellington)	French (Joseph/Jourdan)
25 July	Roncesvalles	Anglo-Portuguese (Wellington)	French (Soult)
25 July	Maya	Anglo-Portuguese (Wellington)	French (Soult)
28–30 July	Sorauren	Anglo-Portuguese (Wellington)	French (Soult)

Date	Action	Victors	Defeated
(Battles of the period 25 July to 2 August known also as 'the Pyrenees')			
31 August	San Sebastian	Anglo-Portuguese (Wellington)	French (Rey)
31 August	San Marcial	Anglo-Portuguese (Wellington)	French (Soult)
7 October	Vera	Anglo-Portuguese/Spanish (Wellington)	French (Taupin)
9 November	St. Jean de Luz	Anglo-Portuguese (Hope)	French (Soult)
10 November	Nivelle	Anglo-Portuguese (Wellington)	French (Soult)
9–12 December	Nive	Anglo-Portuguese (Wellington)	French (Soult)
13 December	St. Pierre	Anglo-Portuguese (Hill)	French (Soult)

1814

Defence of France

Date	Action	Victors	Defeated
29 January	Brienne	French (Napoleon)	Allies (Blücher)
30 January	La Rothière	French (Napoleon)	Allies (Blücher)
10 February	Champaubert	French (Napoleon)	Russians (Olssufiev)
11 February	Montmirail	French (Napoleon)	Allies (Yorck/Sacken)
12 February	Château-Thierry	French (Napoleon)	Allies (Yorck)
14 February	Vauchamps	French (Napoleon)	Allies (Blücher)
17 February	Valjouan	French (Grouchy/Gérard)	Allies (Wrede)
18 February	Montereau	French (Napoleon)	Allies (Schwarzenberg)
27 February	Bar-sur-Aube	Allies (Wittgenstein/Wrede)	French (Oudinot)
7 March	Craonne	French (Napoleon)	Allies (Blücher)
9–10 March	Lâon	Allies (Blücher)	French (Napoleon)
13 March	Rheims	French (Napoleon)	Allies (St.-Priest)
17 March	Fismes	Allies (Blücher)	French (Marmont)
20–21 March	Arcis-su-Aube	Allies (Schwarzenberg)	French (Napoleon)
25 March	La Fère-Champenoise	Allies (Schwarzenberg)	French (Marmont/Mortier)
30 March	Paris (or Montmartre)	Allies (Schwarzenberg)	French (Marmont)

Peninsular War

Date	Action	Victors	Defeated
27 February	Orthez	Anglo-Portuguese (Wellington)	French (Soult)
10 April	Toulouse	Anglo-Portuguese (Wellington)	French (Soult)
14 April	Bayonne	Anglo-Portuguese (Hope)	French (Thouvenot)

War of 1812

Date	Action	Victors	Defeated
5 July	Chippewa	US (Brown)	British (Riall)
25 July	Lundy's Lane	British (Riall)	US (Brown/Scott)
24 August	Bladensburg	British (Ross)	US (Winder)
11 September	Plattsburg	US (Macomb)	British (Prevost)
13 September	Baltimore	US (Stricker)	British (Ross)

1815

War of 1812

Date	Action	Victors	Defeated
8 January	New Orleans	US (Jackson)	British (Pakenham)

Italy

Date	Action	Victors	Defeated
2 May	Tolentino	Austrians (Bianchi)	Italians (Murat)

The Hundred Days

Date	Action	Victors	Defeated
16 June	Quatre Bras	Anglo-Allied (Wellington)	French (Ney)
16 June	Ligny	French (Napoleon)	Prussians (Blücher)
18 June	Wavre	Inconclusive engagement between French (Grouchy) and Prussians (Thielmann)	
18 June	Waterloo	Anglo-Allied (Wellington) and Prussians (Blücher)	French (Napoleon)

ACTIONS AT SEA

Date	Action	Victors	Defeated
1794			
29 May–1 June	Glorious First of June	British (Howe)	French (Villaret de Joyeuse)
1797			
14 February	St. Vincent	British (Jervis)	Spanish (Cordova)
11 October	Camperdown	British (Duncan)	Batavian (de Winter)
1798			
1 August	Aboukir Bay (or 'Battle of the Nile')	British (Nelson)	French (Brueys)
1801			
2 April	Copenhagen	British (Nelson)	Danish (Fischer)
6 July	Algeciras (1st battle)	Inconclusive engagement between British (Saumarez) and Franco-Spanish (Linois)	
13 July	Algeciras (2nd battle)	British (Saumarez)	Franco-Spanish (Moreno)
1805			
22 July	Cape Finisterre	Inconclusive engagement between British (Calder) and Franco-Spanish (Villeneuve)	
21 October	Trafalgar	British (Nelson)	Franco-Spanish (Villeneuve)
1806			
6 February	Santo Domingo	British (Duckworth)	French (Laissaque)
1807			
30 June	Lemnos	Russian (Seniavin)	Ottoman
1809			
11–12 April	Basque Roads	British (Gambier/Cochrane)	French (Allemand)
1811			
13 March	Lissa	British (Hoste)	Franco-Venetians (Dubourdieu)
1812			
13 August	*Constitution/Guerrière*	US (Hull)	British (Dacres)
25 August	*United States/Macedonian*	US (Decatur)	British (Carden)
29 December	*Constitution/Java*	US (Bainbridge)	British (Lambert)
1813			
1 June	*Shannon/Chesapeake*	British (Broke)	US (Lawrence)
10 September	Lake Erie	US (Perry)	British (Barclay)
1814			
11 September	Lake Champlain	US (Macdonough)	British (Downie)

TREATIES AND CONVENTIONS OF THE
REVOLUTIONARY AND NAPOLEONIC ERA

Alessandria, Convention of: between French and Austrian armies, declaring armistice after Marengo; preliminary to Lunéville. 15 June 1800.

Alkmaar, Convention of: between French and Allied armies, for the evacuation of Anglo-Russian forces from the Netherlands. 18 October 1799.

Amiens, Peace of: treaty bringing cessation of hostilities between Britain and France. 27 March 1802.

Basel, Treaty of: peace between France and Prussia. 16 May 1795.

Bologna, Armistice of: between France and the Vatican. 23 June 1796.

Bucharest, Treaty of: peace between Russia and the Ottoman Empire, encouraged by Britain, to free Russia for military action against France. 28 May 1812.

Campo Formio, Treaty of: confirmation of the Peace of Leoben, by which Austria recognized the Cisalpine Republic, surrendered the Austrian Netherlands and received the Republic of Venice. 17 October 1797.

Chaumont, Treaty of: agreement between Britain, Russia, Austria and Prussia to pursue the war against Napoleon to the end, should he refuse peace on terms that limited France to her 1792 boundaries. 9 March 1814.

Cherasco, Armistice of: peace between France and Piedmont following the latter's defeat. 28 April 1796.

Cintra, Convention of: agreement between British and French forces to allow Junot's army to be evacuated from Portugal, causing great indignation in Britain. 22 August 1808.

Concordat: treaty between France and the Papacy normalizing relationships after the break with the Catholic church after the revolution. 15 July 1801; finalized 8 April 1802.

Dresden, Conference of: Napoleon's attempt to solidify the support of his allies for the approaching attack on Russia. 17–28 May 1812.

El Arish, Convention of: preliminary peace between the French Army of the Orient and the Ottoman Empire and allies: rejected by Britain. 21 January 1800.

Erfurt, Convention of: agreement between France and Russia, reinforcing the alliance of Tilsit. 12 October 1808.

Fontainebleau, Treaty of: alliance between France and Spain against Portugal. 27 October 1807.

Fontainebleau, Treaty of: confirmation of Napoleon's abdication. 11 April 1814.

Frederikshavn, Treaty of: ending the Russo-Swedish War by ceding Finland to Russia. 17 September 1809.

Ghent, Treaty of: ending the War of 1812 between Britain and the USA. 24 December 1814.

Gulistan, Treaty of: ending the Russo-Persian War of 1804–13, by the ceding to Russia of Georgia and other Transcaucasian provinces. 12 October 1813.

Jassy, Treaty of: ending the Russo-Turkish War of 1787–92. 9 January 1792.

Kalisch, Convention of: Russo-Prussian alliance. 28 February 1813.

Leoben, Peace of: preliminary peace between France and Austria. 18 April 1797.

Louisiana Purchase: transfer from French to US ownership of Louisiana territory. 20 December 1803.

Lunéville, Peace of: peace between France and Austria, confirming Campo Formio. 9 February 1801.

Madrid, Treaty of: confirming the second Treaty of San Ildefonso, of October 1800. 21 March 1801.

Northern Convention: reviving of the Armed Neutrality of the North against British blockade of the Baltic, between Russia, Sweden, Denmark and Prussia, the latter completing the alliance when joining on 18 December 1800.

Paris, First Treaty of: between France and the Allies, restoring the Bourbon monarchy and France's 1792 boundaries. 30 May 1814.

Paris, Second Treaty of: ending the hostilities after Napoleon's final abdication, and reducing France's boundaries to those of 1790. 20 November 1815.

Pillnitz, Declaration of: declaration of Emperor Leopold II and King Frederick William II of Prussia to collaborate with other European sovereigns to restore the power of the French monarchy. 2 August 1792.

Pleischwitz, Armistice of: temporary cessation of hostilities between France and the Allies after Bautzen. 2 June 1813.

Posen, Treaty of: between France and Saxony, the Elector of Saxony becoming King. 10 December 1806.

Potsdam, Treaty of: alliance between Russia and Prussia against France, which Prussia never acted upon and thus did not join the Third Coalition. 3 November 1805.

Pressburg, Treaty of: peace between France and Austria, the latter surrendering territory. 26 December 1805.

Quadruple Alliance: between Britain, Austria, Prussia and Russia, to ensure that the terms of the Second Treaty of Paris would be obeyed. 20 November 1815.

Reichenbach, Convention of: between Austria and France in an attempt to prevent the resumption of hostilities after the Armistice of Pleischwitz if Napoleon accepted Austria's terms; he rejected them. 19 July 1813.

St. Petersburg, Convention of: agreement between Russia and Sweden for mutual aid in event of Russo-French or Swedish-Danish conflict. 5–9 April 1812.

San Ildefonso, First Treaty of: alliance between France and Spain. 19 August 1796. ('First Treaty' in this period; treaties with this name had existed as early as 1762).

San Ildefonso, Second Treaty of: Spanish ceding of Louisiana to France. 7 October 1800.

Schönbrunn, Treaty of: peace between France and Austria, the latter surrendering much territory and joining the Continental System. 14 October 1809.

Sistova, Treaty of: ending the Austro-Turkish War of 1787–91. 4 August 1791.

Tauroggen, Convention of: between the Prussian contingent of

'. . . we were climbing the Guadarrama with such difficulty . . . The soldiers of Lapisse's division gave loud expression to the most sinister designs against the Emperor's person, stirring up each other to fire a shot at him, and bandying accusations of cowardice for not doing it. He heard it all as plainly as we did, and seemed as if he did not care a bit for it . . . At a short distance from the spot where I had left the Emperor, there was an infantry division . . . I turned sharply at the unanimous acclamations with which this body saluted the Emperor on his appearance . . . Enthusiasm was at its height! It was Lapisse's division! the same that the evening before in crossing the Guadarrama had used the seditious language I have mentioned. In the village where they had spent the night, they had found food and wine – and this was the explanation of the sudden change . . .'

(*Recollections of Colonel de Gonneville*, ed. C. M. Yonge, London 1875, I, pp. 190–3.)

Napoleon's army and Russia, by which the former agreed to be neutral, leading to the entry of Prussia into the 'war of liberation' on the Allied side. 30 December 1812.

Tilsit, Treaty of: peace between France and Russia/Prussia, Russia agreeing to join the Continental System and recognize the Duchy of Warsaw, the latter losing much territory and paying a huge idemnity. 7–9 July 1807.

Tolentino, Treaty of: between France and the Vatican, whereby the latter agreed to pay an indemnity to prevent French occupation. 19 February 1797.

Treviso, Armistice of: between France and Austria. 15 January 1801.

Troyes, Treaty of: between Austria, Russia and Prussia, to determine the conduct of the war. 22 February 1814.

Ulm, Convention of: armistice between Napoleon and Mack's army, preceding the surrender of the Austrian forces. 17 October 1805.

Valençay, Treaty of: between Napoleon and Ferdinand VII of Spain, intended to disentangle France from the Peninsular War; rejected by the Spanish Council of Regency. 11 December 1813.

Vienna, Treaty of: alternative name for Schönbrunn.

Vienna, Congress of: between the Allied powers to settle the affairs of Europe after Napoleon's first abdication; interrupted by the 'Hundred Days' campaign and reconvened after Napoleon's final defeat. First session, 1 November 1814–9 June 1815.

Wereloe, Treaty of: ending the Russo-Swedish War of 1788–90. 15 August 1790.

Znaim, Armistice of: temporary ceasefire agreed between Napoleon and the Archduke Charles preceding the Treaty of Schönbrunn. 12 July 1809.

'Coquin de Temps!': *the French Imperial Guard on campaign in atrocious weather. (Lithograph by Delpesch after Horace Vernet, typical of that artist's superb and realistic style). The grenadiers' plumes are covered with oilskin, but otherwise their uniforms have little concessions to the rigours of active service.*

II
WEAPONS AND THE PRACTICE OF WAR

WEAPONS AND THE PRACTICE OF WAR

WEAPONRY

The 'Art of War' was to a large extent governed by the capabilities of the available weaponry, the basic principles of which had changed little throughout the previous century. Although some national peculiarities existed – for example British 'spherical case-shot' and the Russian 'unicorn' or 'licorn' fieldpiece – it is valid to discuss 'the musket' as a genus rather than to separate each national pattern, as all weapons of one type were technologically very similar, given a reasonable standard of manufacture. Some weapons were better-made than those of other nations, and thus in theory were more efficient, but a greater effect on performance was the competence of the user. In the following sections, therefore, the classifications are those of weapon types rather than national patterns; though where necessary examples of national varieties or particular examples of national usage are noted.

The Musket

The most basic element of Napoleonic warfare was the infantryman and his musket, which operated on a universal principle: a smooth-bored weapon with ignition by the flintlock system. (The only firearm that did not utilize this system was the air-rifle, the propellant of which was compressed air; Austria possessed the 1779–80 pattern Girardoni air-rifle, a 20-shot repeater carried by *Jäger* in 1792–7 and 1799, but its use was very limited and though it remained on official inventories until 1815 it was withdrawn from service in 1800, and may virtually be discounted for the purpose in hand.) All muskets were muzzle-loading, requiring the charge to be inserted via the muzzle; breech-loading weapons existed only in very small numbers, virtually the only one to see service being the Austrian Crespi, equipped with a somewhat bizarre spear-ended bayonet, but again its use was very limited.

The musket consisted of an iron tube affixed to a wooden stock, with a small 'touch-hole' in the right side of the barrel at the end nearest the firer, through which the ignition-spark penetrated from outside to the propellant charge in the tube. This spark was provided by the striking of a lump of flint upon a hinged steel plate termed a 'frizzen' or 'steel', the flint held in the screw-tightened jaws of the 'hammer' or 'cock', which was connected via an internal spring to the trigger on the underside of the stock. The projectile was a lead ball of approximately one ounce in weight; exact size varied with the calibre of firearm but was generally termed 'musket-bore', the narrower barrels being styled 'carbine-bore'. Although loose gunpowder and balls could be used, this method was generally restricted to rifled weapons; for the ordinary musket 'prepared cartridges' were used, consisting of the ball and sufficient powder for one shot contained in a greased paper tube, carried in the infantryman's cartridge-box or *cartouche*, a flapped leather pouch with wooden or tin interior, slung over one shoulder.

To load the musket, the infantryman removed a single cartridge from his pouch and bit off the end, often retaining the ball in his mouth (hence the blackened lips and raging thirst caused by gunpowder in the mouth which afflicted most soldiers in battle). Then, holding the musket horizontally, he drew the hammer back one notch until it rested on 'half-cock', in which state pressure on the trigger would have no effect, thus preventing a premature discharge. The frizzen (hinged with a spring) was pushed in the direction of the muzzle, opening the priming-pan, a depression affixed to the metal 'lock-plate' at the right side of the musket-stock upon which the working parts were positioned. A small amount of powder was then poured into the pan from the cartridge, and the frizzen moved into the vertical position, sealing the powder in the pan. The musket was then moved into the vertical and the butt grounded. The remaining powder was then poured down the muzzle, and the ball spat or dropped after it. The infantryman then removed the iron ramrod from its channel beneath the barrel and reversed it so that its bulbous end fitted into the muzzle; and with it rammed the paper tube of the cartridge down the barrel after the powder and ball, forming a 'wad' to hold them in place. The ramrod was then replaced and the musket returned to the horizontal. At this moment the hammer was drawn back an additional notch on to 'full-cock', when the trigger became operational (though a weak spring might cause it to 'go off at half-cock', potentially lethal for both the firer and those in the direction of the muzzle!). The musket was then raised to the right shoulder; it could not be fired from the left as the ignition of the powder in the pan would burn the firer's eye. Aiming was unusually restricted to pointing the musket in the general direction of the enemy, at which time the trigger was depressed, sending the hammer crashing forwards so that the flint struck sparks upon the frizzen; as the frizzen was forced back on its hinge, the priming-pan was uncovered and the sparks fell on to the powder, which burst into flame. The spark was communicated via the touch-hole to the powder in the barrel, which exploded with a loud report, a cloud of thick smoke and a vicious recoil as the ball was fired. The musket was then lowered and the whole process begun anew.

The projectile was merely a lead sphere with slight differences in size; British muskets, for example, commonly used a No. 11 bore barrel (0.76in calibre) and a No. 14 bore ball (0.71in); the standard French ball was 0.70in, resulting in French bullets weighing 20 to the pound as against the British 14 to the pound, but in combat the difference was negligible. Simple though the ammunition was, it was capable of inflicting the most appalling injury, the ball flattening upon impact and often fragmenting if it hit bone, creating terrible wounds. At the very end of its trajectory, however, a 'spent ball' might hit but not penetrate, causing only a bruise; both Wellington and Napoleon suffered from these with little ill-effect. The flash from the muzzle was such that it might set alight the clothing of anyone in the immediate vicinity, and such was the velocity upon discharge that any projectile could cause fatal injury: buttons or stones might be fired if ammunition ran out (one Englishman fired his cut-throat razor at the French!) and contemporary accounts include such bizarre deaths as those killed by a wooden ruler or a lump of chewed tobacco!

Although the firing drill or 'Manual exercise' varied between armies, it usually followed a standard procedure which was drilled into the recruit with such precision that he would stand his ground, load and fire to order almost oblivious of the destruction around him, operating virtually as an automaton; it was this discipline rather than the quality of the musket which resulted in the great victories of the eighteenth century, particularly those of Frederick the Great whose infantry's discipline was legendary. Firing was usually by volley, muskets being discharged to order rather than at the speed of the individual (except when operating as light infantry in 'open order' when each man fired when ready), though there were different ways of firing volley: either the entire battalion, or in succession of ranks, or by platoons so that a 'rolling volley' resulted, fire beginning at one end of the line and passing along, recommencing when the first platoon had re-loaded. The latter was probably the most effective as it gave an opportunity for siting the target as the smoke drifted away; but there were few old-fashioned protracted fire-fights of mid-eighteenth century style, two lines blasting at each other at close range, due to the development in tactics since the days of Frederick. The rate of fire depended upon several factors, not least the proficiency of the troops; though an experienced man could discharge five shots per minute, this usually declined when firing volley or two or three shots per minute. Under combat conditions this might fall even lower, especially after a protracted fire-fight, when the soldier was tired, the touch-hole became clogged with burned powder (to clear which each man carried a wire 'picker' and often a wire brush to clear residue from the priming-pan, though cases are recorded of men urinating down the barrel as the only way of unblocking it), and when the flint became chipped and worn (each man carried several spares). Heavy rain could render the musket completely inoperable by soaking the cartridge. There were a number of short-cuts to increase the rate of fire, such as ramming the entire cartridge down the barrel and striking the butt upon the ground, hoping to force sufficient powder through the touch-hole to obviate the necessity of filling the priming-pan separately; by sticking the ramrod in the ground to circumvent its repeated drawing and returning (not recommended as a rapid change of position might result in the loss of the ramrod); or by dispensing with ramming altogether, not inserting the paper in the barrel but using just powder and ball, a process known as 'running ball' (i.e., the ball would run out of the barrel if it were angled downwards), a load sometimes used by sentries.

A major factor in assessing the effectiveness of musketry was the misfire rate, calculated at one in 6½ under ordinary conditions, rising to a quarter in wet weather. Other factors affecting the performance included the inexperience or panic of the soldiers: under the stress of battle men might forget to remove their ramrod and fire it away, or in panic continue to ram in cartridge after cartridge so that the musket would explode if they then tried to fire it.

The main disadvantage of the musket was its inaccuracy; but it should be remembered that in the context of a Napoleonic battle it was only necessary that a musket be

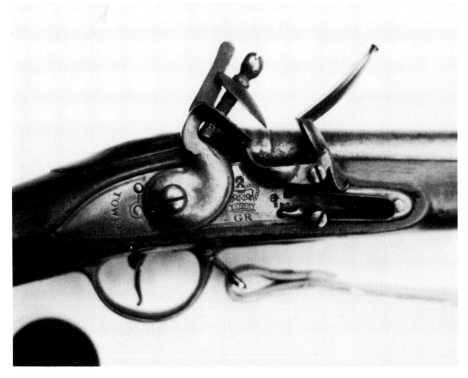

The flintlock mechanism: a British 'Brown Bess' musket-lock, minus the flint which was inserted into the jaws of the 'cock'. The frizzen here is angled forward and the pan open.

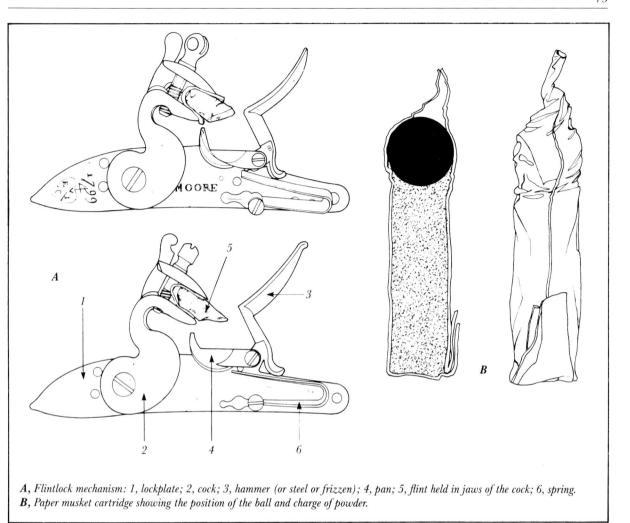

A, *Flintlock mechanism: 1, lockplate; 2, cock; 3, hammer (or steel or frizzen); 4, pan; 5, flint held in jaws of the cock; 6, spring.*
B, *Paper musket cartridge showing the position of the ball and charge of powder.*

capable of registering a hit anywhere on a huge target like a line of men; there was basically no need for the accuracy to hit an individual, and indeed in some circles it was still regarded as faintly dishonourable to mark an individual target. George Napier recorded that at the Coa he called to a French officer to go back, 'not liking to fire at a single man';[1] the Frenchman bravely pressed on so Napier had to shoot him, to his eternal regret! The tactics of the period had been formulated because of the very inaccuracy of the musket, though it is questionable whether they would have been amended had a more accurate musket been widely available. Certainly the lack of accuracy was in no way due to lack of technological development: gunsmiths were capable of producing rifled guns of astonishing accuracy, and even the British so-called 'Duke of Richmond's' smooth-bore musket would have been an immeasurable improvement had its inventor, Henry Nock, been capable of mass-producing them in large quanitites. (Uniquely, this weapon incorporated Nock's 'screwless lock' in which all moving parts were internal, producing a gun much less prone to damage.)

The poor performance of the musket is perhaps best described by Colonel George Hanger, a somewhat eccentric advocate of light infantry tactics and himself a champion rifle-shot:

'A soldier's musket, if not exceedingly ill-bored (as many are), will strike the figure of a man at 80 yards; it may even at a hundred; but a soldier must be very unfortunate indeed who shall be wounded by a common musket at 150 yards, provided his antagonist aims at him; and as to firing at a man at 200 yards with a common musket, you may as well fire at the moon and have the same hope of hitting your object. I do maintain and will prove. . .that no man was ever killed at 200 yards, by a common musket, by the person who aimed at him.'[2] In *Reflections on the Menaced Invasion* (London, 1804) Hanger thought that in combat one hit per 200 shots was a reasonable expectation, such a low striking-rate being caused not by men firing 'at the word of command' and thus unable to take aim, but because the muskets were either crooked or 'bent in soldering the loops on'.[3] He might have added the effect of 'windage', the gap between barrel and ball

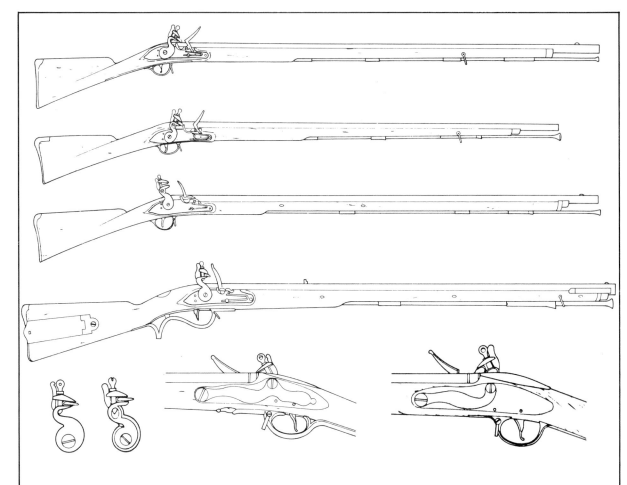

British Muskets. From top to bottom: New Short Land Pattern; India Pattern used in the British service after 1809; New Land Service; Baker Rifle (not drawn to scale with first three muskets). Bottom Row: Baker Rifle cock; Baker Rifle reinforced cock; Short Land Pattern with flat sideplate; India Pattern with convex sideplate.

(about 1/20th of an inch); the greater the windage, the easier to load but the less accuracy. (Thus a British musket firing the smaller French ball might be expected to be less accurate still; though such considerations were probably of negligible effect when assessing what actually occurred in the field.) Bad though these opinions are, they refer to the best-quality mass-produced musket of the era, the British 'Brown Bess'.

Existing statistics for the performance of the musket were almost all conducted under 'ideal' conditions; in the field, when the target was often moving and usually obscured by smoke, not even these results would be obtained. British tests in 1841 established the range of the 'Brown Bess' at 100–700 yards (dependent upon elevation), though at *every* elevation there could be a variation of 100–300 yards. Against a target twice as high and twice as broad as a man, at 150 yards three shots out of four registered; at any greater range not one hit. At 250 yards against a target twice as wide, not one hit was made. Against a target representing a line of cavalry, the

artillerist Müller recorded the following statistics, including a distinction between trained and 'ordinary' soldiers:

Range (yards)	Percentage hits by 'well trained'	'ordinary'
100	53	40
200	30	18
300	23	15[4]

Similar results were obtained by tests of the muskets of other nationalities, usually averaging somewhere between the two sets of statistics recorded by Müller; Prussian tests went to longer range so that the striking-rate against a target 100 feet long by six feet high was only one per cent at 600 yards.

The inaccuracy of the musket meant that a few armies paid much attention to target-practice (except among light troops); in 1805, with the parsimony characteristic of the Austrian military establishment, Archduke Ferdinand attempted to train recruits on an allowance of six rounds

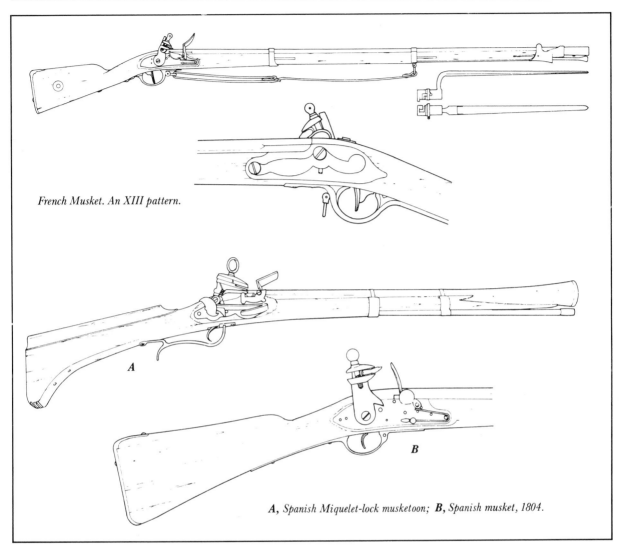

French Musket. An XIII pattern.

A, Spanish Miquelet-lock musketoon; B, Spanish musket, 1804.

each, though in the more enlightened British service the annual rations was 30 rounds ball and 70 blank per man (the blank to practise volley-firing), but only the light infantry (50 and 60 rounds respectively) were drilled in 'firing ball at a mark'. One of the innovations introduced into Russian service by Barclay de Tolly was the design of a target bearing horizontal lines, to aid elevation or depression of barrel according to distance.

Under combat conditions the efficiency of the musket was much less than that attained under controlled conditions, when misfires were usually disregarded in the assembly of statistics. With a misfire rate rising from 15 to 25 per cent in damp weather, with partially obscured and moving targets, and with the failings of the soldiers (ranging from panic to the habit of pouring some of the cartridge's powder on to the ground, lessening the recoil but also the striking-power), musketry could be very wasteful and perhaps confirmed the traditional belief that on the battlefield it required seven times his weight of shot for each enemy killed. The head of the British field train department in the Peninsular War calculated that if all the French casualties at Vittoria were caused by musketry (i.e., not taking into account the fact that many would have fallen to artillery fire), only one hit per 459 shots would register. This seems an exceptionally low rate, though Henegan (the official in question) claimed that similar expenditure occurred in every Peninsular battle except Barossa. In Müller's opinion, under controlled tests as much as 50 per cent of shots hit the target at 100 yards; with misfires and combat conditions taken into consideration, perhaps 15 per cent hits would be a more realistic figure. In tightly packed formations many men would be hit more than once by a volley at close range, so that the average casualty-rate at 200 yards would be perhaps 3 or 4 per cent (which figure Hughes calculates for the casualties at Talavera), rising to 5 per cent or more at 100 yards or less.

The available statistics are distorted by a number of additional factors which cannot be assessed, such as the amount of cover or 'dead ground' available to the defenders, or the experience of the troops. In the latter case, partly trained men could be as dangerous to themselves as to their enemies: when Baron Larrey was instructed to investigate almost 3,000 cases of 'self-inflicted wounds' in the French army in 1813, he discovered that almost all the hand- and forearm-injuries had been caused by men shielding their faces with their hands or being shot accidentally by men in the rank behind them.

All muskets were equipped with bayonets, turning the firearm into a short pike. Almost without exception the bayonets were triangular-sectioned blades with a tubular socket at the end, fitting over the muzzle and locking into place by a zigzag slot over the foresight of the barrel. (Sword-bayonets or German *Hirshfänger* weapons – hunting-swords – which fitted on to the side of the barrel were normally restricted to rifles.) The socket-bayonet allowed the musket to be fired while the bayonet was fixed (some nations, including Russia and Prussia, kept the bayonets fixed almost permanently, dispensing with bayonet-scabbards), though a fixed bayonet could be a hazard to loading from the risk of impaling the hand when ramming down the charge. The socket-fitting was such that the bayonet might be wrenched off the musket without great difficulty, necessitating a number of devices to keep it in place, ranging from the attachment of spring-clips to the socket, locking-rings such as carried on French bayonets from 1763, to tying the bayonet on with string.

A number of nations made much of the bayonet being 'their' national weapon against which no enemy could stand: Britain, France and Russia all regarded it in this light, and numerous colourful declarations by generals are recorded to emphasize the point. Yet, leaving aside the storming of fortified positions (both fortresses and fieldworks like the redoubts at Borodino), examples of bayonet-fights can hardly be found. Bayonet-charges were not uncommon; but as they were almost always executed when the enemy had been shattered by musketry or artillery-fire and was already wavering, one side or the other almost invariably broke and ran before bayonets could actually be brought into play, the resulting fights being simply to hasten the fleeing troops on their way: in effect, it was the pyschological effect of the bayonet-charge which brought results, rather than the physical effect. In the whole of the Peninsular War, though there are accounts of bayonet-duels between individuals (while skirmishing), there appears to be only one example of a mass bayonet-fight, which so impressed those who saw it that they made much of it; and interestingly it occurred totally by chance, when a company of the British 20th Foot was driving away some French skirmishers at Roncesvalles on 25 July 1813. After driving in the skirmishers the company breasted a ridge to find the French 6th *Léger* ten yards away; the British commander, George Tovey, immediately cried 'Bayonet away, bayonet away!' and their dash upon the head of the French column made it recoil,

giving Tovey's men time to regain their own lines. A Brunswick officer who witnessed it compared it to bayonet-drill (the men fencing at each other), which emphasizes its difference from the normal bayonet charge in which one side charged and the other fled before contact. So singular was this fight that Tovey even recalled one 'reckless and intrepid' member of his company, named Budworth, who returned with only the socket on his musket, reeking with blood, declaring that 'he had killed away until his bayonet broke'.[5] One Peninsular surgeon (G.J. Guthrie, Deputy Inspector-General of Hospitals) stated that troops *never* fought hand-to-hand 'for the best possible reason, that one side turns and runs away as soon as the other comes close enough to do mischief'.[6]

Two varieties of musket were especially famous, those of France and Britain. The French musket, styled (unofficially) the 'Charleville' after one of the main factories, was a version of the 1777-pattern, modified slightly in Years 9 and 13 of the republican calendar (hence models termed *An IX* and *An XIII*), a weapon of good quality though hindered by the coarsely ground French gunpowder which tended to clog the barrel which might require washing about every 50 shots. More than two million such weapons were produced, with a noted variety with a much superior finish (costing 10 francs more per musket) produced for the Imperial Guard.

The British musket was known by the generic term 'Brown Bess', a nickname either of endearment or a corruption of the German *Büsche* (gun) and the 'browning' or rustproofing of the barrel. This term covered a multitude of patterns, a number of variations of the 'Land Pattern' (Long and Short) and the 'India Pattern' instituted in the mid-1790s, copying the muskets acquired from the East India Company from 1794 in an attempt to fulfil the requirements that could not be met from official sources. From 1797, ordnance gunsmiths were ordered to produce only the India Pattern though a New Land Service musket with the 42-inch barrel of the old Short Land Service was produced from 1803, and from 1803–10 a Light Infantry musket which had the 39-inch barrel of the India Pattern plus a backsight to assist the aiming necessary for light troops. The 'Brown Bess' was in general a weapon of good quality, and vast numbers were exported to Britain's allies (from 1804 until 1815 some 1,603,711 India Pattern muskets were manufactured), including 113,000 to Prussia and 60,000 to Russia, where they were so prized that their issue was made as a reward to distinguished soldiers. This is hardly surprising given the often atrocious quality of weapons produced by the Russian factory at Tula: 'the name of musket is degraded by such things as they produce; it is wonderful that any troops can use them; besides being clumsy and heavy, they miss fire five times out of six, and are liable to burst whenever they are discharged' according to the contemporary traveller Dr. Clarke (*Travels in Various Countries of Europe*, 1810), a somewhat over-harsh verdict!

The Rifle

Rifled muskets were in a minority, and were only entrusted to the most skilled marksmen. They operated on the same principle as the smooth-bore musket, except that the internal rifling of the barrel imparted spin to the spherical ball, thus giving greatly enhanced accuracy. Feats of marksmanship were such that it was possible to target the officers and NCOs of an approaching enemy formation, or even silence artillery batteries: George Simmons of the British 95th Rifles knocked over the gunners of a French battery at Badajoz; Kincaid of the same regiment performed the same feat at Waterloo, yet these were regarded as almost commonplace feats. The engineer Landmann recorded speaking to a German rifleman at Vimeiro who was declining to shoot a French marksman 60 to 80 yards away, because 'I want de officer; pecause ter pe more plunder.'[7] When such accuracy was possible in combat, it is easy to believe test statistics, such as those produced by the gunsmith Ezekiel Baker who fired 34 shots at 100 yards and 24 at 200 yards at a man-sized target with one of the rifles he designed for the British army, and every shot hit the target. So skilful were the trained riflemen that in British service men would even hold a target above their head for their fellows to aim at!

The rifle was largely a German weapon, civilian hunting-rifles being used before military patterns were produced, so that the concept of 'rifle' tactics was markedly the province of the German *Jäger*, large numbers of whom operated in most German armies. Rifles were slow to be adopted in other armies, partly due to their disadvantages: slower rate of fire due to the tight fit of the ball (British riflemen were originally issued with mallets to force the ball down the barrel!) and the extra training required to produce a proficient rifleman, so that the first rifle-armed troops employed by Britain, for example (exclusive of Ferguson's small corps in the American War of Independence), were units of German mercenaries, and of the four British rifles battalions employed in the Peninsular War (excluding the King's German Legion and 'foreign corps'), three were British in composition (95th Foot) and the other (5th Battalion, 60th) largely German. It was usual for riflemen to be concentrated in their own units (even if these were ultimately distributed throughout the army in separate companies as occurred with the British 5/60th, and in the Prussian army), though an alternative was for selected marksmen of units armed with muskets to be issued with rifles; Russia, for example, armed the twelve best shots of each *Jäger* company (equating with light infantry in other armies) with rifles, and sixteen men per squadron of heavy cavalry. Rifles never found favour in the French army, the original issue to officers and selected NCOs of *voltigeur* companies being withdrawn completely in 1807.

Although 'prepared' cartridges were used with the rifle, many riflemen carried in addition loose musket-balls and flasks of powder to obviate the use of cartridges, the 'wadding' often being carried in the form of ready-greased patches of parchment or linen carried in hinged-lidded 'patch-boxes' hollowed in the butt of the rifle. As riflemen were expected to take advantage of natural cover, the rifle's short barrel allowed it to be loaded in a prone position (very difficult with a musket), and several unique postures were

adopted for aiming, including that used by the British marksman Tom Plunkett when he shot General Colbert at Astorga: 'To fire laying [sic] on the back, the sling must be sufficiently loosened to let it be passed on the ball of the right foot, and as the leg is kept stiff, so, on the contrary, the butt is pulled towards the breast, the head is raised up, till the front sight is brought into the notch in the usual way. . .the position is not only awkward but painful. . .'[8]

Probably the most famous rifle of the period was the British 'Baker', of which more than 30,000 were produced from 1800 to 1815, equipping not only the regular rifle corps but such allied formations as the Portuguese *Caçadores* too.

The Sabre

The principal cavalry weapon was the sabre which, though it existed in a huge variety of patterns, was governed in use and design by two basic theories regarding its employment. Some held that the most effective blow was the cut or slash, in which the edge of the blade was used; others believed that the most effective blow was the thrust, in which the blade jabbed forward like a pointing finger, using the sharpened tip to run through the victim.

The thrust had to be executed with a sharply pointed weapon with a relatively thin blade; no less an authority than Maurice de Saxe declared this to be the most effective design, and to compel its use that the length of the blade should be blunted '. . . that the soldier may be effectually prevented cutting with it in action, which method of using the sword never does execution'.[9] The British *Rules and Regulations for the Sword Exercise of Cavalry* (1796) (originated by John Gaspard Le Marchant, killed at Salamanca) took the opposite view and instituted the cut as the most efficient blow, highlighting the weakness of the thrust: that, if it missed, the opponent had an opportunity of a free strike before the sword could be recovered, whereas with a cut it was much easier to recover the sword into a 'guard' posture. (Although against infantry, the *Rules* noted, the cavalryman's elevated position made the thrust as safely executed as the cut.) These conflicting views determined the national patterns of sabre; the French heavy and medium cavalry, for example, were equipped exclusively with narrow, straight blades suitable for the thrust, with heavy brass hilts to act as a counter-balance to raise the point (with the cut, the weight of blade was more important). The German-style *Pallasch* was used by the heavy cavalry of many other nations, a straight-bladed weapon with a heavy blade suitable to execute the cut. When British swords compared very ill with those encountered in Austrian service in the Netherlands, Le Marchant was responsible for designing new weapons; the 1796-pattern heavy cavalry sword he copied almost exactly from the Austrian 1775 *Pallasch*, having a massive, heavy straight blade with 'hatchet' point which made the thrust virtually impossible, though latterly some regiments ground their blades to produce operable points. It was used throughout the Napoleonic Wars, but was a fearful implement which compared ill with the thrusting-sword of the French; its chopper-like blade could cause dreadful injury but unless the head were targeted far fewer fatalities resulted than from injuries caused by the thrust. One officer wrote of it being a 'lumbering, clumsy, ill-contrived machine. It is too heavy, too short, too broad, too much like the sort of weapon which we have seen Grimaldi cut off the heads of a line of urchins on the stage,'[10] and experience in the Peninsular War emphasized the superiority of the thrusting-weapon; it provides a perfect illustration of the differing theories about the most effective design of sabre, yet not until 1908 did Britain fully accept the point and produce a truly effective cavalry weapon.

The light cavalry of most nations carried the curved-bladed sabre, with which it was possible to thrust but which was designed principally for the cut. The reason for the adoption of such weapons may have been largely traditional: the central European light horse from which most light cavalry was copied had always carried curved sabres, and these were retained even by those nations which realized that the thrust was most effective. French curved weapons could be used to thrust; the corresponding British 1796-pattern light dragoon sabre was so curved and heavily-bladed that only the slash was practicable, the aforementioned critic

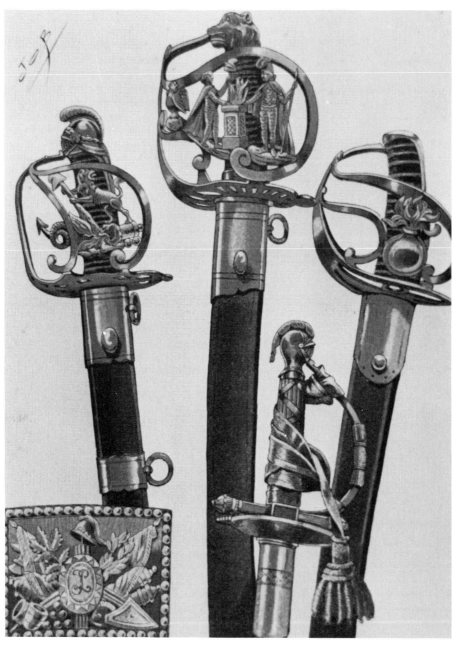

Swords of the French revolutionary armies, those at the centre and left bearing republican symbols incorporated into the basket-hilts (and also borne on the belt-plate, bottom left). The sabre at the right bears the grenade-badge of carabiniers upon the triple-bar guard, and the lighter-bladed weapon at the bottom, with helmet-shaped pommel, is an officer's épée as carried by the infantry. (Print after 'Job')

noting that he could only 'answer for its utility in making billets for the fire'![11]

In cavalry training, swordmanship was often restricted to the practice of a number of set poses or 'cuts', executed with the elbow stiff (movement coming from wrist and shoulder), or with a bent arm against infantry (necessary to obtain sufficient leverage for a downward strike; a bent elbow against cavalry exposed the forearm to a counter-blow). Cavalry combat was frequently very confused, though accounts tell of units approaching each other, opening their files and fencing at each other as the two bodies passed through each other. A confused mêlée might devolve into a multitude of individual combats, 'absolutely like a game at prison bars, which you must have seen at school', as one British officer wrote![12]

Body Armour

Armour was worn by the heavy cavalry of several European armies. France is best-known for its regiments of cuirassiers, who wore immensely heavy iron plates on the breast and lighter plates on the back; a relic of medieval warfare, they had been common to the mid-eighteenth century, but had generally declined in use, as the disadvantages of heavy armour came to outweigh its efficacy in combat: no longer proof against musketry at short range and even less against artillery, the cuirass was of greatest use in close-quarter mêlée, proof against sabre- and bayonet-blows; yet its weight was so prodigious that an unhorsed cuirassier might have difficulty regaining his feet, but in heavy ground might struggle like a 'turned turtle' (in Wellington's words). Such was the decline of the cuirass that in some armies – for example the Russian – regiments retained the name 'cuirassiers' even after discarding their armour, though it is interesting to note that in the latter case, cuirasses were again issued to the Russian heavy cavalry from 1812, emulating the French (from 1809 French-style thrusting swords were also introduced, as preferable to the previous heavy-bladed *Pallasch*; not all armies were sufficiently sensible to adopt better foreign styles in this way!).

The immense weight of the cuirass also restricted the choice of mounts, as only the largest horses could be truly effective for cuirassiers. An attempt to counter the weight problem was to dispense with the rear plate, as in most German armies (and to a lesser extent in the Russian), so that only the breast was protected; but this tended to negate the entire purpose of body-armour. The resolution of the conflicting theories about the best style of armour was made at Eckmühl when two bodies of cuirassiers came into conflict, the French with armoured breast and back and the Austrians with protection only at the front: in the confused mêlée which ensued the Austrians suffered a fatal disadvantage when the French were able to thrust at their backs, so that the proportion of Austrian killed and wounded amounted to thirteen and eight respectively for each French casualty. In such circumstances, the single cuirass was probably no more effective than the common expedient of protecting the body by wearing a rolled cloak bandolier-fashion, protecting against a cut to the left shoulder, the principal stroke of an enemy cavalryman. This practice was so common that the order 'Roll cloaks!' became almost synonymous in the French army with a sign that combat was imminent, while similar defences were improvised by the greatcoats of the Prussian infantry among others.

The Lance

One of the most ancient cavalry weapons, by the mid-seventeenth century the lance had virtually disappeared from western European warfare, being 'a thing of much labour and industry to learn'.[13] After that it was primarily a Polish weapon, which accounts for the Polish-style costume adopted by most lancer regiments when these were formed in the later Revolutionary Wars and early Napoleonic period, by France, Austria, Russia, etc., all of which originally employed Poles in this role. The number of units remained small, however, only France and Russia forming appreciable quantities of lancers after 1811, as the lance required peculiar skill and exceptional circumstances to be truly effective. Against cavalry, a closely packed body of lancers could remain impervious to injury, as their opponents would be unable to come within sabre-range (as demonstrated briefly at Genappe in 1815 when French lancers held off British hussars attempting to penetrate a narrow street), but once the lance-point was 'turned' in an open mêlée the lancer was almost incapable of defending himself as his opponent closed in. William Swabey noted in 1812 that lancers 'made a very pretty tournament appearance . . . but as to their being formidable to formed troops it is quite ridiculous; a dragoon with his broadsword is worth two of them'.[14] Against infantry, however, or in a scouting or skirmishing role (as the lance was used by 'irregular' cavalry such as Russian Cossacks and Spanish guerrillas) it was potentially lethal; the most convincing demonstration of its prowess was at Albuera, where the Polish Lancers of the Vistula Legion massacred Colborne's brigade of British infantry which had failed to form square, the approach of the lancers having been concealed by a hail-storm. A further advantage was demonstrated at the Katzbach where a Prussian infantry square was unable to fire because of heavy rain, but held off the French cavalry with its bayonets until the arrival of lancers who were able to spear the infantry without coming within bayonet-range. A very similar event happened at Dresden, where Austrian infantry resisted cuirassiers successfully until General Latour-Maubourg's escort of fifty lancers was ordered up, who broke the infantry and allowed the cuirassiers to get among them; this contributed to Marmont's recommendation that the best arrangement was to have the front rank of every regiment armed with lances.

Pikes were used by infantry only in time of great shortage, as for the Prussian *Landwehr* in 1813–14, Russian *opolchenie* (militia) in 1812 and the Portuguese *ordenança* in the early Peninsular War, but the pike was never effective and was replaced by muskets at the first opportunity. Half-pikes were used as symbols of NCO rank in some armies, such as the spontoons of British infantry sergeants, the partizans of

Russians or the halberds with which the French flag-escorts were equipped.

The Carbine

Carbines were short-barrelled, lighter versions of the infantry musket with which most cavalry was equipped, for use when the cavalry acted as skirmishers, enabling them to fire from foot or horseback. Their use was primarily as a skirmish-weapon, though a noted exception occurred at Eylau when the French 20th *Chasseurs à Cheval* met a Russian cavalry charge with a volley at six yards' range, knocking down the first line before charging the remainder with the sabre. However, the short barrel – very markedly short in some cases, such as the Austrian carbine or the British 'Paget' pattern – resulted in a very limited range and even less accuracy than the infantry musket; for only a few carbines were produced with rifled barrels. The inefficiency of such weapons led to their withdrawal from some units, especially from those that were not normally expected to skirmish (such as the withdrawal of carbines from the British Household Cavalry in 1813), or their issue to only a small number of troopers, such as to the sixteen 'flankers' of each Russian hussar squadron.

An exception was the French cavalry, whose carbines were longer and generally superior to those of other nations; and there existed in addition the 'dragoon musket', a slightly shorter version of the infantry weapon, designed to allow dragoons to operate as infantry, and was even issued to some *voltigeurs* in place of the more unwieldly long musket without reducing their effectiveness. Thus, French cavalry skirmishers generally enjoyed a considerable advantage over those of other nations, as exemplified in the Peninsular War: 'The French dragoons and chasseurs à cheval were armed with a long fusée, which could throw a ball as far as the musket of an infantry soldier, and that our dragoons, on the contrary, both light and heavy, were armed with a little pop-gun . . . the French dragoons often dismounted . . . and shot at our dragoons at a distance which rendered our short carbines almost useless';[15] 'Our light dragoon carbine is so decidedly bad in all respects, that we have only patience to say, the sooner it is got rid of the better.'[16]

The Pistol

Most cavalrymen carried one or two pistols in their holsters at the front of the saddle, though their effectiveness in combat was virtually nil; in general the pistol was more of an

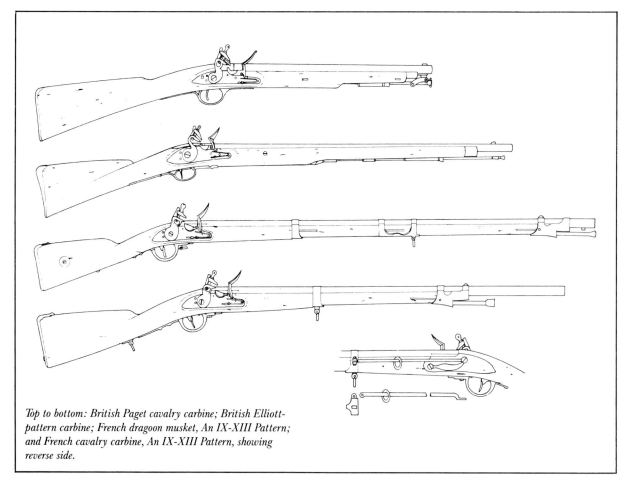

Top to bottom: British Paget cavalry carbine; British Elliott-pattern carbine; French dragoon musket, An IX-XIII Pattern; and French cavalry carbine, An IX-XIII Pattern, showing reverse side.

encumbrance than an asset, especially if it required a different calibre of ammunition from the carbine. (When both carbine and pistol were of equal bore, additional care was necessary not to use the full charge of powder in the pistol: a carbine-load would have blown the pistol from the hand). In combat, the pistol's range was so limited that its discharge was almost pointless 'till you feel your antagonist's ribs with the muzzle',[17] at which range it was safer to use the sword; as an experienced cavalry officer wrote, 'We never saw a pistol made use of except to shoot a glandered horse.'[18]

Artillery

Each nation possessed its own pattern of artillery, but basic design and employment was very similar. There were two principal types of artillery piece: cannon (termed 'guns'), which had a length of twelve calibres or more (i.e., twelve bore-diameters in length); and shorter-barrelled weapons or

A typical piece of field artillery: a 3-pounder on a double-bracket carriage. (Thomas E. DeVoe)

howitzers which were intended for high-angle fire rather than the 'direct' fire of ordinary cannon. The different sizes of piece were classified into 'natures', types usually defined by the weight of shot fired by a cannon or by the bore-diameter of a howitzer; hence '9-pounder' cannon and '5½-inch' howitzers, etc. All weapons were smooth-bored and muzzle-loading, the hollow inside of the barrel being bored out of the cast tube; manufacture was either in iron (which corroded and was prone to splitting after much use), or in 'brass' or 'gun-metal', a version of bronze which was less likely to crack but might suffer from distortion caused by the heat of discharge, known as 'muzzle-droop'.

Guns were produced in sizes ranging from small and light 3pdrs up to immense 32pdr guns and even larger. In general, the heaviest guns used in a mobile field role were the 12pdrs, with 18- and 24pdrs (of much greater weight) being restricted to the slow-moving siege-trains, used for battering holes in fortress-walls; the very heaviest were confined to static defences and were known as 'garrison artillery'. Apart from these, which were generally mounted on large wooden or iron 'garrison cartridges', sometimes with tiny wheels or 'trucks', all artillery was mounted on a standard type of carriage, a wooden framework bound with iron, supporting

two large wheels, with a 'trail' at the rear to stabilize the gun and to enable it to be attached to its two-wheeled limber, the ammunition-container with shafts to which the team of horses was harnessed. Construction of the carriage was either a 'bracket trail' (a framework of two baulks of timber with connecting struts) or a 'block trail' of a single baulk. Slots or iron brackets on the trail allowed the gun-carriage to be traversed by means of iron levers or 'handspikes', motive-power being provided by the muscles of the gun-crew. Aiming in the vertical plane was achieved by the elevation or depression of the barrel by a 'quoin' (a wooden chock upon which the sealed end of the barrel rested) or (more commonly) by a screw-elevator, an adjustable iron rod under the sealed end of the barrel; or by a combination of the two, as in the Russian 1805 System which had an elevator-screw passing horizontally through a quoin.

The principal projectile of the cannon was the roundshot, an iron ball which cut a swathe through whatever it passed en route from the muzzle to where it first pitched ('first graze'), from where (unless the ground was so soft that it sank in) it ricocheted and continued to bounce until its force was spent; when just trundling along the ground like a cricket-ball it was still capable of striking off a foot. Though muzzle-velocities of cannon were similar, the increasing weight of shot greatly increased the effectiveness of the round; thus the artillerist Müller calculated that a 6lb shot was 50 per cent more effective than a 3lb, and a 12lb twice as effective. All fire from cannon had to be 'direct'; indirect fire (over the heads of friendly troops) was impossible. Ranges varied with the amount of propellant charge (each 'nature' had a specified amount) and the elevation of the barrel; though as accuracy declined markedly with the longer range, it was usual for fire not to be opened until it might take reasonable effect. Many complex tables were published to guide artillery officers, of which the following (tests conducted with brass guns in 1793) is typical:

Nature	Charge		Distance of 1st graze (yds)				
		point-blank 1°	2°	3°	4°	5°	
Medium 24pdr 8lb	488		757	1103	1425	1557	1745
Medium 12pdr 4lb		705	973	1189			
Light 12pdr 3lb		601	816	1063			
Medium 6pdr 2lb		775	1003	144			
Short 6pdr 24oz		628	804	991			
(length 54 inches)							
3pdr 1lb		679	883	918[19]			

At closer range, 'canister' or 'case-shot' would be fired, turning the cannon into a gigantic shotgun. Canister consisted of a tin case packed with musket-balls which ruptured as it left the muzzle; with a maximum effective range of 600 yards, it was restricted to repelling a charge or supporting an attack when the enemy was within close range. Two varieties existed, 'light' and 'heavy case'; for example, for a British 6pdr the former consisted of 85 1½oz balls and for the latter 41 3½oz balls. Light case was effective only to about 250 yards; British artillery restricted the firing

of canister to about 350 yards' range, whereas the French fired their heavy case up to its maximum effective range. The 'spread' of shot from the muzzle was calculated by Müller as a circle of 32 feet diameter per 100 yards of range. Frequent references are found to the use of 'grapeshot' on land, though true grapeshot (a number of larger iron balls arranged around an iron column, covered with painted or tarred canvas) was restricted to use at sea; on land, the term 'grapeshot' was (incorrectly) used to describe heavy case.

The other variety of projectile was explosive shot or 'common shell', an iron sphere of combustible material which exploded by means of a fuze ignited by the discharge of the gun. 'Common shell' was the principal projectile of the howitzer, the high-angle fire of which enabled shells to be lobbed over obstacles and friendly troops. A development, used only by Britain, was 'spherical case' or shrapnel, named after its inventor, Henry Shrapnel, R.A., which was first used in 1804. It resembled an ordinary shell but with a thinner casing and filled with a bursting-charge of gunpowder plus musket-balls, so that when the fuze was trimmed correctly the shot could be timed to burst in the air over the heads of the enemy troops, raining balls and shell-casing upon them, and when correctly fuzed (which required some experience) was a most formidable 'secret weapon'; it represented up to 15 per cent of all British ammunition and 50 per cent of howitzer ammunition.

Although each nation had its own gun-drill and numbers of gun-crew (the non-specialist members, who provided the muscle-power for positioning the gun, increased in number with the size of piece), the method of 'serving' a gun was reasonably standard and usually involved five specialist crewmen, though in action some of their duties could be combined. By this period 'prepared cartridges' had replaced the previous use of loose powder, the cartridges consisting of the propellant gunpowder in a sealed fabric or paper bag, the former preferable for leaving fewer unburnt fragments in the barrel after firing. A further development was 'fixed ammunition' in which the projectile had a wooden 'sabot' or shoe affixed, which rested upon the powder of the cartridge.

After unlimbering the gun was aimed, the duty of the senior gunner. Direction of shot was achieved by 'traversing', manoeuvring the gun-trail by means of handspikes and brute force; the barrel was then aligned in the vertical plane to allow for the target being above or below the level of the gun, with an additional 'tangent' elevation to compensate the fall of shot in flight. This calculation was revolutionized by the invention of the 'tangent sight', an adjustable, notched cross-bar at the sealed end of the barrel which was aligned with the fore-sight; perfected, like the screw-elevator, before 1780, it turned the previous haphazard gun-laying into a more precise science, though an element of skill was still required in the gun-captain's assessment of the 'fall of shot' and the consequent adjustments until the target was hit.

When the gun was aimed, the second specialist crewman or 'spongeman' swabbed out the barrel with a wet 'sponge', a rammer with a fleece or similar material nailed on to the head, to clear the barrel of any smouldering residue from the previous shot which might prematurely ignite the next charge. While the sponging was in progress the third crewman or 'ventsman' put his thumb (in a leather stall) over the vent at the sealed end of the barrel to prevent the ingress of air which might cause smouldering material to blow back at the spongeman. The fourth gunner or 'loader' then inserted the cartridge and projectile into the muzzle of the gun, whereupon the spongeman reversed his sponge and pushed the charge down the barrel with the 'rammer' end of the sponge. The ventsman then inserted a 'pricker' down the vent to puncture the cartridge, and then filled the vent with either a length of 'quick-match' (cotton soaked in saltpetre and spirits of wine) or (after about 1800) with a quill or paper tube of mealed powder, to establish conctact between the charge in the barrel and the spark which would ignite it. The fifth member of the crew, the 'firer', then waited until the others had stepped clear before igniting the charge in the vent with a portfire, a length of burning slow-match in a holder. This communicated with the gunpowder in the barrel which exploded with a loud roar, sending the projectile on its course and causing the gun to recoil sharply.

The whole process was then begun anew, as the gun had to be re-aligned after every shot unless the enemy were at virtually point-blank range. (The other method of ignition, by a flintlock bolted to the barrel, was used only at sea.) Rate of fire depended upon the time needed to re-lay the gun after recoil. In a test in 1777 twelve to fourteen unaimed shots per minute were achieved, but this represented a useless waste of ammunition; in practice two roundshot or three canister per minute would seem to have been about the average, gunners being careful not to waste ammunition (there would seem to be no recorded instances of guns running short in combat) and to fire generally only when the target was visible and not obscured by smoke.

Artillery was usually transported by means of the limber, though two other methods were available to save time on the battlefield: by attaching a rope or 'prolonge' to the limber from the gun-trail, to allow the gun to move forward without the time-consuming business of limbering-up and unlimbering again; or it could be dragged forward manually by 'bricole', the gunners hauling on ropes or straps attached to the gun-carriage. (The Swedish invention dating from the later campaigns of Charles XII, known as 'Cronstedt's

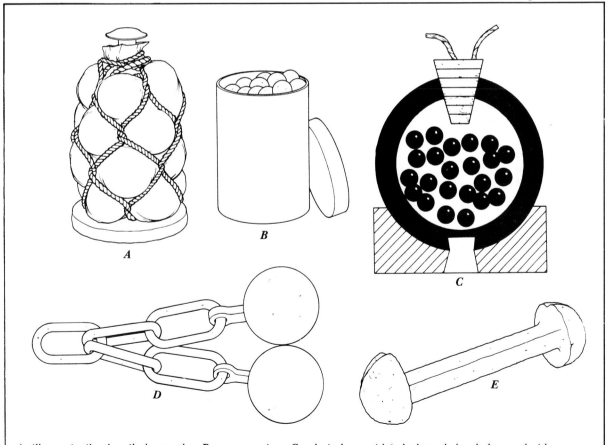

Artillery projectiles. *A*, quilted grape-shot; *B*, case, or canister; *C*, spherical case with 'sabot' attached to the base, and with a wooden fuze in the top; *D*, chain-shot; *E*, bar shot.

advance-rods' (*anmarschbommer*), handspikes at right-angles to the barrel which could be pushed by the gunners, were adopted by few other nations save Austria.)

The heavier guns were restricted to siege-work, the 'battering-train' moving at a ponderous pace, hauled by immense teams of horses or oxen. Included in the siege artillery was the mortar, a short-barrelled shell-gun intended only for high-angle fire, used exclusively for siege and garrison work due to the immense weight (the British 13in mortar, only 43½ inches in length, weighed 36cwt!). Their short barrels were affixed to wooden 'beds' (the recoil would have destroyed an ordinary carriage), with quoin elevation, though in practice it was usual for the mortar to be set permanently at 45° elevation and range varied by the amount of propellant used: the mortar already quoted had a range of 245 yards with a 14oz powder charge and 2,706 yards with 8lb. There were in addition smaller mortars known as 'Coehorns' or 'Coehoorns' (after the designer), small enough to be carried by two men but alarming to fire because they jumped in the air as the projectile left the

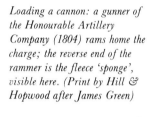

Loading a cannon: a gunner of the Honourable Artillery Company (1804) rams home the charge; the reverse end of the rammer is the fleece 'sponge', visible here. (Print by Hill & Hopwood after James Green)

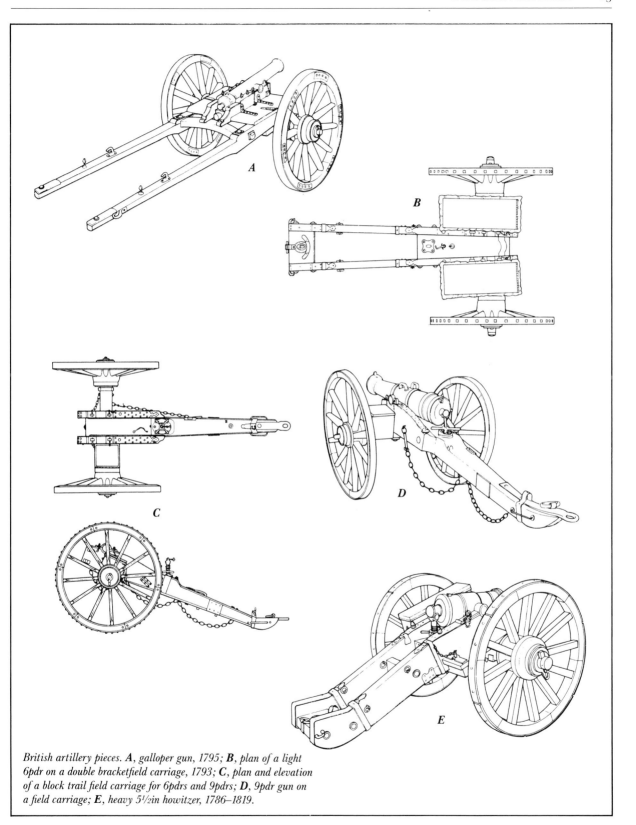

British artillery pieces. **A**, *galloper gun, 1795;* **B**, *plan of a light
6pdr on a double bracketfield carriage, 1793;* **C**, *plan and elevation
of a block trail field carriage for 6pdrs and 9pdrs;* **D**, *9pdr gun on
a field carriage;* **E**, *heavy 5½in howitzer, 1786–1819.*

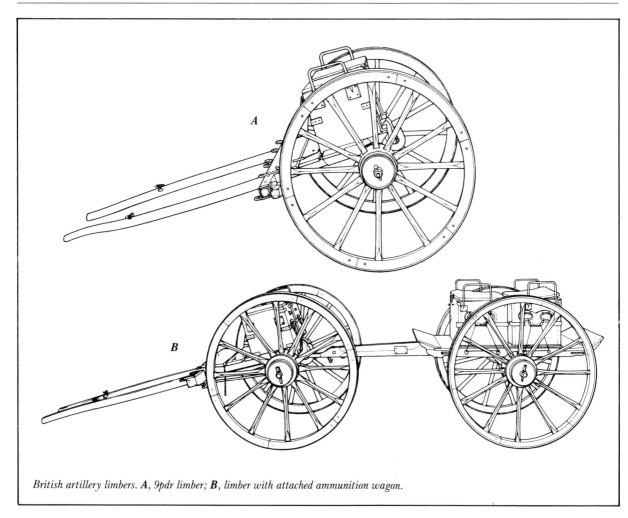

British artillery limbers. **A**, *9pdr limber;* **B**, *limber with attached ammunition wagon.*

barrel. Mortars fired explosive shells, similar to howitzer-shells but often with thicker bases to ensure that they landed fuze-uppermost and were not extinguished when they fell. Falling almost vertically from their immensely high trajectory, bombs could have startling effects, such as that which exploded the Almeida magazine.

An artillery piece used almost exclusively at sea or in garrison was the carronade, a wide-bore, short gun intended to fire round or grapeshot at comparatively short range; named from the Carron foundry in Scotland where first manufactured, it was adopted by several nations and used especially as bow- or stern-chasers aboard ships-of-the-line, or to supplement the main armament of frigates, though an experiment conducted by the British navy was to arm HMS *Glatton* (which fought at Copenhagen under the command of William Bligh of *Bounty* fame) exclusively with 56 carronades. The effect of a carronade at short range was such that it confirmed its nickname, the 'smasher'.

Projectiles used as incendiaries were known by the generic term 'carcasses', resembling shells with three or five fuze-holes and filled with combustible mixture; and for illum-ination, 'light balls' or 'Chinese lights', similar shells with three fuze-holes.

Rockets were employed only by Britain and Austria, of the pattern devised by Sir William Congreve and bearing his name, consisting of a head of various sizes (explosive, case-shot or incendiary) affixed to a stick and launched from a small tripod. The largest had a stick 24 feet long, carrying a head 8 inches in diameter and weighing 3cwt, with a max-imum range of 2,500 yards; but the heaviest field rocket (and lightest bombardment rocket) was the 32pdr, with the 12pdr being recommended for the commonest use on the battlefield. It was an extremely inaccurate and unreliable weapon with a habit of flying off-course or even doubling back upon the firer. For siege-work it was considerably effective (40,000 were fired at Copenhagen in 1807) though Wellington in particular was most unimpressed, stating that as he had no wish to burn any town he thus had no use for rockets, only accepting the proffered rocket troop in the later Peninsular War as a way of acquiring their horses, of which there was a constant shortage. However, the rocket's very unreliability was its main asset. Gleig of the British 85th

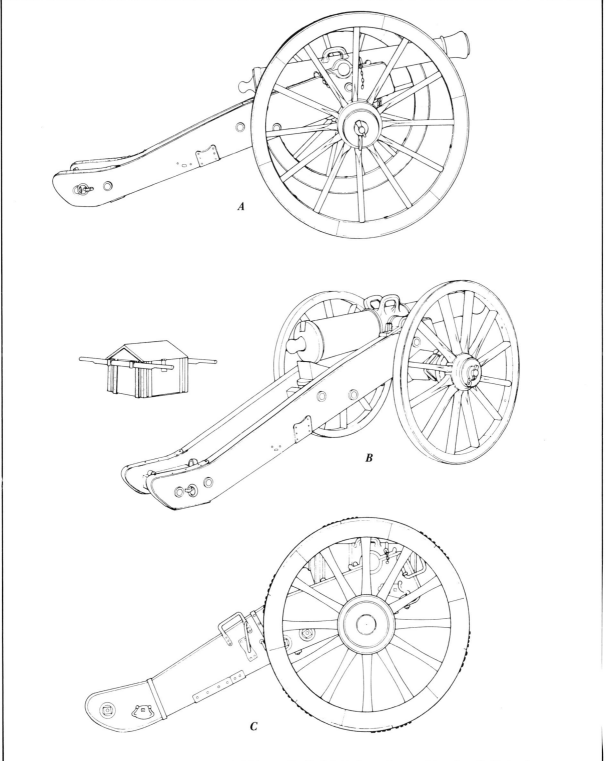

*French artillery pieces, Gribeauval System. **A**, 8pdr field piece; **B**, 12pdr field piece and ammunition chest; **C**, 6in howitzer.*

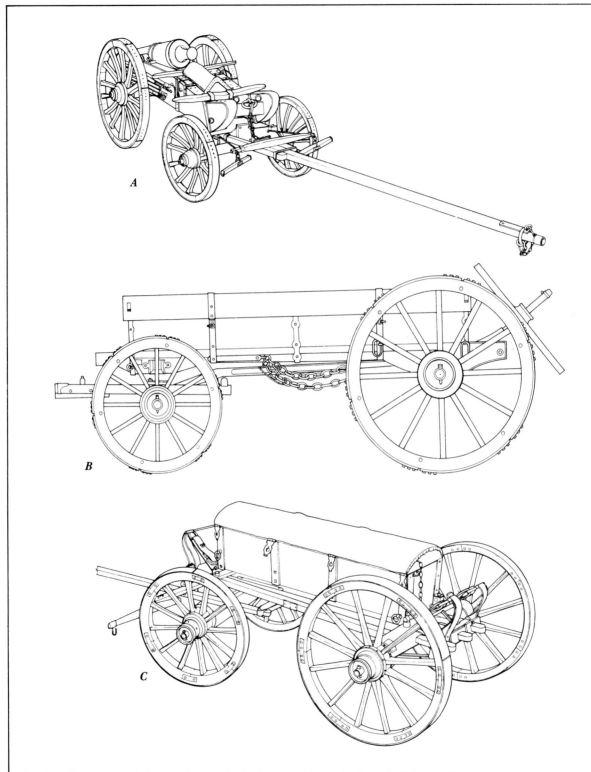

French artillery wagons. **A**, *Gribeauval cannon limbered up;* **B**, *Gribeauval caisson;* **C**, *Gribeauval horse artillery caisson.*

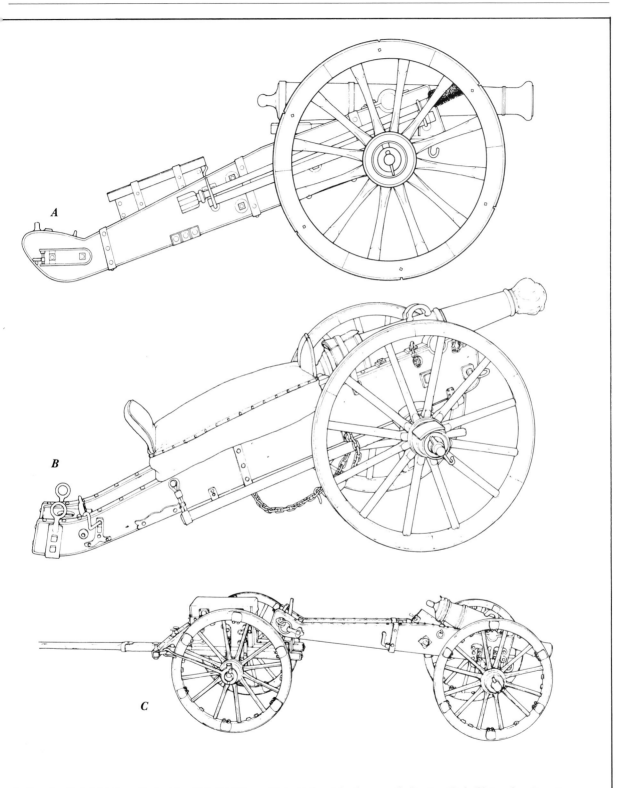

A, Prussian 6pdr field piece; *B*, Austrian 6pdr field piece with padded seat for the crew; *C*, Russian 10pdr 'Unicorn' equipment.

◄ The 'whiff of grapeshot':
Bonaparte defends the
Convention in Paris and makes
his name in the process, 5
October 1795. This provides an
excellent view of the operation of
Gribeauval fieldpieces; note the
handspike being used to traverse
the gun in the centre, and the
open coffret (ammunition-box)
in the right foreground. The
gunner at the left inserts a quill
of powder into the vent of his
cannon. (Print after F. de
Myrbach)

◄ Below left:
A piece of artillery being
manhandled by 'bricole';
apparently a 'battalion gun' as
the crew appear to be light
infantrymen, with a Royal
Artillery instructor with a fur-
crested 'round hat' at extreme
left. (Print after W. H. Pyne,
1802)

▼ A fieldpiece with horse
harnessed directly to it. a form
of 'prolonge' to obviate repeated
unlimbering; note the handspike
inserted in the trail. (Print after
W. H. Pyne, 1802)

described 'the confusion in the ranks of the enemy' which 'beggars description . . . you see it coming yet know not how to avoid it. It skips and starts from place to place in so strange a manner, that the chances are, when you are running to the right or left to get out of the way, that you run directly against it; and hence the absolute rout which a fire of ten or twelve rockets can create'.[20] Such a psychological effect was inflicted upon the French attempting to prevent the crossing of the Adour in 1814: rockets were fired to cover the crossing, and 'the second that let off carried away the legs of one man, set the knapsack of another on fire, and knocked about many more throwing them into great confusion and wounded several. An old serjeant, whom we made prisoner, said, during all his service, he had not known what fear was before; but these machines were devils, running up and down, and picking out and destroying particular victims . . . The rockets were discharged at the time when they produced the greatest effect, in a battery ten abreast.'[21] As the Russian general Wittgenstein remarked, having seen them used by the British at Leipzig, 'They look as if they were made in hell, and surely are the devil's own artillery.'[22]

Notes

1. *Passages in the Early Military Life of General Sir George T. Napier*, ed. W. C. E. Napier, London 1884, pp. 131–2.
2. *To All Sportsmen*, Colonel G. Hanger, London 1814, p. 205.
3. *Reflections on the Menaced Invasion*, Colonel G. Hanger, London 1804, pp. 195–6.
4. See *Firepower*, General B. P. Hughes, London 1974, p. 27.
5. *United Service Journal*, 1839; see *History of the XX Regiment*, B. Smyth, London 1889, pp. 406–9.
6. *Commentaries on the Surgery of War*, G. J. Guthrie, London 1853, p. 16.
7. *Recollections of my Military Life*, G. Landmann, London 1854, II, p. 221.
8. *Scloppetaria, or Considerations on the Nature and Use of Rifle Barrel Guns*, 'A Corporal of Riflemen' (actually Captain H. Beaufroy), London 1808, p. 189.
9. See *United Service Journal*, 1831, II, p. 61.
10. ibid.
11. ibid.
12. Account of Campo Mayor in *The Courier*, 20 April 1811.
13. *Militarie Instructions for the Cavallrie*, J. Cruso, Cambridge 1632, p. 30.
14. *Diary of Campaigns in the Peninsula*, W. Swabey, ed. F. A. Whinyates, orig. pub. in *Proceedings of the Royal Artillery Institution*, 1984 edn (London), p. 114.
15. *Rough Sketches of the Life of an Old Soldier*, J. Leach, London 1831, pp. 268–9.
16. *United Service Journal*, 1831, II, p. 61.
17. ibid.
18. ibid.
19. *The Bombardier and Pocket Gunner*, R. W. Adye, London 1802, p. 163.
20. *The Subaltern*, G. R. Gleig, Edinburgh 1872, pp. 290–1.
21. *Edinburgh Evening Courant*, 11 April 1814.
22. ibid. 20 January 1814.

References

The following includes some of the most significant and/or most accessible titles:

Adye, R. W. *The Bombardier and Pocket Gunner*, London 1802 (invaluable source: the artilleryman's *vade mecum* of the period).

Blackmore, H. L. *British Military Firearms 1650–1850*, London 1961.

Darling, A. D. *Red Coat and Brown Bess*, Ottawa 1970 (detailed study of the most famous and widely used musket of the period).

Ffoulkes, C., and Hopkinson, E. C. *Sword, Lance and Bayonet*, Cambridge 1938, reprinted New York 1967 (concentrates on British weapons but makes 'general' points as well).

Gooding, S. J. *An Introduction to British Artillery in North America*, Ottawa 1972 (of wider relevance than the title suggests).

Haythornthwaite, P. J. *Weapons and Equipment of the Napoleonic Wars*, Poole 1979.

Hicks, J. E. *French Military Weapons 1717–1938*, New Milford, Connecticut, 1964.

Hogg, I. V. *A History of Artillery*, London 1974 (general account of the subject throughout history).

Howard, F. *Sailing Ships of War 1400–1860*, London 1979.

Hughes, Major-General B. P. *British Smoothbore Artillery*, Harrisburg, Pennsylvania, 1969.

— *Firepower, Weapons Effectiveness on the Battlefield 1630–1850*, London 1974.

— *Open Fire: Artillery Tactics from Marlborough to Wellington*, Chicester 1983.

Lavery, B. *The Arming and Fitting of English Ships of War 1600–1815*, London 1987 (much of relevance for other nations as well).

Peterson, H. L. *Round Shot and Rammers*, Harrisburg, Pennsylvania, 1969 (concentrates on artillery used in North America but is an excellent guide to the subject in general).

Robson, B. *Swords of the British Army*, London 1975.

Wagner, E. *Cut and Thrust Weapons*, Prague and London 1967 (covers many of the 'regulation' patterns of the principal nations).

Wilkinson-Latham, R. *British Artillery on Land and Sea 1790–1820*, Newton Abbot 1973.

THE ART OF WAR ON LAND

The art of war in the Revolutionary and Napoleonic age cannot comprehensively be compressed into a few pages; indeed, to cover all aspects and the various national peculiarities, and to evaluate the methods of the leading personalities, would require a work probably as large as this entire book. However, it is possible to recount the basic tenets of what might be termed 'minor tactics' as they applied in general and which would have been recognized by almost any military officer of the period, though these were amended with the experience gained in the campaigns. For reasons of space, what follows includes 'generalizations' about which contradictory examples may be found, and for more extensive and specific references the reader is directed to the works listed at the end of this section.

Infantry

The evolution of 'minor tactics' was dependent initially upon the characteristics of the weaponry available, though it is debatable how quickly tactical theory would have altered had more advanced weapons been widely available, given the inherent conservatism of many of the military establishments. For the infantry, the principal weapon was the smooth-bore flintlock musket, and though some national patterns were superior to others, the general standard of efficiency meant that fire was most effective at 100 yards and below. Rifled muskets were more accurate, but there was little incentive to make them universal as within ordinary tactics there was no necessity to hit any individual; due to the compact blocks in which infantry manoeuvred, provided the shot neither hit the ground nor went over the heads of the target, an error of five or ten yards right or left was relatively unimportant, as damage would be caused to the enemy no matter where along his line the shot struck. (It is interesting to reflect that in 1798 a study was published[1] which advocated a return to the longbow and pike as a way of combating France, to overcome the fact that all armies used muskets of generally equal efficiency, thus putting armies theoretically on parity; a similar plan had been advanced in Charles I's reign[2] and had been rejected as outdated even then! Nevertheless, the longbow in the hands of a trained man would certainly have out-shot any musket, though it was rendered quite impractical by the fact that whereas a recruit could be trained to use a musket adequately in a matter of hours, it required many years of practise to produce a truly effective archer.)

Infantry manoeuvred in closely packed formations out of necessity, even though it rendered them vulnerable to artillery- and musket-fire which would have had reduced effect upon widespread formations; because in order to retain cohesion, compact and disciplined bodies were the only option, for a disordered unit was not only prey to marauding cavalry but could not respond to orders or change its formation as required. It was this which caused the troops of

most nations to be subjected to endless drilling and often draconian discipline; it was unpleasant to endure but not only rendered them an effective unit but might very probably save their lives in combat.

The organization of the basic infantry unit was similar in most armies, and determined largely by what was practicable on the field of battle. Although each nation had its own organization, the basic tactical unit of all was the battalion, with a maximum practicable strength of about 1,000 men. (On active service a battalion with an establishment of 1,000 might often drop to half or even a quarter of that; but what follows applied in theory at least.) The battalion was subdivided into a number of companies, generally between six and ten, with a maximum practicable strength of between 100 and 130 men; anything in excess of that could cause problems of unwieldly sized subdivisions on the battlefield. (The company was originally an administrative rather than tactical unit, in the seventeenth century being virtually the personal possession of the captain who was responsible for its pay, recruiting and provisions; by the later eighteenth century these duties had been taken over by the battalion or regimental administration, leaving the company as one of a number of tactical units.) As the battalion was an autonomous entity, the parent regiment (two or more battalions) was largely an administrative

The action at Boussu, 3 November 1792; the combat in the background demonstrates the French tactic of columnar attack (left) against the static Austrian line (right). (Print after Hippolyte Lecomte)

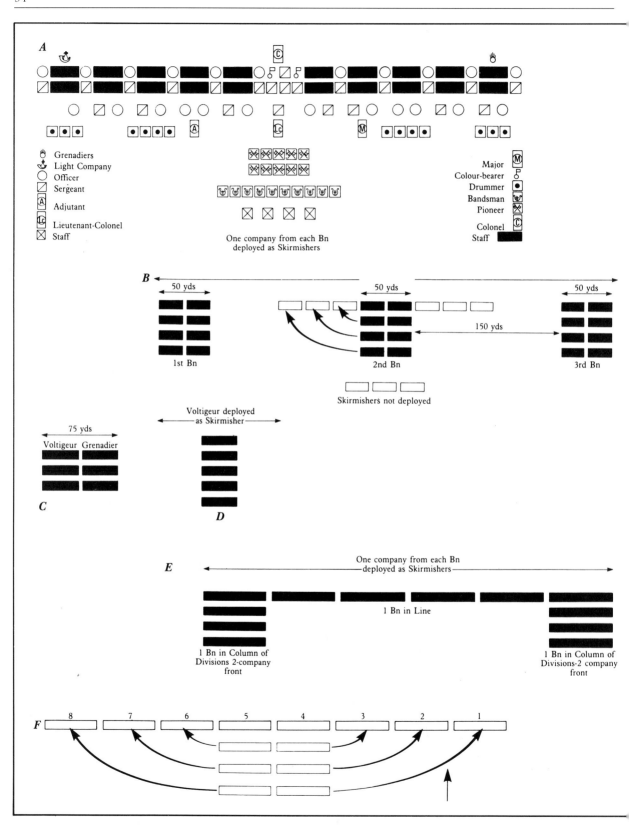

A

Grenadiers
Light Company
Officer
Sergeant
Adjutant
Lieutenant-Colonel
Staff

Major
Colour-bearer
Drummer
Bandsman
Pioneer
Colonel
Staff

One company from each Bn
deployed as Skirmishers

B

50 yds   50 yds   50 yds

1st Bn   2nd Bn   3rd Bn

150 yds

Skirmishers not deployed

Voltigeur deployed
as Skirmisher

75 yds

Voltigeur Grenadier

C   *D*

E

One company from each Bn
deployed as Skirmishers

1 Bn in Line

1 Bn in Column of
Divisions 2-company
front

1 Bn in Column of
Divisions-2 company
front

F   8   7   6   5   4   3   2   1

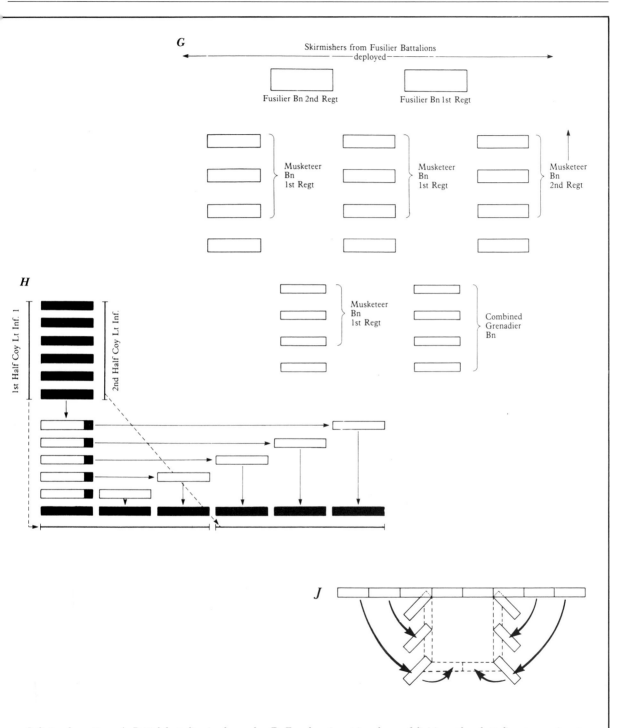

G

Skirmishers from Fusilier Battalions deployed

Fusilier Bn 2nd Regt

Fusilier Bn 1st Regt

Musketeer Bn 1st Regt

Musketeer Bn 1st Regt

Musketeer Bn 2nd Regt

Musketeer Bn 1st Regt

Combined Grenadier Bn

H

1st Half Coy Lt Inf.

2nd Half Coy Lt Inf.

J

*Infantry formations: **A**, British battalion in close order; **B**, French regiment in column of divisions, three battalions to a regiment; **C** and **D**, alternative formations for single-battalion deployments after the 1809 reorganization; **E**, 'l'ordre mixte', showing a three-battalion regiment deployed partly in line and partly in column; **F**, Prussian four-company battalion (1812) moving from columns into line; **G**, Prussian brigade of two regiments deployed for attack (1812); **H**, seven-company battalion moving from column into line; **J**, an eight-company battalion forming square from line.*

Raising the siege of Thionville, 16 October 1792. This depicts the use of what came to be styled 'l'ordre mixte': battalions charging in column (left foreground) with the support of the musketry of the battalion in line (left mid-ground). The Austrians (right) are Hungarian grenadiers (foreground, in fur caps and sky-blue pantaloons) and 'German' fusiliers (right mid-ground, in the squat 'Casquet' cap and white breeches). (Print after Hippolyte Lecomte)

grouping, as it was by no means the usual practice for the several battalions of a regiment to serve together.

Although the company was the battalion's principal subdivision, others existed: the company could be further divided into platoons, half-companies or (German) *Zügen*; or could be combined with another company to produce a manoeuvre-unit termed a 'division'. Within a battalion, it was common practice for one company to be designated as 'grenadiers' and another as light infantry, these forming the élite or 'flank' companies, the former appellation used because most prestige attached to them, and the latter term arising from the fact that when a battalion assembled in line, its élite companies usually stood on the flanks, the most vulnerable part of the line. Apart from distinctions in uniform, however, there was often little difference between the élite companies and the remainder, the latter sometimes termed 'battalion' or 'centre' companies, often fusiliers or, especially in German armies, musketeers. The grenadiers were named from their being equipped in the late seventeenth and early eighteenth centuries with hand-grenades, a weapon which had totally fallen from use by the late eighteenth century; supposedly they were composed of the most stalwart or veteran members of the battalion, or at least those with the largest physique. Conversely, the light infantry supposedly were the most nimble, smallest men, trained in skirmish-tactics; though in some armies they differed little in practice from the ordinary 'line' companies.

The French Revolutionary Wars caused a major change in tactics. Before the Revolution, although light infantry had grown to great competence as a result of experience in the Seven Years War or in colonial warfare (respectively Austria and Britain in particular), tactics were based upon the infantry line, a manoeuvrable though somewhat rigid formation three or four deep, which enabled most if not all of the battalion's muskets to be fired simultaneously. The successes of the disciplined firepower and linear attacks of Frederick the Great's Prussians had a considerable influence throughout Europe, so that although battalions might use columns for manoeuvre (an easier formation to keep when moving at speed), for combat the line was pre-eminent. The French armies of the Revolutionary period introduced a totally new mode of tactics, not originally intended to be innovative but adopted simply out of necessity. The rapid expansion of the French forces at the beginning of the Revolutionary Wars, sweeping into the ranks thousands of untrained men, rendered the old-style tactics no longer feasible, there being insufficient time to drill or instruct the

conscripts. The solution was not new, for column-manoeuvre had been advocated before the Revolution, but was adopted basically to utilize the respective qualities of the units which comprised the early French armies. Those trained battalions which could operate in the conventional way were allowed to retain their linear formations to utilize their firepower; the untrained battalions were paired with them and used their only tactic, a headlong rush to fall upon an enemy line already disordered by the musketry of their better-trained colleagues. The rapid advance in column proved so successful in the early Revolutionary Wars that it was retained even when time was available for the men to be properly trained, evolving into the French formation of *l'ordre mixte* ('mixed order'), in which units in column were arrayed with units in line. Latterly, it seems as if the intention was for column-attacks to move rapidly to within musket-range and then deploy into line for an old-style linear 'firefight'; but for various reasons, not least the counter-measures adopted by some of the more capable opponents, such deployment rarely happened before the column was repelled.

Allied to the development of the columnar attack was the re-birth of light infantry tactics, though some of the more conservative military establishments regarded light infantry service as anything from a minor consideration to an unnecessary and even anarchic development; and in some armies (for example those of Austria and Russia) light infantry never achieved the proficiency of the 'expert' nations such as France and Britain. In the earlier eighteenth century, light infantry had been used as an adjunct to the conventional line, except in terrain peculiarly suited for more extensive light infantry service, such as North America; the light troops were used as skirmishers on the flanks or in the van of an army, as scouts or as a way of harassing the enemy, but had never supplanted the line as the principal formation.

From the earliest stages of the Revolutionary Wars it became customary for French column attacks to be preceded

---

'On seeing this leading column marching in such good order, the enemy confined itself to attacking it with their bullets, which it despised, and soon left behind it. When it came to the lot of the grenadiers of the old guard to pass through this fire, they closed their ranks around Napoleon like a moving fortress, proud of having to protect him. Their band of music expressed this pride. When the danger was greatest, they played the well-known air, *"Où peut-on être mieux qu'au sein de sa famille?"* ("Where can we be happier than in the bosom of our family?"). But the Emperor, whom nothing escaped, stopped them with an exclamation, "Rather play, *'Veillons au salut de l'Empire!'* ("Let us watch for the safety of the Empire!") words much better suited to his preoccupation, and to the general situation.'

(*History of the Expedition to Russia*, Count Philippe de Segur, London 1825, II, p. 206.)

by hosts of skirmishers; indeed, so prolific were these troops that on occasion the skirmish-screen was so thick that it was mistaken by the enemy for a first line of regularly arrayed infantry. The ability to skirmish in this manner, especially in the French army, was not restricted to those troops designated as 'light' (i.e., the regimental light companies or light infantry battalions); on occasion, whole battalions or brigades might be deployed in this manner, so that light infantry tactics were no longer the preserve of 'specialists'. The effect of a host of skirmishers or *tirailleurs* deployed (*en débandade*) in front of the main body was two-fold. Firstly, its musketry, delivered not in volley but 'at will' and often 'aimed', galled and disordered the enemy line, which was largely powerless to reply, as artillery-fire was less effective against skirmishers (they being not so tightly packed as a line or column), and for the same reason musketry delivered in volley would strike many fewer men than if the target had been in line. Secondly, the cloud of *tirailleurs* would screen from the enemy's gaze the manoeuvres of the main body which followed them, so that they would burst upon the enemy line with a degree of surprise, especially if the attack were delivered with the rapid pace which columnar formation allowed, without sacrificing cohesion.

Although light infantry tactics came into prominence with the French army, the essence is described excellently in the privately issued British publication, *A Manual for Volunteer Corps of Infantry* (anon., London 1803):

'Vigilance, activity, and intelligence, are particularly requisite amongst those corps which are ordered upon the service of light infantry. The first duty of these troops is to guard against surprise . . . Rapidity of movement is one of the chief characteristics of light infantry. It is this which establishes their own security, at the same time that it renders them the terror of the enemy . . . they can change their situation without difficulty, in the most rugged and intersected country; and they can appear suddenly upon points where they are the least expected, and the most to be dreaded. The intelligence chiefly required in a light infantry man is, that he should know how to take advantage of every circumstance of ground which can enable him to harass and annoy an enemy, without exposing himself . . . In some situations they must conceal themselves by stooping, in others they must kneel, or lie flat upon the ground . . . Light infantry must know how to gain upon an enemy along hedges, through corn fields, amongst gardens and ditches, almost without being perceived . . . Against regular infantry . . . they must hover round these continually in every quarter. If the regulars advance rapidly upon them, the light troops must recede; and when the enemy is exhausted . . . they must again line the hedges and ditches round him on every side. In such a situation light infantry can be opposed not otherwise than by men acting in the same manner with themselves . . . light troops should all be expert marksmen. *To fire seldom and always with effect* should be their chief study . . . Noise and smoke is not sufficient to stop the advance of soldiers accustomed to war . . . It is a first principle in the war of light troops, that a considerable proportion of their

force should at all times be kept in reserve. The men who are scattered in front ought to be supported by small parties a little way in their rear; and these again should depend upon, and communicate with stronger bodies, further removed from the point of attack . . . In advancing the reserves must not be too eager to press forward. They must give time for those in their front to feel their way with caution, that they may avoid coming unexpectedly upon a superior force of the enemy. In retiring, the skirmishers must keep a good countenance, and avoid hurry. They must endeavour to gall the enemy from every favourable situation, and make him pay dearly for the ground he acquires.'[3]

The maintenance of a reserve (troops held in formed platoons, not in open order) behind the skirmish-screen was vital for any protracted firefight or reconnaissance, but it is doubtful whether such was maintained when the skirmishers were acting immediately in advance of an attacking column, or when the skirmishers were thrown forward only a short distance from the main line; when retiring, the skirmishers

---

William Grattan recounts a rare description of hand-to-hand combat:

'Sergeant Pat Brazil – the brave Brazil of the Grenadier company, who saved his captain's life at Busaco – called out to his two companions, Swan and Kelly, to unscrew their bayonets and follow him; the three men passed the trench in a moment, and engaged the French cannoniers hand to hand; a terrific but short combat was the consequence. Swan was the first, and was met by the two gunners on the right of the gun, but, no way daunted, he engaged them, and plunged his bayonet into the breast of one; he was about to repeat the blow upon the other, but before he could disentangle the weapon from his bleeding adversary, the second Frenchman closed upon him, and by a *coup de sabre* severed his left arm from his body a little above the elbow; he fell from the shock, and was on the eve of being massacred, when Kelly, after having scrambled under the gun, rushed onward to succour his comrade. He bayonetted two Frenchmen on the spot, and at this instant Brazil came up; three of the five gunners lay lifeless, while Swan, resting against an ammunition chest, was bleeding to death. It was now equal numbers, two against two, but Brazil in his over-anxiety to engage was near losing his life at the onset; in making a lunge at the man next to him, his foot slipped upon the bloody platform, and he fell forward against his antagonist, but as both rolled under the gun, Brazil felt the socket of his bayonet strike hard against the buttons of the Frenchman's coat. The remaining gunner, in attempting to escape under the carriage from Kelly, was killed by some soldiers of the 5th . . .'

(*Adventures with the Connaught Rangers*, W. Grattan, London 1847; 1902 edn., ed. Sir Charles Oman; pp. 154–5.)

Infantry combat: a British line (left) prepares to counter-charge a French attack by column (right) in this illustration of Corunna, 1809. (Print by Clarke after William Heath)

would pass through gaps in the line and usually reassemble in two or more parties in the rear of the line, ready to issue out again when required. (It was preferable to collect a battalion's skirmishers in one company, to act together; other systems, such as having a number of skirmishers attached to each company, were not successful. Until 1810, for example, Russia's battalion *Jäger* platoon was normally spread as an extra rank at the rear of the the battalion, negating their supposed 'specialist' skills.) The only counter to vast clouds of *tirailleurs* was for the attacked body to advance its own skirmishers; in armies where these were adequately trained the French skirmishers could be neutralized, but in the early Revolutionary Wars, when even those armies which had once been proficient at light infantry tactics (e.g., Austria and Britain) had allowed their skills to decline, their opponents had little answer to the French *tirailleurs*. Some armies developed effective light infantry as a direct consequence; others never attained the requisite standard. In many armies there were entire regiments designated as light infantry, though in most cases they differed little from the line, and all were equally capable of

fighting in the conventional line-of-battle. In the French army, for example, the *Infanterie légère* was virtually indistinguishable from the line except in uniform and *esprit de corps* (light troops traditionally having the attributes of élite units), which is not to suggest that the light infantry was unskilled, but that the line regiments were equally capable of operating as light infantry. The same is true to a lesser degree of the qualities of the British light and line regiments, Britain being the only nation that eventually equalled the French in the proficiency of its light infantry.

Different skills were required of rifle corps, however. The use of sharpshooters armed with rifled muskets, capable of very great feats of marksmanship, was basically a German invention, hence the common use of the term *Jäger* to describe such troops. As it usually took longer to load a rifle than a musket, due to the tighter fit of the ball in the barrel, such troops were usually employed only as skirmishers, as their volley-firing would be slower and their employment in line a waste of their skill; they were often deployed in small detachments, frequently as single companies, to supplement the ordinary skirmishers of an infantry brigade or division; or, as in Prussian service, were attached to individual regiments. Though riflemen were capable of devastating an enemy by singling out and dropping the officers and NCOs, they never existed in large numbers; even in the British Army, in which 'rifle' tactics probably reached their peak,

British light infantry private, 1791, showing the uniform-features characteristic to the light troops of many nations: short (often cut-down) jacket, short gaiters, and a small leather cap, more suitable to light infantry service than the bicorn. (Engraving by F. D. Soiron after H. Bunbury)

there existed no more than two rifle-armed regiments, albeit of more than the usual number of battalions.

A common practice in many armies was to detach the regimental flank companies and amalgamate those of several units into composite battalions. This had a double purpose: first, it created additional battalions in armies that were short of units (for though the parent battalions were thus reduced in strength they still functioned as tactical units, the creation of extra units more than compensating the weakening of the whole); and secondly, being composed of flank companies, the units thus created were (at least in

theory) of veteran or élite status. This practice was rarely employed in the French army (Oudinot's grenadiers were the really notable exception), and only occasionally in the British (where the units thus formed were almost always light infantry rather than grenadiers); but in other armies the practice was not used merely on an *ad hoc* basis, but the entire design of regimental establishments was directed towards the assembly of such units in wartime: Prussia, Austria, Russia and Sweden all employed the practice.

Much has been made of the respective tactical attributes of the column against the line, though the matter is not, perhaps, as clearly defined as it might appear. The most common misconception concerns the formation of a column: except in unusual circumstances (such as an assault upon a defile or down a street) a column of attack did not resemble a column of march, with a frontage of perhaps six or eight men and an immense length. Although each nation employed its own formation, in general a column's frontage was usually of greater length than its depth; indeed, when two companies were deployed in line at the head of a column, seconded by a further two companies in line and then a further two, the formation might be regarded as a succession of lines rather than the common perception of a column. However, this does not alter the basic fact that with a column, the only muskets that could be brought to bear upon the enemy were those of the first two or three ranks of the leading company (hence the apparent French intention – frequently not achieved – of deploying the column into line before the enemy was engaged). With so few muskets effective at the head of a column, the disparity between them and a battalion in line, when all muskets could be brought to bear simultaneously, is obvious; and thus if the line remained steady and unshaken by the skirmish-fire which ideally preceded a column, the concentrated musketry directed against the head of the column could virtually destroy the leading ranks. Yet the attack in column when mounted by the French failed repeatedly only against the British, the cause being the system adopted by Wellington and copied by his subordinates as the 'correct' way of repelling an enemy column.

Perfected during the Peninsular War, the system involved the shielding of the line from the view of the column, which was achieved in two ways. Most importantly, the ideal position of a line was upon the crest of a hill or a rise in terrain, but not upon the very top; instead, the troops would be arrayed just over the crest, on the reverse slope to that up which the column had to ascend. An added advantage to this disposition was that the troops would also be shielded from enemy artillery, which would have to fire 'blind' over the crest of the hill, not knowing where the target (if any) was; and the effect of roundshot coming over the hill-crest, even if this were possible to achieve, might be reduced greatly if the men sat or lay down instead of standing up. Secondly, the position of the line would be screened by a host of British skirmishers in opposition to those of the French, and again this skirmish-screen was sometimes so dense as to be mistaken for the line itself; this screen would run in before the line engaged the approaching column. As the line was concealed behind the reverse slope, the column would have no clear idea of when it should deploy into line; so that on numerous occasions an advancing French column would be startled by the appearance of the British line advancing from the reverse slope on to the crest. With no chance to deploy, the column's head would be destroyed by musketry and the whole body thrown back down the slope, with the British seconding their volley with a limited bayonet-charge, retiring back behind the crest when the column's rout was complete.

'A man of ours was flogged for breaking into a church and stealing some silver candlesticks. By some neglect his back festered. Being in the hospital one morning, I saw the poor fellow brought in to have his back dressed. He was laid upon the floor, and a large poultice taken off the wound. O! what a sickening sight! The wound was perhaps eight inches by six, full of matter, in which were a number of black-headed maggots striving to hide themselves. At this scene those who looked on were horrified . . . Many were lashed into insensibility, and one who was a Brunswicker, into insanity. It required strong nerves to look on . . . It has frequently been stated that the Duke of Wellington was severe. In answer to this I would say, he could not be otherwise. His army was composed of the lowest orders. Many, if not the most of them, were ignorant, idle, and drunken . . . By the discipline he enforced, the British army became more than a match, even at great odds, for the best of Napoleon's boasted legions. Soldiering at the present is mere child's play compared with what it was from 1800 to 1815 . . .'
(*Rough Notes of Seven Campaigns*, J. S. Cooper, 1869; Carlisle edn. 1914, pp. 14–15.)

(It is easy to over-estimate the 'firepower' effect, however; an unruffled demeanour and the advance of the line with the bayonet was probably equally or even more responsible for the destruction of the column's morale and its consequent rout than was the difference between the line's firepower and that of the column.) This tactic explains why the French (to use Wellington's expression) continued to come on in the old style and be beaten off in the old style; it may not necessarily be evidence that the French continued to rely unimaginatively upon the impetus of the column which had been successful in the Revolutionary Wars, but simply that their lack of knowledge about the position of their target prevented them from deploying into line as they may have intended. The 'reverse slope' tactic was the only effective counter to the French column attack, yet was employed by other armies: before Ligny Wellington tried to persuade the Prussian command to shelter their troops from French fire, but to no avail, and as he expected they were severely mauled as a result. (Incredibly, it was sometimes regarded as not honourable to be sheltered from fire; in 1796 Sir Thomas Graham described an Austrian regiment at Borghetto being shot to pieces when a withdrawal of six yards would have saved them, had regimental honour not demanded that they stood where they were; it was, as Graham observed, nothing more than stupid bravado.)

The column's main weakness was its vulnerability to fire; its depth compared to that of the line resulted in a doubling or trebling of casualties when hit by artillery fire. The Russian army learned this lesson at great cost, when columns were ravaged at Borodino by the French artillery; thereafter, they tended to make greater use of the line or to keep their dispositions shielded wherever possible.

The line was formed either three- or four-deep; each formation had its advantages and adherents. The three-deep line could bring all its muskets into play at once, the front rank kneeling to fire and the others firing standing, the third rank through the gaps in the second; but the discharge of muskets so near to the men in the second rank could injure them, and it was usual for the third rank not to fire simultaneously, but to remain in reserve to replace casualties that occurred in the first two ranks. This reserving of the third rank's fire reduced the efficiency of the line by one-third, and led to its eventual abandonment. Although the British regulations strongly recommended the use of a third rank, by the turn of the century the two-rank line was almost universal, though in French service the third rank was only dispensed with towards the end of the period. By forming the line in two ranks the frontage of the battalion increased by one-third, increasing firepower but leading to 'shrinkage' in action, when the gaps caused by casualties were closed by the men moving in towards the centre of the line; thus spaces could appear between battalions or even between the companies of a battalion, which if they became too great could cause a weakness in the line-of-battle.

Fire could be delivered in several ways: either a massed volley by the entire battalion, not popular as the line would be undefended until all had reloaded; or by ranks, in which case one rank would be loaded at all times; or by sub-division, either company or platoon, so that musketry would be issuing from some part of the line at all times. This was sometimes termed 'rolling volley', as alternate companies or platoons fired in succession from one end of the line to the other.

The flanks of a line were most vulnerable, virtually indefensible against an attack delivered at right-angles to the line, so two basic formations were adopted to secure the flanks. (This was unnecessary if another battalion were in line in close proximity; the outermost ends of a line-of-battle were the vulnerable points.) First, a company at the extreme end of the line could be 'refused', i.e., remaining in line but thrown back at an angle to cover the flank; or a company could be deployed in column on the flank, or in the case of a long battle-line an entire battalion could be arrayed in column, ready to form square in the event of a threat by cavalry.

Infantry in line were extremely vulnerable to a cavalry charge pressed home. Although there are cases of troops in line successfully repelling cavalry – El Bodon in the Peninsular War is perhaps the most famous example – if cavalry could catch a unit in line, especially from a flank, a massacre could ensue as the line was 'rolled up' and trampled beneath the charge. An extreme example of such destruction was the case of Colborne's brigade at Albuera, three battalions of which were destroyed and only one escaped, being farthest from the point of impact and thus having time to form square. This formation was the universal solution to the threat from cavalry, in which the companies of the line folded back upon those in the centre to produce a rectangular formation, each side facing outwards and presenting an almost impenetrable hedge of bayonets against which the cavalry was powerless. The term 'square' should not be taken literally, as 'rectangle' might be more appropriate, for various formations could be adopted; in fact the British regulations always referred to 'the square or oblong'. To form a square of equal faces took up to twice as long as forming an oblong; the British 3rd Division at Waterloo, for example, formed its 'squares' as very elongated oblongs with front and rear faces four companies wide and the sides of only one company. (An interesting dissertation on the merits of this formation over the true 'square' can be found in *Notes on the Battle of Waterloo*, General Sir James Shaw Kennedy, London 1865, pp. 99–101.)

The weakness of the square was its vulnerability to artillery fire, enforcing the dictum that cavalry attacks should ideally always be accompanied by horse artillery otherwise, except in most unusual circumstances, it was almost invulnerable. The only cavalry capable of inflicting much harm were lancers, who if they survived the square's musketry could reach over the hedge of bayonets and poke at the infantry with their lances, or if (as happened to some Prussian squares in 1813) the weather was so wet that the muskets became useless. Very few examples exist of squares being broken by cavalry, and then only if the infantry were demoralized or if, as happened to the French at Garcia Hernandez, a horse crashed dead into one face of the square crushing the infantry beneath and opening a gap into which succeeding horsemen could ride. Under normal circumstances the square was hollow, though a 'rallying square' would be solidly-packed, formed from a broken battalion by men running in upon a central marker. A formation using the same system was the 'mass', adopted by Austria and deriving from formations used in wars against the Turks: a column packed together so tightly that it was virtually impossible to break unless the men became completely demoralized and fled. It had similar attributes to the square except that it was less flexible.

Cavalry

Cavalry comprised three basic categories: heavy, light and 'medium', though exactly of what the latter consisted is debatable. The heavy cavalry was that mounted upon large horses, used to make the decisive charge upon the battlefield; the light cavalry, though able to act similarly, in addition formed the eyes and ears of the army, scouting, skirmishing, raiding and providing the chain of 'outposts' which separated one army from another, fulfilling not only a reconnaissance facility but equally giving first warning and response to any enemy advance upon the encampments of the army. In theory, the 'medium' cavalry was capable of fulfilling both roles.

The disposition of the types of cavalry depended to a degree upon the size of the army of which they formed a part, the terrain over which the campaign was waged, and upon the number of cavalrymen available. In armies where the cavalry was not numerous, it was not possible to make a wide separation between the various types; in the Anglo-

Portuguese Peninsular Army, for example, cavalry was never so prolific for a divisional organization to be anything more than an administrative grouping, units being deployed instead in brigades. Conversely, with armies possessing a large quanity of cavalry, such as Napoleon's *Grande Armée* of 1812, it was possible to form divisions of 'heavies' intended specifically to execute the charge in a pitched battle, with the light and medium cavalry performing the other duties, including the provision of cavalry for corps composed principally of infantry.

Cavalry that comprised the 'heavies' included cuirassiers (both those regiments equipped with body-armour as the name implies, and others retaining the name but without cuirasses, like the Prussian and Russian cuirassiers for much of the period), carabiniers, and heavy dragoons. The light cavalry comprised the hussars (the 'lights' *par excellence*), light dragoons, lancers, *chevau-léger* and the hordes of irregular and Cossack cavalry employed by Russia. Reconnaissance and 'outpost' duty was largely the preserve of these corps – in fact the original French *chevau-léger-lanciers*

were formed specifically to provide a 'light' capacity for divisions of cuirassiers and carabiniers, demonstrating that these latter were never intended to act in any way save to charge in battle. The role of the 'medium' cavalry is less easy to define, as is any criterion to determine what constituted 'medium' cavalry.

Dragoons are often described as 'medium' cavalry, though by the Napoleonic era their original function (troops who rode into action but then usually dismounted and fought on foot, in effect what would later be termed 'mounted infantry') had long since passed. The only dragoons of the Napoleonic period in any way resembling the original concept were those of the French army, who for a time provided dismounted units for active service as infantry; yet it is these same dragoons that stand against the classification of them as 'medium' cavalry. In the later campaigns, the French dragoons became the backbone of Napoleon's cavalry, as cuirassiers were both expensive and difficult to maintain (armoured troopers requiring horses of great strength and size), and following the losses in the Russian campaign the 'heavy' arm was reduced greatly, the dragoons stepping up to compensate. Conversely, at the same time as dragoons were acting as heavy cavalry in northern Europe, other regiments were continuing to fulfill the role of lightish cavalry or mounted infantry in anti-guerrilla operations in

Alexandria: French dragoons charge British infantry, who run into square formation to save themselves. The crested 'round hats' were commonly worn in tropical climates. (Print after A. Dupray)

A sergeant of the British 18th Hussars captures two French officers at Albuera; though the British uniform is shown with passable accuracy, including the shako which replaced the busby for the 1813 campaign, in fact it *depicts an event which never happened, the 18th not being present at Albuera, which illustrates some of the failings of contemporary popular prints! (Print by M. Dubourg after William Heath)*

Spain. The utility of such troops was immense, but it becomes extremely difficult to categorize them, being neither light nor heavy in the conventional sense but capable of performing both roles. Similar problems exist in other armies: the British dragoons and dragoon guards (the latter the same as dragoons, the differing title resulting from regimental history rather than from any difference in function) were not 'light', but being able to perform outpost duty were not 'heavy' in the sense implied by cuirassiers. Austria's dragoons were more heavy than light, though for a time regiments switched titles from dragoons to light dragoons without any change in function; Prussia's truly 'heavy' arm (cuirassiers) was very small, so that their dragoons fulfilled this role; Russia's dragoons were lighter than their large cuirassier arm, yet were not light cavalry. The problem becomes even more complex when heavy regiments had detachments of 'flankers' attached, to skirmish on the extremities of the unit in action, a practice confined to Germanic and Russian armies.

In the early eighteenth century the cavalry's major role was almost wholly offensive, founded upon the aggressive use of cavalry which characterized the campaigns of Gustavus Adolphus and Marlborough, and continued in the armies of Frederick the Great and Maria Theresa. To this end, cavalry was concentrated into massed formations capable of launching immense charges to break or overwhelm an enemy softened by the infantry and artillery. Frederick used his cavalry in this way, but his development of infantry tactics swung the balance away from the cavalry towards the foot-soldier, so that in some armies cavalry was reduced to a supporting arm rather than forming the main weapon of offence. During the Napoleonic Wars, some armies were supplied with comparatively so few cavalry that this was inevitable, though Napoleon's use of massed charges (exemplified by the immense assaults of Eylau) to some degree continued the old process, even though in Napoleon's armies the cavalry formed part of an integrated system rather than being regarded as the main strike-force as they had a century earlier. This change in emphasis is reflected by the tactical deployment of cavalry brigades:

frequently they were attached to infantry corps rather than being concentrated in autonomous cavalry formations. The four cavalry corps of the 1812 *Grande Armée* were a significant departure from the usual system, there being sufficient numbers of cavalry available to Napoleon to provide both cavalry support for the infantry corps and to maintain a central striking-force of horsemen. An example of the decline of the cavalry as a primary weapon is its deployment in Austrian service: from being a main force under Maria Theresa, by 1813 it was distributed throughout the armies' formations in comparatively small detachments, making immense cavalry operations of the old style extremely unlikely.

The techniques of the charge varied from army to army, but a number of general rules applied to most. The preferred formation was the line, though latterly attacks in column became more common, if for no other reason than that it was easier to retain formation in column than in a long, thin line. (By 1812, for example, both the Russian and Prussian manuals officially recommended attack by column of platoons or squadrons.) Cavalry regiments were commonly subdivided into squadrons, and the squadrons into troops (commonly two per squadron), each of these subdivisions being capable of acting independently or of supporting one another. A number of rules were generally applicable, not least that the speed at which the charge was delivered should reach its maximum immediately before the impact with the enemy: to this end, a formation would begin its motion at a walk, building up through a trot and canter to a gallop, and only attain full speed, the charge *à outrance*, for the last 50 yards before impact; the alternative was to arrive at the target with the horses 'blown' which would be disastrous. Similarly, when cavalry received a charge from another mounted formation, it was regarded as potentially catastrophic to meet it at the halt, when the entire impetus would be on the side of the attacker; if being charged was inevitable, the attacked unit would ideally advance to meet the charge and itself be in motion at the moment of impact. Another vital factor was the maintenance of a reserve and the fact that the charge should not get out of hand, but that the troops would rally on command, to re-form and thus protect themselves against a counter-charge.

Failures of the British cavalry to obey the latter rule, which caused a number of defeats in the Peninsular War, led Wellington to issue a number of directives concerning cavalry service, incorporating rules that were universally valid. First, to Hill in June 1812, following 'Jack' Slade's disaster at Maguilla: 'All cavalry should charge in two lines, of which one should be in reserve; if obliged to charge in one line, part of the line, at least one-third, should be ordered beforehand to pull up, and form in second line, as soon as the charge should be given, and the enemy has been broken and has retired.'[4] Secondly, after charges had again rolled on uncontrollably at Waterloo, he issued *Instruction to Officers commanding Brigades of Cavalry in the Army of Occupation* which elaborates further on the principles of cavalry service, and which may be summarized as follows:

1. A reserve should always be kept to second a success or cover a repulse of the first line; the reserve should be half or even two-thirds of the whole.
2. The cavalry should be arrayed in three bodies, the first two in line and the reserve in column, but capable of swinging easily into line.
3. Against cavalry, the distance between the first and second lines and the second line and the reserve should be 400–500 yards, sufficient to enable the supports to second the attack and allow a defeated first line to retire through the spaces in the support without disordering them.
4. Against infantry the second line should be only 200 yards behind the first, to enable them to engage the infantry before the latter had opportunity to re-load after firing at the first line.
5. When the first line charged, the supportng line should follow at a walk only, and the reserves remain still, to prevent the supports from being carried away by the enthusiasm of the first line's charge.

(When considering cavalry it is important not to confuse the term 'line' with 'rank'; each line would normally consist of two ranks, the older three-rank system being recognized as an encumbrance as the third rank restricted changes of direction and was potentially dangerous in being less able to avoid fallers from the first two ranks. Even the 1796 Russian regulations, a result of Tsar Paul's backward-looking 'reforms', recognized this fact.)

'Wear Jersey shirts or flannel waistcoats and drawers, next to the skin; but in Spring and Summer, cotton and calico. In the night, always wear a double cotton or worsted nightcap, either in camp or cantonments.

'Bread, meat, and potatoes give and preserve robust muscular strength. Greens and fruits should be sparingly used, lest they produce fluxes. Good malt liquor well hopped is excellent, but in cold weather, an addition of a little brandy, rum or gin, will be expedient.

'Smoking tobacco in cold weather, and in the night is useful and an excellent preservative. In case of putrid infection, disease or fever, free air and vitriolic acid, bark and snakeroot are most certain remedies.'

(*Military Card for Preserving Health*, Dorset Volunteer Rangers, *c.* 1795.)

Only rarely would firearms be used in a charge, except in the hands of the 'flankers' which might fan out on either side of the charge to gall the enemy, as in Prussian and Russian service. A platoon of skirmishers might often ride out in advance of the main body, to engage the enemy with carbine-fire, but these would move out of the way of a full-blown charge. Carbines were also used on outpost duty and for engaging enemy skirmishers, and would often be fired from the saddle; but their range was limited and accuracy poor, unless they were some of the few rifled weapons in use or more like an infantry musket, such as the French 'dragoon musket'. Instances of the carbine's use in a full-scale action were rare, though did occur, such as the French 20th *Chasseurs à Cheval* at Eylau, a case already quoted. Even the issue of carbines was not universal, and many regiments (especially 'heavies') were provided only with pistols, which were of even less use. Typical of the general practice was Stapleton Cotton's order withdrawing the carbines of the British Household Cavalry in 1813 (save six per troop), as being 'heavies' they would never be called upon to skirmish, and the horses had enough to carry without being further encumbered!

Skirmishing and outpost duty was normally the preserve of the light cavalry, though the 'medium' variety could also be called upon to perform this duty, as sometimes happened with the British heavy dragoons in the Peninsular War. 'Outpost', reconnaissance and raids upon the enemy demanded a high level of training, though this was not recognized by some armies; British regiments, for example, had to learn this craft on campaign, as the duty was totally neglected in training at home. The French and Austrian hussars, Cossacks and German troops in British service were probably the most proficient in such tasks. In outpost duty, a number of sentry-posts would be established, inter-communicating and linked to one or more central points. Messages could be transmitted by rider or by visual signal, which with experienced troops could achieve a very high standard of excellence; exemplifying the best 'outpost' service, the 1st Hussars of the King's German Legion (generally better-trained than their British comrades) held a 40-mile line against four times their number of French cavalry from March to May 1811, without letting through a single French patrol, losing a vedette or transmitting a single piece of incorrect information.

Artillery

Artillery tactics were governed largely by the number of guns available to an army and the resulting disposition of batteries, but a number of basic tenets were applicable to all artillery service.

Chief among these was the practice of bringing a battery into action. With the general 'militarization' of drivers and teams, guns were no longer unlimbered away from the battle-line and manhandled into position by the gunners, but driven up to the site selected for their opening fire. It was common practice for guns to operate in pairs – theoretically

The singular cannon with which the Austrian Cavallerie-Batterien *were equipped, having an elongated trail with a* padded seat, upon which the gunners rode, in the manner of a Würst-Wagen. *(Print after R. von Ottenfeld)*

so that one gun of a pair would at all times be loaded, firing alternately, though this did not always apply in practice – but though each gun had its allocated ammunition-vehicles, they did not usually attend the gun in action. When a site had been selected for the battery's position, the guns would be drawn up in an irregular line, the alignment ideally staggered so that any enfilade fire would strike only one gun-team at a time. The limber (often with a few rounds in a 'limber-box' or trail-chest to enable the gun to open fire immediately) would be kept in reasonably close proximity to the gun, ready for a rapid limbering to advance or retreat, and at least two lines of caissons drawn up in the rear of the battery. The first line would be about 50 yards from the gun-line, and the second line of caissons a further 50 yards or more to the rear, with additional battery vehicles at least a further 100 yards back, so as to gain the maximum protection by distance from the enemy fire. For supply of the guns, it was usual for only one caisson to be driven forward at any one time, to replenish the ammunition of several guns (or the entire battery), so as to expose as few caissons as possible to the dangers of the gun-line, not so much from the enemy's fire as from stray sparks from the battery's discharge; an exploding caisson could wreak the most dreadful havoc. First-line caissons when empty would either be replenished from the second line of caissons, or would allow a second-line caisson to take their place in the first line; thus a continual shuttle of ammunition serviced the battery.

The 'ideal' artillery position was achieved rarely, but included a number of distinctive features. As indirect fire was virtually impossible, guns had to be positioned alongside or in front of their infantry, or 'masked' behind formations capable of rapid movement, e.g., cavalry, which could unc-over the battery and reveal it to the enemy only a moment before it opened fire. The best situation was just over the crest of gently rising ground, allowing the gun to sweep the slope but without 'dead ground' in its front in which enemy troops could be shielded by folds in the terrain. A very elevated position was not ideal due to the difficulty of depressing the guns sufficiently to register on the enemy; Adye thought that 'the greatest effects may be produced from a height of 30 or 40 yards at a distance of about 600; and about 16 yards of height to 200 of distance'.[5] Being thus positioned, the reverse slope would shield the caisson-lines from enemy fire. The favoured ground upon which to establish a battery was soft or miry, to absorb enemy roundshot; conversely, the 'target' ground would ideally be stony, so that landing roundshot would not only bounce but would throw up stone splinters to act as shrapnel upon the enemy.

The employment of artillery and its disposition throughout the army were factors closely linked. There existed two basic theories of employment: as a support to other 'arms' or as an offensive weapon in itself. At the beginning of the period the former was adopted by all armies, evidenced by the common practice of allocating light field-pieces to each infantry unit, a system best described by its British term, 'battalion guns'. Such guns (often crewed by

On Waterloo:
'Never, indeed, had the national bravery of the French people been more nobly shown. One soldier in the French ranks was seen, when his arm was shattered by a cannon-ball, to wrench if off with the other; and throwing it up in the air, he exclaimed to his comrades, "Vive l'Empereur jusqu' à la mort!" . . . at the beginning of the action, a French soldier who had both legs carried off by a cannon-ball, was borne past the front of Foy's division, and called out to them, "Ce n'est rien, camarades; Vive l'Empereur! Gloire à la France." The same officer, at the end of the battle, when all hope was lost, tells us that he saw a French grenadier, blackened with powder, and with his clothes torn and stained, leaning on his musket, and immov-able as a statue. The colonel called to him to join his comrades and retreat; but the grenadier showed him his musket and his hands; and said "These hands have with this musket used to-day more than twenty packets of cartridges: it was more than my share: I supplied myself with ammunition from the dead. Leave me to die here on the field of battle. It is not courage that fails me, but strength." '
(*The Fifteen Decisive Battles of the World*, Sir Edward Creasy, London 1851; 1877 edn., p. 614.)

members of the infantry unit) would accompany the battalion into action to provide immediate fire-support, but the disadvantages outweighed the assets, in restricting the rate of movement of the infantry, and being in any case of such light 'nature' that the shot was not fully effective. Nevertheless, though the system was abandoned by most armies, Napoleon re-issued regimental artillery as late as 1809 in the belief that as the calibre of infantry declined (in this case caused by the attritional losses of his campaigns) the more artillery they required in support.

Otherwise, artillery companies were deployed either on attachment to brigades or divisions, or as a central 'reserve'. This depended upon the quantity of guns available to a general; an army with a comparatively small amount of artillery might not be able to form a reserve at all, as happened with the British Army during the Peninsular War, or at least a reserve so small that it had to be committed to action as a supporting element rather than as an offensive one. With larger armies, however, an extremely powerful reserve could be assembled to perform what was known as 'massed battery' fire. It was a common belief that a concentration of artillery was more powerful than the sum of its parts, in its ability to amass its fire upon a specific point in the enemy's force, to batter a hole in his line to be exploited by an advance of cavalry or infantry; in this way artillery ceased to be a support arm but became a primary offensive element. The most outstanding example of this tactic was probably the French gunner Sénarmont's 'charge' at Fried-land which turned the course of the battle, though some other examples of 'massed battery' fire were less successful

A typical baggage-wagon, with British light infantrymen and their families: women and children 'camp-followers' were present with virtually every army. (Print after W. H. Pyne, 1802)

due largely to failures of co-ordination, such as the French barrages at Wagram and Leipzig, or to the better preparation of the enemy, as at Waterloo. Nevertheless, despite the advantages of 'massed battery' fire, even those possessed of enough artillery to make it feasible were somewhat reticent in emulating the Napoleonic policy; Archduke Charles, for example, recognized the value of concentration of artillery-fire but did no more than recommend its use by the Austrian artillery in those situations where individual artillery commanders thought it feasible. Otherwise, the guns concentrated in the divisional or corps reserve or 'park' would be held back from the initial fighting and committed as and when required to bolster a line or help exploit a breakthrough.

Certain basic rules were applied to targeting. Artillery fire was normally reserved for use against the enemy infantry and cavalry; firing at enemy artillery ('counter-battery fire') was normally discouraged both for being wasteful of shot for limited effect, and dangerous in attracting the enemy's fire. A converse view was advanced by a writer in the *British Military Library* (1801) who stated that as trained gunners were more valuable, it would harm the enemy to a greater degree if they were killed instead of infantry; but this policy was rarely followed except in those cases where an enemy battery was clearly causing great damage to friendly troops. Otherwise, the targeting of artillery is perhaps best summarized by Adye:

'The guns must be so placed as to produce a cross-fire upon the position of the enemy, and upon all the ground

'I was at Hesse Cassel in the summer of 1795, and through military curiosity, went to the Sunday parade, where the Prince was to inspect and manoeuvre his guards. I expected a treat, nor was I disappointed, and I may say, that I never saw a finer body of men; but when I observed His Most Serene Highness galloping down the front of the parade, *caning* indiscriminately the non-commissioned officer and the private, and swearing most cavalierly at the officers, my admiration was soon converted into pity for the brave men (the officers deserved all they got), and into unequivocal contempt for the ruffian Landgrave, the *worthy* and *accomplished* representative of the herd of petty despots, who *then* infested Germany.'

(*Leisure-Moments in the Camp and in the Guard-Room*, J. F. Neville, alias 'A Veteran British Officer', York 1812, pp. 41–2.)

which he must pass over in an attack . . . the fire . . . may at any time be united to produce a decided effect against any particular points. These points are the *débouchés* of the enemy, the heads of their columns, and the weakest points in the front. In an attack of the enemy's position, the cross-fire of

The Prussian army crosses the Rhine, 1 August 1792. This appears to demonstrate the use of pontoons as boats, forming a 'flying bridge'. (Print after J. Volz)

the guns must become *direct*, before it can impede the advance of the troops; and must annoy the enemy's positions nearest to the point attacked, when it is no longer safe to continue the fire upon that point itself. The shot from artillery should always take an enemy in the direction of its greatest dimension; it should therefore take a line obliquely or in flank; but a column in front.'[6]

'Several millions of buck-shot are shipping at Portsmouth, in the Leonidas frigate for America. This description of shot has been in common use with the Americans in the present war and the mangling wounds they inflict are found (when not attached with death) so to protract the recovery of our soldiers that their services are lost to the Army for a considerable time.'
(*Public Ledger*, 24 October 1814.)

Commissariat

Napoleon's famous assertion that an army marched upon its stomach conceals the fact that throughout the Napoleonic era, the ordinary soldier on campaign was likely to be, if not literally starving, at least in a state of almost permanent hunger; as one wrote, 'When a man entered on a soldier's life . . . he should have parted with half his stomach . . . Picking of teeth was not at that time much practised, or wanted.'[7]

There were two basic methods of supply of victuals to an army: either from a central depot or depots, or by allowing the soldiers to forage for their own sustenance (though even in armies with comparatively successful systems of supply, the exigencies of campaigns might well result in units receiving no rations for many days, throwing the men on to their own initiative). The system of 'living off the land' had advantages and many drawbacks, and originated in the early Revolutionary Wars when the French establishment had simply no means of supplying their armies even if food had been available centrally, which it rarely was. Thus, the French soldier was to a considerable degree dependent upon his own skill in foraging (in this case a euphemism for stealing or 'requisitioning' from the unfortunate civilians through whose lands the army was passing), and thus the French army became the most skilled foragers in Europe. The advantages of the system were such (in having no supply-trains or communication-lines to be protected, and the freedom of movement which resulted) that even when France was able to feed its armies, the system of foraging was to a large extent retained. Its major disadvantage concerned the limits it placed upon the disposition of an army, as the component parts would have to scatter widely to find sufficient provisions. Napoleon expressed this system by the remark that the army had to separate to live but unite to fight, though without proper reconnaissance the practice was

fraught with danger if the army were not united when the enemy arrived; Marengo is an example. Ideally, the army was supplied with provisions only during the immediate period before contact with the enemy (when foraging would not be possible), but after the French almost starved to death in the 1806–7 campaign a more orthodox system of supply was instituted, though throughout the period foraging remained an important part of the French system.

The alternative method of supply was similar to that which had operated earlier in the eighteenth century, by which an army was supplied from a number of depots, with trains of wagons or pack-animals operating a continual shuttle-system between the army and the supply-dumps. Although this ensured a supply of provisions (under the ideal conditions which often did not exist), there were disadvantages: lines of communication had to be maintained at all cost, and the movement of an army was restricted to the speed of its supply-trains. An example of the comparative systems occurred in the Valmy campaign, when the French forces were freed of such restrictions but the Prussians were subject to very regular halts while the army's bakers pre-

pared the bread for the following few days. However, to change such a system without having troops used to the alternative was almost impossible; Austria tried briefly to institute a system of 'living off the land' but it was abandoned when it was realized that their forces were very inferior in this regard when compared with the French. In some armies, notably the Russian, commissariat arrangements were always poor; and even in the best-organized, such as Wellington's Peninsular army (dependent though it was upon hired Portuguese muleteers and their teams), the occasions were many when troops were reduced to eating whatever they could scavenge from the countryside, even if that were no more than acorns and leaves.

Siegecraft

Sieges and lines of fortification had declined in importance since the time of Marlborough when campaigns had tended to revolve around the possession of fortified bases; Napoleon's insistence that the primary target of a campaign should be the destruction of the enemy's field army only tended to confirm the decline in fortifications. There were a number of significant operations dependent upon fortified places during the Napoleonic era; notable are the Austrian attempts to relieve Mantua, and the operations in the Peninsular War which produced perhaps the most effective defence-work ever devised, the Lines of Torres Vedras; but these were the exceptions to the general trend.

A fortified enemy garrison could not safely be by-passed by an army, for the presence of a garrison in an army's rear, capable of sallying out to disrupt communications and supply-lines, could be disastrous. There were two basic methods of countering the threat of such garrisons: blockade and siege. In the former, a sufficient number of troops had to be allocated not only to prevent re-supply reaching the enemy garrison, but equally sufficient to contain any offensive moves by the garrison. This policy could keep a large number of troops occupied for an indefinite period; more

convenient, but more costly, was a full siege leading to a breaching of the enemy defences followed by an assault.

The first step in conducting a siege was to impose a blockade to isolate the garrison from support, and then begin work on a circumvallation – encompassing the fortress with trenches and artillery-positions which could be pushed ever closer to the walls. The first of such 'parallels' (so called because the trenches ran approximately parallel to the enemy wall or *enceinte*) were commenced with what was termed 'breaking ground', and having constructed the first of such trenches, saps would be pushed forward until a second parallel could be begun, nearer the walls; then a third, a fourth and so on until it was possible to establish an artillery battery at close range near the point on the enemy wall selected for an assault. The guns employed were generally those of the army's siege- or battering-train, pieces of much

◄ *A French artillery battery at Frankfurt, October 1793. This depicts a typical 'position battery' constructed for fire upon a besieged town, with Gribeauval fieldpieces in position behind a brushwood 'blind' or screen. Note the two handspikes inserted in the trail of the gun in the centre, and the neat pile of shot just out of the path of the gun's recoil. In the left mid-ground is an artillery caisson. (Print after Hippolyte Lecomte)*

Garrison artillery: a heavy gun mounted on a wooden 'garrison carriage' with iron 'truck' wheels, and two gunners of the British Royal Artillery. This aquatint by I. C. Stadler after Charles Hamilton Smith was published on 1 February 1815 as part of the latter's Costume of the Army of the British Empire, *illustrating the uniform introduced in 1812, the jacket in the standard artillery colouring of blue with red facings and yellow lace, and the false-fronted 'Belgic' shako.*

Siege of Toulon, 1793. This depicts a besieging-battery established behind an earthwork rampart, designed to absorb such of the enemy's shot which attempted 'counter-battery fire'. (Print after Jung)

▼ *Siege of Toulon, 1793. This shows a typical earthwork fortification, the earth supported by hurdles and apparently plastered on the outer face, into which 'storm-poles' are inserted. British 'floating batteries' are moored offshore. Note the red 'bonnet of liberty' on the fort's flag-pole.*

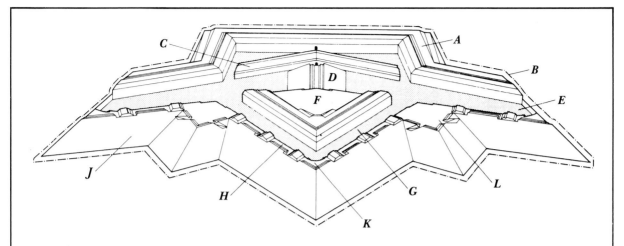

*Vauban's First System of Fortification: **A**, curtain; **B**, part of bastion; **C**, tenaille; **D**, caponier; **E**, main ditch; **F**, ravelin; **G**, ditch of ravelin; **H**, Covered way; **J**, glucis; **K**, salient place of arms; **L**, re-entrant place of arms.*

*Cross section of a fortification: **1**, talus; **2**, terreplein; **3**, banquette; **4**, parapet; **5**, tablette; **6**, cordon; **7**, scarp revetment; **8**, cuvette; **9**, counterscarp revetment; **10**, covered way; **11**, palisade; **12**, glacis; **13**, counterfort. **Below**: Plan and elevation of part of a battery constructed on a wooden foundation.*

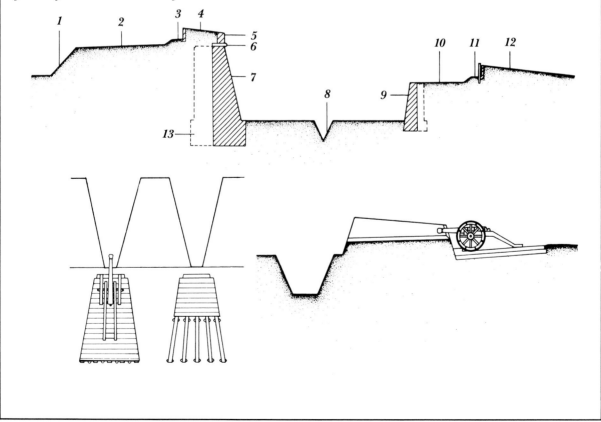

greater weight than those normally employed in the field (24pdrs were favoured), supplemented by mortars which dropped explosive shells almost vertically upon the enemy. The process of pushing the parallels near to the walls was hazardous in the extreme, from the enemy's fire and from possible sallies by the garrison, to kill the engineers and dismount the artillery batteries, so that the greatest vigilance was required on the part of the besiegers both night and day. The immense amount of earth removed from such trenches was usually too great for the small engineer corps to deal with, so that it was usual for large numbers of infantry to be employed as labourers to perform the less-skilled tasks.

The duty of the artillery was to blast a gap in the enemy's wall (usually requiring phenomenal amounts of ammunition: in the 1812 siege of Badajoz, more than 400 tons of shot and powder were used, exclusive of shells and canister-rounds), through which an assault could gain access. Attacks by ladder (escalade) were doubly perilous though at times were carried through with great determination despite the casualties, as at Ratisbon or Badajoz. Once a breach was deemed 'practicable', i.e., capable of being stormed, it was generally regarded that the governor of the fortress could surrender without impugning his honour; to resist after the opening of a practicable breach risked a time-honoured practice whereby the garrison could be refused quarter and

The bombardment of Lille, September 1792. This Austrian battery demonstrates the use of mortars, lobbing their bombs with a high trajectory into the besieged city. The lady at the right (who gave the signal to open fire) was the Duchess of Saxe-Teschen, wife of Duke Albert who commanded the Austrian forces, and sister of Marie Antoinette. (Print after Bertaux)

the fortress sacked by the stormers in 'punishment' for the garrison's forcing them to suffer heavy casualties in carrying the breach. An assault of a defended breach, which the garrison would have attempted to repair or have established an inner defensive-line, was the most hazardous operation in all warfare, guaranteed to cause immense casualties. Full-blown assaults were rare, and where they occurred, as at Ciudad Rodrigo and Badajoz, they slaughtered the attacking troops to such a degree that the most common analogy given by survivors of the storm of the latter fortress is that the breaches resembled nothing so much as the very mouth of hell. Despite this, there was never any shortage of volunteers to form the first storming-parties or 'forlorn hope'. The storm of a breach would often be accompanied by diversionary attacks mounted simultaneously at other points on the defences, not so much to confuse the garrison (for a breach was the obvious target for assault) as to force them to

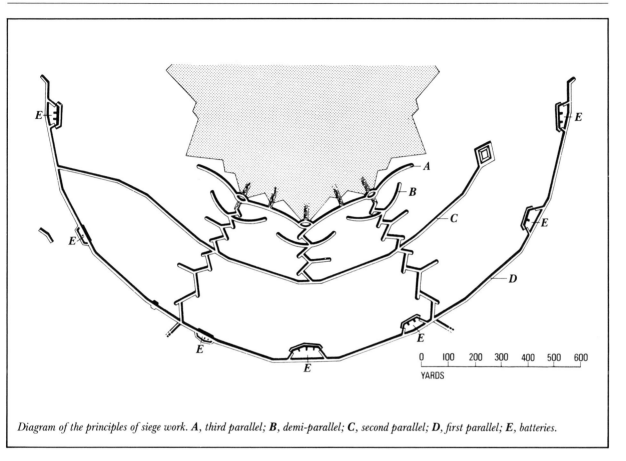

Diagram of the principles of siege work. **A**, *third parallel;* **B**, *demi-parallel;* **C**, *second parallel;* **D**, *first parallel;* **E**, *batteries.*

dissipate their resources around the *enceinte*. One of the great ironies of the 1812 assault of Badajoz, the most concentrated carnage of the age, was that while the breaches were found to be impenetrable despite the most hideous loss of life, it was the diversionary attacks by escalade which succeeded.

Higher Formations

Although there is insufficient space here to detail the many national variations of higher organizations, and the use to which they were put, a few general facts can be ennumerated.

The most fundamental of higher formations was the brigade, a combination of two or more battalions of infantry or regiments of cavalry. These were necessary for reasons of administration and to facilitate both supply and command in battle, though it is surprising that some armies resisted the formation of permanent administrative units until haphazard organization resulted in chaos on campaign; the lack of such properly organized formations was a fatal hindrance to the Allied army in the Austerlitz campaign, for example. A brigade would be commanded either by a general officer appointed for the task, or the senior battalion-commander of the component units (when his own battalion would pass to his second in command). Brigade staff was usually small, no more than a handful of ADCs and administrative officers (such as a British brigade-major) to maintain communica-

tion with higher authority and to conduct the brigade's commissariat matters.

Two or more brigades formed a division, commanded by a general officer, again with his own staff, and with other 'arms' attached: usually artillery was assigned at divisional level (though it could be at brigade level), the divisional artillery 'park' being available to support whichever component parts of the division required it; a division might also include a small cavalry detachment (to perform escort and reconnaissance duty) and an engineer 'park'. In some armies, no higher formation existed than the division, but where larger numbers of troops were involved it was generally not sufficiently capable of co-ordinating all their movements.

This resulted in the creation of the corps or *corps d'armée*, in effect a miniature army with all the necessary component parts included. The corps was commanded by a senior general officer and comprised two or more divisions, a cavalry brigade or division, and a corps artillery park (separate from the divisional parks), with all necessary engineer and commissariat facilities and a considerable corps staff to transmit the directions of the commander and oversee the necessary logistical duties. Not all armies were sufficiently large to operate a corps system: Wellington's Peninsular army, for example, never contained corps *per se* though each division was capable of operating independently in the manner of a corps; and others eschewed the terminology 'corps' while operating the system, for example the Austrian so-called *Armee Abtheilungen* of 1813. Some manner of 'corps' system was necessary when the number of troops increased, however, if duplication of some and omission of other staff duties were to be avoided, if supplies were to be managed competently and if orders were to be transmitted and acted upon without delay.

Allied to the existence of higher formations was the necessity wherever possible to co-ordinate the operations of the various 'arms', of securing the flanks of a line-of-battle with cavalry, or deploying cavalry in the rear of the infantry to exploit a wavering in the enemy line or to counter-attack an enemy breakthrough, and of supporting both defence and attack with artillery. While not universally true, most successful actions or episodes within a more general battle either resulted from, or depended to some degree upon, a successful co-ordination of 'arms' and supports. Conversely, lack of such co-ordination could be disastrous; the destruction of Colborne's brigade at Albuera could have been prevented by having the flanks covered by cavalry, but perhaps the best example is the repeated, heroic but ultimately unavailing French cavalry charges at Waterloo. Had they been accompanied by horse artillery from the outset, the infantry squares which resisted them could have been ravaged by artillery fire and perhaps made vulnerable to cavalry attack. The precariousness of a square assailed in this manner is emphasized by the language used by the normally staid Dundas manual: '. . . such situation would be critical indeed, and from which nothing but the most

determined resistance could extricate them'.[8] Nothing demonstrates so clearly the penalties for the failure to ensure co-ordination of 'arms' than the slaughter of the gallant French cavalry around the immovable red squares along the ridge of Mont St. Jean.

THE ART OF WAR AT SEA

Naval tactics were governed by the design of the ships, and by the fact that naval vessels were essentially floating gun-platforms whose armament was concentrated on their sides, not at the bow or stern. A few guns might be mounted on the bow to fire forwards ('bow-chasers') and a larger number to protrude through the stern, but the vast preponderance of the armament was mounted to fire through ports in the sides of the vessel; thus the most effective mode of combat was by the firing of 'broadsides' against the enemy. From this developed the theory of the 'line-of-battle', by which fleets would be arrayed in line astern, gradually drawing nearer before opening fire and pounding each other with their broadsides, until one or the other broke off combat. Its great advantage was that it prevented part of a fleet from being cut off and overwhelmed by the enemy, and thus its maintenance became something of a shibboleth among naval commanders, even to the extent of threatening death to captains who deliberately broke the 'line-of-battle'. Its disadvantage, however, was that its nature prevented large-scale fleet actions from ending in decisive victory, making combat between fleets a somewhat negative if expensive exercise.

◄ *Below left:*
The 'line of battle': the French fleet at Trafalgar, with British ships 'crossing the "T"' in the

background. Note the condition of the sails, with holes blasted through by roundshot.
(Engraving after Robert Dodd)

▲ *A naval artillery carriage: the barrel supported upon a stepped*

wooden framework, with wooden 'truck' wheels.

It had long been recognized that the most effective broadside could be delivered not upon the sides of the enemy vessel but against either the bow or stern, and manoeuvring a ship into this position (known from the respective situations of the ships as 'crossing the "T"') was a prime tactic in single-ship actions or those involving only a few vessels. By pouring a broadside into the enemy's bow or stern, not only was the attacker rendered largely immune from fire (only the enemy bow- or stern-chasers being able to reply), but shot delivered would pass down the entire length of the ship, the absence of bulkheads resulting in the most appalling damage to a ship thus 'raked' from bow or stern; a single broadside might be sufficient to transform the interior of the enemy vessel into a shambles and cause such confusion that the vessel might surrender or be unable to resist boarding. The problem facing naval commanders was how to combine 'crossing the "T"' with the conventional line-of-battle.

It is sometimes stated that the manoeuvre which effected this – 'breaking the line' – was devised by Horatio Nelson, but although he gave it a new dimension, its roots may be traced to a pamphlet by one John Clerk, an English theorist who had not himself been to sea but who had a clear view of what was required. His idea was that the attacking fleet should approach the enemy in conventional 'line-of-battle',

but that each ship should then interpose itself between two of the enemy ships, or that the fleet should pass through the enemy line, 'and cutting off one division of his fleet from another, so as to prevent the enemy from being able to extricate himself',[9] thus causing the isolated division to be overwhelmed, or at least forcing the enemy to stand and fight at close range and not, as the French usually did when engaging British ships, to damage their rigging and then make off. Clerk printed a few copies of his *Essay on Naval Tactics* in 1782, for private circulation. One of these, given to General Debbeig, was lent to Sir John Jervis who enquired where he might buy a copy. 'It is not to be bought,' answered the General, 'I had this copy from the author, who is a particular friend of mine; he had but a few copies printed, all of which he has given away among his friends.' 'Since that is the case,' said Sir John Jervis, 'you shall not have this copy back again; it is too good a thing for you, who are a landsman, I will keep it to myself.'[10]

The results of the distillation of Clerk's pamphlet seem to have been profound, as the tactic of 'breaking the line' was put into effect as early as the Battle of the Saints (1782), while Duncan, who apparently advised Clerk to re-print his *Essay* as naval officers were eagerly circulating hand-written copies among themselves, followed the scheme at Camperdown with great success. It did require a considerable competency in ship-handling, however; as the *Morning Chronicle* reported, 'The manoeuvre of *breaking the line*, formerly considered as the most desperate system, appears now to be reduced to a system . . . with certainty and success. The skill of our seamen in working their ships, is said to give our fleets a superiority in their performance of which the fleets of no other nation have presumed to emulate.'[11] One of the consequences of 'breaking the line' was to reduce naval battles from a sterile bombardment to a number of individual ship-to-ship actions at close quarters, where the superior ship-handling and gunnery of one side (invariably the British) would be able to make itself felt. Furthermore, it allowed a numerically inferior force to defeat a larger one, if by breaking the line the whole weight of the smaller attacking force could be concentrated upon only part of the larger fleet; the ships ahead of the 'break' would take so long to reverse their course and return to the fight that those astern of the break could be overwhelmed before assistance could be rendered. This was the essence of Nelson's extension of the tactic, by which he attacked at Trafalgar in two columns,

breaking the line twice and bringing about the 'pell-mell battle' which was his stated desire. When the tactic was performed with 'dauntless intrepidity', the results 'must ever command the admiration of the whole World'.[12]

Within the range of naval combat there were two contrasting theories about the targeting of the enemy, dependent upon the overall strategic policy adopted. To French admirals, naval combat (excluding single-ship encounters) was only justified if there were a wider strategic purpose in view; to the British, the destruction of enemy naval elements was an end in itself, and this determined the manner in which battles were fought. French policy was to concentrate fire upon the enemy's masts and rigging, preventing a pursuit if the French decided to make off during the battle; conversely, British tactics were to concentrate fire upon the enemy's deck and hull, dismounting the guns and killing the crew, and hence the British almost always inflicted far heavier casualties than they sustained. Few ships were sunk in battle, however, only those which caught fire and blew up, greatly hazardous to any ship in the vicinity. In some cases such destruction was caused by accident rather

Battle of the 'Glorious First of June': ships-of-the-line fire broadsides at each other, the British ship (left) raking the Frenchman's hull, while the French shot dismasts the British ship. (Engraving by A. Le Petit after P. J. De Loutherbourg)

than by enemy fire; one account of the explosion of the French flagship *L'Orient* at Aboukir Bay stated that the fire was due to flammable paint-buckets, left on deck by a negligent crew, being ignited by sparks from her own guns; while *Achille* was set ablaze at Trafalgar by the flashes of the muskets of her own marksmen in the fighting-tops. Though ships might be riddled with shot-holes they usually stayed afloat until after the action (though were prey to bad weather, like that which sank most of the captured Franco-Spanish fleet after Trafalgar); so that the almost universal method of neutralizing an enemy ship was by capture. If a ship were terribly battered or badly outnumbered, a captain could strike his colours in a gesture of surrender without impugning his honour; alternatively, a ship might be boarded. It is perhaps ironic that the most severe hand-to-hand fighting occurred not on land, where large-scale bayonet-fights were rare, but at sea. Having battered a ship with broadsides, a captain might lay his vessel alongside and lash it close to the enemy, continuing to pound the hull with gunnery at point-blank range if possible; and then send his boarding-party across either on to the enemy's deck or into the hull via the gun-ports. The boarding-parties consisted not only of marines, who might be expected to lead the charge, but also of seamen, armed with pistols, cutlasses, dirks, boarding-pikes and hatchets, and most bitter conflict would ensue until the boarders were killed or ejected, or the crew of the boarded vessel surrendered. Great epics of heroism occurred in such actions, yet were frequently unrewarded, and such tactics were employed as much in single-ship actions as in fleet battles. The primacy of gunnery and ship-handling should not be overlooked, however; in general, boarding only occurred after a vessel had been thoroughly raked by broadsides on the approach.

Notes

1. *Pro Aris et Focis*, R. O. Mason, London 1798.
2. *The Double-Armed Man, By the New Invention*, W. Neade, London 1625.
3. *A Manual for Volunteer Corps of Infantry*, anon. London 1803, pp. 30–3.
4. 18 June 1812; *Dispatches of Field Marshal the Duke of Wellington*, ed. J. Gurwood, London 1834–9, IX, p. 240.
5. *The Bombardier and Pocket Gunner*, R. W. Adye, London 1802, p. 27.
6. ibid. p. 26.
7. *Rough Notes of Seven Campaigns in Portugal, Spain, France and America*, J. S. Cooper, Carlisle 1869, p. 157.
8. *Rules & Regulations for the Formations, Field-Exercise and Movements of His Majesty's Forces*, London (new edn) 1798, p. 353.
9. *Morning Chronicle*, 3 November 1798, which contains a lengthy analysis.
10. ibid.
11. ibid. 9 October 1798.
12. ibid. 3 November 1798.

References

Chandler, D. G. *The Campaigns of Napoleon*, London 1967 (invaluable study relevant to all aspects of Napoleonic warfare).
Glover, M. *Warfare in the Age of Bonaparte*, London 1980.
Griffith, P. *Forward into Battle: Fighting Tactics from Waterloo to Vietnam*, Chichester 1981.
Hughes, Major-General B. P. *Firepower*, London 1974.
—*Open fire: Artillery Tactics from Marlborough to Wellington*, Chichester 1983.
Rothenberg, G.E. *The Art of War in the Age of Napoleon*, London 1977.
Siege-warfare is covered in:
Belmas, J. *Journaux des Siéges faits ou soutenus par les Français dans la Peninsula de 1807 à 1814*, Paris 1836 (the converse view to that of Jones, below).
Duffy, C. *Fire and Stone: the Science of Fortress Warfare 1660–1860*, Newton Abbot 1975.
Jones, Lieutenant-Colonel J. T. *Journals of the Sieges undertaken by the Allies in Spain*, London 1814.
Myatt, F. *British Sieges of the Peninsular War*, Tunbridge Wells 1987.
Viollet-le-Duc, E. *Annals of a Fortress* (trans. E. Bucknall), London 1875 (describes the progression of fortification from the earliest period).
An important survey of the most effective fortification of the period, the Lines of Torres Vedras, is *Memoranda relative to the Lines thrown up to cover Lisbon in 1810*, Colonel J. T. Jones, in *Papers on Subjects connected with the Duties of the Corps of Royal Engineers*, III, London 1839.

MEDICAL SERVICES

Two constraints acted against the health of the soldiers of the Napoleonic Wars: first, the limits of medical knowledge which, before the invention of anaesthetics or the knowledge of the existence of bacteria, had progressed only a limited way over the previous several centuries; and secondly, from military establishments which placed medical services very low on the scale of priorities. As the great French surgeon Percy remarked, 'One would believe that the sick and wounded cease to be men when they can no longer be soldiers.'[1]

There were few units in any European army that could be termed 'medical corps', and even where these existed (such as the *infirmiers* of the French army in the later campaigns) they were hopelessly few in number to make any real impact upon the appalling numbers of maimed and wounded who lay on every battlefield. Instead, medical service devolved upon the small number of officers attached to each battalion or regiment, who rarely had any trained orderlies to assist them; in those armies where non-commissioned medical staff existed, at best they received rudimentary training with the battalion, and at worst were totally unskilled in any duty more demanding than stretcher-bearing. In many armies there existed no rank-and-file medical personnel at all, bearers being recruited *ad hoc* from the lightly wounded or from any unit in the vicinity. In some armies the allocation of medical officers was equally poor, though the dearth in Russian service was extreme; in fact it was said that Platov refused additional medical officers to supplement the one he had on the grounds that all the enemy's fire was less dangerous than a single drug! Under normal circumstances, each battalion would have one surgeon and one or two assistants, though even these officers might not be adequately trained; in the Austrian army, for example, the 120-odd regimental surgeons were trained doctors, but the battalion surgeons (*Ober-Chirugen*) had less training, and the company medical assistants (*Unter-Chirugen* or *Feldschers*) hardly any at all. Even in an army as comparatively sophisticated as the British, John Moore's 51st Foot boasted a surgeon 'completely ignorant, devoid of humanity, and a

---

'The Emperor has no faith in medicine, or its remedies, of which he makes no use. "Doctor," he said, "our body is like a machine for the purpose of life: it is organized to that end – that is its nature. Leave the life there at its ease, let it take care of itself, it will do better than if you paralyze it by loading it with medicines. It is like a well-made watch, destined to go for a certain time; the watch-maker has not the power of opening it, he cannot meddle with it but at random, and with his eyes bandaged. For one who, by dint of racking it with his ill-formed instruments, succeeds in doing it any good, how many blockheads destroy it altogether!" '

(*Memoir of the Life, Exile, and Conversations of the Emperor Napoleon*, Count de Las Cases, London 1836, I, p. 391.)

---

rogue . . . against his ignorance I have no remedy, tho' I have daily the grossest instances of it'.[2] Higher organization was equally of mixed merit: Austria possessed a military medical academy, the Josephinium (named after the emperor who established it in Vienna in 1785), but Britain's 'Medical Board' (Surgeon-General, Physician-General and Inspector-General of Hospitals), 'improved' by being replaced by a single Director-General, was still in the hands of one termed by the Duke of York 'an old driveller'. In France, the insanity of 'revolutionary fervour' had led to the closure of medical schools in 1792 ('privileged' institutions being anathema), so that until they were re-established in 1803 only the most rudimentary training was possible. It is a measure of the wretchedness of central direction as a whole that great renown became attached to the really capable, humanitarian officers such as the French Pierre François Percy, the Physician-General René Desgenettes (the ci-devant Baron des Genettes) and above all Dominique-Jean Larrey, surgeon-general of the Imperial Guard; and the British Inspector-General of Hospitals in the Peninsula, Dr. James McGrigor.

Treatment of injuries was rudimentary. Bullet-wounds that had avoided smashing a bone were 'probed' (often by the surgeon's fingers) in the hope of locating the ball, but otherwise the missile might be left to stay there or work out of its own volition, as preferable to attempted extraction. (When Harry Smith went to Lisbon in 1810 to have a ball removed from his knee, he was advised to keep his stiff leg rather than risk an extraction). Especial danger arose if part of the uniform were carried into the wound, as it was believed this would promote festering (hence the habit of changing into clean clothes immediately before an action, if possible: usually this applied only to officers at sea), and especially feared were pieces of wire epaulette-bullion being carried into a wound, as these were almost impossible to extract.

Where a limb was damaged, either by ball or sabre-cut, amputation was the universal remedy, at times performed with a speed truly astonishing, to reduce the shock to the system caused by a protracted operation. So inadequate was the medical staff after Borodino that Larrey himself had to perform 200 amputations in 24 hours, and stories exist of surgeons operating with such speed that assistant's fingers were amputated accidentally along with the patient's limb; conversely, a tired surgeon with a blunt knife might take twenty minutes to remove an injured limb. Gangrene or 'mortification' was a permanent danger, especially where the process of *débridement* had not been performed, i.e., the excision of all dead tissue from around the wound. Nevertheless, there existed many capable surgeons who were able to perform exceptional feats of surgery, given the prevailing conditions: Purefoy Lockwood of the British 30th Foot was dreadfully wounded at Waterloo, but survived after a silver plate was set into his skull to replace a missing portion, the plate engraved 'bomb proof' to demonstrate that the injury had not deprived him of his spirit! Brutal though the practice of universal amputation might appear, however, under the conditions of the time it was probably the salvation of many, by removing damaged tissue and bone which would otherwise have been the cause of fatal infections.

Speed of treatment was a major factor in assisting the recovery of the wounded, but hardly any facility existed for the evacuation of the injured to the emergency casualty-stations which were established behind the line-of-battle. Wounded men had often to make their own way to such refuges, or be helped by their fellows, though the latter practice was discouraged as giving an excuse for men to absent themselves from the firing-line (a practice which greatly weakened the Netherlandish army in the 1815 campaign, for example); the alternative was for the wounded to lie where they fell until after the action, when parties of the victorious army would be dispatched to succour and gather up those of the wounded as were still alive after the battle. Many lay for several days before their injuries were attended, while the policy of non-evacuation of casualties might have even more terrible consequences, as at Talavera, if dry grass were set alight by the flash of muskets and the helpless wounded burned to death where they lay.

After initial battlefield treatment, casualties would be

The following reports a side of the Napoleonic Wars often overlooked in 'general' histories:

'A little farther on, in an inner court, were the surgeons. They were stripped to their shirts and bloody. Curiosity led me forward; a number of doors, placed on barrels, served as temporary tables, and on these lay the different subjects upon whom the surgeons were operating; to the right and left were arms and legs, flung here and there, without distinction, and the ground was dyed with blood. Dr. Bell was going to take off the thigh of a soldier of the 50th, and he requested I would hold down the man for him. He was one of the best-hearted men I ever met with, but, such is the force of habit, he seemed insensible to the scene that was passing around him, and with much composure was eating almonds out of his waistcoat-pockets, which he offered to share with me, but, if I got the universe for it, I could not have swallowed a morsel of anything. The operation on the man of the 50th was the most shocking sight I ever witnessed; it lasted nearly half an hour, but his life was saved . . . Outside of this place was an immense pit to receive the dead from the general hospital, which was close by. Twelve or fifteen bodies were flung in at a time, and covered with a layer of earth, and so on, in succession, until the pit was filled. Flocks of vultures already began to hover over this spot . . . This was my first and last visit to an amputating hospital, and I advise young gentlemen, such as I was then, to avoid going near a place of the kind, unless obliged to do so – mine was an accidental visit.'

(*Adventures with the Connaught Rangers*, William Grattan, 1847; 1902 edn., ed. Sir Charles Oman, pp. 76–8.)

---

conveyed to improvised hospitals established in a nearby town. A few armies had ambulance units organized for the purpose (Lacy had devised 'flying ambulances' for the Austrian army as early as just after the Seven Years War, and most famous were Larrey's ambulance-trains from 1797), but the majority of casualties were conveyed in ordinary unsprung wagons, at best causing excruciating agony and at worst rendering their injuries fatal; in some cases the lack of organized ambulance-trains was deliberate as with the British in the Peninsula. Hardly any use was made of *cacolets* (panniers slung on either side of a mule or horse in which the injured could ride), though Larrey devised camel-litters of this style in Egypt. So poor was the system of casualty-evacuation that wheelbarrows had to be used in Germany in 1813. Wounded officers were usually billeted in private houses and thus received the best treatment available, but the majority of hospitals to which the 'other ranks' were confined were virtual charnel-houses, ill-ventilated, smoky and generally filthy, with men deposited two to a bed or simply laid upon the floor.[3] Perhaps the greatest improvement introduced by McGrigor in the Peninsula was the establishment of prefabricated hospitals to accompany the army, saving casualties the agonies of transportation and being deposited in the in-sanitary, decrepit buildings and cellars which masqueraded as 'hospitals'. Nevertheless, many wounded men not only survived but returned to their duty, and the casualty-statistics of the Imperial Guard after Aspern-Essling demonstrate what could be achieved even with the limited medical knowledge of the time: out of 1,200 wounded, by August 1809 600 had returned to their units, 250 had been evacuated to France and only 45 had died, testimony to the care and capability of the greatest humanitarian of the age, the surgical genius Larrey.

Injuries in battle were only a portion of the army's casualties; very often a far greater proportion of losses was by sickness. Certain areas and situations were notorious for the prevalence of fever: low-lying and marshy ground was avoided as a camping-site where possible, due to the chance of malarial fevers in hot weather, but in many cases these were unavoidable; 'trench-fever' from stagnant water was an accepted hazard of besieging fortresses, while 'Guadiana fever' and 'Walcheren fever' were endemic in those areas, the latter so severe that battalions which caught it remained sickly for years (Wellington even requested that no more 'Walcheren regiments' be sent to him, their sickness-rate was so bad). The problem afflicted all theatres of war: in 1807, for example, three-quarters of French hospital patients were admitted for reasons other than wounds. The West Indies in particular was a graveyard for European troops, destroying both French and British armies. Statistics for the British losses are almost unbelievable: as many as 80,000 troops died or were invalided between 1794 and 1796; in the Windward and Leeward Islands in 1796 41.3 per cent of the troops *died*, and the average mortality-rate between 1796 and 1828 was 13.4 per cent per annum.[4] Against such infections and 'putrid fevers' the medical establishment had no cure,

> 'On Sunday and Monday last were disembarked at Mount Wise, Plymouth Dock, 200 wounded soldiers from the peninsula. Many of the brave fellows were dreadfully mutilated, yet evinced a cheerfulness truly astonishing. Among them were several of the life guards. One fine fellow, a serjeant, who had both his legs shot away, facetiously desired those who carried him out of the boat not to *wet his feet*. Besides this, many were the jibes and jokes that occurred on their again touching British ground; and the whole party hobbled off to the Royal Military Hospital, with a gaiety of heart that surprised the spectators.'
>
> (*Edinburgh Evening Courant*, 14 February 1814.)

having little conception of the causes (the British Physician-General declined to visit Walcheren in 1809 as he claimed to have no knowledge of the diseases of the camp!); 'remedies' included bleeding, drenching with water, wearing a bag of camphor on the stomach, washing with 'Marseilles vinegar' or drinking a jug of boiled claret. A gauge of the lack of knowledge about such illnesses is the anecdote regarding 21 European officers who went to the West Indies, ten deciding to drink only water and eleven to drink only wine, to determine which was the most healthy. 'Each individual accordingly adhered to the principal we had decided on. But the water drinkers, poor fellows, all died out long since.'

'And what became of the wine drinkers? . . .'
'They somehow or other dropped off one by one, until I alone remain alive . . .'[5]

Notes

1. *Journal des Campagnes de Baron Percy*, Paris 1904, p. 16; quoted in *Larrey: Surgeon to Napoleon's Imperial Guard*, R. G. Richardson, London 1974, p. 2.
2. *Sir John Moore*, Carola Oman, London 1953, p. 73.
3. Few accounts exist of the state of the hospitals of the rank-and-file, but for a summary of those in the Peninsula, see Cooper's *Rough Notes of Seven Campaigns*.
4. These statistic seem incredible; but see, for example, *Contribution to Statistics of the British Army*, Deputy Inspector-General H. Marshall, *Edinburgh Medical & Surgical Journal* No. 125, and reprinted as a pamphlet, Edinburgh n.d. (1836?).
5. *Colburn's United Service Magazine*, London 1849, II, p. 452.

References

Blanco, R. L. *Wellington's Surgeon General: Sir James McGrigor*, Durham, North Carolina, 1974.

Richardson, R. G. *Larrey: Surgeon to Napoleon's Imperial Guard*, London 1974.

Vansittart, J. (ed.). *Surgeon James's Journal*, London 1964 (journal of a typical regimental surgeon, Haddy James of the Life Guards, in the Waterloo campaign).

For the medical techniques of the period, the following are of use:

Chaplin, A. *Medicine in the Age of George III*, London 1919.

Guthrie, J. G. *Treatise on Gun-Shot Wounds*. London 1820.

Macleod, G. H. B. *Notes on the Surgery of the War in the Crimea with Remarks on the Treatment of Gunshot Wounds*, London 1858 (post-dates the Napoleonic Wars but is an interesting study from the battlefield-surgeon's viewpoint, much of which is relevant to the earlier period; the author was Lecturer on Military Surgery at Glasgow University).

Mamelukes: a print after Horace Vernet which, though not contemporary, is typical of Vernet's accurate portrayal of military costume. Entitled 'Retreat of the Mamelukes', when published in The Cavalry Journal *(VI, London 1911) it was ascribed to the Battle of the Pyramids (note the French infantry in the background), though it could apply to any action in Egypt in 1798–9.*

III
THE NATIONS
INVOLVED IN THE
NAPOLEONIC
WARS

THE NATIONS INVOLVED IN THE NAPOLEONIC WARS

The section which follows covers in some depth the history of the many nations involved in the Napoleonic Wars, and gives an outline of the composition and uniform of their military and naval forces. This is necessarily contracted for reasons of space, but for most nationalities references are quoted which will provide more information. In general these are selected for their availability for further reading, and much of what precedes these references may not be covered by those listed.

In addition there are several works that cover more than one nationality, which are listed separately below:

Haythornthwaite, P. J. *Uniforms of the French Revolutionary Wars*, Poole 1981
— *Uniforms of the Peninsular War*, Poole 1978
— *Uniforms of the Retreat from Moscow*, Poole 1976
— *Uniforms of Waterloo*, London 1975
Knötel, R., Knötel, H., and Sieg, H. *Handbuch der Uniformkunde*, Hamburg 1937, reprinted Hamburg 1964 (the 'standard' work on the history of military uniforms of all nations)
Martin, P. *European Military Uniforms: A Short History*, London 1967; originally published as *Der Bunte Rock*, Stuttgart 1963 (reproduces many valuable contemporary prints)
Mollo, J. *Military Fashion*, London 1972 (illustrates many contemporary relics)
Müller, H., and Kunter, F. *Europäische Helme*, Berlin 1984 (a general survey with many Napoleonic items illustrated)
Pivka, Otto von. *Armies of 1812*, Cambridge 1977 (covering the nations comprising the *Grande Armée* for the Russian campaign)
— *Armies of the Napoleonic Era*, Newton Abbot 1979
— *Navies of the Napoleonic Era*, Newton Abbot 1980 (together with the previous title, a good introduction to the uniforms and tactics of the period)

ANHALT

History

Anhalt comprised three minor German duchies neighbouring Prussia: Anhalt-Dessau, Anhalt-Bernburg and Anhalt-Köthen. (A fourth, Anhalt-Zerbst, was absorbed by the other three in 1793 following the death of its prince, Frederick Augustus). In 1806 Alexius of Anhalt-Bernburg was created a duke by the Emperor Francis I, and following the dissolution of the Holy Roman Empire the other princes also took a similar title. All joined the Confederation of the Rhine in 1807; Augustus II of Anhalt-Köthen was especially Francophile, emulating the French internal organization of 'departments' and introducing the *Code Napoléon*. Anhalt-Bernburg was partitioned briefly, but the extinction of the family's cadet branch led to its reunification in 1812. Anhalt-Dessau was the most overtly military of the three, its rulers including Prince Leopold I (1676–1747, alias 'the old Dessauer'), and Leopold II Maximilian (1700–51) who, like the other sons of 'the old Dessauer' (Prince Moritz, 1712–60, and Prince Dietrich, d. 1769), was greatly distinguished as a general under Frederick the Great. The three states joined the Allies in 1813.

Army (cockade: green)

Despite the military traditions of the ruling family of Anhalt-Dessau, the military contribution of Anhalt was slight, the three states combining to form a single infantry battalion of the 5th (Anhalt-Lippe) Regiment of the Confederation, which served in Prussia (1807), the Tyrol (1809), Spain (1809–11), Russia (1812) and Danzig (1813); uniform comprised a shako with white-metal Anhalt arms, green jacket faced rose-pink, and grey breeches. In 1813 a *chasseurs à cheval* regiment was formed briefly, wearing the same colouring, but was captured almost immediately.

ARGENTINA

History

Argentina was not a combatant in the Napoleonic Wars proper, but only in the abortive British expedition of 1806–7; though the political turmoil in Spain during the Peninsular War had profound repercussions in Spain's overseas colonies.

In 1776 Buenos Aires was made the seat of a Spanish viceroyalty covering the territories which are now Argentina, Bolivia, Paraguay and Uruguay. The British expedition of 1806, initiated without governmental authority, hoped to encourage internal dissent which favoured independence from Spain; but, following the initial capture of Buenos Aires, the colonists (led by Santiago de Liniers, a French officer in Spanish service) opposed the British force and compelled it to surrender. In July 1807 a second British landing was also forced to capitulate (caused largely by the ineptitude of the leadership), ending the disastrous foray into South America. Elated at their success, achieved without Spanish assistance, the colonists were filled with a self-confidence which led to open revolt. Liniers was viceroy when news was received of the establishment of the Bonapartist regime in Spain; despite his previous good service, Liniers was mistrusted (as a Frenchman) and deposed by supporters of Ferdinand VII. Acting in Ferdinand's name, the central *junta* at Seville appointed Balthasar de Cisneros as viceroy, a position he took up in July 1809. Opposition to him increased and on 25 May 1810 an armed multitude overthrew his authority and established a provisional *junta* in the name of Ferdinand VII; an attempt by the pro-Spanish faction to make Cisneros president of the *junta* failed, and he retired to Montevideo. Civil war followed between the 'revolutionary' (independence) party and the pro-Spanish faction, the leaders of the former including General Manuel Belgrano (whose name was to become widely known in 1982) and General José de San Martin (who had fought against the French in the Peninsular War), and though civil war continued in the provinces, Argentinian independence was assured from 1816 when the separation of the united provinces of the Rio de la Plata was declared, with Buenos Aires its capital. Spain did not formally acknowledge independence until 1842, after several abortive attempts at reconquest by force; but it may fairly be said that the Peninsular War was the spark which changed the political geography of South America.

Army

The forces that resisted the British invasion consisted primarily of locally raised corps, including a small number of 'veteran' units, provincial militia and volunteers. The veterans wore Spanish uniform, the infantry (*Fijo de Buenos Aires*) with white coats faced red (yellow collar), white-laced bicorns, white breeches and buttons; and the dragoons yellow coats with red facings (yellow lapels piped red), yellow buttons and hat-lace, and white waistcoat and breeches. The militia included four artillery corps: the *Artilleros Provinciales* (100 strong), in blue jackets and breeches, red collar and cuffs, black lapels and a red-plumed 'round hat'; the Union Artillery (395 strong), uniformed similarly but with red lapels, yellow lace and a fur-crested hat; with two cadet companies attached, dressed similarly but with red lapels and, for the *Jóvenes de la Reconquista*, white breeches. The other artillery units were the *Naturales* (Indian labourers, 426 strong), wearing a white-crested 'round hat', blue sleeved waistcoat, and white collar, cuffs, breeches and buttons; and the *Real Maestranza de Artilleria*, a mounted corps with 'round hat' with red, white and blue feathers, blue coat, breeches and lapels, with red facings, lapel-piping and lace on the breeches.

The majority of the infantry corps wore blue coats with red facings, 'round hat' and white breeches; divergences from this colouring are listed below, with details of the various units: Provincial Grenadiers (fur caps with brass plate, red plume and white corps); *Patricios* (white plume, jacket with white hussar braid, red sash); *Montañenses* (red plume);

Asturian or Biscayan corps (blue sash, plume white with red base and red central band); *Cazadores* (green faced yellow, green plume with red tip); Andalusian corps (red plume with green centre); Catalonian corps (blue jacket and breeches, white braid, buff collar and cuffs, fur-crested hat); *Arribeños* (formed in the provinces of the interior: black plume with red tip, light blue sash); *Morenos* (Negroes: red dolman faced white, white-crested leather helmet with red plume); *Pardos* (mulattos: light blue dolman, black facings piped white, fur-crested leather helmet with red plume).

The cavalry included three hussar squadrons: 1st, with blue dolman and breeches, red collar and cuffs, white braid, shako with white cords and red plume; 2nd, similar but white facings, breeches and plume, yellow braid; and 3rd, with green dolman and breeches, yellow collar and braid, shako with yellow cords, yellow plume with green tip. The 4th hussar squadron was the *Cazadores de la Reina* (red dolman, blue breeches, yellow braid, white-crested 'round hat' with black plume). The other cavalry comprised the *Migueletes de Castex* (red dolman, white braid, blue breeches, white-crested helmet with black plume, or 'round hat' with red-tipped yellow plume); *Carabineros de Carlos IV* (red coat with buff collar, cuffs, lapels and turnbacks, blue breeches, buff-crested helmet with red plume and buff band inscribed 'Carlos IV'); and the *Quinteros* (blue dolman faced red, white braid and breeches, plain 'round hat' with red plume; armed with lances or pikes).

There was in addition a corps of naval infantry, in blue short jackets with three rows of white buttons, red collar (bearing an anchor) and cuffs, red-plumed 'round hat' and long, blue nautical trousers. The strength of all these corps varied from less than 200 to above 500, plus the Patricios (1,350); the cavalry units averaged about 200 men each.

Reference

Álzaga, E. W. *Iconografía de los Uniformes Militaires: Invasiones Inglesas*, Buenos Aires 1967.

'At a General Court Martial . . . the trial of private William Green, of the 66th Regiment, for unsoldier-like conduct, and insolence, in using disrespectful language, threatening and striking Ensign Fox, when ordered to be taken to the guard-house by him, on the evening of the 13th April, 1809; and the Court having maturely weighed and considered the evidence against the prisoner, together with what he has urged in his defence, is of the opinion, that he, the said William Green, is guilty of the first part of the charge, viz. in using disrespectful language to Ensign Fox, 66th Foot, which being a breach of the Articles of War, do sentence him to receive 500 lashes, in such manner, and at such a time and place as his Excellency the Commander of the Forces shall direct.'

(General Order, Adjutant General's Office, Abrantes, 24 June 1809; *General Orders: Spain and Portugal*, London 1811, I, p. 82.)

AUSTRIA

The Austrian Empire (initially the Holy Roman Empire) was ruled throughout the period by the Habsburg Emperor Francis II (1768–1835) who succeeded Leopold II in 1792. On 11 August 1804 he assumed the title of Emperor Francis I of Austria, and following the defeat of 1805 the Holy Roman Empire was officially dissolved and the title renounced on 6 August 1806. The Empire spread from Italy to the Netherlands and from Poland to the Balkans, incorporating in 1793 some 6,500,000 Germans, 3,360,000 Czechs, 2,000,000 Walloons and Flemings, 1,000,000 Poles, 900,000 Croats, 700,000 Serbs and numerous smaller nationalities. The Emperor ruled Austria as Emperor, but the 'Hungarian' possessions (including Transylvania) as King of Hungary; thus the Empire's multi-national army was styled the

Francis II, Holy Roman Emperor; Francis I, Emperor of Austria (1768–1835). Prominently displayed are the collar of the Order of the Golden Fleece, and the cross of the Order of Maria Theresa. (Engraving by Meyer after A. Dumont)

Clemens Wenzel Nepomuk
Lothar von Metternich-
Winneburg, Prince Metternich
(1773–1859); the leading Allied
statesman, certainly after the
death of William Pitt.
(Lithograph by Maurin)

Kaiserlich-königliche Armee ('Imperial and Royal'). The central administration ruled the 'German' parts of the Empire; Hungary was ruled by its own Diet (parliament) which enjoyed a degree of independence, as did the Netherlands, Italian duchies and the Tyrol. Foreign policy, like other aspects of government, was nominally decided by the Emperor, but later in the period enormous influence was exercised by the foreign minister, Count (later Prince) Clemens Wenzel Lothar Metternich-Winneburg (1773–1859). He first supported an alliance with France, helping to arrange the diplomatic marriage between Napoleon and the Emperor's daughter, Marie-Louise, but after the 1812 campaign he realized that Napoleon was doomed and took Austria into the war against France. Metternich's influence at the Congress of Vienna was profound, and he became not only the leading statesman in Europe but virtual ruler of the Empire until he was undone by the 'year of revolutions' (1848), the liberal political thought that he had attempted to suppress. Military affairs were run by a combined civil-

military council, the *Hofkriegsrat*, which issued a vast amount of unnecessary and burdensome directives.

The Empire lost territory progressively through the Revolutionary and Napoleonic Wars, each defeat costing land; the Austrian Netherlands went by the Treaty of Campo Formio (1797), though Austria gained Venice by consolation; the Italian duchies were taken by conquest, Venice and the Tyrol went by the Treaty of Pressburg (1806), and the Treaty of Schönbrunn (1809) completed the humiliation of the Empire. Despite such defeats, Austria remained Napoleon's most persistent continental adversary, and not even defeats of the magnitude of Marengo, Ulm, Austerlitz and Wagram caused a total abandonment of the fight. After a brief period of service under French direction (the 'Reserve Corps' for the 1812 campaign), in 1813–14 Austria played a leading part in the overthrow of Napoleon.

Army (cockade: black and yellow)
The Austrian army was multi-national, being divided into 'German' and 'Hungarian' regiments; the latter included Hungary, Croatia and Transylvania, and the former included troops from the Netherlands, Italy and Poland. Recruiting in the 'German' areas was partly by voluntary enlistment, with perhaps half coming from the smaller south German states, lured by high enlistment-bounties; and due to the greater degree of literacy in these areas, an even greater proportion of NCOs were non-Austrian nationals. There was a supplementary conscription (lifetime service until 1802, ten years thereafter), though Italy, Hungary and the Netherlands were exempted; Hungarian recruits were provided by a 'quota' organized by the Diet. Although each regiment had its own recruiting-area, the Poles of Galicia were regarded as untrustworthy and were usually distributed among regiments from other areas. Regiments were nominally commanded by an *Inhaber* (colonel-in-chief or 'colonel-proprietor'), whose title the regiment bore (hence the frequent changes of regimental titles throughout the period) and who exercised great power, even to the appointment of officers below field rank. Officers were largely from the lesser aristocracy whose commissions depended on 'influence', though especially in wartime limited promotion from the ranks was permitted. Training was inconsistent, wartime expansions often resulting in proportions of untrained men in every battalion, and the army was beset by constant governmental parsimony and unnecessary and confusing orders and reorganizations. Although some regiments were disbanded in 1809 following the loss of their recruiting-grounds, others were allocated new areas but kept their old designations, for example the six Walloon regiments whose recruiting areas were transferred

Austrian fusiliers, 1809,
wearing the 1806 shako which
was not in universal use even in
the 1809 campaign. Left to
right: Hungarian private with
light blue breeches; Hungarian
officer; 'German' officer,
'German' N.C.O. (Print after
R. von Ottenfeld)

Austrian Jäger 1809: pike-grey uniform with green facings, black leather equipment and the 'Corsican hat' (Corséhut) which was a feature of many Austrian uniforms of the era. (Print after R. von Ottenfeld)

to Bohemia. The most influential figure in the Austrian Army was the Archduke Charles (1771–1847) who instituted the most comprehensive and modern reforms in the Austrian army especially after Austerlitz; and though he administered to Napoleon his first real defeat at Aspern-Essling, he retired from active command after being crushed at Wagram.

Infantry

At the beginning of the war there were 57 numbered line regiments, 18 *Grenz* regiments (border infantry: see below), three garrison regiments, the *Stabs-Infanterie-Regiment* (for garrison and HQ duties) and irregular *Frei-Corps* (light infantry) raised in wartime. The line regiments usually comprised two field battalions (named the *Leib-* and *Oberst-Bataillon*), each of six fusilier companies; one garrison or *Oberstleutnant-Bataillon* of four companies, which served as a depot; and a grenadier 'division' of two companies, usually detached and formed with the grenadiers of two other regiments into a composite grenadier battalion. 'Hungarian' regiments had three field battalions and a nominal establishment of 5,508 men against the 4,575 of 'German' regiments, but especially in peacetime this number was rarely attained, regimental strength often being between 2,000 and 3,000 men. Establishments were normally increased in wartime by the recalling of men on leave and the assembly of those officially enlisted but untrained. Typical company establishment was four officers (*Hauptmann* or captain, *Oberleutnant* or 1st lieutenant, *Unterleutnant* or 2nd lieutenant and *Fähnrich* or ensign), *Feldwebel* (sergeant-major), four *Corporals* (sergeants), a *Fourierschützen* (quarter-master), three musicians, eight *Gefreiter* (corporals) and a *Zimmermann* (pioneer). (*Feldwebel* and *Fourier* were *Prima Plana* ranks, i.e., senior NCOs.) Company-strength of 230 other ranks in wartime was often as low as 120; grenadier companies were nominally 112 strong, 140 in wartime, and had no *Fähnrich* or *Gefreiter*.

The most important of many organizational changes were the reforms of 1798–9 which removed the *Grenzer* from the numbered sequence, and formed two new line regiments. Hasty reforms introduced immediately before the 1805 campaign caused only confusion (each infantry regiment to consist of one grenadier and four fusilier battalions, each of four companies of 160 men), and in 1807 the old organization was restored, save for the wartime augmentation of the 3rd battalion to six companies, with 'German' companies henceforth 180 strong and 'Hungarian' 200. After 1809 eight regiments were disbanded following the loss of recruiting-grounds, and 3rd battalions were reduced to cadre strength, German companies now being about 60 strong and Hungarian 100. From 1811 4th battalions were formed by integrating the *Landwehr* into the line.

Despite the introduction of new regulations in 1805 and 1807, the infantry maintained the traditional three-rank line, using 'battalion columns' for manoeuvre; though some emphasis was put on the utility of the third rank as skirmishers, light infantry tactics remained largely the preserve of the *Grenzer* and *Jäger*. The most famous of the

1807 innovations was the 'mass', a closely-packed variation of the square, originally used against the Turks: in effect a tight column with depth not exceeding double its width, variants being the 'division mass' (two-company frontage) and 'battalion mass' (single-company frontage). Although vulnerable to artillery they were as proof against cavalry as a square, and more capable of manoeuvre.

The traditional infantry uniform was a practical, single-breasted white jacket with facing-coloured collar, cuffs and turnbacks, very innovative for its time; but for the introduction of an upright collar and less voluminous skirts in 1798, the pattern was similar throughout, German regiments having round cuffs and Hungarians pointed with a fringed lace loop known as a *Bärentatzen* or 'bear's paw'. White breeches and black knee-gaiters were worn by 'German' regiments, Hungarians having light-blue ankle-length pantaloons with mixed black and yellow braid and low, laced shoes. The original head-dress of the *Casquet*, a squat, false-fronted cap with large brass plate, was replaced in 1798 by a large, combed black leather helmet with a black and yellow woollen crest and a brass plate bearing the Emperor's cipher. In 1806 this was replaced by a shako, but this did not become universal until after the 1809 campaign. Grenadiers wore a distinctive fur cap with low back, peaked from c. 1798, its shape giving rise to its French nickname *fauteuil* ('armchair'). Almost uniquely among European armies, officers wore neither epaulettes nor lace (the only lace was that used to indicate NCO rank), and on campaign officers commonly wore a grey-black *Oberrock* or frock-coat, the only mark of rank being the universal gold-and-black waist-sash or *Feldbinde*.

Uniform distinctions consisted of a wide range of facing-colours and white or yellow buttons, as in the following table; though the changes of title are too extensive to be ennumerated here:

Regt	Nationality	Facings	Buttons
1	Moravian	dark red	Y
2	Hungarian	yellow	Y
3	Lower Austrian	sky-blue	W
4	Lower Austrian	sky-blue	Y
5	1st Garrison Regiment	dark blue; then black	W
6	2nd Garrison Regiment	black; then dark brown	W
7	Moravian	dark blue; then dark brown	W
8	Moravian	poppy-red; then grass-green	Y
9	Walloon; then Galician	apple-green	Y
10	Bohemian	parrot-green	W
11	Bohemian	pink; then dark blue	W; then Y
12	Moravian	dark brown	Y
13	Inner Austrian	grass-green	Y
14	Upper Austrian	black	Y
15	Bohemian	madder	Y

Regt	Nationality	Facings	Buttons
16	Styrian	violet; then dark yellow	Y
17	Bohemian	light brown	W
18	Bohemian	dark red	W
19	Hungarian	light blue	W
20	Silesian	crab-red	W
21	Bohemian	sea-green	Y
22	Illyrian; then Moravian	yellow	W
23	Lower Austrian; then Galician	poppy-red	W
24	Lower Austrian; then Galician	dark blue	W
25	Bohemian	sea-green	W
26	Carinthian	parrot-green	Y
27	Styrian; then Inner Austrian	yellow	Y
28	Bohemian	grass-green	W
29	Moravian	pale blue	W
30	Walloon	light grey	Y
31	Transylvanian	yellow	W
32	Hungarian	light blue	Y
33	Hungarian	dark blue	W
34	Hungarian	madder	W
35	Bohemian	crab-red	Y
36	Bohemian	mauve	W
37	Hungarian	poppy-red	Y
38	Walloon	pink	Y
39	Hungarian	poppy-red	Y
40	Moravian	carmine; then pale blue	W
41	Galician	dark yellow	W
42	Bohemian	orange-yellow	W
43	Carinthian/ Inner Austrian	dark yellow; then carmine	Y
44	Italian; then German	madder	W
45	Lower Austrian/ Styrian; then Italian	poppy-red	Y
46	Galician	dark blue	Y
47	Bohemian	steel-green	W
48	Hungarian	steel-green	Y
49	Lower Austrian	light grey	W
50	Upper Austrian	violet	W; then Y
51	Transylvanian	dark blue	Y
52	Hungarian	dark red	Y
53	Slavonian	dark red	W
54	Bohemian	apple-green	W
55	Walloon; then Galician	pale blue	Y
56	Moravian	steel-green	Y
57	Bohemian	mauve	Y
58	Walloon	black	W
59	Upper Austrian	orange-yellow	Y; then W
60	Hungarian	steel-green	W
61	Hungarian	grass-green	W
62	Hungarian	grass-green	W
63	Walloon; then Galician	light brown	Y
64	Tyrolean *Jäger*	(see below)	

Light Infantry

Light infantry battalions were formed only in 1798, wearing infantry uniform but in pike-grey, with 'German' legwear for the Italian units (nos. 2–4, 11 and 14) and 'Hungarian' for the rest; all were disbanded in 1801. Facings as follows, with white (W) or yellow (Y) buttons: Nos. 1 (Y), 2 (W): crab-red; 3 (Y), 4 (W): brick-red; 5 (Y), 6 (Y): orange-yellow; 7 (Y), 12 (W): steel-green; 8 (W), 13 (Y): dark yellow; 9 (Y): carmine; 10 (W), 11 (Y): dark blue; 14 (W), 15 (Y): black.

Jägers

Jäger (riflemen) existed before 1801 (recruits from the Tyrol, used to rifle-shooting, were especially valuable), with the 46th Regiment having two 'rifle' battalions; but in that year, to replace the light infantry, a *Tiroler-Jäger-Regiment* was formed, numbered 64, dressed like the light infantry but with green facings and helmet-crest. Nine 6-company battalions were formed in 1808, wearing pike-grey with green facings and a 'Corsican hat' (*Korséhut*), a 'round hat' with one high, upturned brim.

Frei-Corps

Prior to 1801 almost the entire light infantry duty rested upon the *Frei-Corps* and *Grenzer*. The former were raised in the provinces almost exclusively only in wartime, the most famous including the Grün-Laudon Regiment, the Le Loup *Jäger* (*Niederlandische Feld-Jäger*) and Wurmser's Corps; their uniforms were often exotically Slavonic and variously coloured. Most were transformed into the light infantry in 1798. Some of these corps both looked and behaved in a manner more expected of Balkan bandits, though the opinions of their allies must be viewed with circumspection; Harry Calvert described them in the Netherlands: 'The drawings which Captain Cook brought back from the South Sea are nothing to some of our friends.'[1] One corps, alias the 'Red Mantles', '. . . besides being bad soldiers, disgraced the Austrian army by frequent robberies and assassination. At the commencement of the war they received a florin for the head of every Frenchman they brought into the advanced posts; but it was found that these banditti used to cut off the heads of unfortunate peasants whom they met with in the fields, in order to obtain the promised reward.'[2]

Grenz Infantry

In the 'Military Borders' of Hungary, Croatia, Slavonia and Transylvania every able-bodied man was a peasant-soldier guarding against Turkish incursions. In wartime they were assembled in light battalions of mixed quality; an attempt to make them into proper infantry tended to reduce their natural capabilities as skirmishers. There were seventeen regiments, from which composite battalions were formed in wartime for field service, the majority having always to be left behind to defend the borders. The defeat of 1809 led to six regiments being transferred to French service with the ceding of their territory, but these were all recovered by 1814. Despite official complaints of indiscipline, the *Grenzer* performed well on occasion and were a useful asset to the Austrian army. Their uniform was of Hungarian style, their everyday dress being a brown coat with regimental facings, a shako and blue Hungarian breeches, replaced on campaign by a white coat; from 1808 dark brown uniforms became the regulation dress for all occasions.

Landwehr

The concept of a national militia (*Landwehr*) was regarded with circumspection, in case of political disaffection; but by spring 1808 the need was realized and a mass conscription organized of all men between ages 18 and 45 (excepting exempted categories and army reservists), but the planned numbers were never attained, as the Hungarian Diet refused to sanction the formation units in that country, and it was regarded as too dangerous to arm the Poles of Galicia. Their use in the 1809 campaign was small and effectiveness low, and the force was de-activated until 1813, when the efficiency was improved by incorporating *Landwehr* as the 4th battalions of line regiments. Their uniform was originally varied, often virtually civilian dress, and from 1813 of infantry style but in iron-grey, with the *Korséhut*.

Volunteers

Units of Viennese volunteers existed from 1796 when a few saw active service, but the main formation was in 1797 to oppose the advance of the French; they saw no action and were not of any great proficiency. Small units also existed in 1805 and 1809.

Cavalry

Recruitment for the cavalry was similar to that for the infantry, except that as the mounted service was more popular, bounties were lower. The Austrian cavalry formed one of the most formidable forces of the Napoleonic period: there were almost 45,000 with the field army in March 1809, for example. There was a sharp division between the national elements: all Hungarian cavalry were hussars, the 'German' regiments were all heavy or medium cavalry, and the *Uhlans*, the traditional Polish light cavalry, were raised in Galicia.

In 1792 the cavalry comprised two regiments of carabiniers, nine of cuirassiers, six of dragoons, seven of *Chevauxleger* (officially the 'light' element of the German cavalry: actually they were more like 'medium' dragoons), nine of hussars, one of *Uhlans*, one of *Grenz* hussars and the 'staff dragoons' (*Stabs-Dragoner-Regiment*). Organization was similar for all: each carabinier and hussar regiment comprised four 'divisions' of two squadrons each, the remainder three divisions (the *Grenz* hussars five and the *Uhlans* two), each squadron of two 'wings' (*Flügel*) and two platoons (*Zügen*) each. For carabiniers and cuirassiers, each squadron was about 150 strong; 170–180 in the other regiments. In 1798 the cuirassiers were increased to twelve regiments by the formation of one new unit and the conversion of the carabiniers, the dragoons and *Chevauxleger* were merged into a new category of 'light dragoons', the hussars were increased to twelve regiments, the *Uhlans* to two and a corps of Mounted *Jäger* was formed (*Jäger zu Pferd*). In 1801 the Mounted *Jäger*, three cuirassier, three dragoon and one hussar regiment were disbanded; a new *Grenz* hussar regiment was created, the 12th Cuirassiers converted to dragoons, the light dragoons again split into dragoons and *Chevauxleger*, and a third *Uhlan* regiment was formed. In 1813 a fourth *Uhlan* regiment and a new 7th *Chevauxleger* were formed. A brief re-structuring of all regiments into eight squadrons in 1805 caused only confusion, and almost immediately the heavy regiments and *Grenz* hussars were reduced to six squadrons of 135 men, and the light regiments established at eight squadrons of 150. In addition, a number of supernumerary dismounted troopers were mobilized in wartime to form a reserve squadron of sixty men in the 'heavies' and ninety in the 'lights'. The Staff Dragoons were re-formed in 1805 as one squadron plus ten independent 'wings'; providing guards for headquarters and escorts, the corps was usually newly formed before every campaign by detaching reliable men from the cavalry regiments. One 'division' was formed in 1812, another in 1813 and a third in 1814. After the 1809 campaign, heavy regiments were reduced to four squadrons and light to six.

Cuirassiers

Throughout the period, the cuirassiers wore a short-tailed white coat like the infantry, with facing-coloured collar-patches (*Parolis*), cuffs and edging on the turnbacks; initially with a bicorn. The cuirass was enamelled black and consisted of a front-plate only; and initially officers wore a long white coat over the cuirass. In 1798 a less voluminous jacket was introduced, and the crested helmet like that of the infantry. Rank-distinctions resembled those of the infantry, NCOs having lace on the facings and officers the universal waist-sash. Facing-colours and buttons (white or yellow, W or Y) were as follows:

Regiment	1798		1820	
	facings	buttons	facings	buttons
1	dark red	W	dark red	W
2	black	W	black	W
3	dark red	Y	dark red	Y
4	dark blue	Y	grass-green	W
5	grass-green	Y	light blue	W
6	light blue	Y	black	Y
7	dark blue	W	dark blue	W
8	light blue	W	scarlet	Y
9	light blue	W		
10	black	Y		
11	scarlet	Y		
12	grass-green	W		

Dragoons and Chevauxlegers

Dragoons were initially dressed like the cuirassiers, minus the cuirass and with facing-coloured collars; *Chevauxlegers* had similar uniform, except that the first two and the Latour Regiment (the old 14th Dragoons) wore bottle-green jackets. In 1798 the uniform-changes resembled those of the cuirassiers, but all the new 'light dragoon' regiments had dark green jackets. When the two branches were again split in 1801 the dragoons were ordered to wear white and the *Chevauxlegers* green, but until the old clothing wore out some dragoons wore green and some *Chevauxlegers* white, until ultimately all wore white save the green-clad 1st, 2nd, 4th and ultimately 7th *Chevauxlegers*; buttons were white for dragoons and yellow for *Chevauxlegers*. Regimental facing-colours were:

Dragoons			Chevauxlegers		
	1801	1820		1801	1820
1st	black	black	1st	dark red	bright red
2nd	dark blue	dark blue	2nd	dark green	bright red
3rd	dark red	bright red	3rd	light red	bright red
4th	light red	bright red	4th	dark blue	dark red
5th	dark green	dark green	5th	light blue	light blue
6th	light blue	light blue	6th	black	dark red
			7th	-	crimson

Hussars

The hussars wore a Hungarian-style uniform of tight breeches, braided dolman, and a cylindrical felt cap, replaced in 1798 by a peaked shako; the head-dress had black-and-yellow cords and a black-over-yellow plume. Dolman, collar, cuffs and pelisse were always the same colour, and the braid mixed black-and-yellow. Regimental colours were as follows:

Reg	Dolman/Pelisse	Breeches	Shako	Buttons
1	dark blue	dark blue	black	yellow
2	light blue	light blue	light red	yellow
3	dark blue	dark blue	pike-grey	yellow
4	parrot-green	poppy-red	bright blue	white
5	dark green	carmine	bright red	white
6	light blue	light blue	black	yellow
7	light blue	light blue	grass-green	yellow
8	parrot-green	poppy-red	black	yellow
9	dark green	carmine	black	yellow
10	light blue	light blue	grass-green	yellow
11	dark blue	dark blue	black	white
12	pike-grey	light blue	black	white

Uhlans

From their inception the *Uhlans* wore the traditional Polish square-topped *czapka*, increasing in height in 1801, a green *kurtka* with red facings (including the typically Polish 'plastron' lapels), yellow buttons and green overalls with red stripes; regimental distinctions were limited to the top of the *czapka*, yellow, dark green, scarlet and white for the 1st–4th Regiments respectively. Horse-furniture was of a similar style for all Austrian regiments, the shabraque red with rounded front corners, the Emperor's cipher in the rear corners and an edging of yellow and black lace; the rear corners were almost rectangular for 'German' regiments, pointed for hussars and rounded for *Uhlans*. The lance was carried only by the *Uhlans*, but this traditional Polish weapon was at first carried only by part of the corps, the 'flank divisions' (*Flügeldivisionen*) being armed with carbines, to gall the enemy with musketry while the central divisions charged with the lance. Pennons were in the national colours of black over yellow.

Mounted Jägers

The unit wore dragoon uniform in pike-grey with green facings, pike-grey breeches instead of the white of the other 'German' regiments, and the 1798 helmet with green crest. For the Austrian cavalry in general, the prescribed legwear (white breeches and knee-boots for 'German' regiments, hussar boots and breeches for 'Hungarian') were commonly replaced by grey overalls, buttoned on the outer seam, for campaign.

Auxiliary cavalry

A number of mounted *Frei-Corps* existed, usually attached to the respective infantry units; most wore hussar uniform save for Degelmann's *Uhlans*, which wore ordinary *Uhlan* uniform save for white buttons; it became the 2nd *Uhlans* in 1798.

Insurrectio

Although there was no *Landwehr* in the areas controlled by the Hungarian Diet, the feudal levy or *Insurrectio* existed, though its effectiveness is doubtful (in 1800 it refused to muster!). The infantry units wore a blue 'spencer' (jacket) and Hungarian breeches, and a tall black shako, and the cavalry wore hussar uniform in a variety of colours, principally light or dark blue. Leather equipment in Austrian service was commonly white for regular regiments and black for *Jäger* and *Landwehr*, but the *Insurrectio* usually wore brown. The *Insurrectio* cavalry formed a considerable proportion of the army's total mounted strength – almost 8 per cent at Wagram, for example – though could not be compared with the regulars in terms of proficiency and reliability.

Artillery

The organization of the artillery was centred around the tactical role it was assigned. There were initially three field artillery regiments, a Bombardier Corps of men with additional training, and an Artillery Fusilier Battalion which provided the unskilled labour. A fourth field regiment was created in February 1802, partly from the now-disbanded Artillery Fusiliers, and the number of companies per regiment increased during the period. From 1807 the field regiments received territorial designations: 1st Bohemian, 2nd Lower Austrian, 3rd Moravian and 4th Inner Austrian.

In wartime, the artillery regiments were split into small detachments to serve the 'battalion guns' (*Liniengeschütze*) attached to each regiment, with infantrymen providing the

Austrian cuirassiers, 1815. The officer's black-enamelled cuirass has the gilt 'dart' at the front for troop-officers. The trumpeter (right) has the normal distinctions of his rank, no cuirass and a red helmet-crest. (Print after R. von Ottenfeld)

Austrian Uhlan, *c.1815: green uniform faced red, green overalls and* czapka *with yellow top and the national black-over-yellow plume. (Print after R. von Ottenfeld)*

Austrian artillery c.1800, showing the tobacco-brown coat with red facings which distinguished that branch of the Austrian army, here with the combed 1798 helmet of infantry style, except that the rank-and file of the artillery wore a red comb instead of the black-and-yellow of the infantry. The officer (left) wears the universal Austrian gold sash with black interweaving; the gunner (right) has his artillery tools in a 'holster' on a shoulder-belt. The central figure is a driver of the Fuhrwesencorps, *in light grey with yellow facings and yellow-over-black plume. (Print after R. von Ottenfeld)* ▶*

untrained artillery labourers; the guns were usually 3pdrs. The artillery reserve was crewed by the Bombardier Corps and personnel from the garrison or fortress artillery; reserve batteries usually comprised four guns and two howitzers. There were in addition 'cavalry batteries' of light 6pdrs whose officers and NCOs were mounted but whose gunners sat astride a caisson or *Wurst-wagen*, and were thus much less mobile than proper horse artillery. The guns (24-, 18-, 12-, 6- and 3pdrs, 7- and 10pdr howitzers, mostly bronze) had been superb when introduced in 1753, but had been overtaken in efficiency and striking-power by more modern systems, like that of France.

The allocation of so great a proportion of guns to the infantry meant that concentration of fire by 'massed battery' was almost impossible to achieve, even though as early as 1795 Archduke Charles had written of its utility. In the 1805 campaign, even though the four regiments had 16 companies each, the establishment was still inadequate, and following the defeat of that year an overhaul was instituted, which at last withdrew most of the 'battalion guns'; and as by so doing the gunners lost their infantry manual labourers, a new *Artillerie Handlanger Corps* was formed in June 1808 to perform this duty, each *Handlanger* company being split to provide sufficient untrained crew for three batteries. Throughout the period, the artillery transport service remained a separate unit, the *Fuhrwesencorps*, which was only 'militarized' in 1808. Charles's reforms, accomplished prior to the 1809 campaign, assembled the 'battalion guns' into 8-gun 'brigade batteries', usually deployed at brigade level; the heavier guns were reorganized into 'support' and 'position batteries' of the artillery reserve, the former assigned at divisional or corps level and the latter forming the corps reserve. Support batteries (*Unterstützungs Batterien*) usually consisted of four 6pdrs and two 7pdr howitzers; the cavalry batteries (*Cavalleriebatterien*) of four light 6pdrs and two short 7pdr howitzers; and the 'position' batteries usually of four 12pdrs (occasionally 18- or 6pdrs) and two 7pdr howitzers. With the abandoning of the corps system after 1809, the support and position batteries were concentrated into a reserve park, and allocated to the *Armee Abtheilungen* of 1813–14 much as to the previous corps, with the 8-gun brigade batteries remaining as before, except that the ineffective 3pdr was replaced wherever possible by the 6pdr. These reforms ended the dissipation of fire resulting from the 'battalion guns' system, though even after 1809 concentrated or 'massed battery' fire was only recommended, not made compulsory by the regulations.

The artillery uniform was styled on that of the infantry, including the use of the combed helmet 1798–1803 (with a red crest for the rank-and-file), the jackets brown with red facings (light blue facings for the *Handlanger Corps*); prior to 1798 a low 'round hat' was worn, and from 1803 the *Korséhut* was the official head-dress, but bicorns were permitted officially from 1806 (having been worn at least since 1802), and these continued to be the most common head-dress throughout the remaining campaigns. The *Fuhrwesencorps* wore light grey with yellow facings, and the infantry *Casquet*

until the introduction of a 'round hat' in 1798; from 1803–5 the jacket became white for drivers and grey for craftsmen, with a *Korséhut* worn until the introduction of the shako at about the same time as for the infantry, but the former hat was retained in many cases throughout the period.

Engineers

A number of different engineer corps existed. The *Ingenieurs-Corps* was composed exclusively of officers; they controlled two battalions of rank-and-file, the Sappers (*Sappeur-Corps*) responsible for field fortification, and the Miners (*Mineur-Corps*) trained in siege techniques. In wartime they were supplemented by units of Pioneers, less-skilled units generally disbanded at the close of hostilities. The first pioneer battalion was raised in 1792; three battalions existed in 1805, seven 'divisions' in 1809, and the single battalion left after the defeat of that year was enlarged to three battalions by August 1813. There was in addition a Pontooneer Corps, supplemented by a similar *Grenz* unit styled *Czaikisten*. Uniforms were basically of infantry style, the engineer services wearing light blue-grey faced dark red, and pioneers light grey faced light green; head-dress was originally the 'round hat', and later the *Korséhut*. The Pontooneers wore 'cornflower blue' (sometimes depicted as a dark shade), initially with a distinctive, tail-less jacket with the red facings of the engineers; by 1803 the *Korséhut* had adopted the corps' anchor-badge. The *Czaikisten* wore a uniform like that of the Pontooneers, initially with pointed 'Hungarian' cuffs and a *Casquet* instead of the 'round hat', and by 1809 a blue infantry jacket with red collar-patch, sky-blue Hungarian breeches and the infantry shako with brass anchor badge.

Commissariat and Administration

Staff duties of most types were handled by the 'Quartermaster-General-Staff' (*Generalquartiermeister*), which was recognized as being among the most efficient in Europe; thus Austrian staff officers often ran the affairs of allied forces as well, such as those of the Russians in the Austerlitz campaign. Commissariat duties were the responsibility of the 'field train' (*Militärverpflegungsfuhrwesencorps*) whose war establishment of more than 17,000 men and 34,000 horses served the commissariat, transport, artillery-drivers' and administrative departments. A constant complaint was that the transport corps was too small for its purpose, but that a vast number of unofficial vehicles encumbered every army and hindered movement: in 1809 each infantry regiment should have had thirteen wheeled vehicles and 26 pack-horses, but officers' baggage and other vehicles accumulated

Austrian artillery c.1809, showing the jacket and Oberrock of 'roe-deer brown' and the bicorn hat usually worn at this period in preference to the Corséhut; the black-over-yellow plume was the national insignia, as was the

Feldzeichen *(green sprig) behind the cockade. The driver of the* Fuhrwesencorps *(right) wears his with yellow facings and the shako, though the latter was never universal. (Print after R. von Ottenfeld)*

by a regiment usually vastly exceeded this number. The dependence upon mobile field bakeries and the need to draw supplies from magazines, with only limited requisitioning from the countryside, never allowed the Austrian forces the freedom of movement permitted by the French system.

Higher Organization

There was initially no higher tactical organization established permanently: units were assigned to subordinate commanders in *ad hoc* brigades (two regiments) or divisions (normally two brigades); advanced-guard divisions were formed of light troops (infantry and cavalry), and reserve divisions from grenadiers and heavy cavalry. All these formations lacked the practice of co-operating to form a cohesive operation. A *corps d'armée* system was instituted on 2 February 1809, each corps of three divisions (including one 'advance guard' division of light troops), with artillery concentrated at corps level instead of permanently with the divisions; but as with the 1805 regimental re-organizations, the system was introduced too soon before a campaign for it to be used properly, and the Archduke Charles abandoned the corps organization during the campaign, though he retained the terminology. In 1813 the Army of Bohemia was organized into a 'Main Body' and an 'Advance Guard', but the number of troops involved required something more functional, so in September 1813 the corps system was reintroduced, though not in name: the formations were designated *Armee Abtheilungen*, though the term 'corps' was sometimes used even officially. Normally each comprised one light and one line division, the former of a brigade of two line regiments, a brigade of two *Grenz* or *Jäger* battalions, and light cavalry; line divisions had two brigades of two line regiments each. Each brigade had a battery of artillery (normally 6pdrs, 3pdrs for light divisions), with a 6pdr cavalry battery and two 12pdr batteries as corps reserve. The grenadier battalions, heavy cavalry and artillery reserve (about one-third of the total guns) were concentrated in the Army Reserve.

Navy

Austrian maritime forces were minimal, due to the geographical location of the territory. A few small vessels operating from Trieste and the 'Hungarian Littoral' (Dalmatia) were combined with the small Venetian navy in 1798, upon Austrian possession of that state, though nothing larger than three ships-of-the-line existed, and command was vested in a number of foreign officers, 'von' Williams (British), de l'Espine and Crenneville (French *émigrés*) and Querini (Italian). After the defeat of 1805 only Trieste remained and no naval units existed larger than brigs; after the defeat of 1809 even these coastal possessions were lost and the navy ceased to exist. The Adriatic provinces were recovered in early 1814 and with them some Venetian ships, but these saw no further service.

Notes
1. *Journals and Correspondence of Sir Harry Calvert*, London 1853,

p. 80.
2. *Weekly Dispatch*, 27 September 1801.

References
The outstanding modern work on the Austrian army in English is *Napoleon's Great Adversaries: The Archduke Charles and the Austrian Army 1792–1814*, G. E. Rothenberg, London 1982, which is the starting-point for any study of the subject. *Die Oesterreichische Armee*, R. von Ottenfeld and O. Teuber, Vienna 1895, remains the best-illustrated work on uniforms and organization. See also:
Duffy, C. *Austerlitz 1805*, London 1977.
Haythornthwaite, P. J. *Austrian Army of the Napoleonic Wars (I): Infantry* and *II: Cavalry*, London 1986.
— *Austrian Specialist Troops of the Napoleonic Wars*, London 1990.

BADEN

History

Baden was a minor German principality created in 1771 by the union of Baden-Baden and Baden-Durlach under the Margrave Charles Frederick of Baden-Durlach, the most notable of the rulers of Baden, who had succeeded as a child in 1738. He supported Austria in the Revolutionary Wars, during which Baden was devastated, and in 1796 the Margrave was compelled to pay France an indemnity and surrender his territory on the left bank of the Rhine. The support of the Tsar enabled Baden to accumulate more territory, however, and for Charles Frederick to assume the status of Prince-Elector. Baden sided with Napoleon in 1805 and was rewarded by the grant of ex-Austrian territory at the Peace of Pressburg. In 1806 Baden joined the Confederation of the Rhine, Charles Frederick declaring himself a sovereign prince and grand-duke. Baden's assistance to France in 1809 brought more territorial acquisitions (from Württemberg), and having thus quadrupled his territory Charles Frederick died in June 1811, being succeeded by his grandson Charles, who was married to Napoleon's step-daughter Stephanie de Beauharnais. Baden continued to support Napoleon until after Leipzig, then joined the Allies. The succession caused considerable conflict in the 1816-19 period before finally passing to the line of a morganatic marriage between Charles Frederick and the Countess Hochberg.

Army (cockade: yellow with red centre)

Although small, the Baden army was regarded as being of excellent quality; in the 1812 Russian campaign, for example, it has been described as the best German contingent of the *Grande Armée*. Initially, Prussian uniform and organization were copied; from 1806 France was copied, even to the adoption of French rank-insignia.

In the Revolutionary Wars there were two infantry regiments, the *Leib-Regiment* and the Erbprinz Fusilier Battalion, both wearing Prussian-style uniform in blue with red facings for the former and yellow for the latter, musketeers with the bicorn, grenadiers with tall brass-fronted mitres and fusiliers with smaller mitres, the caps bearing the Margrave's cipher, 'CF'. Officers' sashes were silver, red and yellow. The cavalry consisted of a Garde du Corps of three companies, one of guards, one of dragoons and one of cuirassiers. The Guard Company wore the red and yellow livery of the ruling house (yellow coats faced red with mixed red-

The breast-star of the Order of Military Merit of Baden, established by Grand Duke Charles Frederick on 4 April 1807, for officers who displayed the greatest heroism.

Baden of ex-Bavarian territory; it was re-titled as the Baden Light Dragoon squadron, later regiment, serving in Prussia in 1806, at Eckmühl, Aspern, Wagram, Lützen, Bautzen, Hanau and Leipzig, and with the Allies in 1814. Its uniform was light blue with red facings and white lace loops (discontinued 1808), with the Bavarian *Raupenhelm* until 1804, then a bicorn, until the re-adoption of the *Raupenhelm* with Baden 'CF' plate. A hussar regiment was formed in 1802, wearing dark green with red facings, green pelisse with black fur (white for officers) and gold lace, initially with mirliton caps but shakos from 1806. The 9,000-strong Baden contingent of the *Grande Armée* was virtually destroyed in Russia, but the Hussars won undying fame at Studianka, where they helped cover the passage of the Berezina with the celebrated 'charge of death' in concert with the Hessian *Chevauxlegers*, from which only 100 men returned; in the process it created the outstanding Baden hero of the war, the NCO Martin Springer, who saved the life of the unit's replacement colonel, von Laroche (Colonel von Cancrin having been killed two weeks previously).

The artillery (both foot and horse batteries) wore blue with black facings and yellow buttons, and originally the bicorn, replaced by the *Raupenhelm*; the gunners who served in Spain wore French-style shakos. In French fashion, the personnel of the artillery train wore grey uniforms with light blue facings and white buttons.

and-yellow lace and red girdles); officers' *Gala* dress was a silver-laced red coat with yellow facings and waistcoat, silver-laced bicorn with white plume. The other companies wore white coats with red facings, the same lace, and white-over-red plume.

The Army in the Confederation

After entering the Confederation of the Rhine, the enlarged Baden forces served against Prussia in 1806, at Friedland (X Corps), Aspern and Wagram (IV Corps) and in IX Corps in the 1812 Russian campaign. There were four infantry regiments, all wearing dark blue coats with red facings (white lace loops for the 1st or *Leib-Regiment*); and silver lace and epaulettes, and black-plumed bicorns, for officers. Other ranks had combed black leather helmets with a black crest, with white-metal fittings for the 1st and 3rd and yellow for the others; the 1st Regiment had a star-shaped helmet-plate and the others crowned ovals bearing 'CF'. The 4th Regiment (and an artillery battery) served in Spain, at Medellin, Talavera and Vittoria, and was disarmed and interned after attempting to defect; apparently it wore blue with white facings and red turnbacks. The single *Jäger* battalion wore the infantry uniform in green with black facings, and a combed helmet with green plume and crest.

The Garde du Corps wore white with red facings, with 'Guard'-style lace of Prusso-Russian fashion from 1813; the bicorn was replaced by a combed, Bavarian-style *Raupenhelm* in 1806, with white plume. In 1803 a Bavarian *Chevauxleger* squadron entered Baden service as a result of the ceding to

BAVARIA

History

One of the most important German states, Bavaria had been a significant power during the earlier part of the eighteenth century, especially in the War of the Spanish Succession. In 1777 the direct succession of the Electors of the Wittelsbach dynasty became extinct, and lordship of Bavaria passed to Charles Theodore, Elector Palatine, whose primary concern seems to have been arranging an exchange of Bavaria for the Austrian Netherlands (which never materialized). In 1792 Bavarian forces were mobilized in support of Austria, in accord with Bavaria's responsibility to the Holy Roman Empire; but Moreau drove Charles Theodore into Saxony and an armistice and heavy contribution allowed Bavaria to quit the war. Charles Theodore died in February 1799 and his successor, Maximilian IV Joseph of Zweibrücken, though French in sympathy (and the son of a French general), was compelled by the presence of Austrian troops to oppose France; but after the defeat of Hohenlinden Maximilian Joseph and his chief minister, Max Joseph von Montgelas, concluded a separate peace with France greatly to Bavaria's advantage, which over the next several years resulted in the ceding to Bavaria territories which compensated for those lost by the Treaty of Lunéville. In the following campaigns Montgelas never allowed Bavaria to be a mere French puppet, but more like a weaker partner, and Bavarian troops supported France in 1805, against Prussia in 1806, in the Tyrol in 1809, at Aspern, Wagram, in the 1812

Russian campaign, and in Saxony in 1813; though the French tended to view the Bavarians with unjustified contempt and failed to appreciate their services. In 1805 Maximilian Joseph took the title of King Maximilian I; his daughter Augusta married Eugène de Beauharnais, forging a family link with Napoleon. In 1813, under pressure from Crown Prince Louis and Field Marshal Wrede, Bavaria's most distinguished soldier of the era, Maximilian and Bavaria changed sides and joined the Allies, fighting against their erstwhile comrades at Hanau. Maximilian ruled until his death in 1825, granting the nation its first liberal constitution in May 1818.

Army (cockade: white with light blue centre)
The Bavarian army had been 'improved' by the reforms of Benjamin Thompson, an emigrant American loyalist and

suspected homosexual associate of the British Minister, Lord George Germain; Thompson was created Graf von Rumford by the Elector for his service as Bavarian adjutant-general and war minister. The efforts of this eccentric scientist – most renowned as a chemist – radically altered the appearance of the army and introduced a new fieldpiece, the 'Rumford 3pdr', but by 1799 his influence had waned; Rumford retired to pursue a brief marriage with the wife of the guillotined chemist Lavoisier and to live in seclusion in Paris, where his most lasting achievement was the invention of the coffee percolator.

At the beginning of the Revolutionary Wars, the Bavarian army consisted of two ceremonial guard units; four grenadier, fourteen fusilier and two *Jäger* regiments; two cuirassier, two dragoon and three *Chevauxleger* regiments; artillery and engineers.

2nd Fusiliers red, 3rd–4th Fusiliers brick-red, 5th–6th Fusiliers yellow, 7th–8th Fusiliers green, 9th–10th Fusiliers peach, 11th–12th Fusiliers crimson, 13th–14th Fusiliers black. An unusual addition were black leather fringeless epaulettes with brass 'crescent' and chain edging, intended as shoulder-protection; breeches were grey and the head-dress the 'Rumford *Kasket*', a low-crowned, peaked black leather helmet with brass plate and black horsehair mane (white for grenadiers).

In 1799 a major re-organization abolished the 'Rumford' uniform and reduced the number of regiments which henceforth used titles rather than numbers, though numbers were reintroduced as the official mode of identity in 1806. The new regiments were as follows:

Regiment	Formed from	Facings	Buttons
1st (Leib)	1st Grenadiers	black (red from 1802)	white
2nd	2nd Grenadiers	black (red from 1802)	yellow
3rd	2nd Fusiliers	red (piped white 1806)	yellow
4th	5th Fusiliers	sulphur yellow (piped red 1806)	white
5th	9th Fusiliers	pink, piped red	white
6th	1st Fusiliers	red (piped white 1806)	white
7th	8th Fusiliers	white (piped red 1806)	yellow
8th	6th Fusiliers	sulphur yellow (piped red 1806)	yellow
9th	3rd Fusiliers	scarlet (yellow facings piped red, red collar 1806)	yellow
10th	11th Fusiliers	crimson (yellow facings piped red, red collar 1806	white
11th	4th Fusiliers	black (green facings piped red, red collar 1806)	yellow

The new uniform was sky-blue with the above facings (including full lapels), with white breeches and the *Raupenhelm*, a tall, black leather helmet with black woollen crest (bearskin crest for sergeants and above), with a brass crowned oval plate bearing the Elector's cipher, 'MJ' ('MJK' – '*König*' – from 1806), a red plume for grenadiers, green for light companies and woollen pompoms on the left for fusiliers, coloured white, white/yellow, green and green/yellow for 1st–4th companies respectively. Officers' rank had been distinguished by lace loops in the button-colour, but from 1806 was transferrered to the collar, colonels and captains with three collar-loops, lieutenant-colonel and lieutenant two, major and 2nd lieutenant one, the higher rank of each pair having lace collar-edging in addition. Officers adopted the *Raupenhelm* in 1805, the previous bicorn continuing to be worn by field ranks. From 1800 to 1812 officers wore waist-sashes of light blue and silver.

In 1806 the 11th Regiment was transferred to Berg, and a new 11th raised in 1807, disbanded in 1811 and re-formed in 1813. A 12th Regiment was raised in 1803 (orange facings, white buttons) but disbanded in 1806; a 13th (black facings, red collar and piping, white buttons) and 14th (same, with yellow buttons) were formed in 1807, the 13th being re-

Napoleon reviews the Bavarian contingent of his army, 1809. The Bavarian infantry in the foreground wear their distinctive leather 'Raupenhelm'. (Print after F. de Myrbach)

Infantry

Initially each regiment had two battalions of four companies each, each company 150 strong (168 in wartime); two battalions formed a brigade, the basic tactical unit. The uniform was a white jacket with coloured facings (including half-lapels), with a white waistcoat visible on the abdomen, though in fact it was all one garment, real waistcoats having been abolished by Rumford as an economy. Each pair of regiments had matching facings, with white buttons for the first of each pair and yellow for the others: 1st–2nd Grenadiers light blue, 2nd–3rd Grenadiers dark blue, 1st–

The breast-star of the Military Order of Maximilian Joseph of Bavaria, founded on 8 June 1797 and reformed on 1 March 1806; each award brought a pension and a patent of nobility. (Gold cross with white arms, blue centre, upon a silver star.)

numbered the 11th in 1811, and the 14th as the 13th. In 1813–14 new 12th and 14th Regiments and the Guard Grenadiers were raised, but uniform-details are omitted as they post-dated Bavaria's active participation in the Napoleonic Wars. In 1809 twelve Reserve Battalions were formed, one for each line regiment; from this date regimental strength comprised two battalions of six companies each (one of grenadiers and one of *Schützen* or light infantry), and a reserve battalion of four fusilier companies. After the losses of the 1812 campaign the 1st Battalions were brought up to strength and the 2nd and Reserve Battalions amalgamated.

Light infantry

There were originally two regiments of *Feldjäger*, both wearing the 'Rumford' uniform in green with black facings, with white and yellow buttons for the 1st and 2nd respectively. In 1799 they were split to form four independent battalions, wearing light green (dark green from 1809) with black facings piped red, the *Raupenhelm* with green plume for the élite company, red plume for the carabinier company (formed 1811) and pompoms of white, green, red, blue and yellow for the 1st–5th companies respectively. The 1st Battalion had red collar and white buttons (yellow from 1804), 2nd red collar, white buttons; 3rd black collar, yellow buttons (white from 1804), and was converted to the 12th Line in 1813; 4th black collar, yellow buttons; 5th (raised 1803) crimson facings (black facings with lemon collar, red piping from 1806) and white buttons;

6th (raised 1803), as 5th but yellow buttons; 7th (formed 1808) light blue collar, white buttons. A Tyrolean *Jäger* battalion was formed in 1807 and disbanded in 1811, wearing dark grey or green faced light blue, a shako and black leather equipment (all other infantry wore white belts).

Cuirassiers

The two cuirassier regiments wore the 'Rumford *Kasket*' with white mane, and an infantry-style uniform in white with scarlet facings and white and yellow buttons respectively (white collars and white turnbacks edged scarlet). Cuirasses were not worn. In 1799 the 2nd Cuirassiers was converted to the 4th *Chevauxleger*, and in 1804 the 1st became the 1st Dragoons; no further regiments were formed until 1815.

Dragoons

The dragoons wore the same uniform as the cuirassiers, with black facings and white and yellow buttons for the 1st and 2nd Regiments respectively. The 1st was disbanded in 1803 and replaced by the converted 1st Cuirassiers, with scarlet facings and white buttons, and became the 1st *Chevauxlegers* in 1811. In 1800 these and the extant 1st Cuirassiers received the *Raupenhelm* with white plume, and coats coloured as before but with full lapels. In 1811 the dragoons were converted to *Chevauxlegers*.

Chevauxlegers

Initially the *Chevauxlegers* wore the 'Rumford *Kasket*' with white mane, and a green infantry-style coat with green collar and facings: 1st Regiment black, white buttons; 2nd black, yellow buttons; 3rd apple-green, white buttons. As for all cavalry at this period, each regiment comprised four squadrons of 150 men (180 in wartime) but with horses sufficient for only one squadron; thus in 1793 it was possible only to field a 'combined' cavalry regiment, two squadrons from the 1st, one from the 2nd and 50 men from the 3rd. In 1799 the *Raupenhelm* was adopted, and light green coats (dark green from late 1809), and a reorganization renumbered the 1st Regiment 4th, the 2nd, 3rd; the 3rd, 2nd; and added the 4th, converted from the 2nd Cuirassiers. In 1801 the 3rd was disbanded, and in 1803 the 4th re-numbered 3rd, with a new 4th Regiment formed from the Würzburg cavalry (black facings, white buttons). In 1811 all the cavalry became *Chevauxlegers*, the new 1st and 2nd Regiments previously the 1st and 2nd Dragoons; the new 3rd *Chevauxlegers* was the old 1st Regiment, the 4th the old 2nd, 5th the old 3rd and 6th the old 4th. In 1813 were raised the National *Chevauxlegers* (later 7th), with poppy-red facings, white buttons and a shako; and the *Uhlans*, who had Austrian lancer uniform of dark green with light blue facings (red from 1814) and white buttons (yellow 1814), and yellow-topped *czapkas*. The 7th *Chevauxlegers* were unique in that they resulted from the mobilization of the National Guard 2nd Class (28 February 1813) in response to losses suffered in Russia, though they were not liable for service outside Bavaria. In each of the country's nine administrative regions a 'Mobile Legion' was

The Military Medal of Honour of Bavaria, founded 22 November 1794, in gold and silver versions, to reward NCOs and privates for bravery. Black ribbon with white stripes and light blue edges.

formed, and when enough volunteers were forthcoming for general service, the National *Chevauxlegers* were taken into the line.

Artillery

The artillery battalion was increased to regimental strength in 1791, of two battalions of four companies each, each with 150 men, six guns and two howitzers. Rumford was colonel-in-chief, and his own 3pdr was introduced in 1794; in 1795 Austrian 6pdrs and 7pdr howitzers came into service, and in 1797 12pdrs. Gun-carriages were painted grey with black metalwork, and it was usual at this period for the guns to be attached to the infantry (two per battalion). The artillery uniform was pike-grey, faced blue, but from 1791 dark blue faced black, with the 'Rumford *Kasket*'. From 1801 the *Raupenhelm* was worn, with a red plume; the uniform-colours were the same save for scarlet collar and cuffs; yellow buttons; the rank-and-file carried short swords and pistols until 1811 when muskets were issued, though horse artillery personnel carried cavalry sabres. There was no organized train, civilian teams and drivers being hired in wartime, wearing grey uniforms faced light blue, and white buttons and a 'round hat'; in 1806 the train was 'militarized' and adopted the *Raupenhelm*, and from 1808 cavalry sabres on black shoulder-belts; leatherwork for gunners was white.

References

The most modern illustrated source in English is *Napoleon's German Allies (4): Bavaria*, Otto von Pivka, London 1980.

BERG

History

An independent duchy on the right bank of the Rhine from 1380, Berg remained the property of the family of the Counts Palatine of Neuberg from 1614 to 1742, when it passed to the Sulzbach branch of the house of Wittelsbach. Upon the death of the last of the line, Charles Theodore, it passed to Maximilian Joseph of Zweibrücken (later Maximilian I of Bavaria) who in 1806 ceded it and the Duchy of Jülich to Napoleon. The neighbouring Duchy of Cleves (German *Kleve* or *Cleve*) had been independent until 1614 when it passed to the Electorate of Brandenburg. It was held by the French from 1757 to 1762, and in 1795 part was ceded to France; the remainder followed in 1805. Uniting the two duchies, Napoleon appointed Murat as Grand Duke, which title he held until translated to the throne of Naples; Napoleon himself became Grand Duke on 15 July 1808, until on 3 March 1809 the title was transferred to Louis Bonaparte, eldest son of the King of Holland and Napoleon's nephew, with Napoleon becoming regent during the boy's childhood. On 14 November 1808 Napoleon divided the state into four French-style 'departments' (Rhine, Sieg, Ruhr and Ems), with Düsseldorf as the capital; in December 1810 the department of the Ems and its capital, Münster, was transferred to France, with an increase in territory made in 1811 for compensation. After the collapse of the Confederation of the Rhine, the Berg troops served with the Allies, and the Congress of Vienna transferred Berg and Cleves to Prussian ownership.

Army (cockade: white with red centre; with the Allies, white with light blue centre or edge)

The creation of the Grand Duchy brought with it troops that had previously belonged to the previous states, notably the Bavarian 12th Line. In April 1806 a new regiment was raised in Düsseldorf, of four battalions of eight companies each, with a stiffening of French personnel; conscription was introduced in October 1806. In August 1808 it was reorganized into the 1st and 2nd Berg Regiments, each of three battalions of six companies, plus a four-company depot battalion to service both. In October 1808 a 3rd Regiment was formed (three battalions), and in August 1811 a 4th Regiment by the reorganization of the others into two battalions of eight companies each (one grenadier, one light infantry and six fusilier), each regiment with a depot company. The original regiment served in 1806 against Prussia, and in 1809 the 3rd served in Germany. The 1st and 2nd went to Spain in 1809, suffering 50 per cent casualties at Gerona, and were joined in 1810 by the 3rd Regiment; by late 1811 their strength had declined so markedly that the survivors were concentrated into the 2nd Battalion, 3rd Regiment and the cadre of the remainder sent home to recruit. All save the 2/3rd were virtually annihilated in Russia in 1812; only about 200 survived the retreat from Moscow, though throughout the campaign they were noted for their good conduct, and as late as Kovno the remnant was seen still marching around their colours. A single regiment was formed from the debris, and later a 2nd, which became the 28th and 29th Prussian Line when Berg passed into Prussian ownership. Initially the infantry retained the old Bavarian uniform (light blue with *Raupenhelm*), but in 1806 a white French-style uniform was introduced, with white waistcoat and breeches, light blue facings and yellow buttons, and French shakos with brass plate (either the French eagle-on-lozenge, or oval with either the lion of Berg or Murat's cipher 'J'); organization and company-distinctions were French, grenadiers having fur caps with red cords and plume and light infantry green plumes and green epaulettes with red crescents. The reconstructed 1st Regiment wore the old colours but the 2nd had white faced red, grey trousers piped red, and white shako-cords and white plume with black tip and base. A composite grenadier battalion apparently wore the same, but with dark blue lapels with red piping and yellow loops, and shakos with white cords, black plume over red pompom and brass grenade badge. In December 1813 a volunteer *Jäger* battalion was formed, wearing dark green Prussian-style uniform with red facings, yellow buttons, grey overalls striped red, shakos with green cords and plume and brass cross, and black leather equipment. The Berg *Landwehr* wore dark blue with light blue facings, yellow buttons, white overalls and plain shakos bearing a white-metal cross.

Cavalry

The *Chevau-Léger de Berg* were formed by Murat in 1807, reconstituted as the *Chasseurs à Cheval* de Berg in 1808, and re-titled in December 1809 as the *Lanciers de Berg*. Two squadrons went to Spain in February 1808, and from that November were attached to the Imperial Guard. In April 1812 a regiment of *Chevau-léger-Lanciers* was formed, ultimately titled the 2nd *Chevau-Légers*, three squadrons of which served in the 1812 campaign, most being captured at Borisov; two companies escaped to join the 4th squadron until wiped out in an ambush at Possendorf in 1813. The initial uniform was of French *chasseur* style, dark green with amaranth facings and white buttons; later of lancer style, the colouring was retained, the *czapka* having an amaranth top. The squadrons that served in Spain wore dark green *surtouts* with amaranth shakos and facings. The original unit, including the first squadron which acted as Murat's Garde du Corps (and which was disbanded in 1809, after service in Spain), wore a lancer uniform in white with amaranth facings and amaranth *czapka*, though unlike the ultimate lancer regiment the unit was not armed with lances.

In December 1813 a hussar regiment of four squadrons was formed for service with the Allies, three squadrons becoming the Prussian 11th Hussars and the fourth going to the Prussian 5th *Uhlans*; they wore dark green hussar uniform with red facings, lighter green braid and white buttons, grey overalls and plain shakos with light green cords; the attached volunteer *Jägers* had the same but with yellow buttons, collar-loops and cross on the shako.

Artillery

The artillery battalion comprised a company of horse artillery, one of foot, one of engineers and one of train; they were wiped out in Russia. The artillery wore dark blue French-style uniform with red facings and piping, dark blue breeches and yellow buttons, and shakos with red plume and cords; the train wore grey jackets and breeches, light blue facings, and infantry shakos with oval lion plate and light blue pompom.

References

Pivka, Otto von. *Napoleon's*

German Allies: Westfalia and Kleve-Berg, London 1975.

BRUNSWICK

History

The Duchy of Brunswick was closely connected with Prussia, and to a lesser extent to Britain. In the Seven Years War members of its ruling house rose to the highest rank in Frederick the Great's service, including Duke Ferdinard of Brunswick (1721–92), the brilliant victor of Minden; Duke August Wilhelm of Brunswick-Bevern (1715–81), and Duke Karl Wilhelm Ferdinand (1735–1806). The latter, schooled under his uncle the great Ferdinand, was appointed Allied commander-in-chief for the invasions of France in 1792, but retired after his defeat at Valmy, to be re-appointed to a senior command in the Prussian army in 1806, when he was mortally wounded at Auerstädt. As Duke, he had brought order to the chaotic finance left by his predecessor Karl I, but after the 1806 campaign Napoleon declared the new duke deposed and incorporated Brunswick into the Kingdom of Westphalia. The dispossessed Duke, Freidrich Wilhelm,

The 'Black Legion': hussar (left) and infantrymen of the Duke of Brunswick's corps, wearing their distinctive black uniforms with death's-head shako-badge; the infantry sergeant (centre) wears a British-style waist-sash with his thigh-length litewka. *(Aquatint by I. C. Stadler after Charles Hamilton Smith)*

enlisted his emigrant 'Black Legion' in Austrian service to continue the fight, and after the defeat of 1809 made a remarkable march across Germany to join the British fleet at the mouth of the Weser, continuing his vendetta against Napoleon in British service. Brunswick was restored as an independent state in 1813, Duke Friedrich Wilhelm leading his new 'national' army in the 1815 campaign, where he was killed at Quatre Bras. The close ties with Britain were confirmed by the fact that the Duke's son, Karl II, who succeeded him as a minor, ruled until he came of age under the regency of the Prince Regent, later King George IV of Britain.

Army (cockade: black)

Initially, Brunswick's troops were modelled closely upon Prussian lines, the two infantry regiments (1st Warmstedt, 2nd Griesheim) wearing dark blue Prussian uniform with red facings and yellow or white buttons respectively. In 1809 the Duke raised his 'Black Legion' for Austrian service, recruited from citizens of the now dissolved duchy, consisting of two infantry battalions of four companies each, a hussar regiment of eight squadrons, and a horse artillery battery of two 6pdrs and two 7pdr howitzers. As a token of his hatred and desire for revenge against the French, the Duke clothed his corps in black, with large white metal death's-head badges on their shakos and accoutrements (hence the nickname 'Black Legion'), which colouring was

retained throughout so that in the Waterloo campaign Lady de Lancey described the army as resembling 'an immense moving hearse'. In 1809 the Legion was expanded to three infantry battalions, wearing shakos and black *Litewka*s (frock coats) faced light blue, a *Jäger* company (green jackets faced red, green-laced Austrian *Korséhut*), a hussar regiment (black hussar uniform faced light blue, shako), an *Uhlan* squadron (green Austrian *Uhlan* uniform faced red, yellow-topped *czapka*) and the artillery battery (as infantry but short jackets instead of *Litewka*s).

After the remarkable march to the Weser the 'Black Legion' entered British service, its members sharing their leader's grudge against France: 'English and Brunswickers shook each other by the hand as if they had been long acquainted; the difference of language prevented indeed mutual explanations, but so much at least was understood, that all united in the common cause for the support of liberty and independence...'[1] The same writer expressed the Brunswick prejudice by describing Napoleon as 'a monster, whose only happiness consists in murder, and who never smiles but when his ill-gotten purple is stained with the blood of a foreign people!'[2] However, it was impossible to retain this standard of recruit in British service, and other ill-assorted foreigners were drafted in, so that the calibre declined. Though the Brunswickers continued to perform well in action, they had an appalling record of desertion in the Peninsula, to the extent that Leach of the British 95th

The Brunswick Waterloo medal, cast in bronze from captured cannon, and bearing the portrait of the Duke killed at Quatre Bras, wearing his characteristic field-cap. Yellow ribbon with blue stripes.

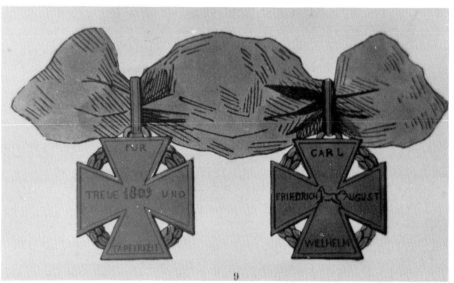

The Medal of Honour for the 1809 campaign, instituted by Duke Charles II of Brunswick on 30 October 1824, for those veterans who had followed 'the Black Duke' from Austrian to British service; in gold for officers and bronze for other ranks, with a sky-blue ribbon.

remarked that 'we had a *lease* of them but for a few weeks,'[3] while 'Black Bob' Craufurd announced when pardoning a British sergeant who had beaten-up a Brunswick officer he suspected of intending to desert, 'If any of those gentlemen have a wish to go over to the enemy, let them express it, and I give them my word of honour I will grant them a pass to that effect instantly, for we are better without such.'[4]

In British service the infantry formed a 12-company regiment of 'Brunswick-Oels Jäger', apparently still wearing black faced light blue, but with short jackets instead of the *Litewka*; but some remained dressed as riflemen, in green jackets faced light blue, and all wore the shako with skull badge, hence their British nickname of 'death or glory men'. The unit was originally sent to the Light Division but transferred to the 7th (with detached rifle companies in the 4th and 5th); the cavalry formed a 6-squadron hussar

regiment, four of which served in eastern Spain from 1813, and then in Sicily.

Having regained his duchy in 1813–14 the Duke raised a new national army, comprising a *Leib-Bataillon* (the cadre of the old 'Black Legion'), three light and three line battalions, five 'Reserve' battalions (*Landwehr*), the *Avantgarde* Battalion (*Jägers*), a hussar regiment (including an *Uhlan* squadron), and horse and foot artillery batteries with associated train. The infantry wore black dolman with black braid, black trousers, with facings light blue for the *Leib-Battalion*, buff (later pink), yellow, orange, red, green and white respectively for the 1st–3rd Light and 1st–3rd Line Battalions, with shakos either of the previous Austrian style or the scuttle-shaped Russian 1812 *kiwer*, with plumes of light blue over yellow for the line and vice versa for the light; white-metal hunting-horn shako-badge for the light and shields for the remainder, the *Leib-Battalion* retaining the old death's head. The hussars retained their old uniform, but the *Uhlans* now wore black faced light blue, with light blue *czapka* (officers yellow with blue-over-yellow plume); the artillery dressed in hussar style with black facings piped yellow, the horse artillery train wearing a similar uniform but the foot train having grey uniforms faced black. The *Avantgarde* comprised *Jägers* and light infantry, the former in grey faced dark green and the latter in black with green collars; both wore the Austrian *Korséhut* with green lace and plume. The Reserve infantry wore black with black facings piped white, and the *Korséhut* without plume.

The Brunswick Corps fought reasonably well at Waterloo, but as most were young and inexperienced the death of the Duke tended to undermine their morale; Mercer of the Royal Horse Artillery noted that the sound of his battery's approach caused one battalion to panic, 'poor lads' who 'in order to run lighter, away went arms and knapsacks in all directions, and a general race ensued, the whole corps being in the most horrid confusion'.[5] Although in the battle Mercer dare not leave his position for fear that his withdrawal would cause the Brunswickers to panic, they held their ground and acquitted themselves well. Captain John Ross of the British 51st noted that around Hougoumont 'There were some straggling Brunswickers, who joined our ranks at this place, and a few of their old soldiers remained during the day with my Company, as they recollected me when serving with them in the 7th Division,'[6]: evidently Peninsular veterans who chose to stand with the 51st rather than retire like their younger and inexperienced comrades.

Notes

1. *Account of the Operations of the Corps under the Duke of Brunswick . . .*, anon., London 1810, p. 50.
2. *ibid.* p. 37.
3. *Rough Sketches of the Life of an Old Soldier*, J. Leach, London 1831, p. 191.
4. *Adventures of a Soldier; written by himself*, E. Costello, London 1852; 1967 edn, p. 47.
5. *Journal of the Waterloo Campaign*, C. Mercer, Edinburgh & London 1870, I, p. 281.
6. *Waterloo Letters*, ed. H. T. Siborne, London 1891, p. 317.

References

The principal modern work in English is *Brunswick Troops 1809–15*, Otto von Pivka, London 1985, being a revision of the same author's *The Black Brunswickers*, London 1973.

CISALPINE REPUBLIC

History

The Cisalpine Republic was formed from the previous Austrian provinces in the area of Milan, 'liberated' by the French campaigns in northern Italy. It was largely the creation of Bonaparte, who was appointed by the French Directory to oversee the establishment of the satellite republic, to ensure that the government would be moderate by excluding Italian Jacobins. The state was organized on 29 June 1797 and proclaimed on 9 July as the Transpadane Republic; its name was soon changed to Cisalpine. It was joined by the Cispadane Republic, and by the Treaty of Campo Formio it received the ex-Venetian territories west of

the River Adige (October 1797), and in the following month the Swiss district of the Valtelline was incorporated, so that the state embraced all the lands between Como and Verona in the north and Rimini in the south. Its existence recognized by the Treaty of Lunéville, in 1802 it was named the Italian Republic, and in 1805 formed the basis of the Kingdom of Italy.

Army (cockade: red with white edge and green centre)
The first native military force after the ingress of the French was the Lombard Legion (Lombardy being the area on both banks of the Po around which the state was constructed), wearing dark green *surtout* with red facings and white buttons, dark green breeches with red stripe and the 'Corsican hat' with upturned left brim, with white-over-red-over-green plume and a square brass plate inscribed 'VIVA/LA LIBERTA'. The artillery wore the same with black facings. The cavalry wore a dark green dolman and breeches with white lace, and a shako with white trim and the same plume as above. The local forces wore French-style uniform: the Milanese National Guard, for example, wore green faced red with white piping and buttons, and bicorns with the plume as above.

From 1797 the Cisalpine forces were organized and uniformed completely in French style, with the substitution of green for blue as the uniform-colour: infantry had red facings, white piping and buttons, green waistcoat and breeches, and bicorns; light infantry yellow facings and waistcoat in French light infantry style, and the French light infantry shako with green plume, and from 1800 a carabinier battalion dressed as before but with red facings. The hussars wore red dolman and breeches, light green facings and pelisse, white buttons and a French shako with red-over-green plume and white cords. The foot artillery wore line infantry uniform with black facings, and the horse artillery green dolman and breeches with red lace and black facings, and a red-corded shako like that of the hussars but minus the hussars' lozenge-shaped plate. The engineer services wore infantry uniform with green facings piped red for sappers, pink facings (green cuffs and collar) for artificers, light blue facings piped red for miners, and pink lapels, turnbacks and shoulder-straps and red piping for artificers of the artillery.

Included in the Cisalpine army were the Polish Legions, formed of Polish *émigrés* who had fought for the French in northern Italy. They wore uniforms of Polish style: dark blue *kurtka* and breeches with crimson facings and piping, white waistcoat and buttons, and *czapka* with dark blue top, white lace, red plume and the French tricolor cockade. The Legion cavalry were lancers, in the same uniform with yellow and crimson facings to distinguish the two regiments. In 1800 a grenadier battalion was formed, in infantry uniform plus red epaulettes and red drooping horsehair plume.

Added to the Cisalpine forces after Marengo was the Italian Legion, a Franco-Polish 'foreign corps' originally formed in September 1799, of four infantry battalions of ten companies each (including a grenadier and a *chasseur* company), four squadrons of *chasseurs à cheval* and a company of light (horse) artillery. They wore French-style uniform in dark green with yellow facings and piping, in light infantry cut (hence green lapels), dark green waistcoat and breeches, white buttons, and bicorns with green and red plumes respectively for fusiliers and grenadiers, and light infantry shakos with green plume and epaulettes for *chasseurs*. The *chasseurs à cheval* wore a similar uniform, with green-plumed shakos minus the white-metal lozenge-plate of the dismounted *chasseurs*.

In 1803 a presidential guard was formed comprising a battalion of grenadiers and *chasseurs à pied* (eight companies), a squadron of *grenadiers à cheval*, a squadron of *chasseurs à cheval*, a company of horse artillery and a company of artillery train; they were dressed exactly as the French Consular Guard, but with green substituting for the blue of the principal uniform-colour, with red facings, and formed the nucleus of the Royal Guard of the Kingdom of Italy when that state succeeded the Italian Republic.

References

Brandani, M., Crociani, P., and Fiorentino, M. *Uniformi Militari Italiane dell'ottocento: periodo Napoleonico*, Rome 1978.
Bucquoy, E. L. *Les Uniformes du Ier Empire: Gardes d'Honneur et Troupes Etrangères*, ed.

Devautour, G., Paris 1977 (covers the Italian Legion briefly).
Pivka, Otto von. *Napoleon's Italian and Neapolitan Troops*, London 1979 (principal modern source in English).

Under the republic, the Cispadane Legion wore a French-style uniform of dark green *surtout* and breeches, red facings and white buttons, and a bicorn with yellow loop and white-over-red-over-green plume. The artillery wore the same as the infantry with black facings, and the engineers as infantry but with red lapels and white waistcoat and breeches. In 1800 a carabinier battalion was added, in infantry uniform with a light infantry shako, red plume and epaulettes. The Cispadane *Chasseurs à Cheval* had dark green dolman and breeches with white braid and buttons, and a peaked black mirliton cap with white upper band and yellow 'wing'. There were in addition French-style National Guard formations; that of Modena (1797) wore dark green faced red, piped white, lapels closed to the waist, with dark green breeches piped red. The artillery company had bicorns, grenadiers black fur caps with red plume and bag and white-metal grenade badge, and the light infantry leather caps of British style, with white-metal plate, green plume and yellow mane.

References

Brandani, M., Crociani, P., and Fiorentino, M. *Uniformi Miliari Italiane del Settecento*, Rome 1976.
Pivka, Otto von. *Napoleon's Italian and Neapolitan Troops*, London 1979.

(An article on the Modena National Guard by P. Crociani and M. Brandani appeared in *Tradition* magazine (London), issue 74.)

CISPADANE REPUBLIC

History

The Cispadane Republic arose out of the French campaigns to 'liberate' northern Italy from Austrian rule, giving encouragement to liberal sympathizers already agitating in Italy. An assembly which met at Modena in October 1796 abolished feudalism, declared universal male suffrage and established the Cispadane Republic. The previous ruler of Modena, Duke Hercules III (1727–1803) was offered the principality of Breisgau and Ortenau in compensation for the loss of his lands, but he declined and died in exile in Treviso. In 1805 the state was incorporated into the Kingdom of Italy, and upon the dissolution of the kingdom Hercules' grandson received back the Modena state as Duke Francis IV, a return to despotic rule.

Army (cockade: red/white/green)

The Duchy of Modena maintained a small army, the cavalry wearing blue coats with white lace and buttons, buff breeches and facings buff for the Garde du Corps (*Guardia del Corpo*) and white for the line cavalry, and bicorns. The infantry comprised a 'division' of guards, a 'division' of volunteers and four of provincial troops. The Guards wore blue coats with white facings and buttons, and the volunteers red facings, with bicorns (bearskin caps with white plumes tipped blue for grenadiers); the provincial units wore white coats with blue, red, green and yellow facings for the four corps.

CONFEDERATION OF THE RHINE

History

The *Rheinbund* was formed by Napoleon to create a buffer of satellite states between France and his mainland European enemies; it originated on 12 July 1806 when some sixteen German princes pledged their allegiance to France and their departure from the Holy Roman Empire, and additional German states joined later. The organization fell apart after Leipzig as the member states abandoned Napoleon and joined the Allies in the 'war of liberation'. Although the smaller states provided composite 'Confederation regiments' to Napoleon's forces, most retained an independent military establishment, those with military forces being covered here individually. The member states were the French empire; the kingdoms of Bavaria, Saxony, Westphalia and Württemberg; the duchies of Baden, Cleve-Berg, Hesse-Darmstadt, Oldenburg and Warsaw; the principalities of Anhalt-Bernburg, Anhalt-Dessau, Anhalt-Köthen, Hohenzollern-Hechingen, Hohenzollern-Sigmaringen, Isenburg, Leyen, Leichtenstein, Lippe-Detmold, Mecklenburg-Schwerin, Mecklenburg-Strelitz, the five houses of Reuss (Ebersdorf, Gera, Greiz, Lobenstein and Schleiz), Saxe-Coburg-Saalfeld, Saxe-Gotha-Altenburg, Saxe-Hildburghausen, Saxe-Meiningen, Saxe-Weimar, Schaumburg-Lippe, Schwarzburg-Rudolstadt, Schwarzburg-Sonderhausen, Waldeck and Würzburg; and the city-states of Erfurt and Frankfurt.

DANZIG

History
Danzig enjoyed only a brief existence as an independent state. One of the chief towns of the Hanseatic League, it was the capital of West Prussia, passing into Prussian control in 1793. In the 1806 war between France and Prussia, despite Russian attempts to relieve General Kalkreuth and his Prussian garrison, Danzig was bombarded and captured (27 May 1807) by Lefebvre, who was accorded the title of Duke of Danzig, and at the Peace of Tilsit Napoleon declared it a free city. Despite this status and the joint guarantee of sovereignty by France, Prussia and Saxony, a French governor remained in the city and by compelling adherence to the 'continental system' almost ruined it as a major trading centre. In 1814 it reverted to Prussian control.

Army
Danzig's battalion of infantry was uniformed in French style, blue with white facings and French shakos (fur caps for grenadiers); their only service was in the siege of Danzig by the Allies in 1813.

DENMARK

History
Denmark had been one of the most influential powers in northern Europe, but had remained neutral in the wars of the mid-eighteenth century, save for a brief but costly war with Sweden in 1788. The long reign of King Christian VII (1766–1808) was an eventful period, but the king's own influence was limited, as he was described as a semi-idiot; thus most influence was exerted by the crown prince and ministers such as Andreas Bernstorff, who controlled foreign policy from 1773 to 1778 and 1784 to 1797. Denmark remained out of the early conflicts, the regime being so 'enlightened' as to arouse suspicions of Jacobinism; but under the influence of the Tsar a small degree of repression was introduced from 1799. Relations with the Tsar led to Denmark's entry into the second 'Armed Neutrality' to exclude British trade; Britain responded by sending a fleet which destroyed the Danish fleet at Copenhagen in April 1801, after a most gallant resistance. Abandoned by Russia and compelled to acquiesce in a disadvantageous peace, Denmark remained neutral until 1807, when Britain sent an expedition to impound the Danish fleet to prevent it from falling into Napoleon's grasp. Denmark had favoured an alliance with Britain, but now resisted, the prince regent objecting to a compulsory British alliance, and some combat ensued before Denmark surrendered and her fleet was captured. Even though Denmark had intended to oppose Napoleon, this propelled her into a French alliance, which was maintained to the end of the war; Christian VII was succeeded in 1808 by Frederick VI, whose support of Napoleon cost Denmark the province of Norway, which by the Treaty of Kiel (January 1814) was transferred to Sweden

Badge of the Order of the Dannebrog of Denmark, an institution of great antiquity re-modelled as an order of merit on 28 June 1808; gold medal, white cross with red edges; white ribbon with red edges.

in revenge for Danish support of France. This diminution of her territory caused considerable economic distress during the period 1815 to 1830.

Army (cockade: black)
The Danish army's active service was mostly restricted to the period 1807 to 1814, in opposition to the British landing in 1807 and in northern Europe, for example at Stralsund in 1809 (against von Schill's uprising: it appears that the Danish hussar Jasper Crohn killed von Schill after the latter had surrendered, yet Crohn was decorated for the act); and in 1813 in support of the retiring French and their allies.

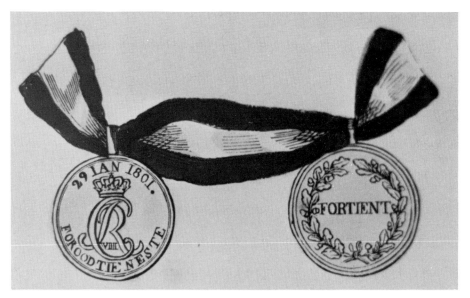

Medal of Merit at the Dockyards of Denmark, an award for long or distinguished service for seamen, naval artificers and artillery, founded 29 January 1801 by Christian VII; white ribbon with red edges.

Infantry

From 1789 the infantry wore a short-tailed jacket similar to the Russian 'Potemkin' uniform of 1786, in the Danish national colour of red, with facings prescribed in 1785 and which remained largely unchanged to 1842:

Regiment	Facings	Buttons
Guards (*Livgarden til Fods*)	light blue	white
Danish Life Regiment (*Danske Livregiment*)	light yellow	white
Norwegian Life Regiment (*Norske Livregiment*	light yellow piped white	white
King's (*Kongens*)	light blue	white
Queen's (*Dronningens*)	light blue	yellow
Crown Prince (*Kronprinsens*)	light blue piped white	white
Prince Frederick	green	white
Fyenen (*Fynske*)	white	white
Seeland	green piped white	white
1st Jutland (*Jyske*)	black piped white	yellow
2nd Jutland	white	yellow
3rd Jutland	black piped white	white
Oldenburg (*Oldenborgske*)	green	white
Schleswig (*Slesvigske*)	light blue piped white	yellow
Holstein (*Holstenske*)	green piped white	yellow

Head-dress was a tall 'round hat' with upturned left brim and white plume; grenadiers wore peaked leather caps with brass front-plate, transverse white crest, facing-coloured bag and white plume with facing-coloured tip; legwear was light grey one-piece gaiter-trousers of Russian style. Shakos were adopted by musketeers and light troops in 1801, and in 1803 Austrian-style bearskin caps were adopted by grenadiers, with legwear grey or blue gaiter-trousers for winter and white for summer; the Guards wore bearskins. Officers had long-skirted coats and bicorns, breeches and long boots

(replaced by hessians in 1801); they adopted epaulettes in 1803, but these were restricted to field ranks in 1812, rank-insignia henceforth being chevrons and rosettes above the cuff. In 1813 grenadiers adopted the shako. Each regiment comprised two battalions, increased to four by the incorporation of the militia (*landevaernet*) which failed against the British in 1807; total regimental strength was sixteen musketeer companies, three of *Jägers* and one of grenadiers, the grenadiers in the 1st Battalion, each of the others having a *Jäger* company. *Jägers* had green plumes and shako-cords and black belts; the remainder had white belts. In 1813 company-strength was regulated at four officers and 163 other ranks.

Light Infantry

The *Jäger* battalions (*Skarpskyttebataillon*) wore infantry uniform in dark green with black facings and battalion-piping, black belts, grey or white breeches, and green plumes; their grenadiers wore the bearskin with green bag and green plume with red tip. They were armed with rifles and sword-bayonets. Most distinguished of the *Jäger* corps was a volunteer unit, the King's Life-Rifles (*Kongens Livjaeger Corps*), formed in 1801 from middle-class inhabitants of Copenhagen, wearing green faced black, grey breeches, 'rifle' equipment and a singular, six-cornered black leather *czapka* with green turban and plume; prior to 1806 officers had 'Tarleton' helmets. In the 1807 British invasion they fought with great gallantry, losing more than a quarter of their strength, and later helped oppose La Romana's mutinous Spaniards. As a reward for their heroic conduct in 1807 they were the only volunteer unit not disbanded in 1814, and ranked in the army list below none but the Guards.

Cavalry

The senior cavalry regiment was the Lifeguard (*Kongelige Livgarde til Hest*), the sovereign's bodyguard of two squadrons of 74 men each; they served only in the 1807 campaign. They wore a pale yellow short jacket faced red, yellow breeches and long boots for guard and parade and blue breeches and short boots on other occasions; their helmet was a variation of the 'Tarleton' with a fur crest or horsehair mane which extended down the wearer's back, and leatherwork was black, the sabretache with a white-metal 'C7' cipher. The four heavy cavalry regiments (*Ryttere*) wore white-plumed bicorns, red infantry-style jacket with facings: Life-Regiment yellow, Seeland dark blue, Schleswig light blue, Holstein light green piped yellow; belts were white, and legwear buff breeches and long boots or blue overalls. The three light dragoon regiments (*Lette Dragoner*) wore Tarletons (introduced 1794) with facing-coloured turban (Life-Regiment red); red jacket with facings: Life-Regiment black piped yellow, Jutland green piped white, Fyenen light blue piped yellow; white belts; white or blue breeches with hussar boots, or grey or blue overalls. (The blue overalls adopted for ordinary dress by all cavalry in 1797 had to be replaced by grey after 1810, due to the economic strictures of war preventing the acquisition of blue dye. The general disappearance of uniform-decoration after 1807 reflected Denmark's approaching bankruptcy caused by the war.) Twelve members of each squadron were armed with rifles and trained as skirmishers; regimental strength was officially four squadrons of four officers and 173 other ranks, but this establishment was never reached, sometimes being less than a third of the regulated number.

The remaining cavalry were hussars, mounted *Jägers* and 'Bosniaks'. The hussars wore Prussian-style uniform of a black mirliton with white lace and plume, light blue dolman faced crimson, crimson pelisse with black fur, white lace and buttons, leather breeches, crimson *Scharawaden* trimmed white (thigh-length stockings), and hussar boots; latterly they wore peaked mirlitons and were permitted to use French-style black busbies. The Mounted *Jägers* wore the uniform of the foot *Jägers*, plus yellow turnbacks. The Bosniaks wore eastern-European costume of a light blue tail-less jacket with crimson cuffs, light blue trousers and crimson girdle (a long red coat with white trim in winter), and a red fez with white turban and light blue feather; officers had a crimson *Konfederatka* with black fur head-band. In 1808 the Bosniaks were converted to lancers, wearing light blue lancer uniform with red facings and *czapka* and white buttons. Lance-pennons were red-over-white, but an illustration of *c*. 1801 shows the Bosniaks with red.

Artillery
The artillery wore line infantry-style uniform with dark blue facings and breeches and yellow buttons. Both foot and horse batteries wore the same, though the horse artillery had cavalry overalls; their shakos, when adopted, had white plumes and a lozenge plate bearing 'R.I.' (*Ridende Artilleri*), and they carried cavalry sabres. The foot batteries had blue shako-pompoms and no plates. Gun-carriages were painted red with yellow metalwork.

Militia
The territorial militia (*Landevaern*) was disbanded in 1807 after failing against the British invasion; they wore infantry uniform in red with blue facings piped white, yellow buttons, a tall 'round hat' with green plume, and beneath the jacket a civilian, long-skirted waistcoat or jerkin of no prescribed colour.

Norwegian Regiments
The majority of units raised in the Norwegian province were volunteer corps, though there were two line and four dragoon regiments. Most unusual were the two ski-borne rifle corps (*Skiløberkorpsene*), originally formed in 1747 and in 1769 attached to infantry regiments, the Soedenfjeldske to the Oplanske Regiment, and the Nordenfjeldske to the Trond-hjemske. Originally they wore blue with yellow facings and braid, blue breeches, a red pelisse with grey fur and a peakless black leather cap like an Austrian *Casquet*, bearing a brass lion on the front; by 1800 they are shown wearing *Jäger* uniform, dark green with black facings piped white, white gaiter-trousers and the same cap. In summer they served as ordinary *Jägers*.

Navy
At the beginning of the Revolutionary Wars the navy was a powerful force, with 38 ships-of-the-line (50–90 guns), 20 frigates (40–42) and numerous coasters. The high quality of both ships and crews was demonstrated by their sterling resistance to the British fleet in 1801 – tougher opponents than the British had ever faced – but after the battle of Copenhagen the fleet was reduced to 20 ships-of-the-line and seventeen frigates. The capture of the fleet in 1807 resulted in the loss of nineteen ships-of-the-line, sixteen smaller vessels of 20 guns or more, ten sloops and 25 gunboats, which virtually annihilated the navy; one further ship-of-the-line, *Prinds Christian Frederik*, was destroyed by the Royal Navy in 1808. Thereafter Danish naval resources were a fleet of sloops and gunboats which were used in the Baltic with considerable effect and the usual courage.

Marines
The Marine Corps was formed in 1798, initially six companies, increased to four battalions in 1803 and reduced to one in 1801; it wore red infantry uniform with blue facings and a white-laced 'round hat' with white plume.

References
The only modern work in English is *Scandinavian Armies in the Napoleonic Wars* (J. Cassin-Scott, London 1976), which includes material on the Danish army; good coverage also appears in *Armies of the Napoleonic Era* and *Navies of the Napoleonic Era*, Otto von Pivka, Newton Abbot 1979 and 1980. The Danish uniform-plates by C. W. Hansen are also extremely valuable.

EGYPT

History

It is not strictly correct to regard Egypt as an independent state, because it was part of the Ottoman Empire; but to all intents it was semi-independent and often defied the will of the Sultan. The ruling body were the Mamelukes (from Turkish *mamlūk, a servant*), who had originally been 'imported' in the thirteenth century to provide an élite body of troops, originally Georgians and Circassians, and who had subsequently imposed their rule over the native inhabitants so that they were in complete control of the territory which was finally acquired by the Ottoman Empire in 1517. The sheiks Ibrahim Bey and Murad Bey had declared their independence from the empire until forced to flee by a Turkish expedition in 1786 which re-asserted Ottoman rule; but after the plague of 1791 had carried off the Ottoman representative Isma'il Bey, Ibrahim and Murad were recalled to resume their government in the name of the Sultan, and were still in power when Bonaparte landed in 1798.

Although the Egyptian regime collaborated with Ottoman troops in the fight against the French, severe disturbances broke out after the French evacuation as the Turks attempted to regain their authority, including an attempted massacre of the Mameluke leaders. The British forces still in Egypt took the part of the Mamelukes and secured the release of those captured by the Ottoman forces. Much confusion followed the appointment, as Ottoman governor, of Mohammed Khosrev, who suffered a defeat at the hands of the Mamelukes and was then driven from Egypt by a mutiny of his own Albanian troops. With the flight of Khosrev, the Albanians' commander, Tahir Pasha, assumed the government, but after 23 days he was killed by his own men for refusing to pay them. The Albanians, now led by Mehmet Ali, one of their regimental commanders, allied with Ibrahim and Osman Bey al-Bardisi of the Mamelukes, in opposition first to a new governor, Achmed Pasha, and then to Khosrev who returned with an Ottoman army; both were defeated. Another Ottoman governor, Ali Pasha Jazairli, attempted to re-establish Turkish rule by separating the Albanians from the Mamelukes; but his forces were unwilling to fight and retired to Syria, and Ali Pasha was reported killed by his own men.

The return from Britain (where he had been endeavouring to enlist support) of Mahommed Bey al-Alfi ('al-Alfi the Great') in February 1804 caused a schism in the Mameluke ranks as his old rivalry with al-Bardisi was revived, and amid scenes of rapine and terrible bloodshed the Albanians under Mehmet Ali appointed themselves the guardians of the Egyptian civilians against the brutality of the Mamelukes. Al-Alfi the Great was forced to flee, Ibrahim and al-Bardisi were driven out, and Mehmet Ali proclaimed Khosrev as Pasha and leader of the government; he was deposed within two days and the Albanians appointed Achmed Pasha Khorshid instead. Heavy fighting continued between the Mamelukes and the Albanian-Egyptians, and the

importation by Khorshid of 3,000 Kurdish *Delis* from Syria (to protect him from his allies!) raised popular feeling against him, the Kurds treating the civilians even worse than the Mamelukes had. The result was a popular revolt during which Mehmet Ali was proclaimed pasha (an appointment later made official by Ottoman decree) and Khorshid was driven away, some of his troops joining the Mamelukes. Mehmet Ali perpetrated a massacre of his Mameluke opponents (83 heads, skinned and stuffed with straw, were sent to Constantinople as proof of his victory!), but he was relieved of his governorship by the Sultan (who with British encouragement favoured al-Alfi); bribery regained his appointment, however, and the death in 1806 of both al-Alfi and al-Bardisi removed his main rivals. The British expedition of 1807, intended originally to support al-Alfi, split the Egyptian support, some favouring the British and others Mehmet Ali; but it was the latter who emerged triumphant after the British withdrew in September 1807. From this point Mehmet Ali was virtually unchallenged; inviting the Mamelukes to the ceremony of appointing his son as commander of an expedition against the Wahhabis in Arabia (see the section 'Ottoman Empire') on 1 March 1811, he massacred them, and though the Mamelukes settled at Dunkulah in the south (where Ibrahim Bey died in 1816, aged 80), their power was destroyed. Mehmet was involved in further campaigns but founded an Egyptian dynasty which continued after his death in 1849 at the age of 80, after a career which had gained virtual (if not official) independence for Egypt from the Ottoman Empire, and which by his later campaigns and conquest of the Sudan brought a degree of stability (albeit by atrocity and slaughter) which Egypt had not enjoyed for some considerable time.

Army

The forces of the Egyptian province were raised and fought in much the same way as those of the remainder of the Ottoman Empire (q.v.), with locally raised forces of little training whose sole tactic was an uncontrolled, headlong rush. The Albanian and Moroccan infantry were by far the best and could perform with resolution, but as with the main Ottoman forces the whole together more resembled (in John Moore's words) a wild, ungovernable mob. Unique to Egypt were the Mamelukes, exclusively cavalry, armed and fighting in a manner little changed from the Middle Ages, whose tactic was simply a valiant charge, during which the Mameluke would fire his carbine and several pairs of pistols, throw his javelins and finally close with the sword upon the enemy. Each Mameluke had a number of servants who acted as a kind of infantry, whose main duty was to recover their master's firearms (thrown aside after firing) and finish off any survivors of the charge. Against formed troops, as proved by Bonaparte, they could easily be driven away. Among the local forces were impressed mobs of peasants or *fellahin*, often armed with no more than clubs, and bands of mounted Arabs; neither were of any real combat value except as semi-guerrillas in a harassing role. Jannissaries served in Egypt but they were restricted to the 'official' expeditions dispatched thence by the Ottoman Empire.

References

Paton, A. A. *History of the Egyptian Revolution*, 1870.

Barthorp, M. J. *Napoleon's Egyptian Campaigns 1798–1801*,

London 1978.

Muir, Sir W. *The Mameluke or Slave Dynasty of Egypt*, London 1896.

FINLAND

History

Finland was a Swedish province from the twelfth century, and was a cause of friction between Sweden and Russia at various periods, despite the boundary between Russia and the Swedish province being settled as early as 1323. Part of Finland was lost to Russia in the wars of Charles XII, and Gustavus III attempted in 1788 to recapture the lost territory. Gustavus's attempts at internal reform had more success, commerce and science being encouraged, and Swedish replaced Latin as the academic language. In the Russo-Swedish war of 1808, however, Sweden finally relinquished possession of Finland by the Treaty of Fredrikshavn (17 September 1809). Finland, however, was not only simply engulfed by Russia but became a semi-independent grand duchy with the Tsar as grand duke; she retained her free constitution and laws, a senate was created and a governor-general appointed. The province of Viborg (ceded to Russia by the Peace of Nystad in 1721) was reunited with Finland in 1811, and Åbo remained the capital until 1821. Not until the very end of the nineteenth century did Russian influence pervade to such an extent as to cause disquiet.

Until 1809 the province had its own regiments as part of the Swedish army, including the 3rd Guard Regiment; these were disbanded upon the Russian acquisition and are covered here in the section on Sweden.

'FOREIGN CORPS'

Though not truly appropriate for inclusion in an account of 'national' participation in the period, the so-called 'foreign corps' should not be overlooked. This contemporary term described men serving in an army of another nationality than their own, though it is not correct to regard all such as mere mercenaries. Mercenary service was common, especially in the earlier years of the eighteenth century, a tradition extended into the Napoleonic Wars by such corps as the Swiss in Spanish service; but the Revolutionary Wars occasioned a new category of 'foreign corps', the patriot-refugee. Especially pre-1801 the political opponents of the French republicans fled abroad to join units of *émigrés* or 'emigrant corps' in the pay of one or other of the opponents of the republicans. Some of these units became integral parts of the army whose pay they accepted (the originally Hanoverian King's German Legion is the most outstanding

example, albeit a late one); others maintained a degree of autonomy, such as the *Armée de Condé* and the so-called 'white cockade corps' which, though paid by an 'Allied' government, retained their allegiance to the French monarchy, signified by their white Royalist cockades. Although many *émigré* units were formed of genuine political refugees, their reputation has suffered by the dilution of many corps by the enlisting of mercenaries or ex-prisoners of war, turncoats who enrolled simply to escape captivity. This was not necessarily damaging, if the ex-prisoners had been serving their original masters unwillingly (for example the German members of the *Grande Armée* captured by the Russians and formed into the Russo-German Legion), but at worst it was a desperate process and created units whose main desire was to desert at the first opportunity and return to their original side.

It was not unusual for such emigrant soldiers to serve in the armies of three or more nations. If the following case is not exactly typical, it demonstrates how wide the service of one man could be. Antoine Lutz was born at Rosheim in Alsace in July 1777, the son of a vineyard labourer, German by descent but French by birth and appearance ('a little, young, smooth-faced Frenchman; well-set, indeed, and of a manly countenance and deportment, but only five feet six inches high').[1] Lutz's family fled to Germany after the execution of Louis XVI, but Lutz himself was conscripted into the French army, deserting once but being forcibly returned to his regiment. After fighting with the French army he again deserted and joined the *Armée de Condé* at Fribourg, and after serving in Mirabeau's Legion and in ten battles he transferred to Russian service with other members of the *Armée de Condé* in 1797. He later transferred to the Grün-Laudon *Freikorps* of the Austrian army, and fought with them against the French in Italy, where he was taken prisoner. He escaped from custody and joined a unit of Germans who were forcibly conscripted into Spanish service; but in May 1799 on a voyage to Barcelona he was captured by a British ship and taken to Minorca, where he enlisted in Stuart's Minorca Regiment, later the Queen's Germans (and later still the 97th Foot) in British service. As a member of the Minorca Regiment Lutz performed the deed which made him famous, capturing the colour of the 3rd Battalion, 21st *Demi-Brigade Légère* at Alexandria. Including his kidnapping into Spanish service, Lutz had therefore served in five national armies plus the French royalist *Armée de Condé* in five years, illustrating how a man might change his paymaster a number of times yet still remain a good, brave, professional soldier.

Note

1. *Cobbett's Weekly Political Register*, 25 December 1802.

References

The leading study is Vicomte Grouvel's *Corps de Troupes de l'Emigration Français*, but important works in English

include *History of the Uniforms of the British Army*, vol. IV, C. C. P. Lawson, London 1966, and a series of papers by C. T. Atkinson in the *Journal of the Society for Army Historical Research*, vols. XXI/XXII, London, 1942–4.

Napoleon Bonaparte, First Consul, in state dress. (Engraving by T. Johnson after Ingres)

FRANCE

History

The political turmoil in France was the cause of the entire Napoleonic Wars. At the beginning of the period the country was an absolute monarchy, with King Louis XVI (1754–93) at its head, having succeeded his grandfather Louis XV in 1774. Faced with growing discontent with the feudal system operating in France and a realization of the need for reform and desperate for funds, Louis acceded to the assembly of a parliament, the States-General, in May 1789. Granted legislative power, the States-General was swept away by an increasing tide of radicalism as the lower elements of the social structure made their presence ever more apparent (demonstrated by the storm of the Bastille prison on 14 July 1789). The more responsible, middle-class legislators realized that the process of reform was getting out of hand, and formed the National Guard under the hero Lafayette in an attempt to keep control, but the decent and honourable aspirations of the instigators were swallowed by the tide of anarchy. The honest Mirabeau attempted to create a constitutional monarchy on British lines, but his noble attempt was engulfed by the tide of communal violence fanned by political agitators such as the Jacobin club, the most fanatical element in the National Convention (parliament). As the situation deteriorated, many aristocrats emigrated; the King's attempt to flee was intercepted and henceforth he was merely a puppet in the hands of anarchy. On 21 September 1791 the monarchy was abolished, a republic proclaimed and 'The Terror' began, a countrywide judicial slaughter of all whose political philosophy did not accord with that of the Committee of Public Safety, the ruling council led by the ruthless republican Maximilien de Robespierre (1758–94). Louis XVI was condemned and guillotined in January 1793, followed by his Queen, Marie Antoinette; his successor, the child Louis XVII (1785–95) died of neglect in prison.

The deposition of the monarchy and the effusion of blood in France not only alarmed the other major European sovereigns but determined them to crush the republican government lest their ideas spread, and the attack on France not only created an internal patriotic reaction to the cry *la patrie en danger*, but placed additional pressures upon the ruling bodies. After attempting to exterminate his opponents, Robespierre was himself unseated by a *coup d'état* and was guillotined on 28 July 1794, which ended 'The Terror' and its policy of mass slaughter. The new administration which replaced the National Convention on 27 October 1795 was the Directory, a five-man executive body which successfully suppressed resistance both from royalist counter-revolutionaries and extremist Jacobins; its original members were La Révellière-Lépeaux, Reubell, Letourneur, Barras and Carnot, the latter being the only really worthwhile member. The Directory imposed a period of comparative stability, though it was inherently corrupt and beset with *coups d'état* and internal plotting; military defeats and economic chaos finally caused its downfall, and it was replaced by the three-man Consulate in the *coup d'état* of 18 Brumaire (9 November) 1799.

The Consulate was planned by two Directors, the Jacobin Abbé Emmanuel Siéyès (1748–1836) and an ex-officer of the royal army, Paul Barras (1755–1820), a man whose immorality did much to influence the corrupt atmosphere of the Directory; they were assisted by the rising star of the French army, Napoleon Bonaparte. On 10 November 'Provisional Consuls' were appointed, Bonaparte, Siéyès and Roger Ducos (1747–1816), a lawyer who had been a member of the Directory; Barras voluntarily retired to enjoy his ill-acquired wealth. Siéyès and Ducos were soon replaced by Jean Cambacérès (1753–1824) as Second Consul, a lawyer and under the Empire one of Napoleon's trusted advisers, and Charles Lebrun (1739–1824), the Consulate's financial organizer. Bonaparte's status as First Consul was unchallenged, and in May 1802 he was appointed Consul for Life. His popularity was such that referenda overwhelmingly elected him Emperor of the French in November 1804. From that date, Napoleon's rule was absolute; the net result of the butchery which characterized the French Revolution had been to replace one autocracy with another, though certain advances had been made. The Empire collapsed with Napoleon's abdication on 6 April 1814, and government devolved upon the newly returned King Louis XVIII (1755–1824), brother of the executed Louis XVI and uncle of Louis XVII. His entourage of ex-*émigrés* intent on revenge did nothing to increase his popularity, which partly explains the ease with which Napoleon returned in 1815 for the brief 'Hundred Days' which marked the end of his rule, Louis XVIII fleeing to the Netherlands with his court. After Waterloo he was again restored to his throne.

Army (cockade: red, white and blue)

The French army enjoyed a high reputation in the mid-eighteenth century, despite a number of severe defeats in the Seven Years War; but their assisting of the American colonies to secure independence from Britain had resurrected their reputation. Much of the army, however, suffered from the malaise which affected society, power being concentrated in the hands of the aristocracy, so that only the nobility could reasonably expect to rise above the rank of captain, with less than one-third of officers actually serving with their regiments; consequently the rank-and-file (recruited by voluntary enlistment for between eight and 24 years) was open to the spread of republican sentiments. The army was virtually destroyed in the early revolutionary period, principally by the emigration of a large proportion of officers and the purging of others, and by the rapid expansion which swept into the army recruits with no time to be trained and unwilling to accept the previous severe discipline. The infantry and especially cavalry suffered most from emigration (the entire hussar Régiment de Saxe defected *en masse*), these having the largest proportion of aristocratic officers; the more 'technical' services (artillery, etc.), which required more extensive training, had never attracted the nobility, so they suffered least from emigration and consequently were a major asset in the early campaigns. The regular ex-royal infantry regiments retained their traditions and discipline despite the effects of the Revolution, and provided the nucleus of the early republican armies; without them, the infant French republic would probably have been crushed, and they formed the cornerstone of the re-organizations of Lazare Carnot which put the French army on a victory footing and paved the way for Napoleon.

Recruitment

To fulfil the enormous requirement of manpower, conscription was used. Based on the 1798 Conscription Laws, all men between ages 18 and 40 had to register, and those between 18 and 25 (later 30) were liable to be called, being selected by ballot. Annual 'classes' could be conscripted before or after their official date; in 1809, for example, men from the classes of 1806–7 and 1810 were called. The practice of anticipating the classes led to the teenaged conscripts or 'Marie-Louises' of 1813–14. As military service became increasingly unpopular, many conscripts never reported for duty (the 'réfractaires') which gave the police an enormous problem. From January 1791 to July 1799 the republic conscripted 1,570,000 men; after that date Napoleon called up 2,545,357 men, of whom about 1,350,000 actually served. Annual levies varied from 500 men in 1810 (all in Italy) to 1,005,000 from 11 January 1813 to 7 January 1814 (the 300,000 men called up on 16 November 1813 included classes as far apart as 1805 and 1814). About three-quarters of the whole were from 'old France'; the remainder came from 'foreign' territories incorporated in the Empire, so that some regiments were French only in name; in 1812, for example, the 14th Cuirassiers, 11th Hussars, 33rd Light Infantry and 123rd–126th Line were Dutch; the 28th *Chasseurs à Cheval*, 11th Light Infantry and 111th and 113th Line were Italian; the 8th *Chevau-Léger-Lanciers* Polish and the 9th from Hamburg, and so on.

Administration

The organization of self-contained formations was originated by Marshal Broglie in 1761, though it was instituted only on campaign; it was the basis of Napoleon's *corps d'armée* system which was a vital part of his method of war, but its essence was thus inherited rather than invented. The smallest tactical formation was the brigade of two or more infantry battalions or cavalry regiments, commanded by a general officer, usually a *général de brigade* (though such appellations were indicative of rank rather than appointment: a brigade might be commanded by the senior colonel of its component battalions, while a *général de brigade* might very well not have a brigade to command). Two or more brigades formed a division, usually commanded by a *général de division*, and including divisional artillery and transport; brigades also had their attached transport, and sometimes an artillery battery. Two or more infantry divisions formed a *corps*

An anecdote which even if apocyphal appears to be characteristic: Napoleon was shown a portrait of himself, painted by David, which had been commissioned by a British nobleman. Napoleon then tried to buy it himself:

' "Sire, I cannot yield it to your majesty: it is already paid for." The Emperor, growing each moment more excited, said to the artist, "David, I will not suffer this portrait to be sent into England. Do you understand me? It shall not go! I will return this marquis of yours his money."

' "Sire," stammered out David, "your majesty would not wish to dishonour me?" On hearing these words, the Emperor grew pallid with rage, and his lips quivered with emotion. "No, certainly; I would not do so, even if it were in my power; but I am equally resolved that those who glory in being the enemies of France, shall never boast of having me in their power – not even in effigy! They shall not have this picture, I tell you!" And at the same moment Napoleon raised his foot, and kicked the painting so furiously, that he broke through the canvas, repeating at the same time in an exasperated tone, "Never shall they have it!" So saying, he instantly left the apartment, leaving every one behind him stupified and terrified by the violence of his conduct.'

(*Chambers' Edinburgh Journal*, 15 September 1849, p. 173.)

(David repaired the picture and sent it to its rightful owner.)

d'armée, usually commanded by a Marshal, a complete army in miniature capable of sustaining independent action, with cavalry division, corps artillery, transport and engineers.

The direction of the army was controlled by General Headquarters, which by Napoleon's time was probably more comprehensive than that of any other nation, numbering by 1812 no less than 3,500 officers and 10,000 other ranks. By 1805 the system was extremely sophisticated, though probably it did not run as smoothly as the vast resources might have suggested it should. Napoleon's *Grand-Quartier-Général* was divided into his personal household or *Maison*, the *Quartier-Général de la Grande Armée* (chief-of-staff, records, clerical and topographical sections), and the General Commissary of Army Stores, responsible for supply and distribution. The *Maison* was the nerve-centre of the army, Napoleon's personal staff or 'little headquarters' (battlefield HQ of aides, equerries and escort), the *Bureau Topographique* which under Bacler d'Albe provided Napoleon with maps and topographical information, and the *Cabinet* or secretarial organization which kept the army's campaign records, most especially the *Carnets* (notebooks) recording in minute detail all known statistics about Napoleon's and his enemies' armies. Fortunately discarded after the early revolutionary campaigns were the *Représentants du Peuple* or *en Mission*, sinister political commissars who interfered with the plans of

A trophy of war: an oriental cloak removed from Napoleon's carriage by a Prussian officer at the end of the Battle of Waterloo, the cloak itself probably an earlier trophy taken by Napoleon in Egypt. (Print after W. Gibb)

THE GREAT RAFT now Afloat in BREST HARBOUR.
2100 FEET LONG, and 1050 BROAD.

every commander in the interests of the political purity of the general's intentions.

Infantry

At the beginning of the Revolution the infantry comprised 79 French and 23 foreign regiments, each of two battalions (the 28th Regiment had four), including the artillery and provincial regiments, ranking as the 64th and 97th Line respectively. Each battalion comprised five companies, four of fusiliers, plus a grenadier company in the 1st Battalion and a *chasseur* (light) company in the 2nd, each company about 120 strong. Beginning in January 1791 the organization was reformed: old regimental titles were abolished and each battalion increased to eight fusilier and one grenadier company. Vast numbers of new battalions were formed, ranging from *Garde Nationale* (reasonably proficient) to the untrained rabble of volunteer and conscript battalions swept up by the *levée en masse* of 1793. As these untrained hordes were incapable of manoeuvre, to utilize their only tactic (an uncontrolled rush on the enemy) the *amalgame* was devised in Carnot's reforms, by which each regular battalion (known as *les blancs* from their old white uniform) was allied to two new battalions (alias *les bleus* from their new blue clothing), to combine the steadiness and disciplined musketry of the regulars with the patriotic but untrained fervour of the new. The resulting formations were styled *demi-brigades de bataille*,

'The Great Raft': a somewhat fanciful view of one of the French invasion-barges which threatened the south coast of England. At the top of the tower is a flag-pole crowned by a 'red bonnet of liberty', and below that a semaphore device.

the term 'regiment' being politically unacceptable (as was the rank 'colonel', implying aristocratic privilege; *chef de bataillon* was used instead). The original 198 *demi-brigades* increased to 211, were reduced to 100 in January 1796 and increased to 110 in that March, the title now being *demi-brigade de ligne*. Official company-establishment of 104 fusiliers, two drummers, fifteen NCOs and three officers (grenadier companies likewise but with fourteen NCOs and 64 grenadiers) was rarely attained, so that instead of the regulation 96 officers and 3,300 men, a *demi-brigade* might have as few as 1,200.

On 24 September 1803 the term 'regiment' was reinstated (*demi-brigade* being used henceforth to describe provisional units); 90 regiments then existed, nineteen with four battalions and the remainder with three, and on 20 September 1804 each battalion converted a fusilier company to *voltigeurs* (lit. 'vaulters') or light infantry, though some units had possessed such as early as 1800. On 18 February 1808 a new organization was made official (having been in progress already) by which each regiment comprised one depot battalion of four companies, and four *bataillons de guerre*, each of four fusilier, one grenadier and one *voltigeur* company; total regimental establishment was 108 officers and 3,862 other ranks. In the later campaigns further battalions were formed, up to seven per regiment, and new regiments: the 113th–120th in 1808, 121st and 122nd 1809, 123rd–126th 1810, 127th–130th 1811, 131st–133rd 1812, 134th–156th 1813; some of these were from already formed provisional or foreign regiments, and the 135th–156th from the *Garde Nationale*.

The initial infantry uniform was the white coat of the *ancien régime* with coloured facings, and the 1791 'Tarleton' helmet which was never universal and most unpopular, the bicorn being much preferred. In 1793 a universal blue coat with red facings and white lapels was introduced, though the white was allowed to wear out; chronic shortages of equipment were endemic during the early period, lack of cloth leading to multi-coloured uniforms worn in the Egyptian campaign, including scarlet, crimson or brown jackets with regimental facings, worn with a peaked leather cap with coloured woollen tuft or *casquette à pouf*. The dark blue coat remained regulation until 1806, gradually becoming tighter-fitting with skirts of reduced length, until shortages of indigo dye caused the re-introduction of the previous white coat with regimentally coloured facings; but perhaps as few as twelve regiments actually received the white, which was regarded as an unserviceable colour and was not approved by Napoleon, who traditionally was sickened by the sight of blood-stained white uniforms at Eylau. Blue was restored in October 1807, but the white was allowed to wear out until late 1809. The coat remained unchanged (though regimental variations were legion) until the introduction by the 1812 regulations of a short-skirted jacket, for the first time with lapels closed to the waist, in the same colours. In February 1806 the bicorn was replaced by a shako which widened slightly towards the top; a slightly taller one was ordered in November 1810, and in 1812 a new pattern replaced the previous lozenge-shaped plate worn by most regiments with a brass eagle above an Amazon's shield or crescent. Company-distinctions (which to a large extent were copied by most of the French satellite nations) consisted of red epaulettes for grenadiers, with either the traditional fur cap (which was not universal) or a shako with red lace, cords and plume; *voltigeurs* commonly had a *chamois* or yellow collar, and shako-ornaments and epaulettes principally yellow but with red and green often added. Fusiliers had plain shoulder-straps and company-coloured pompoms in the head-dress, usually green, sky-blue, yellow and violet for the 1st–4th companies respectively. Legwear throughout the period consisted of white breeches and black gaiters, with white, grey or buff overalls often worn on campaign; equipment was in white leather, with only NCOs, grenadiers and *voltigeurs* carrying the short *sabre-briquet* in addition to the musket and bayonet. In common with the remainder of the army, green 'Imperial livery' with yellow and green lace was ordered for drummers and musicians in 1812, to replace the multi-coloured band uniforms of the previous years, but the green was probably never adopted universally.

Macaulay's lines from *Lays of Ancient Rome* concerning the conflicting emotions dependent upon the individual's position on the battlefield ('Was none who would be foremost/To lead such dire attack;/But those behind cried "Forward!"/And those before cried "Back!"') is reflected in Archduke Charles's order of the day to the Austrian Army on 7 July 1809 following the defeat of Wagram:

'On the evening of the 5th the regiment of Argontier made such bad dispositions, that in the disadvantageous retreat to Neusiedel, the 2d line fired on the 1st, and occasioned great disorder. The regiment of Hesse-Nemburgh, did nothing but wander here and there; sometimes the cry of "forward" was heard, where there was no enemy . . .'

(*Relation of the Operation and Battles of the Austrian and French Armies in the Year 1809*, W. Müller, London 1810, p. 97.)

A common fashion at the period was for the striking of commemorative or souvenir medals imitating those of classical antiquity; this example by J. P. Droz c.1804 is one of the finest depictions of Napoleon, in the guise of a Roman emperor.

Reverse of the medal: an allegorical scene suggesting subjugation of the British lion, and celebrating the construction of 2,000 invasion-barges.

Grenadier of the Régiment Colonel-Général, *1790, the senior infantry regiment of the French army; the retention of the white uniform of the* ancien régime *by the regular troops in the early Revolutionary Wars led to their nickname 'les blancs'. In this case the facings are crimson and lace yellow, the cap-plate brass and the plume white with a crimson tip. (Print after 'Job')*

Shortages of cloth led to the French army in Egypt wearing uniforms of most unusual colours: here, red with light green facings, worn by the 9me Demi-Brigade de Bataille. *The officer (centre) has adopted an oriental sabre and horse-furniture; the grenadier (left) wears the drooping red plume very popular at this period. (Print after 'Job')* ▶

9ᴹᴱ DEMI. BRIGADE DE BATAILLE 1798

Charles Maurice de Talleyrand-Périgord (1754–1838). One of the ablest diplomats of the era, his capacity for self-preservation was legendary, which enabled him to prosper under republican government, Empire and monarchy. Although his influence as foreign minister was immense, Napoleon was right never to trust him completely. (Engraving by W. H. Egleton after Gérard)

'. . . my friend Captain Mein . . . asked the captain commanding the enemy's pickets to have some supper with him, which the poor fellow, who had been half-starved for some months, was delighted to accept. So he came to Mein's house, and after a good supper . . . and an hour or two of conversation, it was time for him to go back to his own picket . . . there is never any personal animosity between soldiers opposed to each other in war . . . and I hope always will be the case. I should hate to fight out of personal malice or revenge, but have no objection to fight for *"fun and glory"*.'

(*Passages in the early life of General Sir George T. Napier*, ed. W. C. E. Napier, London 1884, pp. 176–7.)

Officers' rank was regulated universally throughout the army and through the period, shown by epaulettes and latterly the design of the shako-trim; in gold for line regiments, colonels had epaulettes with bullion fringes on both shoulders; majors the same with silver straps; *chef de bataillon* with thin fringe; captain, fringe on left only; *capitaine-adjutant-major* fringe on right only; lieutenant as captain but a red stripe on the strap; *sous-lieutenant* with two red stripes; and *adjutant-sous-officier* red straps with two gold stripes and red-and-gold fringe on the left only. NCO rank was carried in the form of lace bars above the cuff, in orange or red for corporals and one or two gold bars for sergeants and sergeant-majors, who also had gold thread interwoven in their shako-cords, epaulettes and sword-knot.

French grenadiers, c.1800, a
contemporary watercolour
showing a number of 'campaign'
items: loose trousers with draw-
strings around the ankles, a
yellow and white striped civilian
waistcoat, and a handkerchief
tucked into the pocket of the
standing figure.

The Times, 4 May 1814, carries a story which even if apocryphal illustrates the difference between professional and amateur soldiers; it compares the anecdote with the philosopher Phormio's lecture on military science to Hannibal, which led Hannibal to remark that of all the silly old men he had ever heard, this man who sought to teach him (Hannibal) what he had practised all his life, was by far the silliest:

'A Field officer of a yeomanry corps purchased Arrowsmith's map of the Pyrenees to enable him to follow the reported course of the Peninsular War. After long study he discovered a danger to the Allied army of which Wellington was unaware; so he journeyed to St. Jean de Luz and, Arrowsmith in hand, waited upon Wellington. Spreading the map he pointed to a mountain pass and asked, "What do you think would happen if the French should attack you in this direction?" Wellington replied, "Why, they would get a good drubbing." "Aye, but, my Lord, only see the danger you would be in, if they should make this movement," describing the remainder of the supposed plan. "No, no," replied Wellington. "Be assured the French are not such great fools as to do that." '

Light Infantry

Light infantry tactics played a vital role in the French system of warfare, but were not the preserve of the light infantry regiments alone; line regiments were equally adept at skirmishing, so that the actual difference between light infantry was largely one of uniform and the enhanced *esprit de corps* of the light regiments.

In 1791 there were twelve battalions of *chasseurs à pied*, each of eight companies of forty *chasseurs* (equating to fusiliers in the line) and six carabiniers (the light equivalent of line grenadiers); in 1792 the battalions were enlarged, and in practice the carabiniers appear to have been gathered into a single company. There were in addition many 'irregular' corps of light infantry, most of which were transformed by the *amalgame* into the 22 *demi-brigades légères*, each of one carabinier and eight *chasseur* companies. The number of *demi-brigades* rose to 32, reduced to 30 by January 1796, 26 by September 1799 (four battalions each), and rose to 30 of three battalions each by August 1800. Nine of these were reduced to two battalions, and in August 1801 there were 30 units (numbered 1–31; '30' was vacant), re-titled as *Régiments d'Infanterie Légère*, usually contracted to '— *Léger*'. *Voltigeur* companies were added officially in March 1801 ('scout' sections had existed before), and other changes in establishment followed those of the line. 32nd and 33rd Regiments were formed in 1808, the 34th in 1811 and the 35th–37th in 1812. As before, additional 'irregular' units existed such as the *Tirailleurs Corses* (Corsican *tirailleurs*) and the *Chasseurs des Montagnes* (Pyrenean mountain-troops).

Light infantry uniform was similar to that of the line, but imitated light cavalry styles (even to the wearing of busbies by some élite companies), and included a number of

distinctive features: prior to the adoption of the 1812 jacket, light regiments had worn short-tailed coatees with pointed-ended lapels and frequently pointed cuffs, and lapels and breeches were always dark blue instead of the white of the line. Company-distinctions were generally like those of the line, but many *chasseurs* wore green epaulettes (sometimes with red trim); buttons were white-metal and officers'

epaulettes silver, unlike the yellow and gold respectively of the line.

Cavalry

The cavalry was divided into 'heavy' and 'light', the former used primarily in mass formations to execute the charge, and the latter as divisional cavalry more adept at skirmishing,

◀ *One of the most distinguished Swiss soldiers in the French army was Jean Louis Ebénézer Reynier (1771–1814), born in Lausanne; perhaps best-known for his defeat at Maida by Stuart, he was Minister of War and Marine for the Kingdom of Naples, and commanded VII (Saxon) Corps in the 1812 campaign.*

Musicians of all armies were traditionally dressed in uniform much more elaborate than those of the ordinary troops; in this case one French musician wears a head-dress somewhat akin to a czapka. Both wear the single-breasted surtout (as very popular with officers for campaign dress), 'hussar boots' (often worn by infantry musicians) and have the pointed cuffs characteristic of light infantry uniform. (Print after 'Job') ▶

◀

The eagle became the symbol of Napoleonic France: it was borne upon most military insignia. This shows a shako-plate of the 1812 pattern, the eagle above a crescent or 'Amazon's shield' bearing the number of the 43rd Régiment de Ligne.

though equally capable of executing the charge. Between the two were the dragoons, originally mounted infantry but latterly the backbone of the heavy cavalry. Suffering the worst from emigration of officers, not until about 1796 did the cavalry become even reasonably proficient.

Cuirassiers

The original heavy regiments were simply styled *cavalerie*, of which there were 25 (29 from 1793–9). The 8th Regiment

was equipped with cuirasses and was thus titled *Cavalerie-Cuirassiers*, which formed a model for the rest of the arm, in that between 1801 and 1803 the *Cavalerie* was converted to cuirassiers or dragoons or disbanded, leaving a total of twelve cuirassier regiments, increased by a 13th formed from provisional troops in Spain in 1808, a 14th by the conversion of the Dutch 2nd Cuirassiers in 1810, and a 15th created briefly in 1814; at the Restoration only the original twelve were retained. Organization fluctuated: in 1806 each

French grenadier drummer, c.1800. The uniform is like that of the ordinary grenadiers, distinguished by the red epaulettes and red-plumed fur cap with brass plate bearing an embossed grenade, with the addition of the lace chevrons on the sleeves which were peculiar to the appointment of drummer in many armies. (Print after Maurice Orange)

comprised a headquarters and four squadrons of two companies each, totalling 820 men; from October 1806 to late 1809 a fifth squadron was carried, before the previous establishment was reintroduced. A major problem in maintaining the numbers was the provision of horses sufficiently large and strong to carry a trooper, his cuirass and iron helmet with bearskin turban, leather peak, brass comb and horsehair mane. Because of their ponderous weight, cuirassiers were used almost exclusively for the massed charge on the battlefield, though the 13th, as the sole regiment serving in Spain, could not be employed with a 'cavalry reserve' as were the others. The uniform was blue for all regiments (the 13th wore makeshift brown jackets in Spain and the 14th initially retained their white Dutch uniform faced light blue), with regimental facings as follows: Regiments 1–3 scarlet, 4–6 *aurore* (pinkish-orange), 7–9 pale yellow, 10–12 pink, 13 and 14 *lie-de-vin* ('wine dregs': a dull claret); with blue cuffs for Regiments 3, 6, 9 and 12, and blue cuff-flaps for Regiments 2, 5, 8, 11 and 14. White breeches (grey for active service) were worn with long boots, and shabraques were rectangular, dark blue with white lace edging and a grenade in the rear corners.

Carabiniers

The two carabinier regiments originally wore blue uniform with scarlet facings (blue collars; scarlet cuff-flaps for the 1st Regiment and blue for the 2nd), and bearskin grenadier-caps; in December 1807 the uniform was changed to white with sky-blue facings and armour was introduced, copper cuirasses and helmets, the latter with a scarlet crest instead of the black mane of the cuirassiers, whom they resembled in other matters.

Dragoons

The original eighteen dragoon regiments which existed at the beginning of the Revolutionary Wars were increased to 30 regiments by 1803, forming the backbone of the French

cavalry and virtually sustaining the Peninsular armies single-handed. Organization varied, prior to 1807 including dismounted companies intended for amalgamation into units of *dragons à pied*. From 1807 the organization became more like that of ordinary cavalry, four squadrons of two mounted companies each per regiment (each company officially four officers and 123 other ranks), though some regiments were expanded to five squadrons with a total of 1,200 men. Even after the discontinuance of the unpopular dismounted service, dragoons continued to carry muskets and bayonets to enable them to fight as infantry if required; such combined infantry/cavalry role was invaluable in the Peninsular anti-guerrilla operations.

Dragoons wore a uniform similar to that of the cuirassiers, but with green coats with lapels (closed to the waist after 1812), similar legwear, green shabraques of cuirassier style and the following facing-colours: Regiments 1–6 scarlet, 7–12 crimson, 13–18 dark pink, 19–24 light yellow and 25–30 *aurore*; green collar and cuff-flaps for Regiments 2, 5, 8, 11, 14, 17, 20, 23, 26 and 29; and green cuffs for Regiments 3, 6, 9, 12, 15, 18, 21, 24, 27 and 30.

Hussars

Most flamboyant of the cavalry were the hussars, whose exotic costume (imitating that of the original hussars, Hungarian light cavalry) reflected the 'hussar spirit' exemplified by the hussar general Antoine Lasalle, who declared that any hussar who wasn't dead by thirty was a blackguard! There were six hussar regiments at the beginning of the Revolutionary Wars (less the Régiment de Saxe which defected in 1792) and many small, independent units which were regimented by 1795 to produce fourteen regiments, numbered 1–13 and *7 bis* ('7 again'). The 13th was disbanded in 1796 and in 1803 the *7 bis*, 11th and 12th were converted to dragoons, leaving ten regiments; a new 11th was formed in 1810 from the 2nd Hussars of the Kingdom of Holland, and in 1813 the 12th, 13th and 14th Regiments, the former from a *9 bis* (provisional) regiment raised in Spain in 1811. Two regiments bore the number 13: one of brief existence, replaced by the Regiment 'Joseph-Napoleon' of the Westphalian Guard. Organization throughout the period was reasonable standard for all light cavalry regiments, four squadrons of two companies each (six squadrons 1793–6), with an establishment of about 1,000 (in 1807, for example, each company numbered four officers and 124 men).

Hussar uniform comprised a braided dolman, a furred pelisse, and either tight breeches and 'hussar boots' or campaign overalls; other items originally unique to hussars were the girdle (generally but not always of the facing-colour with 'barrels' of the button-colour), and the sabretache, which existed in elaborate embroidered versions for dress, and plain leather with number or crowned eagle badge for campaign. In the early period the head-dress was usually a mirliton cap with a coloured cloth 'wing' wound around it, which was transformed into a shako by the addition of a peak. True shakos without the wing resembled those of the

'Two or three days ago, an officer of rank in a distinguished cavalry regiment took opium, and destroyed himself. He has been for some time deranged from the effects of a desperate sabre-wound in the head, received at the battle of Waterloo. This unfortunate gentleman, who was but 31 years old, has left a young widow and an aged mother to lament his loss ...

'The inquest on the body of the cavalry officer (Lieutenant-Colonel POOLE) whose self-inflicted death we noticed on Monday, returned a verdict of *Insanity*. It appeared on the clearest evidence, that he had been deranged by reason of severe wounds to the head received at the battle of Waterloo.'

(*Edinburgh Evening Courant*, 25 and 27 September 1817.)

(This sad, late casualty of Waterloo was James Poole of the 2nd Dragoons, Royal Scots Greys.)

infantry, with a wider top, but in 1812 a cylindrical cap known as the *rouleau* shako began to come into use, but was probably not universal until 1814. Basic uniform-colouring (*c*. 1812) was:

Regiment	Buttons		
Dolman	and Lace	Pelisse	Breeches
1 deep sky-blue, red cuffs	white	deep sky-blue	deep sky-blue
2 chestnut, sky-blue cuffs	white	chestnut	sky-blue
3 grey, red cuffs	white	grey (red lace)	grey
4 dark blue, scarlet cuffs	yellow	scarlet	dark blue
5 sky-blue, white cuffs	yellow	white	sky-blue
6 red	yellow	dark blue	dark blue
7 dark green, red collar and cuffs	yellow	dark green	red
8 dark green, red collar and cuffs	white	dark green	red
9 red, sky-blue collar and cuffs	yellow	sky-blue	sky-blue
10 sky-blue, scarlet collar and cuffs	white	sky-blue	sky-blue
11 dark blue, scarlet collar and cuffs	yellow	dark blue	dark blue

The later regiments were:

12 red, sky-blue collar and cuffs	white	sky-blue	sky-blue
13 chestnut, sky-blue collar and cuffs	white	chestnut	sky-blue

14 initially as 13th; when re-formed January 1813 as 8th

Shakos were black (sky-blue for the 5th and red for the 6th) with cords of the lace-colour; but each regiment's élite company and some officers often wore busbies with red plumes. Shako-plumes varied during the period (the *rouleau* had only a pompom) but Martinet shows the following *c.* 1808: 1st, red over black; 2nd blue over black; 3rd and 4th yellow over black; 5th white over blue; 6th royal blue over red; 7th green over red; 8th green with red tip; 9th black with red tip; 10th and 11th black over red. Cloth shabraques with pointed rear corners were sometimes used, but more common for the rank-and-file were shabraques of sheepskin.

Chasseurs à Cheval

Organized like the hussars, the *chasseurs à cheval* formed the bulk of the ordinary light cavalry, the original twelve regiments increasing to 24 by 1801, the 27th–29th Regiments being formed in 1808, and four more in 1811 (17th and 18th, numbers vacant since 1794, 30th and 31st). Less flamboyant than the hussars, they were equally proficient and in fact many regiments adopted items of hussar uniform: the 27th (originally the Belgian *Chevau-légers d'Arenberg*) in fact wore full hussar uniform at one period, while the 30th initially wore red lancer uniform. *Chasseurs* generally wore jackets of light infantry cut, green hussar breeches or campaign overalls, with shakos (originally they had worn the Tarleton helmet), the jackets green with facings as follows: Regiments 1–3 scarlet, 4–6 light yellow, 7–9 rose-pink, 10–12 crimson,

An officer and patrol of the 5th Hussars in campaign dress, c.1807, wearing the scarlet pelisse as an over-jacket and with plume and cords removed from the busbies (generally restricted to the élite company of each regiment). (Détaille)

In his *Mémoires*, published posthumously in 1856, Marshal Marmont recounts an incident at Champaubert, exemplifying the teenaged conscripts ('Marie-Louises') of 1813–14:

'Among the tirailleurs were two conscripts . . . I noticed one who, very calm amid the hissing musket-balls, nevertheless wasn't using his musket. I said, "Why don't you shoot?" He replied somewhat naïvely, "I can shoot as well as the next man, if I have someone to load my musket." The poor child was so ignorant of his business.

'Another I saw had realized his uselessness and asked his lieutenant, "Sir, you're used to this business, take my musket, fire, and I'll give you the cartridges." The lieutenant accepted the proposition and the conscript, exposed to a deadly fire, didn't show a trace of fear throughout the action.'

13–15 orange, 16–18 sky-blue, 19–21 *aurore*, 22–24 *capucine* (bright red), 25–27 *garance* (madder), 28–30 amaranth, 31 chamois. Green collars with facing-coloured piping were worn by Regiments 2, 5, 8, 11, 14, 17, 20, 23, 26 and 29. Horse-furniture was like that of the hussars (the shabraque green), and though lapelled jackets were worn, single-breasted *surtouts* were also used.

Chevau-Léger-Lanciers

Excepting the Polish troops in French service, no regular French cavalry were armed with lances until 1811, when six dragoon regiments (numbers 1, 3, 8, 9, 10 and 29) were converted to *Chevau-léger-lanciers* (light-horse-lancers), to which three 'Polish' units were added by the conversion of the two lancer regiments of the Vistula Legion and the 30th *Chasseurs à Cheval*. They were intended to be the light cavalry of the heavy cavalry corps, but were employed as such only in 1812. The six 'French' regiments wore a uniform similar to that of the dragoons, of green jackets with closed lapels and facings: 1st scarlet, 2nd *aurore*, 3rd rose-pink, 4th crimson, 5th sky-blue, 6th *garance*; green breeches or campaign overalls, brass helmets with brown fur turban and a black crest instead of the loose mane of the dragoons, and horse-furniture like the *chasseurs*. The three 'Polish' regiments wore blue lancer uniform, with facings: 7th pale yellow, 8th blue piped pale yellow, 9th chamois; all had *czapkas* with blue tops. Lance-pennons were of the universal red and white.

Artillery

The artillery was one of the most powerful parts of the army, the number of guns available being sufficient to be used as an offensive weapon by the assembly of 'massed batteries'. As the quality of the army declined over years of attritional warfare, the proportion of artillery was increased to compensate, rising from a ratio of two guns per 1,000 men in 1800 to almost five per 1,000 in 1812. The ordnance was of splendid quality, the 'System' designed by Jean-Baptiste

◄ *Overleaf:*
French artillery overtaken by
Prussian cuirassiers at Hanau;
the artillery mostly wear
greatcoats but the drivers have
their distinctive grey-blue jackets
with dark blue facings. (Print
after R. Knötel)

Action at Dierhoff, 18 April
1797. This demonstrates the
ideal collaboration between
cavalry and horse artillery:
French hussars ford the river
under covering-fire from the
light artillery in the mid-
ground. (Print after Coignet &
Girardet)

Vacquette de Gribeauval introduced under the *ancien régime* remaining in use throughout, fieldpieces being standardized into three 'natures', 4-, 8-, and 12pdrs, plus howitzers, the lighter 4pdrs eventually being withdrawn from the artillery and allocated to infantry regiments during the period when 'battalion guns' were re-issued to provide permanently attached fire-support (not a satisfactory system and one discarded after a number of attempts). A new artillery design was introduced from 1803 ('System of *An XI*') but it never became universal and was generally inferior, so that the original Gribeauval System was re-introduced in 1818. The main alteration was the replacement of the 4pdrs and some 8pdrs with 6pdrs (most captured Prussian and Austrian pieces), and increasing the 12pdrs at the expense of the less-effective 8pdrs. With the 4pdrs relegated to regimental artillery, it was usual to allocate 6- and 8pdrs at brigade or divisional level, with the 12pdrs in corps and army reserves. Batteries normally comprised six guns of one 'nature' and

two howitzers, but in the early period it was not unusual to have more than one 'nature' of gun in a battery. Ordnance usually had brass barrels and olive-green carriages.

There were initially seven regiments of foot artillery, eight by 1799; and though the arm expanded enormously in subsequent years, only one new regiment was formed (the 9th in 1810, from the Foot Artillery of the Kingdom of Holland), the expansion coming by the creation of additional companies in the existing regiments; by 1813 each regiment had 28 instead of the original 20 companies. Each company manned one battery of eight guns and about 30 vehicles, the typical establishment being four officers, ten NCOs and 79 other ranks. Horse artillery was formed in 1791, nine regiments of six or eight companies each existing by 1794; in 1801 the number was reduced to six regiments, a 7th existing briefly in 1810 (from the Horse Artillery of the Kingdom of Holland) before being absorbed by the 1st and 4th Regiments. Each regiment had three squadrons of two companies (batteries) each, plus a depot; from August 1813 the 1st and 3rd Regiments each had a seventh field company. Each battery had six or eight pieces, including one or two howitzers, often 6- or 8pdrs. Their tactical employment was to provide fire-support for the cavalry formations, possible as all gunners were mounted and the guns sufficiently light to keep pace.

Artillery drivers were originally civilians, hired with their teams when required; the system was thoroughly unsatisfactory but not until 1800 was the 'train' militarized by enlisting drivers in the army; thus they could be ordered to take the guns up to the battle-line, instead of unlimbering some distance away and leaving the gunners to drag the pieces by hand into position. Originally eight battalions of five companies each of *train d'artillerie* was formed, enlarged to thirteen battalions of six companies by 1808, and in 1810 the whole force was doubled and a new 14th Battalion raised in Holland, making 27 battalions in all. Battalions were split into separate companies (two officers and 76 men), each of which was attached semi-permanently to an artillery battery.

The foot artillery wore uniforms based on those of the infantry and the horse artillery on those of the hussars or *chasseurs*, in the artillery colouring of dark blue jacket and breeches with red facings and piping, though lapels and usually collar were also dark blue; shako-ornaments were red and buttons and insignia yellow metal. The train personnel wore infantry-style uniform in iron-grey or sky-blue with dark blue facings and white metalwork, often with leather breeches and long boots or campaign overalls.

Engineers

The engineer services were originally part of the artillery, comprising six companies of sappers, six of miners and a small number of engineer officers. In 1793 a proper Engineer Corps was formed, incorporating all branches, its establishment fluctuating until in 1799 there existed two *sapeur* battalions and six miner companies; the latter were reorganized in 1808 into two battalions of five companies each, later six. In 1806 a separate engineer train was formed (*Train du Génie*) to provide transport, and in November 1811 a company of specialist artisans (*ouvriers*). In 1812 there were eight *sapeur* battalions and two of miners, the former reduced to five after losses in Russia; and there existed in addition a number of separate labour corps, some formed from foreigners and others from impressed prisoners of war. All were employed as separate companies, not in battalions; in 1809, for example, each *corps d'armée* had two *sapeur* and one pontoon company (the pontooneer service was a separate formation which came under the aegis of the artillery) plus an additional 6,000 tools with which to equip infantrymen as manual labourers; with the remainder organized into a

'Walking with Disraeli, he told me the following story. I have never made up my mind whether he believed it to be true or not. He spoke as if he implicitly believed it. Speaking of the small circle in which even the greatest move, he told me that the first Napoleon, a year after he became Emperor, was determined to find out if there was any one in the world who had not heard of him. Within a fortnight the Police of Paris had discovered a wood-chopper at Montmartre, within Paris, who had never heard of the Revolution, nor the death of Louis XVIth, nor of the Emperor.'

(*Words on Wellington*, Sir William Fraser Bt., London 1902 edn. p. 179 (orig. pub. 1889).)

Music was a powerful morale-booster on the battle-fields, its effects never better expressed than by Coignet's description of the Imperial Guard at Austerlitz as the musicians played *On va leur percer le flanc/Ran, ran, ran, rantaplan, tirelire . . .*:

'While this air was played, the drums, under the direction of M. Sénot, their major, an accomplished man, beat a charge loud enough to break their drumheads in. The drums and music mingled together. It was enough to make a paralytic move forward!'

(*The Note-Books of Captain Coignet*, J.-R. Coignet, intro. Hon. Sir John Fortescue, London 1928, p. 124.)

central 'park' of nine *sapeur*, three miner, three pontoon and four pioneer companies, four ambulance and two artillery companies, and three battalions of seamen as labourers. Both in training and quality of equipment, the French engineer services were probably the best in Europe. Uniform was based upon that of the artillery, but with black facings piped red.

In addition there existed a small unit of expert topographers, the *Ingénieurs Géographes*, which had existed prior to 1791 but was resurrected in January 1809 with a strength of 90 officers; they wore blue with red facings.

Commissariat

During the early Revolutionary Wars it was impossible for France to feed its armies, so foraging was adopted out of necessity; its strategic effect was such (armies being freed of being tied to slow-moving supply-trains) that even when the Empire could have fed its troops, the previous system was retained, armies normally carrying only between four and seven days' rations for issue when the enemy was so close as to preclude foraging. What transport was required was provided by the Breidt Company, a civilian organization of wagons, teams and drivers; but this was so inefficient that after the army's almost literal starvation in the Eylau campaign, Napoleon formed a military transport service, the *Train des Équipages*, originally eight battalions of four companies and about 140 wagons each. By 1812 there were 22 battalions of six companies, but even these were insufficient, and losses in Russia reduced the number to nine, later twelve battalions. Despite the earnest hard work of Intendant-General Daru, responsible for the army's supplies, the system remained inadequate throughout, perhaps the worst part of the entire French system. Personnel wore uniform like the *train d'artillerie*, but in iron-grey with brown facings.

In addition to the small number of medical officers attached to each unit, in April 1809 a company of medical orderlies (*infirmiers*) was authorized for each corps to assist with the evacuation of casulties; ambulance-companies with vehicles had existed before but were never very prolific. The *infirmiers* wore infantry-style uniform in chestnut-brown with *garance* facings, white piping and buttons, and white or chestnut breeches.

The Napoleonic era was proverbial for the magnificence of its military uniforms, and even in an army as comparatively undecorous as the British, it was possible for Captain Hobkirk of the 43rd Light Infantry to spend a reputed almost £1,000 per annum on his uniform. It is interesting to note, however, how little precious metal was required to produce the appearance of opulence: one pennyweight of gold would gild 700 copper buttons, and thus one ounce of gold would gild 14,000 buttons.

Imperial Guard

Napoleon's Imperial Guard is probably the most celebrated corps of the period, achieving legendary status and in the later campaigns shouldering much of the war's burden. The corps originated with the élite escort formed for members of the Directory, and was expanded hugely into the Consular Guard in November 1799, formed of the army's most stalwart veterans whose allegiance was more to the First Consul than to the nation. Organization fluctuated greatly, but the initial regiments of grenadiers (formed 1799) and *chasseurs à pied* (expanded from company strength in 1800) remained 'Old Guard' throughout, i.e., the *vieux des vieux* or the most indomitable veterans in the army. In May 1804 the title changed to *Garde Impériale*, and from this period it was usual to regard them as the army's reserve: enjoying vastly higher standards of pay, living-conditions, uniform and prestige, it was thought wasteful to expose them unnecessarily and so they were often held back out of combat, much to the troops' disgust (hence the grenadiers' nickname, *grognards* or 'grumblers'). Uncommitted in many battles, they were finally extinguished at Waterloo, vainly attempting to halt the pursuing Allied forces to allow the remainder of the army to escape.

The expansion of the Guard began in earnest in 1804, until by 1813 they represented almost one-third of the army, and in the 1813–14 campaigns were the most effective force available to Napoleon. Second regiments of *chasseurs* and 2nd and 3rd Grenadiers were added (the latter from the Royal Guard of the Kingdom of Holland), plus a host of other corps, regiments of fusiliers-grenadiers and fusiliers-*chasseurs*, two regiments each of *tirailleurs-grenadiers* and *conscrits-grenadiers* (which became the 1st–4th *Tirailleurs* in 1811, to which further regiments were added in 1811–14 to take the number to nineteen *tirailleur* regiments); two regiments of *tirailleurs-chasseurs* and *conscrits-chasseurs*, which became the 1st–4th *Voltigeurs* in 1811, to which Regiments 5–19 were formed 1811–14, the 7th from the previous National Guards of the Guard (raised 1810) and the 14th and 15th from the Spanish Royal Guard. The distinctions between the 'Old

◄

Officer of the Chasseurs à Pied *of the Imperial Guard, a uniform similar to that worn by the Grenadiers but with pointed-* *ended light infantry-style lapels, and a plate-less fur cap with a red-tipped green plume. (Print by Martinet)*

A grenadier of the Old Guard, 1814. Perhaps no other illustration so ideally represents 'the old of the Old', Napoleon's most loyal and devoted troops, here wearing the usual campaign uniform of blue greatcoat with red epaulettes and long-service chevrons on the upper arm, blue overall trousers over white gaiters, the famous bonnet à poil or bearskin cap with plume and cords removed and the cross of the Légion d'honneur on the left breast.

Fusilier of the National Guards of Napoleon's Imperial Guard, a 'Young Guard' formation created in 1810. But for the pointed lapels of light infantry style, the uniform in other respects is like that worn by the ordinary French line infantry in the period before the adoption of the closed lapels of 1812, including the loose overall-trousers commonly worn on campaign.

Engineers of the Imperial Guard, in full dress with 'Old Guard' steel helmet with brass comb and fittings and red plume, blue coat and breeches with black facings, red epaulettes and piping and white gaiters (right); and with iron 'trench-armour', rudimentary protection against enemy fire (left). It is interesting to compare this engraving by Lacoste after Hippolyte Bellangé with a contemporary view of the same uniform, p. 381. ▶

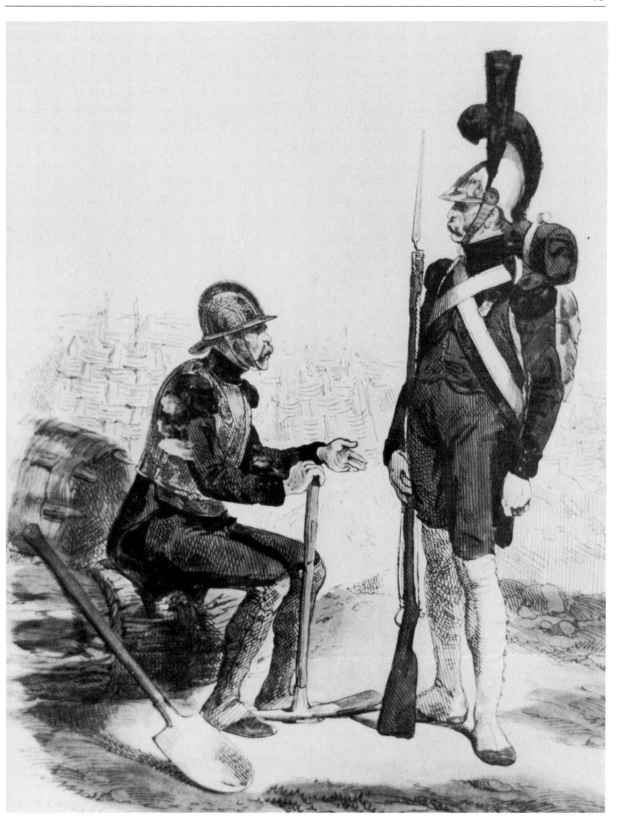

Drum-majors were traditionally the most gorgeously dressed members of the army, none more so than those of the Grenadiers of the Imperial Guard, the most famous being the giant Sénot. (Engraving by Colin after Raffet)

Private of the Conscrits-Grenadiers *of the Imperial Guard, a Young Guard corps formed in March 1809. The red-plumed shako bears the white side-chevrons of the Fusiliers-Grenadiers of the Guard, but the general appearance is that of the ordinary line infantry, with the white breeches and black gaiters often replaced by overalls for campaign. (Lithograph by Villain)*

Guard', 'Middle Guard' and 'Young Guard' were formalized only in 1812, not on unit lines but by length of service; generally the fusiliers were 'Middle Guard' and the junior regiments 'Young Guard', but field officers and captains of the *voltigeurs* and *tirailleurs* were ranked as Old Guard, for example. All the Guard infantry wore infantry-style uniform, but the grenadiers and *chasseurs* were distinguished by wearing the fur cap (the former with brass front-plate and red plume, the latter with red over green plume); alone of the French army the Old Guard retained the 'queue' and powdered hair, and only the Young Guard adopted the 1812-pattern jacket with closed lapels; most of the 'Young' regiments wore light infantry distinctions (blue lapels, pointed pre-1812, and sometimes blue breeches); the Old Guard and fusiliers had line infantry-style distinctions of white lapels.

The cavalry of the Guard originated with the *chasseurs à cheval*, formed from Bonaparte's corps of Guides; they served as Napoleon's escort throughout his campaigns, wearing green *chasseur* uniform with red facings and orange lace, pelisse and fur busby. Other units included the *grenadiers à cheval* (formed 1799), wearing a uniform similar to that of the *grenadiers à pied*, including fur caps, but with cavalry breeches and long boots, and cuirassier-style horse-furniture; the *gendarmerie d'élite*, formed 1801 as the police and security corps, dressed similarly but with peaked fur caps; and the dragoons, formed 1806, in green dragoon uniform with white lapels, and brass helmets with brown fur turban and black horsehair mane, and green shabraques; all had yellow buttons. The light cavalry of the Guard included the *chasseurs*; the *gendarmes d'ordonnance*, a bodyguard corps which existed only in 1806–7, attached to the *chasseurs*; three regiments of lancers, the 1st and 3rd Polish and the 2nd converted from the Hussars of the Kingdom of Holland in 1810, the former wearing blue lancer uniform with crimson facings and *czapka* and silver accoutrements (the 3rd Regiment was wiped out after about a month's active service in 1812), and the 2nd scarlet lancer uniform with blue facings and scarlet-topped *czapkas*; four regiments of *gardes d'honneur*, created in April 1813, dressed in green hussar uniform; and three regiments of 'scout-lancers' (*éclaireurs*) formed in 1813, wearing *chasseur* uniform with the *rouleau* shako, the 3rd Regiment incorporating the squadron of Lithuanian tartars raised in 1812 and wearing an oriental/Cossack uniform. A further squadron attached to the *chasseurs* were the Mamelukes, originally enlisted in the Egyptian campaign and retaining oriental costume until their disbandment in 1814, even after Frenchmen were drafted in to keep up the numbers.

▶

In the 1814 campaign the Imperial Guard formed the Empire's most valuable resource; here the 'marching rampart' is a column of the Old Guard Grenadiers. Napoleon is in the right background, his telescope resting upon the shoulder of an orderly from his escort of Guard Chasseurs à Cheval. (Print after A. Bligny)

Hanau, a battle fought by the Bavarians against their recent allies, the French. A battery of the Imperial Guard Foot Artillery is almost overrun in this print after Horace Vernet.

The Guard possessed its own supporting services so that it resembled an army in miniature; the Guard artillery (six companies of foot and a corps of horse of fluctuating size) was augmented by Young Guard companies from 1809, increasing the number of guns from 96 in May 1811 to 196 in April 1813, so that in the later campaigns it was used as the central army reserve, the most powerful artillery formation under Napoleon's command. It had its own artillery train and *train des équipages*, and its own engineer service; uniforms were based on those of the equivalent line formations but with additional decorations as appropriate to 'Guard' status, and some singular features such as the bearskin bonnets of the foot artillery (peaked, with red plume and no plate), the busbies of the horse artillery, the sky-blue uniform with dark blue facings of the *train des équipages* and the steel dragoon-style helmet with brass eagle-plate and comb supporting a red crest worn by the Old Guard element of the engineers. There was in addition a corps of *Marins* (seamen, not 'marines') of the Guard, intended originally to crew inshore vessels but which was employed both as excellent infantry and as engineers; their uniform was a mixture of hussar and nautical styles, a red-plumed shako, braided blue dolman (or tail-less blue double-breasted jacket) and blue maritime trousers.

At Tilsit the French Guard entertained their Russian counterparts, and were appalled at the outcome:

'After the Emperors were gone, the Russians, who were now at their ease, began to eat again, as hard as they could. We stuffed them with meat and drink, and when they found that they could not eat all that was on the table, what do you suppose they did? They poked their fingers down their throats, threw up their dinner in a heap between their legs, and began all over again. It was a disgusting orgie. That evening we accompanied those who could be taken away, to their quarters, and left the rest of them in their vomit, under the table.'

(*The Note-Books of Captain Coignet*, J.-R. Coignet, intro. by Hon. Sir John Fortescue, London 1928, p. 124.)

The baton of Marshal Jourdan and a sword of Joseph Bonaparte (made during his tenure as King of Naples), both captured at Vittoria. In return for Jourdan's baton which Wellington sent to England as a trophy, the Prince Regent sent Wellington the baton of a field marshal of Britain. (Print after W. Gibb)

Foreign Corps

In addition to those 'French' regiments that contained foreigners, a number of regiments were composed exclusively of foreign personnel. The best were the Swiss regiments, Switzerland having a long tradition of service in France: four Swiss regiments were formed by Napoleon in 1805–6, not mercenaries but supplied under treaty by Switzerland; they served with great distinction, and were remarkable in the French army for their uniforms, in infantry style but coloured red with yellow, royal blue, black and sky-blue facings for the 1st–4th Regiments respectively. (Red coats were also worn by another 'foreign' corps, the Hanoverian Legion). Other Swiss corps included the Valais and Neuchâtel Battalions, the former wearing red and incorporated in the 11th *Léger* in 1811, and the latter famous for their yellow coats with red facings which gave rise to their nickname of 'canaries'. Italy provided a number of corps throughout the period, such as the *Tirailleurs du Po* and *Tirailleurs Corses*; Portugal contributed the Portuguese Legion, clad in brown with red facings and white piping, the infantry (uniquely in French service) wearing the Portuguese *barretina* cap. A Polish legion had been formed in 1799 from Polish exiles endeavouring to obtain an independent Polish state, which corps was transformed into the *Légion Polacco-Italienne* for Westphalian service in 1807. In 1808 this became the Vistula Legion of four infantry and two lancer regiments, which served in the French army with great distinction, the lancers becoming the 7th and 8th *Chevau-Léger-Lanciers* in 1811. They wore Polish-style lancer uniform in dark blue with yellow facings; the infantry wore a mixture of French infantry and Polish styles, their shakos bearing the 'sunburst' plate normally worn on the *czapka*, and dark blue *kurtkas* with yellow facings. Many German recruits were concentrated into the four numbered *régiments étrangers* formed in 1811, the 1st from the *Régiment de la Tour d'Auvergne* (raised 1805), the 2nd from the *Régiment d'Isembourg* (raised 1805), the 3rd from the Irish Legion (raised 1803, including some refugees from the 1798 rebellion) and the 4th from the *Régiment de Prusse* (raised 1806); all wore light infantry-style uniform in dark green. Other corps, small units of Albanians, Greeks and Egyptians, and those recruited from ex-prisoners of war as were some of the above units, were generally of mediocre quality.

Auxiliaries

The *Garde Nationale* was largely merged with the regular army in the early Revolutionary Wars, and then disarmed by the Directory. Only isolated formations existed under the early empire, for example the *Garde de Paris*, raised for internal security duties in 1802 but which served at

'. . . I must confess I did not bear the amputation of my arm as well as I ought to have done, for I made noise enough when the knife cut through my skin and flesh. It is no joke I assure you, but still it was a shame to say a word, and is of no use . . . his instruments were blunted, so it was a long time before the thing was finished, at least twenty minutes, and the pain was great. I then thanked him for his kindness, having sworn at him like a trooper while he was at it, to his great amusement, and I proceeded to find some place to lie down and rest, and after wandering and stumbling about the suburbs for upwards of an hour, I saw a light in a house, and on entering I found it full of soldiers, and a good fire blazing in the kitchen . . .'
(*Passages in the early life of General Sir George T. Napier,* ed. W. C. E. Napier, London 1884, pp. 156, 218–19.)

At the battle of Egmont-op-Zee (1799), Private Ewen McMillan (foster-brother of John Cameron of Fassiefern, commander of the 92nd killed at Quatre Bras) had an ear hacked off:

'Rendered furious by the wound, regardless of Cameron's orders, he rushed among the French, and drove his bayonet, with a ball at the same moment, through the body of the soldier who had wounded him. Returning to his company, he said in Gaelic, to Cameron, "You see what yonder son of the devil has done to me," and pointed to his ear, which was dripping with blood. "He served you rightly," said Cameron, in the same language, "why did you skirmish so far in front?"

"Dioul!" muttered Ewen, "he won't take my other ear." '

(*British Heroes in Foreign Wars*, J. Grant, London 1893, p. 51; the account first appeared in the *Dublin University Magazine*, 1854.)

Friedland and in the Peninsular War, wearing infantry uniform in green with red facings (1st Regiment) or red with green facings (2nd); from 1808 they wore white uniform with green and red facings respectively. In March 1812 a new *Garde Nationale* was formed in three *bans* (categories), the first of men aged 20–26, the second 26–40 and the third 40–60. One hundred departmental 'cohorts' were authorized originally, later reduced to 88, each comprising six fusilier, one artillery and one depot company; uniform was like that of the regular infantry and artillery but with white-metal buttons and insignia. In January 1813 they were converted to line regiments, but there continued to exist twelve 'legions' of Parisian national guard and provincial units, some of which fought during the defence of France in 1814.

Other auxiliary corps included the 'departmental reserve companies' (28 'legions' of infantry, wearing light grey-blue uniform with departmentally-coloured facings); garrison artillery (*canonniers sédentaires* and *canonniers vétérans*, in artillery-style uniform); local *gardes d'honneurs*, mounted and foot bodyguard units to provide escorts for dignitaries who passed through their town (wearing a variety of styles and colours); *canonniers gardes-côtes* (coastal artillery, who wore blue with sea-green facings, waistcoats and breeches); and the *gendarmerie*, the quasi-military police and internal security corps based on the *départments* of the Empire, some of which were used in a military role, such as the *lanciers-gendarmes* who served in the Peninsular War, wearing blue *chasseur*-style uniform with red facings, shakos and armed with lances; the ordinary *gendarmes* wore heavy-cavalry style uniform in blue with red facings, and bicorn hats.

Bonaparte and the monks of St. Bernard during his crossing of the Alps; note the improvised method of transporting artillery through this impossible terrain, gun-barrels being dragged in a hollowed-out log. (Print after Jules Girardet)

Navy

Despite the best efforts of some of its admirals and administrators, the French navy never reached a standard of efficiency that would have allowed it seriously to challenge the domination of the British navy. This was not the result of any inherent weakness of the quality of vessel; indeed, French warships were generally superbly built, and in competent hands their frigates in particular were both swifter and more manoeuvrable than their British

counterparts, and an ambitious building programme was maintained by Napoleon to the very end of the Empire; but repairing and provisioning of warships was a constant and insurmountable problem. It was especially serious for squadrons operating from the main naval base of Brest; generations of ship-builders had stripped the usable timber for many miles, and food was an equal problem; in 1797, for example, when advantage could have been taken of the British naval mutinies, the Brest fleet could only scrape up

provisions for fifteen days at sea instead of the usual six months. In the Trafalgar campaign the French had great difficulty extracting supplies from their Spanish allies at Cadiz (whose resources were equally limited), and such must have been the reputation of the French naval commissariat that even the most basic supplies were only released by the Spanish after Villeneuve had paid in cash!

Napoleon made great efforts to increase French naval power with the aim of outnumbering the British; but though

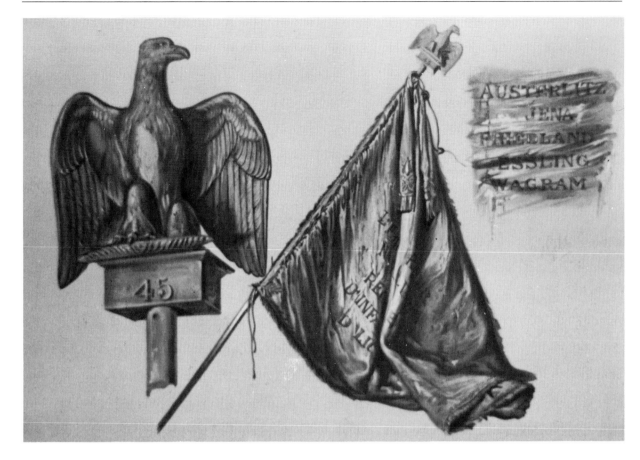

The French army's standards after 1804 were mostly in the form of 'Eagles', but unlike the flags of other armies the important part was the sculpted bronze eagle on top of the pole, not the banner; on campaign the flag was often removed and the eagle alone carried. This shows the 'Eagle' of the 45th Line, perhaps the most famous of all due to its capture at Waterloo by Sergeant Charles Ewart of the British 2nd Dragoons. (Print after W. Gibb)

the ships were of high quality, the calibre of crew was greatly inferior to those of the British. The origin of the problem lay in the *ancien régime* when officers were either aristocrats or recruited from the merchant service, the former having only a theoretical knowledge of seamanship and the latter (contemptuously known as 'blue officers') having practical skill but unwilling to take orders from their socially superior commanders. This led to appalling confusion at sea, a problem greatly exacerbated during the early Revolutionary Wars by the emigration of many of the aristocrats, and by political purges which senselessly removed from command the most loyal and able officers of all ranks; of those serving in 1790, perhaps as few as a quarter were still on duty in June 1791. The stupidity of such purges is demonstrated by the disbanding of the highly efficient Marine Artillery, whose specialist gunnery training was regarded as 'élitist' and

therefore politically unacceptable! The result was a rapid decline in seamanship (even earlier French ships had a reputation of being dirty and ill-kept when compared with the impeccable condition of British vessels), and even the restoration to command of some 'purged' officers never fully remedied the situation.

As France was primarily a land-based power, the navy had taken second place in the queue for resources, and the situation was not improved by the fact that Napoleon had little understanding of the realities of war at sea, or the difficulties presented to admirals who had to execute difficult orders with inferior crews and ill-supplied ships. A further complication was the interference by military officers (Napoleon included); in the Trafalgar campaign, for example, Admiral Villeneuve (an experienced and quite capable seaman) was continually harassed by General Lauriston, nominally his subordinate, who sent libellous reports regarding the admiral to Napoleon, while protocol demanded that Villeneuve's own channel of communication had to be via the Minister of Marine, Admiral Decrès. Despite the expending of large sums on the navy, the French never overcame these difficulties, and a measure of the lack of success in French naval policy is the fact that during the entire period, they lost 90 capital ships to British action; whereas Britain only lost one which was not subsequently

'On the 31st of last August, was arrested in the Commune of Cour and Buis (Isere) a man named Mathieu Felix, ex-soldier of the 31st regiment of light infantry, who had made himself pass for Buonaparte, and announced the pretended arrival of several corps destined to cut off the Allied Troops. He has just been condemned by the tribunal of Vienne to six months imprisonment, to the payment of fifty francs, and to be afterwards placed at the disposal of the government.'
(*The Times*, 2 November 1815.)

recovered. By the time the French navy finally began to improve in training and efficiency, it was too late to affect the outcome of the Napoleonic Wars.

French naval officers wore a military-style uniform in dark blue with gold lace; there was no regulated uniform for seamen, but generally they wore tail-less blue jackets, loose blue or white trousers and a tarred 'round hat'.

Marines
France had no corps of marines *per se* (the 'naval infantry' which existed during the early Revolutionary Wars were

Prince Camille Borghese (1775–1832), second husband of Pauline Bonaparte (1780–1825), Napoleon's second sister. He was governor-general of the French départements au delà des Alpes. Engraving by T. Johnson after Gérard, illustrating the archaic costume of the Napoleonic court.

Rampon and the 32nd Demi-Brigade *at Montelegino, 10 April 1796: a typical example of a commander inspiring his men by exhorting them to defend their Colours. (Print after Berthon)*

'Mutual instruction': the Young Guard (left) and Old Guard (right) stand shoulder-to- shoulder in defence of France, 1813–14. (Print after Charlet)

formed only to garrison naval shore installations), but the stupidity of disbanding the Marine Artillery was recognized and a new naval gunnery corps of seven *demi-brigades* was formed in October 1795, reconstructed as the *Artillerie de Marine* in 1803, four regiments of three battalions each. Although some served aboard ship (at Trafalgar, for example), they were employed increasingly on land, in the Peninsula and Russia, and in 1813 were transferred from the Ministry of Marine to the War Ministry, and were virtually annihilated fighting as infantry in the 1813 campaign. They wore basically artillery uniform with the addition of anchor-badges on their insignia. Other naval formations employed on land were the *ad hoc* battalions of seamen employed as pioneers in a number of campaigns, equipped with a uniform similar to the undress of the Seamen of the Imperial Guard plus a black 'round hat' instead of a shako.

References

Sources for the French army of the period are immense in number; the following are some of the most accessible and/or most significant:

Bucquoy, E. L. *Les Uniformes du Premier Empire* (ed. Lieutenant-Colonel Bucquoy and Devautour, G.): series of books which re-print many of the Bucquoy uniform-cards, a most valuable coverage. Volumes include the following, all published in Paris: *Dragons et Guides* (1980); *Etat-Major et Service de Santé* (1982); *Gardes d'Honneur et Troupes Etrangères* (1983); *La Cavalerie Légère* (1980); *La Garde Impériale: Troupes à Cheval* (1977) and *Troupes à Pied* (1977); *La Maison de l'Empéreur* (1984); *L'Infanterie* (1979); *Les Cuirassiers* (1978).

Blondieau, C. *Aigles et Shakos du Premier Empire*, Paris 1980 (a study primarily of head-dress but including many details of unit-lineage).

Bukhari, E. *Napoleon's Cuirassiers and Carabiniers*, London 1977.

— *Napoleon's Line Chasseurs*, London 1977.

Chandler, D. G. *The Campaigns of Napoleon*, London 1967 (invaluable study of all aspects of Napoleon's system of war).

Elting, J. R. *Swords around a Throne: Napoleon's Grande Armée*, London 1989 (very important modern study of the French army: with Chandler (above) essential reading).

Griffith, P. *French Artillery*, London 1976.

Haythornthwaite, P. J. *Napoleon's Guard Infantry*, I and II, London 1984–5.

— *Napoleon's Light Infantry*, London 1983.
— *Napoleon's Line Infantry*, London 1983.
— *Napoleon's Military Machine*, Tunbridge Wells 1988.
— *Napoleon's Specialist Troops*, London 1988.
Johnson, D. *Napoleon's Cavalry and its Leaders*, London 1978.
Lachouque, H., and Brown, A. S. K. *The Anatomy of Glory*, London 1962 (study of the Imperial Guard, with a vast number of contemporary illustrations).
Malibran, H. *Guide . . . des Uniformes de l'Armée français*, Paris 1904, reprinted Krefeld 1972 (primarily concerned with uniform-regulations but including much on organization and unit-lineage).
Quennevat, J. C. *Les Vrais Soldats de Napoléon*, Paris 1968 (collection of contemporary llustrations and text, a valuable introduction).
Rogers, H. C. B. *Napoleon's Army*, London 1974.

A civilian sightseer describes a battlefield:

'. . . I had not proceeded far before I stumbled over the dead body of a Frenchman, which was lying on its face amongst the grass. The corpse was so frightfully disfigured, and so smeared with mud and gore, that I felt horror-struck; but when, on advancing a little further, I saw hundreds, and in less than an hour, thousands of slain, I found my pity for individuals merge in the general mass, and that the more I saw the less I felt; so true is it, that habit reconciles everything. The dead required no help; but thousands of wounded, who could not help themselves, were in want of everything; their features, swollen by the sun, looked livid and bloated . . . The anxiety for water was indeed most distressing. The German "Wasser! wasser!" and the French "De l'eau! de l'eau!" still seem sounding in my ears. I am convinced that hundreds must have perished from thirst alone . . .

'The general burying was truly horrible; large square holes were dug about six feet deep, and thirty or forty fine young fellows, stripped to their skins, were thrown into each, pell mell, and then covered over in so slovenly a manner, that sometimes a hand or foot peeped through the earth. One of these holes was preparing as I passed, and the followers of the army were stripping the bodies before throwing them into it, whilst some Russian Jews were assisting in the spoilation of the dead by chiselling out their teeth, an operation which they performed with the most brutal indifference. The clinking hammers of these wretches jarred horribly on my ears, and mingled strangely with the occasional reports of pistols, which seemed echoing each other at stated intervals, from different corners of the field. I could not divine the meaning of these shots, till I was informed that they preceeded from the Belgians, who were killing the wounded horses . . .'

('Waterloo, the Day after the Battle', in *With Fife and Drum*, ed. A. H. Miles, London, n. d., pp. 14–15.)

The Frankfurt War Medal for the campaign of 1813; silver with red-and-white ribbon.

FRANKFURT

History

Frankfurt-am-Main was a 'free city' and as such played little part in the political affairs of the earlier Napoleonic era, though in 1792 Custine extracted some 2,000,000 *gulden* from its citizens, and in 1796 Kléber took a further 8,000,000 francs. Its independence was ended in 1806 with the formation of the Confederation of the Rhine, and in 1810 it was made the capital of the newly created Grand Duchy of Frankfurt, which comprised the four districts of Frankfurt, Aschaffenburg, Fulda and Hanau; Eugène de Beauharnais was appointed Grand-Duke. In 1815 it again became a free city, the seat of the German Confederation; but siding with Austria in the 1866 war, it fell to Prussian troops and was incorporated in that state.

Army (cockade: black, later white with red centre)
Upon joining the Confederation of the Rhine, Frankfurt was forced to raise an infantry unit, ranking as the 3rd Confederation Regiment. It served in 1806 against Prussia, and from 1809 one battalion served in the Peninsula, defecting to the British in December 1813. Three other battalions served in Russia in 1812 (34th Division, XI Corps), and in 1813 formed part of the Danzig garrison. In 1814 the 1st and 2nd Battalions were transformed into the 14th Bavarian Line. The initial uniform was of Austrian style, white with red facings, initially with bicorns and later shakos; the *Jäger* companies wore green uniform with red piping, green shako and black plume. In 1808–9 dark blue French light infantry uniform was introduced, with red facings. There also existed a small *gendarmerie*-type unit dressed in blue hussar costume with yellow braid.

GREAT BRITAIN

History

Almost from the outbreak of the Napoleonic Wars, Britain was France's most implacable enemy, and one of the main causes of Napoleon's eventual defeat. The only cessation of hostilities between the two countries was during the brief Peace of Amiens; for the remainder of the period Britain remained steadfastly committed to the struggle against French domination of Europe. Not only did Britain commit her own forces – most effectively in the strangulation of French maritime trade and in the Peninsular War which drained France of military strength – but perhaps equally importantly acted as 'paymaster' to other states allied to Britain by virtue of their opposition to France. In Portugal's case this took the form of Britain assuming command of the country's entire military resources, but more commonly Britain's assistance was in the form of *matériel* (vast quantities of British supplies were poured into the armouries of her allies) and cash, the amount of which in loans and subsidies was enormous. In 1800, for example, almost 7.6 per cent of the Treasury's *total* revenue was spent on subsidies to allied states (3 million pounds out of £39,512,000, £2,500,000 of which went to Austria), while in 1813 assistance to the allies represented more than the amount spent on the Royal Navy (£11,294,416 of the military budget as advances to allied nations, and £11,335,412 in direct loans). By these efforts alone, Britain's contribution to the defeat of France was invaluable, and gives some relevance to the title of Fitchett's Victorian study of the Napoleonic Wars: *How England Saved Europe*.

Britain was essentially a parliamentary democracy, so that the King's influence and position – though still of great importance – was no longer paramount as in other European states. King George III (George William Frederick, 1738–1820) reigned throughout the period, having succeeded his grandfather George II in 1760. George III exerted a beneficial influence in the main and was regarded by his subjects generally with affection, the embodiment of solid, moral values with a dislike of innovation and especially of revolutionary upheavals such as that suffered by France. In the winter of 1788–9 he was treated for what was believed to be insanity (though his illness may actually have had physiological causes), but he made a complete recovery. In 1811, however, his perceived 'mental' health broke down completely and from that date until his death he played no function in government, his son George Augustus Frederick (1762–1830), Prince of Wales, ruling in his stead as Prince Regent, and succeeding as King George IV in 1820.

With one brief interlude (Grenville's coalition government) the Tory party ruled from 1783 to 1830,

William Pitt the younger presiding as chief minister from 1783 until his death in 1806, excepting the period from March 1801 to May 1804 when Addington led the Ministry. After Pitt's death (hastened, it was said, by the catastrophic news of Ulm and Austerlitz) Grenville's brief administration lasted until 1807, when the Tories re-assumed power under chief ministers Portland (1807–9), Spencer Percival (from 1809 until his assassination in the House of Commons lobby by the maniac Bellingham in 1812), and from 1812 to 1827 Lord Liverpool. The parliamentary opposition to the war was largely based upon its financial burden rather than upon moral principle, and though vociferous in its criticism of the conduct of the war never achieved a position in which it could jeopardize seriously the Ministry's determination to prosecute hostilities. The political opposition was equally vociferous outside Parliament in the likes of William Cobbett's *Weekly Political Register*, though in retrospect his opinions appear misguided, as when he wrote of the Peninsular War as 'nothing but a drain on this country, without the smallest chance of any ultimate benefit . . . there exist not the means of final success; and, therefore, the sooner we abandon the undertaking the better.'[1] Typical of the ill-informed comments raised by the radical opposition in Parliament was Sir Francis Burdett's attempt to block the annuity of £2,000 granted to Wellington for his successes in 1812, his denying of Wellington's achievements demonstrating only Burdett's complete ignorance of the subject. When the division upon the measure was called he was the only member to vote against it. In the long term, Britain's participation in the Napoleonic Wars fulfilled Pitt's hope expressed in his last great speech on 9 November 1805: 'England has saved herself by her exertions; and will, I trust, save Europe by her example.'

Army (cockade; black)

Administration was split into two branches: the 'Horse Guards' (so called from the location of the Commander-in-Chief's office) and the Board of Ordnance headed by the Master-General of the Ordnance; the former was responsible for all matters except artillery and engineers, which were administered by the Ordnance and thus were not officially part of the army.

The army's head was the Commander-in-Chief: Jeffrey, 1st Lord Amherst, 1793–5 and thereafter until 1827 the Duke of York, save for a hiatus (1809-11) when Sir David Dundas, Bt. fulfilled the position, the Duke having left office temporarily following a scandal involving his mistress' influence over the granting of commissions. This apart, the Duke was an earnest and valuable occupant of the position. The Commander-in-Chief was assisted by the Adjutant-General (Lieutenant-General Sir William Fawcett, 1781–9, thereafter until 1820 Lieutenant-General Sir Harry Calvert, Bt.), and by the Quartermaster-General (Colonel George Morrison 1761–96, David Dundas 1796–1803, Lieutenant-General Robert Brownrigg, 1803–11, and thereafter until

Britain's perception of her role during the Napoleonic Wars: a typically classical allegory of 'Britannia protecting Europe from the horrors of War and Slavery & triumphing over Discord'. (Engraving by Neagle after Shepperson, published in Bungay, 1815)

1851 General Sir James Willoughby Gordon, Bt.). The Master-General of the Ordnance was Charles, 3rd Duke of Richmond (1784–95), Charles, 1st Marquis Cornwallis (1795–1801), John, 2nd Earl of Chatham (1801–6 and 1807–10), Francis, 2nd Earl of Moira (1806–7) and Henry, 1st Earl of Mulgrave (1810–18).

Officers were appointed by the purchase or granting of a commission. The old belief that all commissions were bought is erroneous: though the purchase of 'steps' (successive promotions) continued throughout the period, only a minority of commissions were bought (involving large sums: a captaincy in the line cost £1,500 in 1814, for example), other promotions being granted by seniority (filling gaps caused by death or retirement), or commissions given freely upon application with a testimonial to the effect that the applicant was of suitable character and education; and when the demand for recruits was at its height, commissions were awarded freely to those enlisting a requisite number of men, a system applying most commonly to officers transferring from the Militia and bringing with them a number of militiamen). The system was open to abuse, especially in the early years of the period, though the worst aspects (such as the granting of commissions to children) were removed when a lower age-limit of 16 was introduced; but even after 1802

'During the time that the British Army occupied its positions along the Spanish bank of the Bidassoa a vast number of desertions took place. As this was an event which had but rarely occurred before, many opinions were hazarded as to its cause. For my own part, I attributed it entirely to the operation of superstitious terror on the minds of the men . . . Rugged as the country was . . . almost every foot of it had been contested; and the dead, falling among rocks and cliffs, were left in various instances, from necessity, un-buried. It was exactly in those parts where the dead lay unburied that single sentinels were planted. That soldiers and sailors are often superstitious everybody knows; nor can it be pleasant for the strongest-minded among them to spend two or three hours of a stormy night beside a mangled and half-devoured carcass. Indeed, I have been myself more than once remon-strated with for desiring as brave a fellow as any in the corps to keep guard near one of his fallen comrades. "I don't care for living men," said the soldier; "but, for Godsake, sir, don't keep me beside *him*." And wherever I could yield to the remonstrance, I invariably did so. My own opinion, therefore, was that many of our sentries became so unmanned by superstitious dread, that they could not keep their ground. They knew that if they returned to the picket a severe punishment awaited them; and hence they went over to the enemy rather than endure the pangs of a diseased imagination.'

(*The Subaltern*, G. A. Gleig, London 1823; Edinburgh edn., 1872, pp. 106–8.)

half the new appointments were under 18 years. The system of 'purchase' was introduced originally to provide a retiring officer with funds from the sale of his commission, avoiding the necessity of government providing a pension for his retirement, though this in fact did exist in the system of 'half pay', by which officers forcibly retired upon the reduction of their unit were paid a small wage to enable them to live until their services should be required again. Open to the abuse of 'patronage' – influential friends or wealth were a great advantage to an officer – the purchase system at least allowed officers of ability to reach high rank at an early age; Wellington, for example, commanded his battalion at age 24. On balance, the system worked remarkably well.

The rank-and-file was recruited exclusively by voluntary enlistment: unlike the majority of European states, no conscription existed. The result was that only the most desperate were induced to enlist, either from lack of civilian employment, fugitives from justice (a minority) or those enveigled by the recruiting-sergeants who guaranteed a life of ease and quick promotion. Recruits received a cash bounty on enlistment – in 1812 as much as £23. 17s. 6d. for lifetime enlistment, five guineas less for seven years – which was a powerful incentive to a labourer enjoying a life of poverty; and the additional sum paid to the recruiter was an incentive for sharp practice. Wellington's oft-misunderstood remark about 'the scum of the earth' referred to the background from which the average recruit was drawn; it was a plea for recruits to be taken from a wider social background rather than purely a criticism of the troops that were enlisted, whom Wellington then described as 'fine fellows'. Once enrolled, the soldier had a hard life, but no worse than the grinding poverty in which many had lived as civilians. Discipline was strict and terrible for malefactors: flogging was the commonest punishment, ranging from 1,200 strokes to the more usual 1,000 and even commonplace 3–700. Appalling though it was, even the simple private soldiers generally accepted it as a necessary way of curbing the lawlessness of the hard core of 'incorrigibles' which existed in every battalion. The calibre of recruit improved markedly after 1805 when Militiamen were at last encouraged to transfer to regular service, from when about half the army's recruits came from the Militia, entering their regular units already trained in the use of arms and used to military discipline.

Cavalry

Three basic types of cavalry existed: Household, heavy, and light dragoons. The Household regiments (two of Life Guards and the Royal Horse Guards, whose 'Household' status was not clearly defined at the time) were heavy dragoons, the sovereign's personal bodyguard and thus uncommitted to many campaigns: only in 1812 were two squadrons of each sent to the Peninsula, but their most lasting fame came at Waterloo. The heavy cavalry comprised seven regiments of dragoon guards and six of dragoons, the difference between them being merely in the minutiae of uniform; the appellation 'Guards' was nothing more than tradition dating from their conversion from

William Pitt (1759–1806), British chief minister from 1783 until his death, less a brief interlude 1801–4, in a suitably martial pose for the politician who prosecuted the war against France with great vigour, as colonel-commandant of the Cinque Ports Volunteers, which in 1803 numbered three battalions of twelve companies each, and a total establishment of 3,168. (Print by Stadler, after Humbert)

regiments of Horse in 1746. From 1799 the number '5' in the list of dragoons was vacant, following that regiment's attempted mutiny in 1798 in support of the Irish rebellion, rebels having been enlisted unknowingly. The remaining regiments were light dragoons, numbered successively after the 6th Dragoons, running to the 25th Regiment in 1815; regiments with numbers up to 33 were of ephemeral duration. From 1806 the 7th, 10th, 15th and 18th Light Dragoons were converted to hussars, necessitating only a change in uniform.

Establishment was generally similar for all the regiments of one type: ten troops of about 90 men each was the standard after 1800, in five squadrons of two troops each, of which one squadron was usually retained at home as a depot, giving a field strength of eight troops in four squadrons. In September 1813 light regiments were increased to twelve troops. Strength on campaign was usually much below establishment, often averaging 400 or less; of the cavalry with the army at the start of the 1809 campaign in the Peninsula, regimental strength averaged 614, but at

One of the most handsome head-dress ever devised was the Tarleton helmet, named after the British cavalry leader of the American War of Independence, Banastre Tarleton (though only in France was it accorded the name officially); it comprised a leather skull with turban around the base and a fur crest running from front to back; this example belonged to the Dunbar troop of East Lothian Yeomanry.

'classical'-style helmets of black leather with brass comb and horsehair mane were introduced, and a new short jacket without the breast-loops; the 2nd Dragoons wore their traditional fur caps throughout, and Household regiments adopted a black-over-red 'caterpillar' helmet-crest in 1814. The light dragoons wore dark blue braided dolmans and 'Tarleton' crested helmets until the adoption of Polish-style plastroned jacket (in the same colour, with epaulettes of the button-colour) and French-style shakos from 1812, generally an unpopular change as it made them appear to be Frenchmen! The hussars wore light dragoon uniform but retained the braided dolman throughout, worn with the pelisse and fur cap (latterly shakos) associated with their 'arm'. Legwear for all regiments was originally white or buff breeches and knee-boots, replaced on campaign by grey overalls generally from *c.* 1810. Regiments existing in 1815 were:

Regiment	Facings	Officers' Lace and Buttons*
1st Life Guards	blue	gold
2nd Life Guards	blue	gold
Royal Horse Guards (blue coats)	scarlet	gold
1st (King's) Dragoon Guards	blue	gold
2nd (Queen's) Dragoon Guards	blue	silver
3rd (Prince of Wales's) Dragoon Guards	white	gold
4th (Royal Irish) Dragoon Guards	blue	silver
5th (Princess Charlotte of Wales's) Dragoon Guards	green	gold
6th Dragoon Guards (Carabiniers)	white	silver
7th (Princess Royal's) Dragoon Guards	black	gold
1st (Royal) Dragoons	blue	gold
2nd (Royal North British) Dragoons (Royal Scots Greys)	blue	gold
3rd (King's Own) Dragoons	blue	gold
4th (Queen's Own) Dragoons	green	silver
6th (Inniskilling) Dragoons	yellow	silver
7th (Queen's Own) Light Dragoons (Hussars)	white	silver
8th (King's Royal Irish) Light Dragoons	scarlet	gold
9th Light Dragoons	crimson	gold
10th (Prince of Wales's Own Royal) Light Dragoons (Hussars)	scarlet	silver
11th Light Dragoons	buff	silver
12th (Prince of Wales's) Light Dragoons	yellow	silver
13th Light Dragoons	buff	gold
14th (Duchess of York's Own) Light Dragoons	orange	silver
15th (King's) Light Dragoons (Hussars)	scarlet	silver

Salamanca was only 354 and was only 412 at the beginning of the Vittoria campaign. Numbers remained very small when compared with the vast cavalry forces fielded by other armies, to a degree because the main sphere of operations, Spain and Portugal, was not truly suitable for the deployment of huge cavalry contingents.

Training was a perennial problem, for regiments were sent on active service with no idea of how to conduct themselves in a war, training at home consisting of elaborate parade-ground manoeuvres, 'which, like Chinese puzzles, only engross time and labour to the unprofitable end of forming useless combinations'.[2] Consequently, tactics and especially the techniques of the 'outpost' (scouting and skirmishing) had to be learned on campaign, the result being a number of catastrophic actions when British charges achieved success but were then turned to disaster by the inability of regiments to control their enthusiasm and rally to resist counter-charges. Such behaviour annoyed Wellington uncontrollably: 'I considered our cavalry so inferior to the French from want of order, that although I considered one of our squadrons a match for two French, yet I did not care to see four British opposed to four French, and still more as their numbers increased . . . They could gallop, but could not preserve their order.'[3]

The heavy regiments wore the national red coat with bars of lace on the breast and bicorn hats, until 1812 when

Regiment	Facings	Officer' Lace and Buttons
16th (Queen's) Light Dragoons	scarlet	silver
17th Light Dragoons	white	silver
18th Light Dragoons (Hussars)	white	silver
19th Light Dragoons	yellow	gold
20th Light Dragoons	orange	gold
21st Light Dragoons	black	silver
22nd Light Dragoons	white	gold
23rd Light Dragoons	crimson	silver
24th Light Dragoons	light grey	gold
25th Light Dragoons	light grey	silver

*White or yellow for other ranks accordingly.

Infantry

The British infantry was the most reliable military force in Europe, exhibiting throughout a determined stoicism which was never bettered. The best summary of their worth is Wellington's reply to Creevey's inquiry about the outcome of the coming Waterloo campaign: pointing to a British infantryman wandering around a Brussels park the Duke declared: 'There, it all depends upon that article whether we do the business or not. Give me enough of it, and I am sure.'[4]

There were two basic types of infantry, Foot Guards and line; the former were the élite of the army, both in the aristocratic background of the officers and the calibre of the men; but in terms of organization, though Guards battalions were almost invariably stronger, they resembled the ordinary line regiments. These consisted of one or two battalions (a small number raised a 3rd or 4th battalion), each of ten companies, including one company of grenadiers and one of light infantry, with an establishment of about 100 rank-and-file per company, though only on the rarest occasions were battalions ever up to strength. It was intended that one battalion should go on active service while the other remained at home, the 'service' battalion exchanging its 'ineffectives' (sick and headquarters personnel) with the 'home' battalion, so that it would be as strong as possible for campaign. The result was that when a 2nd battalion was ordered abroad, it left behind not only its own ineffectives but those of the 1st battalion as well, so that 2nd battalions (and single-battalion regiments) were invariably weaker than 1st battalions, and lucky to embark on campaign with much above 750 men. Attrition on campaign reduced the strength even more drastically: at the end of the 1811 campaign, for example, of the 46 battalions in Wellington's army (excluding the Foot Guards which were always unusually strong), average battalion-strength was only 550, with only nine having in excess of 700 , and the 2/38th having but 263. Reinforcements on campaign were received in drafts from the depot at home or by the return of convalescents from hospital, but as battalions were rarely withdrawn even when so weak as to be unable to operate as separate entities, two very weak battalions might be combined to form a 'provisional battalion' as employed in the later Peninsular War. During the earlier period, a further

'Some years ago I heard of an old pensioner who had been at the Battle of Waterloo, and who hung about the "Ditch" in Manchester. He had the reputation of being very reticent on the subject of the battle. I heard that he was usually to be found at the Old Boar's Head in the evening, so strolling in, I was fortunate enough to find him and get into conversation with him. After standing him three pints of "strong and bitter" I got him to admit that he was present at the battle. After two or three more he got more loquacious and commenced, "Aye, I reckon I wur theer an' it wur a pretty big do. You see it 'appened this way, a danged big Frenchman cum i'front ov me, and I macks a pass at 'im and then he macks a pass at me." With that he paused. "What happened next?" I asked. "You'd a know wot 'appened next if ye'd got as big a chump at side ov t'yed as I got." And so ended the only true account of the Battle of Waterloo.'
(Walter Gibbons, in *The Return*, Blackpool, V no. 143, 6 December 1918, p. 7.)

variation was the detaching of flank companies (grenadiers and light infantry) and forming them into composite 'flank battalions', but this practice was much rarer in British service than in other armies. For tactical purposes each company was styled a platoon, within which were two subdivisions each of two 'sections', though a very weak company might form three sections instead of four. Two companies formed a 'grand division' and a battalion might be divided into two 'wings', but these terms were applied only loosely.

Each regiment bore a number and most a territorial designation, but though the latter had been instituted in 1782 in many cases they bore little relation to the areas from which the regiment drew its recruits, as recruiting-parties were sent far and wide and the later widespread practice of encouraging large drafts from Militia regiments resulted in territorial composition quite different from that of the regimental title, for example English county regiments with a preponderance of Irish rank-and-file due to enthusiastic recruiting among Irish Militia regiments. Only the native Irish and Scottish regiments had a preponderance of men from their designated areas, though in 1809 the 71st, 72nd, 73rd, 74th, 75th and 91st Highland Regiments were re-uniformed, relinquishing their highland dress, as it was thought that kilts would discourage the enrollment of Englishmen. By 1815 the number of regiments had risen to 104, though in the 1790s a host of ephemeral corps had taken this number to 135; and there were in addition a large number of corps of even shorter duration, known only by the name of their colonel, formed as 'recruiting regiments' with the specific intention of breaking them up and drafting the personnel to other units. The formation of new regiments was not found to be very effective, it being more practical to utilize existing depots and *espirit de corps* by raising additional battalions for existing regiments.

The British uniform prior to the adoption of the 'stovepipe' shako: an officer of a battalion company of the 2nd (Queen's) Regiment, 1799, wearing the regimental dark blue facings and silver lace, with the white-over-red plume worn by all save grenadiers and light infantry. (Print from the 'British Military Library' series, published by J. Carpenter)

Initially the infantry wore the red, lapelled coat with long tails, and bicorn hats, much as used in the late American War. In 1800-1 a new uniform was introduced, including a short-tailed, single-breasted red jacket closed to the waist, retaining the coloured facings and regimental lace as before, and a cylindrical shako with large brass plate, replaced in 1812 by a false-fronted ('Belgic') shako, though the introduction of the latter was generally delayed until the end of the Peninsular War. The old white breeches and black gaiters were replaced on active service by loose overalls of several styles and colours, until the introduction in 1812 of uniform grey overalls; all leatherwork was white, or buff for regiments with buff facings. Company-distinctions consisted of 'wings' edged with white worsted for flank companies, and tufted shoulder-straps for 'battalion' companies; with white-over-red plumes for battalion, white for grenadier and green for light companies. Officers of all but light companies retained the long-tailed coat and bicorn until 1812; commissioned rank was indicated by the universal crimson waist-sash and epaulettes of the regimental lace-colour, a single epaulette worn on the left by company officers and two by field ranks; grenadiers and light infantry officers wore laced 'wings' with epaulettes for field ranks. Sergeants' sashes were generally crimson with a stripe of the facing-colour.

Light infantry regiments were formed from 1803 by the conversion of line regiments; though trained to high standards of skirmishing and marksmanship, they were equally capable of fighting as line infantry. They never adopted the 'Belgic' cap, and all wore light-company

A company of British infantry at drill, 1806, wearing the pre-1812 'stovepipe' shako; the officers (right) retained long-tailed coats until 1812, the NCOs illustrated wearing the ordinary short red jacket and the rank-and-file white sleeved waistcoats, breeches and stockings, the usual uniform for drill. Note the 'fugelman' in advance of the front rank. (Print after J. A. Atkinson)

distinctions. The Highland corps (only the 42nd, 78th, 79th, 92nd and 93rd Regiments after 1809) wore feathered bonnets and kilts; and three regiments were styled 'fuzileers' from their being armed in the distant past with light muskets or 'fusils', though by this period they were virtually indistinguishable from the ordinary line infantry except in matters of dress and perhaps *esprit de corps*, wearing fur caps in full dress like the grenadier companies of line regiments.

Some changes of title occurred throughout the period, but the regiments existing in 1815 were as follows, with details of facings and lace:

Regiment	Facings	Lace (officers)	Remarks
1st Foot Guards	blue	gold	
2nd (Coldstream) Foot Guards	blue	gold	
3rd (Scots) Foot Guards	blue	gold	
1st (Royal Scots)	blue	gold	
2nd (Queen's Royal)	blue	silver	
3rd (East Kent)(Buffs)	buff	silver	
4th (King's Own)	blue	gold	

Regiment	Facings	Lace (officers)	Remarks	Regiment	Facings	Lace (officers)	Remarks
5th (Northumberland)	gosling-green	silver		33rd (1st Yorkshire West Riding)	red	silver	
6th (1st Warwickshire)	deep yellow	silver		34th (Cumberland)	bright yellow	silver	
7th (Royal Fuzileers)	blue	gold		35th (Sussex)	orange	silver	Dorsetshire pre-1805
8th (King's)	blue	gold		36th (Herefordshire)	gosling-green	gold	
9th (East Norfolk)	yellow	silver		37th (North Hampshire)	yellow	silver	
10th (North Lincoln)	bright yellow	silver		38th (1st Staffordshire)	yellow	silver	
11th (North Devon)	full green	gold		39th (Dorsetshire)	pea-green	gold	East Middlesex pre-1807
12th (East Suffolk)	yellow	gold		40th (2nd Somersetshire)	buff	gold	
13th (1st Somersetshire)	philemot-yellow	silver		41st	white	silver	
14th (Buckinghamshire)	buff	silver	Bedfordshire pre-1809	42nd (Royal Highland) (Black Watch)	blue	gold	
15th (York East Riding)	yellow	silver		43rd (Monmouthshire Light Infantry)	white	silver	Light Infantry 1803
16th (Bedfordshire)	yellow	silver	Buckinghamshire pre-1809	44th (East Essex)	yellow	silver	
17th (Leicestershire)	greyish-white	silver		45th (Nottinghamshire)	deep-green	silver	
18th (Royal Irish)	blue	gold		46th (South Devonshire)	pale yellow	silver	
19th (1st Yorkshire North Riding)	deep green	gold		47th (Lancashire)	white	silver	
20th (East Devonshire)	pale yellow	silver		48th (Northamptonshire)	buff	gold	
21st (Royal North British Fuzileers)	blue	gold		49th (Hertfordshire)	full-green	gold	
				50th (West Kent)	black	silver	
22nd (Cheshire)	pale buff	gold		51st (2nd Yorkshire West Riding Light Infantry)	grass-green	gold	Light Infantry 1809
23rd (Royal Welch Fuzileers)	blue	gold		52nd (Oxfordshire Light Infantry)	buff	silver	Light Infantry 1809
24th (2nd Warwickshire)	willow-green	silver		53rd (Shropshire)	red	gold	
25th (King's Own Borderers)	blue	gold		54th (West Norfolk)	popinjay-green	silver	
26th (Cameronians)	pale yellow	silver		55th (Westmoreland)	dark green	gold	
				56th (West Essex)	purple	silver	
28th (North Gloucestershire)	bright yellow	silver		57th (West Middlesex)	yellow	gold	
29th (Worcestershire)	yellow	silver		58th (Rutlandshire)	black	gold	
30th (Cambridgeshire)	pale yellow	silver		59th (2nd Nottinghamshire)	white	gold	
31st (Huntingdonshire)	buff	silver		60th (Royal American)	blue	silver	not including rifles
32nd (Cornwall)	white	gold		61st (South Gloucestershire)	buff	silver	
				62nd (Wiltshire)	yellowish buff	silver	
				63rd (West Suffolk)	deep-green	silver	
				64th (2nd Staffordshire)	black	gold	
				65th (2nd Yorkshire North Riding)	white	gold	

Drum-major, pioneer and drummers of the British 66th Foot, in the 'reversed colours' (green faced red) worn by musicians prior to 1812. Beards, aprons and fur caps were symbols of pioneer appointment in many European armies. (Aquatint by I. C. Stadler after Charles Hamilton Smith, from the latter's Costume of the Army of the British Empire*)*

Regiment	Facings	Lace (officers)	Remarks
66th (Berkshire)	gosling-green	silver	
67th (South Hampshire)	pale yellow	silver	
68th (Durham Light Infantry)	deep-green	silver	Light Infantry 1808
69th (South Lincoln-shire)	willow-green	gold	
70th (Glasgow Lowland)	black	gold	Surrey pre-1812
71st (Highland Light Infantry)	buff	silver	Light Infantry 1809)
72nd (Highland)	yellow	silver	
73rd	dark green	gold	
74th (Highland)	white	gold	
75th	deep-yellow	silver	
76th	red	silver	'Hindoostan Regiment' 1807–12
77th (East Middlesex)	yellow	silver	
78th (Highland, Ross-shire Buffs)	buff	gold	raised 1793
79th (Cameron Highlanders)	dark green	gold	raised 1793
80th (Staffordshire Volunteers)	yellow	gold	raised 1793
81st	buff	silver	raised 1793
82nd (Prince of Wales's Volunteers)	yellow	silver	raised 1793
83rd	yellow	gold	raised 1793
84th (York and Lancaster)	yellow	silver	raised 1793
85th (Bucks Volunteers Light Infantry)	yellow	silver	raised 1793; Light Infantry 1808
86th (Royal County Down)	blue	silver	raised 1793; Leinster 1809–12
87th (Prince of Wales's Own Irish)	green	gold	raised 1793
88th (Connaught Rangers)	pale yellow	silver	raised 1793
89th	black	gold	raised 1794
90th (Perthshire Volunteers)	deep-buff	gold	raised 1794
91st (Argyllshire Highlanders)	yellow	silver	numbered 98th 1794–8
92nd (Highland)	yellow	silver	raised 1798
93rd (Highland)	yellow	silver	raised 1800

Regiment	Facings	Lace (officers)	Remarks
94th (Scotch Brigade)	green	gold	brought into line 1802
95th (Rifles)	black	black	
96th	buff	silver	numbered 2/52nd 1798–1802
97th (Queen's Own Germans)	blue	silver	brought into line 1804
98th	buff	silver	
99th (Prince of Wales's Tipperary)	pale yellow	silver	raised 1804
100th (Prince Regent's County of Dublin)	deep-yellow	silver	raised 1804
101st (Duke of York's Irish)	white	silver	raised 1806
102nd	yellow	silver	New South Wales Corps; brought line 1808
103rd	white	silver	9th Garrison Battalion, brought into line 1808
104th	buff	silver	New Brunswick Fencibles, brought into line 1810

Rifle Corps

In an attempt to provide the British Army with a facility for 'rifle' and light infantry tactics, which had required the employment of German mercenaries in the early Revolutionary Wars, a 5th battalion was added to the 60th Royal Americans in 1797, by enrolling principally German recruits with experience of rifle-shooting. These companies were dressed in green, as were the additional 60th battalions raised subsequently, though the original four battalions retained their red uniform. The Duke of York considered adding a rifle company to each line regiment, for which purpose he formed in 1800 an 'Experimental Corps of Riflemen' of personnel from fourteen regiments, to be trained by Colonels Coote Manningham (41st) and William Stewart (67th), both exponents of light infantry tactics. This experimental formation was deployed in the operation against Ferrol, and was then enlarged by drafts from 26 Fencible regiments to create a new line regiment, numbered the 95th, which became one of the most élite formations in the army and won undying fame in the Peninsular War.

The 5/60th was usually deployed as individual companies, allowing each division to have its 'rifle' detachment; the 95th's three battalions usually served complete, forming one of the most valuable elements of the Peninsular Light Division. They wore rudimentary camouflage of 'rifle-green'

The British infantry uniform introduced in 1812, most notably including the false-fronted 'Belgic' shako, is shown in this engraving by the French print-producer Genty, 1815, the 'wings' on the shoulders and the green plume and cap-cords indicate the battalion light company. Note the painted device on the rear of the knapsack, bearing the regimental number.

The French General SIMON, styling himself a baron of the empire, and decorated with the grand cross of the legion of honour, one of BONAPARTE'S accomplished generals, who in violation of his parole of honour absconded from Odiham, and is charged with being concerned with others in carrying on a traitorous correspondence, has been taken by VICKERY, the active Bow Street officer. He was taken in the coal-hole of a house in Kentish Town.'
(*Edinburgh Evening Courant*, 20 January 1812.)

The 95th Rifles were among the most famous and proficient troops in Europe: this print by Genty illustrates their rifle-green uniform with black facings, white piping, black leather equipment, 'stovepipe' light infantry shako and the superb 'Baker' rifle.

with black facings; the 5/60th had red facings and blue breeches, and both retained the 'stovepipe' cap to the end of the period, never adopting the 'Belgic' pattern. Both had black leather equipment and the magnificent Baker rifle.

Other rifle corps included most notably the light battalions of the King's German Legion (also uniformed in green with black facings), and foreign units like the Brunswick Oels *Jägers*; and though 'rifle' tactics did not find universal favour with the more conservative military theorists, a large proportion of the volunteer forces were trained similarly, as 'rifle' tactics of the 'hit-and-run' variety were more practicable for use with troops inexperienced in fighting in line.

Artillery
Compared to the vast artillery forces fielded by other nations, Britain's was small, and remained so despite the expansion which occurred throughout the period, caused more by the difficulty of training a large number of officers than from any inability to produce a sufficient quantity of guns. So meagre were the resources in the early Peninsular War that artillery could not even be deployed in batteries but was divided into two- or three-gun sections; but the worst of these shortages were remedied reasonably quickly. Personnel were highly trained, especially the officers, but the higher ranks were less effective: Wellington only achieved the good artillery commander he required by appointing a junior lieutenant-colonel, Alexander Dickson, over the heads of the senior gunners by virtue of Dickson's Portuguese commission; no 'purchase' existed in the Royal Artillery, promotion being decided by seniority.

Organized in 'brigades' or companies, each an independent entity controlling its ordnance and vehicles, the Royal Artillery was composed of ten-company battalions, eight in 1803, with a 9th Battalion formed in 1806 and a 10th in 1808. Prior to 1802 the guns were grouped for administrative purposes into 'brigades' of about twelve guns, but from then each company consisted of six pieces, usually five guns and one howitzer. Foot artillery comprised companies of five officers, seventeen NCOs, three drummers and 116 gunners, though the drivers of the battery vehicles were officially part of a separate formation, the Corps of Drivers. Orginally artillery transport had depended upon hired civilian carters and teams – a most unsatisfactory arrangement – but the formation of the Corps of Drivers in 1794 still presented problems. By 1808 the corps comprised eight troops of five sections of 90 drivers and craftsmen, the troops being split up and allocated to the various artillery companies; thus the drivers had little supervision from their own officers and became known as a most unreliable body: 'that nest of infamy'[5] as one artillery officer described them!

Horse artillery (styled 'horse brigades' or more commonly troops) was created in 1793 to provide fast-moving fire-support for cavalry, all personnel either mounted or riding on the limbers; by 1801 there were seven troops, and twelve by 1806. Foot companies were originally armed with light 6pdrs and 3pdrs, which proved greatly inferior to the French artillery, so as soon as possible after the commencement of the Peninsular War the more effective 9pdr was introduced, but only by 1815 had the 6pdr been replaced completely. The older howitzers were withdrawn and replaced during the Peninsular War by the 5½in and 4²/₅in models. Horse brigades were initially armed with the 6pdr, which had not

An officer of the Royal Artillery, 1799, wearing the regimental colouring of dark blue coat, red facings and gold lace with the white plume which identified grenadiers and artillerymen. The crimson waist-sash was a national distinction of commissioned rank. (Print from the 'British Military Library' series)

been replaced completely by the end of the war: at Waterloo three troops had 9pdrs, three light 6pdrs, one exclusively 5½in howitzers and one troop with light 6pdrs and rockets. The latter were invented by William Congreve and first deployed in action in 1805, though not until 1813 did the 'Mounted Rocket Corps' see action, one troop in the Peninsula and one with the Allied army in Germany. The concept of 'battalion guns' in British service was soon realized to be flawed, and guns attached to infantry regiments were virtually unknown after 1800 except in a few cases.

The foot artillery wore uniforms of infantry style, and the horse artillery of light dragoon pattern, but in the Royal

The following is perhaps the most celebrated passage in the annals of military writing of the Napoleonic era, and perhaps rivals Xenophon's account of the Ten Thousand's sighting of the sea as the most emotive in all military history: William Napier describes the advance of the Fusilier Brigade at Albuera:

'. . . a fearful discharge of grape from all their artillery whistled through the British ranks. Myers was killed; Cole and the three colonels, Ellis, Blakeney, and Hawkshawe, fell wounded, and the fuzileer battalions, struck by the iron tempest, reeled, and staggered like sinking ships. Suddenly and sternly recovering, they closed on their terrible enemies, and then was seen with what a strength and majesty the British soldier fights. In vain did Soult, by voice and gesture, animate his Frenchmen; in vain did the hardiest veterans, extricating themselves from the crowded columns, sacrifice their lives to gain time for the mass to open out on such a fair field; in vain did the mass itself bear up, and fiercely striving, fire indiscriminately upon friends and foes, while the horsemen hovering on the flank threatened to charge the advancing line. Nothing could stop that astonishing infantry. No sudden burst of undisciplined valour, no nervous enthusiasm, weakened the stability of their order; their flashing eyes were bent on the dark columns in their front; their measured tread shook the ground; their dreadful volleys swept away the head of every formation; their deafening shouts overpowered the dissonant cries that broke from all parts of the tumultuous crowd, as foot by foot and with a horrid carnage it was driven by the incessant vigour of the attack to the farthest edge of the hill. In vain did the French reserves, joining with the struggling multitude, endeavour to sustain the fight; their efforts only increased the irremediable confusion, and the mighty mass giving way like a loosened cliff, went headlong down the ascent. The rain flowed after in streams discoloured with blood, and fifteen hundred unwounded men, the remnant of six thousand unconquerable British soldiers, stood triumphant on that fatal hill!'

(History of the War in the Peninsula, W. F. P. Napier, London 1831, III, pp. 540–1.)

Artillery colouring of blue jackets with red facings and yellow lace; though unlike the light dragoons, the Royal Horse Artillery never adopted the shako and plastroned jacket, but retained the braided dolman and Tarleton throughout. Most field ordnance was 'brass', iron guns being restricted to the siege-train and garrisons, and carriages were painted the 'common colour', grey with black metalwork.

Engineers

Like the artillery, the engineer service was administered by the Board of Ordnance and comprised the small Corps of Royal Engineers, exclusively highly trained officers, and the rank-and-file of the Royal Military Artificers and Labourers (Royal Military Artificers from 1798). The artificers were not field engineers but carpenters and builders who maintained fortresses; eight companies were stationed in Britain, one in Nova Scotia, one in the West Indies and two semi-autonomous companies in Gibraltar. When engineers were required for campaign, detachments were sent from these static companies, usually the most inefficient men who could best be spared, with little or no experience of field service; at Ciudad Rodrigo, for example, only eighteen artificers could be mustered to conduct the siege, so that the manual labour was provided by untrained infantrymen. The wretchedness of this system culminated with the slaughters of Rodrigo and Badajoz, and compelled the government to heed Wellington's plea for a competent engineer corps, which was established as the Royal Military Artificers or Sappers and Miners in April 1812 (Royal Sappers and Miners from 1813), a corps 2,800 strong which was properly trained and which had a great influence in the later stages of the Peninsular War. Not until the Waterloo campaign was the engineer service self-supporting with its own transport and vehicles, however, as previously they had to make do with whatever vehicles and teams could be spared by the Royal Artillery. The engineer corps wore uniforms of infantry style, in the Ordnance colouring of dark blue with black facings and yellow lace, until 1811 when the Royal Engineers changed to scarlet coats with blue facings and gold lace (to prevent their being mistaken for Frenchmen!), and the Sappers and Miners from 1812 wore the same colouring.

An additional unit was the Royal Staff Corps, formed as part of the army (which the other engineer services officially were not, being controlled by the Board of Ordnance) to provide the Horse Guards with its own engineer service. Formed in 1798, the Staff Corps attained battalion size in 1809, but its personnel were usually deployed in small detachments or even individually to superintend the working-parties drawn from the infantry. The unit wore infantry uniform in red with blue facings.

Commissariat and Transport

Commissariat affairs were run by the Treasury, so that commissariat officials were officially civilian employees outside the scope of military discipline, and were in many cases merely untrained clerks. Assistant-commissaries, deputies and clerks were attached to each infantry brigade or cavalry regiment, superintended by the Commissary-General and his Assistants and Deputies, but though many were inefficient their tasks were complicated by the lack of a military transport service. Previously relying exclusively upon hired civilians, a military 'Corps of Royal Waggoners' was formed in 1794 but was a total failure; it was replaced in August 1799 by the Royal Waggon Train, which increased to fourteen troops of wagons and teams by 1814, but even this formation could do no more than merely dent the surface of the army's commissariat problem, so that throughout the period resort had to be made to vast numbers of often unreliable carters hired from the areas in which the campaigning occurred, such as the enormous, inefficient and slow-moving mule-trains and ox-cart convoys of the Peninsular War. Commissaries wore blue infantry-style uniform with black facings, and the Royal Waggon Train a red uniform faced blue, with shakos.

Administration

Compared to the sophisticated staff organizations of other armies, Britain's General Staff was tiny; exclusive of general officers and their personal aides, there were but ten full-time staff officers, the Permanent Assistants of the Quartermaster-General's Department; all other staff officers were detached temporarily from regimental duty. The main organizations were the departments of the Quartermaster-General and Adjutant-General, the former responsible for marches, quarters and the conveyance of troops and the latter for equipment and discipline, though their duties frequently overlapped, and the Quartermaster-General's department became the dominant body during the Peninsular War for no more logical reason than Wellington's finding its head (George Murray) more efficient than that of the Adjutant-General's department, William Stewart. Each general maintained a personal staff of ADCs (two for a lieutenant-general, three for the commander of the forces, who also had a military secretary; any additional ADCs had

to be supported out of the general's own pocket and thus were usually the sons or relations of the general's friends). They conveyed the general's instructions to the units under his command, each brigade having a 'brigade major' who attended to its staff tasks, these officers being detached temporarily from their regiments. Few doctors or surgeons were attached to a central medical staff, save the Inspector-General of Hospitals and his assistants, all other medical officers being attached permanently to their own battalion or cavalry regiment, each possessing one surgeon (ranking as a captain) and two assistants (lieutenants). Until the great humanitarian Doctor James McGrigor was appointed Inspector-General of hospitals in the Peninsula, conditions in these establishments were frightful beyond comprehension. At the head of the army medical service was the Medical Board, comprising the Surgeon General, Physician General and Inspector-General of Hospitals who, being civilians with private practices, devoted little time to their military duties.

Foreign Corps

As late as 1813 one member in eight of the British army was a foreigner, ranging from earnest Germans or French royalists who enlisted as a way of attempting to free their country, to ex-prisoners of war who had enrolled to escape the prison-camps. During the Revolutionary Wars Britain had supported a vast number of 'emigrant corps', some of excellent quality but others quite wretched. Almost all units

A popular art-form, commemorative medals were struck in many countries. This fine specimen depicts 'Lord Wellington' in the pre-1811 British staff uniform, with battle-honours on the reverse up to 1812.

'Last Monday the Buckinghamshire Militia, with their wives and children, were entertained with a plentiful dinner of roasted beef and plum pudding, in the barrack-yard, at Eastbourne, by their Colonel, Earl Temple, according to annual custom. The allowance of strong beer to each man was three pints; to their wives two pints each; and a pint to each of their children. Grinning through a horse-collar, and a variety of other rustic sports, formed the amusement of the afternoon.'
(*Public Ledger*, 4 October 1808.)

were dissolved by the Peace of Amiens, but other 'foreign corps' were enrolled at a later date: excellent Swiss units such as the Regiments de Meuron, de Roll and de Watteville, the Minorca Regiment (taken into the line as the 97th Queen's Germans), the Anglo-Portuguese Loyal Lusitanian Legion (transferred to Portuguese service in 1811), the Chasseurs Britanniques (a relic of the older emigrant corps), but most importantly the superb King's German Legion. This corps was formed from George III's exiled Hanoverian subjects in 1803, eventually growing in size to include ten line battalions, two light battalions (riflemen), five cavalry regiments and both foot and horse artillery. Throughout the Peninsular War and at Waterloo the Legion maintained a record as good as any part of the army, despite the dilution of its original national composition by the enrollment of many nationalities, as new recruits from Hanover could not be obtained due to the French occupation.

Militia

The statutory home-defence force was the Militia, a series of county infantry battalions embodied in wartime and recruited partially by voluntary enlistment and, when insufficient volunteers were forthcoming, by a ballot from among the county's able-bodied male inhabitants (men thus conscripted did not *have* to serve: they could avoid it by providing a 'substitute', i.e., hiring a man to serve in their place). In wartime the Militia was embodied permanently, and almost always served in garrisons away from the county in which it was raised, to avoid any conflict of loyalty if called upon to act against rioting civilians; and from 1805 militiamen were encouraged to volunteer for regular service, providing the army with recruits of a generally higher standard and who were already experienced with arms and used to discipline. The size of each county's regiment was calculated from the population, which related to the 'quota' of men required; in Scotland the Militia was not embodied until 1797. Uniforms were like those of the regular infantry.

Fencibles

Fencible corps (a term derived from 'de-fencible') were in effect regular infantry battalions and light cavalry regiments, recruited in the ordinary way, but for home service only; they could not be sent out of the country without the consent of all concerned. The fears of some fencibles that they were to be 'drafted', exacerbated by governmental indifference and lack

Grenadier of the Gloucestershire Militia, c.1805. Sergeant Hooper, shown here in a contemporary watercolour portrait, wears typical British infantry uniform with 'flank company' wings and a grenadier cap with white plume.

The King's German Legion: Hanoverians in British service. From left to right: grenadier of a line battalion; private of a light battalion; trooper of 3rd Hussars, all in the post-1812 uniform. (Aquatint by I. C. Stadler after Charles Hamilton Smith, from the latter's Costume of the Army of the British Empire, *this print published on 2 April 1815. The uniforms are like those of the respective branches of the British army of which the K.G.L. was an integral part.)* ▶

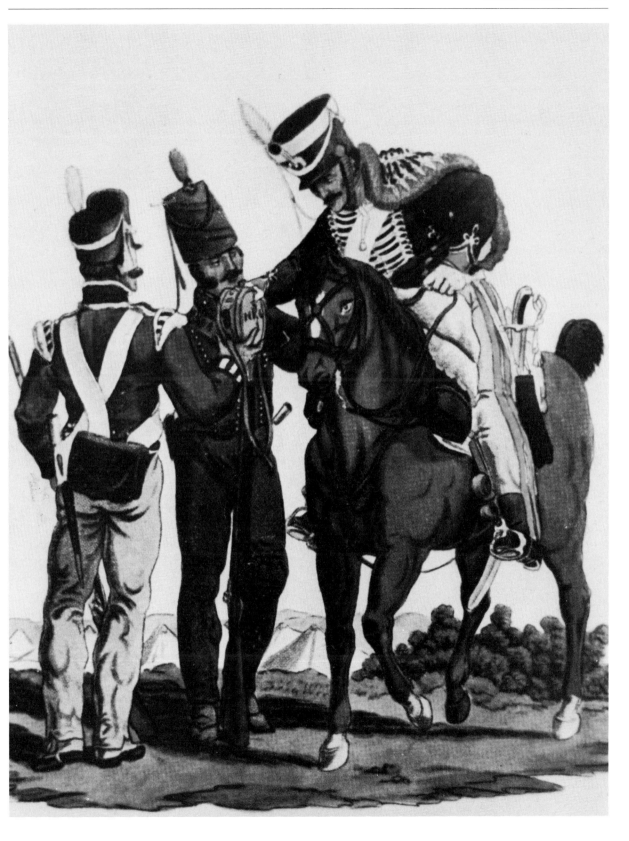

A feature of several European armies was the formation of units of amateur soldiers, generally for home defence. This illustrates a typical corps: Sergeant-Major Patrick Gould of the Royal Edinburgh Volunteers, one of the most famous units of 'gentlemen'-soldiers. The social status of the ordinary 'rankers' caused the earnest Gould infinite trouble, and once in exasperation he told a professional gentlemen that it was easier to drill five fools than one philospher! In this illustration he wears the blue regimental uniform with scarlet collar and cuff-flaps and a fur-crested 'round hat' with black and white plumes. (Mezzotint after George Watson)

A grenadier of the Bank of England Volunteers, 1804, a corps formed from the employees of that institution, wearing red coats with green facings. The strange and expansive gesture is in fact merely one of the poses of the musket-drill or 'Manual Exercise': 'Order Arms!' (Print by John Wallis Jnr.)

of understanding, led to a number of 'mutinies' or bouts of unrest in some corps, though most served with considerable distinction and did indeed volunteer for 'foreign' service, many in the 1798 rebellion in Ireland and even in Portugal and Egypt. The majority of corps were Scottish, though many English and some Welsh and Irish units existed, and all except the Royal Manx Fencibles (enrolled only for service in the Isle of Man) were disbanded by the time of the Peace of Amiens.

Volunteers

Defence of each locality was entrusted to the voluntarily formed military associations, part-time 'home guards' who drilled for one or two hours per week, but who filled an important role in their availability to assist the civil powers to suppress the periodic bouts of unrest which occurred, especially in the 1790s and at the time of the Luddite troubles of 1812. Initially the volunteers were predominantly middle-class and self-financing, serving without governmental assistance; but after almost all were disbanded upon the Peace of Amiens, a much larger and more supervised force was instituted by the government in 1803, and by late summer as an insufficient number of volunteers were thought to have enrolled, the Levy en Masse Act was passed to institute the compulsory training of every able-bodied man. It was never necessary to enact this, as under its slight threat of compulsion volunteers flooded to enroll so that by December 1803 the total numbered 380,193. County 'quotas' were set according to the population (thus Yorkshire had 22,580 men and Bute 90), most receiving pay, arms and financial assistance from the government, though some continued to be self-supporting. In 1808, in an attempt to abolish the very different 'terms of service' under which the corps had agreed to serve (some not willing to leave their own parish!), the force was largely replaced by the new Local

An officer's shoulder-belt plate of William Pitt's Cinque Ports Volunteers, 1803; the maker, the silversmith William Welch, was himself a member of the Exeter Volunteers at this time.

Militia, battalion-sized infantry units, though some volunteer corps existed until 1814. The mounted version, generally styled 'yeomanry', continued independent throughout and in many cases were not disbanded in 1814, as being mostly rurally based they were regarded as valuable for use in the suppression of civil discontent caused by the hardships of the agricultural working population. A smaller number of artillery units existed, but almost without exception they possessed no fieldpieces, but were trained instead to man the guns of the permanent shore-batteries around the coast.

Higher Organizations

Initially, the largest unit was the brigade of two or more infantry battalions, under the command of a 'brigadier' (not a rank but an appointment: a brigadier might be a general officer or the senior battalion-commander, when his battalion would be led by the second in command). Brigade staff consisted only of the brigadier's ADC and his brigade-major. When more than one brigade acted together, the senior brigadier took command. No higher structure existed: the Duke of York in the Netherlands divided his army into 'columns' of several brigades, but only on an *ad hoc* basis, while in Egypt Abercromby used the eighteenth-century practice of referring to 'lines'. The organization of two or more brigades into divisions, complete with artillery and commissariat, only appeared in the Danish expedition of 1807. Moore formed his army into four divisions of two infantry brigades, plus a cavalry brigade, and one of Wellesley's first acts on being given independent command in the Peninsula was to institute a fixed divisional system (18 June 1809), which was maintained throughout the war. Organization depended upon circumstances, but each division included two, three or four infantry brigades and their commissariat; artillery was not at first sufficiently plentiful to make permanent allocations, though companies became associated with particular divisions. An important feature of Wellington's system was the mixing of strong and weak, veteran and raw units, so that the presence of the strong, tried units raised the standard of the weaker. This was especially significant in 1815, when so much of Wellington's force was of mediocre quality. Initially in the Peninsula, Portuguese units were integrated at brigade level; this was not found satisfactory so thereafter the Portuguese formed their own brigades, and the brigades were integrated at divisional level. To supplement the division's own light companies, a rifle company (principally 5/60th but including foreign units) was attached to each division. Although a 'corps' system was never applied, each of Wellington's divisions resembled a French *corps d'armée* in that it was a self-supporting entity complete with staff, artillery, commissariat and reconnaissance facility, though but 6,000 strong.

Royal Navy

As Britain regarded itself as primarily a maritime nation, it was usual for the Royal Navy to take precedence in the allocation of resources, and only rarely (as at the height of

The Patriotic Fund at Lloyd's of London was established to raise revenue for the war, and is most famous for the presentation of superb quality swords to officers who had distinguished themselves in action. Accompanying each sword was a belt with a gilded clasp like that illustrated, bearing an allegorical scene of Britannia slaying serpents representing France and her allies.

the Peninsular War) did military expenditure exceed that on the Royal Navy. It is difficult to describe the Royal Navy as anything other than perhaps the most successful force of its era; for such was the excellence of its operation that even with ships that were not always the equal of their opponents', the navy's campaigns were a series of triumphs, to the extent that when outgunned frigates were defeated by the more powerful Americans in a series of comparatively minor 'single-ship' actions in the War of 1812, their defeats were greeted by almost hysterical outbursts in the press and Parliament: the navy had become so used to victory that they were believed to be virtually invulnerable. When it is considered that during the Revolutionary and Napoleonic Wars, only one British ship-of-the-line was lost and not retaken, as against the French loss in combat of some 90 capital ships, there appears validity in this belief.

The navy was administered by the Lords Commissioners of the Admiralty, headed by the 'First Lord' (usually a politician) and the 'First professional Lord' (a senior admiral), who with a tiny staff ran successfully the entire naval forces, the most invaluable member of staff being the Board Secretary from whom all orders were issued; the most famous and capable of these was Evan Nepean. All naval officers had to be adjudged competent before they were granted commissions, and had to have spent time at sea gaining a thorough grounding in their profession as midshipmen or master's mates; this was different from the commissioning procedures of other nations, whose officers were in many cases not half so well trained, and therein lies a major reason for the excellence of the British navy. Discipline was strict, enforced by the cat-o'-nine-tails, but it is interesting to note that even during the unrest of the mutinies at Spithead and the Nore, the seamen's complaints were directed towards their pay and living conditions rather than against the harshness of the discipline.

The Royal Navy expanded hugely during the period, especially in the number of frigates and smaller craft (in 1793 there were 160 ships-of-the-line and 230 smaller vessels; in 1815 the number was 208 and 633 respectively), and consequently the personnel rose in proportion, from 45,000 at the outbreak of war to 110,000 seamen and 20,000 marines in 1800, for example; though losses in action were comparatively small, disease and shipwreck accounted for some 85,000, necessitating a constant flow of new recruits. These were best obtained by volunteers enrolling for a cash bounty, but as this could not supply all requirements the Impress Service continued to be used, by which 'press-gangs' were permitted to seize any able-bodied man between the ages of 18 and 55, excluding apprentices. Although such

'I availed myself of this opportunity to write to my inestimable friend Mrs. B. At dusk the same Evening I lost sight of the Land's End. How torpid the Bosom, and how unworthy the name of Britain must be he, who can quit his country without offering up a fervent Prayer for its welfare. In taking a last look of its fading shores a variety of Sensations occupied my Mind, some of them painful; but I think the contrary predominated. A thousand instances of its many blessings and general Superiority over other Nations rushed upon my recollection, and it was not without a feeling of conscious pride that I called myself an Englishman.'
(*The Journal of an Army Surgeon during the Peninsular War* – Charles Boutflower, 40th Foot – privately published, n.d. Entry 18 August 1809.)

Cuthbert Collingwood, 1st Baron (1750–1810), Nelson's friend and deputy commander at Trafalagar, assuming control of the British fleet after Nelson's death, wearing admiral's uniform. (Engraving by W. Hogg after H. Howard)

The Trafalgar prayer of Horatio Nelson:

'May the great God whom I worship, grant to my country, and for the benefit of Europe in general, a great and glorious victory; and may no misconduct in any one tarnish it; and may humanity, after victory, be the predominant feature in the British fleet. For myself individually, I commit my life to him who made me, and may his blessing light upon my endeavours for serving my country faithfully. To him I resign myself, and the just cause which is entrusted me to defend. Amen.'

(*The Life and Service of Horatio Viscount Nelson*, Revd. J. Stanier Clarke and J. McArthur, London 1809, 1840 edn., III, p. 145.)

press-gangs preyed upon 'landsmen', trained seamen were the prime target, and naval ships commonly resorted to the interception of merchantmen at sea and the forcible enlistment of their best hands; the abduction of seamen from American vessels was one of the causes of the Anglo-American war. Although the impressment of land-dwellers was highly unpopular, professional seamen often found their duties in the Royal Navy lighter than in the merchant service, as naval ships had vastly larger crews giving less work for each man, though this was perhaps offset by the added dangers of combat and rigorous discipline. The equivalent of the non-commissioned officers of the army ranged from the men of special skills (sailmakers, assistant-carpenters, etc.) who were termed 'idlers' (as their skills precluded their standing watch), to 'petty officers' appointed

Seamen's uniform in many nations was unregulated, so that the ordinary nautical styles prevailed. This British bluejacket ot 1813 wears a typical blue tail-less jacket or 'roundabout', loose trousers and a straw 'round hat', which (especially in northern climes) was frequently tarred.

Death of Lieutenant Grant of the British Rifle Corps at Copenhagen, while detachments of the corps were serving as marines aboard the British fleet. Shown in the background is the usual protective screen of hammocks and netting positioned above the bulwarks of the ship, in this case HMS Isis. This print (after T. Crowther), executed almost a century after the event, shows how events were often sanitized in artworks; in actual fact J. A. Grant was killed when 'his head was taken off by a cannon ball as clean as if severed by a scimitar' (quoted in 'The Rifle Brigade', P. Groves, in Navy & Army Illustrated, London 1898, v, p. 322).

by the captain and to the 'warrant' officers appointed by the Admiralty or Navy Board, gunner, carpenter, boatswain, master-at-arms, etc. Still higher were those of 'wardroom rank', i.e., who shared the officers' quarters: the purser (who was financially responsible for the victuals and clothing aboard ship), the surgeon and master (or 'sailing master'), the latter the most important man after the captain, being responsible for all navigation and production of charts, etc.

Officers of the Royal Navy wore dark blue uniforms with white facings, breeches and waistcoat and gold lace, and bicorn hats; the ordinary sailors had no regulated uniform but generally wore civilian seafarers' clothing, often including a blue tail-less jacket and the universal 'round hat', either in plain straw (for hot climates) or with a covering of tar. Each ship had a complement of Royal Marines, the navy's military force, who wore an infantry-style uniform in

Roderick Murchison, founder of British geology and propounder of the Silurian system, recounts from his service in the 36th Foot:

'When halting at a bivouac before we reached Vimieira [sic], a Portuguese volunteer on horseback coolly unfolded before myself and others a large piece of brown paper, in which he had carefully folded up like a sandwich several pairs of *Frenchmen's ears*, his occupation having been to follow us, and to cut off all these appendages from men who were thoroughly well "kilt" – doubtless to produce them in coffee-houses in Lisbon as proofs of the number of the enemy he had slain!'

(*Life of Sir Roderick I. Murchison Bart.*, A. Geike, London 1875, I, pp. 35–6.)

Many photographs of Napoleonic veterans exhibit in old age the character and clear gaze of youth. The 10th Earl of Dundonald (1775–1860), better-known as Thomas Cochrane, was perhaps the most audacious and successful frigate-captain in history, whose career with the Royal Navy led to his nickname 'The Sea Wolf'. Despite a career of unrelieved success, his radical political views earned the resentment of the Ministry and he was stripped of rank after being unjustly convicted of complicity in the great 'Stock Exchange Fraud' of 1814. He was not pardoned until 1832, having in the intervening period commanded the navies of several infant South American states, with equal success.

red with blue facings (which replaced the original white facings when the corps was granted the title 'Royal' in 1802), and a black 'round hat'. They acted as sharpshooters in action, or led the hand-to-hand combat which occurred when ships were boarded, and formed the nucleus of the landing-parties which were frequently deployed (to great effect) when naval personnel executed raids on the enemy coastline.

The navy's role in the victory over France was crucial; best-known are the great battles, culminating with Trafalgar, in which the British consistently out-fought their opponents; but of equal significance was the 'war of commerce' which destroyed almost completely France's maritime trade. Whereas Napoleon's 'Continental System', aimed at strangling British trade, was a colossal failure, the British 'Orders in Council' which responded, enforced by the

naval blockade of enemy ports, were a total success, and dependent almost entirely upon the Royal Navy. Equally important was their support for the land operations; for geographical reason Britain had to transport its armies to the seat of war by sea, for which naval escorts were required, and the maintenance of maritime supply-routes to Lisbon and latterly Santander was vital for the successful conclusion of the Peninsular War. Without the Royal Navy, the army's victories would not have been possible.

Notes
1. *Weekly Political Register*, 9 November 1811.
2. *Lectures on the Tactics of Cavalry*, Count von Bismarck, 1827; note by the translator, Ludlow Beamish, an experienced officer of the King's German Legion, London edn, p. 134.
3. Wellington to Lord John Russell, 31 July 1826; see *Wellington's Army*, Sir Charles Oman, London 1912, p. 104.

4. *The Creevey Papers*, Thomas Creevey, ed. J. Gore, London 1934, p. 404.
5. *Diary of Campaigns in the Peninsula*, W. Swabey, orig. in *Proceedings of the Royal Artillery Institution*; reprinted London 1984, p. 176.

References
From the vast literature concerning Britain during the Napoleonic Wars, the following are among the most accessible and relevant:
Barthorp, M. J. *British Cavalry Uniforms*, Poole 1984.
— *British Infantry Uniforms*, Poole 1982.
Emsley, C. *British Society and the French Wars*, London 1979.
Fortescue, Hon. Sir John. *History of the British Army*, London, from 1899.
Fosten, B. *Wellington's Heavy Cavalry*, London 1982.
— *Wellington's Infantry I* and *II*, London 1981–2.
— *Wellington's Light Cavalry*, London 1982.
Fox, K. O. *Making Life Possible*, Kineton 1982 (military aid to civil power).
Gates, D. *The British Light Infantry Arm 1790–1815*, London 1987.
Glover, M. *Wellington as Military Commander*, London 1968 (much on the army in general in addition to Wellington's generalship).

— *Wellington's Army in the Peninsula*, Newton Abbot 1977.
— Glover, R. *Britain at Bay*, London 1973 (defence against invasion).
— *Peninsular Preparation: the Reform of the British Army 1795–1809*, Cambridge 1963.
Haythornthwaite, P. J. *British Infantry in the Napoleonic Wars*, London 1987.
— *Wellington's Military Machine*, Tunbridge Wells 1989.
— *Wellington's Specialist Troops*, London 1988.
Lavery, B. *Nelson's Navy: The Ships, Men and Organisation 1793–1815*, London 1989.
Lawson, C. C. P. *History of the Uniforms of the British Army*, vols. IV, London 1966, V, London 1967.
Oman, Sir Charles. *Wellington's Army*, London 1912 (very important: a companion to the same author's *History of the Peninsular War*).
Pope, D. *Life in Nelson's Navy*, London 1981 (the best modern study).
Rogers, H. C. B. *Wellington's Army*, London 1979.

HANOVER

History

Hanover occupied a unique position among the German states by virtue of the accession of the Elector of Hanover to the throne of Great Britain in 1714. Despite the close connection, however, the two states were united but remained separate entities, linked by a common ruler. Hanoverian troops fought alongside the British in the campaigns of the mid-eighteenth century (as they had under Marlborough's command before the Hanoverian succession to the British throne), and the existence of Hanover as a possession of the king had considerable bearing upon the foreign policy of British governments. The main factors that affected Hanover during the Revolutionary and Napoleonic Wars were the status of the Electorate as a vulnerable outpost of the British royal family, and the jealousy felt by Prussia over its increasing prestige. Hanoverian troops served with the Allied forces in the early campaigns, but the withdrawal of Prussia from the war by the Treaty of Basel in 1795 compelled Hanoverian neutrality, as its position was untenable without support. At Bonaparte's instigation Hanover was occupied briefly by Prussia in 1801, but at the

peace which ended the Revolutionary Wars Hanover was actually increased in size by the addition of the bishopric of Osnabrück. After the collapse of the Peace of Amiens Hanover was indefensible and was occupied by France under the Convention of Sulingen. Napoleon used Hanover to tempt the Prussians into neutrality, suggesting that they take over the Electorate, but after the defeat of Prussia in 1806 southern Hanover was incorporated into the new kingdom of Westphalia, and the northern portion added to France in 1810. The Hanoverian leaders and people were resentful of their loss of independence and many thousands emigrated to continue the fight against Napoleon in foreign armies, principally in the superb King's German Legion of the British Army; and when the 'war of liberation' followed Napoleon's defeat in Russia, Hanover was freed and formed an army which assisted in Napoleon's final overthrow. At the Congress of Vienna British ministers were concerned to keep British interests separate from those of Hanover (from the beginning of the joint sovereignity there had been political friction in Britain about Hanoverian interests deciding British foreign policy), and at the Congress Hanover was raised from the status of electorate to that of a kingdom. Not until 1819 was a parliamentary-style government instituted, the 85-member estate established in 1814 merely acting as a façade for rule by the leading families, as had occurred before the collapse of 1803, executive power being concentrated in the hands of a *Statthalter* or viceroy appointed to rule in Hanover in the British king's stead. The close connection between Britain and Hanover was ended in 1837 with the death of William IV, who was succeeded in Britain by Queen Victoria; as under Hanoverian law a woman could not succeed, the throne passed to Ernest Augustus, Duke of Cumberland, George III's fifth and most unstable son.

Army (cockade: black)

There were in effect two Hanoverian armies, that existing before 1803 and that formed after the liberation; there was no continuity of unit-lineage between the two. Although Hanoverian uniform and equipment in both periods resembled those of the British army (save for the yellow sashes worn by officers instead of the British crimson), the Hanoverian army was totally separate, having its own administration, establishment and commanders.

Infantry: pre-1803

The infantry originally comprised the foot guards and line regiments, each of two battalions of one grenadier and five musketeer companies; when deployed in the Netherlands in the first campaign the grenadiers were detached and united into composite battalions, and the regiments were organized for field service into two battalions of four musketeer companies each, about 150 strong. Other regiments retained their grenadiers but had five-company battalions plus a regimental depot company. From 1798 each battalion had one grenadier and three musketeer companies. There had been fifteen line regiments, but in 1787 the 14th and 15th were transferred to the service of the British East India Company, and a new 14th was raised as light infantry in 1793; there also existed *Jäger* companies. The 9th and 12th Regiments were disbanded upon the reduction of the army in 1798.

Infantry uniform was of British style, red coats with coloured facings and bicorn hats; British-style closed jackets and the 'stovepipe' shako were adopted in 1800–01. Grenadiers wore fur caps, as in the British army; officers' lace was silver for all but the foot guards, which had gold. Facing-colours were: foot guards, 2nd Regiment: blue; 1st and 10th Regiments dark green; 3rd and 11th black; 4th and 13th light blue; 5th and 12th yellow; 6th and 7th light green; 8th and 9th white. The new 14th Light Infantry wore grey faced light green with yellow buttons, and Austrian-style *Korséhuts* (which also appear to have been worn by the line regiments in the Netherlands); *Jägers* had similar hats and green uniforms with yellow or buff breeches and black leather equipment. The *Landwehr* (militia) battalions wore ordinary infantry uniform with white facings, and garrison battalions red facings.

Cavalry: pre-1803

The cavalry, equipped with Hanoverian horses which enjoyed a high reputation, was especially known for the excellence of its training and discipline. The regiments comprised the Lifeguard (*Leib-Regiment*) and ten line regiments, each of four squadrons of two companies each. In the Netherlands in 1794 the regiments deployed each contributed two field squadrons, each about 150 strong; four squadrons were united to form each 'Combined Regiment' for active service. After Hanover's withdrawal from the war, all regiments were reduced to two squadrons each. The uniform comprised blue coats with regimental facings (the *Leib-Regiment* wore red coats in imitation of the British Life Guards), with bicorn hats with white plumes with yellow base for the rank-and-file, and yellow tip for officers. Facings-colours were: *Leib-Regiment*, 1st, 9th and 10th red, 2nd, 4th, 5th and 8th white; 3rd, 6th and 7th yellow; buttons were white for the 1st, 3rd–7th and 10th and yellow for the remainder. Regiments 1–4 were styled 'Cavalry' and 5–8 Dragoons; the 9th (Queen's) Light Dragoons and 10th (Prince of Wales's) Light Dragoons bore titles like those of the British cavalry regiments bearing the same numbers, and had the peak-less, false-fronted light dragoon cap as worn by the British light dragoons in the 1770s, though it is possible that the British Tarleton helmet was adopted towards the end of the period. Horse-furniture was blue with white lace edging for all except the *Leib-Regiment*, which had red.

Artillery and Engineers: pre-1803

The Artillery Regiment originally comprised two battalions of five companies each; in the Netherlands the artillery was organized in three 'divisions', two of fourteen guns (ten 6pdrs, the rest 4pdrs) and two heavy howitzers, and a 'horse division' of four 3pdrs and two 7pdr howitzers. In addition

Hanoverian Waterloo Medal, silver with dark red ribbon with light blue edges; this example named to Soldat *(private)*

Johann Jürgen Brammer of the Lüneburg Landwehr *Battalion.*

Bronze Medal for veterans of the King's German Legion, awarded by Hanover for those in

British service from 1803–14. White ribbon with yellow edges.

each infantry regiment had a battery of six light guns. Organization varied until by the end of the Revolutionary Wars the artillery comprised three foot batteries (six 6pdrs and two 7pdr howitzers each), two horse batteries (six 6pdrs, four 3pdrs and two 7pdr howitzers) and one reserve battery (six 12pdrs).

The artillery wore British-style uniform of lightish blue coats with red facings, yellow lace and bicorn hats. The engineers (a corps of officers) wore the same but with darker blue coats and gold lace; the rank-and-file of the engineer services had the same colouring but with yellow epaulettes and distinctive head-dress: pontooneer and pioneer companies with black 'round hats' upturned at the back and bearing crossed-anchors and crossed-axes badges respectively, and the Sapper and Miner company with peak-less light infantry caps with either a black plume or drooping red horsehair mane at one side in the fashion of British light dragoons. Artificers wore plain 'round hats' and dark blue jackets with collars coloured to indicate their duties: tool-keepers red, coppersmiths straw-yellow, blacksmiths and saddlers blue. Drivers of the train service wore scarlet coats and breeches, either a short-skirted double-breasted jacket or long-skirted single-breasted coat, with blue facings and brassard on the left arm (bearing white 'GR') and either a plain black 'round hat' or a peaked cap with red crown and green band.

The Re-formed Army
Disbanded in July 1803, the Hanoverian army was not re-formed until the 'war of liberation'. It comprised ten regular battalions and a large number of *Landwehr* battalions, many of which served in the Waterloo campaign; they officially became independent of British control in February 1814. The King's German Legion discharged its non-Hanoverian personnel at the conclusion of the war in 1814, the remainder being intended to serve as the nucleus of the new Hanoverian army, but the onset of the 1815 campaign forestalled this process and the KGL was still part of the British Army at Waterloo.

Infantry: post-1813
The new regular units were styled 'field-battalions' (*Feld-Bataillone*), of which the Bremen, Verden, York, Lüneburg, Grubenhagen, Lauenburg, Calenburg and Hoya were present at Waterloo. From February 1815 each was linked with three *Landwehr* battalions to form new regiments (e.g.,

---

Garrison Orders, Bristol, 1811:
'The soldiers are again directed to avoid spitting on the pavement of the Cathedral during Divine Service; the Royal North Gloucester are reported the only regiment who pay attention to the previous orders on the subject.'
(*The Royal North Gloucester*, W. J. Cripps, London 1875, p. 129.)

Feld-Bataillon Verden was associated with *Landwehr* Battalions Verden, Bremelehe and Harburg), but in the field battalions continued to act independently. (Some confusion exists over the title of the field-battalion: the second unit in seniority raised in 1813 was titled 'Bremen-Verden', and was re-named 'Bremen' in early 1815. The new Battalion Verden was originally fourth in seniority, raised in 1813 under the title of Battalion Bennigsen.) The majority of field-battalions wore British infantry uniform of red jacket with coloured facings (blue for Bremen, green for Verden, etc.) and the 'Belgic' shako; the Lüneburg and Grubenhagen were 'light battalions' and were dressed in green with black facings, the former with 'stovepipe' shakos and cornflower-blue trousers for officers (the ordinary grey for other ranks), and the latter apparently with peak-less 'stovepipes' (or with folding peaks?) and grey trousers. Initially uniforms had been much more rudimentary: the Lüneburg, for example, wore a uniform like that of the Prussian *Landwehr*, a peaked cap and thigh-length *litewka* in dark green, with sky-blue cap-band and facings, and prior to the adoption of the 'stovepipe' light infantry cap the 'Belgic' shako was worn as the first replacement of the peaked cap. (Battalion Bennigsen was issued with white 'Belgic' shakos manufactured for the British Army in India!) There was also a *Jäger* corps (*Feldjägerkorps von Kielmannsegge*), formed in spring 1813, its two original companies increasing to four by October 1813; it was disbanded in September 1814 but was reformed in 1815 and fought at Waterloo. It wore dark green jackets and peaked caps with light green facings, grey trousers and black belts, and was armed with rifles.

In 1814 27 (later 30) *Landwehr* battalions were raised, each of four companies (without grenadiers or light infantry), titled Münden, Northeim, Osterode, Hanover, Hameln, Alfeld (later Einbeck), Hildesheim, Peine, Goslar (later Salzgitter), Celle, Gifhorn, Ulzen, Lüneburg, Harburg, Lüchow, Stade, Ottendorf, Bremervörde, Verden, Bremerlehe (later Osterholz), Hoya, Osnabrück, Bentheim, Meppen, Nienburg, Quackenbrück, Iburg (later Melle); and later Springe, Diepholz and Ratzeburg. These were intended to wear British-style infantry uniform in red with blue facings, 'Belgic' shakos for officers and 'stovepipes' for the other ranks, but because of shortages of the correct uniforms blue uniforms faced red were used, and even as late as Waterloo the Bremervörde, for example, appears to have worn green jackets with dark blue trousers.

Cavalry: post-1813
Whereas the re-formed infantry acquitted themselves with credit at Waterloo, the cavalry was less distinguished and in one case brought shame upon the army. There were three hussar regiments: Lüneburg (Prince Regent's), Bremen and Verden, and Duke of Cumberland's, formed in 1813; they wore British-style hussar uniform, the former with blue dolmans faced scarlet, scarlet pelisses and white lace, and the other two regiments dark green dolmans faced scarlet with yellow lace, the Bremen and Verden with scarlet pelisses and the Duke of Cumberland's with dark green; the latter wore

yellow-laced shakos and the others brown busbies with blue (Prince Regent's) or green bags. Each was composed initially of three squadrons, later four, each of about 150 men in two companies. When ordered to advance at Waterloo the Duke of Cumberland's declined to obey and the whole regiment marched off to Brussels spreading news of Wellington's defeat. As a punishment the corps, composed of wealthy volunteers who had supplied their own horses, was dispersed and the men distributed among the various Allied formations as forage-escorts and to perform other mundane tasks.

Artillery: post-1813

The re-formed artillery wore a uniform like that of the British Royal Artillery (blue with red facings, yellow lace and 'Belgic' shako), with only their red-over-white plumes and yellow sashes (officers) distinguishing them from the British. Two foot batteries were present at Waterloo.

References

Hofschröer, P. *The Hanoverian Army of the Napoleonic Wars*, London 1989.
Lawson, C. C. P. *History of the*

Uniforms of the British Army, vol. VI, London 1966 (contains an account of the Hanoverian army pre-1803).

THE HANSEATIC STATES

History

The Hanse Ports of the north German seaboard were the last vestige of the powerful medieval trading confederation of the Hanseatic League, an alliance of independent city-states. Hamburg, Bremen and Lübeck retained their independence as 'free cities' despite the eclipse of their power, and even when the archbishopric of Bremen was acquired by the Elector of Hanover (King George I of Great Britain) in 1720 the independence of Bremen city was recognized, and its lands even increased in 1803. Their independence ended with annexation by France in 1806, but the city-states were restored to their previous freedom by the Congress of Vienna. During the period of French occupation, personnel and resources were impressed by the French (the French 127th Line was formed in Hamburg, for example), but during the 'war of liberation' the city-states formed units for the Allied forces.

Army (cockade: white with red cross)

Until 1810 the Hanseatic cities maintained small units for their own internal security; Hamburg, for example, had an infantry regiment of ten companies of between 1,400 and 1,900 men, and small dragoon and artillery contingents, the city uniform-colour being red with blue facings; the artillery wore dark blue faced red. (Red cloth intended for their uniform was appropriated for the French 9th *Chevau-Léger-Lanciers*, hence the unit's nickname, 'Red Lancers of Hamburg'.)

Hamburg was liberated by a Russian force on 18 March 1815, and two days later the city was asked to raise a corps in

War Medal of the Hanse Towns for the 1813 campaign: silver, with red-and-white ribbon.

the Allied interest: the result was the Hanseatic Legion (*Hanseatische Legion*) of three infantry battalions (two of volunteers from Hamburg, the 3rd from Lübeck, liberated some days before Hamburg), two artillery batteries and two *Jäger* companies (one incorporated in each of the 1st and 2nd infantry battalions); the total strength was about 3,800. Though Hamburg was re-occupied by the French, the Hanseatic Legion remained with the Army of the North and served throughout the 1813–14 campaign; on 5 December 1813 Lübeck was again recaptured, and Hamburg remained in French hands until the armistice of April 1814. The Russians liberated Bremen on 5 October 1813; on the 28th a Bremen corps was raised by two officers, von Eelking and von Weddig, comprising an infantry battalion, a *Jäger* company and a volunteer cavalry squadron, which served with Wallmoden's Corps in the Netherlands and northern France; in 1815 the cavalry was attached to the Prussian 6th *Uhlans*. There existed in addition home-defence units of the previous style, the Hamburg *Burgergarde*, which in later 1813 was enlarged by volunteers from the outer Hanse towns and rechristened the *Hanseatische Burgergarde*.

Initially the Hanseatic Legion wore simple soft caps, *litewkas* and overalls in dark green, and later a mixture of Prussian and Russian styles. The cavalry were *Uhlans* in green faced crimson and *czapkas*; the infantry ultimately wore

green Russian infantry uniform with red facings, the Russian 1812 *kiwer* and white-over-red plume; the foot artillery the same with black plume and sky-blue facings; and the horse artillery dark green hussar uniform faced sky-blue, with red-plumed French shako. The Bremen infantry wore black or dark grey Russian infantry uniform with red facings and shakos like the Hanseatic Legion; the *Jägers* dark green faced light green, and a 'round hat' with light green woollen crest; and the cavalry a black or dark grey *litewka* faced red, and black *czapka*, which colouring was retained in the Prussian 6th *Uhlans*. The *Hanseatische Burgergarde* wore light grey greatcoats, dark blue trousers with light blue stripe and the British 'Belgic' shako. The cavalry of the *Hamburger Burgergarde* wore dark blue *litewka* and overalls, light blue facings and dark blue *czapka*; the Lübeck contingent of the *Burgergarde* had dark green *litweka* and overalls with red piping, and dark green cloth caps, their cavalry having similar caps in dark blue with light blue band, dark blue pelisse and overalls, and were armed with lances bearing white pennons with the red Hanseatic cross, a design worn on the cockade of all these troops.

References

The uniform of the Hanseatic troops may be found most conveniently in the *Bulletin of the British Model Soldier Society* (London), issue 3/1986.

HESSE-CASSEL

History

Hesse-Cassel (German, *Hessen-Kassel*) was a landgraviate south of Hanover of some military pretentions: an ally of Britain in the Seven Years War, Landgrave Frederick II (ruling 1760–85) hired some 17,000 of his troops to Britain to fight in the American War of Independence, the payment for which he used to improve the economic and intellectual resources of the state. The next landgrave, William IX (ruling 1785–1821) joined the Revolutionary War against France, but made peace by the Treaty of Basel in 1795. For the loss in 1801 of his possessions on the left bank of the Rhine he received in return some ex-French territory around Mainz, and was elevated to the rank of elector as William I. In 1806 he made a treaty of neutrality with Napoleon but the latter, suspecting William's intentions, invaded Hesse-Cassel, expelled the elector and added the state of Westphalia. In 1809 the dispossessed elector raised a military force for Austrian service, the *Kur-Hessen Freikorps* (*Kur-Hessen* = electoral Hesse), of very mixed composition,

▲ *Badge of the Order of Military Virtue of Hesse-Cassel, founded by Frederick II on 25 February 1769 and re-titled as the Military Order of Merit on 22 October 1820: a reward for military distinction restricted to officers. Gold with white enamel cross; ribbon sky-blue with silver lace edging.*

◄

Breast-star of the Order of the Golden Lion of Hesse-Cassel, founded on 14 August 1790 by Frederick II, and enlarged by William I on 1 January 1818.Silver star with red-and-white striped lion on a blue disc, surrounded by a scarlet circlet.

which saw some service in the 1809 campaign and was then disbanded. In November 1813 the 'war of liberation' allowed William I to return to his capital and his lands were restored by the Congress of Vienna, but the restoration was in many ways a retrograde step as both William I and his son William II (who succeeded in 1821) were determined to return Hesse-Cassel to its previous condition, abolishing all French reforms and dissolving all representative assemblies until a revolt in 1830 which compelled William II to adopt a liberal constitution and retire to Hanau, appointing as regent his son Frederick William, whose reign was only slightly less troubled and repressive than his father's.

Army: pre-1806 (cockade: white with red centre)

The Hesse-Cassel army wore a uniform very like that of Prussia, except for the national distinctions of cockade and the officers' mixed silver and crimson sashes. Grenadiers had metal-fronted mitre caps, fusiliers similar caps but smaller, and musketeers bicorns; the infantry wore dark blue coats with regimental facings, the eighteenth-century open-fronted coat being changed to one with closed lapels prior to 1806. Regiments comprised one grenadier and two musketeer battalions, each of four companies; the grenadiers were often detached and combined into composite grenadier units in wartime, those existing in the early Revolutionary Wars being dispersed in October 1795. Regimental details were as follows: *Garde*: red facings, white buttons, lace and grenadier-cap fronts; *Garde Grenadiers*: red facings, white buttons and lace, musketeers with yellow mitres with white-metal plate, grenadiers with fur caps with yellow bag; *Leib-Regiment* (re-named Kurfurst 1803): yellow facings, white buttons and lace; *Erbprinz* (re-named Kurprinz 1803, von Wurmb 1805): light crimson facings, white buttons, crimson grenadier caps with brass plate; *Prinz Karl* (Landgraf Karl 1805): red facings, yellow buttons, red grenadier caps with brass plate; *Von Kospoth Fusiliers* (von Biesenrodt 1801, Kurprinz 1805): white facings, yellow buttons, buff fusilier caps with brass plate, black fur grenadier caps with buff bag; *Von Lossberg Fusiliers* (von Linsingen 1799, von Biesenrodt 1805): orange facings, white buttons, black fur grenadier caps with orange bag; *Von Ditfurth* (von Hanstein 1792, disbanded 1795): yellow facings and buttons, black fur grenadier caps with yellow bag; *Schlotheim Fusiliers* (raised 1799 from depot companies): green uniform faced red, white buttons; *Jägers*: green uniform faced crimson, white buttons; garrison regiments uniformed as infantry in blue with facings: Regiments von Porbeck and Matthias red, von Colson crimson, von Knoblauch yellow, Köhler white.

Cavalry regiments also wore Prussian-style uniform, all with bicorns save the hussars: *Garde du Corps*: straw-yellow coat faced crimson, silver lace, iron cuirass; *Gendarmes*: white coat faced poppy-red, yellow buttons, black cuirass; *Leib-Dragoons*: light blue faced poppy-red, yellow buttons; *Prinz Friedrich Dragoons*: light blue faced yellow, white buttons; *hussars*: yellow dolman and breeches, light blue facings and pelisse, white buttons and braid, black busby with yellow bag.

Artillery wore infantry-style uniform with crimson facings and yellow lace. *Land-Regiments* (Militia) were raised in 1794, named after the towns in which they were recruited, wearing unlaced infantry uniform with facings: Cassel poppy-red, Eschwege crimson, Hersfeld white, Hanau red, Marburg yellow, Ziegenhain black, Rinteln buff, Rheinfels (disbanded 1794) and Geismer; all had white waistcoats and breeches save Ziegenhain and Rinteln (buff) and Marburg (yellow). White waistcoat, breeches and leather equipment were common to the rest of the army.

Kur-Hessen Freikorps

The Kur-Hessen 'Legion' was only nine companies strong, numbering less than a thousand, of whom almost a quarter were Saxons, a quarter Prussians, 100 Bavarians and among other nationalities included were Bohemians, Poles, French and even one British officer; only fourteen officers and 99 other ranks were Hessian. The Garde Grenadier Battalion (3 companies) wore Austrian grenadier caps with red bag, dark blue uniform with red facings and white buttons; the light infantry battalion (3 companies) had Austrian shakos, dark green jacket and breeches with red facings and white buttons; the *Leib*-Dragoons (one squadron) Austrian cavalry helmets with red-over-white crest, light blue jacket, poppy-red facings and white buttons; the hussars (one squadron) Austrian infantry shakos, yellow dolman, light blue pelisse and facings, and white buttons; the artillery (one company) infantry uniform in dark blue with crimson facings and yellow buttons.

The 1813 Army

The re-created army was dressed in Prussian style, though the regulations could not be implemented fully until after the war. Indicative of the Elector's desire to turn back the clock was the re-introduction of the 'queue' as late as 1816, long abandoned by every other army in Europe. The infantry wore Prussian shakos and dark blue jackets; each line regiment comprised one fusilier and two musketeer battalions, each of four companies, the former with black belts instead of the white of the remainder, plus two grenadier companies (detached to form composite grenadier battalions). Regimental details were: *Schweizer Leibgarde*: light blue coat, poppy-red facings and white buttons; *Leib-Grenadier-Garde*: poppy-red facings, white buttons, bearskin caps with white-metal plate; *Garde Grenadiers*: as *Leib-Grenadier-Garde*, but the two grenadier companies only with bearskins, the musketeers with shakos; *Regiment Kurfurst*: yellow facings and buttons; *Regiment Kurprinz*: white facings, yellow buttons; *Regiment Landgraf Karl*: red facings, yellow buttons; *Regiment von Solms*, crimson facings, white buttons; *Jägers*: as line but green coats faced red, white buttons, black belts.

The cavalry comprised the following: *Garde du Corps* (one squadron): straw-yellow jacket faced poppy-red, white buttons, black leather Bavarian-style *Raupenhelm* with black crest; *Garde Hussars* (one squadron): dark blue dolman and pelisse, poppy-red facings, white breeches, buttons and lace, black busby with red bag; *Leib-Dragoons* (four squadrons): light blue jacket faced poppy-red, white buttons, Prussian shako; *Hussars* (four squadrons): as *Garde Hussars* but with shakos.

The artillery comprised two and a half batteries of foot and a half-battery of horse, wearing infantry-style uniform in dark blue with crimson facings, yellow buttons, shakos with brass crossed-cannon insignia, white breeches and black belts. Two *Landwehr* battalions were raised in each of the provinces in November 1813, forming three regiments; they wore plain Prussian shakos with an oilskin cover bearing a white *Landwehr* cross, dark blue *litewkas* with facings crimson, black and red for the 1st–3rd regiments respectively, white buttons and grey overalls.

Plumes throughout the army were coloured according to rank: white with red base for officers, white with red tip for rank-and-file, and white with red tip and base for NCOs.

References

Pivka, Otto von. *Napoleon's German Allies: Hessen-Darmstadt and Hessen-Kassel*, London 1982.

HESSE-DARMSTADT

History

The landgraviate of Hesse-Darmstadt had remained loyal to the Holy Roman Empire during the wars of the mid-eighteenth century, so in 1792 the landgrave, Louis X (1753–1830, son of Caroline 'the great landgravine') entered the war against France in the Imperial interest. In 1799 he was compelled to sign a treaty of neutrality, and in 1803 (having formally surrendered part of Hesse on the left bank of the Rhine which had been captured from him during the Revolutionary Wars) he received a much larger grant of land from the Duchy of Westphalia, including the bishopric of Worms and the Electorate of Mainz. Louis took Hesse-Darmstadt into the Confederation of the Rhine and adopted the title of Grand Duke of Hesse as Louis I. He joined the Allies after Leipzig, which enabled him to retain his title at the Congress of Vienna, though he was forced to concede some territory to Prussia and Bavaria, and to recognize the independence of Hesse-Homburg which had recently been incorporated into his possessions.

Army (cockade: black; white with red centre after 1807)

Initially, organization and uniform closely resembled those of the Prussian army. In the Revolutionary Wars two Hesse-Darmstadt contingents were deployed, one with the Austrians on the upper Rhine and one in the Netherlands; and in 1796–7 an infantry brigade served in British pay in the Trieste area. Facing-colours to the blue infantry uniform were: 1st *Leib-Battalion* crimson, 2nd orange, *Regiment Landgraf* white, *Regiment Erbprinz* pink, infantry depot battalion yellow, *Landregiment* light blue; yellow buttons save for the 1st *Leib* and *Regiment Landgraf*, white.

The military establishment was reconstructed in June 1803 following the acquisition of new territory, by which one infantry brigade was established from each of the three provinces (Starkenburg, Upper Hesse and Westphalia). Each brigade comprised two infantry battalions (in dark blue coats) and one fusilier battalion (light infantry in green coats), each battalion of four companies. Titles and composition of the brigades were: *Leib-Brigade*: *Leib*-Regiment, *Leib*-Fusilier Battalion, red facings; *Landgraf-Brigade*: Regiment Landgraf, Fusilier Battalion Landgraf, light blue facings; *Erbprinz-Brigade*: Regiment Erbprinz, Fusilier Battalion Erbprinz, pale yellow facings. Each province also formed a 'reserve brigade' bearing the provincial name, composed of a *Landregiment* (militia) and a garrison regiment.

Breast-star of a Commander of the Order of Louis of Hesse-Darmstadt, founded in 1807 by Grand Duke Louis I as the Order of Merit. Silver star with black centre bearing gold inscription, gold cross with arms enamelled black (inside) and red (outside), with green wreath.

When the state was elevated to a grand duchy the units were retitled: *Leib-Garde Brigade*: *Leib-Garde* Regiment, *Garde-Fusilier* Battalion; *Leib-Brigade*: *Leib*-Regiment, 1st *Leib*-Fusilier Battalion; *Brigade Gross- und Erbprinz*: Regiment Gross- und Erbprinz, 2nd *Leib*-Fusilier Battalion. In March 1812 a light infantry regiment was formed from the Garde- and 1st *Leib*-Fusilier Battalions, designated the *Garde-Fusilier* Regiment from June 1813; and in January 1814 a new infantry regiment, Prinz Emil, was formed (pink facings). The Leib-Garde and *Leib*-Regiment served with the French in 1806–7 (the 1st Leib-Fusiliers at Jena) and in 1809 at Aspern and Wagram; Regiment Gross- und Erbprinz served in 1806 and then in the Peninsula, at Talavera and as part of the garrison at the final assault of Badajoz. The *Leib-Garde* and *Leib*-Regiment served in the Russian campaign (the former being destroyed) and in 1813; the re-formed *Leib-Garde* and *Garde* Fusiliers served with the Allies after Leipzig. In December 1813 a volunteer *Jäger* corps was created, four companies strong, and disbanded at the end of the 1814 campaign; they wore green with red facings. (An earlier *Jäger* corps, dressed in Prussian style in green faced black, had been disbanded about 1796). Bicorns continued to be worn by all infantry until 1809–10, when French-style shakos were adopted.

Hesse-Darmstadt raised a cavalry regiment of three squadrons in April 1790, these *Chevauxlegers* wearing dark green with red collar and otherwise black facings, and until about 1806 a peak-less cap with asymmetrical false front and black horsehair crest, similar to that worn by the British light dragoons in the third quarter of the eighteenth century. This was replaced by a Bavarian-style *Raupenhelm* with black crest and plume, and at the same time (in common with the rest of the army) the old open-fronted coats were replaced by shorter jackets with closed lapels. The *Chevauxlegers* participated in the famous 'charge of death' at Studianka, and were virtually destroyed in the 1812 campaign. The army's other cavalry units were not truly combatant units: the Grand Duke's ceremonial *Garde du Corps* troop, wearing bicorns and straw-yellow uniforms faced red; and a hussar-style gendarmerie unit wearing white dolman and mirliton, red facings, and light blue pelisse and breeches. The original two artillery companies were expanded to three in 1803, dressed in infantry uniform with black facings piped red.

References

Pivka, Otto von. *Napoleon's German Allies: Hessen-Darmstadt and Hessen-Kassel*, London 1982.

HOHENZOLLERN

History

The two principalities of Hohenzollern were among the most minor of German states, connected to the branch of the Hohenzollern family which ruled Prussia and ultimately the German Empire. In 1576 the Hohenzollern lands were divided to form the states of Hohenzollern-Hechingen and Hohenzollern-Sigmaringen, and from 1695 entered into a compact with Brandenburg that should either branch become extinct, rights to the territory were to revert to the other Hohenzollern prince and then to Brandenburg. Both states joined the Confederation of the Rhine, but not until the political unrest of 1848 did the princes Frederick William of Hohenzollern-Hechingen and Charles Anton of Hohenzollern-Sigmaringen abdicate in favour of the King of Prussia, which state absorbed the principalities. The most distinguished member of the families of the two Hohenzollern states was Prince Charles of Hohenzollern-Sigmaringen who became King of Roumania in 1881.

KINGDOM OF ITALY

History

Napoleon's disregard for the conditions of the Treaty of Lunéville was nowhere more evident than in northern Italy; instead of guaranteeing the independence of the Ligurian and Cisalpine (later Italian) Republics, both became satellites of France. After his coronation as Emperor of the French, Napoleon proposed to make his brother Joseph ruler of the Italian state, but on Joseph's declining the crown of the new kingdom, Napoleon took it himself and on 26 May 1805 in Milan Cathedral crowned himself King of Italy with the ancient iron crown of the Lombard kings, with the traditional words '*Dio mi l'ha dato; guai à chi la tocca!*' ('God hath given it to me; woe to him that touches it!'). On 7 June he appointed his stepson, Eugène de Beauharnais, as Viceroy of Italy to implement his commands: republicanism was henceforth suppressed, having been encouraged by France before the foundation of the Empire. The Kingdom of Italy was increased in size, Austria ceding part of Venezia, Istria and Dalmatia after Austerlitz, and in 1808 the border was extended south to the boundary of the Kingdom of Naples after the partition of the Papal States. Under Napoleon, Italy benefited by the adoption of French-style administration and law, but had her trade strangled by the consequences of the 'continental system' and was compelled to provide troops to Napoleon's army. The Italian forces served Napoleon with distinction, most notably at Maloyaroslavets; but the destruction of the Italian contingent in Russia precipitated the downfall of the French regime in Italy. As Napoleon's fortunes declined, Bavaria permitted Austrian forces to march through the Tyrol and down the valley of the Adige, not even Eugène's heroic defence being able to overcome the defection of Murat and a renewed growth of republicanism. Lord William Bentinck's landing at Leghorn on 8 March 1814 and his proclamation to the Italian people to rise and assert their freedom was the final blow; on 14 April Eugène signed an armistice at Mantua. The end of the Kingdom of Italy meant a return to the old order to a large extent; only the most beneficial aspects of Napoleonic administration were never completely extinguished.

'Repeated depredations have been recently committed, or attempted, by military invalids quartered in the
neighbourhood of Chelsea. James Moornson, invalid,
late of the 29th regiment, was charged on suspicion of
having committed divers felonies.

'Mr. M. Newland, Seymour-place, Chelsea, stated,
that about eight o'clock the preceding evening the
female servant came into his sitting room, and said
that men were attempting to get in at the back door.
Having provided himself with fire-arms, he went to the
back first floor window, and saw a man at the door,
which turned out to be the prisoner. Mr. N. threatened
to shoot him, and fired over his head, when prisoner
exclaimed that he cared for neither shot nor powder.
He was, however, secured; and some neighbours stated
they saw two others in the garden in his company.

'Prisoner said he had been drinking. Remanded.'
(*The Times*, 7 November 1814.)

Army (cockade: red, white and green)

The army was organized entirely on French lines, and
uniformed in virtually the same manner, substituting the
dark blue of France for dark green. Based upon the forces of
the Italian (ex-Cisalpine) Republic, Italian contingents
fought against Austria in 1805 and 1809, against Prussia in
1806, in the Peninsular War, in the 1812 campaign and in
Saxony in 1813; they were a solid, reliable body, markedly
different from the universally criticized Neapolitans. The
total force in 1812 amounted to some 90,000 men; of the
27,000 that went to Russia, some 25,000 perished, and by
1814 only a skeleton remained. After the surrender of 1814
the Austrians disbanded the army, rightly believing that its
remnant harboured dissidents clinging to the ideals of
Italian independence.

Royal Guard

Built upon the Presidential Guard of the Italian Republic, by
1808 the Italian Royal Guard comprised a battalion of
grenadiers, one of carabiniers, one of marines, a regiment of
vélites, two dragoon squadrons, four Guards of Honour
companies, and a company of horse artillery and artillery
train. By 1812 this had been expanded by an extra Guards of
Honour company (from Venice), a conscript regiment, a
corps of gendarmerie and a company of foot artillery and
train.

The infantry originally comprised a battalion of five
companies of grenadiers and a similar unit of *Cacciatori* (light
infantry, re-titled Carabiniers in 1809). Both wore uniforms
like those of the French Guard Grenadiers and *Chasseurs à
Pied*, with dark green replacing dark blue (long-skirted coat
with red cuffs and turnbacks, white lapels, buttons,
waistcoat and breeches, fur caps with plate, red plume and
epaulettes and white cap-cords for Grenadiers; red-fringed
green epaulettes, red over green plume and red-and-green
cap-cords for Carabiniers). The *Vélites*, a training-school for
men of good family to provide NCOs and officers for the line

in French style, comprised a battalion of Grenadier *Vélites*
and one of *Cacciatori Veliti* (later Carabiniers); their uniforms
and company-distinctions were like those of their parent
corps, but the coats white with green facings. The four-
battalion conscript regiment was the equivalent of the
French Young Guard; their conduct in Russia so impressed
Eugène that he re-titled them *Cacciatori*. They wore dark
green short jackets with red facings, green lapels, white
buttons and green-plumed shakos.

The Guard Dragoons (which generally accompanied
Eugène) were dressed exactly as the Dragoons of the French
Imperial Guard, but for white lace and buttons. The Guards
of Honour were recruited from noble families as a form of
cadet corps from which the rank-and-file graduated as
lieutenants after two years' service; officers held double rank,
so that (for example) lieutenants ranked as captains in the
other corps. Their dark green dragoon uniform had facings of
the company-colour, companies being titled from the areas
from which their recruits were drawn: Milan pink, Bologna
yellow, Brescia buff, Romagna scarlet and Venice orange.
Their brass dragoon helmets had a comb in the form of an
eagle, supporting a black caterpillar crest, with a white
turban bearing crowned 'N' on the front and a white plume;
white waistcoat and breeches. The Gendarmerie was dressed
like the French Elite Gendarmes, in blue coat with crimson
facings and a red-plumed peaked bearskin cap. The horse
artillery was dressed exactly as that of the French Imperial
Guard, but the train wore a grey jacket with dark green
facings and lace breast-loops, and a black *czapka* bearing
brass crossed cannon-barrels under the Iron Crown, and a
red plume. The foot artillery wore green coats with black
facings piped red, and bearskin caps with red plume and
cords; the train was dressed like that of the horse artillery but
with green-flapped cuffs instead of pointed cuffs. The
Marines (mostly Venetians and Dalmatians) wore dark
green *surtout* and breeches, red facings and waistcoat, white
buttons, and green plume and epaulettes for 2nd class
marines and red for 1st class, with a black 'round hat'
bearing a brass lozenge plate.

Infantry

Each of the seven line regiments comprised a depot and four
field battalions, each of four fusilier, one grenadier and one
voltigeur company; organization and company-distinctions
were like those of the French army, as were officers' rank-
markings except that metalwork was in silver. In 1806 the
original green uniform was replaced by white with facings as
below:

Regiment	Lapels	Collar	Cuffs	Cuff-flaps
1st	white	green	white	scarlet
2nd	scarlet	white	white	green
3rd	green	scarlet	green	scarlet
4th	white	scarlet	white	green
5th	scarlet	green	scarlet	green
6th	green	white	white	scarlet
7th	scarlet	scarlet	green	green

Voltigeurs had green plumes and epaulettes and grenadiers red; the latter could also wear a bearskin cap with red plume and cords and often a brass plate. In 1808 the original bicorn was replaced by a French shako with brass lozenge plate. In November 1811 two guns were attached to each unit, the gunners wearing a uniform like that of the regiment but in dark green with red facings and plume, with the transport platoon having dark green *surtouts* piped red, and green plumes.

The three (later four) light infantry regiments were organized like the line, in French style, the fusiliers being termed *chasseurs* (*cacciatori*) and the grenadiers, carabiniers. Their uniform was like that of the French light infantry but in dark green: short jacket with pointed lapels, green waistcoat and breeches, and facings: 1st Regiment yellow (including waistcoat), 2nd red, 3rd orange and 4th (formed 1811) crimson or wine-red. The shako was like that of the line with cords white for *chasseurs*, red for carabiniers and green for *voltigeurs*; company-distinctions as for the line, but carabiniers' bearskins had no plates. In 1806 a further light regiment was formed from the newly acquired territory, the Dalmatian Legion, later Regiment; it wore an Austrian-style single-breasted green jacket and Hungarian breeches, red facings (yellow collar for *voltigeurs*), white waistcoat, native sandals cross-gartered on the lower leg, and a 'Corsican hat' with green plume (red for carabiniers, yellow for *voltigeurs*), which colouring was retained when the infantry shako was adopted in 1808. Another unit formed in light infantry style was the Colonial Regiment, raised in 1803 as the *Legione Italiana*, virtually a penal corps into which vagrants and foreigners were conscripted; consisting only of fusiliers, it wore grey jackets with light green facings and shako-pompom.

Cavalry

In 1805 the Italian Repbulic's two hussar regiments were converted to the dragoon regiments *Napoleone* and *Regina*, each of four squadrons of two companies plus a depot company. Their French dragoon uniform was dark green with crimson and pink facings respectively, though in Spain the former wore coats of brown local cloth, faced red. Their brass dragoon helmets had a black horsehair mane and a green plume with facing-coloured tip. The *chasseur* regiments (*cacciatori a cavallo*) wore green long-tailed coats with white breast-loops with facings: 1st Regiment (*Real Italiano*) yellow, 2nd (*Principe Reale*, raised 1808) scarlet, 3rd (raised 1810) orange and 4th (raised 1811) crimson or wine-red. Waistcoat and breeches were dark green, and the head-dress initially

czapkas with black fur turban, replaced in 1811 by shakos with green plume with facing-coloured tip; élite companies wore black busbies with red plumes and white-metal shoulder-scales with white fringes. The Gendarmerie was organized on French lines, in three 'legions' of two squadrons, each of two companies; they wore dark green dragoon uniform with crimson facings, white buttons, buff waistcoat and breeches and red-plumed bicorns. Mounted companies had cavalry boots and dismounted companies white waistcoat and breeches and infantry gaiters.

Artillery and Supporting Services

The horse artillery regiment was uniformed like the light cavalry, in green with black facings, red piping and lace and green-over-black *czapka*-pompom; in 1811 they adopted red-plumed shakos. The three foot artillery battalions wore the uniform of the Guard foot artillery but with shakos, from 1810 with red plume and cords, and red cuffs; the train of both horse and foot artillery wore the uniform of the Guard train, adopting the shako in 1811. The engineer battalion comprised two miner and seven sapper companies, in foot artillery uniform save for cuffs piped red; they replaced the bicorn with the shako in 1812, and epaulettes and plume were yellow for sappers and red for miners. A train battalion of four (late six) companies was formed in 1808, dressed in reddish-brown jackets faced crimson; the 2nd Battalion (formed 1812 and annihilated in Russia) wore yellow facings. The original 'Corsican hat' was replaced by the shako in 1810. The engineer train company (formed 1807) which transported the siege-train wore a dark green *surtout* with black facings, white buttons and yellow lace and epaulettes, with a yellow-plumed bicorn; from about 1813 they adopted the uniform of the artillery train. Ambulance companies (formed 1811) wore red-brown jackets with dark grey facings, waistcoats and breeches with white buttons and a plain shako.

Auxiliaries

From December 1811 each province was authorized to form a French-style departmental reserve company, wearing infantry uniform in dark green with red facings, white lapels, breeches and waistcoat, and shako. The existing Invalid and Veteran battalions were amalgamated into a regiment (1st and 2nd battalions respectively) in 1811, in infantry uniform in dark green with white facings, red breeches, waistcoat, lapels, and the shako. The garrison units comprised the Coast Guard Artillery and the Milan and Venetian Guard. The former (seven, later eight companies) was raised in July 1810 from coastal inhabitants as protection against British raids, and wore infantry-style uniform in dark green with black lapels, white buttons, grey turnbacks, waistcoat and breeches, and bicorns with tricoloured plume. The Venetian Guard comprised two infantry battalions and an artillery company, in infantry uniform of dark green (including lapels) with red facings and piping, white waistcoat, breeches and buttons and infantry shako, the artillery with the same uniform with green facings piped red. The Milan

Guard battalion (raised 1811), though officially a 'garrison' corps, served in Germany and in the 1814 Italian campaign; its light blue infantry-style uniform had red facings (light blue lapels), white buttons, breeches and waistcoat, and the infantry shako.

Navy

The navy originally consisted of a battalion of artillery raised in 1803 to man shore-defences and gunboats, but the acquisition of Venice and Dalmatia in 1806 brought the need for a much greater maritime capacity, supplied by Venetian ships which passed into Italian hands. The navy was never large and included nothing larger than frigates, but fought a number of minor actions against the British, most notably that off Lissa (13 March 1811), one of the largest 'frigate actions' of the period. Four British vessels under Captain William Hoste of HMS *Amphion* engaged eleven Franco-Italian craft, including four frigates; the Franco-Italians were totally defeated (nothing larger than a brig escaped, plus the frigate *Flora* which made off after having struck her colours, an act regarded as so dishonourable that Hoste wrote to her captain demanding restitution of the escaped vessel!); but the captain of the Venetian frigate *Corona* (44 guns), Commander Pasqualigo, was accorded great praise for his conduct by the victors. In 1814 the Italian navy was transferred to Austria, the ships and crews remaining Venetian as they had been all along.

The naval gunnery corps (which in 1812 comprised a battalion of eight artillery companies, one ordnance, one bombardier and one cadet company) wore a green jacket, waistcoat and 'gaiter-trousers', scarlet epaulettes and piping, white buttons, and a curious black 'round hat' with triangular brass front-plate edged with black fur, with a strip of fur down the back of the cap and a red plume. The *Battaglione di flottiglia* was a six-company cadet-corps used to train young seamen, based at Venice and manning light *xebecs*; it wore green *surtouts* with white buttons, grey trousers and 'round hats' bearing the national cockade. Seamen appear to have worn uniform (though perhaps this was not regulated) of dark green jacket piped white, green trousers and a black 'round hat'; officers probably wore dark green *surtouts* with silver buttons and epaulettes, and either a bicorn or a 'round hat', though conceivably red facings were also worn.

References

Ales, S. *L'Escercito del Regno Italico*, Milan 1974.
Brandani, M., Crociani, P., and Fiorentino, M. *Uniformi Militari Italiane dell'Ottocento: Periodo Napoleonico*, Rome 1978.
Pivka, Otto von. *Napoleon's Italian and Neapolitan Troops*, London 1979.
A comprehensive series of articles, *Napoleon's Italian Army* and *Napoleon's Italian Navy*, P. Crociani and M. Brandani, appeared in the magazine *Tradition* (London), issues 43–4, 46–8 and 53.

LIECHTENSTEIN

History

The most minor of European states, Liechtenstein was a territory sold by the Count of Hohenems in 1713 to the Liechtenstein family which from the twelfth century had owned castles of the name in Styria and near Vienna. In 1719 the territory was raised to the status of principality by the Emperor and officially titled Liechtenstein, forming a dependent part of the Empire until 1806. From 1806 to 1815 it was a sovereign state, joining the Confederation of the Rhine; it was part of the German Confederation from 1815 to 1866 and once again became a truly sovereign state after that date. During the Napoleonic Wars Prince Johann Liechtenstein was a field marshal in the Austrian army, and Prince Moritz a general; the former was described as 'the Pappenheim of the Austrian Cavalry during the war with Revolutionary France.'[1]

Note

1. 'Avesne-le-Sec and Le Cateau Cambresis', H. C. Wylly, in *Cavalry Journal*, vol. VIII, Aldershot 1913, p. 250.

LIGURIAN REPUBLIC

History

A French satellite established in northern Italy, the Ligurian Republic was based upoon the previous independent republic of Genoa and her territory along the Mediterranean seaboard. Genoa was occupied by the French and in June 1797 was transformed into the Ligurian Republic, modelled on the French state; after the succeeding campaigns (including the siege of 1800 in which the city of Genoa suffered appalling privations), in 1805 the republic was taken into France as the 28th military district, of three *départements*. In 1809 the 27th and 28th districts were united into a separate province (*le Gouvernement général des départements au delà des Alpes*) under the governorship of Prince Borghese, resident in Turin. In 1814 discontent with the French regime was precipitated into revolt by the assurance of Lord William Bentinck that the Allies would restore the Genoese Republic; but the intention was actually that Genoa should be incorporated into the restored kingdom of Sardinia, which duly happened. Republic ferment remained and broke into a brief rebellion in 1848.

Army (cockade for both Genoese and Ligurian Republics: red with white edge)

The Genoese army comprised a number of infantry regiments and associated services, dressed in the usual style of lapelled, open-fronted coat with black knee-gaiters and bicorn. Typical details were (1793): Regiment Sarzana, blue coat, pink facings, white buttons, breeches and waistcoat, Bavarian-style leather helmet with brass plate; Regiment Savona, blue faced red, white buttons, waistcoat and breeches, bicorn; Regiment Corso the same with yellow buttons; Regiment *Real* Palazzo, scarlet coat, blue facings, waistcoat and breeches, yellow buttons, bicorn; Regiment Raustrumb the same with white breeches and waistcoat. The Cadet Battalion wore blue faced black with white piping, waistcoat and breeches, and the artillery blue faced white.

The Ligurian Republic's forces wore French-style uniform, initially a green *surtout* with red facings and waistcoat, yellow buttons, green breeches and bicorn. In 1798 this was replaced by a blue uniform of similar style with the facing-colour only visible as the collar and piping, white, red, blue and sky-blue for the 1st–4th Battalions respectively; with blue breeches and company-distinctions as for the French army, red epaulettes and plume for grenadiers, green for chasseurs, etc. The artillery wore blue with red facings and piping, blue breeches and green-plumed bicorns. The National Guard wore long blue jackets with red piping, white cuff-flaps and waistcoats, blue breeches, and bicorns.

Although the Ligurian forces passed into the French army when the state was absorbed by France in 1805, a separate light infantry unit was formed in November 1805, the *Chasseurs auxiliaires*, 200 strong, in French blue light infantry uniform with red collar and cuffs, white piping, waistcoat and buttons, blue breeches and a shako with white-metal lozenge plate.

References

Brandani, M., Crociani, P., and Fiorentino, M., *Uniformi Militari Italiane dell'Ottocento: Periodo Napoleonico*, Rome 1978.
— *Uniformi Militari Italiane del Settecento*, Rome 1976.

Bucquoy, E. L. *Les Uniformes du Premier Empire: Gardes d'Honneur et Troupes Etrangères*, ed. G. Devautour, Paris 1983.

LIPPE

History

The German principality of Lippe comprised two states: the principality of Lippe-Detmold and the countship of Schaumburg-Lippe, both with rulers descended from Simon VII of Lippe (1587–1627); the holder of the main line, Frederick William Leopold of Lippe, officially received the title of Prince of the Empire in 1789, this originally having been conferred but not confirmed in 1720. In 1762 the associated countships of Lippe-Biesterfeld and Lippe-Weissenfeld passed to the main line; the count of Schaumburg-Lippe (whose domain included Bückeburg) was elevated to a prince in 1807. Following the death of Frederick William Leopold in 1802, management of the state passed into the capable hands of his widow, Princess Pauline (ruled 1802–20 and was succeeded by her equally capable son, Paul Alexander Leopold), under whom the state enjoyed great prosperity. Both Lippe and Schaumburg-Lippe joined the Confederation of the Rhine in 1807, and in 1813 the German Confederation, Lippe leaving the *Rheinbund* in November 1813 and Schaumburg-Lippe in December.

Parr Kingsmill recounts an example of compassion for a wounded enemy which he witnessed at Badajoz. Having disarmed a wounded French officer who had slashed him, a Connaught Ranger removed the Frenchman's calebash of wine,

'and gravely addressing the wounded man, said (while reloading his piece): "Now, my fine fellow, you see what you have lost by your contrariness." "Ah, monsieur," said the Frenchman, "je suis grievement blessé, rendez moi mon calabache, je vous en prie." "Grieving for your calebash – is it that you mane?" said Pat. "Why, then, I'll tell you what – no man shall say that Pat Donovan ever deprived either friend or foe of his little dhrop of dhrink – and there 'tis for you." "Grand merci, grand merci!" said the officer. "Oh, don't bother yourself axing mercy from me," said Pat; "but take my advice," said he, as he bawled loudly and slowly in his ear, so as, he thought, he must understand him; "keep roaring, 'Mercy, mercy, mercy' to all our fellows as they come up, and, by Gor, they'll not take the least notice in life of you." '

('In Badajoz's Breaches', in *With Fife and Drum*, ed. A. H. Miles, London, n.d., pp. 265–6.)

Army (cockade: Lippe-Detmold red and white, Schaumburg-Lippe red and yellow)

Lippe had no standing army and no military tradition until joining the Confederation of the Rhine, though the most famous member of the dynasty was probably Marshal Count Frederick of Lippe-Bückeburg who commanded the Portuguese army in the war with Spain in 1762 and who was responsible for the complete reconstruction of the Portuguese army. Under the Confederation of the Rhine Lippe and Schaumburg-Lippe were required to provide an infantry unit of 500 men from Lippe and 150 from Schaumburg-Lippe; with the Anhalt contingent they formed part of the 5th Confederation Regiment, serving in the 1807 campaign, in the Tyrol in 1809, in Spain 1809–11 and against Russia in 1812; in 1813 they formed part of the Danzig garrison. Their uniform was white with green facings and white buttons, and French company-distinctions; originally with green-plumed bicorns, they wore black 'rounds hats' with upturned left brim in Spain, and in 1812 French shakos were adopted, with jackets now closed to the waist, in the same colouring.

MECKLENBURG

History

The territory of Mecklenburg on the Baltic coast of north Germany comprised the duchies of Mecklenburg-Schwerin and Mecklenburg-Strelitz, which were divided as the solution to a dynastic dispute by the Treaty of Hamburg (8 March 1701). Duke Frederick of Mecklenburg-Schwerin opposed Frederick the Great and thus his duchy was occupied temporarily by the Prussians, but his successor Duke Frederick Francis I (1756–1837) remained neutral in the Revolutionary Wars. In 1806, however, his territory was

Silver Medal of the Military Medal of Merit of Mecklenburg-Schwerin, founded by Duke Frederick Francis I on 23 July 1814 as a reward for distinguished service in the 1813–14 campaigns; the higher award was in gold. Ribbon bright blue with red (inner) and yellow (outer) edging.

overrun by the French and in April 1808 he joined the Confederation of the Rhine. Though he had contributed troops towards the Confederation forces, the duke was the first member to abandon the French alliance in March 1813, and his troops fought against France in 1813–14; in 1815 he joined the German Confederation and took the title of Grand Duke. The much smaller state of Mecklenburg-Strelitz, comprising the separate areas of the duchy of Strelitz and the principality of Ratzeburg, was spared French occupation due to the benign influence of the King of Bavaria. Duke Charles of Mecklenburg-Strelitz joined the Confederation of the Rhine in February 1808 but withdrew in 1813; he joined the German Confederation in 1815 and assumed the title Grand Duke, and died in 1816.

Army (cockade: blue with yellow centre and red edge)
The original uniform of the Mecklenburg-Schwerin infantry battalion was in Prussian style, blue with red facings, white buttons, waistcoat and breeches, and white-laced bicorn with red-over-white pompom; officers' sashes were in the national colours of mixed red, blue and gold. Both states combined to form the 8th Confederation Regiment, 1,900

men from Mecklenburg-Schwerin and 400 from Mecklenburg-Strelitz, organized and uniformed like the French, in dark blue with red facings, white buttons, grey breeches and French shako. A Guard Grenadier battalion was dressed similarly but with bearskin caps with red plume and white cords, red epaulettes and white loops on collar and cuffs; an artillery battery wore the infantry uniform with black facings and plume. Mecklenburg-Schwerin had a Guard cavalry unit wearing straw-yellow with red facings, and in 1813 formed a volunteer mounted rifle corps (*Freiwilliger Jäger zu Pferd*) in dark green Prussian uniform with red facings, yellow buttons, grey overalls with red stripe and shako with black falling plume and a star-plate in brass bearing the state arms in the centre. In 1813 Mecklenburg-Strelitz raised a hussar regiment (which captured the 'Eagle' of the French Seamen of the Imperial Guard at Leipzig), dressed in black hussar uniform with yellow lace, light blue breeches laced yellow, black and yellow sash, shako with yellow cords and yellow 'Wendish cross' badge, and a black sabretache bearing a brass crowned 'C'; the volunteer *Jäger* company attached wore the same uniform but with dark green dolman, pelisse and shako-cords and black facings.

NAPLES

History

The term 'Naples' is used here to cover a number of states which existed in southern Italy. In 1738 Charles of Bourbon, son of Philip V of Spain, was recognized as 'King of the Two Sicilies', Sicily and the Neapolitan territory which covered the whole of southern Italy up to the Papal States. Charles abdicated in 1759 when he succeeded to the throne of Spain, passing Naples to his 8-year-old son who became King Ferdinand IV of Naples and III of Sicily, and in 1770 married Maria Carolina, daughter of Maria Theresa of Austria. Ferdinand was a somewhat boorish character known as *il rè lazzarone*, the *lazzaroni* being the lowest class of peasantry; thus the ambitious Maria Carolina was the dominant member of the partnership, and with the help of her English minister John Acton she freed Naples from Spanish influence. Naples violently opposed the deposition of the French monarchy and in 1793 joined the First Coalition, and republicanism in Naples was suppressed; but it gained ground and peace was made with France in 1796. In 1798 Maria Carolina induced Ferdinard to declare war again and Neapolitan forces briefly occupied Rome, before retreating in haste at the approach of the French. Despite the support of Horatio Nelson (who was received ecstatically by the Neapolitan court), Ferdinand fled to Sicily while the *lazzarone*, devoted to his dynasty, began to massacre all those suspected of republican sympathies. Faced with anarchy the middle and upper classes, deserted by their king, turned to the French to restore order, and on 20 January the French General Championnet fought his way into Naples in the face of fierce opposition from the royalists. The republicans established the Parthenopean Republic (23 January), but the state was ill-organized and in financial difficulty. Meanwhile, from safety in Palermo, Ferdinand sent Cardinal Fabrizio Ruffo (a man of wealth and influence) to Calabria to organize a counter-revolution, which succeeded beyond expectations. With some Russian and Turkish assistance, Ruffo's 'Christian Army of the Holy Faith' (*Esercito Cristiano della Sante Fede*) of brigands, peasants and some soldiers ravaged the Parthenopean Republic, defeated the republicans and eventually persuaded the French defenders of Naples to leave under an armistice. In July 1799 Ferdinand returned from Palermo and began executing republicans. War with France continued until March 1801.

Upon the renewal of hostilities, Ferdinand negotiated with Britain while appearing to accede to Napoleon's wishes; consequently Napoleon sent an army under his brother Joseph to occupy Naples, and Ferdinand and his queen again fled to Palermo. In February 1806 Joseph Bonaparte entered Naples as the new king, but though he introduced some welcome reforms his rule was never universal in the provinces where brigandage held sway, and the unrest was exacerbated by Sir John Stuart's British expedition to Calabria which defeated a French army at Maida before it withdrew. In 1808 Napoleon removed Joseph to the throne of Spain and appointed Murat as king of Naples; he proved a more popular monarch by favouring Neapolitans and by crushing the Calabrian brigands. His drift from Napoleon and towards Italian independence led to his downfall, and after several defeats by the Austrians he fled to France; the Neapolitan generals Pepe and Carrascosa concluded a treaty with Austria and on 23 May 1815 Austrian troops entered Naples to restore the Bourbons.

Meanwhile, Ferdinand and Maria Carolina had continued to reign in Sicily, supported by British subsidies and protected by a British garrison; Murat's attempted invasion ended in disaster. Their rule was obnoxious and oppressive, and after conflict with their parliament in which the British minister, Lord William Bentinck, backed the opposition, Ferdinand was compelled to resign his authority, appoint his son as regent and introduce a liberal constitution; the queen was exiled in 1813 after perpetual intrigue against Bentinck and even negotiation with the French. After the fall of Napoleon the British retired, Ferdinand reasserted his authority, dissolved parliament and arranged for Austrian support in regaining his mainland possessions; Murat's attempt to re-possess his kingdom under the delusion that he still enjoyed popular support ended with his arrest and execution. Ferdinand proclaimed himself King of the Two Sicilies at the Congress of Vienna, uniting Naples and Sicily and abolishing the Sicilian constitution, heralding an era of repression, violence and foreign occupation which was not improved by the accession

Neapolitan uniforms were often extremely ornate, perhaps more than the combat value of the troops deserved, as with this member of the royal bodyguard, including the crimson and white cockade worn after the expulsion of the Bourbons and the establishment of the Kingdom of Naples.

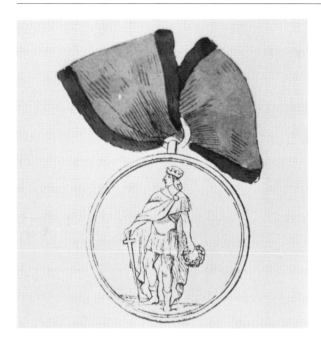

Silver Medal of the Order of St. Ferdinand and of Merit of the Two Sicilies, instituted 25 July 1810 as a reward for military distinction for NCOs and privates; blue ribbon with red edges.

of the corrupt libertine Francis I upon Ferdinand's death in 1825.

Army: Kingdom of the Two Sicilies (cockade: red)

By general consent, throughout the period the Neapolitan troops remained perhaps the worst in Europe in every respect, in combat, for discipline and for desertion. The remark reputedly made by the king during discussions about the army's dress is well-known, to the effect that no matter what colour the uniform, the troops would still run away; such opinions were echoed by almost everyone who came into contact with them. Marshal Macdonald almost had apoplexy when it was suggested that he be transferred to Neapolitan service; even when composing his memoirs long after, he wrote: 'My blood boils even now, and my fury rises, as I write these lines, and think to what a degree of abasement I should have fallen had I been desired to command Neapolitan soldiers. I, who had fought and annihilated them ... I, who had been witness of their cowardice, their desertion, and their flight!'[1] Napoleon, writing of Neapolitans sent to the Peninsula, was equally scathing: 'Let the King of Naples know that all his troops in Spain desert, and are in a wretched state, and that I will have no more of them. Order Marshal Perignon not to send any more, and General Miollis to let none pass. They are a gang of thieves, and poison the country through which they pass.[2] I have no wish to crowd Catalonia with bad soldiers, or to increase the troops of banditti ... I do not want any more Neapolitan troops in Spain ... I will have no more.'[3]

In the one action in which the Neapolitan regulars served creditably, the defence of Gaeta against the French in February–June 1806, their resolution was due largely to the spirit of their German commander, the Prince of Hesse-Philippsthal, who would shout abuse at the French from the ramparts; the fortress surrendered after he was wounded and left.

The infantry of the Kingdom of the Two Sicilies wore a blue coat with short tails, and facings to indicate the brigade: 1st Brigade (Regiments *Re* and *Regina*) red, 2nd (*Real Borbone* and *Real Farnese*) crimson, 3rd (*Real Napoli* and *Real Palermo*) pale yellow, 4th (*Real Italiano* and *Real Campagna*) orange, 5th (*Puglia* and *Lucania*) jonquil, 6th (*Sannio* and *Messapia*) dark

Medal of the Order of St. Ferdinand and of Merit of the Two Sicilies, founded on 1 April 1800 to commemorate the recapture of Naples. Abolished by Joseph Bonaparte, it remained in vogue with King Ferdinand in Sicily. Gold medal with silver lilies and blue circlet, blue ribbon with red edges.

green, 7th (*Calabria* and *Agrigento*) black, and 8th (*Siracusa* and *Borgogna*) light blue. Waistcoat and breeches were white, and the head-dress a white-laced bicorn, or for grenadiers a narrow-brimmed 'round hat' with red turban and a brass badge of the royal cipher and a trophy of arms on the front. Officers' sashes were mixed silver and red. There were also two 'foreign' brigades: *Brigata Straniera* ('foreign brigade') of the 1st and 2nd Foreign Regiments, mostly German in composition, in infantry uniform with red facings and white loops on cuffs and breast; and the *Illirico* Brigade of the 1st and 2nd *Illirico* Regiments, formed of Albanians, in blue with red facings, white loops, red girdle and pale yellow waistcoat.

The cavalry wore bicorns, white coat, waistcoat and breeches in German style, with broad lace on the cuffs, skirts and down the breast, and facings again according to brigade: 1st Brigade (Regiments *Re* and *Regina*) red, 2nd (*Rossiglione* and *Tarragona*) crimson, 3rd (*Borbone* and *Principe*) yellow, and 4th (*Napoli* and *Sicilia*) orange; the first of each pair of regiments had yellow lace and the second light blue, both edged with the facing-colour, save Regiment *Borbone*, whose red lace was edged yellow.

There were also volunteer light infantry regiments which wore brown coats with yellow buttons, grey waistcoat and breeches, and bicorns with green plume tipped with the facing-colour; facings were: Regiment *Truentini* red, *Amiternini* black, *Marsii* apple-green, *de Liri* yellow, and *Formiani* light blue.

Army: Parthenopean Republic (cockade: red with blue centre, yellow edge)

The Parthenopean Republic's troops were National Guard, wearing French-style uniform of blue coat with yellow collar and cuffs piped red, and red lapels and cuff-flaps piped yellow; buff waistcoat and breeches, and white-laced bicorn with red over yellow over blue plume.

Army: Kingdom of Naples (cockade: white with crimson centre)

After the establishment of the French regime in 1806 the army was organized on French lines, with French-style uniform and equipment; it consisted of a Royal Guard and line regiments, both of which were increased progressively.

Royal Guard

The infantry comprised a ceremonial company of halbardiers (in blue single-breasted coats with red facings, silver lace, white breeches and silver-laced bicorn), regiments of grenadiers, *voltigeurs*, and two of *vélites*. The grenadiers wore dark blue coats with light crimson facings, yellow buttons and loops on the collar, lapels and cuffs, red epaulettes, white breeches, and a plate-less bearskin cap with red cords and plume; the Guard *Voltigeur* regiment wore the same but with yellow collars and shakos. The *Vélite* regiments wore Guard Grenadier uniform but in white with red and amaranth facings respectively for the 1st and 2nd regiments, green epaulettes with red crescents and bearskins with green plume and cords. In 1811 the *Voltigeurs* were

converted to a 2nd Grenadier Regiment, uniformed like the first, and when the *Voltigeurs* were re-formed in 1814 they wore *vélite* uniform plus shako and yellow collar.

Included in the Royal Guard was a company of dragoons, expanded to form the *Guardie d'Onore* (*Gardes d'Honneur*), which after the Russian campaign was divided to form the *Garde du Corps* and a cuirassier unit. The original uniform was green, but in 1809 Murat introduced a uniform coloured like that of his ex-Berg cavalry, in white lancer uniform with amaranth facings, and *czapka*. The *Garde du Corps* wore a scarlet single-breasted coat faced yellow, white epaulettes, lace loops and breeches, and bicorn with white loop and plume; the Cuirassiers wore French cuirassier uniform in blue with white lace and epaulettes and amaranth facings. Also in the Royal Guard was a corps of gendarmerie, and a regiment of mounted *Vélites*. The latter originally wore blue jackets and breeches, yellow facings and lace loops, and either a yellow-topped *czapka* or a shako with white-over-yellow plume, yellow cords and white-metal or brass sunburst-plate; by 1809 it had altered to hussar style, of white dolman, amaranth facings, breeches and pelisse, yellow lace, and a shako or black busby with yellow-laced amaranth bag and white plume over amaranth ball. In 1813 the unit was converted to the Hussars of the Guard, wearing a similar uniform but in green with amaranth cuffs and yellow lace. The Guard artillery consisted of a company of foot and one of horse artillery, increased by 1811 to two companies of each, with attendant train; uniform was in French style, the foot artillery in dark blue with crimson facings, yellow buttons and shako with crimson cords and plume, the horse artillery in busbies with crimson bag and plume, dark blue coatee and breeches, crimson facings and lace and yellow buttons, and the train in medium-blue jacket and breeches, amaranth facings, and shakos with amaranth cords and plume.

Infantry

The infantry wore French-style uniform, initially long-tailed coats with open lapels and bicorns, changing to French-style shakos which were ordered in 1809 but it was probably 1810–11 before the change was fully implemented, at which date a short-tailed jacket with closed lapels was introduced. Organization was in French style, each regiment of two battalions, later three, of one grenadier, one light infantry and six fusiliers companies each, plus a depot company; later the regiments were increased so that each had three battalions exclusive of those serving abroad, so that by August 1813, for example, the 5th–8th Regiments had five battalions each. (Although Napoleon was not impressed with the calibre of the Neapolitans, the government was eager to send units abroad, which, as such troops were paid by France, was a relief to the continually hard-pressed Neapolitan finances.) As Joseph Bonaparte had to create his army from scratch, there was no existing regimental framework or nucleus of trained men; recruits were impressed Neapolitan peasants (many of whom only wished to desert at the first opportunity), the indigent or criminals, and thus the French and German professional officers had little chance of moulding this rabble into an effective force. The 1st and 2nd Regiments were authorized in June 1806 (titles were only granted from December 1810); the 3rd in March 1810, its officers ex-prisoners or members of an ephemeral battalion formed of officers with no commands (a return to the 'reformado' system of the seventeenth century); the 4th in August 1809 and the 5th and 6th in September 1809. The 7th Regiment was converted from the French *Pioniers Noirs*, a unit of Haitian and other Negroes created in 1803, and it is a significant pointer to the character of the Neapolitan army that in French service the unit had been reckoned the worst in the army, whereas they were the best in the Neapolitan forces! The 8th Regiment was formed in

Order of St Januarius of the Two Sicilies, founded in July 1738 and abolished when Joseph Bonaparte became King of Naples; it continued to be

awarded by King Ferdinand during his sojourn in Sicily. Gold cross with red and white enamelling, red ribbon.

Spain in 1810 from the debris of the 1st and 2nd Line and 1st Light battalions serving in the Peninsula; the 9th was formed in 1812 from apprehended deserters and the sweepings of the prisons, and the 10th in March 1814 from the 4th and 5th Battalions of the 9th; thus it is not surprising that a battalion of the 10th mutinied in 1815. The 11th was created in May 1814 and the 12th in June from the remnant of the Neapolitan troops in Germany, the latter almost immediately being converted to the new *Voltigeurs* of the Royal Guard, whereupon a new 12th was raised in ex-Papal territory.

Uniform-distinctions were in French style (grenadiers with red plume and epaulettes, *voltigeurs* yellow collar, yellow-tipped green plume, etc.); the uniform was originally white, but succeeding regiments were dressed in different colours: 1st Regiment white faced sky-blue; 2nd white faced sky-blue, later scarlet; 3rd blue faced black; 4th blue faced amaranth; 5th blue faced orange (green from *c.* 1811), 6th sky-blue faced crimson, 7th brown faced scarlet. In 1811 a universal white uniform with closed lapels was ordered, with facings as follows: 1st Regiment (*Re*) and 10th sky-blue; 2nd (*Regina*) and 11th scarlet, 3rd (*Principe*) black, 4th (*Real Sannita*) amaranth, 5th (*Real Calabria*) and 12th (*della Marca*) green, 6th (*Napoli*) orange, 7th (*Real Africano*) yellow, 8th pink and 9th sky-blue, later violet.

The 1st Light Infantry was formed in 1806, uniformed in French style (short-tailed dark blue jacket and lapels, red collar, white piping and buttons); the 2nd Light Infantry was formed with yellow facings. In 1813 the previous Royal Corsican Regiment became the 1st Light Infantry, whereupon the existing 1st and 2nd Light were re-numbered 2nd and 3rd, and a new 4th Regiment raised; facings were black, yellow, red and orange respectively. A rifle corps was formed by Joseph Bonaparte as an anti-guerrilla force (*Cacciatori di Montagna*), in Austrian-style brown *surtout* and overalls, green facings, and a 'Corsican hat' with green band and hunting-horn badge on the front.

Cavalry

In February and March 1806 the 1st and 2nd *Chasseurs* were formed (*Cacciatori a Cavallo*), in French chasseur uniform of dark green with red and yellow facings respectively, white buttons, green-plumed French shakos, red breeches in full dress and grey overalls on other occasions. In December 1806 the Naples Municipal Guard was converted to the 1st *Chevau-Légers*, in light blue jacket and breeches, amaranth piping, white buttons and French shako; in March 1813 Murat converted the *Chasseurs* to the 1st and 2nd *Chevau-Légers*, the previous 1st Regiment becoming the 3rd and a new 4th raised. The uniform prescribed was sky-blue (it may have been darker in some cases) with facings red, yellow, yellow and orange for the 1st–4th respectively, though the 2nd may have retained their old green uniform; all carried lances with crimson-over-white pennon, and in French style élite companies wore hussar busbies. The provincial cavalry wore French-style uniform and shako, coloured as follows: *Calabria Citra*, *Calabria Ultra* and *Basilicata*, black coat faced red, white buttons; *Bari, Lecce, Lucera*, brown faced yellow, white buttons; *Chieti, l'Aquila, Teramo*, brown faced light blue, yellow buttons; *Principato Citra, Principato Ultra, Terra di Livorno*, blue faced white, yellow buttons; waistcoats were of the facing-colour.

Artillery

The line artillery was dressed like that of the Guard, but with red facings, and the train as that of the Guard but with black facings. Engineers wore foot artillery uniform with white buttons. Ordnance was painted in French style, green with black metalwork.

Army: Kingdom of Sicily (cockade: red)

The army remaining loyal to the Bourbons and which for most of the period was based in Sicily was reorganized in 1800; the coat-colour was now white, in Austrian style, with 'round hats' and black leatherwork. Infantry brigades and facing-colours were: 1st Brigade (Regiments *Real Ferdinando* and *Real Carolina I*) red, 2nd (*Real Principe II* and *Real Principessa*) sky-blue, 3rd (*Calabria* and *Abruzzi*) black, 5th (*Real Principe I* and *Real Carolina*) ash-grey, 6th (*Reali Sanniti, Reali Presidi*) light yellow. Provincial light infantry units wore leather caps, short dark green jackets with facings: *Campani* orange, *Calabri* black, *Apuli* yellow, *Aprutini* white, *Sanniti* red, *Marsi* crimson. The Albanian battalion wore an Austrian-style uniform in scarlet with blue facings, white piping, blue or white 'gaiter-trousers' and a peakless, cylindrical cap with a red bag and the royal cipher in brass on the front. The cavalry wore white Austrian-style uniform with broad facing-coloured lace down the breast and around the turnbacks, bicorns, and grey overalls with facing-coloured stripe; regiments and facings were: Regiments *Re* red, *Regina* sky-blue, *Principe I* yellow, *Principe II* green, *Principessa* crimson and *Valdemone* aquamarine. The artillery wore peakless leather caps and blue uniforms with red facings, grey waistcoat and breeches and yellow buttons. Provincial infantry and cavalry units were formed in July 1800, uniformed like the regulars, but the infantry with red jackets and the cavalry blue.

The army was reorganized again after the final retreat to Sicily, and a British-style uniform introduced in 1808, for infantry a single-breasted blue jacket, white overalls, 'stovepipe' shako, and plume and 'wings' in white, red or green for fusiliers, grenadiers and *chasseurs* respectively. Facings were: Regiments *Sanniti, Presidi* and *Estero* red, *Valdemone* and *Valdinoto* green, garrison regiments aquamarine, with white buttons (*Presidi* and *Valdemone* yellow). The Royal Guard Grenadier corps wore scarlet with blue facings, white overalls, yellow buttons and British 'stovepipe' caps with rectangular brass plate (fur caps in full dress); the artillery wore blue with red facings. The cavalry also wore shakos, blue jackets and breeches with facings: Regiments *Principe* yellow, *Valdemone* crimson, *Valdinoto* green. From 1808 regiments of Sicilian volunteers were raised: eight garrison regiments wore green British-style uniform with facings scarlet for the Mazzara district,

Demone sky-blue and Noto black. Four light regiments wore green dolman and breeches with 'provincial' facing-colours, or green jacket and sky-blue gaiter-trousers, with a crested leather helmet similar to a 'Tarleton', with green plume; the one artillery and one engineer regiment wore grey with green facings and white and yellow buttons respectively. These Sicilian volunteer corps existed until 1818, but others were absorbed into the regular army in 1812, for example the Queen's *Voltigeurs* which wore sky-blue dolmans with red facings, white hussar-braid and overalls, and Tarletons. One of the few units to follow the king to Sicily was the Albanian *chasseur* battalion (*Cacciatori Albanesi*), which fought at Gaeta; it wore a blue bolero with red facings over a white vest, a squat black busby with red bag, and white overalls, or alternatively a blue shell-jacket faced red, white skull-cap and *fustanella* (skirt) over blue-grey trousers. Among the reforms forced upon the king by the 1812 constitution was the elimination of 'foreign' units, so the Albanian corps was disbanded and not reformed until 1817.

Navy

The navy of the Kingdom of the Two Sicilies in 1792 comprised only some ten ships-of-the-line (four 74s, six 50s), ten frigates and some smaller craft. When the king fled to Sicily he took part of the fleet with him and ordered the remainder to be destroyed; their contribution to the Allied war effort was minimal. Officers wore dark blue coats with gold lace; marines wore Austrian-style peakless leather caps bearing the royal 'FR' cipher, short, double-breasted blue jackets and trousers, red facings and yellow buttons.

The navy of the Kingdom of Naples was very small, virtually what the royal navy had left behind with a few larger vessels added later. The services of Murat's navy were unimpressive: for example, in May 1810 twelve vessels attempted to drive away the British frigate HMS *Spartan* which had been cruising off the coast; the British captain, Jahleel Brenton, repelled this apparently overwhelming attack with some comfort! Among the personnel of the Neapolitan navy was a unit of Guard Marines, dressed like the Guard Grenadiers but with red facings.

Notes
1. *Recollections of Marshal Macdonald*, ed. C. Rousset, trans. S. L. Simon, London 1892, I, pp. 293–4.
2. *Confidential Correspondence of Napoleon Bonaparte with his Brother Joseph*, London 1855, II, p. 131.
3. ibid, II, p. 134.

Crociani, P., and Brandani, M. *Cavalleria di Linea di Murat*, Rome 1978.
— *L'Esercito Napoletano 1806–15: Fanteria di Linea*, Milan 1987.
Pivka, Otto von. *Napoleon's Italian and Neapolitan Troops*, London 1979.

References
Brandani, M., Crociani, P., and Fiorentino, M. *Uniformi Militari Italiane dell'Ottocento: Periodo Napoleonico*, Rome 1978.
— *Uniformi Militari Italiane del Settecento*, Rome 1976.

NASSAU

History

The German Duchy of Nassau, independent until 1866, had a ruling family split into two branches as early as 1255. The junior or Ottonian branch (named from Otto, grandson of Count Walram of Nassau, d. 1198) was connected to the fortunes of the Netherlands, as a descendant of this family was William the Silent, whose successors were granted the title of Prince of Orange-Nassau. William IV of Orange-Nassau was deprived of his Nassau and Netherlands heritage in 1806 by his refusal to join the Confederation of the Rhine, but upon becoming William I of the Netherlands in 1815 his possession of the Netherlands was assured, and his Nassau possessions passed to the head of the Walramian line. This, named from Otto's brother Walram, did not rule a unified Nassau as the territory was partitioned a number of times, but at the beginning of the nineteenth century only two states existed, Nassau-Usingen, ruled by Prince Charles William, and Nassau-Weiburg, ruled by Prince Frederick William. Both lost their territory on the left bank of the Rhine to France in 1801, but were compensated by grants of other land. In 1806 Frederick William and Charles William's successor, his brother Frederick Augustus, both joined the Confederation of the Rhine (the former becoming Prince of Nassau and the latter Duke of Nassau), but changed sides after Leipzig and thus held their territories after the collapse of the Empire. In 1815 Frederick Augustus of Nassau-Usingen ceded some of his lands to Prussia, receiving in return the greater part of the German possessions of the Ottonian branch, and when he died without a son in 1816 the whole of Nassau was united under Frederick William of Nassau-Weilburg as Duke of Nassau. He granted his subjects a constitution and representative assembly in 1814, and was succeeded by his son William in 1816, heralding a period of some dissention between the assembly and the duke which was not fully resolved until 1836.

Army (cockade: black)

As part of the Holy Roman Empire the states of Nassau provided personnel towards a combined *Oberrheinisches* regiment, which in 1792 wore bicorns, blue coats and white facings and breeches. In 1803 four Nassau infantry battalions were formed, split into two regiments in 1808, the 1st (Nassau-Usingen, the old 1st and 4th Battalions) and 2nd (Nassau-Weilburg, the old 2nd and 3rd). Each battalion originally consisted of four companies, but upon reorganization in 1808 French-style establishment was introduced, each regiment of two battalions of one grenadier, one light and four fusilier companies. All wore green uniforms with red facings and yellow buttons (3rd and 4th Battalions white), grey breeches (2nd green) and buff belts (3rd, classed as *Jägers*, black). The 2nd and 4th Battalions wore black and green shakos respectively (the 4th's grenadiers with red-plumed black shakos), the 1st Battalion black-plumed Bavarian *Raupenhelms* (red plume for grenadiers), and the 3rd Battalion bicorns. In 1808 French shakos and rank-insignia were adopted, the grenadiers of the 1st battalions of the two new regiments initially retaining the *Raupenhelm* of the old 1st battalion, but by 1810 all grenadiers wore brown busbies with red bag, cords and plume. Facings became black with yellow piping for all, and legwear either grey breeches or green trousers.

The infantry served with considerable distinction in the Peninsular War, but upon the state's change of allegiance to the Allies the 2nd Regiment defected to the British, and the 1st was disarmed and interned by the French. In 1813 a 3rd Battalion was raised for the Allies (absorbed by the 1st in 1814), plus a *Jäger* corps and *Landwehr* regiment, both disbanded in June 1814. In 1815 the Nassau regiments formed part of the Netherlands army and were acknowledged to be among the best of Wellington's forces, fighting with distinction at Quatre Bras and Waterloo.

Nassau's cavalry regiment was formed in 1804, two squadrons serving the Confederation of the Rhine: styled *Reitende Jäger* (mounted *Jägers*), it served in Spain and was disarmed with the 1st Infantry Regiment, and was not re-formed after 1814. The uniform was green with silver lace, with a black-crested *Raupenhelm* with green plume and white-metal fittings.

References

Pivka, Otto von. *Napoleon's German Allies: Nassau and Oldenburg*, London 1976.

Rumour abounds in wartime; Cavalié Mercer remembered how a mass of Netherlandish fugitives streamed from Quatre Bras crying '*Tout est perdu! les Anglais sont abimés, en déroute, abimés, tous! tous! tous!*' Among this panic-stricken mass was a single British soldier.

'. . . a private of the 92nd (Gordon Highlanders), a short, rough, hardy-looking fellow, with the national high cheek-bones, and a complexion that spoke of many a bivouac. He came limping along, evidently with difficulty and suffering. I stopped him to ask news of the battle, telling him what I had heard from the others. "Na, na, sir, it's aw a damned lee; they war fechtin' yat an I left 'em; but it's a bludy business, and thar's na saying fat may be the end on't. Oor ragiment was nigh clean swapt off, and oor Colonel kilt jist as I cam awa'." Upon enquiring about his own wound, we found that a musket-ball had lodged in his knee, or near it; accordingly Hitchins, dismounting, seated him on the parapet of a little bridge we happened to be on, extracted the ball in a few minutes, and, binding up the wound, sent him hobbling along towards Nivelle, not having extracted a single exclamation from the poor man, who gratefully thanked him as he resumed his way.'

(*Journal of the Waterloo Campaign*, C. Mercer, Edinburgh & London 1870, I, p. 251.)

THE NETHERLANDS

Although in 1815 the forces of both Belgium and Holland served in the army of the Kingdom of the Netherlands, it was an uneasy and recent alliance between two states which had been separate for more than two centuries. The split between the northern and southern Netherlands might be dated from the signing of the League of Arras in January 1579, by which the southern Walloons proclaimed their adherence to Catholicism and the Spanish monarchy in defiance of the northern provinces whose Union of Utrecht announced their determination to defend their liberty and Protestant religion against all outside influences. The southern provinces remained under Habsburg control, becoming the Austrian, rather than Spanish, Netherlands by the Peace of Utrecht (1713). In 1789 the Brabancon revolt defeated the Austrians at Turnhout and the 'Belgian United States' declared their independence under the leadership of the advocate Van der Noot, but the arrival of a powerful Austrian force in November 1790 caused the collapse of the revolt and the provinces reverted to Imperial control, albeit only briefly: in the early Revolutionary Wars the provinces were over-run and for the rest of the Napoleonic era were absorbed as integral parts of France.

The northern Netherlands were a federated republic, the 'United Provinces', administered by a States-General with the ruling prince bearing the title *Stadholder*, an elective office made hereditary to the House of Orange from the mid-eighteenth century. The anti-Orange faction exerted such influence that in 1787 a Prussian army had to re-impose the Orange rule of William V; a hereditary kingdom might have replaced the somewhat unsteady republic had not the Revolutionary Wars occurred, though despite William V's alliance with Britain and Prussia the Provinces remained neutral as long as possible. Only after the Austrian Netherlands had been over-run did the United Provinces enter the war against France, though the 'patriot party' – opponents of the house of Orange – favoured the French. In late 1794 the Provinces were invaded, the *Stadholder* fled to England, and the 'patriot party' established the French satellite of the Batavian Republic, having abolished all the traditional aspects of the *Stadholderate* and United Provinces organization. The French alliance became French domination, however, bringing the ruination of Dutch trade and overseas empire, and a succession of governments changed the States-General into a National Convention, a Constituent Assembly and in 1801 a central Commission with eight provincial 'parliaments'. In 1805 Rutger J. Schimmelpenninck (1765–1825) was appointed Napoleon's viceroy with the ancient title of Grand Pensionary, and in 1806 the state was transformed into the Kingdom of Holland, with Napoleon's brother Louis as sovereign. Though perhaps the most worthy of the Bonaparte brothers, Louis was an unwilling king of a resentful people, and abdicated in 1810 after refusing to bend completely to Napoleon's demands. The Kingdom of Holland was then incorporated completely into France, until a general revolt

after Leipzig in which the Prince of Orange (William VI, son of William V) was recalled amid general rejoicing to accept the title 'sovereign prince' under a free constitution (1 December 1813). The Treaty of London (14 June 1814) amalgamated the old United Provinces and Austrian Netherlands under William VI to form a new Kingdom of the Netherlands, William taking the title King William I on 15 March 1815; he surrendered his Nassau lands in exchange for Luxembourg, of which state he became Grand Duke. Confirmed by the Congress of Vienna, he was crowned in Brussels on 27 September 1815, but the Belgians were always unwilling subjects and after the Belgian revolt of 1830 the two states became separate in 1831. William I abdicated in the following year and was replaced by his son, William II, who as Prince of Orange had served on Wellington's staff in the Peninsular War and was nominally in deputy command of the Anglo-Allied army in the Hundred Days campaign.

Army: Batavian Republic (cockade: black)

The Batavian forces were organized and uniformed in French style, with black cockades replacing the traditional Dutch orange from 1795. Although they served under French command, there was not at this period any attempt to integrate the units into the French forces.

Cavalry

Batavia had two regiments of heavy cavalry, one of dragoons and one of hussars. The heavy regiments wore white-plumed bicorns, white coats with crimson turnbacks, black collar, cuffs and lapels for the 1st Regiment and light blue for the 2nd, white waistcoat, breeches and buttons, and crimson and yellow shabraques respectively, laced white. In 1802 they were converted to light dragoons, wearing a white short-tailed jacket with closed lapels, facings and shabraques as before, plus white lace loops, and a 'Tarleton' helmet with crimson turban and white plume, replaced by French brass dragoon helmets about 1805; in 1804 the jackets became dark blue with pink facings. The dragoons wore a uniform like that of the heavy regiments but in blue with pink facings, and brass dragoon helmets. The hussars wore French-style hussar uniform of dark blue throughout with red facings, yellow braid, black mirliton cap with red wing, red-and-white cords and red, white and blue plume. The 2nd Light Dragoons were disbanded in 1805, the dragoon regiments being re-styled the 1st Light Dragoons and the previous 1st being re-numbered as the 2nd.

Infantry

The infantry was organized in a series of French-style *demi-brigades*, each of three battalions, with uniform and company-distinctions of the French model (though with longer coat-tails), white breeches, waistcoat and buttons. There were seven *demi-brigades* plus two 'foreign' regiments, *Waldeck* and *Sachsen-Gotha*; facings were red (1st and *Sachsen-Gotha*), crimson (2nd), white (3rd and 4th), light blue (5th and 6th)

and yellow (*Waldeck* and 7th); the 4th had red collars. Turnbacks were white except for the 1st, 4th and *Sachsen-Gotha* (red), 5th light blue, 7th and *Waldeck* yellow; piping was white for all except for the 4th and *Sachsen-Gotha*, red, though the 4th's collars were piped white.

In 1803 the *demi-brigades* were reorganized into 23 numbered battalions, three from each *demi-brigade* plus one from each foreign regiment, with the same uniform but changed facings, which were red but for the following exceptions:

Collars: blue (Battalions 2, 6, 8, 11, 14, 17, 21), white (3, 7, 12, 22, 23), crimson (4), white piped crimson (5), light blue (13, 16), white piped light blue (15) or yellow (19);
Cuffs and lapels: crimson (4–6), white (7–9, 12, 23), white piped red (10, 11), light blue (13–18), yellow (19–21);
Cuff-flaps: blue (2, 6, 8, 11, 14, 17, 20, 21), white (3, 7, 12, 23), white piped crimson (4), crimson (5), light blue (13, 16), white piped light blue (15), yellow (19);
Turnbacks: white (4–8, 16–18, 23), light blue (13–15), yellow (19–21).

Light *demi-brigades* wore French-style dark blue jackets with red collar and sometimes cuffs, red-laced blue breeches and cylindrical shakos with a drooping plume at the right, cords and plume green for *chasseurs* and red for carabiniers. The four *Jäger* battalions wore infantry uniform in dark green, including waistcoat and breeches, green-plumed bicorn, black leather equipment and facings red, black, black and crimson for the 1st–4th Battalions respectively; the 2nd had black lapels and buttons were yellow for the 1st and 3rd and white for the others.

Artillery
Foot artillery wore infantry-style uniform of blue coat, waistcoat and breeches, red facings and yellow buttons; the horse artillery wore dragoon uniform with bicorn, blue coat and lapels, red collar and cuffs, straw-yellow breeches and long boots.

Army: Kingdom of Holland (cockade: black)
The Batavian army was re-organized for the Kingdom of Holland, and though internal organization and insignia continued to be of French pattern, a distinctive national uniform was adopted. When the kingdom was incorporated into France in 1810 the Dutch regiments were absorbed by the respective branches of the French army, though continued to wear their Dutch uniform for some time.

'Dutch' grenadier of the French Imperial Guard: the Royal Guard of the Kingdom of Holland absorbed in the French army in 1810, retaining the same basic colouring as worn as part of the Dutch army: white with crimson facings, red epaulettes and plume, and a plate-less fur cap. (Print by Pierre Martinet)

Cavalry

Among the organizational changes was the creation of a Royal Guard, and from September 1806 the cavalry comprised the 1st (Guard) Hussars (2 squadrons), 1st (Guard) Cavalry (horse grenadiers) (3 squadrons), the 2nd Hussars, 3rd Hussars and 2nd Cavalry (ex-Batavian Hussars and 1st and 2nd Light Dragoons respectively), all of 5 squadrons. The 2nd Cavalry was re-titled as Cuirassiers (though not equipped with cuirasses), and in 1807 the 1st (Guard) Cavalry was disbanded and its personnel transferred to the 2nd and 3rd Hussars, and the 1st (Guard) Hussars converted to the *Régiment de la Garde à Cheval* comprising both hussars and cuirassiers. As a reward for distinguished service in the Peninsular War, in 1809 the 3rd Hussars became the Hussars of the Guard. When the Dutch army was absorbed into that of France, the 2nd Cavalry became the French 14th Cuirassiers, the 2nd Hussars the French 11th Hussars, and the Guard Hussars became the 2nd *Chevau-Légers* of the Imperial Guard, the famous 'Red Lancers'.

Uniform remained of French style. The 1st (Guard) Hussars wore scarlet dolman and breeches with blue facings, yellow braid, white pelisse, black busby with red bag, yellow lace and white plume, dark blue shabraque with yellow lace and red piping. The 1st (Guard) Cavalry wore white coats, waistcoats and breeches, crimson facings, yellow loops and trefoil epaulettes, and a plate-less bearskin cap with red plume and cords, or a busby with white cords and crimson-tipped white plume; and gold-laced crimson shabraque. The later Guard cuirassier detachment wore the same but with red-plumed French cuirassier helmets. The 2nd Hussars wore dark blue dolman, breeches and pelisse, scarlet facings, yellow lace, yellow-laced blue shabraque and French hussar shako with yellow cords, black plume and brass numeral '2' on the front. The 3rd Hussars wore a similar costume in dark sky-blue, with the numeral '3' on the shako changing to the royal cipher 'L' in 1809. The 2nd Cavalry wore a uniform like that of the 1st (Guard) but with dark sky-blue facings and no lace, scarlet epaulettes and French cuirassier helmets; horse-furniture was of French cuirassier style, dark sky-blue with yellow lace and grenades in the rear corners.

Infantry

In 1809 the infantry was reorganized into nine regiments, the 1st being a Guard unit initially of one grenadier and one *chasseur* battalion. The Guard grenadiers became the 2nd (later 3rd) Grenadiers of the French Imperial Guard, and the first four line regiments the 123rd–126th French Line, with the remaining Dutch corps disbanded and the personnel distributed among them. All wore white coats with medium-length tails and lapels closed to the waist, white breeches and waistcoats, short black gaiters, French company-distinctions and facings: 1st crimson, 2nd light blue, 3rd red, 4th pink, 5th dark green, 6th grass-green, 7th yellow, 8th violet and 9th black. Head-dress was a shako with white-metal numeral on the front, white cords and carrot-shaped, facing-coloured pompom on the left (white

with coloured centre for fusiliers); grenadiers had bearskin caps with brass plates bearing a grenade, white cords and red plume. The 1st (Guard) Regiment had white coats with open lapels (pointed-ended for the *chasseurs*), crimson facings, yellow loops, crimson epaulettes for grenadiers and green with crimson crescent for *chasseurs*; they had plate-less bearskin caps with white cords and scarlet plume (green-tipped for *chasseurs*). Metalwork and officers' epaulettes were gold for the 1st and silver for the remainder. The *Jägers* wore infantry uniform in the previous Batavian colouring; the 1st Battalion was the light infantry of the Royal Guard, and facings were light blue and yellow for the 2nd and 3rd respectively, with yellow buttons; in 1810 they were amalgamated to form the French 33rd *Léger*.

Artillery

The four foot artillery battalions wore French-style uniform of dark blue coat, breeches and lapels, red collar, cuffs and shako-cords, shakos with brass badges of crowned crossed cannon-barrels, and pompom of red, white, blue and yellow for the 1st–4th Battalions respectively; in 1810 they became the French 9th Artillery. The horse artillery wore hussar uniform of dark blue dolman and breeches, red facings and braid, shako with red upper band, cords and plume and brass company-numeral; they were intended to form the French 7th Horse Artillery but in the event were absorbed by the 1st. The artillery train was uniformed like the foot or horse branches, but with grey jackets and legwear, black facings, red piping and trouser-stripe, white buttons and shako-badge and black leatherwork; they became the 14th Battalion of the French artillery train. The engineer corps was dressed like the artillery but with white buttons instead of yellow, and in 1810 was integrated with the French engineers.

The Belgian Legion (cockade: Austrian)

During the brief resumption of Austrian control in 1814, prior to the establishment of the Kingdom of the Netherlands, a Belgian Legion was formed of four infantry regiments and one of *Chevau-Légers*. The latter wore Austrian cavalry helmets with yellow crest and white metal plate bearing 'LB', dark green jacket and breeches, yellow facings and white buttons. The infantry wore Austrian-style jackets in white with pointed cuffs, facings green, yellow, light blue and red respectively for the 1st–4th Regiments, white or dark grey breeches with facing-coloured stripe, and a French shako with facing-coloured pompom, black and yellow Austrian cockade and brass letters 'LB' on the front, and black leather equipment.

Army: Kingdom of the Netherlands (cockade: orange)

The Netherlands army was a somewhat reluctant alliance of Dutch and Belgian units (such appellations were not used in 1815, but 'North Netherlands' and 'South Netherlands' respectively). Many of the Belgians had been fighting on the French side barely a year before, and having expected independence were very unenthusiastic about their new king

Louis Bonaparte, King of Holland (1778–1846), wearing the distinctive white uniform of the army of the Kingdom of Holland, 1806–10. (Engraving by W. Miller)

and the Dutch alliance, which explains in great part the disappointing performance of many Netherlandish troops in the 1815 campaign. The unusual nature of the alliance is demonstrated by the careers of several of the leading generals in 1815: the Prince of Orange (commander of the Allied 1st Corps) and the Quartermaster-General, Constant de Rebecque, had both served Wellington in the Peninsula; General Janssens, head of the War Ministry, had fought against the British at the Cape and in Java, and General David Chassé, probably the best of the Netherlandish commanders, had gained considerable distinction with the French in the Peninsula, becoming both a general and a Baron of the Empire; he fought against his erstwhile allies in 1815 with as much distinction as he had served them. Relations between the King and Wellington were strained, as William I endeavoured to interfere in Allied planning; the conflict was not resolved until 4 May 1815 when Wellington was appointed Field Marshal of the Netherlands, giving him supreme command over the Netherlands army.

Cavalry

The eight cavalry regiments were numbered consecutively, all of four squadrons of two companies each: the 1st and 3rd Carabiniers, 4th Light Dragoons and 6th and 7th Hussars were Dutch, the latter East Indian, and the 2nd Carabiniers, 5th Light Dragoons and 8th Hussars were Belgian. The carabiniers wore dark blue jackets with red facings (it is likely that the 1st retained their earlier pink facings during the Waterloo compaign), white buttons and grey breeches; the 3rd had yellow turnbacks. Head-dress was a brass-combed iron helmet with black woollen crest, brass lion-mask on the front, and white plume, though it is possible that the older bicorns were worn at Waterloo. The 4th Light Dragoons wore dark blue jackets with red facings, white hussar braid, grey trousers and a French-style shako with white lace band and cords, black plume and white-metal crowned shield-plate; the 5th wore green jackets, yellow facings and similar green shakos with white-metal crowned 'W' badge and yellow-tipped white plume, officers having cylindrical green shakos of the French *rouleau* design. The hussars wore sky-blue hussar-style uniform (dark blue pelisse for the 6th), red facings for the 7th and 8th, white buttons (6th yellow) and braid (6th mixed yellow and black), and shakos like those of the 4th Light Dragoons with white lace (6th yellow), the shako of the 7th being red. There was also a corps of Guides (*Guides te Paard*) in dark blue jackets faced crimson, with a shako like that of the 4th Light Dragoons but without lace and with an upright or drooping black plume; the unit carried lances with red over white over blue pennons, but these were apparently not issued until September 1815.

Infantry

The infantry was numbered consecutively and consisted of 36 regiments, mostly of single battalions: 1st, 2nd, 4th and 7th Belgian; 5th, 10th and 11th Dutch East Indian, 16th–18th and 27th Dutch *Jägers*, 19th–26th and 33rd Dutch, 28th

Nassau, 29th–32nd Swiss mercenaries, 34th a garrison battalion, and the 35th and 36th Belgian *Jägers*; there was in addition the 2nd Nassau Regiment (not numbered in the line) and 45 Militia battalions, nos. 1–20 Dutch and the remainder Belgian. Each battalion comprised six fusilier companies (eight in the Swiss regiments) and two of *flanquers*, one 'heavy' (grenadiers) and one light. The uniform was of British infantry style in dark blue with white facings (orange for militia), the head-dress a British 'Belgic' pattern with brass plate for Belgian units and wider-topped Austrian-style shakos for Dutch; *flanquers* had blue cloth rolls on the shoulders, piped white. Plumes were white, with red or green tip for grenadiers and light infantry respectively; equipment was a mixture of British and French styles, white belts, British canteens and French hide knapsacks. The *Jägers* had green jackets, yellow facings and green plumes tipped red or yellow for the flank companies. Officers had longer-tailed coats, gold lace and orange sashes. The colonial infantry (of which the 5th Regiment served in the Waterloo campaign) wore blue with sky-blue facings and red piping, and white plumes tipped sky-blue; the Nassau regiments (by general consent the best units of the army) retained their green uniforms worn under the Confederation of the Rhine. Some

William Frederick, Prince of Orange, from 1815 King

William I of the Netherlands (1772–1843).

of the militia wore British-style 'stovepipe' caps instead of the Austrian shako.

Artillery

The artillery consisted of six foot battalions (4th Belgian, 5th and 6th colonial) each of six companies (the 4th had five); six horse companies (two Belgian) and six six-company militia battalions (2nd and 6th Belgian). The foot artillery wore

Cross of a Knight of the Military Order of William of the Netherlands, instituted by William I on 30 April 1815; gold cross with green foliage, white cross, and orange ribbon with blue stripes.

> Fraternization could occur on campaign when no personal animosity existed between the opposing forces:
>
> 'One fine moonlight night our advanced sentry called the attention of Colonel Alexander to the French sentry in his front, who was distinctly seen in the moonlight leaning against a tree, and fast asleep with his musket by his side. Alexander went quietly up to him, and took possession of the musket, and then awoke him. The man was at first much frightened upon finding himself disarmed, and in the hands of an English officer. Alexander gave him back his firelock, merely remarking, that it was fortunate for him that he had found him asleep on his post, instead of one of his own officers. The poor fellow expressed the greatest gratitude . . . Shortly after the battle of the Nive, Colonel Alexander, in returning from the front on a very dark, stormy night, missed his way, and his horse falling over a bank, both horse and rider came clattering down heels over head into a lane, and close to a French sentry, who instantly challenged. Alexander hearing the *qui vive*, and the click of his musket, thought that he was going to fire, and called out "*C'est l'officier du poste Anglais – ne tirez pas!*" "*Non, non, mon Colonel*," replied he, "*J'espere que vous n'êtes pas blessé!*" '
>
> ('Out-Post Anecdotes' by 'Green Feather', *United Service Journal*, London 1840, I, pp. 223–4.)

infantry-style uniform of a dark blue jacket, black facings, red piping, light grey trousers and Austrian-style shako with red-tipped black plume; the horse artillery wore the same with yellow-laced red shoulder-rolls and shakos with black plume, red cords and brass crowned cannon-barrels badge. Engineers wore the foot artillery uniform with sky-blue facings, and sky-blue plume with black tip.

Navy

The main attraction to France of the acquisition of the Netherlands was their very considerable fleet, Holland having been one of the world's major trading nations. Consequently the capture of the Dutch fleet – largely achieved by French cavalry who took possession of the ships when they were icebound – augmented the French naval forces with good ships and seamen of a higher overall calibre than those of the French navy. The Batavian fleet was considerable (some 36 ships-of-the-line, eighteen frigates and a host of smaller craft in 1795) and despite major losses (especially the defeat at Camperdown and the surrender of a squadron off the Cape in 1796) the Dutch remained a considerable threat to the British navy, though by 1801 the number of ships in service had declined to ten ships-of-the-line and five frigates, eight and twelve respectively upon the creation of the Kingdom of Holland, and thirteen and ten when the Dutch fleet was incorporated into the French navy in 1810. Equally important was the presence of good harbours in the Netherlands, which Napoleon incorporated in his plan for the invasion of England, and which prompted the Allied expeditions to Holland in 1795, 1799 and 1814 (in all of which the inhabitants showed only lukewarm support for the Allied incursions), as well as lesser operations such as the disastrous Ostend expedition and the landing at Walcheren, both designed wholly or in part to dislocate French plans for the utilization of Netherlandish ports. After

Camperdown the Dutch navy's main actions were in the East Indies (where they generally suffered at British hands) and in small coastal skirmishes, a considerable part of the navy consisting of coasters and gunboats, and a vast number

The capture of the Dutch fleet, 21 January 1795, by French cavalry, which crossed the ice in which the Dutch ships were held fast. (Print after C. Mozin)

Figurehead of the Dutch flagship Vryheid, *captured at Camperdown; the scale is evident from the bell-mouthed* blunderbuss *(sometimes used in 'boarding actions' aboard ship). (Print after W. Gibb)*

of invasion-craft prior to the abandonment of Napoleon's descent on England in 1805.

The navy included two marine regiments which were absorbed into the Batavian line and replaced by a marine unit styled *Korps Mariners*, augmented in August 1806 by a grenadier detachment. Naval officers wore dark blue uniforms with light blue collar and cuffs from 1807 for petty officers and above. The seamen's dark blue jacket had yellow buttons, worn with a 'round hat', red waistcoat and white or dark blue trousers (summer and winter respectively); yellow-laced seams were adopted in 1807, with light blue collars and piping on the white trousers. The marines wore infantry-

style uniform in dark blue with red facings, infantry shako with brass anchor badge and black-tipped red plume; the grenadiers wore Corsican hats with brass grenade badge and red plume, red jackets faced light blue, yellow buttons, red epaulettes and light blue trousers.

References

The series *De Nederlandse Armee* (Bussum 1963–8) covers the Dutch army branch by branch, though is not restricted to the Napoleonic period. *The Dutch-Belgian Army at Waterloo* (C. A. Norman, in the periodical *Tradition*, London, issues 46–8 and 60) is a comprehensive study.

NORWAY

History

Although Norway had long been a sovereign state, from 1397 it was part of a triple kingdom with Denmark and Sweden; and from 1449 became virtually a province under the Danish crown. Not until 1807 did agitation for Norwegian nationality result in the establishment of an administration separate from Denmark, though Danish overlordship remained until the Treaty of Kiel (14 January 1814) by which Norway was ceded to Sweden as 'punishment' for Denmark's support for Napoleon, and as a condition of Sweden's entry into the coalition against France. King Frederick VI of Denmark acceded to Sweden's territorial demands but never consulted the Norwegian people, who rebelled, framed a constitution (17 May 1814) and elected as king the previous Danish governor of Norway, Prince Christian Frederick. Bernadotte immediately invaded Norway, but after barely two weeks' hostilities negotiations ensured that Norway remained under the Swedish crown, but with the maintenance of the constitution. Christian Frederick resigned his crown and quit the country; Norway remained a Swedish possession until 1905.

OLDENBURG

History

The German state of Oldenburg had been ruled by the kings of Denmark from 1702, until in 1773 it was exchanged by Christian VII of Denmark with Duke Paul of Holstein-Gottorp (later Tsar of Russia), who handed it to his kinsman Frederick Augustus, Bishop of Lübeck, and in 1777 the state was elevated to the rank of duchy. The bishop's son William succeeded as duke in 1785, but being weak-minded the state was administered by his cousin Peter Frederick Louis, Bishop of Lübeck, who eventually succeeded as duke in 1823. In 1806 Oldenburg was occupied by the French and Dutch and the duke and regent fled; but in 1807 William was restored and the state joined the Confederation of the Rhine in October 1808. When William and Peter refused to exchange Oldenburg for Erfurt in 1810, Napoleon seized the state, joined it to Hanover and incorporated it into metropolitan France. The Tsar being related to the ruling house, possession of Oldenburg was a cause of Franco-

Russian friction, and following liberation in 1813 the Tsar's good offices ensured that William was not only restored but granted the principality of Birkenfeld, and the whole accorded the status of grand-duchy, though the title 'grand duke' was not assumed until the accession of Peter's son Augustus in 1829.

Army (cockade: blue with red cross)

Oldenburg possessed a small infantry unit wearing Prussian uniform in dark blue with red facings, and bicorns, until in 1808 a battalion of infantry was required by the Confederation of the Rhine, of four fusilier, one grenadier and one *voltigeur* company. The uniform was still in Prussian style, blue with red facings, with Corsican hats with white plume for fusiliers and green for *voltigeurs*; grenadiers had bearskin caps, and an unusual feature for so small a contingent was the employment of Negro drummers. After annexation by France the unit was absorbed into the French 129th Line. After liberation, in November 1813 the Oldenburg Regiment was formed for service with the Allies, comprising one regular and one *Landwehr* battalion, in Prussian-style uniform in blue with red facings, white

> 'This day was the anniversary of the battle of Waterloo. The circumstance was mentioned by some one present, and the recollection of it produced a visible impression on the Emperor. "Incomprehensible day!" said he in a tone of sorrow; "Concurrence of unheard of fatalities! Grouchy! Ney! d'Erlon! Was there treachery, or only misfortune? Alas! poor France!" Here he covered his eyes with his hands.'
>
> (*Memoir of the Life, Exile and Conversations of the Emperor Napoleon*, Count de Las Cases, London 1836, II, p. 334.)

buttons, white or blue trousers (summer and winter respectively), and black-plumed French shakos with white cords and a shield badge; the volunteer *Jäger* company of the *Landwehr* battalion had green facings, grey cloth caps with green piping with white cross badge, grey overalls and black belts.

References

Pivka, Otto von. *Napoleon's German Allies: Nassau and Oldenburg*, London 1976.

The Medal of Honour of Oldenburg, founded 30 April 1815 at the suggestion of Blücher, for service in the 1813– 14 campaigns. Silver medal with dark blue ribbon with red stripes.

OTTOMAN EMPIRE

History

Although not strictly a European power, the Ottoman Empire (or 'Sublime Porte') played a not inconsiderable part in the Napoleonic Wars in its conflicts with other states. The empire consisted of a number of provinces stretching from Greece and the Balkans to the Middle East, all with governors but which (as in the case of Egypt) almost assumed the status of independent states. Nominally all were under the repressive rule of the Sultan, but his chief minister or Grand Vizier wielded immense power and headed the government. The state was still administered on medieval lines, and atrocity, rebellion and murder were endemic.

At the beginning of the Revolutionary Wars, the weak Sultan Abd-ul-Hamid (ruled 1773–89) had recently been succeeded by his son, Selim III (ruled 1789–1807), who continued the war declared against Austria and Russia in 1788, waged in the Balkans and along the frontier provinces. Peace with both states (August 1791 and January 1792 respectively) established the Dniester as the frontier, surrendered the Crimea to Russia and restored to the empire Austrian conquests such as Belgrade. The empire became involved with the war against France as a result of Bonaparte's Egyptian expedition, but probably more significant was internal reaction to the Sultan's attempts at reform, and provincial revolts like that of Serbia where the inhabitants rose in protest against the brutality of the Ottoman governor of Vidin, the bandit Pasvan Oglu. The rebel leader George Petrovich, alias Kara Georgi ('Black George') captured Belgrade, and though an imperial army suppressed the tyranny of Oglu he was reinstated into the government. Other serious revolts occurred at Adrianople in 1804 and with the Wahhabi movement in Nejd, a religious sect which attacked those not conforming to its tenets (a strict adherence to the original laws of Islam, with puritan-like aversion to luxury and to the worship of saints and even Mohammed, instead of to God). The movement's founder, Ibn 'Abd ul-Wahhab, is said to have died in 1791.

In late 1806 disputes over the principalities of Wallachia, Moldavia and Bessarabia caused the Ottoman Empire to declare war on Russia (encouraged by France via her ambassador, General Sébastiani), Russian forces invading Moldavia and Wallachia; British unease at the French influence caused a brief period of Anglo-Ottoman hostility, a British naval foray to Constantinople being repulsed in early 1807. During the war with Russia internal unrest increased as the empire's élite military force of Janissaries saw its pre-eminence threatened by the Sultan's creation of a new military force. Enlisting the support of reactionary elements equally suspicious of European-style reforms, and taking advantage of the army's need to march to the Danube, the Black Sea garrisons rose in revolt in 1807 and unrest spread to the Janissaries. Selim attempted to appease them but was dethroned in favour of his nephew, Sultan Mustafa IV (1807–8). The Treaty of Tilsit resulted in a suspension of hostilities with Russia, and the returning army attempted to restore Selim III, but he was murdered before they could achieve their purpose. Instead, they killed Mustafa IV and the sole survivor of the imperial family became Sultan, Mahmud II (1808–39). Selim's chief supporter, Mustafa Baïrakdar (who had led the attempt to restore him, was

equally reform-minded and who had been distinguished in the Russian war) was appointed Mahmud's Grand Vizier and succeeded in overaweing the Janissaries by virtue of his personal corps of 10,000 irregulars (*kirjalis*). The remnant of Selim's new troops were assembled into regiments of *seymen-i-jedid*, affiliated to the Janissaries in an attempt to gain their co-operation. It was a vain attempt; unwisely dispersing the *kirjalis*, the Vizier was attacked by the Janissaries and blew himself up in the arsenal at Constantinople; fighting spread to the fleet, which bombarded the capital, and the Janissaries, having massacred all the 'new troops' they could find, extorted an amnesty from the helpless government.

After Tilsit the Ottoman Empire remained neutral in the Napoleonic conflict, though desultory hostilities occurred with Russia from 1809 until 1812 when, due to the mediation of the British diplomat, Stratford Canning, peace was achieved by the Treaty of Bucharest (28 May 1812), by which Russia received Bessarabia but the Empire kept Moldavia and Wallachia. Serbia was restored to Ottoman rule but was given internal autonomy, but the situation was so ill-defined that unrest continued, the new Serbian leader Milosh Obrenovich eventually leading a general revolt which restored Serbian independence. Having murdered Kara Georgi on his return from Austria (whence he had fled in 1812), Obrenovich was proclaimed hereditary prince of Serbia. Relations between Russia and the Ottoman Empire remained strained despite the treaty of Bucharest, and were to cause much conflict in succeeding years.

Army

The Ottoman army was composed of two main branches, the 'regulars' (who received pay) and the irregulars, unpaid and assembled only in wartime, both infantry and cavalry, though the distinction is somewhat blurred and complicated by the existence of provincial forces. The irregulars had no training; the mounted volunteers or *akindjis*, for example, had no tactic whatever save a headlong rush. Although the Sultan maintained a cadre of officers for employment in wartime, the principal 'regular' forces were the Janissaries, a corps founded in 1330 by the enforced enrollment of Christian children from the European provinces (Albania, Bosnia and Bulgaria were preferred) by a system of conscription known as *devshurmé*. They were trained as warriors and throughout the succeeding centuries became renowned as the most feared and fearsome of the Sultan's servants; although it appears that their adoption of the Muslim religion was not compulsory, they were Islam's most staunch defenders. They were styled *yeni chéri* ('new troops') and initially were blessed by the venerable Haji Bektash, who ever after was the corps' patron saint. The whole corps was known as the *ojak* (hearth), and divided into *ortas* (regiments) and again into *odas* (lit. 'rooms': the barracks occupied by the Janissaries). After the reorganization of Suleiman I there were three classes of *orta*: the *jemaat* (101 *ortas*), the *beuluk* (61) and the *sekban* or *seimen* (34), plus 34 *ortas* of apprentices or *ajami*. The difference between the three classes was generally only of name, though the *beuluk* had the

The Napoleonic Wars produced very few recorded examples of what the twentieth century came to know as 'shell shock', psychological damage or derangement caused by exposure to enemy fire and the attendant sights of horror. It has been stated that 'shell shock' is produced less by a traumatic event of brief duration than by protracted exposure to danger, which slowly drains the human will like withdrawals from a bank-account, to use Lord Moran's comparison; perhaps because Napoleonic battles were of short duration there was not the same danger of mental damage. Nevertheless, an interesting example concerns Admiral Louis Antoine de Bouganville (1729–1811), navigator and the officer who saved part of the French fleet after the defeat of de Grasse by Rodney in 1782, who was made a senator, count and member of the *Légion d'honneur* by Napoleon; he is probably best remembered by the name of the largest of the Solomon Islands and by the plant *Bougainvillea glabra*. His favourite parrot, which had been present at the battle, afterwards 'could never be induced to be talkative as before, but to every question or endearment answered in one only word, "Bomm! bomm!! bomm!!!" '

('Another Chapter on Parrots', in *The Leisure Hour*, 1 May 1869, p. 284.)

privilege of guarding the Sultan, and the *jemaat* (or *yaya beiler*) were tasked with guarding the frontiers. The strength of *orta* varied greatly, sometimes with only 100 men, or in excess of the war footing of 500; by 1805 the total strength of the *ojak* had reached more than 112,000. *Ortas* were normally assigned to a permanent garrison, promotion being from within the *orta*, personnel only transferring when given command of another *orta*. They were unpaid in peacetime but received rations, supplemented by earnings from whatever craft they practised (though this was contrary to regulations), and had no regulated uniform, the tall cap (originally white, later red) being their distinctive mark, with officers distinguished by the colour of their boots, commanders of *beuluks* wearing red, the others yellow, and subordinate officers black. Discipline was enforced rigidly and loyalty was given first to their officers; an inviolable regulation was that they should neither marry nor grow beards.

The Janissaries' method of combat was a combination of modern and medieval: they used firearms but were equally practised with the sword. Though they were the Empire's best troops, like the Praetorian Guard they became the bane of the Empire; customarily brutal in the extreme, they were lawless and treated civilians with great cruelty, and threatened successive Sultans from their earliest revolt in 1443. Their usual method of protest was to set fire to Constantinople; 140 fires were said to have been raised in the 28 years of Ahmed III's reign, for example! Used as the tool of unscrupulous ministers for personal gain, they were the reason why Selim III attempted to form his new 'regular' army of *nizam-i-jedid*, which the Janissary revolt against the Vizier Baïrakdar caused to be suppressed. In the next two decades the lawlessnesss and want of respect to the Sultan grew to such a degree that Mahmud II was determined to be rid of them, and in 1825 established a corps of properly drilled troops; as expected, the Janissaries rose in revolt in June 1826, whereupon many were exterminated and the corps dissolved, ending a long existence born in glory but closing in lawlessness and banditry.

In addition to their semi-medieval organization, the Ottoman forces had other distinctive characteristics as described by the Archduke Charles, who devoted a special section of his *Principles of War* to them: he characterized them as brave and bold, very adept at weapon-handling, but totally incapable of acting in concert. He described how Ottoman armies would attack with neither fear nor co-ordination, every man rushing forward on his own initiative, cavalry and infantry together; but courage and rapidity of manoeuvre was no substitute for the discipline of European troops, so that if the initial onrush failed they would retire with the same speed and lack of cohesion. This failing, thought Charles, rendered the Turks incapable of awaiting an attack in formation or of defending a position, so that disciplined troops who maintained their cohesion could defeat great numbers of Turks; Austria used squares for this and Bonaparte's tactics in Egypt were very similar and equally successful against such unco-ordinated rushes.

> Reactions to the threat of French invasion recorded by the Constable of Slaithwaite, West Yorkshire, 1798:
> 'John Ramsden, Waterside, engineer. No objection to be enrowled in the Infantry, provided they be trained at Slaithwaite and Government finds arms.
> Joel Hoyle, Highfield, clothier, will be a labourer, and hath no implements. Will work hard.
> John Bamforth: If Dob go, I go alongside her.
> James Sykes, Cophill, is determined to kill a Frenchman, if possible.
> James Sykes, driver with a long whip, will assist all in his power for the French to have their own. Consequently he must be a Jacobin.'
> (*History of the Formation and Development of the Volunteer Infantry*, R. P. Berry, London & Huddersfield 1903, p. 326.)

Navy

The Ottoman Empire possessed a navy of considerable strength, ships-of-the-line, frigates and galleys (in 1790 some 30, 50 and 100 respectively); the principal source of seamen were from the Greek provinces in the Aegean. The design of the main vessels was not dissimilar to those of the European powers, but the smaller craft included many 'native' types. The sailing ability was competent, but tactically they were far behind the European powers and consequently lost heavily when confronted by European opponents, as demonstrated by the annihilation of the Turkish fleet at Navarino in 1827. The naval personnel had no uniform, officers being distinguished largely by boot-colour (as above); and one *orta* of Janissaries was employed as marines. Perhaps the most famous action involving the Ottoman navy during this period was the capture of the frigate *Badere Zaffer* by HMS *Seahorse* in July 1808, after a most fierce action.

Reference

A useful account of the Ottoman forces is 'The Turkish Army of the Napoleonic Wars 1798–1812', D. Sweet, in the journal *Empires, Eagles and Lions*, issue 75, Cambridge, Ontario, 1975.

PARMA AND PIACENZA

History

Ownership of the Italian duchies of Parma and Piacenza had fluctuated between Spain and Austria after the end of the Farnese dynasty in 1731. In 1748 Maria Theresa surrendered the territory to Don Philip, *infante* of Spain, and his son Ferdinand (who succeeded to Parma in 1765) saw his state overrun by the French in 1796; he purchased a lifetime tenure from France for 6,000,000 lire and 25 of the finest paintings in Parma. Upon his death in 1802 the territory passed to France; Ferdinand's son Louis became King of Etruria. The territories were henceforth administered by France under Moreau de Saint-Méry and Junot; and on 24

Cross of the Order of Constantine of Parma, instituted probably in 1190 and abolished by Joseph Bonaparte when he bacame King of   *Naples; it transferred to Sicily with the royal family. Gold with red-enamelled cross and blue ribbon.*

May 1808 they became the French *département* of Taro and its troops were incorporated into the French army. At the Congress of Vienna, Parma, Piacenza and Guastalla were assigned to Napoleon's consort Marie-Louise, and upon her death reverted to Charles II, son of King Louis of Etruria.

Army

At the time of the formation of the *département* of Taro, Parma's troops wore French-style uniform, the infantry in dark blue with yellow facings and buttons, and French shakos with yellow-tipped black plumes; and the cavalry wore a blue single-breasted *surtout* with yellow facings, buff breeches and leatherwork and a similar shako, with yellow cords in place of the infantry's white.

Reference

Bucquoy, E. L. *Les Uniformes du Premier Empire: Gardes d'Honneur et Troupes Etrangères*, ed. G. Devautour, Paris 1983.

PIEDMONT

History

The north Italian state of Piedmont was owned by the House of Savoy, which held the kingship of Sardinia from 1718, and which had produced a noted soldier in Charles Emmanuel III (ruled 1730–73). His son who succeeded, Victor Amadeus III (1773–96), was as incapable and decadent as his ministers, so that upon the outbreak of the Revolutionary Wars the state was not in a fit condition to resist the French. Savoy became a French province and though the Piedmontese troops resisted for four years despite continual defeats, Victor Amadeus capitulated by the armistice of Cherasco and died soon afterwards. His son Charles Emmanuel IV (1796–1802) was induced by Bonaparte to enter a confederation with France and surrender the citadel of Turin, which meant the end of Piedmontese independence; distressed at his error he abdicated in December 1798 and retired to Sardinia while the French occupied the whole of the country. Charles Emmanuel landed at Leghorn in an attempt to regain his territory during Bonaparte's absence in Egypt, but Marengo dashed his hopes and he retired to Naples, abdicated again in 1802, entered the Society of Jesus and died in Rome in 1819. His brother, Victor Emmanuel I (reigned 1802–21) remained in Sardinia until the Congress of Vienna restored his dominions (plus Genoa), and his family eventually succeeded to the kingship of the unified Italy in 1861, in the person of Victor Emmanuel II. After the House of Savoy lost control of Piedmont, a Piedmontese Republic was formed, but in September 1802 the territory was integrated completely with France as the 27th military distict, all resources being directed towards the French army; for example, the French 111th Line was Piedmontese in composition.

Army

See under 'Sardinia' for details of the military forces of the House of Savoy. The debris of the Savoy forces was integrated with those of France in 1799, but a number of Piedmontese units were formed under French rule, the first being the Piedmontese Hussars of 1800; they wore green dolman and breeches, white braid and buttons, red lace edging to collar and cuffs and shako with white metal lozenge plate, and in 1801 became the French 17th *Chasseurs à Cheval*. In May 1803 Napoleon authorized the formation of four 'Legions' in the area of Italy now absorbed by France, each of three line and two light battalions of five companies (including one of grenadiers, carabiniers in the light infantry) and an artillery company; *chasseur* squadrons were proposed but may never have been formed. The initial uniform was of French infantry style in grey with red facings, white buttons, and head-dress and company-distinctions like the French; but in July 1803 a new uniform was authorized, in brown with sky-blue facings and white buttons. The grenadiers retained their red-plumed bearskin caps and the light infantry French shakos with yellow-tipped green plumes, but the fusiliers adopted a curious black leather helmet of dragoon pattern, with brass plate and comb and black horsehair aigrette but no mane; this was probably replaced quite quickly by the shako. Only one legion was actually formed, the *Légion du Midi*, part of which went to San Domingo and was absorbed by the 82nd Line in 1805. The remaining two battalions were reduced to one in November 1808 (one grenadier, one *voltigeur* and three *chasseur* companies), absorbed by the 11th and 31st *Léger* in August 1811. The artillery probably existed no longer than 1805, and wore French artillery uniform. A better-known Piedmontese corps of the French army were the *Tirailleurs du Pô*, raised in 1803 from the 27th military district with the title *Bataillon Expéditionnaire Piémontais*; organized like a French light regiment, it wore dark blue with red facings, white piping and white (or yellow?) buttons, and may have retained the bicorn considerably longer than the French infantry. Its carabiniers wore bearskin caps, red plumes and epaulettes. The unit was absorbed by the 11th *Léger* in 1811.

References

Bucquoy, E. L. *Les Uniformes du Premier Empire: Gardes d'Honneur et Troupes Etrangères*, ed. G. Devautour, Paris 1983.

POLAND

History

The unfortunate kingdom of Poland had been a political football for the adjoining powers (Russia, Prussia and Austria) during the eighteenth century, and lost territory to all of them. The reigning monarch at the beginning of the Revolutionary Wars was Stanislaus II Poniatowski, elected king of Poland under Russian influence in 1764, who had presided over the First Partition (1772) by which the state lost a quarter of its territory to its three great neighbours; in return, Poland was presented with the 1775 constitution devised for it, which achieved a degree of internal stability not enjoyed for a long period. Poland remained an elective monarchy in which real power lay in the hands of a permanent council of 36 elected members; although the king was president of the council, his powers were very limited. Encouraged by Prussia to forsake the Russian alliance, Poland's 'four years' diet' assembled in October 1788 and reformed the constitution, abolishing the permanent council, more than doubling the agreed size of the army (to 65,000), and in May 1791 a new constitution was pushed through under fears of a further partition, converting Poland to a hereditary limited monarchy. This, together with a Prusso-Polish alliance (March 1791), pledging mutual aid, presented a serious threat to Russia, and thus Catherine the Great was receptive to entreaties for help from Polish dissidents desirous of a return to the old constitution. A Russian declaration of war on the new Polish regime was followed by a Prussian repudiation of the alliance, leaving the small Polish army to resist the Russians unaided; only 46,000 strong, under the command of Prince Joseph

Poniatowski and Tadeusz Kościuszko (1746–1817), they held off the Russians for three months until the king and Hugo Kollontaj, a leader of the diet, acceded to the rebel demands. Many Polish commanders resigned in disgust at the surrender; Russian troops poured in, whereupon Prussia invaded to prevent total Russian domination. The Second Partition followed (September 1793) by which Russia and Prussia took more territory, leaving Poland but one-third of her original size.

Nationalism had always been strong in Poland, and now centered upon Kościuszko in Leipzig where a patriot movement assembled, determined but politically naïve. Kościuszko failed to win French support for a rebellion (his aim was an alliance of republics against the monarchies), and unwisely supported a mutiny in the Polish army against a move to incorporate it in the Russian forces. The rising was premature but Kościuskzo joined it in April 1794 in Cracow, and the mass rebellion which followed inflicted defeats upon the Russians and recovered three-quarters of the Polish territory, including Warsaw and Vilna. Kościuszko was appointed dictator with the assistance of a supreme council, but internal dissent neutralized the bravery and resolution of the troops. Warsaw was defended against Russo-Prussian attack (July–September 1794), but the Polish patriot forces were defeated heavily at Maciejowice (10 October) and finally at Praga (29 October); with the rebellion crushed, the Third Partition (1796) removed Poland from the map. This led to mass emigration, most of the Polish patriots taking service with France or French satellites as a way of continuing the fight against the partitioning powers, though Kościuszko wisely remained aloof, rightly suspecting French motives. Wounded and captured at Maciejowice, after his release by the Russians he lived in Philadelphia, and from 1798 in France.

Polish hopes for independence were revived after the Treaty of Tilsit, when Napoleon created the Grand Duchy of Warsaw; but cynically he used it merely as a recruiting-ground for vast numbers of superb troops for his armies. A member of the Confederation of the Rhine and nominally controlled by the King of Saxony (as grand-duke), the Duchy of Warsaw was but a satellite of the French empire, Napoleon deliberately preventing it from becoming sufficiently large to be self-supporting. The Duchy of Warsaw ended with the collapse of French influence after the 1812 campaign and its occupation by Russian forces (Warsaw on 18 February 1813); many Poles retired with the French army, but others hoped the Tsar would re-establish their independence, and the Tsar found it to his advantage to encourage such beliefs. In the event, the Congress of Vienna divided Poland between Russia, Prussia and Austria, plus a tiny republic based on Cracow, with the Russian apportionment having only an ostensible independence by virtue of the Tsar being appointed king of the so-called 'Congress Kingdom'. The story that Kościuszko had cried '*Finis Poloniae!*' as he fell wounded at Maciejowice is apocryphal, but it is an appropriate comment on Polish independence following the collapse of the republic.

Army (cockade: white)

The Polish army's most notable contribution to the evolution of warfare were the lancers which were copied by virtually every European army, the lance being the traditional weapon of Polish cavalry. Polish uniform was copied similarly, in the distinctive square-topped lance-cap (*czapka*) and plastron-fronted, short-tailed jacket (*kurtka*); even in the British Army these features endured until the First World War and are present today in the ceremonial dress of some regiments. Prior to the Third Partition the army wore a Russian-style uniform including a short-tailed, lapelled jacket with small turnbacks. The fourteen infantry regiments wore dark blue with coloured facings (light blue, orange, green, buff, black, pink or yellow) with white overalls or blue with facing-coloured stripe; the most unusual feature was the head-dress, a peaked black felt 'round hat' with white-metal front-plate bearing an eagle and backed with a large black leather plate, and a black plume arching from the back to the rear of the front-plate. Officers wore the traditional Polish *konfederatka*, a low-crowned *czapka*. The cavalry wore a similar jacket (blue faced red) and red or blue overalls, with a 'round hat', *czapka* or mirliton; riflemen wore green jacket and breeches, red facings and white-plumed Corsican hat. Artillery wore grey with black facings and white-plumed 'round hat'.

Kościuszko's army included not only troops in these 'regular' uniforms, but large numbers of 'patriot' personnel wearing civilian clothing, long coats or smocks, 'round hats' or *konfederatkas*, and armed with agricultural tools such as scythes mounted as pikes.

Polish Legion

Many Poles emigrated following the Third Partition and sought refuge in France or states under French control, and under General J. H. Dombrowski (1755–1818) a Polish Legion was formed for service in the pay of the Cisalpine Republic (q.v.). In 1798 a second Legion was formed; each comprised three 10-company infantry battalions and three companies of artillery, with cavalry added that year. The 2nd Legion was captured in Mantua and the Austrians insisted that all Galicians (nominally Austrian subjects) be enlisted or returned to the Austrian army in which many had served before. In 1800 the Poles were reorganized into the *Légion Italique* and a newly formed Danube Legion; it comprised four 10-company infantry battalions, four cavalry squadrons and a horse artillery battery. The Italian Legion

Infantry of the Vistula Legion; fusiliers in the background (plain shoulder-straps, pompom on shako) and élite company men in the foreground, distinguished by their sabre-belts and red plume, shako-lace, epaulettes and gaiter-trim for grenadiers (left) and yellow shako-lace, plume, gaiter-trim

and green epaulettes with yellow crescents for voltigeurs *(right). The jacket is in the cut of the traditional Polish* kurtka, *in dark blue with the yellow collar and cuffs of the 2nd Regiment; the sunburst plate on the shako was styled on that normally carried on a* czapka. *(Print after 'Job')*

comprised seven infantry battalions, five artillery companies and was augmented by cavalry originally from the 1st Polish Legion of the Cisalpine Republic. At the end of 1801 all were absorbed into the French army as the 1st–3rd Foreign *Demi-Brigades*; the 1st was transferred to the Cisalpine army and the others, re-numbered as the 113th and 114th *Demi-Brigades*, were sent to waste away in San Domingo.

Duchy of Warsaw: Army

The forces of the Duchy of Warsaw were largely newly-created, upon cadres which had already served Napoleon; Dombrowski remained a leading figure. In addition to the Duchy's own army, other Polish units served in French pay, most famously the Vistula Legion, founded on the *Légion Polacco-Italienne* of recent Westphalian service (and a descendant of the Cisalpine Poles), which in March 1808 was transferred to French service with an establishment of three infantry and one cavalry regiments, increased by a regiment of each in 1810. In June 1811 the cavalry (lancers) became the French 7th and 8th *Chevau-Léger-Lanciers* (their most famous service was in Spain, being one of the units which destroyed Colborne's brigade at Albuera), and after suffering dreadful casualties the four infantry regiments were amalgamated in June 1813 into the Vistula Regiment, disbanded 1814. The lancers wore classic Polish lancer uniform in dark blue with yellow facings and *czapka*-top, the infantry also in blue with yellow facings (including closed lapels and pointed cuffs) and French shakos with the 'sunburst' plate normally carried on the *czapka*.

Cavalry

There were 20 regiments numbered consecutively (a 21st Lancers was formed in Lithuania in 1812 but it is doubtful if it ever reached establishment), of which the 1st, 4th and 5th were *Chasseurs à Cheval*, the 10th and 13th Hussars, the 14th Cuirassiers and the remainder lancers. The *chasseurs* wore dark green French-style uniform with yellow buttons, shako with white-metal eagle-plate or cockade, facings red, crimson and orange for the 1st, 4th and 5th respectively, and green overalls with facing-coloured stripes; élite companies wore busbies of a distinctive Polish pattern, without the usual 'bag' but with a red cloth top with yellow boss in the centre, red plume and cords. The hussars wore dark blue dolman and pelisse, crimson facings, light blue breeches, shako with white lace and cords, with yellow buttons and braid for the 10th and yellow for the 11th. The cuirassiers wore French cuirassier uniform, in blue with red facings and yellow buttons. The lancers wore a black *czapka* with metal eagle-plate, black plume and white cords, and dark blue *kurtka* with blue lapels (11th and 15th crimson, 19th and 20th yellow, 21st orange). Collars were crimson with white piping except for: 2nd (red piped white), 6th (white piped crimson), 7th (yellow piped red), 8th (red), 9th (red piped blue), 19th and 20th (yellow) and 21st (orange); lapel-piping was crimson except for 2nd, 19th and 20th (yellow), 3rd, 9th, 11th, 12th and 15th (white), 7th and 8th (red), and 21st (orange); cuffs were crimson with white piping except for:

2nd (red piped white), 7th and 8th (yellow piped red), 9th, 11th and 12th (blue piped white), 19th and 20th (yellow) and 21st (orange); the blue overalls had crimson stripes except for the 2nd, 3rd, 7th, 19th and 20th (yellow), 8th and 9th (red) and 21st (orange). Elite companies had peaked fur caps with red plume and cords, and red epaulettes. Lance-pennons were probably red-over-white for the 2nd, 3rd and 16th, and red, white and blue for the remainder, though red-over-yellow or vice-versa are also shown for the 2nd.

Infantry

There were ultimately 21 infantry regiments (18th–21st raised in Lithuania in 1812), organized in French style, each of three battalions of one grenadier, one *voltigeur* and four fusilier companies. All wore black *czapka* with brass 'sunburst' plate bearing the number, and a dark blue *kurtka* with facings according to the division to which regiments were allocated: 1st Division (originally 1st–4th Regiments) yellow lapels, red collar and cuffs; 2nd (5th–8th Regiments) crimson; 3rd (9th–12th Regiments) white, with yellow buttons (2nd Division white). Equipment was of French pattern, with white or blue trousers. From September 1810 all regiments were ordered to adopt uniform facings: white lapels, turnbacks and cuff-flaps, blue collar piped crimson, crimson cuffs and yellow buttons, but regimental variations still existed, most notably for the 13th Regiment which had white *kurtkas* with sky-blue facings; red collars are shown for the 4th, 5th, 16th and 17th at least. Company-distinctions were in French style, *voltigeurs* with yellow collars, green epaulettes (sometimes with red or yellow crescents), green or white *czapka*-cords and yellow-tipped green plumes, but recorded variations include the 2nd's yellow plume with sky-blue tip, the 14th's red-tufted yellow pompom with red horizontal stripe, and many with green or yellow pompoms. Grenadiers wore fur caps, sometimes peaked, sometimes with a sunburst plate or a grenade badge (5th Regiment) with red plume and white or red cords; the 13th's grenadiers wore shakos with a brass grenade over a numbered plate, red cords and pompom. The 4th, 7th and 9th Regiments served with the French in Spain and wore French uniform, even to the adoption of the tricolor cockade in place of the usual Polish white.

Artillery

The Duchy's foot artillery was created in December 1806 and by March 1812 numbered twelve field and four garrison companies; horse artillery was added in 1808, raised and equipped at the personal expense of Count Wladimir Potocki, expanded to a regiment in 1810. For the 1812 campaign 104 guns were deployed, but losses were so severe that only ten guns and four howitzers survived until 1814, including a single company of horse artillery. The foot artillery wore infantry-style uniform (*kurtka* or lapelled French-pattern coat) in dark green with black facings, red piping, green or white trousers, yellow buttons and shako with red plume and cords. The horse artillery initially wore lancer uniform of *czapka* and *kurtka*, but from 1810 *chasseur* uniform in the same colouring: dark green single-breasted jacket with black facings, red piping, dark green overalls with black stripes piped red, and black busby with red cords. The artillery train wore similar jackets in dark blue with yellow facings, white buttons, yellow-striped blue overalls and dark blue *czapka* with red cords and pompom; and the equipment train similar but with grey *kurtka* and legwear. Engineers wore foot artillery uniform plus a gold collar-grenade.

References

Chelminski, J., and Malibran, A. *L'Armée du Duché de Varsovie 1807–15*, Paris 1913.
Gembarzewski, B. *Wojsko Polskie*, Warsaw 1964.
Linder, K. *Wojsko Polskie Miniatury*, Warsaw 1968.

Pivka, Otto von. *Napoleon's Polish Troops*, London 1974 (the most accessible source).
Zygulski, Z., and Wielecki, H. *Polski mundur wojskowy*, Cracow, 1988 (a superb compilation of contemporary pictures and extant relics).

PORTUGAL

History

Portugal's monarch throughout the period was Queen Maria I of the Braganza dynasty, who succeeded her father Joseph in 1777; she was married to her uncle who ruled as her consort, Pedro III. Maria had shown signs of religious mania and became totally insane after 1788, following the deaths of Pedro (1786), her heir Don Joseph, and her confessor, the inquisitor-general. Her second son, Don John, assumed the conduct of affairs but was only confirmed as official regent in 1799; he succeeded as King John VI upon his mother's death in 1816. Partly through the influence of his wife Carlota Joaquina (daughter of Charles IV of Spain) and partly from fear of the Portuguese radicals who sympathized with the French Revolution, Don John led Portugal into a Spanish alliance in March 1793 to join an attack on France. This collapsed in July 1795 when Spain made peace; Portugal, as Britain's traditional ally, was deliberately excluded and a Franco-Spanish plan for the partition of Portugal was devised. Supported by a British expedition under Sir John Stuart, Portugal remained at war with France until in 1799 Don John attempted to make peace. The French terms being unacceptable (a severing of British trade), Portugal declared war on Spain in February 1801, was immediately invaded, forced to close Portuguese harbours to British ships, surrender Olivenza to Spain and pay France a reparation of 20,000,000 francs. Napoleon's behaviour in the following years was calculated to humiliate the Portuguese and goad

<table>
<tr><td>The 1812 campaign:

'Thus great expeditions are crushed by their own weight. Human limits had been surpassed. The genius of Napoleon, in attempting to soar above time, climate, and distances, had, as it were, lost itself in space: great as was its measure, it had been beyond it.'

(History of the Expedition to Russia, Count Philippe de Segur, London 1825, II, p. 180.)</td></tr>
</table>

them into renewing the war (giving France an excuse for conquest), but this only occurred in 1807 when France invaded in an attempt to impose the 'continental system' by force. Lisbon was occupied, and having appointed a Council of Regency headed by the Bishop of Oporto, in November Don John and the royal family sailed for Brazil. He remained in Portugal's south American colony until July 1821, complicating the internal dissent felt throughout the nation in the aftermath of the Napoleonic Wars, which was the cause of civil war in later years. Although the Council of Regency nominally ruled Portugal during the Peninsular War, it was corrupt and unwilling to co-operate fully with Wellington and Beresford (Marshal of the Portuguese army), so that the actual government was conducted largely by Beresford and by Britain's representative on the Council, Sir John Stuart (son of the Sir John named above).

Army (cockade: red and blue, circular or cross-shaped)
Portugal had a tradition of foreign commanders-in-chief, attempting to repeat the success of Count Frederick of Lippe-Bückeburg who commanded the Portuguese forces in the war with Spain in 1762 and who reorganized the army, and that of the Duke of Schomberg (a native of the Palatinate) a century earlier. Subsequent foreign commanders were greatly inferior and enjoyed only brief tenure: in 1796 the Prince of Waldeck (minus an arm lost at the siege of Thionville) who went to Portugal in the hope of making his fortune; the Prussian Count de Golz, formerly Frederick the Great's secretary; and the French *émigrés* de la Rosière (appointed Portuguese quartermaster-general) who had served under Saxe, and the Count de Viomenil, who transferred from British service as Marshal of the Portuguese army. After the collapse of 1807 it required another foreign commander, Marshal Beresford, to reorganize the army and introduce experienced foreign officers before the Portuguese could evolve into the splendid troops they became during the Peninsular War. The army was run officially by the Council of War (established 1643) but its powers were minimal, and the commanding Marshal was virtually omnipotent in organizational matters. Supreme command in the Peninsular War was vested in Wellington as Marshal-General, but he left the ordinary administration in Beresford's capable hands.

At the outset the standard was abysmal: recruitment was by selective conscription (taking only the poorest and least-skilled), with ten-year service. Officers were ill-educated and with wretched prospects of promotion: two-thirds were cadets (for which position only the nobility was eligible) and the remainder uneducated ex-sergeants. There was no authorized method of training; pay, equipment and food was appalling, discipline lax but relieved by impromptu hangings, beatings or shooting, leading to low morale and a general state of inefficiency. The whole army was organized in three 'Grand Divisions': 1st or South, 2nd Central and 3rd Northern.

Prior to reorganization the army included 24 infantry regiments with territorial designations, each of two

Badge of the Order of the Tower and Sword of Portugal, the premier military decoration: gold medal with white-enamelled cross, blue circlet, green oak-leaves and wreath, and blue ribbon.

battalions of five companies, each company 114 strong (though actual strength was generally very much below the establishment); one company of each 1st battalion were grenadiers and a company of each 2nd battalion light infantry. Twelve cavalry regiments each had four squadrons but were so deficient in mounts that no more than half the 9,000 establishment could ever be mobilized for service. The four artillery regiments were in permanent garrison, each of one sapper, one miner and eight artillery companies, with 3- and 6pdr guns and civilian teams and drivers hired when required. The 140 officers of the Engineer Corps received little practical instruction; the principal fortifications were those of Almeida and Elvas, but the remainder were in a state of decrepitude and garrisoned mainly by invalid gunners. The only attempt at modernization prior to 1808 was the Legion d'Alorna (named after the Marquis who commanded it), consisting of eight light infantry companies, two cavalry squadrons and a horse artillery troop. The territorial militia was recruited by selective conscription for life, liable for service on a rota basis (thus spending most of their time in their civil occupations), augmented by a *levée en masse*-style *ordenança*, without uniform and armed only with agricultural tools and vine-poles, of negligible combat value but which perpetrated many atrocities on French stragglers from 1807.

Despite appalling central direction, the calibre of the ordinary recruit was potentially good. Illustrative of this is the conduct of the impressed peasants who built the lines of Torres Vedras: 5,000 to 7,000 were conscripted for work at any one time, up to 40 miles from their homes, paid from 6 to 10 *vintems* per day (1s. to 1s. 8d. in British currency); yet not one example of unwillingness was evident, as Major John Jones of the Royal Engineers described: their excellent conduct was 'more ascribed to regular habits of persevering labour . . . than to the efficiency of the control exercised over them',[1] as they succeeded 'in transporting 12-pounders into situations where wheels had never before rolled' with nothing more than 'their rude means of transport':[2] ox-teams and human muscle. Similar characteristics were remarked of the troops, though one of their officers thought them 'a patient good-tempered people, therefore very susceptible of discipline under good officers; and when so are very steady under arms . . . but they are, in fact, a timid people, and . . . should be brought into such a state of discipline that they will be more afraid of their officers than of the enemy'.[3]

The Reform

The reformation of the Portuguese army was one of the most remarkable organizational feats of the era. The army was virtually disbanded after Junot's invasion and re-assembled in a very poor state. William Beresford was seconded from the British army to be Marshal of Portugal on 2 March 1809, and immediately instituted a complete overhaul while retaining the existing regimental structure. From company level British officers were introduced, which had a profound effect even though no more than 200 ever served at any one time. Useless Portuguese officers were retired and the better ones integrated with the British, so that any Portuguese field-officer had British above and below him, and vice versa: thus a British major would have a Portuguese senior captain and colonel, and a Portuguese brigade-commander would have British colonels under his command, and so on. The improvement in leadership was combined with better pay, food, clothing and discipline, and thus higher morale, which allowed the inherent qualities of the Portuguese soldier to shine through. As the Anglo-Portuguese staff officer William Warre noted, '. . . had they justice done unto them in the common comforts . . . they would make as good soldiers as any in the world. None are certainly more intelligent or willing, or bear hardships and privation more humbly',[4] very different from the 'Portuguese cowards, who won't fight a 1/16th of a Frenchman with arms, but murder and plunder the wounded',[5] which he had described prior to the

Officer's belt-plate of the 5th Regiment (1st Elvas), in gilt with silver star and wreath and blue-enamelled centre; a very rare relic of the Portuguese army, probably of the Peninsular War era.

reformation. Although some officers remained incompetent, by 1812 the Portuguese had a formidable reputation: Wellington termed them 'the fighting cocks of the army'; 'I believe we owe their merits more to the care we have taken of their pockets and bellies than to the instruction we have given them.' He added: 'In the end of the last campaign they behaved in many instances extremely ill, because they were in extreme misery, the Portuguese Government having neglected to pay them. I have forced the Portuguese Government to make arrangements to pay them regularly this year, and everybody knows how they behave.'[6] This transformation of the Portuguese army from a shambles to be among the best in Europe is as much a testimony to the abilities of Beresford and his assistants as to the inherent character of the Portuguese soldier.

Infantry

The 24 infantry regiments were linked in pairs to form eleven brigades (the 20th and 22nd Regiments were never brigaded); regiments had two battalions (the 21st only one), each of seven companies, probably five 'centre', one grenadier and one light, though the light companies were apparently detached in about 1811. Battalion-strength was officially 770, but was often very much less on campaign. The original uniform was a dark blue coat with facing-coloured collar, cuffs, lapels and turnbacks, and a bicorn. The 1806 regulations prescribed a shorter, dark blue jacket (long tails for officers), the *barretina* cap with a false front like the 1812-pattern British 'Belgic' shako, with white plume, brass plate bearing the regimental number and an oval with the national arms above, and cords of mixed blue and the facing-colour (and gold for NCOs), dark blue breeches and white gaiters or white gaiter-trousers in summer, and white leather belts; British weapons and equipment were introduced progressively. A British-style 'stovepipe' shako with the previous plates was introduced in 1811, perhaps because the uniforms were manufactured in Britain or conceivably to regularize the silhouette of the Portuguese uniform to conform with that of the British (important for recognition at a distance). Large blue shoulder-wings were worn by all, with blue and facing-coloured fringe for grenadiers and brass-scaled straps for NCOs and above. Facings were white for Regiments 1 (*La Lippe*), 2 (*Lagos*), 3 (1st *Olivenca*), 13 (*Peniche*), 14 (*Tavira*), 15 (2nd *Olivenca*); red for 4 (*Freire*), 5 (1st *Elvas*), 6 (1st *Oporto*), 16 (*Viera Telles*), 17 (2nd *Elvas*), 18 (2nd *Oporto*); yellow for 7 (*Setubal*), 8 (*Evora*), 9 (*Viana*), 19 (*Cascaes*), 20 (*Campomayor*), 21 (*Valenca*); and light blue for 10 (*Lisbon*), 11 (1st *Almeida*), 12 (*Chaves*), 22 (*Serpa*), 23 (2nd *Almeida*) and 24 (*Braganca*). Blue collars were worn by the 1st–12th. White piping was the distinctive of the 1st 'Grand Division', red the 2nd and yellow the 3rd; this applied throughout the army. Thus piping and turnbacks were white for Regiments 1, 4, 7, 10, 13, 16, 19 and 22; red for Regiments 2, 5, 8, 11, 14, 17, 20 and 23; and yellow for the remainder.

Rank-markings regulated from *c.* 1806 were: colonel, two shoulder-scales with bullions; lieutenant-colonel the same but bullions only on the right; major the same but bullions on the left; captain, scales with fringes; lieutenant with fringe only on the right; 2nd lieutenant with fringe on the left; sergeant, scales with yellow fringes; 2nd sergeant with fringe on the right; *furriel* (quartermaster-corporal) with fringe on the left; corporal, two yellow stripes on the cuff; lance-corporal, one stripe.

Light Infantry

Six battalions of light infantry (*caçadores*) were formed by Beresford in November 1808, trained in British 'rifle' tactics; three more were converted from the Anglo-Portuguese Loyal Lusitanian Legion and three more newly created, bringing the total to twelve. Each comprised 770 men in five companies, of which one were *atiradores* (sharpshooters). Their uniform was dark brown jacket and breeches with yellow loops on the breast, the *barretina* with green cords and plume (black for *atiradores*) and facing-coloured collar and cuffs: 1st Regiment (*Castello de Vide*) and 4th (*Vizeu*) light blue, 2nd (*Moura*) and 5th (*Campomayor*) red, 3rd (*Villa Real*) and 6th (*Oporto*) yellow, the 1st–3rd with brown collars. In about 1811 a British-style 'stovepipe' shako was introduced, and jackets with black braid on the breast; facings were black with the following exceptions: 1st sky-blue collar, 2nd scarlet cuffs, 4th sky-blue collar and cuffs, 5th scarlet collar and cuffs, 6th yellow collar and cuffs, 7th yellow cuffs, 8th sky-blue collar, 9th scarlet collar, 10th yellow collar, 11th sky-blue collar and scarlet cuffs, 12th scarlet collar and sky-blue cuffs. Equipment was black leather; originally armed with short swords and the infantry musket, they later adopted British rifles.

Cavalry

The twelve cavalry regiments remained the weakest element of the army and always needed the support of British troops;

as Wellington commented, ' . . . they behaved infamously, and they must not be employed again alone, or with our cavalry, who gallop too fast for them, but only as they were on the 22nd July [Salamanca] viz., in support of our infantry, and with English dragoons with them'.[7] Regimental establishment was 594 in four squadrons, but actual strength rarely approached 300; no more than 1,300 of the total establishment of more than 7,000 were ever fit for field service simultaneously, and such was the shortage of horses that the 2nd, 3rd and 12th Regiments were never mounted but employed as garrison troops.

The original uniform was lightish blue with bicorn or helmet, and cuirasses; by 1809 it had been regularized to a dark blue jacket and breeches, a combed black leather helmet with black crest and red plume, and facing-coloured collar and cuffs: 1st Regiment (*Alcantara*), 2nd (*Moura*) and 3rd (*Olivenca*) white; 4th (*Principe*), 5th (*Evora*) and 6th (*Braganca*) red; 7th (*Lisbon*), 8th (*Elvas*) and 9th (*Chaves*) yellow; 10th (*Santarem*), 11th (*Almeida*) and 12th (*Miranda*) light blue. Piping was white for Regiments 1, 4, 7 and 10, red for 2, 5, 8 and 11, and yellow for the remainder. In the later Peninsular War shakos appear to have been worn by some regiments, e.g., the 10th.

The Legion d'Alorna wore the uniform of the respective 'arms', the cavalry in lightish blue dolmans and the crested helmet, the infantry with shakos, all with black facings.

Artillery

The four artillery regiments were improved greatly by the superintendance of Alexander Dickson, Wellington's Peninsular artillery chief, and by Beresford's introduction of the superior 9pdr, but the garrison artillery remained poor and very under-strength. They wore infantry-style uniform, changing to the 'stovepipe' cap like the infantry, with black facings and plumes; the four regiments were: 1st (*Corte*), 2nd (*Algarve*), 3rd (*Estemos*) and 4th (*Oporto*). The engineers remained of limited use due to having too many senior officers unwilling to superintend field-works because of their elevated status; they wore infantry uniform with black facings, gold lace, and bicorns with white-tipped black

---

A comment in a Visitors' Book at Waterloo:

'I this day visited the field where Napoleon, by the misconduct of an officer, was obliged to yield the palm of victory to superior numbers; and that his son may one day revenge his death, and shake Europe to its centre, is the sincere wish of an American.

'Junius Brutus Booth, Citizen of the United States, June 3, 1826.'

(Booth, an actor of some little repute, was in fact born in London; he is perhaps best-remembered as the father of John Wilkes Booth, the assassin of Abraham Lincoln.)

('The Waterloo Albums', in *United Service Journal*, London 1839, I, p. 89.)

plumes. The pontoon-train was crewed by landing-parties from British warships, and from 1813 Wellington sanctioned the use of Portuguese naval personnel. The commissariat was especially wretched and attracted censure from all who encountered it; D'Urban's note that it was 'infamous beyond all description'[8] is typical!

Militia

One regiment of conscripted militia was formed in each of Portugal's 48 regions; each regiment had two battalions of six companies each, totalling 1,500 men, though this figure was rarely attained. Units served for two, three or six months, so that only a fraction of the whole was embodied at one time. They had limited value except as garrison troops, to relieve regulars for active duty; as Wellington noted, 'the greater number of this description of men we have, the greater number of the better description we should have to dispose of'.[9] The Torres Vedras fortifications were designed to enable them to be held without depriving the field army of a single brigade, as Jones wrote: the militia were basically

Kincaid makes a perceptive comment on how events can be influenced by chance and the individual:

'Millitary men in battle may be classed under three disproportionate heads – a very small class who consider themselves insignificant – a very large class who content themselves with doing their duty, without going beyond it – and a tolerably large class who do their best, many of which are great men without knowing it. One example in the history of a private soldier will establish all that I have advanced on the subject . . . We were engaged in a very hot skirmish, and had driven the enemy's light troops for a considerable distance with great rapidity, when we were at length stopped by some of their regiments in line . . . We remained inactive for about ten minutes amidst a shower of balls that seemed to be almost like a hailstorm, and when at the very worst, when it appeared to me to be certain death to quit the cover, a young scampish fellow of the name of Priestly, at the adjoining tree, started out from behind it, saying, 'Well! I'll be hanged if I'll be bothered any longer behind a tree, so here's at you,' and with that he banged off his rifle in the face of his foes, reloading very deliberately, while every one right and left followed his example, and the enemy, panic-struck, took to their heels without firing another shot. The action requires no comment, the individual did not seem to be aware that he had any merit in what he did, but it is nevertheless a valuable example for those who are disposed to study causes and effects in the art of war.'

(*Random Shots from a Rifleman*, Sir John Kincaid, London 1835; Maclaren's combined edn. with *Adventures in the Rifle Brigade*, London 1908, p. 211.)

'ill-organized peasantry' but 'being possessed of innate courage, were equal to defend a redoubt'.[10] They were ordered not to engage in combat if possible, and were unreliable when they did, for example the Tomar Militia which fled at Busaco. Their 1806-pattern uniform was depicted as medium green with scarlet facings; latterly they wore blue infantry uniform, but were so short of equipment that even pikes were pressed into service.

Navy

For a state with a considerable maritime tradition and which possessed considerable overseas territory, Portugal played little part in the naval operations of the Napoleonic Wars. The navy possessed eleven ships-of-the-line, ten frigates and other smaller vessels in active use in 1795, and collaborated with the British navy in the Atlantic and Mediterranean; but the chief vessels accompanied the royal family to Brazil and only unserviceable ones were left, some of which were taken into French service. The remainder reverted to Portuguese control by the Convention of Cintra, but apparently engaged in no further active service for the remainder of the period. In the colonial actions in which Portuguese troops were involved – for example the 500 who assisted the British navy in the capture of Cayenne in January 1809 – they were conveyed in British ships, in this case in HMS *Confiance*. The officers' uniform was dark blue with gold lace (though red facings may have been used also); marines wore blue with red facings, white buttons, blue breeches with red stripe, white belts and a *barretina* with a black fur crest running from front to back.

Notes

1. *Memoranda relative to the Lines thrown up to cover Lisbon in 1810*, Colonel J. T. Jones, in *Papers on Subjects connected with the Duties of the Corps of Royal Engineers*, vol. III, London 1839, p. 40.
2. ibid. p. 51.
3. *Adventures in Three Quarters of the Globe*, J. Blakiston, London 1829, II, p. 336.
4. *Letters from the Peninsula*, Sir William Warre, ed. E. Warre, London 1909, p. 239.
5. ibid. p. 28.
6. Wellington to Liverpool, 25 July 1813; *Dispatches of Field Marshal the Duke of Wellington*, ed. J. Gurwood, London 1834–9, X, p. 569.
7. Wellington to Beresford, 8 September 1812; *Dispatches*, IX, p. 402.
8. *The Peninsular Journal of Major-General Sir Benjamin D'Urban 1808–17*, ed. I. J. Rousseau, 1930, p. 153: 4 October 1810.
9. Wellington to Beresford, 9 February 1811; *Dispatches* VII, p. 239.
10. Jones, op. cit., pp. 27–8.

References

Pivka, Otto von. *The Portuguese Army of the Napoleonic Wars*, London 1977.
Ward, S. G. P 'The Portuguese Infantry Brigades 1809–14', in *Journal of the Society for Army Historical Research*, vol. LIII, London 1975, pp. 103–12 (a most important paper on Peninsular War organization).
Accounts by participants which give much information on the progress of the Portuguese army include:
Blakiston, J. *Twenty Years' Military Adventures in Three-Quarters of the Globe*, London 1829.
Bunbury, T. *Reminiscences of a Veteran*, London 1861.
Warre, Sir William. *Letters from the Peninsula*, ed. E. Warre, London 1909.

PRUSSIA

History

Under Frederick II 'the Great' (ruled 1740–86), Prussia was advanced from a German state of medium importance to one of the foremost powers in Europe, due almost entirely to Frederick's campaigning and the excellence of the Prussian army which became a model for many military theorists. Despite Prussian successes in the Seven Years War, however, the army had declined somewhat in effectiveness, believing, perhaps, that as 'Old Fritz's' methods had been successful, modernization was unnecessary. The first signs were evident in Frederick's last campaign, the War of the Bavarian Succession against Austria (1778) in which comparatively little action occurred; and after Frederick's death in 1786 a strong and vigorous monarch was required to re-assert Prussia's position in Germany, a position its size and Frederick's legacy demanded, but such a guiding hand was not forthcoming.

Frederick II was succeeded by his nephew, Frederick William II, in 1786. Lacking the energy and determination of his uncle, he neither pursued the previous vigorous external policy, nor made any attempt to meet the internal discontent by liberal reforms, so that the system of

King Frederick William III of Prussia (1770–1840), wearing staff uniform with the twisted shoulder-cords of full dress, and the breast-star of the Order of the Black Eagle. (Engraving by T. Johnson)

government remained that of absolutism, but perhaps lacking the 'enlightenment' of Frederick the Great. Frederick William II tended to follow Austria's lead in foreign affairs, in direct contrast to his uncle, hence the Austro-Prussian alliance against revolutionary France. The Prussian army had been engaged in a somewhat fruitless but expensive campaign in Holland in 1787, and was not especially distinguished against the French; and in 1795, suspicious of the motives of Austria and Russia, Prussia made a separate peace (of Basel) which virtually split Germany into two camps. The greatest shame was the willingness with which Prussia abandoned German territories along the Rhine, yet was eager to expand eastwards, and though the partitions of Poland virtually doubled the state's area, the eastern provinces added little to her power. The following years of Prussian neutrality cost her prestige, and weakened the army and the previous attitudes of economy and good order.

Frederick William III succeeded his father as king in 1797, and though he tried to remedy the worst aspects of his father's regime by lifting some of the more repressive laws, he lacked the decisiveness required. Not until the formation of the Confederation of the Rhine did Frederick William decide to act against the growing menace from France, and only then after the urgings of his queen, Louise of Mecklenburg-Strelitz, whose determination and hatred of the French led her to be regarded in some quarters as 'the only man in Prussia'. The crushing defeats of Jena and Auerstädt demonstrated the decline of the Prussian army and national resolve; Frederick William lost half his kingdom by the Peace of Tilsit, including all the acquisitions from the second and third partitions of Poland and all land west of the Elbe. Yet this débâcle also resulted in the regeneration of Prussia, for

the humiliation resulted in a rebirth of patriotism and moral regeneration, led by the *Tugenbund* or 'League of Virtue'. Credit for much of the reconstruction lies with Frederick William's two great ministers, Baron Heinrich von Stein (1757–1831) and, after he was forced by French pressure to flee to Austria in 1809, his successor, Prince Karl von Hardenburg (1750–1822). Stein overhauled the government, instituting a new, radical system by which the departmental ministers were both the king's advisers and the executive power for performing his wishes, dispensing with the useless councillors who had provided advice but who had little connection with the respective government departments. Serfdom was abolished and the previous rules prohibiting transition of employment or tenure of land between the three classes of nobles, burghers and peasants were scrapped. Coupled with the educational reforms of Wilhelm von

The death of the Prussian hero Major von Schill at Stralsund, 31 May 1809; a somewhat 'heroic' version by Richard Knötel from Die Königin Luise *(1896). It illustrates to good effect the white uniform of the infantry of the Kingdom of Holland, including a grenadier (left) with fur cap bearing a facing-coloured patch and white cross, light infantry (right), with green epaulettes and shakos bearing a horn-badge, and ordinary fusiliers, including the distinctive shako with side-loop and regimental number on the front.*

Humboldt, and Hardenburg's revolutionary edict which made the peasants the legal and absolute owners of part of their land, these reforms not only modernized the state but encouraged the growth of patriotic sentiment. The army was modernized similarly by the Hanoverian General Gerhard von Scharnhorst (1755–1813) and the Saxon General Augustus Wilhelm von Gneisenau (1760–1831), the former in particular becoming the symbol of rekindled patriotism and the tide of German nationalism which grew to a flood in 1813.

Prussia remained out of the 1809 war, and contributed troops to Napoleon's invasion of Russia in 1812. General Yorck's Prussian contingent concluded an armistice with the Russians by the Convention of Tauroggen (30 December 1812) which, though Frederick William at first disowned it, precipitated Prussia's joining of the Sixth Coalition. With massed popular support, Prussia became a leading participant in the 'war of liberation' which drove the French from Germany, and the francophobe Blücher (always antagonistic towards Prussian friendship with Napoleon) became one of the leading Allied commanders in the 1813–14 campaigns, and led the Prussian forces with equal effect in the Waterloo campaign. Prussia did not receive quite the same amount of territory at the Congress of Vienna as she had lost, but retrieved her old territories west of the Elbe, Swedish Pomerania and parts of Saxony and Westphalia; but her position was infinitely stronger than before, and she led the cause of German nationalism in the following years largely as a result of the campaigns of 1813–15. Frederick William III died on 7 June 1840, popular to the last, and despite the somewhat inauspicious opening of his reign, his later achievements were considerable. From this position Prussia became the leading German state and the foundation of the German Empire, though the upsurge of patriotic sentiment which was so vital in the 1813–14 period might be regarded as having not totally beneficial effects for Europe as a whole in the subsequent century.

Army (cockade: black; after 1808, black with white edge)
Before the disaster of 1806 the Prussian establishment was largely a relic of that dating from the great days of Frederick the Great; after 1806, Napoleon insisted that the army should not exceed 42,000 men (it had been about 200,000 in the 1790s), a restriction evaded by a process of calling to the colours successive batches of recruits and discharging them when fully trained, thus creating a reservoir of trained personnel in addition to those actually under arms. The change in the character of the army was much more than merely a reformation of regiments: whereas prior to 1806 the personnel was either conscripted or mercenary, that of 1813 was fired with patriotic fervour which engendered a hatred of the French and a desire for revenge, with the belief that it was no longer a chore to serve in the army but a privilege to serve the nation. This constituted a considerable part of the reasons for the army's success and to a degree compensated for the often wretched standard of uniform and equipment which resulted in many of the hastily formed units of 1813

Napoleon and Prussia:

'His aversion to Frederick William was remarkable. Napoleon had been frequently heard to speak reproachfully of the cabinet of Prussia for its treaties with the French republic. "It was a desertion of the cause of kings; that the negociations [*sic*] of the court of Berlin with Directory displayed a timid, selfish, and ignoble policy, which sacrificed its dignity, and the general cause of monarchs, to petty aggrandizements." Whenever he followed with his finger the traces of the Prussian frontiers upon the map, he seemed to be angry at seeing them still so extensive, and exclaimed, "Is it possible that I have left this man so large a territory?" '

(*History of the Expedition to Russia*: Count P. de Segur, London 1825, I. p. 6.)

Regiment	Facings	Officers' Lace	Other Ranks' Lace
1	poppy-red	silver	white, 3 red stripes
2	crimson	silver	crimson
3 (*Leib Regiment*)	dark blue	gold	dark blue, white strip
4	black	gold	dark blue and white checks
5	light blue	gold	light blue and white diamonds
6	light brick-red	gold	white and light brick-red mixed
7	lemon	silver	white and yellow strip
8	dark blue	silver	dark blue, 2 white stripes
9	crimson	gold	white and crimson
10	poppy-red	gold	poppy-red
11	light blue	silver	white with light blue chains
12	dark orange	gold	orange, white stripes
13 (Garde du Corps)	poppy-red	silver	silver

receiving only an overcoat and a cloth cap, some barefoot and armed only with pikes, despite immense quantities of munitions supplied to Prussia by Britain. A new command structure ensured that only capable officers prospered (in 1806 more than half the generals and a quarter of regimental and battalion-commanders were aged over 60), and after the reforms it was possible for any citizen to become an officer, whereas before 1806 more than 90 per cent were nobles. On 3 February 1813 a formation of volunteer *Jägers* was decreed, to be raised from middle- and upper-class young volunteers able to buy their own equipment (which formation also provided a training-ground for aspirant officers), and on 9 February a national militia (*Landwehr*) was decreed, 120,000 strong, encompassing men between ages 17 and 40, which could be brought up to strength by conscription if insufficient volunteers were forthcoming. Both of these organizations harnessed the upsurge of patriotic feeling and have been idealized in German history. The spirit of the Prussian army was completely re-born.

Cavalry: pre-1806

Prior to the defeat of 1806 the cavalry comprised twelve cuirassier regiments plus the Garde du Corps, twelve dragoon regiments (thirteen in 1802 and fourteen in 1803), and ten hussar regiments including one of *Bosniaks* (later lancers, raised from Prussia's Polish territory). Under Frederick the Great they had been employed in 'shock' action, but in the 1806 campaign the formation of divisions including a cavalry brigade resulted in the cavalry becoming too scattered to act effectively *en masse*.

Cuirassier regiments comprised five squadrons (the Garde du Corps three until 1798) with a field strength of 841. They wore no cuirass, but a white jacket (the 2nd yellow) with facing-coloured collar, cuffs, turnbacks and girdle, with broad lace down the breast and edging the cuffs, shoulder-straps and white belts; white breeches, long boots and bicorns with white plumes for troopers, with a black tip for NCOs and black base for officers. Regimental distinctions were:

Sabretaches were facing-coloured with edging and 'FWR' cipher in the lace-colour; waistcoats were facing-coloured (10th and 13th dark blue).

Dragoon regiments had five squadrons each (5th and 6th ten), with a field strength of 841 and 1,682 respectively. Initially they wore infantry-style light blue uniform with facing-coloured collar, cuffs, turnbacks and later shoulder-straps; the cavalry jacket (*Kollet*) in the same colours was introduced from 1802, with light blue turnbacks laced in the facing-colour (9th white), a button-coloured aiguillette on the right shoulder, and other items like cuirassiers. Facings were black (Regiments 1 and 12), white (2 and 6), pink (3), straw-yellow (4), dark crimson (5), scarlet (7, 8 and 9), orange (10), crimson (13) and chamois (14); buttons and officers' lace were yellow/gold for Regiments 1, 2, 7, 13 and 14 and white/silver for the remainder.

The nine hussar regiments had 10 squadrons each and a field strength of 1,543, and the tenth (ex-*Bosniaks*, in 1806 the *Towarczy* or lancer regiment) of ten squadrons totalling 1,251, plus the independent hussar battalion (later 11th Hussars) of five squadrons. They wore braided dolman, pelisse, overalls or white breeches and a busby (1st–4th and 9th) or a black mirliton with yellow or white lace trim (a white skull and crossed bones badge for the 5th); busbies were withdrawn for all but the 2nd in 1796, and from 1804 shakos were introduced but were not universal by 1806; with plumes coloured like those of cuirassiers detailed above. Regimental details were: dolmans light green (1st Regiment, dark green from 1800), scarlet (2nd), white (3rd, dark blue from 1800), light blue (4th), black (5th), brown (6th), lemon (7th), dark crimson (8th), yellow (10th, dark blue from 1803 and 11th, dark green from 1806). The pelisse was coloured as the dolman except for: 1st and 11th (dark green), 2nd, 3rd and 10th (dark blue), 7th (light blue); braid and buttons were white except for the 3rd and 6th (yellow), 4th (blue and white braid, officers' silver), 10th (red and white braid pre-1803) and 11th (red and white braid, NCOs' white, officers' silver pre-1806, then yellow); officers' braid of the 2nd was gold. Collar and cuffs of the dolman were green (1st pre-1800, 11th pre-1806), dark blue (2nd, 10th pre-1803), red (1st and 4th post-1800, 5th and 11th post-1806), yellow (3rd, 6th, 10th post-1803), light blue (4th pre-1800, 7th) or black (8th); sashes were in the facing-colour (except 4th yellow, 8th and 11th red, 10th crimson) with barrels in the button-colour (except 3rd, 6th and 11th white, 10th blue). Sabretaches were in the dolman-colour (except 3rd yellow, 4th rank-and-file white, 5th officers' red, 7th light blue, 8th and 10th black, 11th red) with lace of the button-colour (except 3rd white, 4th light blue, 5th, 8th and 9th none save officers' silver, 11th white or yellow post-1806). The 9th Regiment was the Polish *Towarczys* (converted from the *Bosniaks* in 1799) organized in traditional Polish fashion, the first rank (one-third of each squadron) of *Towarczys* or nobles with the second and third ranks of troopers. They originally wore a tail-less red jacket with blue facings, white lace and breeches and a white-plumed astrakhan cap, and in winter a dark blue frock-coat with white fur trim. Officers wore fur caps with the usual officers' plume, red or dark blue frock-coat with blue or red facings respectively, and silver hussar braid. Later the unit wore a dark blue *Kollet* with poppy-red facings, white-edged red girdle and a peakless shako; their lance-pennons were blue over red.

Cavalry: post-1806

After the 1806 campaign the cavalry was reduced to four cuirassier, six dragoon, seven hussar and two *Uhlan* (lancer) regiments, each of four squadrons of two companies each, each company of two troops (*Zügen*), with squadrons 125 strong.

Cuirassiers wore double-breasted white *Kollets* of infantry style (minus cuff-flaps) with regimental facings and turnback-lace: 1st (Silesian) black, 2nd (East Prussian) light blue, 3rd (Garde du Corps) red, 4th (Brandenburg) dark blue (cornflower-blue by 1814). Buttons were yellow (1st and 4th) or white (2nd and 3rd); the 3rd had white 'Guard' loops (*Litzen*) on collar and cuffs. The head-dress was a combed black leather helmet with black hair crest and a brass plate bearing an eagle (a star for the 3rd), and the usual service legwear were grey overalls. For campaign a dark blue *litewka* could be worn with facing-coloured collar (4th scarlet), and though captured French cuirasses were issued in 1814 it is unlikely that they were worn during the campaigning. The red shabraque was square-cut and edged in the facing-colour.

The dragoons wore a similar *Kollet* or *litewka* in light blue, with facings (collar and shoulder-straps only on the *litewka*): 1st (Queen's) crimson, 2nd (1st West Prussian) white, 3rd (Lithuanian) and 4th (2nd West Prussian) scarlet, 5th (Brandenburg) black and 6th (Neumark) pink; yellow buttons for 3rd and 5th and white for the remainder. They wore grey overalls and a shako with cords in the button-colour, normally covered with black oilskin concealing the

eagle-plate (button-colour) and black-and-white national pompom; officers wore a black-and-white cockade instead of the plate. Their light blue shabraques were round-ended and edged in the facing-colour.

The hussars continued to wear the traditional uniform, but with a shako with a black-and-white cockade (1st and 2nd with a white death's head); in March 1815 six new regiments were converted from the previous 'National Cavalry', volunteer units raised in 1813. Regimental details were: dolman and pelisse black for Regiments 1 (1st *Leib*-Hussars), 2 (2nd *Leib*-Hussars) and 7 (West Prussian); dark blue for 3 (Brandenburg), 5 (Pomeranian) and 8 (1st Westphalian); brown for 4 (1st Silesian); green for 6 (2nd Silesian), 10 (1st Magdeburg) and 11 (2nd Westphalian); light blue for 9 (Rhenish). Facings were scarlet (1st–3rd, 6th), yellow (4th), dark blue (5th), red (7th, 11th) and light blue (8th–10th, 12th); buttons and braid yellow (4th–7th, 9th and 10th) and white for the remainder. Sashes were facing-coloured with button-coloured barrels; shabraques of black lambskin with red 'wolf-tooth' edging.

The *Uhlans* wore dark blue *Kollets* with pointed cuffs, red facings, yellow buttons, the standard grey overalls, blue and red girdle, hussar shako with black plume and yellow cords for full dress, and shoulder-straps white, scarlet and yellow respectively for the 1st (West Prussian), 2nd (Silesian) and 3rd (Brandenburg) Regiments. The *Uhlan Leib*-Squadron formed in 1808 and re-titled the Guard *Uhlan* Squadron in 1810 originally wore a blue *kurtka* faced red, but from 1810 the *Uhlan Kollet* in the same colours with yellow 'Guard' loops on the facings; they had an Austrian-style *czapka* with blue top and yellow trim and cords. The *Uhlan* shabraque was dark blue with round ends and red edge (or hussar lambskin); lance-pennons were white-over-blue, red-over-blue and yellow-over-blue for the 1st–3rd Regiments respectively, and white-over-red for the Guard, changing to universal white-over-black from March 1815. Additional *Uhlan* regiments were formed from the 'National Cavalry' in 1815: 4th (Pomeranian), 5th (Westphalian), 6th (2nd West Prussian), 7th (1st Rhineland) and 8th (2nd Rhineland), with shoulder-straps light blue, white, red, yellow and light blue respectively, with white buttons (4th yellow). Some units retained their old uniform to the end of the period, however: the 6th (ex-Lützow's *Freikorps* and Bremen Volunteers) wore black *litewkas* faced red, with the shako and *czapka* respectively; and the 7th (ex-Hellwig's *Streifkorps* and von Schill's Hussars) with red dolman with blue facings and *czapka* and white braid, and black hussar uniform respectively. The 8th Regiment was formed from the hussars of the Russo-German Legion.

Infantry: pre-1806

The infantry comprised the Foot Guards, 52 line regiments (increasing to 54 in 1794, 55 in 1797, 56 in 1803 and 57 in 1804) and twenty fusilier (light infantry) battalions, rising to 21 in 1795 and 24 by 1806. Each regiment comprised one grenadier and two musketeer battalions plus a depot (becoming the 3rd Musketeer battalion in 1796, raised to full

strength only on mobilization), each battalion of four companies of 155 other ranks (with ten riflemen or *Schützen* per company). From June 1799 each regiment comprised two 5-company musketeer battalions, the depot and two grenadier companies, the latter to be detached in wartime to form half of a composite grenadier battalion. In July 1806 new organization gave each regiment three 4-company battalions (the 3rd Battalion fusiliers) and two grenadier companies, but this was only enacted after the war. Each grenadier battalion was drawn from two regiments and was usually named after the commander but could be referred to by the numbers of the regiments from which they were drawn, e.g., Battalion 'Sack' might also be styled 'Nr. 33/47'.

Initially the uniform was like that worn under Frederick the Great: a blue coat with coloured facings, white waistcoat and breeches and black gaiters; in 1788 the tricorn hat and grenadiers' mitre caps were replaced by a bicorn-like cap termed a '*Casquet*' with upturned front and rear flaps, the front bearing a grenade or (for musketeers) the 'FWR II' cipher in the button-colour; officers wore bicorns. Regiments 6 and 21 had straw-yellow waistcoat and breeches, and some had lace loops on the facings. After the accession of Frederick William III the bicorn was re-introduced, the uniform re-styled with closed lapels, and a new grenadier cap devised, a squat head-band of the facing-colour (light blue for those with white facings) edged white, with a tall black leather front-plate with a brass grenade over a brass lower band bearing a black eagle, with a black peak edged with white tape, and a white plume; buff overalls were worn on campaign. Facing-colours in 1806 were: poppy-red Regiments 1, 3, 15 (Guard), 22, 24, 27, 34 and 48; orange 2, 4, 12, 14, 16, 19, 26, 42 and 43; straw-yellow 5; scarlet 6 (Guard Grenadiers), 8, 9, 20, 21, 25, 38, 46, 52, and 56; deep pink 7, 18, 23, 40 and 57; lemon 10, 45, 47, 51 and 60; crimson 11, 29, 37, and 55; dull orange 12, 14, 16 and 26; white 13, 17, 33, 36, 39, 49 and 59; buff 28, 30, 32, 44 and 54; pink 31; deep yellow 35; light crimson 41 and 50; pale yellow 53 and 58. Buttons were white for Regiments 1, 7, 10, 11, 13, 15, 18, 19, 21, 23, 28, 30, 34–37, 40, 43, 48–52, 54, 56 and 58, and yellow for the remainder.

An unusual contemporary depiction of Blücher, wearing the Prussian hussar uniform of the pre-1806 period, presumably that of his 8th Regiment (red with black facings, and mirliton cap). At his neck he wears the Pour le Mérite, *and the star of the Order of the Black Eagle upon his breast.*

'When Blücher, in his hate of France, refused the order of the Holy Ghost, which Louis XVIII wished to confer, and the Duke tried in vain to persuade him to accept, "If I do," said the vengeful Prussian, 'I will hang the order on me behind." "And if you do", observed the Duke, "you will show how much you value it, by hanging it where the enemy will never hit it." '

(*Wellington Anecdotes*, anon., London n.d., p. 35)

The fusiliers had similar uniform but in dark green, the *Casquet* bearing an eagle-badge, with facings light green (Battalions 1 and 8), pink (2, 7), white (3, 11), light blue (4, 17), dark green (5, 20), orange (6, 12), straw-yellow (9, 10), buff (13, 15), black (14, 16) or crimson (18, 19); buttons yellow for 1–6, 10, 14, 15 and 18 and white for the remainder. in 1797 the bicorn was introduced, and in 1801 a cylindrical shako with eagle-badge in the button-colour; and from 1797 a shorter-tailed jacket with facings according to the brigade to which the battalions were attached: crimson (1, 2, 5, 18–20), light green (3, 6, 11 ,21, 23, 24), light blue (4, 8, 9, 12, 16, 17) or black (7, 10, 13–15, 22); white buttons for 7, 9, 10, 12, 17, 18–24 and yellow for the remainder, and black leather equipment.

Infantry: post-1806

The reconstructions by the end of 1808 produced twelve regiments each of two musketeer and one fusilier battalions (the fusiliers no longer separate), plus two grenadier companies to be detached and formed into six composite grenadier battalions (Regiment 8 did not detach its grenadiers, Regiment 9 providing four companies to compensate, these forming the *Leib*-Grenadier Battalion). Each battalion comprised four companies with an expanded wartime strength of about 800 men (often less, occasionally more). They wore a short-tailed, double-breasted dark blue *Kollet* with red turnbacks (long tails for officers), yellow buttons, with an open collar (closed from 1813) and cuffs (with blue patches) in the facing-colour, and shoulder-straps coloured according to the seniority of the regiment within the province, white, poppy-red, yellow and light blue for the 1st–4th Regiments respectively. Black gaiters were worn with white or grey breeches (summer and winter respectively) and a shako bearing a brass royal cipher for musketeers, eagle for grenadiers and a black cockade with white edge for fusiliers, all with an upper white lace band, the white national pompom with black centre, and an immense plume in white (Guards) or black (grenadiers), which became much narrower in 1813, though the shako-ornaments were usually concealed by a black waterproof cover worn on campaign. Guards wore the star of the Order of the Black Eagle on the shako, save their grenadiers who had a 'flying eagle' badge.

Regiments and facing-colours were: 1, 3, 4 and 5 (1st–4th East Prussian) dull orange or brick-red; 2 (1st Pomeranian) white; 6 and 7 (1st and 2nd West Prussian) crimson; 8 (Guard Regiment) scarlet (cuffs without flaps, with white buttons and white loops on facings); 9 (*Leib*-Regiment)

Grenadier of the Foot Guards, Prussian army, c.1809. The uniform is basically that worn from the post-Jena period throughout the remaining campaigns of the Napoleonic Wars, including a double-breasted Kollet in dark blue with red facings and white 'Guard' lace, dark grey breeches, knee-boots, and a shako with 'Guard star' plate and the enormous Busch plume worn by grenadiers, in this case in white. (Print by Wolf & Jügel)

Prussian Landwehr *officer, wearing a uniform like that of the ordinary infantry (instead of the* litewka *of the* Landwehr*), plus the* Landwehr *cap.* Landwehr *officers often wore regular infantry uniform, with the* universal silver and black waist-sash indicative of commissioned rank in all branches of the Prussian army. (Print by Jacquemin after popular prints of the 1814–15 period showing Allied troops in the occupation of Paris)

Prussian Landwehr *private, c.1814–15, wearing the typical* litewka *frock-coat and a cloth cap (here with a waterproof cover) bearing the* Landwehr *cross. The roll worn bandolier-fashion was a common practice among the Prussian infantry in* general. *(Print by Jacquemin after popular prints of the 1814–15 period showing Allied troops in the occupation of Paris)*

poppy-red; 10 (Colberg) white; 11 and 12 (1st and 2nd Silesian) lemon. In June 1813 Regiment 8 (Guards) was taken out of the line and the succeeding regiments re-numbered, with a new 12th (2nd Brandenburg) being formed, with poppy-red facings and shoulder-straps (the *Leib*-Regiment ranked as the 1st Brandenburg). A second Foot Guard regiment was raised at the same time, uniformed like the 1st (ex-Regiment 8) but with flapped cuffs and yellow

buttons, and in 1814 the grenadier battalions were formed into two Guard Grenadier regiments, with red facings and white and red shoulder-straps for the 1st and 2nd Regiments respectively bearing the ciphers of the Allied sovereigns after whom the units were named, 1st (Tsar Alexander) red cipher, and 2nd (Emperor Francis) yellow.

Twelve 'Reserve' regiments and volunteers were formed in 1813 with a wide variety of uniforms ranging from the green of the ex-Russo-German Legion to makeshift grey waistcoats and cloth caps, blue uniforms manufactured in Britain for the Portuguese army, 'stovepipe' caps, green British 'rifle' uniform or white Berg uniform, some of which were retained as late as the Waterloo campaign. In March 1815 the Reserve and volunteer units were numbered as line regiments (13–24 and 25–32 respectively): Regiments 13, 15–17 (1st–4th Westphalian), 14 and 21 (3rd and 4th Pomeranian), 18 and 19 (1st and 2nd Posen), 20 and 24 (3rd and 4th Brandenburg), 22 and 23 (1st and 2nd Upper Silesian). Subsequent numbers were formed from: 25 (Lützow's *Freikorps*), 26 (Elbe Regiment), 27 (Hellwig's *Streifkorps* and others), 28 and 29 (Berg infantry), 30 and 31 (Russo-German Legion) and 32 (Elbe, Saxon and Westphalian). Facing- and shoulder-strap colours were in accordance with the existing system, with three new 'provincial' colours introduced in 1814: Magdeburg light blue, Westphalia pink and Rhineland crab-red.

Jägers

The 10-company *Jäger* Regiment had a wartime strength of almost 2,000, with a green uniform faced red and a green-plumed *Casquet*; the bicorn was introduced in 1797. After 1806 the remnant formed the 1st (Guard) and 2nd (East Prussian) *Jäger* battalions, to which the Silesian *Schützen* (sharpshooter) battalion was added as the 3rd in 1813. They wore infantry uniform in green with red facings (Silesians black piped red) and shakos with cockades; the Guard battalion wore the 'Guard star' badge and yellow loops on collar and cuffs. In 1814 a Guard *Schützen* battalion was formed, uniformed like the Silesian but with 'Guard star' and lace. All had black leather equipment.

Landwehr

The mobilization of the *Landwehr* in 1813 created an immense force including 149 infantry battalions and 113 cavalry squadrons, which though often poorly equipped (at least at the outset) often had a combat capability approaching that of the regulars. Their uniform was usually a dark blue (sometimes grey) cloth cap with leather peak, band in the provincial colour and the '*Landwehr* cross' on the front (from which the German Iron Cross was taken), and a *litewka* in blue with cuff-piping and collar in the provincial colour and shoulder-straps either in that colour or in a seniority-colour as for the regular infantry. Provincial facing-colours were: East Prussia poppy-red, West Prussia black, Brandenburg brick-red, Pomerania white, Silesia yellow, Elbe light blue, Westphalia green and Rhineland crab-red; buttons were yellow for Brandenburg, Pomerania, Elbe and Rhineland and white for the remainder. Equipment was in black leather, and officers often wore the infantry *Kollet*.

Landwehr cavalry were supposed to wear a dark blue *litewka* with provincial distinctions as above, a shako bearing the '*Landwehr* cross', with black sheepskin shabraques and lance-pennons in the provincial colour; in effect a wide variety of styles and colouring existed, including some (like the 7th Silesian) wearing *Uhlan* uniform with *czapka*, others with British 'stovepipes' or captured French shakos, with a wide variety of colouring in the pennons.

Artillery

In 1806 each infantry battalion had an attached 6pdr, and each of the four foot artillery regiments comprised nine companies, each with six 12pdrs and two 10pdr howitzers; the horse artillery comprised twenty troops of six 6pdrs and two 7pdr howitzers. In 1808 a complete reorganization formed three brigades, 1st Prussian, 2nd Silesian and 3rd Brandenburg, each of twelve foot and three horse companies, each with six cannon and two howitzers. The preferred weapon became the 6pdr, so that in August 1813 the field army included 42 companies of 6pdrs, one of 3pdrs, one of 7pdr howitzers and six of 12pdrs, and due to shortages of equipment it was not possible to maintain the correct mix or ordnance, so that some all-gun companies existed. The 4th Foot and 4th Horse Companies were Guard units, and six foot and the 12th Horse companies were *Landwehr*. Despite the establishment of the three 'brigades', in wartime one (light) foot and one horse company were attached to each army brigade, with the remaining guns allocated to corps and army reserves.

The artillery wore blue infantry-style uniform with blue facings, black from 1798, red turnbacks, white breeches and belts, black gaiters and bicorn and yellow buttons; the horse artillery wore a similar uniform with white plume and buff breeches, until in 1802 they adopted dragoon-style jackets with black facings piped red, and white breeches. From 1808 they wore the blue *Kollet* (without cuff-flaps for horse artillery) with red turnbacks, black facings piped scarlet and blue cuff-flaps for the foot artillery, and the same but with blue turnbacks edged with black lace and red piping for the horse, who from 1809 could wear a blue *litewka* with facing-coloured collar. Shoulder-straps were white, yellow and scarlet respectively for the 1st–3rd brigades; the Guard batteries had yellow loops on collar and cuffs (they formed part of the 3rd brigade). The shako had a national pompom and brass three-flamed grenade badge, white upper band for

> The Duke of Wellington was known as a sometimes ascerbic correspondent, hardly surprising when in addition to affairs military and of state he received a vast amount of trivial correspondence, all of which he answered in his own hand though often in the third person and without a signature, so as not to gratify autograph-hunters. This is typically brusque:
>
> 'The Duke of Wellington presents his Compliments to Mr. Briant and can assure him in answer to his Note of the 14th Inst. that he has only to go to the Tower to see what he pleases. An order from the Duke is not necessary. It *must be obvious* to Mr. Briant that an order is not necessary & would be obnoxious to others who should be desirous to see the Tower and might not obtain one.'
>
> (MS, author's possession.)

foot and yellow for horse, who also had yellow cords and white plume in full dress; the Guard companies wore a brass 'Guard star' badge and black plume. Foot companies had infantry equipment in black leather; horse companies were equipped as cavalry, with sabres and white leatherwork. Field ordnance used a double-bracket trail, with woodwork painted light blue.

Engineers and Support

As in most armies, the engineers comprised a corps of officers and units of other ranks. The *Ingenieurkorps* was composed of officers and senior NCOs only, wearing infantry-style uniform in dark blue with red facings, silver loops on the lapels, and bicorns. Manual work was performed by the Pioneer Corps, constituted as three 'fortress' companies in November 1809, raised to four in 1812 and to seven in 1813, when seven 'field' companies were added, plus the Mansfeld *Landwehr* battalion; by 1815 the corps numbered eight fortress and nine field companies plus the Mansfelders. Their uniform was that of the foot artillery minus cuff-flaps, with white buttons, fusilier shako with cockade, black leather equipment and a short carbine in place of the infantry musket. The *Landwehr* battalion wore a black (or dark grey) *Kollet* with red piping and a plain shako bearing a white-metal *Landwehr* cross over an oval plate bearing crossed hammers.

The commissariat was divided into the *Truppentrain* (transport personnel and vehicles attached to regiments) and the 'mobile columns', the central train organization. From 1808 both wore a blue *Kollet* with blue cuffs, grey breeches and black gaiters for those serving dismounted and grey cavalry overalls for mounted personnel; for the *Truppentrain*, collar and shoulder-straps were of the regimental colour, and for the mobile columns light blue collar, red shoulder-straps and white buttons. Head-dress was an unlaced shako with a cockade coloured according to the branch of service: drivers and remount depots dark blue, commissariat and field hospitals bright red, bakeries light blue, paymaster staff bright green, supply depots lemon and postal service orange; after 1813 all wore a black-and-white national cockade instead. Medical officers wore infantry uniform with dark blue facings piped red; medical orderlies had a grey *litewka*, breeches and cap with dark blue collar, shoulder-straps and cap-band.

Rank Marking

Prior to 1808 officers' rank was indicated by the national silver-and-black waist-sash (worn throughout the period), silver-and-black sword-knot and gorget. From 1808 the different grades were differentiated by metallic lace on the shoulder-straps: subalterns with a central stripe, captains with both edges laced, and field officers laced all round. From 1812–14 subalterns adopted the previous captains' pattern and captains a strap with lace on all edges save that at the point of the shoulder. From 1813 metal 'crescents' were added to the straps, fringed for field officers. NCOs had metallic lace of the button-colour on the collar and cuffs (on

the lower edge of the collar until 1813, thereafter on the top) and black-and-white sword-knots; and the tip of the plume in black or white, contrasting with the main colour.

Higher Organization

No fixed divisional system was operated until shortly before Jena, when to up-grade the previous brigade system a new organization was introduced, each division to comprise two infantry brigades (8–10 battalions), a cavalry brigade (10–15 squadrons), two artillery batteries, 5–10 light cavalry squadrons (for reconnaissance) and a light infantry battalion. Its introduction so shortly before a campaign caused only confusion, and the dispersal of the cavalry worked against its ability for shock action. The reduction of the army after the defeat of 1806 allowed for the careful introduction of a new system, brigades now consisting of two infantry regiments (six battalions, with each regiment's fusilier battalion acting as light infantry), one grenadier battalion, one foot and one horse battery and 10–14 cavalry squadrons. Although this continued to relegate the cavalry to a supportive role for the infantry, it worked well in practice. (Although termed 'brigades', these formations actually fulfilled a divisional role; two Prussian brigades combined to form a Corps.)

References

The major source for the history of the Prussian army probably remains C. Jany's *Geschichte der Preussen Armee von 15 Jahrhundert bis 1914*, but the following are more accessible:

Hofschröer, P. *Prussian Cavalry of the Napoleonic Wars*, *I* and *II*, London 1986.
— *Prussian Landwehr and Landsturm*, London 1980.
— *Prussian Light Infantry 1792–1815*, London 1984.
— *Prussian Line Infantry 1792–1815*, London 1984.
— *Prussian Reserve, Militia & Irregular Troops* 1806–15, London 1987.
Nash, D. *The Prussian Army 1808–15*, New Malden 1972.
Ortenburg, G. *Preussische Husarenbilder um 1791*, Copenhagen 1976.
Young, P. *Blücher's Army*, London 1973.

REUSS

History

The Thuringian principalities of Reuss were controlled by two branches of the same family, known as Reuss (elder line) or Reuss-Greiz, and Reuss (younger line) or Reuss-Schleiz-Gera. The division (initially into three states) occurred in 1564, and into two from 1616; the head of the elder line (Reuss-Greiz) became a prince of the Empire in 1778, the heads of both having taken the title 'count' in 1673; the Count of Reuss-Schleiz-Gera became a prince in 1806. In 1807 both states joined the Confederation of the Rhine, and in 1815 the German Confederation. A bizarre and most confusing practice existed by which *all* male members of the ruling house of both states were christened Heinrich (Henry) and distinguished by a number, but in a system that was eccentric in the extreme. In Reuss-Greiz, the numbers continued until 100 was reached, whereupon the next male offspring was titled Henry I; in Reuss-Schleiz-Gera the first prince of a new century was numbered Henry I, and the numbers rose until a new century was reached. Thus Henry XIV (younger line), born 1832, was the fourteenth prince of Reuss-Schleiz-Gera to be born in the nineteenth century, and was the son of Henry LXVII (1789–1867), the 67th prince born in the 18th century!

Army (cockade: red, black and yellow)
The troops maintained by the houses of Reuss prior to the Confederation of the Rhine had been small, bodyguard-style units, latterly wearing blue with red facings, yellow buttons and white breeches, grenadiers having fur caps with brass plates. Upon joining the *Rheinbund*, Reuss had to provide 450 men in three companies to the 2nd Battalion, 6th

The Cross of Honour founded by Prince Henry XIII of Reuss-Greiz in his capacity of governor of Frankfurt-am-Main; awarded for the campaigns of 1813–14. Iron cross with gilded edges and inscription, the arms bearing the ciphers of the three Allied monarchs, Alexander I, Frederick William and Francis I; ribbon white with yellow central stripe and edges black (left) and dark red.

Confederation Regiment (the remainder of the battalion from Waldeck); their Austrian-style uniform was white with light blue facings, yellow buttons, light blue breeches with yellow or yellow/black/red braid, French-style shako bearing an oval brass plate stamped 'R', yellow or yellow/red/black cords and red plume; black gaiters, white belts and gold lace for officers.

ROMAN REPUBLIC

History
The temporal power of the Catholic Church was represented by the Papal States, centered on Rome and even maintaining an army of very dubious worth. Pope Pius VI (ruled 1775–99) presided over a state on the verge of bankruptcy, and opposed the French Revolution with its confiscation of ecclesiastical property. Conflict between France and the Papacy simmered, exacerbated by the murder in Rome of the French diplomatic agent Hugon de Bassville in February 1793; some papal territory was annexed in 1791 (including Avignon) and by the Peace of Tolentino (February 1797) the Pope surrendered his claim to more territory, paid a large indemnity to France and agreed to disband his army. The French encouraged republican agitation in Rome, and after the French general Duphot was killed in a scuffle, the Directory ordered Berthier to march on Rome, where the French were welcomed by the Roman democrats who proclaimed the Roman Republic on 15 February 1798; the French 'liberators' thoroughly ransacked the city, with Massena at their head. Pius VI was taken as a prisoner to Siena and later to Valence, where he died on 29 August 1799; he was succeeded by Pius VII who entered Rome and began to rule, papal government having been restored after the French reverses in Italy. He ruled until 1809 – having been coerced into presiding at Napoleon's coronation – but in that year Napoleon annexed the Papal States and removed the Pope to France, Pius VII having excommunicated the French invaders of his territory. He was allowed to return only in 1814. During the French rule of 1809–14 the Roman territory was governed by a special commission (*consulta straordinaria*) with the municipal and provincial institutions of France.

Army (cockade: Papal States red with yellow edge; Roman Republic, red with black centre and white edge)
The Papal forces comprised infantry corps based in the various fortresses, cavalry, provincial infantry and cavalry militia. The infantry wore white Austrian-style uniform with facings red for the Guard Regiment, Regiment *Corsi* orange, *Romagna* (formed 1793) orange, Regiment *Castel San Angelo* and *Ancajani* Battalion green, yellow for the garrisons of Ancona and Senigallia, and sky-blue for Ferrara and 'Forte Urbano'. The head-dress was a peaked black leather cap with brass papal arms in front and a brass-edged comb supporting a black crest. The cavalry (two, later three companies of dragoons) wore iron-grey (blue from January

1795) with red facings, yellow buttons and white breeches; the artillery wore brown with red facings and waistcoat, white breeches, yellow buttons and red-plumed bicorn. The provincial infantry wore predominantly blue faced red (Romagna white faced red, Cesena white faced sky-blue, etc.) and the militia cavalry blue faced red (Ferrara blue faced white, Urbino blue faced yellow, Umbria white faced blue).

The troops of the Roman Republic wore uniforms in the colours of the national cockade: white coat with red collar and lining, black cuffs, and bicorn.

Under French rule, a battalion of Roman Veterans was formed in April 1810, and in the following August was amalgamated with the Ligurian Veteran Battalion, into the 9th Veteran Battalion. It wore French infantry uniform in light blue with scarlet facings, white lapels, buttons, piping and breeches, and red-laced shakos.

References
Brandani, M., Crociani, P., and Fiorentino, M. *Uniformi Militari Italiane dell'Ottocento: Periodo Napoleonico*, Rome 1978.
— *Uniformi Militari Italiane del Settecento*, Rome 1976.

Bucquoy, E. L. *Les Uniformes du Premier Empire: Gardes d'Honneur et Troupes Etrangères*, ed. G. Devautour, Paris 1983.

Barnabas Luigi Gregorio Chiaramonti, Pope Pius VII (1740–1823; elected Pope in March 1800). (Engraving by T. Johnson after David)

RUSSIA

History

Although the Romanov dynasty had been founded by the Tsar Michael (ruled 1613–45) and despite attempts at modernization by Peter the Great (1682–1725), only in the reign of Catherine II (the Great) was Russia fully recognized as a major European power, albeit (to western eyes) a land of mystery. The formidable Catherine was of German descent, daughter of the Prince of Anhalt-Zerbst, married to Tsar Peter III (himself half-German) who was assassinated by a court conspiracy after only a few months of his reign. Catherine's reign, coming after a succession of ineffectual rulers, enabled Russia to regain its status as a major power, with expansionist aims: she participated in the partitions of Poland, removing that state from the map, and aimed for the same with the Ottoman Empire's European possessions. An ambitious plan for a Russo-Austrian drive against the Turks failed when Austria made peace with the Ottoman Empire, Russia following suit in 1792 by the Peace of Jassy, and though she encouraged the monarchies in their fight against the democratic movement, Catherine remained aloof from the campaigns against republican France. On her death in 1796 she was succeeded by her son, Paul, a simpleton often referred to as 'the mad Tsar', who attempted to reverse all his mother's reforms simply out of spite; and in 1798, partly from a desire to protect Malta after he had declared himself Grand Master of the Order of St. John, he took Russia into the war against France, sending armies to the Netherlands, Switzerland and north Italy. Receiving less support from Austria and Britain than he thought his due, and enraged by British possession of Malta, he then took Bonaparte's side with some ideas of a conquest of British possessions in India; it was perhaps fortunate for the prosperity of his country that he was assassinated by a court conspiracy on 23/24 March 1801, to be succeeded by his son, Tsar Alexander I, whose complicity in the murder was suspected.

Alexander attempted to reverse the worst aspects of his father's policy, the internal organization of the state being modernized, some of the more oppressive measures revoked, a Council of the Empire created, and even some emancipation of the serfs begun; but his liberal intentions had to be subjugated to the interests of foreign policy. Upon Alexander's accession Russia was involved in the Armed Neutrality of the North against Britain, but within a short time Franco-Russian relations worsened to the extent that Alexander came to believe that Russia must resist Napoleon to save Europe from subjection. Consequently Russia participated in the Third and Fourth Coalitions, but defeats from Austerlitz to Friedland and the collapse of Prussia led to the Treaty of Tilsit, by which Russia became France's ally. The Franco-Russian treaty was never regarded with enthusiasm by Russia and foundered when Napoleon launched his invasion of 1812; and in the Sixth Coalition Russia played a leading role in the campaigns of 1813–14 which finally accomplished Napoleon's downfall. Russia also participated in the Seventh Coalition, but Waterloo prevented Russian troops from having to fight yet again.

In addition to the better-known Napoleonic campaigns, Russia was involved in three other wars during this period. A war against the Ottoman Empire was fought 1806–12, ending in the Treaty of Bucharest (28 May 1812) by which the disputed territory of Bessarabia was granted to Russia. After Tilsit, Napoleon and the Tsar attempted to force Sweden to abandon their British alliance and in February 1808 Barclay de Tolly led a Russian army into Finland, which province was wrested from Swedish control, and Russia confirmed in possession (and of the Aland Islands) by the Treaty of Frederikshavn (September 1809). Following the annexation of Georgia (1800), Persian assistance to dissident Georgians resulted in a Russian invasion of Persia in 1804, warfare which dragged on against Shah Fath Ali throughout the Napoleonic period, along the Caspian coast and in the Caucasus region, until after a major Russian victory at Aslanduz (31 October 1812) the Treaty of Gulistan (12 October 1813) ceded Georgia and other trans-Caucasian provinces to Russia.

At the end of the Napoleonic Wars Russia occupied the position desired by Catherine the Great, that of a leading European power and not just one on the fringe of civilization. Having liberated Europe from French domination (as he saw it), Alexander had little sympathy for those who wished to continue the process and liberate themselves from their own repressive institutions; thus, he turned against his academic sympathy for liberalism which had influenced his early years and became a champion of reactionary measures against the democratic movements, leading to some internal dissent and the Decembrist revolt in the early stages of the reign of Tsar Nicholas I, who succeeded his brother when Alexander died on 1 December 1825.

Army (cockade: black, orange and white)

Russia possessed an almost unlimited reservoir of manpower by virtue of the immense territory controlled by the Tsar: at Alexander's accession he ruled some 48,785,000 people, more than half the male population being serfs tied to agricultural estates and thus little more than slaves. These provided the army's rank-and-file, recruited by conscription for 25 years' service (lifetime prior to 1793), levied upon the number of 'souls' entered on the tax rolls, varying from the conscription of one man in 500 in peacetime to one in 20 in wartime. In some years there was no conscription; in 1812 there were three, each of up to five men per 100, and as substitute conscripts could be bought, only the most inefficient serfs were surrendered to the army by their 'owners'. With a most miserable standard of living in civilian life, the conscript was content with conditions and provender equally wretched, enabling the army to be maintained at minimum cost. Despite such terrible condition, and physically beaten by his officers and NCOs, the Russian soldier was possessed of characteristics of stoicism and resilience almost unique in Europe; he retained a devotion to religion, Tsar and country which caused both friends and foes to marvel. The British observer Sir Robert Wilson is often quoted, expressing his admiration for troops who would march for days with only the crudest of provisions but without complaint, but perhaps more illuminating are the views of an enemy. The French cavalryman Marbot wrote of the Russians at Golymin in 1807: ' . . . although our soldiers fired upon them at twenty-five paces, they continued their march without replying . . . every regiment filed past, without saying a word or slackening its pace for a moment. The streets were filled with dying and wounded, but not a groan was heard, for they were forbidden. You might have said that we were firing at shadows. At last our soldiers charged the Russian soldiers with the bayonet, and only when they pierced them could they be convinced that they were dealing with men.'[1] Their stoicism confirmed the belief among some Western observers that they were not really human; prior to the 1812 campaign a British traveller was told by a French officer that the Russians were animals, 'but one can kill an animal'.[2] Accounts of depredations against the Swedes in 1808 led the Russians to be described as 'hordes of barbarians and savages [from whom] every inhumanity that can be named or even thought of, may be expected',[3] and similar beliefs were expressed by British troops who encountered them in the Netherlands in 1799, who described them as idle, plundering drunkards: 'The Russians is people as has not the fear of God before their eyes, for I saw some of them with cheeses and butter and all badly wounded, and in partiklar one man had an eit days clock on his back and fiting all the time which made me to conclude and say all his vanity and vexation of spirit'.[4]

Conversely, the Russian officers were regarded as the worst in Europe; recruited from the minor gentry, they had little chance of promotion and many spent their lives in drink and idleness. This may have been exaggerated by contemporary observers, but there is truth in the assertion, and that it permeated the highest ranks. General Markov was dismissed in 1812 for being unable to distinguish between roads and rivers on a map, and Bunbury's account of General Lacy, Russian commander-in-chief in the Mediterranean, condemns the system which had given him supreme command; of Irish descent and speaking with the strongest Irish brogue imaginable, he *had been*, no doubt, a brave and meritorious officer: but he was now between seventy and eighty years of age, and showed no trace of ever having been a man of talent or information . . . At the councils of war . . . he used to bring his nightcap in his pocket, put it on, and go to sleep while others discussed the business'. His chief of staff, General Oppermann, Bunbury thought 'a clever fellow, but . . . he left an impression on one's mind of his being not too honest.'[5]

This highlights another characteristic of the Russian army, the employment of foreign officers (due to the low quality of native Russian officers). The foreigners were generally disliked and even mistrusted, but the army could

scarcely have operated without them: even the most notable reformer, Barclay de Tolly, War Minister and one of Russia's leading commanders, was a Lithuanian of Scottish descent. The careers of such foreign officers could encompass several armies: typical was 'Captain Fritz' who left a memoir of his services (*Wider Napoleon! Ein deutsches Reiterleben*, 1861): a Mecklenburger, he fought with the Prussians at Auerstädt, briefly joined the Russians, transferred to the Brunswick 'Black Legion' in Austrian service, made two campaigns in the Peninsula with the King's German Legion, returned to the Russian cavalry for the 1812 campaign and rejoined the Prussians in 1813. Some foreigners were mercenaries, some joined the Russians to continue the fight against France after the fall of their own countries, and others simply went for adventure, like the British naval captain on half-pay, Nesbit Willoughby, who served as a Russian colonel in the 1812 campaign, ' . . . a man who thrust his head into every gun, and ran it against every stone wall, he could find from Cape Cormorin to Moscow. When I knew him, his face was cut and hacked in all directions.'[6]

Under Catherine the Great, the reforms of Prince Potemkin had given the Russian army one of the most functional uniforms in Europe; the reaction of Paul I returned to the costume and practice of the mid-eighteenth century, as described by Bunbury: ' . . . exactly the hard, stiff, wooden machines which we have reason to figure to ourselves as the Russians of the Seven Years' War. Their dress and equipments seem to have remained unaltered; they waddled slowly forward to the tap-tap of their monotonous drums; and if they were beaten they waddled slowly back again, without appearing in either case to feel a sense of danger, or the expediency of taking ultra tap-tap steps to better their condition'.[7] Under Alexander I and with the assistance of his minister Arakcheev, the army was modernized with considerable speed: new uniforms, general reforms and modernized tactics, inspired by Suvarov and Kutuzov and rejecting the Frederickian doctrine of linear tactics which Paul had advocated. Barclay de Tolly continued the process of reform so that by the later stages of the war the Russian army operated with reasonable efficiency. As early as 1805 Bunbury discovered ' . . . surprising progress; they were now well-armed and equipped, and had very much the outward character of good German soldiers'.[8] Only the deplorable commissariat and a continued total disregard for the well-being of the ordinary soldier remained as serious deficiencies.

Infantry

On Alexander's accession there were regiments of musketeers, grenadiers and *Jägers* (light infantry), each of two battalions and named after its commander; to give a sense of local identity Alexander reverted to naming regiments after their town or province. In April 1803 3rd battalions were formed, each regiment then having two ordinary battalions and one of grenadiers; in grenadier regiments the former were styled fusiliers and in the *Jägers* the grenadiers were termed carabiniers. Each battalion comprised three musketeer or fusilier companies and one of grenadiers, each regiment with an establishment of 1,692 rank-and-file (1,128 musketeers and 564 grenadiers in musketeer regiments). Until 1806 regiments were grouped in 'Inspections' or inspectorates, there being no permanent organization higher than the regiment, which created an administrative nightmare. In 1805 the infantry comprised 77 regiments (plus two battalions) of musketeers, 13 of grenadiers and 20 of *Jägers* (plus Guard and garrison battalions), with the 'Military Reform Commission' placing all regiments on an establishment of 2,256 men (1,385 for

Jägers). From 1806–8 the Inspections were abolished and replaced by Divisions, each of two musketeer and one *Jäger* brigade, each brigade of two regiments. Barclay de Tolly's reforms of 1811 replaced the term 'musketeers' with 'infantry', and split each battalion's élite company into two platoons, one of grenadiers and one of *tirailleurs*, the latter ostensibly trained as light infantry; but they, like the *Jägers*, were little different from the rest, as the Russians never excelled at skirmish tactics, and no manual for such duties existed until 1818: the mass attack with the bayonet remained the advocated and 'traditional' Russian tactic.

Alexander I, Tsar of Russia (1777–1825).

Russian infantry drummer of grenadiers (left) and NCO musician (right), wearing the 1805 shako with the huge plume of grenadiers. The uniforms are of ordinary infantry style with the addition of white lace for musicians, and lace of NCO rank on shako and collar of the man at right; his red plume with white tip is similarly a rank-distinction. (Print after Viskovatov)

From 1811 grenadier regiments were concentrated into grenadier divisions, and henceforth musketeer regiments no longer had grenadier battalions. In each regiment the 2nd battalion was designated as the reserve or depot, and the 1st and 3rd as the field battalions, though confusingly the 3rd battalion could also be referred to as the 2nd, i.e., 2nd field battalion. The depot battalions formed the 'Supply Army', not a reserve of personnel but a formation which took the field itself, with the grenadier companies of three depot battalions being formed for active service into a single 'combined' or 'converged' grenadier battalion, allocated to the field army on a scale of two battalions per division. In November 1811 many regiments received a 4th battalion which joined the Supply Army. Having reinforced their own field battalions and lost their grenadiers, Supply Army units were invariably much weaker than the others, sometimes with less than half the establishment of 738 per battalion.

The *Jäger* regiments were increased to 22 in 1805 and 32 in 1806; the 33rd to 46th were formed in 1810 by the conversion of line regiments (nine of which were re-formed from the Garrison Regiments), and the 47th–49th *Jägers* in January 1811 also from garrison regiments; the 49th was converted to a line regiment two months later, but a new 49th and 50th formed in October 1811, with four line regiments. In January 1811 the Rostov Regiment was converted to grenadiers (bearing the name of Arakcheev, the only corps with a 'personal' name), and in 1813 Regiments Kexholm and Pernau were converted similarly, replacing the Pavlov Grenadiers in the line, they having joined the Guard. In April 1814 six *Jäger* regiments were designated 'Grenadier-Jägers' but retained their numbers.

Paul I re-introduced a Frederickian uniform of the national dark green coat with coloured facings, bicorns for musketeers, metal-fronted mitres for grenadiers and shorter mitres for fusiliers. Alexander I's reforms introduced a more modern, short-tailed, green double-breasted jacket with red turnbacks, yellow buttons, collar and cuffs of the Inspection colour and shoulder-straps coloured according to the seniority of the regiment within the Inspection, red, white, yellow, raspberry, turquoise, pink, light green and grey for the 1st–8th Regiments respectively (colours were duplicated for Inspections with more regiments). White breeches were worn with black gaiters in summer and knee-boots in winter; belts were white leather and the knapsack was a curious, black canvas or cylindrical valise worn at an angle across the back. In 1805 a black shako was introduced, with a black cockade with orange edge and a tufted pompom, white, yellow or red for 1st–3rd battalions respectively, with regimentally-coloured centre. Grenadiers retained their mitres (with headband in the shoulder-strap colour and rear in the Inspection colour) only until 1805, when they adopted the shako with a brass grenade below the cockade, and an immense black plume; the Pavlov Regiment retained their mitres, handing them to down to successive generations, until 1917, some of the 600 still preserved then bearing the marks of Napoleonic bullet-holes. Facing-colours of Inspections were: St. Petersburg red, Livonia turquoise,

Coignet remarked that in the enemy's country, 'if you don't take anything, you feel you've forgotten something' (*The Note-Books of Captain Coignet*, J.-R. Coignet, ed. Hon. Sir John Fortescue, London 1928, p. 188). This attitude is exemplified by Sergeant Bourgogne of the Imperial Guard who reviewed his knapsack in Moscow:

'I found several pounds of sugar, some rice, some biscuit, half a bottle of liqueur, a woman's Chinese silk dress, embroidered in gold and silver, several gold and silver ornaments, amongst them a little bit of the cross of Ivan the Great – at least, a piece of the outer covering of silver gilt, given me by a man in the company who had helped in taking it down . . . a woman's large riding-cloak (hazel colour, lined with green velvet . . .): then two silver pictures in relief, a foot long and eight inches high; one of them represented the Judgement of Paris on Mount Ida, and the other showed Neptune on a chariot formed by a shell and drawn by sea-horses, all in the finest workmanship. I had, besides, several lockets and a Russian Prince's spittoon set with brilliants . . . a large pouch hung at my side, underneath my cape, by a silver cord. This was full of various things – amongst them, a crucifix in gold and silver, and a little Chinese porcelain vase . . . Add to all this a fair amount of health, good spirits, and the hope of presenting my respects to the Mongol, Chinese and Indian ladies I hoped to meet, and you will have a very good idea of the *Vélite* sergeant of the Imperial Guard.'

(*The Memoirs of Sergeant Bourgogne*, A. J. B. F. Bourgogne, ed. P. Cottin and M. Hénault, London 1899; r/p with introduction by D. G. Chandler, London 1979, pp. 56–7.)

Lithuania light green, Ukraine pink, Dniester lilac pre-1805, then dark green, finally with red cuffs; Caucasus medium blue, Smolensk white, Moscow orange, Finland yellow, Brest straw-yellow, Crimea light ochre, Kiev raspberry, Orenburg buff, Siberia grey. Grenadier regiments were distributed throughout the Inspections.

Officers had longer-tailed jackets, gold-edged shoulder-straps and the universal national waist-sash of silver with black and orange lines; they retained the bicorn unil 1807, and junior ranks carried a spontoon until that date. When the shako was adopted it had a silver pompom, gold upper band and chains hung around from gilt or silver eagle-badges on the sides. NCOs had gold-laced collar, cuffs and shako, pompoms quartered white and mixed black-and-orange, grenadier plumes with a white tip with vertical orange stripe; most carried a partizan.

In November 1807 Inspection colours were abolished and all regiments adopted red facings and shoulder-straps coloured red, white, yellow, green piped red and light blue respectively for the 1st–5th regiments in a division, with the divisional number in red (in yellow on red straps); officers adopted epaulettes with gilt crescents and gold fringe for field ranks, and new legwear comprised white 'gaiter-trousers' for summer and white overalls with black leather 'booting' on the lower leg for winter (loose 'booting' could be buttoned over the gaiter-trousers). In July 1808 brass grenade-badges (with three flames for grenadiers) replaced the shako-cockade, and in April 1809 a black rectangular knapsack replaced the cylindrical pattern. NCO partizans were withdrawn in the same year, and in June shako-cords were adopted, white for all except NCOs (white/black/orange) and officers (silver/black/orange), from 1811 white and silver respectively. In February 1811 grenadiers adopted a thinner plume, and in 1812 a new shako was introduced, with a convex top, though the old pattern continued in use for some years. Throughout the period, the grey-brown greatcoat was often worn on campaign for reasons of comfort.

Jägers wore infantry uniform in light green with regimental facings until November 1811 when a dark green uniform with red cuffs and white collar was introduced, and in 1809 dark green facings piped red; winter legwear was green with red piping. The bicorn was replaced in 1802 by a brimmed 'round hat', and in 1807 the infantry shako was adopted. Equipment was in black leather, and rifled muskets were replaced by the ordinary pattern in June 1808; in 1812 there existed 28 calibres of musket and eleven varieties of carbine or rifle, the productions of the central factories at Tula and Sestrovetsk (more than 150,000 per year) being of an inferior standard to the 60,000 British muskets issued as rewards for deserving soldiers.

Cavalry

The thirteen cuirassier regiments were reduced to six in 1803, increased in 1811 by the addition of the Astrakhan and Novgorod Regiments, and in 1812 by the conversion of the Pskov and Starodub Dragoons; in April 1813 the Emperor Regiment was transferred to the Lifeguard. Regiments initially had five field squadrons (660 rank-and-file) and one depot squadron; 6th and 7th squadrons were formed in 1812. In 1803 bicorns were replaced by black leather combed helmets with a black woollen crest (replaced by horsehair in 1808), a brass front-plate bearing the imperial double-eagle (a star of the Order of St. George for the Military Order Regiment), and brass chinscales from 1808. The short-tailed, double-breasted white jacket had facings light blue (Emperor and Starodub Regiments), raspberry (Empress and Pskov), black (Military Order), dark green (Little Russia: medium green from 1812), medium blue (Gluchov), orange (Ekaterinoslav), yellow (Astrakhan) and pink (Novgorod); buttons were yellow for Military Order, Little Russia, Pskov and Starodub, and white for the remainder. Cuirasses were adopted in 1812–13, black-enamelled for all except the Pskov (French white-metal cuirasses, brass for officers) and Empress (officers at least with white-metal); both complete cuirasses and the German pattern of front-plate only were used. White breeches and long boots were replaced by grey overalls on campaign.

The eleven dragoon regiments were increased by the conversion of seven cuirassier regiments in 1803, plus five newly raised corps, all of five field squadrons (6th and 7th squadrons were formed from 1812); eight more regiments were formed in 1806 and two in 1807, 36 existing by 1812, reduced to eighteen in that year. The dragoons originally wore infantry-style uniform in light green with coloured facings, red turnbacks and legwear like the cuirassiers; in 1803 cuirassier-style helmets replaced the bicorn and cuirassier-style jackets were adopted changing to dark green in 1807. Facing-colours were as follows, (W) and (Y) indicating white or yellow buttons, and * a regiment converted to other cavalry in 1812: facings red: Riga (Y), Starodub* (W), Tiraspol* (Y), Iamburg* (W); orange: Karkov (Y), Sieversk* (W); ultramarine: Tver (Y), Tchernigov* (W); pink: St. Petersburg (Y), Moscow (Y); yellow: Smolensk (Y), Kinburn (W), Serpuchov* (Y), Dorpat* (W); dark orange: Pskov* (Y), Kargopol (W); buff: Vladimir* (Y), Nijegorod (W); grey: Taganrog* (Y), Narva (W); black: Orenburg* (Y), Ingermanland (W); white: Irkhutsk* (Y), Siberia* (W); raspberry: Kazan (Y), Kiev (W); turquoise: Kurland (Y), New Russia (W), Niejine* (Y), Arsamass* (W); violet: Borisoglievsk (Y), Pereiaslav* (W); red piped white: Livonia* (Y), Jitomir* (W); white piped red: Finland (Y), Mita (W).

Eight dragoon regiments were converted to Mounted *Jägers* in November 1812, wearing dragoon uniform with facing-coloured cuffs, shoulder-straps and piping on collar and turnbacks, green overalls with facing-coloured double stripe, and 1812-pattern shako with green cords and white plume; facings: Regiments Arsamass blue, Dorpat pink, Livonia red, Niejine light blue, Pereiaslav raspberry, Sieversk orange, Tchernigov ultramarine and Tiraspol yellow.

Tsar Paul increased the single hussar regiment to eight,

'There was a small green opposite Government House, over which no one was permitted to pass. Not a creature was allowed to approach save the General's cow; and the sentries had particular orders to turn away any one who ventured to cross the forbidden turf. One day Lady D——, having been calling at the General's, wished to make a short cut, and, accordingly, bent her steps across the lawn, when she was arrested by the sentry calling out, and desiring her to return and go the other road. She remonstrated: the man said he could not disobey his orders, which were to prevent anyone from crossing that piece of ground.

"But", said Lady D——, with a stately air, "do you know who I am?"

"I don't know who you be, ma'am," replied the immovable sentry, "but I knows who you b'aint – you b'aint the General's cow." '

(*Recollections of an Old Soldier, by his Daughter* – actually Francis Skelly Tidy, by Mrs. Ward – in *United Service Journal*, London 1840, II, p. 474.)

two more being added in 1803 (one of these, Odessa, converted to *Uhlans* in 1805), one more in 1805 and another in 1807. Each regiment comprised ten field squadrons in two battalions (1,320 rank-and-file) and two depot squadrons; by late 1812 each regiment had six field and one depot squadron. Infantry shakos replaced the original busby or mirliton in 1803, with red and white pompom and cords for 1st and 2nd battalions respectively (though variations existed); otherwise they wore typical hussar uniform with white breeches or grey service overalls. Colours until 1809 were:

Regiment	Dolman	Facings	Pelisse	Buttons/ Braid
Soum	straw-yellow	turquoise	turquoise	white
Elizabeth-grad	straw-yellow	red	straw-yellow	yellow
Pavlograd	dark green	turquoise	turquoise	yellow
Mariupol	white	yellow	dark blue	yellow
Alexandria	black	red	black	white
Olviopol	dark green	dark green	dark green	white
Isum	red	dark blue	dark blue	yellow/ white
Akhtyrsk	chestnut	yellow	chestnut	yellow
White Russia	dark blue	red	dark blue	white/ red-and-white

New colours were adopted in 1809, shako-decorations becoming braid-coloured; in 1812 some units adopted the new shako, and the Irkhutsk Regiment was converted from the dragoons of that name. Post-1809 colours (including breeches) were: Soum grey (red facings and pelisse); Elizabethgrad grey (dark green breeches); Pavlograd dark green (turquoise facings and pelisse); Mariupol dark blue (yellow facings); Alexandria black (red facings); Olviopol dark green (red breeches and facings); Isum dark blue (red dolman); Akhtyrsk chestnut (yellow facings, dark blue breeches); White Russia dark blue (red facings and pelisse); Grodno dark blue (light blue facings); Loubny dark blue (yellow facings); Irkhutsk black (raspberry facings and breeches). Buttons and braid were yellow for the Pavlograd, Elizabethgrad, Mariupol, Akhtyrsk and Irkhutsk, white for the remainder.

The first *Uhlan* regiments were converted in 1803, the original three rising to four (1805), seven (1809) and twelve (1812). Each comprised one depot and ten field squadrons (1,160 lancers and 160 'flankers' armed with carbines); they wore Polish-style lancer uniform of dark blue *kurtka* with red facings, fringless epaulettes of the button-colour, blue girdle

Russian Guards officer wearing the uniform of 1812, including the distinctive scuttle-shaped 'kiwer' (shako) and the one-piece 'gaiter-trousers' worn in summer. Unlike the officers of some nations, on campaign

Russian company officers often carried knapsacks. (Print by Jacquemin after prints of the 1814–15 period showing Allied troops in the occupation of Paris)

edged raspberry and a black leather *czapka* with coloured top. *Czapka*-tops were as follows in 1812: Lithuanian, Taganrog, Siberia and Iamburg Regiments white; Tartar and Orenburg raspberry; Polish, Volhynie, Jitomir and Vladimir blue; Tchougouiev and Serpuchov red. *Czapka*-piping was raspberry (Lithuanian, Polish), white (Tartar, Tchougouiev, Jitomir), red (Taganrog, Siberia, Iamburg) or yellow for the remainder; buttons white (Lithuanian, Tartar, Polish, Tchougouiev, Jitomir, Siberia) and white for the remainder; blue collars were worn by Lithuanian, Tartar, Volhynie, Vladimir, Taganrog and Serpuchov Regiments.

Lifeguard

The Guard or Lifeguard cavalry was originally the Chevalier-Garde Regiment, transformed by Tsar Paul from a ceremonial bodyguard to a cuirassier regiment, with horse guards and hussars added, and later Cossacks, dragoons and *Uhlans* in 1809, Cuirassiers (ex-Emperor Regiment) in 1813 and mounted *Jägers* in 1814. All wore the basic uniform of their line equivalents, plus German-style 'Guard' loops (*petlitzi*) on collar and cuffs. The Chevalier-Garde wore white cuirassier uniform with scarlet facings piped white, yellow lace and the star of the Order of St. Andrew on the helmet; the Horse Guards likewise without the white piping; the cuirassiers retained their 'Emperor' Regiment uniform plus white loops. The dragoons had dragoon uniform with scarlet facings (and uniquely scarlet lapels); the Mounted *Jägers* line uniform with red facings and red-striped white loops; the *Uhlans* line uniform with red facings and *czapka*, red and yellow piping and cords, and yellow loops. The

Field Marshal Alexander Vasilievitch Suvarov, Count Suvarov-Riminsky (1729–1800). One of the greatest Russian soldiers in history, and the leading commander of his age, Suvarov performed prodigies during the 1799 campaign but unfairly fell from favour and died in eclipse. (Engraving by A. Roffe after Hampe)

hussars wore scarlet dolman and pelisse, busby, green pelisse and silver lace, and later the shako (with brass flying-eagle plate from 1809), dark blue dolman and breeches, red facings and pelisse, and yellow braid. From 1811 the cavalry of the Lifeguard was organized in two self-contained divisions.

The foot regiments were acknowledged to be the most impressive-looking troops in Europe, the men carefully selected and officers from the highest aristocracy. There were originally three regiments, the Preobrajenski (four battalions), Semenovski and Izmailovski (three), plus a *Jäger* battalion increasing to a two-battalion regiment in 1806; and in 1808 a Finland Regiment and 1811 a Lithuanian Regiment were formed. Prior to 1811 all were grenadiers, but in that February each battalion was organized in one grenadier and three fusilier companies; in April 1813 the Life and Pavlov Grenadiers were raised to Guard status. Uniform was like that of the line, plus brass eagle shako-plates from 1808, and 'Guard lace' on the facings. Cuffs were red for the three original regiments with collar and shoulder-straps red (Preobrajenski), ultramarine piped red (Semenovski) and dark green piped red (Izmailovski); the Lithuanians wore red lapels, later adopted by the Life and Pavlov Regiments. Collar and cuffs in 1812 were: Preobrajenski and Lithuanian red, Semenovski and Life Grenadiers blue piped red, Izmailovski and Pavlov green piped red. The *Jägers* wore light green with orange facings and yellow loops and the Guard shako; from 1807 dark green with orange piping. The Lifeguard infantry normally served in a self-contained division, two divisions from 1813.

Artillery

There were originally eight artillery regiments (the 8th being horse artillery), reorganized in 1801 into thirteen foot and one horse battalion. The quality drew enthusiastic comments from foreign observers (notably Sir Robert Wilson), and the artillery was extremely powerful, batteries normally consisting of twelve guns; but it was not especially well handled in the Austerlitz campaign and from 1806 the service was reorganized into brigades, by 1814 attaining a strength of 28 field, ten reserve and four depot brigades. Brigade-organization varied, but typically included two 'position' batteries, two or three light batteries, a horse battery and perhaps a company from the Artillery Pontooner Regiment; brigades were normally assigned at divisional level.

In 1805 a major reform was instituted, with Inspector-General of Artillery Alexei Arakcheev playing the part of Russia's Gribeauval. He introduced a new range of guns to replace the previous 3-, 6-, 8- and 12pdr cannon and 9- and 12pdr licornes (or 'unicorns': howitzers firing shells over long range with a flatter trajectory than normal). The '1805 System' restricted field artillery to 6- and 12pdr guns and 3-, 10- and 20pdr licornes (the 3pdr withdrawn in 1810), of improved construction with screw-elevators and from 1811 with a more sophisticated sight. By 1812 Russia possessed 133 batteries; the Guard artillery, 64 (later 80 guns) remained separate. The 'position' batteries normally

consisted of four medium 12pdrs, four short 12pdrs and four 20pdr licornes; horse and light batteries had eight 6pdrs and four 10pdr licornes. New tactical directions included the use of concentrated fire by 'massed battery' and decried the withdrawing of guns in jeopardy, but instead advocating firing until the last moment to inflict such damage on the enemy as to offset the potential loss of the guns. The chief architect of these plans, the young General Kutaisov (who should not be confused with Kutuzov, as he sometimes is) was so energetic that he forgot his duties as artillery chief at Borodino and perished leading a bayonet-charge, so that much of his artillery reserve was never ordered into action.

Foot artillery wore infantry-style uniform in dark green with black facings, red piping and yellow buttons; horse artillery wore dragoon-style uniform in the same colours. The Guard artillery wore the same with the usual Guard distinctions, and unlike most armies Russia did not maintain a separate train organization, drivers being part of the artillery, wearing the same uniform plus cavalry overalls. Engineer services included a pioneer regiment of two battalions, each of one miner and three pioneer companies; by 1806 these had expanded to two three-battalion regiments and a sapper regiment was organized in 1812. They wore artillery uniform plus white buttons; the pontooner corps was part of the artillery.

The commissariat organization was woefully deficient, and the medical services virtually non-existent; indeed, when the Tsar offered the Cossack general Platov extra surgeons to supplement the one his entire force included, Platov refused, saying that not all the enemy's fire was as lethal as a single drug!

Cossacks

The Cossacks formed a virtually inexhaustible supply of irregular light cavalry, whose value as skirmishers, scouts and raiders was incalculable. Descended from outlaws settled in southern Russia, they were wild, undisciplined and rapacious tribesmen, commanded by their tribal chiefs (*atamans*) and organized according to their territory (*voisko*) into squadrons (*sotnias*), and though lacking discipline were unswervingly loyal to the Tsar. Their endurance was legendary: mounted on mean-looking ponies, they could march without respite for days on end, and then charge with all the speed and more fury than the finest cavalry in Europe. Though they rarely charged formed troops, their fearful screaming and legendary skill with the lance could throw even veteran troops into panic; they harried the *Grande Armée* out of existence in the retreat from Moscow, and their very approach caused terror: in 1813 a new prayer was said in Germany, *De Cossaquibus, Domine, libera nos* ('Free us, Lord, from the Cossacks'). Some of their allies regarded them as representing the unspoiled nature of mankind, the 'noble savage' incarnate; a more usual reaction was to view them as *banditti* of the worst variety, their presence evoking descriptions of the entire Russian army as 'rampant bears'.[8] A British naval officer who served alongside them, R. B. James, described them as ' . . . a most extraordinary race of people, very uncouth and barbarous in their appearance and manners . . . all difficulties are overcome by their perseverance; whatever they undertake, they seldom fail to accomplish . . . great gluttons, and greater drunkards. Although scarce able to stand, when once mounted, they seldom fail in their duty . . .'[9] The popular perception was a mixture of these attributes: ' . . . terrible and unsparing . . . In their living, the Cossacks are very gross, and commit great excesses in drinking. The quantity of spirits they swallow without intoxication is truly astonishing';[10] yet so resourceful that they were always capable of ' . . . extricating themselves out of difficulties on all emergencies . . . nothing stops these warriors . . .'[11]

There were numerous tribal units, principally those of the Don, Black Sea, Bug, Siberia, Ukraine, Urals and Orenburg; though most had prescribed uniforms, the commonest costume was either 'native' dress (often including a fur cap) or a dark blue jacket (or long kaftan in winter), with baggy trousers and a peaked blue cloth cap. Facing-colours were carried on the jacket and cap-band (red for the majority), but on campaign there was little uniformity except for the Guard Cossacks, who wore scarlet jackets (summer) or blue kaftans (winter), with dark blue trousers, yellow 'Guard' loops with red stripe on the facings after 1809, and a black busby with red bag. Almost all carried their traditional lance, but also festooned themselves with any other weapons they could acquire, from native long knives to cavalry sabres, several pairs of pistols and carbines; a British officer who saw them in the Netherlands, Thomas Austin (who was advised to remove his epaulettes lest the Cossacks murder him to possess them!) noted that almost all carried highly prized sabres of Birmingham manufacture.

Even more 'irregular' cavalry were the Asiatic tribesmen, Circassians in medieval chain-armour, tartars, bashkirs and kalmucks, who wore 'native' costume and were armed with bows and arrows, which the French regarded with derision, calling them *Amours* (from their cupid-like weapon!). Such tribesmen had no tactic whatever but a mad, mounted dash,

at the end of which they would discharge a shower of arrows. James described them as, 'Ugly beyond every thing; Broad low foreheads: small round black eyes like the Chinese: high cheek bones, large mouths, black teeth, pug noses, small chins, and a beautiful copper complexion. From their being armed with bows and arrows, the French ladies called them les Cupidons du Nord; Bless their ugly faces for setting me at liberty . . . '[12]

Militia

Remembering Pugachev's Serf Revolt, Russia was initially unwilling to institute training of the peasantry, but in November 1806 the militia (*opolchenie*) was created to train 612,000 serfs. In 1812 the force was embodied and 223,361 men enrolled, organized in 'cohorts' of two pike battalions and a musket-armed *Jäger* battalion, plus a grenadier company. More than 70 cohorts were formed, fifteen in St. Petersburg alone, plus six *Jäger* regiments, two pike regiments, and 80 mounted or 'Cossack' regiments. Training was rudimentary and equipment very basic: though some had muskets, many had only pikes or axes, and the cavalry mostly lances. Uniform and equipment varied from some sophistication in the case of some of the cavalry units, to simple grey greatcoats and cloth caps worn by the majority. The militia was used as a reserve for the regulars, some distributed among the line regiments to work as pioneers; in action they stood behind the regulars but executed the charge (virtually their only tactic) with equal resolution. In addition to the *opolchenie* were partisan bands formed in 1812, some with a nucleus of regular hussars but others merely peasant bands armed with agricultural tools, who were responsible for the most hideous atrocities on stragglers encountered during Napoleon's retreat.

Higher Organization

Under the Tsar Paul there was no more sophisticated organization than that of the individual unit, which commanders formed into 'columns' as they saw fit. Not until 1806 was a permanent divisional system introduced; and from 1811 Barclay de Tolly's reforms instituted a Corps system into the First and Second West Armies, a Corps generally comprising two infantry divisions, a regiment or brigade of cavalry and an artillery brigade. Grenadiers were concentrated into élite divisions, and the remaining cavalry into cavalry divisions, two of cuirassiers and eight others of mixed dragoons and light cavalry. The artillery organization in 'brigades' ensured that each contained field, horse and position batteries. Though patterned on the French system,

---

Order from Rostophin, Military Governor of Moscow, to the Russian people, 1812:

'Arm yourselves, it matters not with what arms; but particularly pitchforks, which are so much the more suitable against the French, because in weight they resemble trusses of straw.'

(*Edinburgh Evening Courant*, 16 November 1812.)

the Russian corps remained slower-moving and less flexible in operation despite the great progress made by the 1805 reforms. The staff was not noted for its efficiency, to the extent that the army's affairs were often run by the Austrian staff when the two nations acted in concert.

Navy

Peter the Great began the construction of the Russian navy, and though numerically it was extremely strong the closure of Russian ports in winter due to ice always prevented it from exerting the influence its size suggested. Apart from shallow-draughted vessels (including galleys) employed in the Baltic, Russian ships were constructed on the usual lines and handled competently; like the army, they employed many foreign officers, especially British or British-trained. The main sphere of operations was in the Baltic and Mediterranean, generally in conjunction with other allied navies, but the Russians participated in the blockade of the north European seaboard by the British; prior to Camperdown Russian ships had collaborated with the Royal Navy, but Admiral Duncan found them ill-disciplined and it is perhaps fortunate that they were not present at the battle. Fourteen ships-of-the-line blockaded the Batavian coast in 1798 and won a minor victory, and in the same year a Russo-Turkish fleet collaborated in the capture of Corfu and other islands along the Dalmatian coast, and assisted in the capture of Naples. Operations continued in the Mediterranean from 1805, the Adriatic in 1806–7 and the Aegean, and in 1807 Russo-Turkish hostilities resulted in Russia's major naval success of the period when Admiral Seniavin won a sharp action at Lemnos on 19 June. The Russians withdrew from the Mediterranean in early 1808, and hostilities with Britain in the Baltic during the period of Franco-Russian alliance after Tilsit cost the Russians some minor vessels and the 74-gun *Sewolod*. The war against Sweden produced a number of actions, mainly involving squadrons of smaller vessels in support of land operations.

The navy was organized in three fleets; Baltic, Black Sea and Caspian, but the units into which the seamen were organized were administrative with little significance in relation to the crewing of ships. Officers wore a green uniform in army style, and seamen a green double-breasted short jacket and trousers and 'round hat'. From 1796 the marine and naval artillery battalions were reorganized into twelve marine battalions, and in 1804 into four marine regiments; they were organized and equipped on army lines and in 1813 were transferred to the army establishment. Their uniform was like that of the infantry, with distinctive facing-colours, and from 1803 green facings, white piping and shoulder-straps red, white, yellow and green respectively for the 1st–4th Marines. They fought on land and participated in the 1812 campaign.

Notes

1. *The Memoirs of Baron de Marbot*, ed. A. J. Butler, London 1913, II, p. 200.
2. *Memoirs of Anna Maria Wilhelmina Pickering, Together with extracts from the Journals of her Father, John Spencer Stanhope*, London 1903, p. 530.
3. *Morning Chronicle*, 5 September 1808.
4. 'Recollections of the British Army', in *Colburn's Military Magazine*, February 1836; Hon. Sir John Fortescue (see *History of the British Army* vol. IV, London 1906, p. 677) believed the author to be a member of the British 35th Foot.
5. *Narratives of some passages in the Great War with France*, Sir Henry Bunbury, 1854; 1927 edn, London, p. 127.
6. *Twenty Years' Military Adventures in Three Quarters of the Globe*, J. Blakiston, London 1829, I, p. 347.
7. Bunbury, op. cit., p. 145.
8. *A Boy in the Peninsular War*, R. Blakeney, ed. J. Sturgis, London 1899, p. 341.
9. 'The Naval Officer, or Vicissitudes of a Sea Life', in *Napoleon the Gaoler*, E. Fraser, London 1914, pp. 168–9.
10. *The Times*, 20 January 1814.
11. *Edinburgh Evening Courant*, 3 January 1814.
12. James, in Fraser, op. cit., p. 170.

References

Works on the Russian army in English are limited, but include a number of important sources. More general works include:

Palmer, A. *Russia in War and Peace*, London 1972.

Wilson, Sir Robert. *Brief Remarks on the Character and Composition of the Russian Army*, London 1810.
— *General Wilson's Journal* (ed. Brett-James, A.), London 1964.
— *Narrative of Events during the Invasion of Russia*, London 1860.

Uniforms and organization are covered in:

Falzone, I., and Rava, G. *L'Escercito Russo 1805–15: Fanteria*, Parma n.d.

Hansen, C. W. *The Russian Army 1812–13*, Copenhagen 1977.

Haythornthwaite, P. J. *The Russian Army of the Napoleonic Wars: Infantry* and *Cavalry*, London 1987.

Krijitsky, A., and Gayda, M. *L'Armée Russe sous le Tsar Alexandre Ier de 1805 à 1815*, Paris 1955.

Mollo, B., and Mollo, J. *Uniforms of the Imperial Russian Army*, Poole 1979.

Nafziger, G. *The Russian Army 1800–1815*, Cambridge, Ontario, 1983.

Viskovatov, A. V. *Historical Description of the Uniforms and Armaments of the Russian Army*, St. Petersburg 1844–56 (the most extensive and authoritative work on the subject; some of the superb plates are reproduced in Falzone & Rava, above).

Zweguintzow, W. *L'Armée Russe*, Paris 1973.

SARDINIA

History

A Spanish possession until the Treaty of London (1720) caused it to be exchanged for Sicily, Sardinia was ruled from that time by the dukes of Savoy, to whom it brought a royal title. Details of the tribulations of the family are noted in the section on Piedmont. Sardinia's active participation in the Napoleonic Wars was restricted virtually to the 1792–6 war against republican France. King Victor Emmanuel I, who succeeded on his brother's abdication in 1802, returned to Cagliari in 1806, where he remained until 1814 when he retired, leaving his brother Carlo Felice as viceroy, who himself succeeded to the throne when Victor Emmanuel abdicated in 1821.

Army (cockade: cornflower-blue)

The two heavy cavalry regiments wore yellow-laced bicorns, dark blue coats with red turnbacks, faced red (Regiment Piedmont) and black (Regiment Savoy, without lapels), and yellow and white buttons respectively, brass shoulder-scales from 1789, white or buff breeches and waistcoat and white belts. The infantry was dressed similarly in 'royal blue' coats with regimentally-coloured collar, cuffs, lapels and turnbacks, white waistcoat and breeches, black gaiters, white belts, and bicorns; grenadiers wore fur caps. A modernized uniform was introduced for light troops from the mid-1790s, including an Austrian-style single-breasted blue jacket with short tails and a 'round hat' with upturned brim; for the *Corps Franchi*, for example, it had red turnbacks, yellow collar and cuffs, white loops, blue waistcoat and breeches, and white-laced hat with short blue plume. The modernization continued with the adoption *c.* 1803 of single-breasted jackets for all, blue breeches and combed leather helmet with brass plate and cornflower-blue crest. Facing-colours in 1814 were: Guard Grenadiers red, white loops on the breast and cuffs; Regiment Savoy black, red turnbacks; Piedmont red; Aosta dark red, yellow turnbacks; Cuneo crimson, white turnbacks; Regina white, dark red turnbacks; Sardinia red, with loops as for the Guard. Buttons were white for all except Savoy and Piedmont, yellow; grenadiers had fur caps; and equipment was white leather. Artillery wore infantry uniform in dark blue (including breeches) with black collar, cuffs and lapels and yellow buttons; engineers the same, with white buttons, waistcoat and breeches, crimson facings and yellow turnbacks.

References

Brandani, M., Crociani, P., and
  Fiorentino, M. *Uniformi Militari
  Italiane del Settencento*, Rome
  1976.

SAXE-COBURG-SAALFELD

History

The Thuringian 'Saxon duchy' of Saxe-Coburg-Saalfeld was formed into an independent state in 1680 for Duke Albert, son of Duke Ernest of Saxe-Gotha; the name 'Saxe-Coburg-Saalfeld' was initiated by Duke John Ernest, Albert's younger brother. His sons succeeded him as joint rulers, the survivor, Francis Josiah, introducing the principle of primogeniture for the succession. Under Duke Francis (who died in December 1806) and his son and successor Ernest Frederick, the state became bankrupt and a commission was established to manage its finances. When Duke Francis died, the new duke was serving as an officer in the Russian army, and the state was placed under French military government; only after Tilsit did Saxe-Coburg-Saalfeld enter the Confederation of the Rhine. In 1826, after the ruling family of Saxe-Gotha-Altenburg became extinct in 1825, Duke Ernest exchanged Saalfeld for Gotha, taking the title of Duke of Saxe-Coburg-Gotha, the most famous member of this family being Albert, Prince-Consort of Queen Victoria.

Army

In 1809 Saxe-Coburg-Saalfeld contributed a detachment to the 4th Confederation Regiment, a light company to the 1st

Gold breast-star of the Order of Annunciation of Sardinia.

Battalion (the remainder from Saxe-Gotha-Altenburg) and a light company to the 2nd (the remainder from Saxe-Gotha-Altenburg and Saxe-Meiningen); it served in Spain. The Prussian-style uniform was dark green with yellow collar and cuffs, red turnbacks, white buttons, three white loops on the green cuff-flaps, light blue breeches with yellow stripe and thigh-knot, shako with white cords and brass lozenge plate, and white belts; officers wore bicorns initially. In 1813 the state collaborated with Saxe-Meiningen and Saxe-Hildburghausen in forming a volunteer *Jäger* corps for service with the Allies, wearing green with red facings, yellow piping, grey overalls with green stripe and green-corded shako. A *Landwehr* formation at this time wore green *litewkas* and 'round hat', and the third-line *Landsturm* the same with light blue piping, black belts, and was armed initially with pikes.

SAXE-GOTHA-ALTENBURG

History

Saxe-Gotha was established as an independent Thuringian duchy in 1554, and Saxe-Gotha-Altenburg formed in 1672 when the Duke of Saxe-Gotha inherited Saxe-Altenburg. During the Napoleonic era its dukes were Ernest II (to 1804) and Augustus thereafter; the family became extinct after the death of Duke Frederick IV in 1825, which caused a redistribution of territories within the 'Saxon duchies' in 1826. Ernest, Duke of Saxe-Coburg-Saalfeld, exchanged Saalfeld for Gotha, creating the state of Saxe-Coburg-Gotha; Duke Frederick of Saxe-Hildburghausen exchanged his duchy for Altenburg, re-creating an independent Saxe-Altenburg.

Army (cockade: black and yellow)

Saxe-Gotha-Altenburg joined the Confederation of the Rhine in December 1806, and was compelled to contribute a detachment to the 4th Confederation Regiment, in 1809 providing one grenadier and four musketeer companies of the 1st Battalion (with a Saxe-Coburg-Saalfeld light company), and one grenadier and two musketeer companies of the 2nd Battalion (with a Saxe-Coburg-Saalfeld light company and two musketeer companies from Saxe-Meiningen). Prior to this date Saxe-Gotha Altenburg's infantry unit had worn blue coats with red facings, yellow buttons, white waistcoat and breeches and white-laced bicorn; this colour-scheme was maintained in the 4th Confederation Regiment, the coat with closed lapels, and the bicorn worn until the adoption of a shako in 1812, with red and yellow plumes respectively for grenadiers and light infantry. The French-style shako bore the Saxon arms on a crowned oval plate, red pompom (plume for grenadiers) and white cords; blue trousers with red stripe were adopted from 1809. A small dismounted Garde du Corps company was

> 'By the accidental discharge of a musket, one day last year, the ramrod entered the belly, passed through the body, and the end of it stuck in the back-bone of one of the soliders of our division, from whence it was actually hammered out with a stone. The poor fellow recovered, and joined his regiment, as well as he had ever been, and was, last night, unfortunately drowned, while bathing in the Tormes.'
>
> (*Random Shots from a Rifleman*, Sir John Kincaid, London 1835; Maclaren's combined edn. with *Adventures in the Rifle Brigade*, London 1908, p. 76.)

maintained as the ducal bodyguard, in yellow jackets with red facings and sash, red-and-white diamond-pattern lace, yellow breeches, knee-boots and a brass combed helmet with brown fur turban and black bearskin crest. In early 1813, with the remnant of the 4th Confederation Regiment besieged in Danzig, Napoleon ordered the formation of the Thuringian Battalion (*Thüringisches Marschbataillon*), but it defected to the Allies in April 1813 and fought against the French at the Katzbach. It wore Saxe-Weimar shakos, dark blue coats with red collar and light blue cuffs, and light grey

Medal of Military Merit of Saxe-Coburg-Saalfeld, instituted 1814 by Duke Ernest for troops serving under his command in that year. Gilt with red ribbon with green stripes.

The Iron Medal of Saxe-Coburg-Saalfeld, instituted by Duke Ernest for the volunteers of 1813–14; black ribbon with yellow edges and yellow and green stripes.

War Medal of Saxe-Gotha-Altenburg, instituted in 1816 by Duke Augustus (Emilius Leopold Augustus) for those engaged in the 1814 campaign, *in bronze for rank-and-file and gilded bronze for officers; green ribbon with yellow and black striped edge.*

trousers; later it adopted dark blue jackets of British manufacture with light blue facings. A further battalion formed for Napoleon's service wore blue coats faced red and shakos with red pompoms.

SAXE-HILDBURGHAUSEN

History
Saxe-Hildburghausen was the smallest of the Saxon duchies, which became an independent principality (with capital at Hildburghausen) in 1680, founded by Duke Ernest, son of Duke Ernest the Pious of Saxe-Gotha. Under Duke Frederick (who had ruled since 1780) it joined the Confederation of the Rhine in December 1806, and contributed a single company to the 4th Confederation Regiment, serving in the 3rd Battalion with five companies from Saxe-Weimar-Eisenach. The Hildburghausen company wore the same uniform as those from Saxe-

Weimar-Eisenach, q.v. When the state changed sides in 1813 it contributed troops to the volunteer *Jäger* unit formed with Saxe-Meiningen and Saxe-Coburg-Saalfeld. In 1826 Saxe-Hildburghausen was amalgamated with Saxe-Meiningen, Duke Frederick (who died in 1834) exchanging his duchy for Saxe-Altenburg, which from 1672 had formed part of the Duchy of Saxe-Gotha until the extinction of that state's ruling family in 1825.

SAXE-MEININGEN

History
The Thuringian Duchy of Saxe-Meiningen was founded as an independent state in 1681 by Duke Bernard, son of Duke Ernest the Pious of Saxe-Gotha. Devastation in the Seven Years War and ducal extravagances led to the state's bankruptcy, but under Duke George (who succeeded his brother Charles in 1782, following the regency of his mother Charlotte Amalie), prosperity was restored. George died in 1806 and having introduced succession by primogeniture was succeeded by his son Bernard Ernest Freund (1800–82), his mother Eleanora of Hohenlohe-Langenburg acting as regent until 1821. The Napoleonic Wars caused the return of financial distress, but the death of the last member of the ruling family of Saxe-Gotha-Altenburg in 1825 was beneficial, as the resulting rearrangement of the Saxon duchies more than doubled the size of Saxe-Meiningen by the addition of Saxe-Hildburghausen, Saalfeld and other areas. Alone of the Saxon duchies, Saxe-Meiningen declared for Austria in 1866 and was immediately occupied by Prussian troops; Duke Bernhard abdicated and was succeeded by his son George who took Saxe-Meiningen into the Prussian camp.

Army (cockade: green and white)
Prior to 1807 the state's single military unit was a *Jäger* corps, dressed in green jacket and breeches with red facings, white buttons, black leather equipment and gaiters, and Austrian-style black leather helmets. Joining the Confederation of the Rhine in December 1806, Saxe-Meiningen had to supply two musketeer companies to the 2nd Battalion 4th Confederation Regiment (with three companies from Saxe-Gotha-Altenburg and one from Saxe-Coburg-Saalfeld). The Saxe-Meiningen contingent wore the uniform of Saxe-Gotha-

'When the French were driven out of Saragossa, the Spaniards said it was the statue of the Virgin which stood at their gates that performed the exploit. An Irish Monk, who has lived here* for 20 years, and who told us the story, said: "A fig for their saints – the English have two saints, St. Powder and St. Ball, and when they want to enter a place they use very little ceremony."'
(* 'here' is Corunna)
(*Public Ledger*, 22 November 1808.)

Altenburg, but with black leatherwork and double-breasted jackets without lapels instead of the red lapels of Saxe-Gotha-Altenburg; by 1812 they had adopted Saxe-Gotha-Altenburg uniform completely. In 1813 the state participated with Saxe-Coburg-Saalfeld and Saxe-Hildburghausen in the formation of a volunteer *Jäger* corps for service with the Allies.

SAXE-WEIMAR-EISENACH

History

Saxe-Weimar-Eisenach was the largest and most important of the 'Saxon duchies'. Connected to the ruling house of Saxony, Saxe-Weimar became independent in 1641, enlarged by amalgamation with Saxe-Eisenach in 1644. Duke Charles Augustus (1757–1828) succeeded to the dukedom as an infant upon the death of his father Ernest Augustus II in 1758, his mother Anna Amalia of Brunswick ruling as regent until 1775. Charles Augustus was a man of varied talents and liberal disposition; interested in art and science, he was a patron of Goethe and Schiller, and employed the great Johann Herder to reform his state's education, resulting in Jena University becoming justly famous. Charles Augustus' influence was out of all proportion with the size of his state, and he became the leading mover in the formation of the 'league of princes' (*Fürstenbund*) under Frederick the Great in opposition to the Holy Roman Empire in 1785. A general in Prussian service, Charles Augustus was present at Valmy and Kaiserslautern, and in the Jena campaign. Weimar was sacked on the day after Jena, and to avoid the confiscation of his state Charles Augustus was compelled to join the Confederation of the Rhine; it was said that only the pleading of his duchess, Louise of Hesse-Darmstadt, prevented Napoleon from deposing him. In 1813 Charles Augustus abandoned the French alliance and joined the Allies; he commanded a corps in the Netherlands in 1814, and the Congress of Vienna rewarded him with an extension of his territory and its elevation to grand-duchy. He became the first German prince to grant a liberal constitution (5 May 1816) which aroused the ire of other states which regarded him as a revolutionary, and this curtailed further liberalization. When he died in June 1828 he was mourned universally as one of the most noble and humanitarian men of his age. He was succeeded by his elder son, Bernhard (1792–1862), a professional soldier who served the Netherlands with distinction: he was the 'Prince Bernhard of Saxe-Weimar' who held the French in the early part of the battle of Quatre Bras, and rose to command the Dutch East Indian forces (1847–50). His son, William Augustus Edward, gained much distinction in the British Army during the Crimean War.

Army (cockade: black, green and yellow)

Charles Augustus disbanded his forces except for a small bodyguard, but in 1788 formed a *Jäger* battalion which

The Order of the White Falcon of Saxe-Weimar-Eisenach, founded by the Imperial cavalry general the Duke Ernest Augustus on 2 August 1732, and reconstituted in October 1815 by Duke Charles Augustus. (The white falcon symbol was chosen to represent the state, as a falcon, following the Imperial eagle!) Gold cross enamelled red, with green-enamelled arms and white falcon; red ribbon.

fought with the Prussians at Auerstädt. This unit initially wore green jackets with yellow buttons and collar-patch, white breeches, buff belts and 'Corsican hat' with green plume and red band; belts became black in 1796, and in 1806 the uniform was a green jacket and breeches, yellow collar, turnbacks and buttons, and a head-dress like the Prussian leather grenadier cap with a brass plate, black horsehair mane and green plume; the unit was armed with rifles. The hussar unit wore a black tapering shako with white plume and red-and-white cords, red dolman, and blue cuffs, pelisse and overalls (with red stripe).

Under the Confederation of the Rhine the state furnished five of the six companies of the 3rd Battalion, 4th Confederation Regiment; it suffered heavily in the Peninsular War and in Russia in 1812. Until 1809 they wore the previous uniform with yellow-edged bicorn; in that year

French-style shakos were adopted, with white cords and green plume or pompom (orange-red for the carabinier company created by 1812), green jacket with yellow collar-patch and buttons, grey or white overalls (winter and summer respectively) and black leatherwork; officers had gold epaulettes. This uniform was retained when the battalion served with the Allies. A *Landwehr* unit about 800 strong was formed in 1814, in dark green *litewka* and trousers, black facings, yellow piping, black brassard edged yellow on the left arm, and a green cloth cap with black peak and band. A small volunteer *Jäger* unit (mounted and foot) wore black *litewka* and trousers (with yellow stripe), yellow piping, black equipment and a black-plumed shako with brass cross-badge for the cavalry; and green *litewka*, yellow facings, grey trousers and plume-less shako for the infantry.

SAXONY

History

Saxony emerged from the Seven Years War in a state of devastation. Its ruling family, hereditary electors of Saxony, had recently aspired to kingship when Augustus II was elected to the throne of Poland, but the regal status and the tribulations it brought were lost on his death in 1763. His son and successor as elector, Frederick Christian, survived his father by only two months, leaving the electorate to his 13-year-old son Frederick Augustus III, who ruled through a regent until 1768. During the early part of his reign Saxony's fortunes improved and his care for his subjects brought him the nickname 'the Just'. He supported Prussia in the dispute over the Bavarian Succession, and exchanged his claim to the Bavarian throne for a large sum which helped redeem Saxon territory pawned to other states, and to reduce the immense public debt. In foreign policy he avoided connections that might prove dangerous, declining the throne of Poland in 1791 even though it was offered with a hereditary succession, remembering the cost of the previous Polish involvement; and when the Revolutionary Wars began, he involved Saxony as little as possible beyond the minimum contribution demanded of him as a prince of the empire. In 1796 he concluded a treaty of neutrality with France, but in 1806 supported Prussia, Saxon forces acquitting themselves with some distinction in the war.

Under Napoleon's blandishments, the Elector assumed the title of King of Saxony (as Frederick Augustus I) by the Peace of Posen (11 December 1806), entering the Confederation of the Rhine as an independent sovereign, and undertook to support France with 20,000 men. Saxony's external policy was controlled by Napoleon, but internally the alliance had little effect beyond the emancipation of Roman Catholics, unlike the changes imposed by the French in some of their satellites. In 1807 Frederick Augustus's loyalty to Napoleon was rewarded by the granting of the Duchy of Warsaw. The collapse of French power had a dire effect, however, for even after Saxony was invaded by the Allies in spring 1813 Frederick Augustus refused to abandon

the French alliance; but during the battle of Leipzig popular sentiment was reflected by the desertion of the Saxon forces to the Allies, and Frederick Augustus was made prisoner. For the following year Saxony was governed by Russia, and from November 1814 by Prussia, and only Austria's desire to have a buffer between themselves and Prussia prevented total annexation by Prussia. The wrangle at the Congress of Vienna over the fate of Saxony almost caused a rupture between the Allies, Russia supporting Prussia, and Britain and France taking Austria's part. In the event, Prussia took over half the state (7,800 square miles), Frederick Augustus retaining 5,790 square miles, more than half the population, and his royal title. He governed this rump of his original territory until his death in 1827, ending a reign which had resulted in Saxony's ceasing to be a major power.

Cross of the Military Order of St. Henry of Saxony, founded in October 1739, reformed in September 1768 but largely unused until 1807. Gold cross with blue circlet, green leaves and an enamelled figure of St. Henry in the centre; blue ribbon with yellow edges.

Army (cockade: white; green, black and yellow (1813) and green with white edge thereafter)

It is perhaps unfortunate that the Saxon army is best-remembered for its 'rout' at Wagram, and its defection at Leipzig, events which conceal the fact that in general the Saxons were a steady professional body which performed as well as any of Napoleon's satellite forces. Without belabouring the point unduly, at Wagram the Saxons were under Bernadotte's command, were sent into a position where they were raked by Austrian artillery and assailed by cavalry, and not surprisingly in such circumstances some broke and fled, almost carrying Massena's corps with them. That the reputation of the Saxon army as a whole has suffered is due largely to Napoleon's anger with Bernadotte, who claimed that his Corps was instrumental in the victory; Napoleon denied this by being equally inaccurate, saying that the French were solely responsible and that the 'foreigners' were totally irrelevant. Perhaps Marbot's comment is the fairest: 'The Saxons are brave, but the best of troops are sometimes routed', accounting for the rout by Bernadotte's handling of the attack. (When Napoleon encountered Bernadotte dashing to the rear to halt and reorganize the broken troops he remarked: 'Is that the scientific manoeuvre by which you were going to make the archduke lay down his arms?')[1] That Napoleon's ire with Bernadotte should colour the reputation of the entire Saxon army is unfortunate, as is criticism of their defection at Leipzig, which was a political decision rather than one occasioned by low morale.

Cavalry

The four heavy regiments, each of four squadrons, included the Garde du Corps, a Carabinier regiment (disbanded 1810) and two cuirassier regiments, Kurfürst (retitled in December 1806 as König and June 1807 as *Leib-Kürassier-Garde*) and Kochtitzky (re-titled Zastrow in 1808 and amalgamated with the *Leib*-Cuirassiers after virtual destruction in Russia, to form a new *Kürassier-Regiment*. The Garde du Corps and Zastrow were especially distinguished in 1812, being probably the first to penetrate the Raevsky Redoubt at Borodino and losing half their strength in the process; the combined total of both regiments which survived the campaign was twenty officers and seven other ranks. All the heavy regiments wore a pale straw-coloured *Kollet* closed down the front without buttons, red facings (Garde du Corps dark blue, Zastrow yellow), gold lace for officers (Zastrow silver), and yellow lace for other ranks with coloured edge: Kurfürst red, Carabiniers red-and-black, Zastrow black-and-white and Garde du Corps red-and-blue; white breeches, long boots and white-plumed bicorn. In 1810 the jackets became white or off-white, and brass combed helmets adopted, with black crest, brown fur turban and white plume; cuirasses were adopted only latterly.

The light cavalry included four *chevauxleger* regiments (four squadrons each) and one of hussars (ten squadrons). The former wore bicorns, red coats, yellow buttons, buff waistcoats, white breeches and belts and high boots; in 1810

short jackets were adopted, with closed lapels and pointed cuffs, and the bicorn replaced by a white-plumed shako with brass shield-plate. Officers had longer coat-tails, gold epaulettes and white plumes with black base. Facings were: Regiment Prince Clement light green, Prince Albrecht dark green, Prince Johann black and von Polenz light blue. The two latter regiments were virtually destroyed in 1812 and disbanded in 1813. Regiment Prince Clement had been equipped with lances in 1811 (light green over red pennon) and in 1813 adopted a Polish-style uniform in light blue with black facings and red piping, but reverted to red with light blue facings and the shako in 1815. The hussar regiment (formed 1791) wore a black mirliton with light blue wing and white plume, white dolman, breeches and buttons, and light blue pelisse, facings and braid. From *c*, 1806 the dolman

Medal of the Order of the Rue Crown of Saxony, instituted by Frederick Augustus on 20 July 1807 at the suggestion of Napoleon. Gold medal with green and white enamel and green ribbon.

At Essling:

'I felt an urgent call to relieve nature, but it was strictly against orders to move a step towards the rear. There was no alternative but to go forward in advance of the line, which I did; and, having put down my musket, I began operations with my behind to the enemy. All at once a cannon-ball came along, rico-chetted within a yard of me, and threw a hail of earth and stones all over my back. Luckily for me I still had my pack on, or I should have perished. Picking up my musket with one hand and my trousers with the other, black and blue behind, I . . . was soon back in my place in the ranks. "Well, Coignet," said Captain Renard, "that was a near thing." "It was, sir; their paper's too hard, I couldn't use it. They're a lot of swine." And then followed handshakes all round with my officers and comrades.'

(*The Note-Books of Captain Coignet*, J.-R. Coignet, intro. Hon. Sir John Fortescue, London 1928, p. 124.)

became light blue with black facings, and the *chevauxleger* shako was adopted in 1810. For service with the Allies in 1813 one regiment each of cuirassiers, hussars and Uhlans were constituted from the survivors, three squadrons each.

Infantry

The infantry comprised the Guard Grenadiers and twelve line regiments, each of two battalions of one grenadier and four musketeer companies; on campaign the grenadiers were detached and amalgamated into four-company composite grenadier battalions. In 1806 regimental strength was about 1,750; after the 1810 reorganizations this rose to more than 2,000.

The line regiments wore white coats, waistcoats, breeches and leatherwork, facing-coloured collar, cuffs and lapels, musketeers with bicorns bearing a white pompom and facing-coloured centre. Grenadiers had Austrian-style peakless bearskins with brass plate and facing-coloured rear patch bearing a white cross, and carried sabres; one NCO and eight privates of each company were sharpshooters, wearing musketeer uniform plus a green plume, and carried rifled muskets. Officers had gold or silver hat-lace (according to button-colour), enamelled gilt gorgets, and sash (until 1809) and sword-knot in mixed silver and crimson; grenadier officers had epaulettes, enamelled gilt cap-plate and gold cords, and carried carbines. NCOs had gold or silver hat-lace and until 1809 carried spontoons (carbines for grenadiers).

Regiments bore the name of the colonel, the following titles being appropriate for 1806, with facing-colours and yellow or white buttons respectively for the first and second of each pair of units named: Kurfürst and von Sänger red; Prince Clement and Prince Anton dark blue; Prince Maximilian and von Thümmel yellow; Prince Frederick August and von Low light green; Prince Xaver and von

Bünau light blue; von Rechten and von Niesemeuschel crimson. In December 1806 the Kurfürst Regiment was re-titled König, and in 1810 Regiments von Sänger (from 1808 von Cerrini), von Thümmel (1808 von Burgsdorff), Prince Xaver (1806 von Obschelwitz) and von Bünau (1808 von Dyherrn) were disbanded. A French-style uniform was adopted in 1810, of a short, white jacket with closed lapels and pointed or flapped cuffs, and French-style shakos with brass crowned shield plate bearing 'FA' and white plume and cords. Grenadiers had red plume, cords and epaulettes and NCO rank-distinction was in French style, facing-coloured bars for corporals (and yellow shako-lace) and gold for sergeants. Officers had longer coat-tails, white plume with black base, gold lace shako-band and gold epaulettes in French style. Facings were: König and von Niesemeuschel scarlet, von Low and Prince Anton dark blue, Prince Maximilian and von Rechten yellow, Prince Frederick August and Prince Clement green, with yellow buttons for the first of each pair and white for the others.

The Guard Grenadiers wore infantry uniform but in red with yellow facings and white epaulettes (officers silver), and bearskin caps with yellow rear patch bearing a white cross, and white cords. Garrison battalions wore infantry uniform with black facings and white buttons. In 1809 the skirmishers of the line regiments were formed into the 1st and 2nd *Schützen* battalions, re-titled Light Infantry in 1810; they wore infantry uniform in dark green (including breeches), with black facings (no lapels), yellow buttons, green plume and shako-cords. In 1809 a *Jäger* corps was formed, similarly uniformed but with red piping, green collar with black patch, grey breeches piped red, black equipment and brass horn-badge on the shako.

In 1813 five regular regiments were formed for Allied service from the débris of the previous units: a 'Provisional Guard Regiment' of three battalions, from the previous Guard Grenadiers, Regiment König and the line grenadiers; the 1st and 2nd Provisional Line Regiments (two battalions each), from the old Regiments Prince Anton and Prince Maximilian; and the 1st and 2nd Light Infantry (two battalions each), plus a *Jäger* battalion. A 3rd Provisional Line Regiment was formed from the old Regiment Prince Frederick August, and in 1815 the old titles Prince Anton, Prince Maximilian and Prince Frederick August were restored. Also formed for service with the Allies were four *Landwehr* regiments (three battalions each), in blue jackets faced red, grey overalls, black equipment and shakos bearing a brass cross and the new cockade (green, yellow and black from November 1813). There was also a unit styled 'Volunteers of the Saxon Banner' of five hussar squadrons and two light infantry battalions; the former wore green hussar uniform and plume, red facings, yellow braid, light blue overalls, and shakos bearing the cross badge; and the latter green jackets, red facings, yellow buttons, grey overalls with red stripe, black equipment and Austrian-style 'Corsican hat' with white plume and brass cross-badge.

Artillery

Field batteries were normally only formed upon mobilization for war, the troops being employed on garrison duty in small detachments in peacetime, which tended to diminish their effectiveness. In 1806 sixteen foot or garrison and two horse batteries were employed, each of six guns; 8-gun batteries were employed in 1807, and in 1812 batteries comprised four 6pdrs and two 8pdr howitzers, one foot battery being attached to each infantry division, one horse battery to the cavalry division, and the remainder forming VII Corps' reserve; each line regiment had two 4pdr battalion guns. In the 1813 campaign the horse batteries had six, later four guns; the four foot batteries had eight 6pdrs and the reserve was a single battery of eight 12pdrs. In Allied service the artillery comprised two 6-gun horse batteries, and two 8-gun foot batteries. The artillery wore infantry-style uniform in dark green with red facings, yellow buttons, buff waistcoat and breeches and yellow-laced bicorns with red plume; they adopted re-styled uniforms and the shako with the infantry. The horse batteries wore the same colouring in *chevauxleger* style, with white breeches and hussar boots; the train wore light blue with black facings, red piping and white buttons. Engineers wore artillery uniform with white buttons, and originally red waistcoat and breeches.

Higher Organization

As the Saxon forces formed part of larger armies (with the Prussians in 1806, in IX Corps in 1809 and VII Corps in 1812) their organization conformed to that of the larger formations; typical divisional composition was two infantry brigades of two battalions each, plus a grenadier battalion, foot artillery battery and engineer company.

Note
1. *Memoirs of Baron de Marbot,* ed.
   A. J. Butler, London 1913, II,
   p. 386.

References
Pivka, Otto von. *Napoleon's German Allies: Saxony 1806–15,* London 1979.

SCHWARZBURG

History

The Thuringian principalities of Schwarzburg were possessed by the same family, one of the oldest and most noble in Germany. The senior (smaller) state was Schwarzburg-Sonderhausen, whose count was elevated to the status of prince of the Empire by Leopold I in 1697; the larger, Schwarzburg-Rudolstadt, was the cadet branch descended from Albrecht VII of Schwarzburg (1605), whose count was made a prince in 1710. Both states entered the Confederation of the Rhine in April 1807; in 1816 Schwarzburg-Sonderhausen redeemed Prussian claims by the surrender of some territory, as did Schwarzburg-Rudolstadt in 1819. By an unusual tradition akin to that of the house of Reuss, male members of the house of Schwarzburg bore the name Günther, initially distinguished by numbers and later by prefixing another name.

Army (cockade: blue and white)

In 1792 Schwarzburg provided an infantry contingent for the coalition against France, dressed in blue coats with red collar, cuffs and turnbacks, blue lapels piped red, yellow buttons, white waistcoat, breeches and equipment, black gaiters and white-laced bicorn. For the *Rheinbund,* Schwarzburg-Sonderhausen and Schwarzburg-Rudolstadt each provided two companies for the 6th Confederation Regiment, wearing green with red facings, yellow buttons, grey breeches, black gaiters and leatherwork and a red-plumed shako with white cords; the Schwarzburg-Sonderhausen troops had green cuff-flaps and brass octagonal shako-plate, and those from Schwarzburg-Rudolstadt unflapped cuffs and a brass lozenge-plate. They also provided a company each for the so-called 'Princes' Battalion' (*Fürstenbataillon*) which served in Spain (the other companies from Lippe-Detmold, Lippe-Bückeburg, Reuss

Medal of War of Schwarzburg-Sonderhausen, for veterans of 1814; silver medal, blue ribbon with white edge.

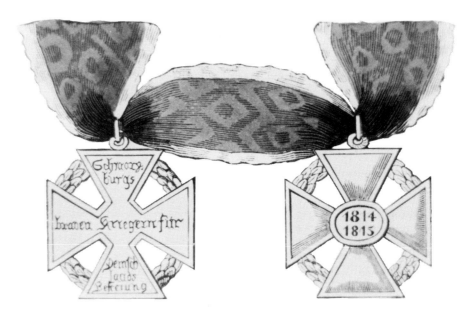

and Waldeck); and in 1813, for service with the Allies, a line battalion, a smaller *Landwehr* battalion and a volunteer *Jäger* company.

Military Decoration of Honour of Schwarzburg-Rudolstadt, a silver cross instituted in 1816 for veterans of the 1814 campaign. Bright blue ribbon with white edges.

SPAIN

History

Spain's prosperity and prestige had declined since the great days of the sixteenth century, which a series of unsuccessful monarchs had done little to prevent. King Charles III (ruled 1759–88) was an 'enlightened despot'; his successor Charles IV was simply a despot, and one of so little intellect that he verged on imbecility, very much under the influence of his wife, the coarse and unscrupulous Maria Louisa of Parma. Foreign policy under Charles III had been governed by the 'Family Compact' with France, but the French Revolution ended the alliance. Charles IV continued to rely upon his father's minister, Don Jose Moñino y Redondo, Count of Floridablanca (1728–1808), who encouraged a coalition of European powers against France. Fearing that a war might limit the revenue she squandered, Maria Louisa persuaded the king to replace Floridablanca with his father's previous finance minister, Pedro Pablo Abarca de Bolea, Count of Aranda (1719–98); but he, attempting to liberalize internal policy and make Spain neutral, was dismissed in November 1792 and replaced as chief minister by the Queen's lover, Manuel de Godoy (1767–1851). Corrupt and of limited talent, Godoy presided over a humiliating start to Spain's participation in the military campaigns of the era.

Spain joined the coalition against France when the execution of Louis XVI aroused Charles IV's fury, and invaded across the Pyrenees. So inept were Spanish operations in 1793–4 that the Pyrenean fortresses were lost and the French penetrated almost to the Ebro; so that Godoy was compelled to conclude peace by the Treaty of Basel in 1795, which brought him the title 'Prince of Peace' but which was very unpopular in Spain. Further humiliation followed, the Franco-Spanish alliance by the Treaty of San Ildefonso (1796) proving desperately disadvantageous to Spain, and the defeat of her fleet at St. Vincent greatly impaired her ability to maintain control over the overseas colonies. Distrusted by both Spanish and French, Godoy was removed from office (upon French insistence) in March 1798 and replaced as chief minister by a member of the pro-reform party, Saavedra. Internal plots and Bonaparte's influence led to Godoy's reinstatement in 1800, with Spain remaining a French puppet, in whose interest they attacked Portugal in 1801. Godoy (commanding in person) extracted a treaty of neutrality from Portugal, but as this was not sufficiently strict for Bonaparte, Charles IV was compelled to repudiate it. This French domination of Spain was confirmed in 1807 when Napoleon sent French troops through Spain to compel Portugal to adopt the 'Continental System'. The Spanish royal family was beset by internal friction: the King's son and heir, Ferdinand (1784–1833) for a time intrigued with Napoleon and was arrested when Godoy learned of the plot, being accused of attempting to dethrone his father and murder his mother. Napoleon used this internal dissent to his own advantage; Charles IV was induced to abdicate and retire to Rome, and pro-French factions allowed Napoleon to proclaim Joseph Bonaparte as new king of Spain. Ferdinand, who had briefly claimed the throne as King Ferdinand VII, was lured to France and interned at Talleyrand's château of Valençay for the next six years.

The bulk of the Spanish population had no thought of accepting Joseph and rebellion spread throughout the country, initiating the Peninsular War. With Godoy and the king in exile, no central political figure emerged to champion the cause of Ferdinand VII, administration devolving upon a number of local *juntas* or committees, with a central *junta* chosen from their members; there was thus little co-ordination of effort which was a major cause of the Spanish routs early in the war. In 1808 old Floridablanca was called upon to take the presidency of the central *junta* (he had been incarcerated after his removal from office and only avoided starvation by the intervention of his brother), but he died on 20 November at Seville. The capture of Seville resulted in the dissolution of the central *junta*, which allowed the liberal reforming parties to concentrate at Cadiz, which became and remained the capital of what was left of independent Spain.

In 1810 a parliament was organized on the lines of the old *Cortes*, a body composed largely of nobles and clerics which under the old system was summoned at the beginning of reigns to swear homage to the king but which had no power. The new *Cortes* had a preponderance of members of the 'third estate' (commoners), but as much of Spain was under French control no systematic process of election could be achieved; but unrepresentative though it was, the *Cortes* determined to institute a new constitution, which it passed on 19 March 1812. Some of the provisions were so liberal and others not conducive to good government that many decided that the *Cortes* must be suppressed after the war, but at the time attention was directed towards the expulsion of the French. The Bonapartist kingdom of Spain, which never received popular support, collapsed as the Peninsular War resulted in the defeat of the French, and Ferdinand VII, released by Napoleon, returned to Madrid in March 1814. Before his return he had accepted the 1812 Constitution, but having returned immediately repudiated it; his attempts to govern despotically failed due to his own lack of capacity and character, and resulted in the 1820 revolution, three years of anarchy and a renewed French invasion, followed by further revolts and the Carlist War. Far from returning France to tranquillity, the end of the Peninsular War merely heralded a further prolonged period of conflict and suffering.

Army (cockade: red)

Years of neglect and corruption had left the Spanish army in an abysmal state, quite unfitted to fight a war, which became obvious almost from the outset. Despite a deep sense of patriotism which infused the population, leading to such feats as the defence of Saragossa, the regular army remained inefficient and as likely to run away as to stand firm, a characteristic which existed to the end of the Peninsular War. On occasion the regulars did fight with determination – the artillery was notably unwilling to relinquish its guns, suffering a succession of heavy casualties in actions when they were left unsupported, and the stand of Zayas' brigade went far to saving Beresford in the early part of the battle of Albuera, for example – but in general neither organization, leadership nor training was conducive to producing an efficient army. Many British observers were totally dismissive of the Spaniards, for example: 'nothing better than mere rabble – no organization, no subordination, but every one evidently pursued that plan which seemed right in his own eyes';[1] 'in their best days . . . more like an armed mob than regularly organized soldiers';[2] 'The loss I most regret on these occasions are the arms, which the fools throw away in their flight, and more irreparable than men of which they ought to have no want'.[3]

Excluding the virtual mercenaries of the 'foreign corps', the Spanish army was recruited partly by voluntary enlistment (and as conditions were so appalling there was little incentive to join save to escape penury) and partly by a selective conscription, the *Quinta* (so termed as it originally was intended to take every fifth man), but as all middle-class artisans were exempt the burden fell upon the most unskilled agricultural labourers. The officer corps was worse; one-third was supposedly appointed from the ranks (but had no chance of rising beyond captain) and the remainder from the nobility and gentry (a patent of nobility was essential to gain a cavalry commission). There was virtually no officer-training (the five military colleges had been reduced to the one at Zamora by Godoy) and no regulated drill, so that each colonel trained his men in his own fashion; and the resulting appalling standard of leadership reduced the Spanish army to the depths. Surtees noted that every officer 'appeared to vie with the other who could make the greatest harlequin of himself, whilst those of them who were mounted would caper and prance about the streets like so many fools . . . the majority of them were the most haughty, and at the same time the most contemptible creatures in the shape of officers, that I ever beheld'.[4]

This lack of leadership explains the difference between the amazing fortitude of the civilian, guerrilla and volunteer forces and the wretched state of the regulars; among the most perceptive comments are those of Blakeney, who declared that, 'Courage was never wanting in Spanish soldiers; but confidence in their chiefs was rare', and that despite the pouring into Spain of vast funds and *matériel* by Britain, such was the corruption of the government and administration that most never reached the army: ' . . . left barefoot, ragged

'Fortunately, some platoons which Davoust [sic] had rallied, and the appearance of another troop of his stragglers, attracted the enemy's attention. Mortier availed himself of it. He gave orders to the three thousand men he had still remaining to retreat slowly in the face of their fifty thousand enemies. "Do you hear, soldiers?" cried General Laborde, "the marshal orders ordinary time! Ordinary time, soldiers!" And this brave and unfortunate troop, dragging with them some of their wounded, under a shower of balls and grapeshot, retired as slowly from this field of carnage, as they would have done from a field of manoeuvre.'

(*History of the Expedition to Russia*, Count Philippe de Segur, London 1825, II, p. 180.)

and half-starved. In this deplorable state they were brought into the field under leaders many of whom were scarcely competent to command a sergeant's outlying picqet';[5] and of John Colborne: 'The privations and misery endured by a large mass of the people of Spain from their patriotism and hatred to their oppressors, were seldom equalled. With a brave, hardy, active, abstemious peasantry, fond of glory, it may appear extraordinary that the struggle of the Spaniards was prolonged for six years without any decided success, but the Central Junta and the presumption and obstinacy of most of the men placed at the head of the armies rendered their perseverence and courage useless.'[6] With only notable exceptions like La Romana and the many officers of foreign descent (principally Irish) who, if they were no military geniuses at least were determined to fight, the Spanish high command was probably the most wretched of any major European state. At the outbreak of the Peninsular War the situation was exacerbated by Godoy's 'lending' of the best elements of the Spanish army to Napoleon, for service under La Romana in Denmark and north Germany. (These troops – the cavalry regiments Rey, Infante and Algarve, the Almansa and Villaviciosa Dragoons, the 1st Barcelona and 2nd Catalonian Light Infantry and the line regiments Asturias, Princesa, Guadalajara and Zamora – rebelled against the French and were shipped home by the British navy to continue their fight against the French in Spain.) Only in the later Peninsular War, when some Spanish brigades were put more closely under British control and they became adequately provisioned as a result, did they become at all reliable.

Cavalry

The cavalry was the worst part of the Spanish army, greatly under-strength and with insufficient horses to mount much above half the regiments; theoretical establishment was in regiments of about 670 men in five squadrons. As the Peninsular War progressed numerous new or local regiments were formed, including cuirassiers, lancers and various types of *chasseurs* and hussars, but their efficiency was never high and their consequence limited. The twelve regular heavy regiments wore white coats until 1806, and blue thereafter, with red turnbacks, facing-coloured collar, lapels and cuffs, bicorns with button-coloured lace edging, yellow or buff breeches, long boots and white leather equipment; the four senior regiments in the following list had lace loops on the lapels. Regiments and facings were: Rey red; Reina sky-blue; Principe red; Infante white; Borbon, Farnesio and Alcantara red; España, Santiago and Montesa crimson; Algarve yellow; Calatrava sky-blue. Buttons were white (Rey and Infante yellow), and piping of the facing-colour except for Rey, Principe and Borbon (white), Reina (red), Infante and Farnesio yellow and Alcantara green; Alcantara had green lapels; España yellow collar and Calatrava red.

The light regiments comprised eight of dragoons and two each of *cazadores* (*chasseurs*) and Hussars. The dragoons wore a uniform similar to that of the heavy regiments but in yellow, with white buttons, piping and lace (including six

loops on each lapel); facings were Regiment Rey crimson, Reina light red, Almansa sky-blue, Villaviciosa and Sagunto green, Pavia red, Numancia and Lusitania black; yellow collars for Pavia, Sagunto and Lusitania. The *cazadores* wore braided green dolmans and breeches, white lace and braid and facings sky-blue for the *Voluntarios de España* and red for the Olivenza Regiment, initially with fur-crested leather helmets and later shakos with red plume and white cords. In 1807–8 the Almansa and Villaviciosa Dragoons (serving with La Romana) also wore *cazadore* uniform with red facings. The hussars wore a similar style, with black mirlitons with red plume and white cords, and pelisses, the latter with contrastingly-coloured collars. Regiment Maria Luisa wore scarlet dolmans faced light blue, scarlet mirliton-wing, sky-blue pelisse with red collar, and white braid; Regiment España had emerald dolmans, sky-blue facings and breeches, sky-blue pelisse with green collar and green mirliton-wing; they are also shown in busbies with green bag, with a green wing and red plume like the mirliton.

Infantry

The infantry originally comprised 35 Spanish line regiments of three battalions each, six Swiss mercenary regiments, three of Irish and one of Italians, and twelve light battalions. The establishment of a line regiment was 2,186 men and 70 officers, each battalion of four companies, with company-strength an extremely unwieldy 180-plus, though in practice units were usually greatly under-strength. The uniform was a white coat with coloured facings, white turnbacks, waistcoat, breeches and leather equipment, and a red-plumed bicorn; grenadiers had tall, plate-less fur caps with a long, facing-coloured cloth bag hanging at the rear, covered in intricate embroidery, and button-coloured lace loops on cuffs. In 1800 the lapels were closed and the coat-tails shortened (officers retained the longer coat), and the hat was supplanted by a metal-fronted mitre-cap in the button-colour, but the bicorn was reintroduced very quickly. In 1806 facing-coloured cuff-flaps were introduced; all facing-coloured items were piped white, and the white collars of some regiments, pockets and turnbacks were piped in the facing-colour. Regiments were organized in eight brigades, each with its own facing-colour: 1st Brigade (Regiments 1 Rey, 2 Reina, 3 Principe, 8 Soria, 27 Princesa) purple; 2nd Brigade (4 Saboya, 5 Corona, 6 Africa, 7 Zamora, 11 Sevilla) black; 3rd Brigade (12 Granada, 13 Valencia, 16 Toledo, 19 Murcia, 21 Cantabria) light blue; 4th Brigade (9 Cordoba, 10 Guadalajara, 17 Mallorca, 20 Leon, 25 Aragon) red; 5th Brigade (14 Zaragoza, 15 España, 18 Burgos, 22 Asturias, 23 Fijo de Ceuta) light green; 6th Brigade (24 Navarra, 26 América, 29 Málaga , 30 Jaén, 31 Ordenes Militares) dark blue; 7th Brigade (28 Estremadura, 32 Voluntarios de Castilla, 33 Voluntarios del Estado, 34 Voluntarios de la Corona, 35 Borbon) crimson. Buttons were white except for regiments numbered above 1, 3, 4, 6, 9, 12, 14, 17, 18, 24, 27–29 and 33, yellow; collars white for nos. 3, 6–8, 16–20, 22, 29, 30, 33 and 34; lapels white for nos. 11, 23, 25, 27, 31 and 35. The 8th Brigade was formed of the foreign regiments, which wore the same uniform but in light blue with yellow facings: 36 Irlanda, 37 Hibernia (light blue collar), 38 Ultonia (light blue lapels) and 39 Nápoles; white buttons for all except Irlanda, yellow. The Swiss regiments wore dark blue with red facings and dark blue cuff-flaps and collar-patch (Swiss regiments 1–5), and the same with red cuff-flap and dark blue collar with no patch (Regiment Preux). For all regiments, officers wore epaulettes of the button-colour and red sashes with gold tassels.

The light infantry wore green faced red, white breeches, waistcoat and leather equipment, bicorn and brown gaiters, until 1800 when the coat became blue. In 1802 they were re-equipped in lightish green hussar uniform with red facings and girdle, yellow lace, and a low black leather 'round hat' with black fur crest, red turban and green plume. In 1806 a line-infantry style uniform was authorized, in dark blue with green-plumed bicorn (latterly shakos) and facings: 1st and 2nd Aragon and Barbastro red; 1st and 2nd Catalonia, Tarragona, Gerona, 1st and 2nd Barcelona yellow; Voluntarios de Valencia, Campo Mayor and Navarra crimson. Blue collars for 2nd Catalonia, 2nd Aragon, 2nd Barcelona and Campo Mayor; blue lapels for Tarragona, 1st Barcelona, Barbastro and Navarra; white buttons for all except 1st and 2nd Catalonia and Tarragona, yellow.

From 1812 the line regiments received a British-style, single-breasted dark blue jacket with red collar, cuffs and turnbacks, a British-style 'stovepipe' shako and light blue overalls (though grey or brown were equally common). The centre companies (fusiliers) had white plumes and shako-lace (a strip around the base and a chinstrap, usually tied up over the top), blue shoulder-straps piped red, and a brass rampant-lion shako-badge; sergeants had white epaulettes. Grenadiers had red shako-lace and plume, blue padded wings with red fringe, brass grenade shako-badge, and sergeants red epaulettes; and *cazadores* (light companies) green plumes and shako-lace, brass hunting-horn shako-badge, blue wings with green fringe, and green epaulettes for sergeants. Officers had longer-tailed coats, gold epaulettes and the universal red sash. Buttons were yellow, and weapons and equipment often of British style. Light regiments wore the same uniform in lightish blue with white piping and the same company-distinctions.

Many variations existed, especially in the locally raised units, many in British-style uniform: Regiment *Muerte*, for example, wore dark green single-breasted jackets with medium blue collar, cuffs and overalls, and a British shako with green plume and white-metal skull and crossed bones as appropriate for its title; Regiment Medina Sidonia wore brown, faced light blue, with French-style shako; Regiment Cortes red faced white; Toledo brown faced yellow; Patria dark green faced red, with red-plumed French-style shako; Santa Fée dark blue faced green, piped red, with French-style shako; Regiment Fernando VII (which served at Talavera) lightish-blue British-style jacket and overalls faced red, piped white, with French-style shako. The diversity of uniform even after the introduction of British-style uniform is evident from a description of Whittingham's

Military Order of St. Ferdinand of Spain, instituted by the Cortes *in 1811, and renewed by Ferdinand VII on his return to Spain. Gold cross for officers, silver for 'other ranks', with white-enamelled arms, green wreaths and blue circlet; red ribbon with yellow edges.*

Division which served in eastern Spain in 1812: Majorca Grenadiers, blue faced sky-blue, blue breeches, buff collar; Murcia Grenadiers blue faced yellow, sky-blue breeches, black belts; 2nd Majorca blue faced red, blue pantaloons; Majorca *Cazadores* like the British 95th Rifles; Cordova blue with buff collar and cuffs and crimson lapels; Guadalajara Grenadiers blue with buff facings and belts; all wore French-style shakos. (Similar differences in uniform were evident in the cavalry: the units present here were the Almansa, dressed like the British 10th Hussars, and the Olivenza, in yellow faced red, with red-plumed Tarleton helmets.)

A sergeant of the light company of the 1/2nd (Cold-stream) Guards recounts a skirmish at Talavera:

'At this time having obtained entrance in the Olive Grove occupied by them the Skirmishers on both sides singled out their objects, & thus for 10 or 15 minutes were amusing outselves shooting at one another as deliberately as if we had been Pigeon Shooting . . . I cannot resist telling you that the object I had singled out, & myself exchanged three rounds each, the second of his, hit me slightly on the right Shoulder, & after my third he disappeared therefore I conclude he went home!'

(MS, author's possession.)

Variations of uniforms continued to the end of the period. 68 line regiments existed in 1815, of which nos. 36–48 were formed in 1808, 49–55 in 1809, 56–61 in 1811, 62–63 in 1812, 65–66 in 1813 and 66–67 in 1814. The majority wore blue with red facings: Regiments 3 Galicia, 4 Saboya, 8 Soria, 11 Sevilla, 12 Granada, 14 Zaragoza, 28 Aragon, 31 Estremadura, 33 Ordenes Militares, 40 Pravia, 42 Castropol, 47 Almansa, 48 Baylen, 53 Carinena, 54 2nd Princesa, 57 San Fernando, 65 Andalusia and 67; variations on this uniform included 17 Mallorca and 20 Leon, with white collar; 35 Baza and 56 2nd Asturias, with light blue collar; 55 Leales Manresanos and 63 Reunion, with light blue lapels; 36 Fernando VII and 66, white lapels, green cuffs; 7 Zamora, buff lapels; 10 Guadalajara, yellow collar; 45 Voluntarios de Madrid, blue collar; 49 1st Guadix, buff collar; 50 Barcelona, green lapels; 51 Alpujares, light blue cuffs; 52 Union, green collar, blue lapels; and 68 Alexandro, blue lapels. Five regiments wore blue with yellow facings: 13 Valencia, 15 España, 16 Toledo (white lapels), 46 Quinto de Granaderos (light blue lapels) and 64 Veteranos de la Patria (blue lapels). Six wore blue with buff facings: 9 Cordoba and 61 Guadalajara, both with red lapels, 29 América, 30 Princesa, 32 Malaga and 39 Almeira. Regiments 6 Africa, 23 Asturias and 44 Benevente wore blue with light blue facings; 2 Principe and 26 Hibernia blue with white facings; 22 Cantabria and 25 Navarra (light blue lapels) wore blue with green facings; and 41 Palma blue with blue facings (white collar). Four regiments wore light blue faced red: 21 Irlanda, 58 Cadiz, 34 Borbon (yellow lapels) and 37 1st Badajoz (white lapels); 18 Burgos and 62 Mataro had light blue faced yellow, and 27 Ultonia light blue faced buff. Five regiments wore brown: 1 Rey (purple facings), 38 Lena (light blue facings, red collar), 43 Cangas de Tineo (green facings, buff collar) and 59 Arlanza and 60 Granaderos de Castilla (red facings). Three retained the old white uniform: 5 Corona (dark blue facings), 19 Murcia (light blue) and 24 Fijo de Ceuta (green).

Artillery

The artillery was probably the best element of the army, though like the others it had been neglected grievously. It comprised various territorial 'departments' and four regiments (1st–4th) based respectively on the departments of Barcelona, Cartagena, Seville and Corunna. Each regiment comprised ten companies, six of the 40 being horse artillery. Each battery was supposed to comprise six guns, but such were the shortages that some had only four, and apart from the four complete batteries with La Romana's corps, all were desperately short of horses, the deficit having to be supplied by hired mules and horses before a campaign began. There were also 62 static companies of veteran artillery and five of labourers. The uniform was infantry-style in dark blue with red facings (blue lapels and cuff-flaps piped red), yellow buttons, yellow-laced bicorn with red plume, blue waistcoat and breeches and yellow grenade-badge on the collar. The horse artillery wore a similar uniform plus a black *cazadore* shako with yellow lace and cords and red plume, their jackets being short-tailed; Goddard & Booth show this uniform with a 'round hat' with upturned front brim. The labourers wore tail-less blue jackets with red collar, cuffs and piping, blue overalls and low shoes, and a plain 'round hat' decorated only with a national cockade at the left; the artillery train was manned by hired civilian drivers who wore civilian dress. There was no organized military train or commissariat corps, all vehicles and personnel being requisitioned when required, a totally haphazard arrangement.

Royal Guard

In addition to the halbardier company (*Guardias Alabaderos*), a ceremonial palace-guard corps, the Royal Guard, included four Garde du Corps companies (*Guardias de Corps*) who wore cavalry uniform in blue with red facings laced white, white hat-lace and blue breeches, and carbine-belts red, purple, dark green and yellow respectively for the *Companias* (companies) Española, América, Italiana and Flamenca. The other Guard cavalry unit was the Royal Carabiniers (*Carabineros Reales*), of two light and four heavy squadrons. The latter wore Garde du Corps uniform but with blue cuffs, no lace on the lapels, and white belts; the light squadrons wore blue hussar uniform, a dolman with red facings over a red waistcoat and blue breeches, all braided white, and a black shako with white cords, blue plume and white-metal oval plate. The Spanish and Walloon Foot Guard regiments, each of three battalions, wore infantry-style uniform in dark blue with scarlet facings, blue breeches and collar, white loops on the lapels and cuffs, white gaiters and white-laced bicorns; they adopted the shako later, like the line regiments. Despite the name the Walloon Guards were no longer all Belgians, but other nationalities were included as well.

Engineers

The engineer corps comprised a small staff of officers, 174 strong in 1808, and a regiment of two battalions of sappers and miners (*Zapadores-Minadores*) 1,000 strong. Officers wore infantry uniform in dark blue with purple facings (red cuffs and turnbacks), silver lace (including lapel-loops) and epaulettes, red waistcoat, blue breeches, silver-laced bicorn and silver castle-badge on the collar. The Sappers and Miners wore a similar uniform, but with shorter-tailed jackets, white lace, blue pantaloons, short black gaiters, and the 1802-pattern light infantry hat with black fur crest, white-laced brim and turban, and red plume; and white leather equipment.

Militia

The Provincial Militia (*Milicias Provinciales*) comprised four grenadier 'divisions' of two battalions each, and 42 single-battalion corps bearing the names of the district in which they were raised – Alcázar de San Juan, Toledo, Burgos, etc. – and officered by members of the leading local families. They were on average stronger than the line battalions and were probably equally as efficient; at the beginning of the Peninsular War, for example, they had been embodied since 1804 and were thus probably as inured to service as the regulars. There were also 114 companies of *Milicias Urbanas*

Nothing so epitomized the resistance to the French by the ordinary Spanish population as the so-called 'Maid of Saragossa', Agostina or Manuela Sanchez, who helped crew a cannon in the defence of Saragossa after her fiancé had been killed. The exploit became almost legendary and was celebrated in poetry by Byron and illustrations by Goya, a very 'romanticized' version by Sir David Wilkie, and in this portrait (mezzotint by H. Meyer), in which she wears a quasi-military uniform including a laced dolman.

(town militia) based in thirteen locations, ranging in strength from the 20 companies in Cadiz to the single company at Alconchel. The Militia wore infantry uniform, principally white with red facings and yellow buttons, but the town militia had a more varied dress, some in blue with coloured facings and others in white. There were also 41 invalid companies distributed throughout the country, the largest garrison being at Madrid (four companies) and Pamplona and Alcántara (three each); the others were stationed singly or occasionally two companies together. They wore blue coats and breeches with white cuffs, buttons and waistcoat, and plain bicorns.

Guerrillas

In contrast to the lacklustre performance of the Spanish regular army, the volunteer and guerrilla forces had a profound effect upon the Peninsular War both in tying-down vast numbers of French troops and in the damage they inflicted: one estimate puts French losses to guerrilla activity at 100 men per day throughout the war. French supply-lines and communications were disrupted, even couriers had to be escorted by large bodies of dragoons, and many dispatches were captured and passed to Wellington. On both sides the guerrilla war was conducted with revolting cruelty, massacre and counter-atrocity being the order of the day, giving rise to comments like Wellington's that when inflamed the Spaniard was an 'undisciplined savage'. In December 1808 the central *junta* ordered the guerrillas to organize in *partidas* or multiples of 100 infantry or 50 cavalry; in effect, bands ranged from a handful to many thousands, so that leaders like Espoz y Mina controlled reasonably sized armies. The guerrilla war was also a excuse for simple banditry, involving not only Spaniards but even French, British and Portuguese deserters, such as the multi-national gang led by a renegade French sergeant known as 'Marshal Stockpot' who was finally captured and shot by the French. The presence of such bands only increased the savagery and butchery with which the guerrilla war was waged. Guerrilla chieftains ranged from ex-regular officers to landowners, priests and peasants; in addition to Mina, the leading characters included Don Julian Sanchez, whose cavalry latterly served in Wellington's Spanish contingent, and Juan Martin Diaz, alias 'El Empecinado' ('Inky Face'), who later entered politics and met the gallows as a result. Even under such popular leaders as Sanchez much banditry occurred: 'He gives no quarter to any who make resistance. His followers sometimes amount to a thousand, at others he cannot muster fifty. They make a great deal by plunder, and absent themselves for the purpose of spending their Money; which having done they again join his Standard.'[7] Although some 'uniforms' are shown in contemporary illustrations, there was actually little 'uniformity' and most guerrillas wore whatever they could loot along with basically civilian costume: 'arrayed in green jackets with slouched hats and long feathers, others in blue, helmeted like our yeomanry or artillery drivers, while not a few wore cuirasses and brazen headpieces such as they had probably plundered from their

slaughtered enemies . . .'[8] Rough and ill-equipped as many were, they contributed greatly to the French defeat, and most Spanish heroes of the period came from other services than the regular army, including the famous 'Maid of Saragossa', Agustina Zaragoza or Sanchez, who during the siege crewed a cannon after her fiancé had been slain manning it; she was portrayed by Goya in an engraving entitled (appropriately) *Que valor!* and even appears in Byron's *Childe Harolde's Pilgrimage*. Unfortunately, however, the lasting impression of the guerrillas is one of horror and brutality; Lejeune, who survived a massacre, wrote that even after the passage of 35 years 'the cracking of their bones, still rings in my ears, and the remembrance of the scene makes me shudder with horror .'[9] (His description of the guerrillas' appearance, 'their pointed white teeth, which looked like those of angry wolves', is probably coloured by his terrible experiences.)

The Bonapartist Army (cockade: red and yellow)

The Spanish army raised from 1808 by Joseph Bonaparte was of little consequence, as the majority of Spaniards were vehemently anti-Bonapartist. The best elements were transferred from the French army into Joseph's Royal Guard, according to Napoleon's instructions ('Admit no one into it except the French conscripts whom I have ordered from Paris or Bayonne, and French soldiers who, either as prisoners with Dupont or otherwise, have been for less than a year in the Spanish service. Of these you may be sure.'[10] The Guard comprised two six-company battalions of grenadiers, expanded in 1809 to two regiments, Grenadiers and *Tirailleurs* of the Guard, augmented by a fusilier regiment, uniformed like the French Imperial Guard's corresponding units but for the red and yellow cockade. The one foot and one horse artillery batteries were dressed similarly in French style, and the Guard hussar regiment wore red dolman and pelisse, sky-blue facings, yellow lace, white breeches and busby with red bag and yellow-tipped red plume.

Joseph's cavalry comprised six heavy and one light regiment, the former in Spanish heavy cavalry-style uniform, yellow-laced bicorn, brown coat with yellow lace and button-loops, white waistcoat and breeches, long boots, and facings red, white, light blue, pink, black and green for the 1st–6th Regiments respectively. The 7th Regiment, Lanceros de la Mancha, wore French-style *chevauleger* uniform in brown with red facings (yellow collar), yellow-laced brown breeches, a red-plumed black leather helmet with black crest, and red lance-pennon with yellow horizontal stripe. Horse-furniture was brown with yellow lace for the heavy regiments and green for the lancers.

The first infantry unit was formed in December 1808, Royal Etranger, of four battalions of six companies each, which Napoleon declared should comprise '. . . all the Austrians, Prussians and Italians who have passed the last ten years in Spain . . . One of the advantages of this will be to clear off the crowd of strangers who swarm in Madrid . . .'[11] This was not an encouraging comment on the merit of the unit, but more so than Napoleon's remark on Joseph's line regiments: 'They should not be allowed to approach within ten leagues of Madrid . . . These regiments are indispensible as a refuge for numbers of people who would otherwise become bandits . . .'[12] Seven two-battalion regiments were planned, but it is doubtful whether all became effective; plus an additional foreign regiment, Royal Irlandais; the Regiment Joseph-Napoleon which served Napoleon in northern Europe; and two light battalions. The line regiments wore French-style uniform with shakos bearing a brass lozenge-plate emblazoned with a crowned 'N', yellow cords and red pompom, brown jacket with yellow buttons, white breeches and gaiters, French equipment and facings: 1st Regiment (Madrid) white, 2nd (Toledo) light blue, 3rd (Seville) black, 4th (Soria) violet, 5th (Granada) blue, 6th (Malaga) dark blue, 7th (Cordova) red. The Regiment Joseph-Napoleon wore French-style uniform in white with light green facings. The 1st (Castile) and 2nd (Murcia) Light Infantry wore the same as the line with light green facings, brown breeches and light green pompom with red tip. The army never proved effective, and at Vittoria only 248 officers and 5,390 men were present as virtually the whole of Joseph's disposable army.

Navy

The Spanish navy had been among the best in Europe, but corruption and maladministration had reduced it to almost as much of a wreck as the army, even though it was a vital contact between Spain and her overseas colonies. At the beginning of the Revolutionary Wars the fleet was powerful in theory with 76 ships-of-the-line, but only 56 of these were serviceable and even these were under-crewed and with resources in desperately short supply; Spanish dockyards were notoriously bad, as the French found to their cost when they attempted to re-fit before Trafalgar, and the administration was corrupt. However, the best ships were extremely powerful (including the largest warships afloat, like the gigantic *Santissima Trinidad* (130 guns), which was the Spanish flagship at Trafalgar) and were often competently handled. Losses at St. Vincent and especially Trafalgar (nine ships-of-the-line at the latter) were grievous blows, but from the beginning of the Peninsular War the Spanish maritime effort virtually ended, when the alliance with Britain prevented the Royal Navy from wreaking any further havoc.

The navy (*Armada*) was organized in three *departmentos*: Cadiz, Ferrol and Cartagena, each with its captain-general and staff, including directors of supply, weapons and engineers. Each *departmento* was subdivided into provinces, into which the sailors were registered; Ferrol had eleven provinces, Cartagena ten and Cadiz nine, though the personnel were most numerous in the Cartagena *departmento*. In 1798 the total establishment included more than 64,000 seamen, 20,000 naval artificers and 16,000 marines. There were no uniform-regulations for seamen, though blue jackets, striped trousers and blue Catalonian stocking-caps were common; officers wore army-style uniform in dark blue with red facings, red or white waistcoat and breeches, and

'The people of England, I am certain, will not believe the horrible and infernal manner in which the French have behaved in their retreat. Nothing that ever I have read or heard of any where since the beginning of the world, has equalled their excesses. You will hear many of these tales; for every body is shocked, and determined to expose them. They have murdered every peasant most wantonly. We see every day bodies of women, who have either been stabbed or shot, young and old. When near Condeixa they sent out regular parties to drive all females above ten years of age into the camp to please the soldiery: and it is said they carry an immense number with them. Every child we meet is bewailing the loss of his parents murdered. The houses are burnt; and every thing they could not make use of they have endeavoured to render useless. They have dug up the bones of the dead in search of plunder. One of our followers entering a village a little off the road, two days ago, found six and thirty of the inhabitants murdered; most of them in their beds . . .'
('Extract of a letter from Lord Wellington's Army, dated March 29'; in *The Courier*, 20 April 1811.)

gold lace. The 20 brigades of naval artillery were distributed throughout the *departmentos*; they wore infantry-style uniform of plain bicorn (sometimes with red plume), blue coat with red facings and piping (blue or red lapels), yellow buttons, white breeches, waistcoat and leather equipment, yellow collar-badge of an anchor and grenade, and were armed with a musket and short sabre. Their shipboard undress consisted of a tail-less brown jacket with red facings and piping, brown waistcoat (piped red) and trousers and a brown stocking-cap with yellow-laced headband. The marines consisted of twelve battalions of six companies each, later reduced to four battalions, two stationed at Cadiz and one each at Ferrol and Cartagena; their officers were from the navy. They wore infantry-style uniform of blue coat, red facings, yellow buttons and anchor on the collar, white waistcoat and leather equipment, white or blue breeches, short gaiters, and a plain bicorn (sometimes with red pompom) and infantry-style fur cap for grenadiers (who had yellow loops on the cuffs); weapons were like those of the naval artillery, and the brown undress uniform was the same with different insignia.

Notes
1. *Twenty-Five Years in the Rifle Brigade*, W. Surtees, London 1833 p. 77.
2. ibid., p. 92.
3. *Letters from the Peninsula 1808–12*, Sir William Warre, ed. Revd. E. Warre, London 1909, p. 100.
4. Surtees, op. cit., pp. 108–9.
5. *A Boy in the Peninsular War*, R. Blakeney, ed. J. Sturgis, London 1899, p. 311, 313.
6. *The Life of John Colborne, Field-Marshal Lord Seaton*, G. C. Moore Smith, London 1903, p. 135.
7. *The Journal of an Army Surgeon during the Peninsular War*, C. Boutflower, privately printed, n.d., p. 54.
8. *The Subaltern*, G. R. Gleig, London 1825, p. 220.
9. *Memoirs of Baron Lejeune*, ed. Mrs. A. Bell, London 1897, II, pp. 91–2.
10. *The Confidential Correspondence*

of Napoleon Bonaparte with
his Brother Joseph, London
1855, I, p. 380.
11. ibid., I, pp. 379–80.
12. ibid., II, p. 26.

References

Bueno, J. M. El Ejercito y la
Armada en 1808, Malaga 1982
(especially well-illustrated
modern work).
Esdaile, C. J. The Spanish Army in
the Peninsular War, Manchester
1988 (the most important work
on the subject).

Glover, M. Legacy of Glory: The
Bonaparte Kingdom of Spain, New
York 1971.
Pivka, Otto von. Spanish Armies of
the Napoleonic Wars, London
1975.
Rudorff, R. War to the Death: the
Sieges of Saragossa 1808–09,
London 1974 (a good account
of the determination which was
characteristic of the ordinary
Spanish population).

SWEDEN

History

Long a major power in the Baltic area, Sweden entered the period of the Revolutionary Wars in some turmoil. King Gustavus III (1746–92) (Frederick the Great's nephew) might be regarded as the last of Sweden's great kings; as befitted a monarch of the 'age of enlightenment' he did much to improve the internal affairs of Sweden, but aroused the anger of the nobility and some resentment from the middle classes, attempting to rule without a parliament, though was able to outmanoeuvre his opponents by the passing of the Act of Unity and Security (17 February 1789) which gave the monarch greater powers. He declared war against Russia in 1788 and won a major naval victory at Svensksund (9–10 July 1790), which led to a peace-treaty a month later, and in October 1791 concluded a defensive pact with Russia greatly to Sweden's advantage. Against the French Revolution he aimed to form an anti-Jacobin alliance, but fell victim to an aristocratic conspiracy and was assassinated at a masquerade at Stockholm opera-house in March 1792. He was succeeded by his 14-year-old son Gustavus IV, whose uncle, Duke Charles of Sudermania (1748–1818), acted as regent during his minority; but real power resided with the minister Baron Gustaf Adolf Reuterholm, who had been imprisoned by Gustavus III and whose vindictive influence caused great damage to Sweden's prestige. Reuterholm instituted close relations with France, only withdrawing from a French alliance under Russian pressure, and an attempt to overthrow the government (with Russian aid) was suppressed. Reuterholm finally achieved his French alliance in April 1795, but in November 1796 Gustavus IV came of age and took over the running of the state himself, the duke-regent fading into the background; Reuterholm was expelled and for the next twelve years lived abroad under the pseudonym of Tempelcrentz.

Gustavus IV's government was a return to autocracy, and was marked by changes of foreign allegiance. In March 1794 a neutrality compact had been agreed with the old adversary Denmark, and in December 1800 Sweden participated in the Armed Neutrality of the North, but was spared British reprisals by the assassination of the Tsar and the resulting collapse of the Armed Neutrality. Napoleon's execution of

the Duc d'Enghien in 1804 determined Gustavus IV to join the coalition against France, but a quarrel with Prussia delayed Swedish military intervention until after the coalition was destroyed by Austerlitz. After Jena only the diplomatic efforts of Gustavus III's old minister, Count Johann Toll (1743–1817) saved the Swedish army from destruction, though Swedish Pomerania was lost. After Tilsit the Tsar was forced by Napoleon to act against Sweden to compel the Swedes to accept the Continental System, and in February 1808 a Russian army invaded the Swedish possession of Finland, with Denmark (under French domination) also declaring war. A British force under Sir John Moore was sent to Sweden's aid, but Gustavus IV, becoming increasingly unstable, had a violent quarrel with Moore and the British withdrew. The immediate consequence was the deposition of Gustavus, who was now clearly insane; a conspiracy of army officers placed him under arrest (13 March 1809), declared his dependents incapable of ruling Sweden and elected the previous duke-regent king as Charles XIII (5 June 1809), who accepted a liberal constitution. Gustavus was transported to Germany in December and lived in exile, settling in Switzerland, under the titles of Count of Gottorp or Colonel Gustafsson; he died indigent in February 1837.

Charles XIII was clearly a temporary leader; infirm and childless, he had no automatic successor. The war against Russia continued until September 1809, when after several serious defeats the Swedes were compelled to accept a humiliating peace, surrendering Finland and the Aland islands to Russia by the Treaty of Frederikshavn (17 September 1809). After the mysterious death of the first elected successor to the ailing Charles XIII, Prince Charles Augustus of Augustenburg, a new candidate was accepted: Napoleon's disgraced Marshal Bernadotte, who took the title of Crown Prince Charles John. Bernadotte soon became the effective ruler of Sweden due to the infirmity of the king, and though in November 1810 Sweden was compelled to declare war on Britain, it was signified to the British that she did so under duress and that it would be merely a token; instead, Bernadotte planned to acquire Norway as compensation for the loss of Finland by taking the Allies' part against his old master, against whom he was now extremely antagonistic.

'The suppression of a riot in the town in 1799, occasioned by a party of Irish rebels, was probably the most formidable service in which the Warrington Volunteers were called upon to engage . . . we might hence expect a certain feeling of anxiety on the part of the relatives of the Volunteers, but certainly not to the extent shown by the wife of Joshua Fletcher, of the Grenadier Company, who as she handed him his cumbrous hat, and gave him a parting kiss, said, "Now Joshua, as soon as ever they begin to be rough, do thee run home again as fast as thee can."'

(Warrington Volunteers 1798–1898, W. Crompton and G. Venn, Warrington 1898, p. 32.)

Medal for Valour in the Field of Sweden, awarded in gold for officers and silver for other ranks; blue and yellow ribbon.

By the Treaty of Petersburg (5 April 1812) Sweden undertook to assist Russia in Germany in return for Norway (then a Danish possession). Bernadotte's ambitious foreign policy invoked some criticism, but the *Riksdag* (parliament) of Orebro (1812) introduced general conscription, giving Bernadotte the means to carry out his plans. Peace was made with Britain, and in 1813–14 Bernadotte led a Swedish army against Napoleon in Germany. In recompense, Britain and Russia agreed to the acquisition of Norway, as punishment for Denmark's support of Napoleon, which was achieved by the Treaty of Kiel (14 January 1814). Charles XIII died on 5 February 1818 and was succeeded by Bernadotte as King Charles XIV John; his reign was in general beneficial and his dynasty continues to rule Sweden.

Army (cockade: yellow with blue centre)

There were two basic types of regiment: a permanent or regular variety were stationed in barracks and fortresses, receiving extra pay for their 'regular' status and including the Lifeguards, the Life or Queen's Infantry, the artillery, the Mörner Hussars, the engineers, one Finnish infantry regiment and two Finnish *Jäger* battalions. The remainder of the army was mobilized for 28 days' training each spring, and in wartime; and in 1813, following the introduction of conscription, a five-year period of service was introduced for which males between the ages of 21 and 25 were eligible. The Finnish regiments were lost when the province was taken by Russia. Uniform-details are confusing, caused by several changes of regulation and uncertainty as to when these actually took effect.

Cavalry

Cavalry regiments were usually organized in two battalions of four squadrons of 125 men each. From 1779 Gustavus III created a 'Swedish national uniform', largely for reasons of economy, a distinctive and functional costume, comprising a 'round hat' with plume at the left and a very short-skirted, single-breasted jacket with very small turnbacks at the front of the skirts. The uniform was dark blue throughout with coloured facings; the dragoons replaced the 'round hat' with a bicorn in 1796, and the heavier regiments of dragoons wore double-breasted jackets with yellow buttons but no lapels, buff breeches, long boots, white leather equipment, white plumes and facings white for the Life Regiment and yellow for the Scanian Regiment. In 1807 the lighter dragoons adopted a peaked leather helmet with a white plume at the front and a falling white mane; the Westgotha (*Väastgöta*) Regiment wore this with a tail-less dark blue jacket with blue 'half-lapels' piped white, red collar and pointed cuffs, and knee-boots. At the same period the Småland Light Dragoons wore a similar light blue uniform with yellow facings, and a shako with white plume and red cords. The two hussar regiments wore conventional hussar costume: the Mörner Regiment (named after its colonel) with dark blue dolman and pelisse, gold braid and white-plumed shako; and the Skånska Regiment, which wore buff with blue facings and yellow lace. The Life Cuirassiers wore a distinctive buff jacket and breeches, blue facings, long boots, white-metal cuirass with gilt fittings and a gilt-mounted black leather helmet with gilt comb and white crest.

The Lifeguard cavalry comprised six squadrons and an attached squadron of mounted *Jägers*. Their uniform was white with light blue facings and breeches, white collar, buttons and lapel-loops, with a light blue service uniform faced white, with no lace and light blue half-lapels piped white. They wore the second pattern of 'round hat', a tall, brimmed head-dress with tall, upturned left brim, a white plume over light blue pompom at the left, a black fur crest over the top, and gold cords for officers and red or yellow and blue for other ranks; with a yellow hussar-style girdle, hussar breeches with white lace in dress uniform or light blue overalls on service, and the light blue sabretache bearing the three gold crowns of Sweden regulated in 1795. The *Jäger* squadron wore light dragoon uniform in dark green with half-lapels and white piping, lapel-lace and breeches; black leather equipment, knee-boots and the leather light dragoon helmet with white plume and mane. The 'round hat' of the Lifeguard cavalry was replaced by a shako in 1813.

Infantry

Regiments were organized in two battalions, each of four companies of 150 men each; in 1814 some regiments formed 3rd battalions. Each regiment had a small grenadier platoon, and each company a *Jäger* detachment, which could be

Cross of the Order of the Sword of Sweden, instituted as a reward for military distinction, revived by Frederick I in 1748 and renewed subsequently, in November 1798 and July 1814. Gold cross with blue centre and white arms; yellow ribbon with blue edges.

withdrawn in wartime and formed into composite grenadier or *Jäger* battalions. (The Queen's Life Regiment apparently retained its grenadiers and *Jägers*.) The Foot Guards had two battalions of six companies each, each company 100 strong, with a similarly-sized *Jäger* company attached.

Gustavus III's 'Swedish national uniform' was adopted from 1779, consisting of a 'round hat' with coloured band (usually white or yellow) and white plume, a short-tailed jacket, and white belts (black for *Jägers*, some of whom appear to have worn green uniforms). The coloured facings included collar, cuffs, shoulder-straps, turnbacks and lapels which did not extend completely to the waist; with white or blue breeches. Regimental colouring from 1797 was a dark blue jacket (Bohuslens and Jönköping Regiments light blue), yellow buttons (Kronoberg Regiment white), white breeches (Närike-Varmland and Västmanland Regiments buff) and facing colours: Regiment Bohuslens yellow (red collar), Dalarnas white (red collar and cuffs), Elfsborg yellow (white collar, cuffs and turnbacks), Helsinge white, Jönköping, Kalmar and Kronoberg yellow (red collar and cuffs), Närike-Varmland and Västmanland yellow piped white, Skaraborg pale yellow piped white, Sodermanland yellow, Uppland yellow (white collar), Vesterbottens white (red collar) and Västgöta-Oals yellow (blue collar piped white). The *Jäger* regiments wore: Jämtland light grey faced green, grey breeches; and Närike-Varmland green with black facings piped white, and green breeches. The Finnish regiments wore similar uniform in grey with grey breeches (Østerbottens Regiment yellow), yellow buttons, and facings: Abo-lens and Nyland Regiments and Kajana Battalion blue, Adlercreutz blue piped yellow (red collar piped yellow, grey turnbacks piped blue), Bjorneborg light blue, Østerbottens and Savolax (grey collar piped yellow) yellow; Tavastehus dark blue piped red. The Finnish *Jägers* wore grey (Karelske green), with facings green piped yellow (Karelske; white turnbacks), green piped white (Savolax) and grey piped blue (Nyland). All the Finnish regiments had yellow buttons save the Savolax *Jägers*, white.

In 1807 a new infantry uniform was introduced, a simpler, short-tailed grey coat with dark blue collar, cuffs and turnbacks for all, with a blue and yellow striped girdle; the hat remained the same, but with a yellow plume, and regimental-distinctions were confined to the colouring of the cockade. Company-identification pompoms were worn under the plume, red, white, blue, yellow, white with red edge, yellow with blue edge, blue with red edge and yellow with red edge respectively for the 1st–8th companies of a regiment. *Jägers* had green facings, plume, pompom and crest on the hat. Not all regiments adopted the grey uniform, however, some apparently retaining the previous pattern. Equipment became black for all save grenadiers, who retained the earlier white. In 1810 a blue uniform was introduced, double-breasted and without lapels, with red cuffs and shoulder-straps and yellow turnbacks; legwear became one-piece gaiter-trousers or overalls, with red stripes and thigh-knots, and equipment reverted to white, though the Kronoberg Regiment apparently retained black; and some regiments seem to have retained the previous grey uniform.

In the 1813–14 campaigns foreign uniform-styles were adopted, often out of necessity, including the use of captured French shakos or the Russian 1812-pattern *kiwer*, and latterly a Swedish shako of French style with a yellow plume and star-badge bearing the Swedish arms. Colours known to have been worn in 1813–14 were generally dark blue jackets (Bohuslens light blue, Kronoberg grey, Västgöta white) with yellow turnbacks (Kronoberg blue, Västgöta light blue, Västmanland yellow) and yellow buttons (Småland and Västgöta white); collar and cuffs red (Småland and Södermanland yellow, Västgöta light blue; Bohuslens and Uppland yellow cuffs; Kronoberg and Västmanland blue cuffs; Kronoberg grey collar, Uppland white); cuff-flaps of the cuff-colour save Elfsborg, Jönköping, North Skånska, South Skånska and Södermanland blue, Uppland white and Västmanland red; shoulder-straps of the uniform colour piped in the cuff-colour except for Västmanland, blue piped red. The Kronoberg Regiment appears to have worn blue trousers instead of the grey of the remainder, and the Småland, Södermanland and Uppland yellow trouser-lace instead of red. *Jägers* wore green with black facings and green shako-cords, but some regimental *Jägers* retained their regimental colours, such as the Bohuslens' light blue with yellow facings and red collar. When the Swedes landed in Germany they formed new units of French and German ex-prisoners, including the *Royal Suedois* (Franco-German) in dark blue single-breasted jacket and overalls, yellow facings and French shako with yellow pompom and brass lozenge plate; the Pomeranian Legion in green jacket and overalls with yellow piping and overall-stripes, Russian shako with green cords and plume; a Pomeranian *Landwehr* unit in a blue *litewka* with yellow facings and 'round hat' with black crest and white plume; and the German Englebrecht Regiment, in blue with red facings (including lapels), blue overalls and Russian shako with yellow cords and white plume.

Guard and grenadier corps also existed. The 1st (Svea) Guard Regiment wore a dark blue long-tailed coat with yellow facings (including half-lapels), white lace loops, breeches and gaiters, and until 1807 a white-plumed bicorn. In 1807 they adopted a coat with white epaulettes, open lapels revealing a white waistcoat, and a 'round hat' with brass band bearing the royal arms, white plume and oblique black crest running from right front to left rear; in 1813 the lapels were closed to the waist. The regimental *Jägers* wore the same in green with yellow collar and piping, green breeches, plume and hat-crest. The 2nd (Andra) Guard Regiment wore the same in a lighter blue, red lapels and piping to the blue facings; in 1813 the facings became red, and the *Jägers* wore the uniform of the 1st Regiment but with orange piping, and later red facings. A 3rd (Finnish) Guard Regiment wore a uniform like that of the 2nd, but like the Finnish line, it was disbanded upon the loss of the province.

The grenadier corps included the Life-Grenadier Brigade, which wore a single-breasted blue jacket with red facings, white epaulettes, collar- and cuff-loops and buttons, blue

breeches with white stripe and thigh-knots, and a 'round hat' with flat brim (not upturned), a brass grenade-badge over a brass band, white plume and black transverse or fore-and-aft crest; lace became yellow *c.* 1813. The *Jäger* detachment wore the same with green plume and black belts. The Life-Grenadier Regiment wore the same uniform with white facings and yellow lace. The Queen's Life Regiment wore blue with yellow facings, white epaulettes, loops and breeches, with the head-dress of the line until the adoption of the Russian 1812-pattern *kiwer* in 1813 with white cords and plume (red for grenadiers and green for *Jägers*, the latter with black belts). The Queen Dowager's Regiment wore infantry uniform with pink facings, white piping and turnbacks; it was disbanded in 1808.

Artillery

There were four artillery regiments (three after the loss of Finland), each of two battalions of three companies and a central park. Each company had four or six 3-, 6- or 12pdr cannon; the two horse batteries had 6pdrs and 8pdr howitzers, and for the Norwegian expedition of 1814 a mountain battery of 3pdrs was created. The horse artillery was formed by Karl von Cardell (colonel of the Vendes Artillery and later Master of the Ordnance); all gunners were mounted and their great mobility was proven at Leipzig. Ordnance was painted blue-green. Uniform was of infantry style, dark blue jackets and yellow buttons, dark blue trousers with yellow stripes, and collars coloured white (Vendes Regiment, with yellow loops), blue (Svea Regiment), yellow (Gotha Regiment) and red (Finnish Regiment). The infantry hat had a brass band and yellow cockade and plume (Vendes white), and by 1813 shakos had been adopted, the Vendes a French-style cap, yellow lace upper band, cords and plume, the Svea with black plume and the Gotha with yellow lace. Belts were buff-leather. An illustration probably depicting horse artillery in 1814 shows a bell-topped shako with black plume, blue dolman with yellow buttons, white collar, blue and yellow girdle and blue overalls with double yellow stripe. Pioneer units had no permanent establishment but were taken as required from the infantry, with only officers and NCOs with engineering training; commissariat personnel were similarly detached from the regiments as required.

Rank Insignia

Officers were distinguished by metallic lace and epaulettes, rank indicated by the number of stars on the epaulette: colonel three, lieutenant-colonel two and major one, with gold collar- and cuff-embroidery; company officers had loops on the collar and epaulette-stars: captain three (epaulette-fringe on right only), lieutenant two and 2nd lieutenant one (fringe on left epaulette only). A white brassard worn by officers on the left upper arm commemorated the 'palace revolution' of 1772.

Navy

Uniquely, Sweden possessed two navies: the 'Army Fleet' (*Armens Flottan*) of inshore craft, and the Admiralty or High Seas Fleet (*Örlogs Flottan*) of seagoing vessels. This was in consequence of the country's geographical position: the Baltic coastline was ideal for amphibious operations and thus the inshore 'Army' fleet was of great importance. Recruits were enrolled either by bounty or under the same militia system which provided the bulk of the army.

As Sweden's maritime aspirations had traditionally been confined to the Baltic, the Admiralty Fleet was not as large as those of other maritime nations: in 1790 she possessed about 27 ships-of-the-line and twelve frigates. The 'Army Fleet' was equipped with shallow-draught vessels combining sails and oars, capable of operating very close to the shore or even of being run aground for amphibious landing, ranging in size from the *hemmema* or frigate to the *pojama*, virtually an oar-powered gunboat. These were designed originally by the British naval architect Chapman (whose name was borne by a Swedish 44-gun frigate) and intended to replace conventional ships-of-the-line in the Baltic, but they were found too small to oppose ordinary ships and less manoeuvrable than the smallest inshore sloops and gunboats. The 'Army Fleet' initially comprised two divisions, a Swedish squadron at Stockholm and a Finnish one at Helsingfors.

Naval officers initially wore Gustavus III's 'national uniform' in dark blue with gold lace, epaulettes and thigh-knots, light blue and yellow sash and 'round hat' with yellow over light blue plume; in 1802 this was replaced by a dark blue coat with less gold embroidery, and a gold-laced bicorn hat with same plume for senior ranks' full dress. In 1810 a single-breasted dark blue coat with gold lace but no longer epaulettes was worn from 1810; officers of the 'Army Fleet' apparently had blue facings piped white, and white-plumed bicorns and 'round hats'. The waist-sash was officially discontinued but its use may have continued throughout. The seamen commonly wore short blue jackets and waistcoats, plain 'round hats' and blue breeches or grey,

white or other colours of trousers; from about 1804 yellow waistcoats and jacket-linings appear to have been introduced, but the seamen's clothing was largely unregulated. The Naval Artillery was equipped in army uniform, dark blue with initially yellow piping, later white, yellow buttons, white breeches and leather equipment, and a 'round hat' with white plume for the 'Army Fleet' and yellow for the Admiralty.

References

Cassin-Scott, J. *Scandinavian Armies in the Napoleonic Wars*, London 1976.
Holmquist, B. M., and Gripstad, B. *Swedish Weaponry Since 1630*, Arlöv 1982.

A valuable series of articles, 'Uniforms and Organization of the Royal Swedish Infantry, Artillery and Navy of the Napoleonic Wars', Dr. W. B. Young, appeared in the periodical *Tradition* (London), issues 59–61.

SWITZERLAND

History

Switzerland consisted of a loose confederation of autonomous states, with close connections with France extending back many years, including the service of the famous Swiss regiments in the French army. The French Revolution thus could not avoid affecting the Swiss, the Helvetian Club of Paris (founded 1790) being the centre of the export of revolutionary ideas which caused several risings within the states of the confederation. Some were suppressed by the authorities of individual states, but in 1791 Porrentruy rose against the prince-bishop of Basel and declared itself the 'Rauracian republic'; it was saved from anarchy only by annexation by France as the *département* of Mont Terrible. This forshadowed later events, as the French cast acquisitive eyes towards the confederation, encouraged by internal dissent and reformist movements under the leadership of such as Peter Ochs (1752–1821), burgomaster of Basel, and the exiled lawyer Frederick Caesar Laharpe (1754–1838), tutor for ten years to the future Tsar Alexander I. Under the invitation from Laharpe and others to protect the liberty of Vaud, a French army marched in (February 1798) and proclaimed the 'Lemanic republic'. The French encountered considerable opposition, especially in Berne where the Bernese forces (with little aid from other members of the confederation) under Johannes Weber actually inflicted a reverse upon General Brune's French army at Neueneck; but the vain attempt at defending Swiss territory ended in capitulation on 5 March 1798. Brune proposed that the defeated confederation be tranformed into three republics, the Tellgau, Rhodanic and Helvetic, but this did not find favour with the Directory and the whole became the 'Helvetic Republic, one and indivisible' on 29 March 1798. Modelled on France, it was divided into 23 cantons, with an executive directory of five members in the capital at Lucerne. The centuries-old independence of the different states was not to be overcome so easily, however, and revolts flared, especially in Schwyz and Unterwalden, and had to be suppressed with brutality, especially in Nidwalden in

September 1798 where the French action was styled 'the days of terror'. With the republic thus imposed by force, in the 1799 campaigns involving Austria and Russia the invaders were greeted with joy by some Swiss who regarded their intervention as an opportunity to throw off French control; an unavailing effort.

Its directors being practically nominated by the French, the Helvetic Republic was compelled to make a close military alliance with France, and in January 1800 the directory was replaced by an executive committee similar to the French Consulate. The centralization of power was not compatible with the independent tradition of the previous states, and internal struggles arose between the 'Unitary' part of Ochs and Laharpe and the 'Federalists' desiring regional autonomy; French troops were withdrawn under the terms of the Peace of Amiens and the Federalists began to gain the upper hand in an open revolt. Bonaparte, who had made the Valais into an independent republic in August 1802, cast himself in the role of mediator and summoned the factions to a conference in Paris in December 1802 which on 19 February 1803 accepted an Act of Mediation which gave the country a federal constitution and, for the first time, the

Salomon Bleuler, a native of Zürich, in the uniform of the 4th Swiss Regiment (red with blue facings) in which he served as company- and battalion-commander in the Peninsular War and in Russia in 1812.

Swiss regiments in British service, a contemporary print depicting the green-uniformed corps with the red facings of Regiment Bachmann, the black of Roverea, and the Jäger companies presumably of Regiment Salis with leopardskin turbans around their shakos. All have light blue-grey breeches.

official name of Switzerland. The thirteen members of the pre-1798 confederation were again established (the three Forest states, Lucerne, Zürich, Glarus, Zug, Berne, Fribourg, Soleure, Basel, Schaffhauzen and Appenzell) to which were added six new cantons, St. Gall, Graubünden, Aargau, Thurgau, Ticino and Vaud. Cantons were granted their own assemblies and the whole was administered by a Diet in which all cantons had a vote (the six most populous, Berne, Zürich, Vaud, Aargau, St. Gall and Graubünden had two votes), the annual meeting of the Diet to gather alternatively at Fribourg, Berne, Soleure, Basel, Zürich and Lucerne. The state's neutrality was guaranteed by France, but a close alliance with France was concluded on 27 November 1803. This arrangement, better suited to the traditional independency of the Swiss, lasted until 1815, Switzerland only becoming involved in the Napoleonic conflicts in the supply of troops to the French forces, a most valuable asset to Napoleon.

France continued to interfere in Swiss affairs; in 1806 the principality of Neuchâtel was awarded to Marshal Berthier, in 1810 the Valais was made into the *département* of the Simplon (to secure the pass), and Ticino was occupied by the French from 1810 to 1813. With the decline of Napoleon Swiss independence was threatened, and an Austrian invasion in December 1813 induced the Diet to repudiate the

1803 constitution. Berne headed a movement for the restoration of the old order, but Zürich led the remainder in a desire to maintain the existing system; which was retained, with three new cantons (Valais, Neuchâtel and Geneva) raised to the status of full members of the Confederation. The Congress of Vienna decided in November 1815 to place Switzerland under the guarantee of the great powers who undertook to maintain Swiss neutrality, thus freeing Switzerland from French influence for the first time in three centuries, which compensated for the somewhat reactionary nature of the constitution of August 1815 when compared to that of 1803.

Army (cockade: red, yellow and green)
Prior to the establishment of the Helvetic Republic, the member states of the Confederation each maintained the capacity for forming a combined army to oppose aggression. These forces were mobilized in 1792, but had no common uniform: their costume and organization varied from state to state, generally dressed in long-skirted coats, bicorn, breeches and gaiters, but including units wearing virtual civilian dress and 'round hats'. Blue or brown were the commonest uniform-colours, and in some cases the colour was determined by the language of the wearer: in the Fribourg contingent German-speakers wore brown and

French-speakers blue, for example. Other uniforms included the light grey, faced blue, of Zürich, and the green uniforms with black belts worn by *Jäger* corps. Berne wore dark blue, but the Watteville Regiment wore the scarlet uniform traditionally associated with Swiss troops in French service.

The Helvetic Republic's forces comprised a 'legion' of infantry, *chasseurs* and artillery, in French-style uniform in the red/yellow/green colouring of the state cockade. In addition, each canton maintained a militia or national guard, the infantry in bicorn or 'round hat' with yellow/red/green plume, and a French-style dark blue coat with red, yellow and green facings, and white breeches. The *Chasseurs à Cheval* wore French hussar uniform of a mirliton cap with red wing edged yellow and yellow-over-red-over-green plume, green dolman faced red and red waistcoat with yellow braid, and green breeches with yellow stripe and thigh-knots; this unit became the French 19th *Chasseurs à Cheval* in 1804. In 1803 the Helvetian *demi-brigades* wore *garance* (red) with facings white piped blue for the 1st, blue piped white for the 2nd and yellow piped sky-blue for the 3rd. Two companies of *Chasseur-Carabiniers* formed in the *département du Leman* in 1800 wore a dark blue single-breasted coat with sky-blue facings, dark blue waistcoat with sky-blue hussar braid, dark blue breeches with sky-blue darts on the thighs, green epaulettes, French light infantry shako with green plume and cords and black belts; they were disbanded in 1804. A dragoon unit at the same time wore red faced green, buff breeches, long boots and bicorn with red plume with green base.

In French service the traditional red uniform was maintained; it was perhaps most famously worn by the Swiss Guard of the *ancien régime* which was massacred at the Tuileries in 1792; but other colours included the yellow coats of Berthier's Neuchâtel Battalion, hence their nickname 'canaries'. The Valais republic's infantry wore dark blue French-style uniform (including breeches) with red facings, but the French army's Valais Battalion wore red with white facings. Not all the Swiss were content to live under French domination, and a number of emigrant corps were formed for British service: the regiments Roverea, Salis, Courten and Bachmann, recruited largely by the British minister in Berne from the remnant of those who had attempted to resist French occupation, were amalgamated in 1801 under the colonel of Roverea's, Frederick de Watteville. Other excellent Swiss corps in British service were the regiments of de Roll (an ex-Swiss guardsman of the French royal army, as were many of his original recruits) and de Meuron, the latter raised originally for Dutch service but transferring to British pay upon the capture of Ceylon in 1795. Not all managed to maintain an entirely Swiss composition, as French, Germans and even Italians were accepted, though de Watteville's and de Meuron's especially remained largely Swiss/German, and served with as much high reliability as did the Swiss regiments in the French army.

References

Boty, J. -R. *Régiments Suisses au Service de France*, Sion 1975.

Calpini, J. *Les Milices Valaisannes*, Sion 1974 (an illustrated account of the forces of a typical single region).

Dändliker, K. *A Short History of Switzerland*, trans. A. Salisbury, London 1899 (still remains a useful guide to the confusing internal history of Switzerland at this period).

de Vallière, Captain. *Honneur et Fidélité: Histoire des Suisses au Service Etranger*, Neuchâtel, n.d. (standard history of the Swiss in foreign service).

Medal of the 10th August of Switzerland, instituted 7 August 1817 for survivors of the Swiss Guard who had defended the Tuileries on 10 August 1792. Cast iron medal, white ribbon with red cross.

TUSCANY

History

The traditional home of the Medici, Tuscany passed into Austrian ownership in 1737, a succession of grand dukes being members of the Imperial family; in 1765 Leopold, son of Emperor Francis II, became Grand Duke, relinquishing the title when he succeeded his brother Joseph II as emperor. His second son was appointed Grand Duke as Ferdinand III, who attempted to remain neutral during the Revolutionary Wars, but in 1799 the French entered Florence, welcomed by a number of Tuscan republicans, and Ferdinand fled. A popular rising in Ferdinand's name and encouraged by Pope Pius VII expelled the French with much brutality, and Florence was recovered with Austrian assistance. The French returned in October 1800 and committed some pillage, but having experienced Austrian rule the population was more prepared to accept them than before. Murat established a provisional government and by the Treaty of Lunéville Tuscany was converted to the Kingdom of Etruria as a part of the Spanish dominions, Duke Louis of Parma being appointed king. He died in 1803,

leaving an infant son, Charles Louis, under the regency of his mother, Marie Louise of Spain, who ruled in a reactionary manner until 1807. By the Treaty of Fontainebleau (27 October 1807) Charles IV of Spain was forced to cede Etruria to France, by which annexation Tuscany was divided into three *départements* as the 29th military distict. Tuscany was ruled by a French administrator-general until

Elisa (Marie-Anne-Elisa) Bonaparte, wife of Felice Pasquale Bacciocchi, Princess of Piombino, Grand Duchess of Tuscany (1777–1820). (Engraving by R. G. Tietze after Pierre Prud'hon)

March 1809 when Napoleon's sister Elisa Baciocchi was made grand-duchess. Following Napoleon's defeat in 1814 Murat occupied Tuscany, which he handed over to Austria, and in September 1814 Ferdinand III was welcomed back by virtually all the population, French rule having been oppressive, heavy taxation and conscription having been especially unpopular. Ferdinand was confirmed in possession of his lands by the Congress of Vienna, but was forced out of Florence temporarily in 1815; after Napoleon's final defeat he returned and ruled until his death in 1824, his policy of benevolent and paternal despotism including the maintenance of much of the French legislation, so that the transition from French rule to the old regime was accomplished without excesses, unlike some other states.

Army (cockade: blue)

The Tuscan army wore an Austrian-style uniform, with a blue single-breasted coat with red facings for the infantry regiment Real Toscano, and a peakless black leather cap with black plume and brass Tuscan arms on the false front, with yellow buttons, white waistcoat and legwear. The dragoon regiment wore the same colouring, with blue breeches and a white-laced bicorn with black plume. A volunteer *Jäger* corps at Livorno (*Cacciatori Volontari di Livorno*) wore a uniform prescribed in July 1794 of green with red facings and yellow buttons. In the same year provincial militia was organized, wearing infantry uniform decreed in December 1795 of black-plumed bicorn, white coat, waistcoat and breeches, yellow buttons and facings green for the Florence battalion, Pisa sky-blue, upper Siena dark blue and lower Siena red.

In 1807 the Etrurian troops passed into French service, the infantry regiment becoming the 113th Line, which continued to be recruited in the Tuscan *départements*. The Etrurian Dragoons, reconstituted as the Tuscan Dragoons in January 1808, became the French 28th *Chasseurs à Cheval* in May, serving in the Peninsula, including at the siege of Gerona; they wore dark blue *surtouts* with red facings and epaulettes, and red-plumed bicorns, which uniform they probably retained initially in French service, perhaps substituting the monogram 'N' for the previous 'CL' (Charles Louis) in yellow lace on the red shabraque.

Shortly after the appointment of Elisa Baciocchi as grand-duchess, on 24 March 1809 two *vélite* battalions were authorized, one as bodyguard for Elisa in Florence and one for Prince Camille Borghèse, governor-general of the *départements au delà des Alpes*; raised by voluntary enlistment from the 27th–29th military districts, they were classed as part of the Imperial Guard and uniformed like the Guard Fusiliers-Grenadiers. Two small companies of Gardes d'Honneur were organized in 1810 in Turin and Florence, wearing scarlet coats with blue facings, white lace, buttons, breeches and waistcoat, and a white-laced bicorn with white plume in full dress and blue and red in ordinary dress (red, pink-over-white and pink-and-blue are also recorded). Largely of young men of good family, the Gardes d'Honneur included both mounted and dismounted men, and after the

Order of St. Joseph of Tuscany, founded by Ferdinand III on 19 March 1807 as Grand Duke of Würzburg, and taken to Tuscany when he regained his dominions in 1814. Gold medal with red enamelling and white-enamelled arms, red ribbon with white stripes.

On Blücher:

'At night the Field Marshal is usually to be found at some of the many tables for high play in Paris, in which he indulges rather too freely. He there sits down, after his usual custom, without his coat, and joins in hazard, or what else is going on, in a sort of business-like manner. He looks old, weather-beaten, and seemingly bending under age. He has, nevertheless, a very soldier-like look, but his eyes have lost a part of their warlike fire – they look at all times dull and somewhat dim; but this may be ascribable to temporary indisposition, or rather fatigue from the campaign, of which he is not apparently wholly refreshed or recovered.'

(*Edinburgh Evening Courant*, 30 May 1814.)

1812 campaign were incorporated in the French 4th Gardes d'Honneur. Also existing was a company of Tuscan Veterans (blue infantry uniform, red facings, white buttons, breeches and waistcoat, red-plumed bicorn), and a gendarmerie corps styled *Sbires Toscans*, four companies created in May 1809, wearing blue-grey *surtout*, waistcoat and breeches with a black 'Corsican hat' with upturned right brim and black belts.

References

Brandani, M., Crociani, P., and Fiorentino, M. *Uniformi Militari Italiane del Settecento*, Rome 1976.

Bucquoy, E. L., ed. Devautour, G. *Les Uniformes du ler Empire: Gardes d'Honneur et Troupes Etrangères*, Paris 1983.

UNITES STATES OF AMERICA

History

The USA did not play an extensive part in the Napoleonic Wars, but the War of 1812 may be considered an offshoot in that it arose to some extent out of British operations against France. The United States were governed by four Presidents during the period: George Washington (1732–99, president 1789–97), John Adams (1735–1826, president 1797–1801), Thomas Jefferson (1743–1826, president 1797–1809) and James Madison (1751–1836, president 1809–17); the first two were Federalists, the others Democratic Republicans. The period saw a considerable expansion of territory, most notably by the 'Louisiana Purchase' which arose as a result of the wars in Europe: this vast tract of land in the south of north America was ceded to France by Spain at the Treaty of Lunéville (9 February 1801), and sold to the USA by Bonaparte in 1803; this one transaction more than doubled

> On the retreat from Moscow:
> 'We walked on, thinking of all that had passed, stumbling over dead and dying men. The cold was even more intense than on the day before. We joined two men of the line who had their teeth in a bit of horseflesh. They said, if they waited any longer, it would be frozen too hard to eat. They assured us as a fact that they had seen foreign soldiers [Croats] of our army dragging corpses out of the fire, cutting them up and eating them. I never saw this sort of thing myself, but I believe it frequently happened during this fatal campaign . . . I am sure that if I had not found any horseflesh myself, I could have turned cannibal. To understand this situation, one must have felt the madness of hunger; failing a man to eat, one could have demolished the devil himself, if he were only cooked.'
> (*The Memoirs of Sergeant Bourgogne*, A. J. B. F. Bourgogne, ed. P. Cottin and M. Hénault, London 1899; r/p with intro. by D. G. Chandler, London 1979; pp. 56–7.)

the area of the United States and gave the country control of all the great river-systems of central north America.

Until the War of 1812 the military operations in which the United States became involved were largely restricted to warfare against the indigenous Indian nations. Chief among these were the actions in the Ohio valley, two expeditions against the hostiles (under generals Harmer and St. Clair) being defeated (October 1790, November 1791); a reorganized army under the Revolutionary War hero 'Mad Anthony' Wayne (1745–96) decisively defeated the Indians at Fallen Timbers (20 August 1794) and brought peace to the frontier for some years. Some minor naval actions occurred in the 'war' with France (1798–1800) sparked by operations in the West Indies and the interruption of American commerce. In 1801–5 the United States rebelled at paying 'protection' money to the Barbary States, principally Tripoli, and minor amphibious and naval actions occurred in the Mediterranean involving US naval and marine personnel, notably the capture of the grounded USS *Philadelphia* and its subsequent destruction by Decatur's amphibious raid (February 1804). The next major campaign against the hostiles was the Shawnee war (1811) against chief Tecumseh, who was defeated by William Henry Harrison at Tippecanoe (8 November 1811); and the Creek War in Florida in 1813–14, the Creek rising being encouraged by Britain in support of the War of 1812. (West Florida had been annexed by the USA in October 1810, though the dispute as to whether it had been included in the Louisiana Purchase was not resolved until renunciation of sovereignty by Spain in 1819.) Andrew Jackson ended the Creek War by his victory at Horseshoe Bend (27 March 1814) and the subsequent Treaty of Fort Jackson (9 August). The other actions involving US forces were the War of 1812 against Britain, and the brief war with Algeria – a resumption of the Barbary troubles – successfully concluded by Decatur's Mediterranean squadron of the US navy in March–June 1815.

Army (cockade: black)

Following victory in the Revolutionary Wars the United States took the unusual step of disbanding the regular army almost completely, relying for defence on the concept of a 'well-regulated militia' as enshrined in the Constitution's 2nd Amendment. The faults of this system were demonstrated by the Harmer and St. Clair defeats, and though the need for a regular military force had become obvious by the abortive Shay's rebellion in New England (August 1786–February 1787), the regular army by 1789 consisted of only one infantry regiment and one artillery battalion, totalling 840 men, and even these were 20 per cent under-strength. From December 1792 the regular army was styled 'The Legion' with a total strength of 5,120 plus staff; it comprised eight infantry and four rifle battalions, four light dragoon troops and four artillery companies. The infantry was organized in 'Sublegions' each of two infantry and one rifle battalion; the cavalry and artillery were separate and allocated as necessary. Their uniform was based on that of the Continental Army of the Revolutionary War, the infantry in blue coats faced red (short jackets for light infantry), white waistcoat and buttons, blue gaiter-trousers and apparently a leather light infantry cap with turban and plume white, red, yellow and green for the 1st–4th Sublegions respectively, and a black horsehair mane for the 1st and 3rd and white for the others. At some date before 1794 the head-dress changed to a fur-crested 'round hat' with Sublegion-coloured turban and plume, though the light companies may have retained the leather cap; officers had bicorns and silver epaulettes. Artillery wore the same uniform with yellow buttons, white or blue gaiter-trousers, gold epaulettes for officers and yellow-laced bicorns with black plume tipped red. The cavalry wore infantry uniform except for Tarleton helmets with turban in the Sublegion colour, white breeches and knee-boots.

The main defence remained the militia which could be mobilized in wartime; for example, during the 'Whisky Rebellion' in Pennsylvania (July-November 1794) some 15,000 militia were assembled and Washington himself took the field; yet they were no substitute for a professional army. In 1796 the regular army was reduced to four 8-company infantry regiments, two light dragoon companies and a combined 'Corps of Artillerists and Engineers'. In 1808 Jefferson persuaded Congress to authorize an expansion, the rank-and-file on a voluntary 5-year enlistment and a 160-acre land-grant on discharge, and though the Military Academy at West Point had been established in 1802 it was not fully developed, so that most officers were trained regimentally. The theory behind the continuing small size of the army is expressed in a letter from Jefferson to Kościuszko in April 1802: 'We keep in service no more men than enough to garrison the small posts dispersed at great distances on our frontiers, which garrisons will generally consist of a Captain's company only, and in no case of more than two or three, in not one of a sufficient number to require a field officer; and no circumstances whatever can bring these garrisons together, because it would be an abandonment of their forts.'[1] With the imminence of war with Britain, the establishment was raised to 35,603, but recruiting was never easy (even when the term of enlistment dropped to 18 and 12 months and the bounty increased and land-grant doubled) so that frequently actual strength was barely half the establishment. Regular regiments were numbered in a universal 'line', and though recruited from specified areas did not bear state designations. The country was divided into nine, later ten, military districts.

Cavalry

The two cavalry companies authorized in 1796 were disbanded in 1802, and though a light dragoon regiment was reformed in 1808 it was not fully mounted or brought up to establishment until 1812, when upon the authorization of a new regiment that January it was numbered as the 1st Light Dragoons, the new corps being the 2nd; establishment was of twelve companies, 80 strong. They were employed only in detachments in the War of 1812 and the two regiments amalgamated in May 1814 as the 1st Light Dragoons, and were disbanded at the end of the war; regular cavalry was not formed again until 1833. Until 1799 they wore the uniform of the Legion cavalry, when a similar style was authorized in green with black facings, yellow loops on cuffs and skirts, and Tarleton. From 1808 the uniform was the Tarleton, blue jacket with three rows of silver buttons and white breeches

US Colours from the War of 1812: right: 4th Infantry Regiment, captured at Fort Detroit; left, New York Militia, captured at Queenston. Both are dark blue with the coats-of-arms in their proper colours. (Print after W. Gibb)

'. . . at the storming of Badajos, in April, 1812, one of our officers got a musket-ball in the right ear, which came out of the back of the neck, and, though after a painful illness, he recovered, yet his head got a twist, and he was compelled to wear it looking over the right shoulder. At the battle of Waterloo, in 1815 (having been upwards of three years with his neck awry), he received a shot in the left ear, which came out within half an inch of his former wound in the back of the neck, and it set his head straight again!'

(*Random Shots from a Rifleman*, Sir John Kincaid, London 1835; Maclaren's combined edn. With *Adventures in the Rifle Brigade*, London 1908, p. 240.)

(The officer in question was Thomas Taylor Worsley, adjutant of the 3/95th at Waterloo.)

for officers, and a similar style with red collar and cuffs and white breast-loops for other ranks, with white overalls with blue stripe. In 1812 a new uniform was specified: a full dress of dark blue dolman with three rows of white buttons, blue hussar-braid on breast and rear seams and white braid and knots on the collar and cuffs, white or blue breeches and long boots, and a peaked black leather helmet with leather comb supporting a white horsehair mane, white-metal fittings and light blue plume with white tip at the left. Undress was the same except that the dolman was replaced by a skirted coatee with similar decorations but with all braid in blue. Officers had silver lace and chain wings and silver cuff- and collar-lace.

Infantry

In January 1812 there were seventeen infantry regiments, the 1st formed in 1789, 2nd 1791, 3rd–7th 1808 and the remainder in 1812. Internal organization varied: the 1st and 2nd Regiments had ten companies of 76 men per company, the 3rd–7th ten companies of 78, and the 8th–17th eighteen companies of 110 men, in two battalions. These strengths were never attained fully (some never formed their 2nd battalions), and in June 1812 new organization gave each regiment one depot and nine field companies of 106 of all ranks; the number of regiments increased to 25 in 1812, and ultimately to 48 line and four rifle regiments. Recruiting was an insuperable problem so that not only were regiments under-strength, but on occasion one or more companies might be detached to operate independently. For example, in July 1814 the infantry based in District No. 7 (New Orleans, Mobile and the Creek Nation) ranged from the 7th Infantry with 670 effectives, to the 44th's 89 men; average regimental strength in this district was 387 (or deducting the 44th detachment, 462), only half the authorized figure. At this date only one regiment was stronger than the 7th; in the 9th District fourteen line regiments were represented, with an average strength of 282. In as far as 'state' indentities existed, the following were the places of recruitment: 1st and 15th New Jersey; 2nd and 44th Louisiana; 3rd Mississippi; 4th New Hampshire; 5th, 16th and 22nd Pennsylvania; 6th,

13th, 23rd, 27th, 29th, 41st and 46th New York; 7th, 17th and 28th Kentucky; 8th Georgia; 9th, 21st, 33rd, 34th, 40th and 45th Massachusetts; 10th and 43rd North Carolina; 11th, 26th, 30th and 31st Vermont; 12th, 20th and 35th Virginia; 14th and 38th Maryland; 18th South Carolina; 19th Ohio; 24th and 39th Tennessee; 25th and 37th Connecticut; 32nd Delaware/Pennsylvania; 36th Maryland/Virginia; 42nd Pennsylvania/New York.

The regulation uniform was the same for all regiments, individual identification being limited to the inscriptions on cap-plate and equipment: a British-style dark blue jacket with red collar and cuffs, white turnbacks, buttons, belts and lace (loops on breast, collar and cuffs), grey gaiter-trousers or overalls and a felt 'stovepipe' shako with white cords and plume and a rectangular white-metal plate with cut corners bearing an eagle, trophy of arms and regimental number. In 1813 a new uniform was introduced, as before but with blue collar and cuffs, lace only on the collar, white breeches and black gaiters, and a false-fronted black leather shako like the British 'Belgic' pattern with rectangular white-metal plate with concave corners, white cords and plume. Officers' lace was silver. Such was the shortage of *matériel*, however, that neither uniform was universal, grey cloth being used for many jackets and some regiments having to use whatever colour was available: early in the War of 1812, for example, the 12th Infantry had drab jackets, the 16th black, and the 17th a mixture of blue, drab, brown (with green or red facings) and black. Other units wore 'summer fatigue uniform' of a plain white linen jacket without lace or skirts, and white linen overalls.

The Rifle Regiment wore an infantry-style uniform of dark green with black facings, yellow buttons and lace, green gaiter-trousers, black leather equipment and the 'stovepipe' cap with yellow cords, green plume and brass lozenge-plate; and in summer a green hunting-shirt and pantaloons fringed with buff or light brown. They carried the Model 1803 rifle. Initially styled the 'Regiment of Riflemen' it became the 1st Regiment officially in 1814 (though the number had been used before) when three more were organized (2nd–4th), but these wore a plain grey uniform and the 1813 leather shako. The 1st Regiment adopted the new cap but apparently retained the green uniform, the new shako having a circular plate bearing a bugle with the regimental number in the 'curl'.

Artillery

From 1802 the artillery was organized in a single 'Regiment of Artillerists', twenty companies strong, the personnel distributed throughout garrisons and coastal fortifications, trained and employed as infantry; only when a campaign was imminent was field artillery issued. When the army was expanded in 1808 in answer to a growing possibility of war with Britain, a regiment of 'light artillery' was authorized, ten companies strong, but only one company was trained experimentally as horse artillery; from 1809 it had no horses and only in February 1812 were more authorized. At the beginning of 1812 the Regiment of Artillerists comprised five battalions of four companies each, and the Light Artillery ten companies, all serving as infantry; in January the former was redesignated the 1st Artillery upon the formation of the 2nd and 3rd Regiments, each of two battalions of ten companies each. In May 1814 the three regiments were amalgamated into a single Corps of Artillery of twelve battalions of four companies each; the light artillery remained separate. They served as individual companies, not in battalions; and there was no separate train service, drivers being part of the central organization.

The artillery continued to wear infantry-style uniform in dark blue with red facings, yellow-laced hats with red plume, and yellow buttons; in 1808 the light artillery was authorized a short-tailed, lapelled jacket in the same colours, blue pantaloons for winter, and a peaked leather cap with upright front and back plates, the front bearing 'USLA' in brass letters, with a transverse bearskin crest and a blue plume with red tip at the left. In 1812 a dark blue single-breasted jacket was introduced, with three rows of buttons, white pantaloons for dress and dark blue for service, and a cylindrical shako with yellow cords, brass plate and red-tipped white plume. The 1st Artillery continued to wear its long-tailed coat and bicorn, but the 2nd and 3rd adopted the light artillery shako with rectangular brass plate, short-tailed jacket (authorized in late 1812) in dark blue with red collar, cuffs and turnbacks, yellow lace on the facings and breast, and white gaiter-trousers with yellow stripe (these were officially replaced by overalls in late 1812 but doubtless remained in use until worn out). By 1814 the differences in uniform had been eliminated, and from this date the corps wore dark blue infantry jackets with dark blue facings, yellow buttons, collar-loops and collar-edging, white or blue overalls, black gaiters, and the 1813 shako with yellow cords, white plume and rectangular brass plate.

Engineers

The engineer corps was established in March 1802 and was closely associated with the West Point Academy where the engineers were trained; the unit was very small and not intended to be used in a combat capacity but to be responsible for coastal defence-works. Most field engineering was performed by the pioneer in each infantry company, with additional 'muscle' provided by the infantry where necessary. In March 1813 a Corps of Topographical Engineers was established, with a strength of sixteen officers; at the end of the War of 1812 it was disbanded and the engineers restricted to training the cadets at West Point and maintaining the coastal fortifications. The engineer corps wore artillery uniform with black facings. In April 1812 a Corps of Artificers was formed, barely of company strength, composed of craftsmen, under the aegis of the Quartermaster-General's Department; it wore green single-breasted coats with red collar laced yellow, yellow buttons, red or white waistcoat (winter and summer), green or white breeches (winter and summer), and the infantry shako with rectangular brass plate, yellow edge to the false front, yellow cords and green plume. Officers did not hold commissions so

had no sash or epaulettes, but had gold lace and red wings laced gold, with stars to differentiate the grades. The unit was disbanded in 1815.

Rank-markings

Universal army rank-insignia was as follows: corporal, white epaulette on the right; sergeant, two epaulettes, scarlet waist-sash and straight-bladed sword with iron hilt (artillery NCOs had yellow epaulettes and brass-hilted swords); lieutenant, silver epaulette on left shoulder; captain, epaulette on right; field officers, two epaulettes. All officers wore crimson waist-sashes.

Militia

The standing militia, intended originally to provide the main body of the country's defence and later to supplement the regulars, consisted of able-bodied men between the ages of 16 and 60, who were required to provide their own muskets and to serve in one or two annual musters. In addition to the state militias were local volunteer companies who were liable to serve to defend their own localities. In neither case was there any great degree of precision in their training, discipline was lax and although on numerous occasions in the War of 1812 they fought well, on other occasions they fled or even refused to obey the orders of their superiors. A fatal weakness in the militia system was the authority under which they operated; when in 1812 the governors of Connecticut and Massachusetts were ordered by the President to mobilize their state militias under central command, both objected, claiming that according to the Constitution they, not the President, were the arbiters of when the situation was sufficiently critical to warrant the assembly of the militia. The supreme court supported the Governor of Massachusetts, and not until 1827 was it finally agreed that it was the President's responsibility alone to assess the need for assembling the militia.

Some of these units, especially the urban volunteer corps, were dressed and equipped most splendidly in all manner of styles and colours, though other units were reduced to wearing virtual civilian or frontier dress, 'round hats' and hunting-shirts included, which one British officer described

'On his return from the disastrous campaigns of Moscow and Leipsic, Napoleon, in order to maintain the appearance of confidence, frequently appeared amidst the multitude with scarcely any attendants . . . One day, at La Halle, a woman with whom he had been holding a little dialogue, bluntly told him he ought to make peace. "Good woman," replied the Emperor, "sell your greens, and leave me to settle my affairs. Let every one attend to his own calling." The bystanders laughed, and applauded him.'

(*Memoir of the Life, Exile and Conversations of the Emperor Napoleon*, Count de Las Cases, London 1836, III, p. 393.)

as giving them the appearance of wild Italian bandits. These forces included artillery, generally in uniforms resembling those of the regulars, and cavalry, some urban units most gorgeously dressed, but others equipped more functionally, such as the Kentucky Mounted Volunteers who had a fine service record. The concept of the 'mounted rifleman' was largely restricted at this period to north America, but one akin to the original dragoons of seventeenth-century Europe: troops who rode into action but generally dismounted and fought as infantry. Those armed with rifled muskets in the War of 1812 enjoyed a distinct advantage over those who carried the ordinary smoothbore firearm.

Navy

The US navy was created only in 1794 with the intention simply of protecting American commerce; even at the end of the War of 1812 there was not a single ship-of-the-line in commission. Latterly, however, frigates such as the USS *Constitution* and *President* (44 guns), *Chesapeake*, *Constellation* and *Congress* (36) and *Essex* (32) were among the most formidable in the world, and were responsible for ravaging British commerce during the War of 1812 and scoring a number of remarkable victories over British naval vessels, the only occasions when the Royal Navy was threatened seriously in 'single-ship' actions throughout the period. Although the ships officially ranked as frigates, they were immensely more powerful in weight of shot than the equivalent British vessels, and more resembled ships-of-the-line in their hitting-power, yet were as manoeuvrable as true frigates; they were so impressive that Napoleon ordered his

An unusual ensign: the blue flag with white letters flown by Oliver Hazard Perry which he flew at the Battle of Lake Erie, bearing the exhortation reputedly made by mortally wounded Lawrence of the USS Chesapeake *in the action with HMS* Shannon.

new frigates to be designed as copies of the US vessels. The second reason for US success was the quality of the crews: unintimidated by the British reputation, well-trained and determined, with competent officers. Given the comparative sizes of the British and US navies in the War of 1812, even taking into account the preoccupation of the Royal Navy with the war against France which resulted in there being few warships in north American waters at the start of the war, the Americans did more than could ever have been expected and with their limited resources damaged British prestige to a greater degree than the combined fleets of the French and their allies had achieved in two decades of war.

In addition to the seagoing frigates and many smaller vessels, squadrons were deployed against corresponding British squadrons on the great lakes, again with considerable success, including not only gunboats but some which equalled the size of the smaller varieties of seagoing warship.

US naval uniform closely resembled that of Britain: officers had blue coats with gold lace, bicorns and white breeches, and the seamen's dress was unregulated, generally a blue short jacket, white or striped trousers and a 'round hat'. Unusual head-dress worn for boarding were Tarleton-style helmets with bearskin crests, and even bearskin-covered chinstraps which added to the ferocious appearance of the men, while the crew of the USS *Constellation* at least

---

The following was compiled as an example of the inconstancy of the popular press ('see how many faces our gallant neighbours the French have!'), and was repeated as late as 1907; it reputedly records the headlines in French newspapers following Napoleon's escape from Elba until his resumption of power prior to the Waterloo campaign:

9 March: The Anthrophagus has quitted his den.
10 March: The Corsican Ogre has landed at Cape Juan.
11 March: The Tiger has arrived at Gap.
12 March: The Monster slept at Grenoble.
13 March: The Tyrant has passed through Lyons.
14 March: The Usurper is directing his steps towards Dijon.
18 March: Bonaparte is only sixty leagues from the capital. He has been fortunate to escape his pursuers.
19 March: Bonaparte is advancing with rapid steps, but he will never enter Paris alive.
20 March: Napoleon will tomorrow be under our ramparts.
21 March: The Emperor is at Fontainebleau.
22 March: His Imperial and Royal Majesty yesterday evening arrived at the Tuileries, amidst the joyful acclamations of his devoted and faithful subjects.

(*A Soldier's Experience, or, A Voice from the Ranks*, T. Gowing, 1907 edn., Nottingham, p. 627.)

were reported as equipped with iron skull-caps, perhaps the same head-dress.

The US Marine Corps was formed in November 1775, but after a major reduction in 1783 it was re-established in battalion strength in 1798. The uniform was of infantry style, initially green with red facings, white waistcoat and legwear and a 'round hat'; later it was blue with red facings and was first officially codified in 1804, with yellow loops and buttons, and 'stovepipe' shakos with brass plate, red plume and yellow cords; linen overalls in summer, white breeches and black gaiters in winter; officers had gold lace and epaulettes, and wore either the bicorn or (especially in summer) a 'round hat'.

Note

1. *Correspondence*, III, p. 498, quoted in *United Service Journal*, 1839, vol. II, p. 37 (London 1839), which includes an interesting account of the development of the US establishment.

References
Elting, J. R. (ed). *Military Uniforms in America: The Era of the American Revolution 1755–95*, San Rafael, California, 1974.
— *Military Uniforms in America: Years of Growth 1796–1851*, San Rafael, California, 1977.
Katcher, P. R. N. *The American War 1812-14*, London 1974.
Steffan, R. *The Horse Soldier 1776–1943: Vol. I 1776–1850*, Norman, Oklahoma, 1977.
Windrow, M., and Embleton, G. A. *Military Dress of North America 1665–1970*, London 1973.

VENICE

History

The state of Venice had declined greatly from her heyday as a leading commercial and military power, the result of an atmosphere of luxury and complaisance on the part of successive doges and councils. Initially opposing the French republicans, the Peace of Leoben left Venice without an ally, and the government resolved to offer no resistance to the French, the doge Lodovico Manin abdicating on 12 May 1797. The treaty of Campo Formio (17 October 1797) partitioned Venetian territory, that west of the River Adige being awarded to the Cisalpine Republic, while that east of the Adige, including Venice, Istria and Dalmatia, went to Austria; Venice's naval resources passed into French control via their Italian satellite. Early in 1798 the Austrians entered Venice, bringing to an end 1,100 years of Venetian independence. For the remainder of the period control varied between France and Austria, until Austria was finally confirmed in ownership in 1814; despite an abortive revolt in 1848, only in 1866 did Prussia's defeat of Austria allow Venice to be incorporated into a united Italy.

Army (cockade: blue; 1797, red with green centre and white edge)
Venice's infantry wore Austrian-style white uniform with blue facings and yellow buttons, the jacket of the Austrian single-breasted, short-tailed pattern, with a peakless Austrian-style black leather cap with a brass plate bearing the lion of St. Mark's; the artillery wore iron-grey jacket and breeches. The infantry of the outlying territories wore a similar uniform in blue, faced white. Venice's 'foreign' regiment, Bubich, wore a Balkan-style costume of red coat with blue facings and crimson lace, blue waistcoat and breeches laced yellow, short yellow Hungarian boots and girdle, and a red beret or black infantry cap with brass plate, and was armed with a basket-hilted broadsword in addition to the ordinary musket and cartridge-box.

In August 1797, prior to the state's assimilation by Austria, the 'liberated' Venetian Republic uniformed its troops in a style similar to that of the Cisalpine Republic: green infantry uniform with red facings and waistcoat, and a curious, squat black leather helmet with front and rear peaks and a shallow brass comb with a white-over-red-over-green plume at the front, and a brass plate bearing a lictor's *fasces* and the inscription '*Liberta O Morte*'.

References
Brandani, M., Crociani, P., and Fiorentino, M. *Uniformi Militari Italiane dell'Ottocento: Periodo Napoleonico*, Rome 1978.
— *Uniformi Militari Italiane del Settecento*, Rome 1976.

WALDECK

History

The German principality of Waldeck consisted of two enclaves, Waldeck and Pyrmont, separated by about thirty miles. In 1438 the Landgrave of Hesse obtained rights of suzerainty over Waldeck, and though the Hesse claim was not finally settled until 1847 (when it was decided that the rights of Hesse had lapsed with the dissolution of the Holy Roman Empire), Waldeck enjoyed independence. Waldeck and Pyrmont were first united in 1631, and for a short time were divided into Wildungen and Eisenburg, but upon the death of the Imperial Field Marshal George Frederick, last of the Wildungen branch, the whole was unified under Christian Louis of Eisenberg, and remained united except for the years 1805–12 when Waldeck and Pyrmont were ruled by two brothers. Christian Louis' son, Frederick Anthony Ulrich (ruled 1706 to his death in 1728) was made a prince of the empire in 1712. In April 1807 Waldeck entered the Confederation of the Rhine, and the German Confederation in 1815; Prince George II (died 1845) granted the state its first constitution in 1816.

Army (cockade: black/red/yellow)
Under its obligations for the Confederation of the Rhine, Waldeck provided three companies to the 6th Confederation Regiment (400 men with the detachment from Reuss to form the 2nd Battalion), and the 6th Company to the *Fürstenbataillon* ('Princes' Battalion'). The contingent wore a French-style shako with brass lozenge plate, white or yellow cords, white jacket with dark blue collar, cuffs and lapels, yellow buttons, grey breeches, black gaiters and white belts.

WESTPHALIA

History

The German Duchy of Westphalia was separated from Saxony when that state's Duke Henry the Lion fell under imperial ban in 1180. Until 1803 it was administered for the archbishopric of Cologne, when the secularization of church lands gave part to Prussia and the greater amount to Hesse-Darmstadt. The Kingdom of Westphalia was created only in December 1807 following the Treaty of Tilsit, as a gift from Napoleon to his brother Jérôme who became king. It was not a duplicate of the old territory of Westphalia, however, but was composed of parts of Hanover, Brunswick, Saxony and most of Hesse-Cassel. The new kingdom's capital was Cassel and it was divided into eight departments, administered on French lines, the constitution granted by Jérôme being virtually inoperative and the state being run by Jérôme's bureaucracy. From the beginning its finances were in a parlous state, and it was reduced to financial ruin by the drain of resources and men for Napoleon's wars, and not helped by Jérôme's somewhat inept leadership. In January 1810 most of Hanover was added to the kingdom but at the end of that year about half, and the city of Minden, was annexed to France. Jérôme was driven from his capital in October 1813 and the kingdom dissolved; at the Congress of Vienna Hesse-Darmstadt surrendered her claims to Westphalia and the whole became a province of Prussia.

Army (cockade: dark blue with white edge)

Although Westphalian troops formed a considerable proportion of Napoleon's German forces, his opinion of them was not flattering, especially as he felt some picque at Jérôme's disregarding of his advice. In 1810 Napoleon accused his brother of '. . . playing at soldiers . . . as for the recruiting of the troops in Catalonia, I will send no more Westphalians thither, to swell the enemy's bands; that of all the German soldiers, they are the least to be depended upon; that in consequence of an old-standing hatred, arising from the fact of these troops having always served with the English, they have more satisfaction in fighting against us, than any others . . . it is a great act of folly to increase troops, whom there is no means of supporting, and which cannot be depended upon . . . I ought to have insisted . . . that no person in the Westphalian army has the command of my troops . . .'[1] Napoleon's criticism was especially fierce for Jérôme's refusal to form French regiments for his personal Guard; in April 1813 he railed that 'The King's great fault is his ignorance of history and principles of politics, and the rash manner in which he behaves. Here is the result – though he has an army of from 15,000 to 20,000 men, he is on the brink of being driven out of his capital, by two or three squadrons . . .'[2] Nevertheless, Westphalian troops served in Spain, in Saxony in 1809, formed the whole of VIII Corps in the Russian campaign (from which Jérôme, initially corps commander, was dismissed by Napoleon after a row over his lethargic behaviour), and in the 1813 campaign. The brigades which went to Russia were virtually annihilated;

only 50 infantry and 60 cavalry struggled back across the Berezina, and as many as 11,000 were lost in the Peninsular War. The army was largely conscripted from its own territory; exceptions were the 1st and 2nd Line Regiments, originally assembled from the debris of the Hessian army, the 1st squadron of the Guard *Chevauxlegers* who were originally Poles who acted as Jérôme's first escort, and the nucleus of the 1st Light Battalion, originally non-Prussians from the Prussian army, captured in 1806. Only with the formation of the Guard Hussars, largely French conscripts, did Jérôme attempt to follow Napoleon's advice regarding the organization of a reliable French element within the army.

Royal Guard

Jérôme formed his Guard entirely from Westphalians, contrary to Napoleon's advice. Napoleon declared that he almost insisted on a French Guard, as he had with Joseph Bonaparte in Spain, '. . . but I was prevented from so doing by the false idea instilled into the King, that such a course would weaken his own independence'.[3] Six hundred French cavalry, 3,000 infantry and one or two artillery companies would, thought Napoleon, have made Jérôme 'lord of his own kingdom, and safe from all attack',[4] but in the event the Westphalian Guard was not regarded as completely reliable. Senior of the three Guard cavalry units was the Garde du Corps, a ceremonial bodyguard squadron which wore a white jacket faced blue with red piping, gold lace and epaulettes, white breeches, long boots, cuirasses and an iron helmet with gilt comb and fittings (with 'JN' – Jérôme Napoleon – on the plate), a black fur crest and white plume; service-dress was the same but with a blue jacket faced red. The Guard *Chevauxlegers* wore a black leather helmet with brass comb and fittings, black crest and red plume, single-breasted green jacket with red facings, yellow loops of breast and facings, green breeches with yellow stripe and thigh-knots, hussar boots and buff leather equipment; the front rank was armed with lances with green and white pennon. The Guard hussar regiment, raised from French conscripts in 1813, wore French hussar uniform of red shako with yellow lace and cords, white plume and brass crowned shield-plate bearing 'JN', red dolman, blue pelisse and breeches, yellow lace and buttons. The unit was ordered to be disbanded upon the collapse of the kingdom, but under Jérôme's pleading Napoleon consented to take it into the French line as the 13th Hussars; its name was retained as the *Hussards Jérôme-Napoleon*. Its three squadrons were virtually destroyed at La Fère-Champenoise and the unit ceased to exist.

Senior of the four Guard infantry units was the Guard Grenadiers, wearing a white coat with red facings and epaulettes, yellow buttons and loops on the facings, white belts, waistcoat, breeches and long gaiters (black gaiters in winter and on campaign), and bearskin caps with red cords, plume and rear patch bearing a yellow grenade. In service dress a single-breasted white jacket was worn, with red facings, shako with brass lozenge plate and red pompom.

The Guard *Jägers* wore a dark green jacket with lemon facings and piping to green lapels, white buttons and loops on the collar, cuffs and lapels, green breeches with white stripe and thigh-knots, black gaiters, white belts, and shako with white cords, plume and eagle-plate. The *Jäger-Carabinier* battalion wore a single-breasted dark green jacket with red piping and loops on collar and cuffs, green epaulettes with red crescents, yellow buttons, green breeches with red stripe and thigh-knots, red-laced black gaiters, black belts, and a shako with brass eagle-plate, red cords and red-tipped green plume; they were armed with rifles. The Guard Fusiliers wore white infantry uniform with dark blue facings, white

Officer of Westphalian Garde du Corps, Jérôme Bonaparte's personal bodyguard, in full dress, c.1810; blue uniform with red facings, iron cuirass with gilt sunburst badge, gilt helmet with bearskin crest and white plume; the horse-furniture is dark blue with gold lace and fringe. Note the 'JN' cipher on the cuirass and holster-caps, signifying 'Jérôme Napoleon'. (Print after Alexander Sauerweid)

buttons and loops on the collar, cuffs and lapels. The Guard horse artillery wore a single-breasted dark blue jacket with red facings, epaulettes and breast-loops, blue breeches with red stripe and thigh-knots, red-laced hussar boots, buff belts, and a shako with brass lozenge plate and red cords and plume.

Cavalry

The cavalry was organized in regiments of four squadrons of 138 men each, plus a depot. The heavy cavalry comprised two cuirassier regiments, much to Napoleon's disgust ('I have told the King, over and over again, that he ought not to have cuirassier regiments, because that branch of the service costs too much money, and the native horses are not adapted for it . . .');[5] the 1st Regiment wore a French cuirassier helmet, white jacket with crimson facings (including lapels), red epaulettes, white breeches and leather equipment, long boots, and French cuirasses adopted in 1810. From 1812 the jacket became single-breasted and dark blue with the same facings, and orange facings for the new 2nd Regiment. The two *Chevauxleger* regiments (the 2nd raised in 1812) had a helmet like that of the Guard *Chevauxlegers* but with white-metal fittings, dark green jacket with orange and chamois facings respectively for the 1st and 2nd Regiments, white buttons, green breeches with facing-coloured stripe and thigh-knots; lances were carried briefly c. 1811, with blue and white pennon. The two hussar regiments wore French-style hussar uniform, the 1st with green dolman, pelisse and breeches, white buttons and braid, and shako with white-metal eagle plate, white cords and green plume; the 2nd wore the same but with light blue dolman, pelisse and breeches, red collar and cuffs, and white plume.

Infantry

Like the rest of the army, the infantry was organized and equipped in French style, with French company-distinctions and rank-markings. The line regiments each had two 6-company battalions (the 2nd and 7th three battalions) plus a depot of four companies of 560 men; each field battalion had one grenadier, one *voltigeur* and four fusilier companies and two 6pdr guns with 32 crew. The French-style uniform comprised a white jacket with facings dark blue for the 1st and 2nd Regiments, 3rd and 4th light blue and 5th and 6th yellow, but were dark blue for all by 1810; in 1812 there were eight regiments. Buttons were yellow and officers' epaulettes gold; white waistcoat, breeches and belts, and French-style shako with brass lozenge plate, white cords and pompom in company colour (light blue, white, yellow or green for the 1st–4th fusilier companies respectively). Fusiliers had white shoulder-straps piped in the facing-colour but from 1812 blue epaulettes with white crescents; plume, shako-cords and epaulettes were red for grenadiers and green for *voltigeurs* (with yellow-tipped plume). Grenadiers of the 1st Regiment had bearskin caps like those of the Guard Grenadiers.

The three single-battalion light infantry corps each had six companies (873 men) and a depot (140); they wore infantry uniform in cornflower-blue with green, later orange facings;

in 1809 this changed to a dark green single-breasted jacket and breeches, light blue facings and piping, white buttons, black belts, and shako with white-metal eagle plate and green plume. The National Guard, based in the main towns, wore long-tailed, dark blue double-breasted coats with red turnbacks and piping, white buttons, plain bicorns, blue breeches, black belts, red epaulettes for grenadiers and green with red crescents for *voltigeurs*; 2nd battalions had the same with white lapels.

Artillery

The artillery was organized and equipped exactly like that of the French army, except for minor insignia: the uniform had red collar, cuffs and turnbacks, blue breeches and lapels piped red, yellow buttons, red shako-cords and plume or pompom and brass lozenge-plate bearing 'JN'. Train personnel wore grey jackets with red collar, cuffs and turnbacks, grey lapels piped red, white-braided red waistcoat, grey breeches with white stripe and thigh-knots, hussar boots, buff belts and French shako with white metal fittings and lozenge plate, white cords and red pompom.

Notes

1. *New Letters of Napoleon I*, Lady M. Lloyd, New York 1894, cccvii.
2. ibid., ccccxxxvi.
3. ibid.
4. ibid.
5. ibid., cccvii.

References

Pivka, Otto von. *Napoleon's German Allies: Westfalia and Kleve-Berg*, London 1975.

WURTTEMBERG

History

The German Duchy of Württemberg had laboured under internal dissatisfaction in the second half of the eighteenth century due to the unpopularity of its spendthrift duke, Charles Eugene (1728–93), who from his coming of age in 1744 (he had succeeded Duke Charles Alexander in 1737 as a minor) used somewhat arbitrary means of raising money to fight Prussia in the Seven Years War, itself unpopular with his Protestant subjects, the duke being a Roman Catholic. Charles Eugene died childless and was succeeded by two brothers, Duke Louis Eugene (died 1795) and Frederick Eugene (died 1797); the latter, related by marriage to Frederick the Great in whose army he had served, educated his children in the Protestant faith, so that the son who succeeded him in 1797, Frederick II (1754–1816) was of the same religion as the majority of his subjects. Frederick Eugene had been compelled to withdraw his support for the Emperor by a French invasion, and when Frederick II entered the war against France, the French invaded again and devastated the country. In March 1802 Frederick signed a private treaty with France, surrendering his possessions on the left bank of the Rhine in return for nine imperial towns, though the new districts were not merged fully into the duchy but styled 'New Württemberg'. The duke accepted the title of elector from Napoleon, and in 1805 joined France in a

Among the most singular of military head-dress of the Napoleonic era was the Raupenhelm *('crested helmet') worn by several German states, notably Bavaria, made of very thick black leather with a metal-reinforced comb, front and rear peaks, generally with a flap between the peaks intended to divert rainwater from the ears, and a bearskin or (as here) woollen crest. This particular example bears the three antlers of Württemberg on its front-plate.*

military alliance; in recognition for this assistance Frederick received some Austrian territory at the Peace of Pressburg, and on 1 January 1806 assumed the title of king, repealed the constitution and united Old and New Württemberg. He joined the Confederation of the Rhine in 1806, and received more territory; and yet more after the peace of 1809. In return, Württemberg provided troops for Napoleon's campaigns, including the near extinction of the 14,000 men who served in III Corps in the 1812 campaign. In November 1813 Frederick switched sides by concluding a treaty at Fulda with Austria, which confirmed his royal title and his newly acquired possessions, after which the Württemberg troops joined the Allies against France. The Congress of Vienna made no readjustment of Frederick's territory despite his years of support for the French; yet despite this successful emergence from the Napoleonic conflict, he died on 30 October 1816 amid internal unrest after his draft of a new constitution had been rejected. His successor, William I, negotiated a new constitution which was granted in September 1819, so that although the 'year of revolution' (1848) did not pass without some internal disquiet, no violence occurred in Württemberg.

Army (cockade: black; then black with yellow edge and red centre)

The Württemberg forces served with considerable distinction throughout the period; even in the catastrophe of the retreat from Moscow, Napoleon remarked upon their remnant, still marching in formation, though only about 30 strong. The army had seen no active service since the Seven Years War, though in 1786 a mercenary regiment was raised for Dutch service; it was captured at the Cape by Britain in 1795 and remained prisoners until the unit was disbanded in Ceylon in 1808. Recruitment was by voluntary enlistment until 1807, when conscription was introduced, infantry serving eight years and cavalry ten.

Cavalry

The lineage of the cavalry is exceptionally complicated, and changes of title can only be summarized here. Initially the cavalry comprised a Lifeguard of one squadron each of hussars, dragoons and mounted *Jägers*, and a horse grenadier unit. The *Husaren-Garde* wore dark red hussar uniform with light blue facings and yellow lace; the *Dragoner-Garde* yellow cuirassier-style uniform with crimson facings and silver-laced hat; and the *Leibjäger-Garde* green with red facings, white waistcoat and breeches, silver lace, and silver-laced hat with white plume. In 1793 a dragoon regiment (*Kreisdragoner*) was created for Imperial service, eight companies strong; and in November 1794 the Guard was disbanded and its personnel used to form the depot for the dragoon regiment. A new *Leibjäger* corps was created in 1796, amalgamated with the dragoons in 1798 to form a regiment composed of Garde du Corps (1st Squadron), *Leibjäger* (2nd) and *Chevauxlegers* (3rd and 4th). In 1801 the Garde du Corps and *Leibjäger* were detached and the *chevauxleger* element expanded to a full regiment. In 1805 two new regiments were formed, the Kurfürst *chevauxlegers* (four squadrons, titled *Leibchevauxlegers* from 1806) and the Prinz Paul *Jägers* (three squadrons, titled Herzog Louis from 1807). The *Jäger* Regiment 'König' was raised in 1806, and in 1807 the original *chevauxleger* regiment was re-titled Herzog Heinrich. In 1809 the Kronprinz Dragoons were created from the depots of the other four regiments. In 1811 numbers were assigned: 1st *Chevauxlegers* (ex-Herzog Heinrich, re-named Prinz Adam *Chevauxlegers* in 1812 and 1st *Leibkavallerie* in 1813), 2nd *Leibchevauxlegers*, 3rd Herzog Louis *Jägers*, 4th König *Jägers* and 5th Kronprinz Dragoons. In 1813 the premature defection to the Allies of the 2nd and 4th led to the re-numbering of the Herzog Louis *Jägers* and Kronprinz Dragoons as 2nd and 3rd respectively, with new 4th (Prinz Adam) and 5th *Jägers* formed. In 1814 the 2nd–4th received the title *Kavallerie-Regiment* but retained their old designations.

From 1798 the uniform was a short-tailed blue jacket with facing-coloured collar, cuffs, turnbacks and half-lapels, white breeches, long boots, and a combed black leather helmet with black plume and horsehair mane and a brass shield-plate bearing the state arms and motto 'Furchtlos und Treu'. By 1811 this had been replaced by a leather Austrian-style combed helmet with yellow-over-black crest. The 1st *Chevauxlegers* wore scarlet facings, from 1811 yellow collar and cuffs and blue lapels and turnbacks piped yellow. The rank-and-file wore a wide, facing-coloured girdle; officers had silver epaulettes and lace, the national silver waist-sash with red and yellow lines interwoven, and a royal arms helmet-plate. The *Leibchevauxlegers* wore scarlet facings, yellow turnbacks piped red, and blue lapels piped scarlet in 1811, with white loops on collar, cuffs and lapels until 1811, and just one collar-loop thereafter. The senior (*Leib*) squadron wore bearskin caps with white cords and black plume, in the fashion of the original horse grenadiers. The Mounted *Jägers* wore green with black belts and the combed helmet with green crest, facings yellow and pink for the 3rd and 4th respectively; the new 4th of 1813 had red facings, and the *Jägers* adopted shakos with brass lozenge-plate from 1813–14. The Dragoons wore green with white facings (and latterly lace loops) and the shako.

The two Lifeguard squadrons (detached 1801) were expanded to a regiment in 1808 by the transfer of one squadron each from the *Leib* and Herzog Heinrich *Chevauxlegers*. The 1st (*Leibjäger*) Squadron wore green faced black, yellow buttons, white breeches and bearskin cap; the 2nd (Garde du Corps) Squadron yellow jackets with a black *supreveste* (imitation cloth cuirass) and the cavalry helmet; and the 3rd and 4th (Horse Grenadier) Squadrons blue jackets with yellow facings, white epaulettes and breeches and bearskin cap. On campaign all wore the Horse Grenadier uniform, though the 1st Squadron retained its green colouring with black facings.

Decoration of Honour for the 1814 Campaign of Württemberg, founded by Frederick I in February and August 1814, in gold for officers and silver for other ranks, in three varieties, bearing the dates for the battles of Brienne (1 February), La Fère-Champenoise (25 March) and Paris (30 March). Poppy-red ribbon.

Infantry

Initially the infantry comprised a Guard regiment, the Saxe-Coburg and von Hügel Regiments of two battalions, a grenadier and a garrison battalion. In 1793 a *Kreisregiment* was formed for Imperial service, of two grenadier and ten musketeer companies. In 1798 a reorganization produced four infantry and two grenadier battalions, one of which became foot guards in 1813; as in the Austrian army regiments were known by the name of their *Inhaber*, so titles often changed, and only in 1811 were numbers introduced. From 1807 battalions consisted of four companies totalling under 700 rank-and-file, though some had five companies by 1813. The reserve or *Landregiments* for internal defence rose to eight regiments by late 1813, each of five companies.

The uniform was initially of Prussian style, dark blue coats with red turnbacks, white waistcoats, breeches and belts, black gaiters, and hat laced in the button-colour. Facings in 1798 were: Regiment Mylius yellow, Obernitz light blue, Seeger red (white shoulder-straps), Beulwitz pink and Perglas white; with white buttons (Mylius yellow). In 1799 the bicorn was replaced by the combed leather helmet as worn by the cavalry, with black mane, and the coat replaced with a short-tailed jacket with half-lapels; in 1806 a crested helmet with white plume and black 'caterpillar' was adopted, and in 1811 the lapels became blue with facing-coloured piping. Eight regiments existed in 1811, with facings: 1st yellow, 2nd orange, 3rd white, 4th pink (white piping), 5th light blue (white piping), 6th white (red piping), 7th red, 8th straw-yellow; buttons yellow for the 6th–8th and white for the remainder. From 1812 Austrian-style shakos were adopted, with brass lozenge-plate bearing 'FR', brass side-chevrons and national cockade at the right.

A single *Jäger* company was formed in 1799, expanded to a battalion in 1801, wearing green coats and breeches, black facings and leather equipment, white piping and buttons and green-plumed Corsican hat, replaced in 1801 by a shako with dark green turban and plume. A 2nd battalion was formed in 1805; both were armed with rifles. In 1805 two light infantry battalions were formed from 5th companies of the line regiments, in infantry uniform in dark green with light blue facings, white piping and yellow buttons, and the combed helmet with black crest. In 1807 *Jägers* and light infantry adopted red-plumed shakos with green turban, and in 1811 Austrian-style shakos with white cords and brass lozenge-plate. In 1813 the *Jäger* battalions were amalgamated to form a new 9th Line, adding yellow lace to the collar and cuffs, with yellow buttons, and the light battalions combined to form a 10th Line (light infantry) regiment. An 11th Line was formed from the *Landregiment* rifle corps.

Artillery

Initially the artillery comprised a Guard horse battery and 'battalion guns' attached to the infantry. In 1792 the former was incorporated into a 12-gun *Kreisartillerie* unit for Imperial service. In 1800 a 'bombardier company', a 'cannonier company' and a depot company were formed, and a new horse battery in 1801, equipped with six 6pdrs and

Military Order of Merit of Württemberg, founded as the Military Order of St. Charles in February 1759, and renewed in 1799 and 1806. Gold cross with white-enamelled arms, blue circlet and green wreath; blue ribbon.

two 7pdr howitzers by 1803. One company of foot artillery was distributed to man the 'battalion guns', the other forming the artillery reserve (seven 6pdrs and four 3pdrs), though by 1806 both appear to have been operating as companies. In 1807 a second 6-gun horse battery and third 10-gun foot company were formed, and a third horse battery in 1808. By 1810 a heavy foot company or park had been formed, equipped with 12pdrs. For the 1812 campaign the foot companies had three 6pdrs and two 7pdr howitzers, and the heavy company six 12pdrs. In May 1814 three battalions were established, the first consisting of four 6-gun horse batteries (one accorded Guard status since 1807) and a 4-gun Guard foot company; the 2nd battalion comprised two 6-gun light foot companies and two heavy foot companies (with 12pdrs); and the 3rd battalion consisting of the reserve and depot. Ordnance was basically of Austrian construction, but French patterns were introduced from 1812; all guns taken to Russia were lost.

Artillery uniform was of infantry style, in light blue with black facings, white piping, breeches, waistcoat and belts, yellow buttons, and bicorn; the half-lapelled jacket was adopted in 1799 and the black-maned helmet. In 1804 the crested helmet was introduced, with black crest and white plume, and breeches and lapels became light blue. The horse batteries wore the same plus a black girdle, metal shoulder-scales and hussar boots instead of the black gaiters of the foot artillery, and yellow turnbacks piped black. Guard units had white loops on collar and cuffs. In 1813 the shako was adopted, with white-metal fittings for the Guard and brass for the remainder; Guard units also wore white buttons. The train personnel wore light blue single-breasted jackets with black collar, cuffs and shoulder-straps (piped yellow), yellow buttons, grey breeches and the shako.

References

The most comprehensive work in English is *The Württemberg Army 1793–1815* (G. F. Nafziger, Leeds 1987), though an important assemblage of German sources, 'Württemberg Line Cavalry 1798–1816' by J. Cook, appeared in the periodical *Empires, Eagles & Lions*, Cambridge, Ontario, 1986.

The responsibility of command weighed heavily. Even after the mass carnage of Waterloo, Cavalié Mercer never forgot the first casualty sustained by his battery, for which he blamed himself by opening fire without orders and attracting a French reply:

'The first man of my troop touched was by one of these confounded long shot. I shall never forget the scream the poor lad gave when struck. It was one of the last they fired, and shattered his left arm to pieces as he stood between the waggons. That scream went to my very soul, for I accused myself as having caused his misfortune. I was, however, obliged to conceal my emotion from the men, who had turned to look at him; so bidding them stand to their front, I continued my walk up and down, whilst Hitchins ran to his assistance.'

Mercer was later somewhat shamefaced to admit that the sight of a wounded horse drove the image of Gunner Hunt from his memory . . .

(*Journal of the Waterloo Campaign*, C. Mercer, Edinburgh & London 1870, I, p. 302.)

WURZBURG

History

The German state of Würzburg, later the capital of the Bavarian province of Lower Franconia, was established as a bishopric in AD 741. The bishops soon assumed political power and ruled the state until its secularization by the Peace of Lunéville, and in 1803 it was granted to Bavaria. By the Peace of Pressburg (1805) it was made into an independent electorate, granted to Ferdinand, former grand-duke of Tuscany, who took the title grand-duke of Würzburg. He joined the Confederation of the Rhine in September 1806 but left in November 1813, and the Congress of Vienna ended the state's independence and returned it to Bavaria.

Army (cockade: red with blue centre and yellow edge)
Würzburg's infantry in the later eighteenth century had worn white uniforms with red or blue facings, but in 1795 the Würzburg *Kreisbataillon* wore blue with red facings, white buttons, waistcoat and breeches, and bicorn. In 1801 it was expanded to three battalions wearing white Austrian-style single-breasted jackets with red, blue and green facings for the 1st–3rd Battalions respectively, white breeches and leather equipment, and the Austrian 1798 combed helmet with black crest, and fur caps for grenadiers. Red or green epaulettes for grenadiers and light infantry were adopted when the state joined the Confederation of the Rhine. A French-style uniform was adopted from *c.* 1809, white with red facings (including lapels), French-pattern shako with brass lozenge-plate bearing a crowned 'F', and yellow and green epaulettes and plume for *voltigeurs*. Officers wore gold sashes with interwoven red and blue lines. The cavalry – the Würzburg *Chevauxlegers* – wore single-breasted green jackets with red facings, white breeches, yellow buttons, knee-boots and the Austrian cavalry helmet with black crest, brass plate bearing crowned 'F', and red-tipped black plume. In 1811 red epaulettes and an infantry-style shako with red cords and the same plume were adopted. The artillery detachment wore infantry uniform in grey-brown (including waistcoat and breeches) with red facings, shako-cords and plume, and yellow buttons and shoulder-scales.

IV
BIOGRAPHIES

BIOGRAPHIES

Abercromby, Sir Ralph (1734–1801)

Sir Ralph Abercromby was Britain's most distinguished general of the Revolutionary Wars period, a skilled and worthy man beloved by the army. Born of Scottish gentry, he studied civil law at Leipzig, but professing more interest in a military career obtained a commission in 1756. He served in the 3rd Dragoon Guards during the Seven Years War (where he attained a great respect for the methods of Frederick the Great), but declined to serve in the American War as he had great sympathy with the colonists and no desire to partake in such a fratricidal conflict. He retired in 1783, serving as Member of Parliament for his native Clackmannanshire, until he surren-dered the seat to his brother and moved to Edinburgh. Upon the outbreak of the Revolutionary Wars he resumed his military career, serving most valuably in the Netherlands, in the West Indies as commander-in-chief in succession to Grey (capturing St. Lucia, St. Vincent and Trinidad), and returning home in 1797 was appointed commander-in-chief in Ireland. A great humanitarian, he attempted to suppress agitation whilst not insti-tuting military oppression, but was thwarted at every turn by over-zealous factions, and resigned before the outbreak of the 1798 rebellion which he had laboured to prevent.

He was one of few to emerge with credit from the 1799 expedition to north Holland, and his talents and experience

Sir Ralph Abercromby, wearing the dress uniform of a lieutenant-general. (Engraving by Finden after Hoppner)

made him the ideal commander of the expedition to Egypt in 1801. Despite the difficulties he encountered from his own government – he noted succinctly that 'there are risks in a British warfare unknown in any other service'[1] – his landing in Egypt was brilliantly successful, and his defeat of Menou at Alexandria was the decisive action of the campaign. Struck in the leg by a ball towards the close of the action, he died aboard ship a week later; carried away in a soldier's blanket, his last order before turning over command to his successor was that he must be given the name of the owner, for 'a soldier's blanket is of great consequence',[2] a gesture abso-lutely typical of this worthy man. The Duke of York's tribute was no more than he deserved: 'His steady obser-vance of discipline, his ever-watchful attention to the health and wants of his troops, the persevering and uncon-querable spirit which marked his military career, the splendour of his actions in the field and the heroism of his death, are worthy the imitation of all who desire, like him, a life of heroism and a death of glory.'

Notes
1. *History of the British Army*, Hon. Sir John Fortescue, (London 1906),. IV, p. 810.
2. ibid. p. 844.

Reference
Lieutenant-General Sir Ralph Abercromby, K. B., a memoir by his son James Abercromby, later Lord Dunfermline, 1861.

Beauharnais, Eugène de (1781–1824)

Eugène de Beauharnais was one of the most worthy and loyal of Napoleon's subordinates, and earned his respect not only as a step-son but for his military abilities and character. Born in Paris on 3 September 1781, he was the child of General Viscount Alexandre de Beauharnais and Josephine Tascher de la Pagerie. His father briefly commanded the Army of the Rhine but was guillotined in June 1794 for failing to relieve Mainz. The young Eugène's first meeting with Napoleon occurred when he went to request the return of the sword belonging to the father he revered; from this meeting Napoleon made the acquaintance of Josephine Beauharnais and although Eugène resented their marriage, he became the most loyal servant of his step-father, whose aide he was in the 1796–7 campaigns and in Egypt (wounded at Acre). Promoted to general in 1804, he received the title of prince and was appointed Viceroy of Italy in 1805. His administration of Italy was entirely beneficial (despite basically performing his step-father's instructions) and be became popular with the Italians for his fair conduct; Napoleon arranged his marriage to the beautiful Princess Auguste Amélie of Bavaria, but it was a true love-match and it was typical of Eugène's character that it was said his first words to the princess were to offer to abandon the marriage and take the blame himself if she had any doubts.

In the 1809 campaign, assisted by Macdonald, Eugène commanded the Army of Italy, and though checked at Sacile won an important victory at Raab and acquitted himself with distinction at Wagram. Equally distinguished was his command of the Italian contingent in the 1812 campaign, especially at Borodino and at Maloyaroslavets (which the

Italians fought largely unaided), and he succeeded to command of the army after Murat's return home. He played an important part in the victory of Lützen and defended Italy with some skill in 1814. Having promised his father-in-law not to become involved in Napoleon's schemes any longer, he did not rally to his step-father in 1815; becoming Duke of Leuchtenberg and Prince of Eichstädt, he lived the remainder of his life in Munich, helping the old soldiers and comrades of Napoleon. A genuinely good man, de Bourrienne's enumeration of his characteristics seems accurate: '... an excellent heart, a fine courage, strict honour, great generosity and frankness, with an obliging and amiable temper'.[1]

Note

1. *Court and Camp of Bonaparte,* anon., London 1831, p. 257.

References

Oman, Carola. *Napoleon's Viceroy,* London 1966.

Ducasse, Baron A. (ed.). *Mémoires et Correspondence politique et militaire du Prince Eugène,* Paris 1858–60.

◄

Eugène de Beauharnais, Viceroy of Italy, in the uniform of the Chasseurs à Cheval *of the Imperial Guard. (Engraving by C. A. Powell after Henri Scheffer)*

▼

Beresford at Albuera. Hand-to-hand combat was relatively rare, and especially so when it involved generals. At Albuera, Beresford was attacked by a Polish lancer; a man of great strength, he grappled with the lancer and pitched him from the saddle. (Engraving by T. Sutherland after William Heath)

William Carr Beresford in the uniform of Marshal of the Portuguese army. (Print after Heaphy)

Beresford, William Carr, Viscount (1768–1854)

The illegitimate son of the 1st Marquess of Waterford, William Beresford entered the British Army in 1785, and lost an eye in a shooting accident in Nova Scotia in the following year. Distinguished at Toulon, he received command of the 88th Foot in 1795, leading them in India, in Baird's expedition to Egypt, and was present at the capture of the Cape in 1806. Captured after the hopeless expedition to Buenos Ayres, he escaped and at the end of 1807 was sent to Madeira as governor and commander-in-chief in the name of the Portuguese monarchy, where he learned Portuguese. He then served under Wellesley and Moore in the Peninsula before being appointed Marshal of the Portuguese army (2 March 1809) with the task of reorganizing and reforming the then very poor army. Though he had limited abilities as a field commander, in the organizational and training role he was supremely successful, initiating the first effective Portuguese light troops (*Caçadores*), integrating a small number of British officers into the service, and by improving the lot of the ordinary soldier caused morale to soar, thus transforming the Portuguese forces into a vital part of the Peninsular army. Awarded a knighthood of the Bath and a Portuguese peerage after Busaco, he commanded at Albuera where his limited generalship was revealed; but he remained an important figure in the Allied organization, and was severely wounded at Salamanca. He served in the later actions with considerable distinction, and was created Baron Beresford of Albuera and Cappoquin at the close of the Peninsular War, upgraded to a viscountcy in 1823.

The Portuguese revolution in 1819 led to the dismissal of British officers, and Beresford refused commands in the civil war, turning to British politics in which he was an ardent supporter of Wellington who appointed him Master-General of the Ordnance in 1828. Following his retirement from politics in 1830 he was involved in a heated dispute with Napier over the latter's Peninsular history, and indeed Beresford's reputation has suffered from Napier's opinions. Wellington recognized his deficiencies as a field commander, but nevertheless regarded him as his most valuable subordinate: 'All I can tell you is that the ablest man I have yet seen with the army, and the one having the largest views, is Beresford. They tell me that when I am not present he wants decision . . . but I am quite certain he is the only person capable of conducting a large concern.' When asked who should assume command in case of an accident to himself, Wellington hesitated and then said 'Beresford'. Some surprise was expressed and then he continued: 'I see what you mean by your looks. If it was a question of handling troops, some of you fellows might do as well, nay, better than he; but what we want now is some one to feed our troops, and I know no one fitter for the purpose than Beresford.'[1] This is a very fitting summary of the skills of the Marshal who died at his country estate at Bedgebury, Kent, on 8 January 1854.

Note

1. *The Wellington Memorial*, A. J. Griffiths, London 1897, p. 308.

The perspective on life depends upon circumstances: the Duc de Fezensac recalled that during the 1805 campaign even scraps of food became prized possessions:

'Another day, a little soldier of my company, who I had helped, secretly gave me a bit of ammunition bread and a scrap of chicken, which he'd wrapped in a dirty shirt. Never in my life did I have a better meal.'

(*Souvenirs militaires de 1804 à 1814*, Duc de Fezensac, Paris 1863.)

Sergeant Fricasse cites examples of republican patriotism from 1795:

'Cailac, one of our captains, who had his leg shattered by a ball, from which he died three weeks later, said: "My life is nothing; I would give it a thousand times for the republic to triumph." Struck in the belly by a shell-splinter, one of the battalion's grenadiers said to those who wished to help, "Leave me, pals, leave me to die! I'm happy, I've served my country"; and he died.'

('Journal de marche du Sergent Fricasse', in *Gloires et Souvenirs Militaires*, C. Bigot, Paris 1894, p. 7.)

Bernadotte, Jean-Baptiste Jules (later Charles-Jean) (1763–1844)

The son of a French lawyer, Jean-Baptiste Bernadotte (who added the name Jules later) enlisted in the French army in 1780, rising to the rank of sergeant-major before the Revolution, after service in the East Indies. A most ardent republican (who had 'Death to Tyrants' tattooed on his arm!), his political leanings and military talents led to a rapid rise in the Revolutionary Wars, achieving the rank of *général de division* by October 1794. After distinguished service along the Rhine he was employed briefly in diplomatic duty (being compelled to quit his post as ambassador in Vienna after riots caused by his hoisting of the tricolor!), and on 16 August 1798 he married Désirée Clary, Joseph Bonaparte's sister-in-law. He had served under Bonaparte in Italy, and though he declined to assist in Bonaparte's *coup d'état* was employed in high office under the Consulate and was among the first creations as marshal in 1804. He handled his Corps with distinction in the Ulm/Austerlitz operations (receiving the title of Prince of Ponte Corvo), but was severely criticized by Napoleon for his delay in supporting Davoût at Auerstädt. Relations with Napoleon deteriorated and after mishandling his Corps at Wagram Napoleon summarily dismissed him from the army in disgrace. He was placed in command of the force to counter the landing at Walcheren, but Napoleon removed him from all his appointments in September 1809; the break was irreversible.

Having shown great kindness to Swedish prisoners in the late war with Denmark, Bernadotte was approached by the Swedish government as a possible successor to the heirless King Charles XIII; he mentioned the offer to Napoleon, who thought it absurd, but on 21 August 1810 he was duly elected as Crown Prince, changing his name to Charles-Jean and his religion to Lutheran, formally becoming Charles XIII's heir on 5 November. From the first he adopted Sweden as his homeland, subjugating all to their interests; as he wrote to Napoleon in 1813, 'I will say to the Swedes, "I fight for you, and with you, and the vows of free nations will accompany your efforts"', 'in this struggle between the liberty of the world and oppression.'[1] Consequently, Napoleon's seizure of Swedish Pomerania in 1812 led to Bernadotte's drawing closer to the Tsar and Allies; he took Sweden into the Sixth

Jean-Baptiste Jules Bernadotte, in the uniform of a French   *Marshal. (Engraving by T. Johnson after F. Kinson)*

Coalition, leading her army in the campaigns of 1813–14 as commander of the Army of the North. He was accused of making deliberate delays in the Leipzig campaign and in France, but such were probably only out of consideration for his native country; he may have entertained some hopes of a French popular rising unseating Napoleon and appointing him in his stead, but such was never possible as most Frenchmen regarded Bernadotte as an unmitigated traitor, which is certainly how Napoleon viewed him, remarking later that 'In his intoxication, he sacrificed both his new and his mother country, his own glory, his true power, the cause of the people, and the welfare of Europe . . . He is now the only upstart sovereign in Europe.'[2] Nevertheless, there is an element of irony in the fact that the once most vehement republican and not the most talented of Napoleon's marshals should be the only one to found his own dynasty, which still exists; for he became King Charles XIV in February 1818, unifying Sweden and Norway and in every way being a moderate and a good king, despite his inherent conservatism which caused some disquiet in the *Riksdag* (parliament) in 1840.

Notes

1. *Court and Camp of Bonaparte*, anon., London 1831, p. 234.
2. *Memoirs of the Life, Exile and Conversations of the Emperor Napoleon*, Count de Las Cases, London 1836, IV, p. 110.

References

Barton, Sir Dunbar *Bernadotte, the First Phase 1763–99*, London 1914.
— *Bernadotte and Napoleon, 1799–1810*, London 1921.
— *Bernadotte, Prince and King 1810–44*, London 1925.
Dewes, S. *Sergeant Belle-Jambe*, London 1943 (concerned primarily with Bernadotte's military career).
Phillipart, Sir John. *The Memoirs and Campaigns of Charles John, Prince Royal of Sweden*, London 1814.
Russell of Liverpool, Lord. *Bernadotte, Marshal of France and King of Sweden*, London 1981.
Shefer, C. *Bernadotte roi*, Paris 1899.

Berthier, Louis Alexandre (1753–1815)

Louis Berthier was a poor general, but was absolutely invaluable to Napoleon as chief of staff. Born at Versailles, he became a military engineer like his father and served under Rochambeau in America; at the Revolution he served in the Versailles National Guard and aided the escape of Louis XVI's aunts. His perceived adherence to royalism led to periods of unemployment, but his administrative skills led to posts as chief of staff under Rochambeau, Lafayette, Lückner and Biron (the latter better-known as Duc de Lauzun). Posted to the Army of Italy as a general, his great experience, capacity for hard work and love of the most painstaking detail made him the ideal assistant to Bonaparte, and thereafter he served as Napoleon's right hand, equally capable in diplomatic tasks as military, and serving as Minister of War 1800–07. Appointed Marshal in the first creation, he was ennobled as Prince of Neuchâtel (1806) and Wagram (1809). He had been nominal commander of the Army of Reserve in the Marengo campaign, but Napoleon had actually been in charge; his only really independent command was at the beginning of the 1809 campaign, when his lack of aptitude for strategy became apparent. Thereafter, he continued to serve as chief of staff, the most vital part of Napoleon's household, though Napoleon seems not to have realized his worth fully; although he regarded Berthier as a friend, he once described him as merely a 'chief clerk' and on at least one occasion beat the poor man's head against a wall in an outburst of rage.

A stout, short man, his often jolly nature grew progressively morose, especially when Napoleon arranged his marriage to a German noblewoman instead of to his beloved mistress, Madame Visconti, whose husband died shortly after his marriage: he said 'To what a miserable condition am I reduced! With a little more constancy, Madame Visconti might have been my wife!'[1] Berthier's misery increased with war-weariness and complaints that he was overworked to the point of death, and upon the Restoration he was favoured by the Bourbons and remained loyal to them in 1815. His name was struck off Napoleon's register of marshals, and he fell to his death from a window at Bamberg on 1 June 1815, perhaps assassinated by a secret society, murdered by Russians who were passing at that moment, or more likely by accident or suicide from remorse at the abandonment of his old master. Perhaps the first professional staff officer in history, Berthier's talents in this role were vast; but as Napoleon remarked, 'Nature has evidently designed many for a subordinate situation; and among these is Berthier. As chief of staff he had no superior; but he was not fit to command five hundred men.'[2]

Notes

1. *Court and Camp of Bonaparte*, anon., London 1831, p. 241.
2. ibid. p. 242.

References

Derrecagaix, General. *Le Maréchal Berthier, Prince de Wagram et de Neuchâtel*, Paris 1905.
Watson, S. J. *By Command of the Emperor: a Life of Marshal Berthier*, London 1957, r/p Cambridge 1989.

Louis Alexandre Berthier, in the early uniform of a republican general officer. (Engraving by H. Davidson after Antoine-Jean Gros)

Bessières, Jean-Baptiste (1768–1813)

Born near Cahors, the son of a surgeon, Bessières intended to follow his father's profession but joined the army on the outbreak of the Revolution, serving as an officer in Louis XVI's Constitutional Guard and participating in the defence of the Tuileries. Re-enlisting as an ordinary soldier, he served as an NCO in the Pyrenees and was re-commissioned in 1793. Distinguished service in Italy brought him to Bonaparte's notice, and he was given command of Bonaparte's Guides, the forerunner of the Consular Guard, whose cavalry he led at Marengo, having earlier distinguished himself further in Egypt. Promoted to general in 1800 and to marshal in 1804, he served in the campaigns of 1805–06–07 as commander of the Guard cavalry; in 1809 he was created Duke of Istria. In the Peninsular War he was given his first independent command, winning the Battle of Medina del Rio Seco; at Essling his repeated charges held back the Austrians, and at Wagram his horse was killed beneath him. He replaced Bernadotte as commander of the Army of the North, then returned to Spain as Massena's second-in-command, before being recalled to lead the Guard cavalry in the Russian campaign. Before the start of the 1813 campaign Bessières remarked that 'at the present crisis, with our young soldiers, we leaders must not spare ourselves';[1] ever in the most dangerous situations, three days into the campaign he was struck by a musket-ball in the breast at Rippach, near Weissenfels, while reconnoitering, and killed on the spot.

A man who worshipped Napoleon, to whom he was a true friend, Bessières was a grievous loss, for not only was he a brave and skilled general but a good and honest man, beloved by his own troops and admired by his opponents. Ever anxious to prevent the worst horrors of war, so well had he treated the people in Spain that even they, his most bitter enemies, offered up masses for his soul; and typical of his humanity was his behaviour at Marengo, when seeing a fallen Austrian in the path of his charge, Bessières commanded his men, 'My friends, open your ranks; let us spare that unfortunate man.'[2]

Notes

1. *Memoirs of the Life, Exile and Conversations of the Emperor Napoleon*, Count de Las Cases, London 1836, I, p. 341.
2. *Court and Camp of Bonaparte*, anon., London 1831, p. 246.

References

Bessières, A. de. *Le Maréchal Bessières, Duc d'Istrie*, Paris 1941.
Rabel, A. *Le Maréchal Bessières*, Paris 1903.

Blücher, Gebhard Leberecht von, Prince of Wahlstadt (1742–1819)

Perhaps the most implacable of Napoleon's opponents, and Prussia's most famous general of the period, Gebhard Blücher was born near Rostock in Mecklenburg, son of a retired officer. His first military service was in the Swedish army at age 14, but after being captured by the Prussians in 1760 he entered the Prussian army, gaining much experience as a hussar officer. Complaining about lack of promotion, his request to Frederick the Great was reputedly answered with 'Captain Blücher can take himself to the devil', and for fifteen years from 1773 he spent his time farming. He returned to the army only after Frederick's death, rising to command a hussar regiment. Greatly distinguished against the French in 1793–4, he rose to the rank of lieutenant-general in 1801 and, a leading member of the 'war party' in Prussia in 1805–6, served as a cavalry commander in the disastrous campaign of the latter year. He fought on until compelled to surrender from want of provisions and ammunition at Ratkau (6 November 1806). Totally opposed to any collaboration with Napoleon, he was a natural leader of the 'patriot party' and was virtually banished from court for his objections to the sending of a Prussian contingent to Napoleon's Russian campaign.

Gerhard Leberecht von Blücher.   after F. C. Gröger)
(Engraving by T. W. Harland

> 'So indecorously was the veteran BLUCHER buffetted about by the crowd at Portsmouth, that the fine enamel of the ornament, presented to him by the PRINCE REGENT, has been cracked from top to bottom.'
>
> (*Edinburgh Evening Courant*, 2 July 1814.)

In the 'war of liberation' in 1813 he was given command of the Army of Silesia with Gneisenau as chief of staff – Blücher had, in fact, assisted Scharnhorst and Gneisenau in the reconstruction of the Prussian army – and in the latter he found a perfect collaborator. Blücher's overriding attribute was his determination and energy; never a brilliant tactician, the nickname bestowed upon him by his men (who worshipped the old warrior), *Marschall Vorwärts* ('Marshal Forward'), epitomizes his temperament. Despite setbacks in 1813–14 Blücher kept up the morale of his troops and, aided by Gneisenau's clear brain, maintained such pressure on Napoleon that the Allies were successful, due in no small part to the old general's determination. Expecting to retire in 1814 (when he was appointed Prince of Wahlstadt, 3 June, and fêted wherever he went, especially in England), he was recalled to command the Prussian forces in the Hundred Days campaign, when his determination and valour were stretched to the limit. Promising to assist Wellington come what may, he was ridden-over at Ligny and thus temporarily lost command to Gneisenau, who favoured retirement for reorganization; but having recovered, Blücher succeeded in convincing his chief of staff that his word must be kept and Wellington assisted, and thus the Allies were successful at Waterloo. (It is interesting to note that Blücher found it necessary to argue his case with Gneisenau, not simply issue an order, a reflection upon their relationship: a genuine partnership rather than the one serving his superior).

Retiring from ill-health and old age, Blücher died on his Silesian estates on 12 September 1819. To the end of his life he retained a somewhat wild streak (as behoved a typical hussar), but his passionate hatred of the French and his loyalty to his cause recompensed him even for the mental instability which at times appeared to be present. Despite his intellectual limitations, he represented the finest type of 'fighting general', personally and morally brave.

References

The leading biography is probably *Blücher*, W. von Unger, Berlin 1907–8; Roger Parkinson's *Hussar General* is the leading biography in English. Blücher's 1793–4 diaries and a paper on his ideas for a national army are in *Campagne Journal 1793–94 von Gl.Lt v. Blücher*, ed. Golz & Ribbentrop.

Bonaparte, Jérôme, King of Westphalia (1784–1860)

Jérôme was the youngest and arguably least talented of the Bonaparte brothers; Napoleon's term for him, *petit polisson* (scamp) is probably not unfair. Wounded in a duel with Davoût's brother, he then trained as a naval officer, but his lack of application caused Napoleon to write: 'Die young, and I shall have some consolation; but if you live to sixty, without having served your country and leaving behind you any honourable recollections, you had better not have been born.'[1] Jérôme quit his ship in America and returned home with an American bride, Elizabeth Patterson of Baltimore; Napoleon refused her admission and the poor girl had to settle in Camberwell, where she gave birth to a son, before returning home. Jérôme spent an undistinguished naval career, though he rose to the rank of admiral, and in 1806 he

Jérôme Bonaparte, King of Westphalia (1784–1860); note the royal cipher on his holster-caps, 'JN' (Jérôme-Napoléon). Engraving by M. Haider after Antoine-Jean Gros)

commanded a Bavarian division. Having had Jérôme's marriage annulled, in August 1807 Napoleon married him to Princess Frederica Catharina, daughter of the King of Württemberg, and appointed him king of the newly created satellite of Westphalia. Jérôme's extravagant lifestyle complicated an already parlous economy, and he was forced to turn to the Jewish moneylender Isaac Jacobson, whose influence grew, much to the chagrin of Jérôme's new subjects; there was an abortive rising in April 1809 led by army officers, and the participation of large numbers of Westphalian troops in Spain and the Russian campaign almost reduced the state to bankruptcy. Jérôme initially commanded the Westphalian Corps in Russia, but was dismissed by Napoleon following a row about his lethargic conduct. Westphalia rose against him in 1813; he was chased from his capital and spent some time in Switzerland and Trieste.

Returning to France during the Hundred Days, he commanded a division at Waterloo and was responsible for the costly and self-defeating attacks throughout the day on Hougoumont; he then threw himself upon the mercy of his father-in-law, who kept him under semi-arrest. Given the title Count of Montfort in 1816, after two years he was allowed to leave, and lived at Trieste, in Italy and Switzerland until returning to France in 1847. His career resurrected, he became Marshal of France and president of the Senate, and died on 24 June 1860. His children included Napoleon Joseph Charles Paul (1822–91), commonly known as 'Plon-Plon', who became direct heir to the Napoleonic succession; and Jérôme Napoleon (1805–70), Elizabeth Patterson's child, who resided in Baltimore. Elizabeth, born 1785, outlived her husband by 19 years; Frederica Catharina died in 1835. Jérôme Napoleon's elder son served with the French army in the Crimea, and his younger son was Roosevelt's navy secretary 1905–6 and later US attorney-general.

Jérôme was not devoid of talent but preferred the luxuries associated with royal status to its duties; good-natured but indolent, he was regarded by Napoleon with some derision: in 1813 he was alleged to have told Jérôme to go away: 'You are hateful to me. Your conduct disgusts me. I know no one so base, so stupid, so cowardly; you are destitute of virtue, talents, and resources. I hate you as much as I hate Lucien ...',[2] which is a thoroughly ungenerous if not entirely unmerited condemnation of the most easy-going of the Bonaparte dynasty.

Notes
1. *Court and Camp of Bonaparte*, anon., London 1831, pp. 76–7.
2. ibid. p. 87.

References
Casse, Baron A. du *Mémoires et correspondance du roi Jérôme et de la reine Cathérine*, Paris 1861–6.
Martinet, A. *Jérôme Napoléon, roi de Westphalie*, Paris 1902.

Bonaparte, Joseph, King of Naples and Spain (1768–1844)

The career of Napoleon's eldest brother was spent very much in Napoleon's shadow, and at the direction of Napoleon's whim. Trained as a barrister, his early services were in the diplomatic sphere: minister to Parma and Rome, member for Corsica in the Council of Five Hundred, member of the Council of State, and negotiator of the Convention of Montfontaine (his country house) with the USA, and of the Treaties of Lunéville and Amiens. Despite disagreeing with Napoleon about the Bonaparte succession (in the event of Napoleon's death Joseph thought it should pass to him and not to Louis Bonaparte's son) and a refusal of the crown of Lombardy, Joseph acted as head of the government when Napoleon was campaigning in 1805, and in 1806 was sent to Naples with a French army. Having expelled the Bourbons, Joseph accepted the crown of Naples (31 March 1806) and proceeded to make as beneficial reforms in the country as his meagre treasury would allow, being genuinely concerned with improving the lot of the ordinary citizen.

In 1808 he very reluctantly surrendered the crown to Murat and took up a new kingdom, Spain, a far less happier territory. Joseph was never accepted by the Spanish people,

Joseph Bonaparte, King of Spain and formerly King of Naples (1768–1844), in Spanish uniform. (Engraving by L. Rados after J. B. Bosio)

At Würschen, 1813:
'. . . Lieutenant Lherault, who was quite near the Emperor, had his leg carried off by a cannon-ball, and was thrown under the feet of Napoleon's horse. In spite of his injuries, no cry escaped his lips, except the words "Vive l'Empéreur!" Napoleon, however, could scarcely contain his grief, and with great emotion he turned to Marshal Duroc, exclaiming, "Fortune is certainly against us to-day." Duroc, in his turn, was mortally wounded on the following day.'
(*Napoleon's Famous 'Guides'*, P. White, in *Cavalry Journal*, VIII, Aldershot 1913, p. 192.)

never controlled much of the country, and was completely under Napoleon's domination; he attempted to abdicate four times, without success. Having few military talents, he was totally subservient to Napoleon and to the generals Napoleon appointed, a serious blow to Joseph's prestige. Defeat in the Peninsular War led him to write to Napoleon: 'I have done no good here, and have no prospect of doing any. I therefore entreat your Majesty to suffer me to resign into your hands the right to the crown of Spain . . .',[1] but only after Joseph's flight from Spain after the crushing defeat of Vittoria did Napoleon accede to his wishes; Napoleon noted in July 1813 that his behaviour never ceased to bring misfortune upon the army, as if all the ills of the Peninsular War were Joseph's fault. In 1814, as Napoleon's deputy, Joseph gave Marmont the power to make a truce, leading to the surrender of Paris, which caused Napoleon further dissatisfaction.

After the Hundred Days, Joseph went to America where he lived under the alias of Comte de Survilliers, leaving to visit England, Genoa and Florence. Finally quitting the United States in 1839, he retired to Florence, where he died on 28 July 1844. A kind-hearted but not very energetic man, his tastes were not for conquest and kingship but more pacific pursuits – fond of literature, he published a romance entitled *Moina* in 1799 – and would have been much happier had he been allowed to live privately with his wife, Julie Clary, whom he married in Marseilles before his diplomatic career began. Napoleon's reflection is probably just: 'He did the best he could. His intentions were good, and therefore the fault rested not so much with him as with me, who raised him above his proper sphere.'[2]

Notes
1. March 1812; *Court and Camp of Bonaparte*, anon., London 1831, p. 32.
2. ibid. p. 34.

References
The most extensive work on Joseph Bonaparte is *Mémoires et correspondance politiques et militaires du roi Joseph*, Baron A. du Casse, in ten volumes, Paris 1854; a good selection is *The Confidential Correspondence of Napoleon Bonaparte with his Brother Joseph*, London 1855. An interesting early biography is *History of Joseph Bonaparte*, J. S. C. Abbott, New York 1869. *The Legacy of Glory: the Bonaparte Kingdom of Spain*, M. Glover, New York 1971, is an excellent coverage of the Spanish adventure.

Brunswick, Friedrich Wilhelm, Duke of (1771–1815)
Son of Duke Karl Wilhelm Ferdinand and grandson of Frederick, Prince of Wales, Duke Friedrich Wilhelm succeeded to his father's title after the latter's death from a wound received at Auerstädt; the new Duke found his lands possessed by the French, and Napoleon reputedly sent a message immediately after Jena that '*Je veux l'écraser lui et toute sa famille*',[1] which was taken as proof of Napoleon's hatred of the Brunswick dynasty resulting from their close kinship with the British royal family. In 1809 the dispossessed Duke raised his famous 'Black Legion' for Austrian service, and after the collapse of Austrian resistance marched across Germany to be evacuated by the British fleet, to continue the fight against France under British colours. Restored to his

Friedrich Wilhelm, Duke of Brunswick (1771–1815): the 'Black Duke' in the uniform of the Brunswick Oels Corps. (*Print from Ackermann's* Repository of Arts)

duchy in 1813–14, 'the black duke' raised a new national army and led it in the Waterloo campaign, being killed at Quatre Bras while rallying his young soldiers. His hatred of the French was exemplified by the death's head badge and black uniforms with which he equipped his troops, and in the anti-French camp he was regarded as the *beau idéal* of a patriot: 'Weak and abject are the German princes who have sacrificed their people to his [Napoleon's] will; who have prostrated themselves before him merely to preserve a miserable existence, an existence suited to their feeble minds. . . . What an example does not the Duke present to them! . . . He is the only German Prince who has shown a determined mind, and a readiness to sacrifice his property; had every one acted as he has done with firmness and disinterestedness in support of independence, the German nation would not have been reduced to the wretched state in which she is at present.'[2]

Notes

1. *Account of the Operations of the Corps under the Duke of Brunswick . . .* anon., London 1810, p. 5.
2. ibid. pp. 37–8.

Brunswick, Karl Wilhelm Ferdinand, Duke of (1735–1806)

Duke Karl Wilhelm Ferdinand learned his military skills in the Seven Years War, under the Duke of Cumberland and later under his uncle, the great Ferdinand of Brunswick; his style of command was thus rooted in the mid-18th century and not truly fitted for the 'modern' wars of the French Revolution. Though a Prussian field marshal respected by both friends and opponents, he was also ruling prince of Brunswick (succeeding his father, Duke Karl I, in 1780) and a model sovereign of the 'enlightened despotism' school, caring for his people and with wide interests: he lived for a time in Rome, studing the antiquities. His connections to the British royal family were close: he married the daughter of Frederick, Prince of Wales. His reputation as the best general in Europe led to his being offered command of the French army in 1792; instead, he commanded the Allied army which invaded France in that year, and was defeated at Valmy. He remained in the army in 1793, but finding his actions confounded by the wishes of the King of Prussia – whose presence in 1792 seems to have placed great constraints upon Brunswick's freedom of action – he resigned. He undertook a diplomatic mission to Russia in 1803, and at the personal request of Queen Louisa of Prussia came out of retirement to lead the Prussian army in the 1806 campaign, though again the presence of the king and his advisers was not beneficial. Mortally wounded at Auerstädt, he died on 10 November 1806 near Hamburg, very possibly having outlived his style of warfare.

References

Fitzmaurice, Lord. *Charles William Ferdinand, Duke of Brunswick*, London 1901.

Carnot, Lazare Nicolas Marguerite (1753–1823)

Lazare Carnot was the most influential French military figure of the Revolutionary period. Born of a middle-class Burgundian family, he was an engineer officer during the *ancien régime* and wrote a number of treatises (including an essay on the use of balloons!) in the pre-revolution era. Embracing the revolution (he was a committed republican and voted for the execution of the king), he was elected to the Assembly and became a prominent figure in domestic politics, but it was his military skills that were of the greatest value. Though he ranked only as a captain, virtually all military administration and organization was his doing, the *levée en masse* and *amalgame* included; as a member of the Committee of Public Safety from August 1793 his role was actually that of combined minister of war and chief of staff.

Lazare Nicolas Marguerite Carnot (1753–1823), 'the organizer of victory'.   (*Engraving by J. Massard*)

His labour was incessant and his abilities vast: his sobriquet 'the organizer of victory' was a literal truth; the army which Napoleon inherited owed more to Carnot than to any other source, and it is doubtful whether the infant French republic could have survived without his assiduous attentions in reconstructing and maintaining the army.

Carnot quarrelled with Robespierre and thus escaped his fall, and in 1795 was appointed a Director; he was twice president of the Directory but forced to flee abroad in 1797. He returned after the *coup d'état* of 18 Brumaire, served as minister of war from early 1800 and took part in the campaigning on the Rhine; he had often accompanied armies in the field, and was so influential at Wattignies that credit for the victory is often accorded to him, rather than to Jourdan who was in command. Carnot continued to effect important reforms in the military establishment, but his republicanism led him into conflict with the growing monarchism of Napoleon, and from early 1801 he retired from active public life, remaining a senator but devoting himself to writing and science. His greatest work (commissioned by Napoleon as a textbook for the Metz engineering-school) was *De la défense des places fortes* (1810) which was translated for the use of almost every army in Europe. The threat of invasion in 1814 led to his return to active command, as *général de division* and governor of Antwerp, his defence of which was a brilliant episode. He rallied to Napoleon in 1815 and served as Minister of the Interior, but was proscribed at the second restoration and spent the remainder of his life in exile, mainly at Magdeburg, still occupied with science and writing.

Once the saviour of France, Carnot was a sincere and incorruptible patriot, whose influence on the French military cannot be over-stated; in military theory, his idea of 'active defence' was highly influential in the science of post-Napoleonic fortification. His progeny was scarcely less influential in their own way: his eldest son Sadi (1796–1832), himself an engineer officer, was a brilliant scientist ('Carnot's principle' is fundamental in the theory of thermodynamics), whose career was tragically curtailed by cholera. The second son, also Lazare (1801–88), was a leading French politician; his son Marie became fourth president of the Third Republic and was assassinated by an Italian anarchist in 1894, and his second son became a distinguished mining engineer and one of France's leading analytical chemists. Few families have contributed so much to their homeland.

References

Carnot, H. *Mémoires sur Carnot*, Paris 1863.

Picaud, A. *Carnot, l'organisateur de la victoire*, Paris 1885–87.

Tissot, P. F. *Mémoires historiques et militaires sur Carnot*, Paris 1824.

Charles, Archduke of Austria, Duke of Teschen (1771–1847)

Among the best of Napoleon's opponents, Charles was the most outstanding Austrian commander of the era. Brother of Emperor Francis II, he trained as a soldier from youth, being adopted by the Duke of Saxe-Teschen, governor of the Austrian Netherlands. He fought at Jemappes, and as governor of the Austrian Netherlands won Neerwinden but was defeated at Wattignies and Fleurus. Promoted to field marshal in 1796, he led the Army of the Rhine against Moreau and Jourdan, winning the actions of Rastadt, Amberg and Würzburg; he then commanded in Italy without success, but returning to the Rhine theatre was victorious at Biberach and Stockach, but was beaten at Zürich. After difficulties co-operating with his Russian callies he retired from command, becoming governor of Bohemia, Minister of War, and in 1805 commanded in Italy. After the defeat of 1805 he led the reorganization and reconstruction of the Austrian army – his most valuable contribution – and in 1809 was in overall command of the Austrian forces. Though defeated at Eckmühl he

Archduke Charles of Austria (1771–1847). (Engraving by T. W. Harland after Kellerhoven)

The Archduke Charles recounts the nature of war:

'War is the greatest evil that can befall a state or nation. The principal need of a sovereign or general-in-chief will this be to assemble from the beginning of the war all disposable forces, and employ them in such a way that the war lasts as short a time as possible and ends quickly in the most favourable manner. The object of all war must be an advantageous peace, because only an advantageous peace lasts, and it is only a lasting peace that can, by making nations happy, accomplish the ends of governments.'
(*Principles of War*, 1808, opening paragraph)

administered the first real defeat on Napoleon at Aspern-Essling, but was overwhelmed at Wagram, his last active command. Defeat at Wagram and his subsequent retirement have tended to obscure his very considerable talents as a reformer, organizer and commander, and the most vivid image of his career – rallying the wavering Regt. No. 15 (Zach) at Aspern-Essling by grasping their Colours – may be apocryphal, for he later joked that a little man like he was could hardly have made off with a heavy flag like that! His military writings were of considerable influence, though his theories were perhaps overly cautious; Clausewitz claimed that he attached more importance to possession of ground than destruction of the enemy, which may have had a bad influence in the 1866 war, yet his activity in action was a strange contrast to his circumspect theorizing.

References
Erzherzog Carl also Feldherr und Heeresorganisator, M. von Angeli, Vienna 1896–7, is an 'official' biography, but the incomparable modern study is *Napoleon's Great Adversaries: The Archduke Charles and the Austrian Army 1792–1814*, G. E. Rothenberg, London 1982. Charles' writings were edited by Archdukes Albert and William in *Ausgewählte Schriften weiland Sr. K. Hoheit Erzh. Carl v. Österreich*, Vienna 1862.

Propaganda (of a very unsubtle nature) operated in most countries. Typical anti-French propaganda (though not, perhaps, without foundation) appeared in the broadsheet *The Contrast, 1792*:

'*British Liberty:* Religion – Morality – Loyalty – Obedience to the Laws – Independence – Personal Security – Justice – Inheritance – Protection [of] Property – Industry – National Prosperity – Happiness.

French Liberty: Atheism – Perjury – Rebellion – Treason – Anarchy – Murder – Equality – Madness – Cruelty – Injustice – Treachery – Ingratitude – Idleness – Famine – National & Private Ruin – Misery.'

(It is interesting to find 'equality' listed with the many evils of 'French Liberty': hardly a view which would arouse any sympathy in the modern world!)

Cuesta, Don Gregorio García de la (1740–1812)

Probably no general attracted such opprobrium from his allies as did Cuesta, one of Spain's best-known generals. A Castilian, he first fought the French in 1793, and in 1808 was appointed Captain-General of Estremadura; having been defeated at Medina de Rio Seco and Medellin, he commanded the Spanish forces supposedly collaborating with Wellesley in the Talavera campaign. In this capacity he was unwilling or unable to perform his obligations, giving Wellesley no assistance to the extent that the Spanish army was virtually unengaged at Talavera while the British had a terrible fight; he refused to provision the British and even abandoned their wounded to the French, having pledged to care for them. Old and immobile, he travelled in a lumbering coach and when mounted had a servant on each side to hold

him in the saddle. British opinion of Cuesta was thus devastating. At Medellin, D'Urban noted that he 'behaved with the fire of five-and-twenty' until ridden down by his own bolting cavalry (D'Urban and Cuesta's nephew rescued him from under the horses); yet after Talavera and the abandonment of the British wounded, D'Urban noted that 'With such Allies it is impossible to act – Treachery or panic?'[1] Others were not so charitable: John Colborne thought him 'a perverse, stupid old blockhead';[2] Edward Costello remarked that 'I also then beheld that deformed-looking lump of pride, ignorance and treachery, General Cuesta. He was the most murderous-looking old man I ever saw.'[3] After a stroke, Cuesta retired in August 1809, which the Portuguese staff officer William Warre greeted with delight that the 'old brute' had gone: 'This obstinate surly old ignorant fellow is, thank God, removed. He was, to say the best of him, quite superannuated, and so violent and obstinate that everybody feared him but his enemies.'[4] Cuesta died in retirement in Majorca.

Notes
1. *The Peninsular Journal of Major-General Sir Benjamin D'Urban 1808–17*, ed. I. J. Rousseau, London 1930, pp. 48, 68–9.
2. *The Life of John Colborne, Field Marshal Lord Seaton*, G. C. Moore Smith, London 1903, p. 130.
3. *Adventures of a Soldier*, E. Costello, London 1852; 1967 (London) edn, ed. A. Brett-James, p. 21.
4. *Letters from the Peninsula 1808–12*, Sir William Warre, ed. Revd. E. Warre, London 1909, p. 74.

Davoût, Louis Nicolas (1770–1823)

Louis Davoût (the name was also spelled Davout and Davoust) was probably the most able of Napoleon's marshals. The offspring of minor nobility, he was commissioned in 1788 but dismissed from his post on account of his over-zealous support of the Revolution. Almost immediately he was elected *chef de bataillon* of the 3rd Yonne Volunteers, but despite good service at Neerwinden was removed from office just after his promotion to *général de brigade* because of his noble antecedents. Nevertheless, he served on the Rhine and in Egypt under Desaix, and demonstrated his abilities to Bonaparte in the Marengo campaign, so that he was appointed a marshal in 1804 and also colonel-general of the Imperial Guard Grenadiers. He conducted a noted forced march to Austerlitz, but his greatest feat was his defeat of Brunswick at Auerstädt, which Napoleon appreciated but perhaps resented as detracting from his own victory of Jena. He was almost equally distinguished in 1807, and ennobled as Duc d'Auerstädt in March 1808; the 1809 campaign brought him the title Prince of Eckmühl. In 1812 he led I Corps, which his stern discipline made the best in the army, but in 1813–14 was concerned only with the defence of Hamburg, which he held with vigour until a month after Napoleon's abdication. In 1815 he rallied to Napoleon and was appointed Minister of War and Governor of Paris, in retrospect a great mistake as he was a more capable field commander than any others who

Louis Nicolas Davoût (1770–1823), wearing the dress uniform of a Marshal of the Empire. (Engraving by R. A. Muller after Marzocchi & Gautherot)

acts were more ruthless and oppressive than those of an open enemy'; 'no despotism could exceed that of this old soldier of liberty: he filled all Poland with dread and brought much disgrace on the French name';[1] yet to be fair, he was always given the most difficult tasks and carried out his instructions with the same minute care with which he expected his own directions to be performed. Though he gathered a large personal fortune he was not a blatant plunderer like other marshals, despite a statement that 'His avarice was equal to his cruelty.'[2] Though he never held a fully independent command, the dour, austere marshal was a very considerable soldier indeed.

Notes
1. Abbé de Pradt, quoted in *Court and Camp of Bonaparte*, anon., London 1831, pp. 248–9.
2. ibid.

References
Blocqueville, Marquise de. *Le Maréchal Davoût raconté par les siens et lui-même*, Paris 1870–80.
Gallagher, J. G. *The Iron Marshal: a Biography of Louis N. Davoût*, Champaign, Illinois, 1976 (the only major work in English).
Vigier, J. *Davout, maréchal d'Empire, duc d'Auerstädt*, Paris 1898.

Desaix, Louis Charles Antoine (called Desaix de Veygoux) (1768–1800)

Louis Desaix was probably the real victor of Marengo, but as he was killed at the moment of victory the credit was all Napoleon's. Born of a noble but impoverished family, he was commissioned in 1783 but embraced the principles of the Revolution. Narrowly escaping the guillotine because of his background, his abilities were recognized and by 1793 he was a general, greatly distinguished in command of Jourdan's right wing in 1795 and under Moreau in the following year, especially in his defence of Kehl. His fame was equal to that of Moreau and Bonaparte, but he fell under the spell of the latter, accompanying him to Egypt. When Bonaparte was away in Syria, Desaix conquered Upper Egypt, and behaved with such fairness to the native inhabitants that he was nicknamed 'the Just Sultan'. He signed the Convention of El Arish but was detained by Lord Keith for some months, and only returned home in time for the climax of the 1800 campaign. Detached from the army with two divisions, he used his initiative and marched to the sound of the gunfire, just in time to rescue Bonaparte at Marengo: with the Austrians victorious all along the line, Desaix remarked that although the battle was lost, 'There is yet time to win another', but was killed leading the decisive attack.

Desaix was admired universally by both friends and enemies for his brave and honest behaviour; even in Britain, the country of his bitterest enemies, he was described in 1804 as 'esteemed by the French soldiers, honoured by the Austrians, and loved by all who knew him'.[1] Napoleon later remarked that his talent was 'entirely the result of education and assiduity . . . he lived only for noble ambition and true glory: his character was formed on the true ancient model', and that such was his nobility that he would never have been a rival but 'would have been satisfied with secondary rank',

served in such capacity, and Davoût commanded the French army in the dying days of Napoleon's regime. After two years of disfavour and internal exile, he was reinstated by the Bourbons.

Davoût was unmilitary in appearance, bald, short-sighted and with strong spectacles, but his military talents were great though ill-used in the later campaigns. A stern disciplinarian, dour and with few gracious attributes, his reputation suffered by his stern behaviour as governor-general of the Duchy of Warsaw (from 1807) and governor of Hamburg, where he was known as 'the terrible Davoût' or 'the Hamburg Robespierre'; 'under the mask of an ally, his

*Louis Charles Antoine Desaix
(1768–1800). (Engraving by R.
G. Tietze after J. Guerin)*

and in 1782 joined the service of the Margrave of Anspach-Bayreuth, taking the name of Gneisenau from some lost family estates in Austria. He gained some experience in British pay during the American War of Independence, and in 1786 was granted a Prussian commission. Ten years of garrison duty provided ample time for the study of the theory of his profession; in 1806 he served in a staff capacity at Jena, but came to prominence over his gallant defence of Colberg in 1807. He was instrumental with Scharnhorst in reconstructing the Prussian army after the disaster of 1806, but the fall of Stein from French suspicion and pressure led to his retirement. After travels to Russia, Sweden and Britain he returned to Berlin to assume a leading role in the 'patriotic' movement, working openly and covertly, and upon the renewal of the war against France in 1813 he was appointed Blücher's chief of staff. This was perhaps the greatest partnership in the history of military command, for the two were perfect foils: Gneisenau the cool, calculating brain, and Blücher the fire and determination to carry out the plans they both formulated. The successful advance on Paris was largely Gneisenau's work, and it is possible to judge the relationship by Blücher's remark to Hardinge after Ligny, that 'Gneisenau has given way', hardly a normal comment from a general nominally in supreme command.

and that his death was 'the greatest loss he could possibly have sustained'.[2] (Napoleon might have thought differently in 1800 had Desaix survived, knowing that Marengo was saved by him!).

(He should not be confused with Joseph Marie Dessaix (1764–1834), the French general who formed the *Légion des Allobroges* in 1792, was one of the few members of the Council of Five Hundred to oppose the *coup d'état* of 18 Brumaire, and was greatly distinguished at Wagram.)

Notes

1. *Monthly Review*, London 1804, p. 541.
2. *Memoirs of the Life, Exile and Conversations of the Emperor*

Napoleon, Count de Las Cases, London 1836, I p. 148.

Reference

Martha-Beker, F. *Le Général L. C. A. Desaix*, Paris 1852.

Gneisenau, August Wilhelm Anton, Count Neithardt von (1760–1831)

Like many leading Prussian commanders, Gneisenau was not of Prussian birth, and indeed was correctly named Neithardt, the son of a Saxon officer, raised in poverty. After two years at Erfurt University he entered Austrian service,

August Wilhelm Anton Gneisenau (1760–1831), wearing the system of rank-marking by epaulettes introduced into the Prussian army from mid–1814. (Lithograph after F. Kruger)

In the Waterloo campaign, Gneisenau for some reason harboured the deepest mistrust of Wellington, and after Ligny (when due to Blücher's incapacity he was temporarily in command, more senior commanders having been passed over to allow the Blücher-Gneisenau partnership to continue), his inclination was to withdraw and leave Wellington to fight unaided; but fortunately for the Allied cause old Blücher insisted that his word to support Wellington be honoured, and the day was won. (Gneisenau's unwillingness to collaborate with Wellington has attracted some vituperative criticism from British authors: 'No intellectual eminence can exalt a nature so essentially low as this, a nature which, from sheer terror of that which is high, abases all others to its own vile and despicable level!'[1] Gneisenau conducted the pursuit after Waterloo with relentless energy, but soon retired from the service from ill-health and for political reasons. He returned in 1818 to become governor of Berlin, field marshal in 1825, and in 1831 was appointed to command the Army of Observation on the Polish frontier, with Clausewitz as chief of staff. Both were stricken by cholera, Gneisenau dying on 24 August and Clausewitz on 18 November. Conceivably the greatest Prussian general since Frederick, Gneisenau was revered by his subordinates but has not, perhaps, received his full due from his political masters or posterity.

Note

1. *History of the British Army*, Hon. Sir John Fortescue. London 1920, vol X, r/p as *The Campaign of Waterloo*, Elstree 1987, p. 134.

References

Das Leben des Feldmarschalls Grafen Neithardt von Gneisenau, first three volumes by G. H. Pertz, Berlin 1864–9, final two by G. Delbrück, 1879–80; *Das Leben des G. F. M. Grafen von Gneisenau*, H. Delbrück, Berlin, 1894.

Hill, Rowland, 1st Viscount (1772–1842).

Rowland Hill was Wellington's second in command in the later Peninsular War, probably the best subordinate commander in the British Army, without aspiring to the greatness of his chief. Born in Shropshire, one of sixteen children of Sir John Hill of Hawkstone and nephew of the famous preacher Revd. Rowland Hill (joint founder of the British and Foreign Bible Society and the London Missionary Society), Rowland Hill was commissioned in 1790 and studied at the Strasbourg military academy. He served with distinction at Toulon, commanded his 90th Foot in Egypt, and served as brigade and divisional commander in the early Peninsular War, surviving an absence with ill-health to be promoted to lieutenant-general, knighted in 1812, and receiving a barony in 1814. Of all Wellington's subordinates he was the most capable in independent command, though Wellington's influence probably prevented his development as a completely independent general. His abilities were proven on every Peninsular battlefield, especially at Arroyo dos Molinos (his own victory), Vittoria, Nivelle and Nive. He commanded the Allied I Corps in the Waterloo campaign, arriving just in time to lead Adam's brigade at the end of the battle. In 1825

Rowland, 1st Viscount Hill (1772–1842), wearing undress uniform of a lieutenant-general, including the Waterloo Medal on the left breast.

Wellington on his opponents:

'When Massena was opposed to me I could not eat, drink or sleep. I never knew what repose or respite from anxiety was. I was kept perpetually on the alert. But, when Soult was opposed to me, then I could eat, drink, sleep, and enjoy myself without fear of surprise. Not that but Soult was a great general. Soult was a wonderful man in his way. Soult would assemble a hundred thousand men at a certain point, on a certain day, but when he had got them there he did not know what in the world to do with them.'

(*Wellington Anecdotes*, anon., London n.d., pp. 36–7.)

The Napoleonic Wars produced a huge array of popular souvenirs, often of little artistic merit. The earthenware jug illustrated is an especially fine example of the genre, made

c.1812, depicting 'General Hill' on one side and Wellington on the other, the same figure used for both personalities and not resembling either one!

the only general to enjoy Wellington's complete trust, the ordinary soldiers worshipped him more for his kindness and assiduous attention to their welfare under all circumstances; known as 'the soldier's friend', their nickname 'Daddy Hill' speaks volumes.

Note

1. *The Wellington Memorial*, A. J. Griffiths, London 1897, p. 295.

References

Sidney, Revd. E. *The Life of Lord Hill*, London 1845.
Teffeteller, G. L. *The Surpriser*, Newark, New Jersey, 1983.

Kellermann, François Etienne (1770–1835).

François Kellermann was the son of Marshal François Christophe de Kellermann, Duc de Valmy, to which title François succeeded in 1820. Originally of Saxon descent, the Marshal was awarded his baton (1804) and dukedom (1808) long after his active career had ended, but his reputation was imperishable following his victory of Valmy which had saved the infant French republic. From 1797 he was employed in purely administrative duties, in which he had considerable skill. Probably his son François Etienne was more famous; he was commissioned at age 15 into the hussars of the *ancien régime*, and surviving a brief period of arrest with his father (because of aristocratic background), he served with great distinction as a cavalry commander in Italy, attracting Bonaparte's especial notice by his forcing of the Tagliamento. At Marengo he executed a cavalry charge which he always believed saved the battle, and was ever afterwards greatly aggrieved that he had not received the rewards he thought he was due. Though not the most famous, Kellermann was probably the most capable of all Napoleon's cavalry commanders, and no matter how much he was criticized Napoleon remarked, 'General, whenever your name is brought before me, I think of nothing but Marengo.' After fighting at Austerlitz he served with distinction in the Peninsular War, but though recalled for the Russian campaign ill-health prevented him from serving before 1813. Keeping his rank under the Bourbons, he rallied to Napoleon in 1815 and was notably distinguished at Quatre Bras and Waterloo, where he received the last of his several wounds. After the second restoration he served in purely administrative posts. The major criticism of Kellermann's career was his unbridled penchant for loot, which was infamous even in a society which accepted a degree of plunder as routine; in Spain he even held rich Spaniards to ransom, behaviour which blighted his name even among his adherents. De Gonneville described him as 'a little man, of unhealthy and insignificant appearance, with a clever look, but false'. After the restoration he assumed an attitude of piety and built a church near his house outside Paris; but 'It is very likely that both house and church were the result of exactions committed in Spain'![1]

Note

1. *Recollections of Colonel De Gonneville*, ed. C. M. Yonge, London 1875, I, pp. 250–1.

he was promoted to full general and was Commander-in-Chief from 1828 until 1842; he was created a viscount shortly before his death. Upon his death Wellington wrote to the nephew who succeeded him (Hill never married) that throughout his long career 'nothing ever occurred to interrupt for one moment the friendly and intimate relations which subsisted between us'.[1] But though he was perhaps

Of the spendthrift Eugène d'Hautefeuille, who was separated from his wife and though only a *sous-lieutenant* was of so haughty a bearing that he acknowledged no-one as his superior:

'Otherwise, he was amiable, of a joyous temper, and sometimes quite charming. General Laroche said to him one day before a battle: "Take care of yourself, for if your wife were a widow I would marry her."

He answered, "I should be very glad, General, if that could be managed without my being killed!" '

(*Recollections of Colonel de Gonneville*, ed. C. M. Yonge, London 1875, I. p. 173.)

François Etienne Kellermann (1770–1835), wearing French staff uniform including the heavily embroidered dress coat.

Mikhail Larionovich Golenishcev-Kutuzov (1745–1813), disciple of Suvarov and the leading Russian commander of the Napoleonic Wars.

Kutuzov, Mikhail Larionovich Golenishcev-Kutuzov, Prince of Smolensk (1745–1813).

Mikhail Kutuzov was Russia's greatest soldier of the era, yet a figure often misrepresented and not given his due in his time. Born at St. Petersburg on 16 September 1745, son of a military engineer, he entered a military career at age 12 as an engineering cadet, and rapidly showed his intelligence; most unusually for a Russian officer he was both well-educated and proficient: he could speak French, German, Polish, Swedish, English, Turkish and some Latin in addition to his native tongue. He saw much active service in Poland (1764–

9), in the Crimea (1770–4) against the Turks (where he was shot though the head and lost an eye), and in the Turkish war he won great renown and benefited from the experience of serving under the great Suvarov, whose heir in some respects he became. He was then employed in a variety of important diplomatic and administrative duties (including as ambassador to Turkey and Prussia) and led the Russian forces in the 1805 campaign. Kutuzov attempted to prevent the Austrians from fighting at Austerlitz, but could not exercise supreme command due to the presence of the Tsar; yet he was able to extricate the Russian survivors despite being wounded in the battle. Never popular with the Tsar, between 1806 and 1811 he was sidelined as governor-general of Lithuania and Kiev, but restored to command in 1811 against the Turks on the Danube, where he again enjoyed great success. The dire events of 1812 compelled his recall as commander-in-chief of the Russian forces in succession to Barclay de Tolly, and despite allowing Moscow to be captured, Kutuzov husbanded the Russian forces and repeatedly thwarted Napoleon's plans. He was criticized for his lethargy in following the retreating *Grande Armée*, but his strategy was correct: he allowed the retreat to decimate Napoleon's army at little cost to the Russians, and planned to trap them at the Berezina, which only just failed to destroy Napoleon completely.

He was created Prince of Smolensk for his success, but ill and ageing, he was removed from command by the Tsar, who had appointed him only with the greatest reluctance. He died shortly after, at Bunzlau in Silesia, on 28 April 1813. Latterly of considerable bulk and over-fond of alcohol and young women, Kutuzov has suffered most from a reputation for lethargy; the British observer Sir Robert Wilson, one of his most fierce critics, noted that 'he died most opportunely for his fame',[1] which is very unfair. Though Kutuzov went to sleep in the council of war after his advice before Austerlitz had been ignored, commanded latterly from his *droshky* and at Borodino remained at the rear and gave few orders, he was a very capable general with the facility for inspiring the ordinary Russian soldier, and like his old master Suvarov, he put effectiveness in combat and the soldier's well-being before appearance of the machine-like minutiae of drill. His was the most important role in the defeat of Napoleon in 1812 and deserved more recognition than was received.

Note

1. *Private Diaries of Travels . . .*, Sir Robert Wilson, ed. Revd. H. Randolph, London 1861, I, p. 356.

Mikhailovsky-Danilevski (St. Petersburg 1850) was issued in a French translation by A. Fizelier in Paris in the same year, but the standard English-language source is *The Fox of the North*, R. Parkinson, London 1976.

References

The Russian biography by

Lannes, Jean (1769–1809)

Of all the marshals, probably none was so esteemed by Napoleon as Jean Lannes, a blunt and outspoken son of a livery-stable keeper. Despite a poor education, Lannes was a strong and adept sportsman, which led to his election as sergeant-major of the Gers volunteer battalion, rising to *chef de battaillon* by his gallantry in the early campaigns. Dismissed for political reasons in 1795, he re-enlisted as a private and again rose by merit, greatly distinguished and much-wounded in Italy, where he became Bonaparte's closest friend and confidant (the only one allowed to address Napoleon as '*tu*'). After service with the Army of the Orient he returned to France and played an important role in the *coup d'état* of 18 Brumaire, and was rewarded by commandancy of the Consular Guard. Commanding the advance-guard in 1800, he won the victory of Montebello

'BUONAPARTE has lately sent medals of French honour to some of the French prisoners in Pennicuick, near Edinburgh; and to others, mere privates, he has transmitted commissions in the French service. As a proof of French rapacity and ingenuity, these prisoners have taught a crow to steal. They set him off from the prison-yard when they hear that clothes are drying in a field contiguous to the prison of Pennicuick, and the creature picks up caps, cloths or other articles, with which it faithfully flies back to the prison! This mode of thieving by proxy has only lately been discovered.'
(*The Times*, 7 January 1814.)

Jean Lannes (1769–1809): an early portrait in regimental uniform. (Engraving by G. Kruell after J. B. P. Guerin)

Lannes at Ratisbon: to inspire the French to the escalade of the city, Lannes seized a ladder and threatened to lead the attack in person (his staff prevented it!). (Print after A. Paris)

(from where he took the title of his dukedom, awarded in 1808), and played a crucial role at Marengo. He commanded his Corps with distinction at Austerlitz, and in the following year won the battle of Saalfeld and was further distinguished at Jena. He served with equal distinction in 1807 and in Spain in 1808–9, when Napoleon summoned him to the German front, leading the storm of Ratisbon (and threatening to be first up the scaling-ladders!). Ever assigned to the most critical position, at Essling he commanded the French defence of the town with his customary courage, but was mortally wounded by a roundshot which smashed both legs, of which the right was amputated; he died nine days later. As Napoleon regarded him as a true friend, he was devastated by Lannes' death and wept in public. Lannes was the ideal battlefield subordinate, capable enough to carry out Napoleon's plans without supervision, and a man of exceptional courage. Napoleon remarked that 'I found him a dwarf, but I lost him a giant',[1] and as a friend he was never replaced.

Note
1. *Memoirs of the Life, Exile, and Conversations of the Emperor Napoleon*, Count de Las Cases, London 1836, I p. 251.

References
Lannes, C. L. *Le maréchal Lannes,*

duc de Montebello, Tours 1900. Thoumas, C. *Maréchal Lannes*, Paris 1891 (the standard biography). Wilette, L. *Le maréchal Lannes, un d'Artagnan sous l'Empire*, Paris 1979.

La Romana, Pedro Caro y Sureda, Marquis of 1761–1811
General La Romana was probably the best of the Spanish commanders during the Napoleonic Wars. He served against France in 1793–5, but was appointed to command the Spanish division 'lent' to Napoleon in 1807, serving in Denmark and northern Germany. He was instrumental in arranging for the defection of these units, escaping from Denmark in British ships (thanks to the efforts of the remarkable British intelligence agent, James Robertson, alias 'Brother Gallus'), and served in the Peninsular War. He was appointed a member of the Seville *junta* and in 1810 became commander of the Spanish army which collaborated with Wellington. Some were critical of his abilities: 'Romana therefore has about 25,000 Men, if he knows how to make use of them – which I doubt – certainly he is wild and fantastic in all his measures, and as far as one can judge from his previous conduct, by no means an able soldier'.[1] He was, however, devoted to his country and unlike some Spanish generals determined to fight. Boutflower repeated the general impression: 'He speaks, I am told, with great confidence of the ultimate triumph of Spain over her oppressors. He is most devoted to his Country, and I really believe determined not to survive the extinction of her liberty. His appearance proves that a very great soul does sometimes inhabit a very mean body.'[2] (*The Times* correspondent, Henry Crabb Robinson, thought that La Romana more resembled a Spanish barber than a general!). Sadly, he died unexpectedly on 23 January 1811 ('he was seized with spasms in his stomach & almost immediately

expired'); 'his death adds another to the many instances of the awful uncertainty of Human Life . . . His zeal in his cause was unquestionable, but his Talents were considerably below par'.[3] He was played to his rest by the 79th Highlanders who struck up *To the land of the leal*; an appropriate tune for this champion of Spanish liberty.

Notes
1. *The Peninsular Journal of Major-General Sir Benjamin D'Urban 1808–17*, ed. I. J. Rousseau, London 1930, p. 92.
2. *The Journal of an Army Surgeon during the Peninsular War*, C. Boutflower, privately published, n.d., p. 50.
3. ibid. p. 74.

'Saturday a detachment of American prisoners arrived at Taunton on their route to the depot at Dartmoor. In the middle of the night they contrived to make their escape, by taking up the flooring of a room in which they were confined in the Old Angel Inn, and digging down to the foundation of the place. Twenty-seven succeeded in getting out, of whom eleven only have been retaken.'
(*The Times*, 1 July 1814.)

Mack, Karl, Freiherr von Leiberich (1752–1828)
A commoner ennobled for bravery, Karl Mack von Leiberich was appointed chief of staff of the Austrian army after distinguished service against the Turks. He proposed the 'plan of annihilation' of the First Coalition against republican France, which failed. Appointed commander-in-chief of the Neapolitan army in 1797, he captured Rome in November 1798 but fled from his mutinous troops, was captured by the French, yet escaped in 1800. His army re-organizations imposed upon the Austrian forces immediately before the 1805 campaign caused only confusion, and in command of the Danube theatre in 1805 he was totally out-manoeuvred by Napoleon and after a somewhat half-hearted resistance surrendered at Ulm. For this he was condemned to death, but instead was imprisoned and ultimately pardoned, but never again held command. Though it appears harsh, there was some foundation for Horatio Nelson's opinions: 'let not General Mack be employed; for I knew him at Naples to be a rascal, a scoundrel, and a coward'.[1]

Note
1. *The Life and Services of Horatio, Viscount Nelson, from his Lordship's Manuscripts*, J. Stanier Clarke and J. McArthur, London 1809; 1840 edn, III, p. 117.

Marmont, Auguste Frédéric Louis Viesse de (1774–1852)
Auguste Marmont was the offspring of minor nobility from Châtillon-sur-Seine, and from an early age was educated in the scientific disciplines of military theory, principally artillery. This education was similar to Bonaparte's, so it was

appropriate that he was appointed Bonaparte's ADC for the Italian and Egyptian campaigns, and became a close friend. After assisting in the *coup d'état* of 18 Brumaire he managed the artillery with such distinction at Marengo that he was immediately promoted to *général de brigade*, but was greatly disappointed in not being one of the first marshals (he received his baton only in 1809), which seems to have been the origin of his dissatisfaction at the way he was treated throughout his career. For five years governor of Dalmatia (from where he took his title, Duke of Ragusa), his regime was greatly beneficial to those in his charge. Appointed as Massena's replacement in command of the Army of Portugal in 1811, he was defeated decisively at Salamanca, where he was wounded so severely by a shell that he was scarcely fit for the command he was given in 1813, when he fought throughout the German campaign. In 1814 he was routed at

Laon and earned Napoleon's wrath, but it was nothing compared to the emperor's rage when Marmont concluded a secret convention with the Allies and surrendered his Corps on 5 April, an act of betrayal which completely overthrew Napoleon's plans; 'Marmont delivered the last blow,' as Napoleon remarked. It was never forgiven by the French nation, and was the origin of a verb used at the time, *raguser*, to betray, from his title.

In 1815 Marmont remained a royalist, but was exiled from France with the king at the 1830 revolution. He spent his remaining years wandering Europe, an embittered man, writing his memoirs (which are a personal defence rather than an unbiased account of his life); oddly, in Vienna he was appointed tutor of the Duke of Reichstadt, Napoleon's son and himself briefly styled Napoleon II. A commander of considerable ability, Marmont's reputation has been

Auguste Frédéric Louis Viesse de Marmont (1774–1852), in the uniform of a Marshal of France, wearing the cross and breast-star of the Légion d'honneur. *(Engraving by T. Johnson after J. B. P. Guerin)*

sublimated to his betrayal of Napoleon. He possessed one of the most illegible hands of the period; when in 1815 he wrote his own orders (fearing a spy in his staff), it was said that the Duke of Mortmart (commanding the royal rearguard) spent all night trying to decipher the route, and was captured before he could unravel Marmont's left-hand calligraphy!

References

Marmont's *Mémoires* were published posthumously in 8 volumes from 1856 (Paris); the modern biography is *Le maréchal Marmont, Duc de Raguse*, R. Christophe, Paris 1968.

Massena, André (1758–1817).

André Massena was one of Napoleon's most able subordinates. Son of a small wine merchant (perhaps of Jewish origin), he went to sea as a cabin-boy until joining the army and rising to the rank of sergeant-major. Leaving the army in 1789 he pursued the trades of fruit-seller and smuggler until his previous military service led to his election as lieutenant-colonel of the 3rd Var Volunteers in 1792. By December of the following year he was *général de division*, and played a leading role under Bonaparte's command in Italy. He took command of the French forces in Switzerland in 1799 (his victory at Zürich proving his ability in independent command), and in early 1800 took over the Army of Italy, defending Genoa amid appalling privations before being compelled to surrender. After being dismissed temporarily from his command for unbridled looting (which dogged his career), he resumed his service in Italy in the 1805 war against Austria, having been appointed a marshal in the first creations of 1804. Having thoroughly looted Naples, he served in Poland in 1807 and in the following year gained a title – Duc de Rivoli, commemorating his services at that battle (1797) – and lost an eye when Napoleon shot him while hunting (typically, poor Berthier was blamed). In 1809 he served with great distinction against Austria, at Aspern-Essling and Wagram, and in January 1810 was created Prince of Essling. The remainder of his active military career was less successful, being sent to the Peninsula to command

André Massena (1758–1817), one of the most able of all Napoleon's marshals. (Engraving by R. G. Tietze after Gros)

Sir John Moore (1761–1809), wearing the 'unlaced' (i.e., service-dress) version of the staff uniform, with buttons in threes, identifying the rank of lieutenant-general. (Engraving by C. Turner after Sir Thomas Lawrence)

the 'Army of Portugal', in which post he was foiled repeatedly by Wellington. (Some of his misfortunes were self-inflicted: apparently he made no attempt to check the reconnaissance at Busaco, being diverted instead by Henriette Leberton, his mistress, who accompanied his HQ disguised as an officer!) Following these defeats Massena was recalled to France and saw no further truly active employment, but was briefly commander of the Paris National Guard in 1815. He refused to sit on the panel which tried Ney, and died in disfavour with the Bourbons on 4 April 1817.

Normally morose, indolent and with an insatiable desire for loot and women, Massena only truly came alive in the presence of the enemy, when his military skill was considerable and his presence inspirational. Recklessly brave (he commanded at Wagram from a carriage when too ill to ride), Lejeune's description at him at Aspern is memorable: 'Throughout this awful struggle Massena stood beneath the great elms on the green opposite the church,

calmly indifferent to the fall of the branches brought down upon his head by the showers of grape-shot and bullets, keenly alive to all that was going on, his look and voice, stern as the *quos ego* of Virgil's angry Neptune, inspiring all who surrounded him with irresistible strength.'[1]

Note
1. *Memoirs of Baron Lejeune*, trans. Nancy Bell, London 1897, I. p. 271.

References
The best biography in English is *Massena*, Sir James Marshall-Cornwall, Oxford 1965; Massena's *Mémoires* were published in Paris, 1848–50.

Moore, Sir John (1761–1809)

Sir John Moore is, after Wellington, the most famous British soldier of the age; yet his career was largely unfulfilled as he died at the end of a successful battle which climaxed a disastrous retreat. The son of a Scottish doctor of high connections, Moore was commissioned in the British army at age 15, having declined the offer of a commission from the Emperor Joseph II; he served in the American war and after sitting as Member of Parliament for Peebles, Lanark, Linlithgow and Selkirk (he was a Whig, which hindered his military advancement under a Tory administration) he purchased command of the 51st Regiment in 1790. Moore led his regiment in the operations on Corsica in 1794, but after a blazing row with the island's viceroy, Sir Gilbert Elliot, he was sent home in disgrace. Promoted to brigadier-general, he survived fever in the West Indies, and as major-general served in Holland in 1799, where he was shot through the head, miraculously with no ill-effects. Abercromby's most valuable subordinate in Egypt, he was again wounded and returned home to command Shorncliffe camp, where he instituted the system of light infantry training which produced the superb Light Division of the Peninsular War; often regarded as the father of British light infantry tactics, Moore was rather a developer and resurrector of previous systems than totally an innovator, but his effect was none the less profound. It was as a leader and trainer of men that Moore was most inspirational, those under his command regarding him with respect verging upon idolatry.

'Lieut. Gen. Prescott's Orders. St. Pierres, 16th June 1794.

'Whereas, Vice-Admiral Sir John Jervis has given orders, I am told, frequently, here on shore, and particularly, by a note dated off Point Petre, June 11th, 1794, which must have arisen from great ignorance, or great presumption and arrogance.

'If from ignorance, poor man! he is to be pitied; but if from presumption and arrogance, he is to be checked.

'It is therefore Lieut. Gen. Prescott's orders, that in future no attention whatever is to be given to such Notes, or Orders, and his signature to such, is to be as little regarded, as that of John Oakes, or Peter Styles.'
(*United Service Journal*, London 1831, II, p. 338.)

A lieutenant-general from 1805, Moore was employed on the abortive expedition to support Sweden, where his quarrel with the mad Swedish king wrecked the operation, and was then appointed to command the British forces in the Peninsula following the recall of Wellesley and his superiors after the débâcle of Cintra. Let down appallingly by his Spanish allies, Moore's advance against enormous odds may well have diverted the French from administering the *coup de grâce* against the Spanish, but in doing so it almost destroyed his army; yet the spirit was such that at the end of this most appalling retreat, the army turned at bay at Corunna and inflicted a heavy defeat on Soult. Terribly wounded by a roundshot in the left shoulder, Moore died during the night. He was buried on the ramparts at Corunna:

'We carved not a line, and we raised not a stone –
But we left him alone with his glory.'

in Wolfe's immortal verse; yet despite attempts by his political opponents to blacken his name, the general impression was that left by George Napier: 'In Sir John Moore's character we have a model for everything that marks the obedient soldier, the persevering, firm, and skilful general; the inflexible and real patriot who sacrificed all personal feeling to his country's weal; the truly virtuous and honourable man; the high-minded, finished, and accomplished gentleman.'[1] His reputation was perhaps best summarized by Wellington, who in later life admitted it likely that Britain would not have won the Peninsular War without him.

Note
1. *Passages in a the Early Military Life of General Sir George T. Napier*, W. C. E. Napier, London 1884, pp. 77–8.

References
Brownrigg, B. *The Life and Letters of Sir John Moore*, London 1921.
Maurice, Sir J. F. *The Diary of Sir John Moore*, London 1904.
Oman, Carola. *Sir John Moore*, London 1953.
Parkinson, R. *Moore of Corunna*, London 1976.

Moreau, Jean Victor Marie (1763–1813)

Jean Moreau was one of the most able French generals of his era. Trained in the family profession of law, he always longed for a military career and at the outbreak of the Revolutionary Wars was elected lieutenant-colonel of the volunteers of Ille-et-Vilaine. His abilities resulted in promotion to *général de division* in early 1794, Carnot recognizing his talents. He succeeded Pichegru as commander of the Army of the North, and in 1796 led the Army of the Rhine and Moselle. He attempted to conceal the treacherous correspondence between Pichegru and the Prince de Condé (having earlier committed himself in Pichegru's defence), and announced his discovery too late to save himself from implication in the plot. Dismissed from command, he was brought back in desperation as commander of the Army of Italy. Dissatisfied with the Directory, he supported Bonaparte's *coup d'état*, receiving in return command of the Army of the Rhine, where his conduct at Hohenlinden won renewed fame. His marriage to the Creole Mademoiselle Hullot (a member of Josephine's circle) compounded his poor political skill, and

Jean Victor Marie Moreau (1763–1813), in the uniform of a general of the Revolutionary Wars. (Engraving by H. B. Hall after J. B. P. Guerin)

under her influence the 'club Moreau' of those disenchanted with Bonaparte led to royalist intrigue. Moreau himself was a sincere republican (despite the fact that his father had been guillotined during 'The Terror') and had no royalist sympathies, but regarded himself as poorly treated and was not averse to the idea of becoming military dictator to restore pure republican government. Recognizing the rivalry, Bonaparte banished him and from 1804 to 1813 Moreau lived in exile in New Jersey.

Thanks to Bernadotte's influence he was induced to return to Europe as the Tsar's military adviser (probably still hoping to be appointed republican dictator of France in place of Napoleon's empire), but he was mortally wounded at the Tsar's side at Dresden and died five days later, on 2 September; he was buried at St. Petersburg and his wife received a Russian pension. It has been said that if Bonaparte had not been Bonaparte, then Moreau would have been; but though he was a brilliant general, his political skill was small and he was manipulated by his over-ambitious wife. His final words, 'Rest easy, gentlemen, it's my destiny', seem to epitomize his career, so brilliant yet so unfulfilled, and ending in opposition to the country he loved.

References

Jochmus, C. *General Moreau – Abriss einer Geschichte seines Lebens und seiner Feldzüge,*

Berlin 1814.
Philippart, Sir John. *Memoirs of General Moreau,* London 1814.

Mortier, Edouard Adolphe Casimir Joseph (1768–1835)
Born the son of a cloth merchant at le Cateau-Cambrésis, Edouard Mortier was the only one of Napoleon's marshals who was half-English. He entered the army as *sous-lieutenant* in 1791, serving on the Meuse and Rhine, and by 1799 had risen to *général de divison* after distinguished service in Switzerland. His conduct in the occupation of Hanover in 1803 led to his appointment as marshal in 1804, and to the

On Waterloo:
'The usual salutation on meeting an acquaintance of another regiment after an action was to ask who had been hit? but on this occasion it was "Who's alive?" Meeting one, next morning, a very little fellow, I asked what had happened to them yesterday? "I'll be hanged", says he, "if I know anything at all about the matter, for I was all day trodden in the mud and galloped over by every scoundrel who had a horse; and, in short, that I only owe my existence to my insignificance." '
(*Random Shots from a Rifleman*, Sir John Kincaid, London 1835; Maclaren's combined edn. with *Adventures in the Rifle Brigade*, London 1908, p. 173.)

colonel-generalcy of the Artillery and Seamen of the Consular Guard; in 1805 he was given command of the infantry of the Guard. In the Ulm campaign he won great distinction at Durrenstein, and took over Lannes' Corps

Edouard Adolphe Casimir Joseph Mortier (1748–1835), as commandant of the Artillery and Seamen of the Imperial Guard. (Engraving by Lacoste after Demoraine)

after Austerlitz; he commanded Napoleon's left at Friedland and in 1808 was ennobled as Duc de Trévise. In the Peninsula from 1808 to 1811, he won the victory of Ocaña under Soult's overall command, where he was wounded. In 1812 he commanded the Young Guard, was made governor of Moscow, and continued to command the 'Young' in 1813, and the Old Guard in 1814, where he exhibited great skills in command of rearguards and detachments. In 1815 he escorted Louis XVIII to the frontier but then joined Napoleon, though fell ill after being allocated a high command. His inactivity in the Waterloo campaign hastened his rehabilitation by the Bourbons; he was re-admitted to the Chamber of Peers in 1819, in 1830–1 was French ambassador to the Tsar, and in 1834–5 minister of war and president of the council of ministers. On 28 July 1835, accompanying Louis Philippe at a review of the National Guard, Mortier was one of twelve persons killed by a bomb thrown at the king by the assassin Fieschi.

Reference

Moreel, I.. *Le Maréchal Mortier,
    duc de Trévise*, Paris 1958.

Murat, Joachim (1767–1815)

Murat was the most colourful character of the Napoleonic age, and one of the most inspirational of cavalry leaders, though patently unfitted for the high offices he held. The son of an innkeeper at la Bastide-Fortunière, he was intended for the church but to escape his creditors he ran away to the army, from which he was dismissed for idleness in 1790. After re-enlisting in Louis XVI's ephemeral Constitutional Guard, he was appointed *sous-lieutenant* in the 21st Chasseurs, where he gained a reputation for swagger and the vehemence of his revolutionary sentiments. Despite good service in the Army of the North he was almost purged for his extreme Jacobin beliefs, but made the acquaintance of Bonaparte and from a position of the latter's aide rose to the rank of general in Italy, where his reputation as a madcap cavalry commander was made, and confirmed in Egypt, especially at Aboukir, where he was severely wounded. He played a leading role in the *coup d'état* of 18 Brumaire, and his close alliance with the Bonapartist faction was confirmed by his marriage to Napoleon's sister Caroline on 20 January 1800. He commanded the cavalry at Marengo, in January 1804 was made governor of Paris (appointing the commission which tried and judicially murdered the Duc d'Enghien), was created a marshal in May 1804 and in the following February was appointed both a prince and the Grand Admiral of France. After Austerlitz, Napoleon rewarded him with the grand-duchy of Berg (15 March 1806); he commanded the cavalry at Jena, Eylau and Friedland, and in 1808 was given overall command of the French armies in Spain. The apogee of his career came on 1 August 1808 when he was created King of Naples in succession to Joseph Bonaparte.

The throne of Naples turned his head; taking his royal status too seriously, he came into conflict with Napoleon (even blaming him for the failure of the attack on Sicily in

*Joachim Murat, King of Naples
and Grand-Duke of Berg
(1767–1815). (Engraving by
H. Wolf after Gérard)*

1810, Murat's own responsibility), and a complete breach was only averted by the Russian campaign, for which Napoleon offered him overall command of the cavalry. His conduct was not impressive (he had little strategic aptitude, and while the ideal *beau sabreur* for leading a charge was unskilled for any higher responsibility); he was as popular with the Cossacks as with his own troopers for his flamboyance and courage, but when Napoleon gave him command of the *Grande Armée* he returned to Naples, fearing that Napoleon and even his wife were plotting to dethrone him. (Davoût once remarked that he was king of Naples only by 'grace of the Emperor and the blood of Frenchmen'; to which Murat replied that he was king in the same way that the Emperor of Austria was emperor, and thus would do what he liked.) Despite negotiating in secret with Austria and Britain (to be confirmed as king of Naples if he changed sides), Murat fought with Napoleon in 1813 until after Leipzig, when he went home. Under Austrian guarantees of his kingdom, he changed sides and engaged the French in early 1814, but when it became obvious that neither Britain nor Austria had any intention of letting him keep Naples he began to plan an Italian national resistance to clear Italy of foreigners. Murat was defeated by the Austrians at Tolentino on 2 May 1815 and fled to France to regain

Napoleon's favour; this was rejected scornfully and eventually Murat landed with a small force in Calabria to attempt to regain his throne. He was arrested immediately, tried under his own law for disturbing the peace and was shot five days later, on 13 October 1815.

Whatever his merits as king (he had many, especially in his desire to improve the lot of his subjects), it is as the most handsome and dashing cavalryman of his or perhaps any age that he is remembered. A man of great vanity and less brains, his greatest delight was in devising outrageous uniforms for himself, so that the public called him 'King Franconi' (director of a Paris theatre), and even Napoleon admitted that he had 'the appearance of a quick operator or a mountebank', yet thought that 'The fault is originally mine. There were several men whom I had made too great; I had raised them above the sphere of their intelligence.'[1] Despite or perhaps because of that, Murat was idolized by his troopers to the end, in whose eyes 'the golden eagle' could do no wrong.

Note

1. *Memoirs of the Life, Exile, and Conversations of the Emperor Napoleon*, Count de Las Cases, London 1836, II, pp. 394–6.

References

Of the many biographical works concerning Murat, those in English include *Interesting Facts Relating to the Fall and Death of Joachim Murat*, F. Macerone, London 1817, and the more modern biography *Marshal Murat*, A. H. Atteridge; worthy of note are *Joachim Murat, seine letzten Kämpfe und sein Ende*, Helfert, Vienna 1878; Chevenon and St.-Yves' *Joachim Murat*, Paris 1905; and the most modern biography, *Murat – Cavalier, Maréchal de France, Prince et Roi*, M. Dupont, Paris 1980.

'. . . a conversation between Napoleon I and Count Flahaut, who was his companion in his flight from Waterloo to Charleroi. Count Flahaut, who was on terms of personal intimacy with the Emperor and his family, said to him, "Is not your Majesty surprised?" [i.e., at the outcome of Waterloo]. Napoleon replied, "No, it has been the same thing since Crecy."'

(*Words on Wellington*, Sir William Fraser Bt., London 1902 edn. p. 250 (orig. pub. 1889).)

Napoleon Bonaparte (1769–1821)

It is usual to regard Napoleon as one of the 'great captains' of history, but to classify him simply as a great general is to overlook the fact that his military skill was far from being his sole talent. Indeed, though he enjoyed an advantage of owing no political master (at least after his elevation to First Consul), his achievements when regarded in the wider context elevate him to a plane higher than that reserved for great commanders. In the breadth of his achievements and his effect upon his own and succeeding ages, he probably deserves a niche at the very pinnacle, alongside Alexander. The fact that one of the most tumultuous eras of history bears his name is confirmation of his unique position.

Napoleone Buonaparte was born on 15 August 1769 at Ajaccio, Corsica, the second son of a lawyer of minor aristocratic connections and little fortune. This in itself sets Napoleon apart from many of his rivals, for the majority of the other 'great captains' enjoyed advantages of birth or wealth in addition to their own skills; whatever Napoleon achieved was accomplished by his own talents, an eye for opportunity and a slice of luck, though the existence of the latter does not denigrate his talents; as he admitted himself, luck was crucial in reaching the very top, and when discussing the merits of a general, he would always ask, 'But is he *lucky*?'

The events of Napoleon's career have been recounted and dissected in innumerable works, so the briefest outline is appropriate here. His military education began at the school at Brienne, and in 1784 at the Military School in Paris, from where he was commissioned into the artillery. The service into which he entered was not determined simply because of a recognized aptitude in mathematics and science, but equally because it was the service which accepted most impoverished gentry and middle-class; the cavalry and to a lesser extent the infantry were the provinces of the aristocracy. He continued to study and in 1793, when the upheaval of the Revolution gave opportunities to those who under the *ancien régime* might have languished for their entire career as subalterns or enlisted men, he came to notice by his successful planning of the recapture of Toulon in his capacity as Dugommier's artillery chief, though only a captain of 24 years of age. In a fashion characteristic of the early revolutionary period, his progress was interrupted by the coups and counter-coups, and even led to his arrest (during which period he continued to study), until his scattering of a royalist mob with his celebrated 'whiff of grapeshot' in Paris, in defence of the Convention, restored his fortunes. With the support of Barras and the Directory, despite his youth and comparative lack of campaign experience, he was appointed to command the 'Army of Italy', having married Barras's ex-mistress, Josephine de Beauharnais, six years his senior, probably the greatest passion of his life but one not reciprocated to the same degree.

Command of the Army of Italy established his reputation as among the leading generals of his age; his achievements were prodigious, transforming a verminous, starving and demoralized army into one which routed the Austrians so completely that he was able to conclude the Peace of Campo Formio virtually without reference to the Directory. So high was his reputation that the Directory feared his growing fame and his standing with the army, so his expedition to Egypt was sanctioned partly on strategic grounds (to menace Britain's commerce with the Middle East and India) and partly to remove him to a theatre where he could pose no direct threat to the Directory itself. Despite the eventual failure of the expedition, and Bonaparte's abandoning of it in mid-campaign, his reputation and influence remained so high that upon the fall of the corrupt and ineffective Directory, Bonaparte was appointed one of three Consuls of the new regime by the coup of Brumaire (November 1799). The political schemers behind the Consulate probably intended to use him simply as a figurehead to gain popular support, but his considerable political skill, not to say low cunning and ruthlessness, soon established him as First Consul and, in effect, master of France; it was by any standards a quite astonishing rise from total obscurity in less than five years.

Bonaparte's position was confirmed by the victory of Marengo and the peace which followed, though here again luck played a considerable part, for it might be said that Marengo was turned from a Napoleonic defeat to a victory not by his own skill but by the fortunate invervention of Desaix, whose death in battle prevented any popular adverse comparison with the First Consul. From here it was but a short step to his proclamation (with overwhelming popular support) as First Consul for Life, and then Emperor of the French, as Napoleon I (2 December 1804). The attainment of this position confirmed that Napoleon had political skills equalling his military abilities: Moreau presents a sharp contrast, for at one time his military reputation made him a rival for Napoleon's popularity, but his political intelligence was flawed. In his internal policies, Napoleon reformed totally both the administration and the economy of France, including his most enduring achievement, the *Code Napoléon*. By removing the spectre of further internal turmoil, by bringing peace to Europe for the first time in a decade, and by restoring France's pride and prosperity, had the Peace of Amiens endured he might still be regarded as the saviour of his country; but his own ambitions and the threat which he presented – or was believed to present – to his enemies, made peace impossible.

At first Napoleon enjoyed spectacular success; indeed, his army probably reached its peak in 1805, and the manoeuvre of Ulm and the victory of Austerlitz were probably his greatest military achievements, scarcely surpassed by anything in military history. The construction of a satellite confederation of German states and the humiliating defeat of Prussia in 1806 confirmed his position of pre-eminence; but even after Russia made peace on Napoleon's terms at Tilsit, his most implacable enemy, Britain, remained unpacified. His attempt to ruin British trade by the 'Continental System' resulted instead in the beginning of his own downfall, for though he again defeated Austria in 1809, in the course of it he received his first serious military reverse, and the attempt to establish Spain as a Bonapartist satellite created a 'running sore' which continued to bleed the Empire of its resources to the last. The first signs of the decline of his own powers, and the collapse of the Empire, were evident even before Napoleon undertook the catastrophic Russian campaign of 1812.

From then, his fortune progressed downhill. Not only was his *Grande Armée* destroyed in Russia, but the 'war of liberation' overturned his barrier of satellite states, so that France itself became the focus for the next campaign. After battles in which Napoleon's powers had appeared to be deserting him, he commanded with renewed vigour in the defence of France in 1814, but the odds against him were overpowering, and his abdication was forced on 6 April after

Josephine de Beauharnais, born Marie Rose Josephine Tascher de la Pagerie (1763–1814), Napoleon's first empress and probably his only true love. (Engraving by H. Wolf after F. Gérard)

Napoleon I, Emperor of the French, in typical campaign uniform of the later period, the redingote grise *over the uniform of the* Chasseurs à Cheval *of the Imperial Guard; and a troubled expression suitable to the campaigns of 1813–15. (Engraving by J. François after P. Delaroche)*

even the marshals turned against him. After chafing with boredom in his new 'kingdom' of Elba, Napoleon made a last attempt to re-establish his old power, and though much of France rallied to him, the combined Allies were determined upon his final defeat; in the event only their forces already present in the Netherlands were required, Wellington's Anglo-Netherlandish and Blücher's Prussians. Napoleon's second abdication was followed by his exile on the inhospitable rock of St. Helena, where he lived for the remaining six years of his life in bitter contemplation of what might have been. He died on 5 May 1821, a sad relic of the days when almost the whole of Europe trembled at his tread.

It is difficult to express in a few paragraphs the reasons for Napoleon's military success, for he was not an innovator in

the sense that some commanders established or developed a totally new system of tactics, but rather one who developed and built upon a system already in vogue. Lazare Carnot was responsible to a considerable degree for the methods in which the French army conducted its 'minor tactics', though the principles of earlier theorists were also utilized. Rather, Napoleon honed these to perfection and put them into practice with a vigour which far outstripped that of his opponents, and to perform his almost *Blitzkrieg* manoeuvres he required an army of the highest calibre. He achieved that by his organization and reformation of its system of operation (some of which he inherited: the practice of 'living off the land', for example, was already well-established before Napoleon); and by channelling the patriotic fervour which arose in the early years of the Revolutionary Wars into a cult of his own person. Napoleon was blessed with a number of capable subordinates who could perform his commands with a will (despite the counter-productive rivalry which existed between his subordinates and which Napoleon actually fostered); yet none was sufficiently talented or energetic to be allowed complete freedom of action. This, perhaps, is where the Empire's greatest weakness lay: while its Emperor may have been a military genius of the first order, he was but one man and could only command in person at one place at a time: with the Empire at war on more than one 'front' at a time, only one could benefit from his presence. It was simply too large to be controlled by one general, even one as great as Napoleon and who enjoyed the advantage not only of carrying out the policies of the state but of setting those policies himself.

In the wider context of strategy, one characteristic appears in almost all Napoleon's campaigns: the ability to contend with more than one enemy force at once, and to defeat much larger opponents by interposing his own army between the component parts of their forces, holding one enemy wing with a minority of his force and falling upon the other wing with the bulk of his army, thus achieving numerical 'local superiority' and defeating the enemy in detail. The existence of French *corps d'armée* capable of sustaining an action independent of support, and the rapid speed of manoeuvre attainable by the French over short distances, made this strategy possible. Another cornerstone of Napoleon's system

Napoleon arrives as a prisoner aboard HMS *Bellerophon*:
'During the time we were heaving the anchor up, and setting the sails, Bonaparte remained on the break of the poop; and was very inquisitive about what was going on. He observed, "Your method of performing this manoeuvre is quite different from the French," and added, "what I admire most in your ship is the extreme silence and orderly conduct of your men. On board a French ship every one calls and gives orders; and they gabble like so many geese." '
(*England's Wooden Walls*, J. Allen, in *United Service Journal*, London 1840, III, p. 27.)

'At the post-mortem examination Dr. Arnott got charge of Napoleon's heart, which was deposited in a hand basin with water. The Doctor took the basin into his bedroom, and placed it on the hob, expecting it to be in perfect safety till morning. During the night he was awoke by hearing a plunge, and, suspecting at once the cause of alarm, started out of bed. Fortunately, there was a lamp burning in the chamber. A rat had seized hold of the heart, but found it so heavy that it dropped from his teeth into the water, and then made his escape. The Doctor took the basin, with its precious contents, into bed with him, along with a good long stick; but his slumbers were at an end for the remainder of that night. The armourer of the 20th Regiment of Foot soldered the silver vase in which the heart of Napoleon was deposited in the presence of Dr. Arnott on the day following.'
(*A Handbook of British and Foreign Orders, War Medals and Decorations*, Dr. A. A. Payne, Sheffield 1911, p. 507.)

of war was his concentration upon the destruction of the enemy's field army, even to the extent of neglecting his own communications in order to bring about the major battle which was the object of all the campaigns. In the attainment of his objectives he depended upon the loyalty of his troops, and it is this aspect which demonstrates perhaps the most remarkable feature of the man's personality.

Napoleon's complex character included a streak of ruthlessness which at times subjugated all other emotions to the triumph of his will for personal attainment, treated his most loyal followers with a degree of callousness and even led to physical assaults upon those who displeased him; yet conversely Napoleon inspired devotion verging upon idolatry on the part of his troops. Some of this was a carefully calculated ploy: the distribution of favours such as the *Légion d'honneur*, the habit of recognizing ordinary soldiers and claiming he remembered them from a previous battle, the appeal to the French army's penchant for emotions of patriotism and glory in theatrical speeches; but these apart, there is no question that he exerted an almost mesmeric effect upon his followers. Some might complain bitterly behind his back – Kellermann always felt cheated of the credit of Marengo, Macdonald recorded Vandamme raging that without him (Vandamme), Napoleon would still be keeping pigs on Corsica; yet such was the effect of Napoleon's presence, whether enhanced by artifice or not, that countless thousands of Frenchmen and even their allies quite willingly laid down their lives for the good of '*le Tondu*' ('the shaven one': from Napoleon's being short-haired and clean-shaven). Napoleon might declare in his most ruthless moments that men like him cared nothing for the lives of a million men; yet on other occasions he mourned, probably with some genuine feeling, the deaths of so many men of which, whatever he might say, he was the principal cause. Few characters in history have inspired on the one hand such adoration, and on the other such hatred, as did Napoleon; the latter verged on a degree of vituperation scarcely ever surpassed, as when a clergyman from Skipton in Yorkshire declared that he wished 'that if he is not assassinated, he may be devoured by the Crocodiles of the Nile'![1]

The image of the ruthless 'Corsican ogre' does not accord with the prisoner on St. Helena who played happily with English children, evidence, according to one, of the 'close affinity between superlative intellect and the warmth of the generous affections'.[2] Even Napoleon's most bitter opponents could not but feel some sympathy with him as he improved his English by reading Aesop's *Fables* to pass the weary hours of captivity. 'In one of the fables the sick lion, after submitting with fortitude to the insults of the many animals who came to exult over his fallen greatness, at last received a kick in the face from the ass. "I could have borne everything but this," the lion said. Napoleon showed the wood-cut, and added, "It is me and your governor."'[3]

The melancholy end of the ex-Emperor, coupled with the remarkable hold he maintained over the affections, even adoration, of his soldiers, contributed to the 'Napoleonic legend' which grew after his death, encouraged by the ceremonial return of his remains to France in 1840 and the annual parade of veterans, growing ever greyer and more bowed in their old uniforms, until in public perception little was evident save the legend of glory and success; the sacrifice of countless thousands of lives in the pursuit of Napoleon's ambition tended to be overlooked or concealed by the dazzling rays of glory emanating from the legend. But for all the ruthlessness of his character, what cannot be denied is that Napoleon changed the course of history and of warfare to a degree equalled by few other personalities in the entire span of recorded history. Yet for all his political skills and attainments, it is as a soldier that Napoleon is principally remembered; and as a final comment it is interesting to consider the opinion of his most skilled adversary and the general who eventually caused his final overthrow, the Duke of Wellington: 'I used to say of him that his presence on the field made a difference of 40,000 men.'[4]

Notes

1. *Morning Chronicle*, 18 January 1799.
2. *Recollections of the Emperor Napoleon on the island of St. Helena*, Mrs. Abell, ed. Mrs. C. Johnstone, London 1873, p. 257.
3. ibid. pp. 264–5.
4. *Conversations with the Duke of Wellington*, Earl Stanhope, London 1899, p. 9.

References

Biographies of Napoleon are legion; the following is merely a brief selection of English-language editions:

Aubry, O. *Napoleon*, London 1964.
Baring Gould, S. *The Life of Napoleon Bonaparte*, London 1897.
Barnett, C. *Bonaparte*, London 1978.
Chandler, D. G. *The Campaigns of Napoleon*, London 1967.
Herold, J. C. *The Age of Napoleon*, London 1963.
Las Cases, Count de. *Memoirs of the Life, Exile, and Conversations of the Emperor Napoleon*, London 1836.
Marshall-Cornwall, Sir J. *Napoleon as Military Commander*, London 1967.
Roseberry, Lord. *Napoleon, the Last Phase*, London 1900.
Sloane, W. M. *The Life of Napoleon Bonaparte*, New York 1906.

Nelson, Horatio, 1st Viscount (1758–1805)

Horatio Nelson was probably the greatest naval tactician and strategist in history, and undisputedly by both his achievements and his personality was one of the outstanding Englishmen of his or any age. The son of a Norfolk clergyman, he entered the Royal Navy in 1770 and after extensive service in the West Indies (where he married a widow) he was a half-pay post-captain at the outbreak of the Revolutionary Wars. In 1793 he was appointed to command the 64-gun HMS *Agamemnon* (known to the seamen as 'old Eggs and Bacon'!), and in the following twelve years established a reputation which has never been surpassed. Serving in the Mediterranean, he was blinded in the right eye at Calvi (Corsica) in 1794, and was largely responsible for Sir John Jervis's victory at St. Vincent (1797) when, in command of HMS *Captain*, he prevented the escape of the Spanish fleet and personally captured two Spanish ships by boarding, for which he received a knighthood and promotion to rear-admiral. He lost his right arm at Santa Cruz (Tenerife) later in the year, but recovered to lead the Mediterranean fleet in a most brilliant action which annihilated Bonaparte's fleet in Aboukir Bay (1798) which isolated the French army in Egypt, earning Nelson a barony and great popularity. In January 1799 he recovered Naples from the French and was rewarded with the Neapolitan dukedom of Brontë, and from this time originated his liaison with Emma Hamilton, wife of the British ambassador at Naples, the antiquary Sir William Hamilton. Nelson accompanied the Hamiltons to England in 1800 and separated from his wife, establishing a curious *ménage à trois* with the Hamiltons. A vice-admiral from 1801, he was sent as Hyde Parker's deputy in the operation against Denmark, and by disobeying Parker's orders won the Battle of Copenhagen, earning a viscountcy and even more fame and popularity. After the death of Sir William Hamilton in April 1803 he continued to live with Emma, who gave birth to his daughter Horatia. Upon the renewal of the war he was sent to blockade Toulon; his fleet pursued Villeneuve's break-out to the West Indies and back, and destroyed French naval hopes for good by the shattering victory of Trafalgar, during which Nelson was shot by a sharpshooter from the French ship *Redoutable* and died on the evening of the battle. He was given a state funeral at St. Paul's.

Horatio Nelson writes of his successes:

'Thus may be exemplified by my life, that Perseverance in any profession will almost probably meet its reward. Without having any inheritance, or having been fortunate in prize-money, I have received all the honours of my profession, been created a peer of Great Britain, and I may say to the reader, "GO THOU, AND DO LIKEWISE."'

(Nelson's 'Memoir of Services', in *The Life and Services of Horatio, Viscount Nelson*, Revd. J. Stanier Clarke and J. McArthur, London 1809; 1840 edn., II, p. 8.)

Richard Brinsley Sheridan's epitaph on Nelson:

'A man amongst the few who appear at different periods to have been created to promote the grandeur and add to the security of Nations; inciting by their high example their fellow-mortals through all succeeding times, to pursue the course that leads to the exaltation of our perfect nature.'

(*The Life and Services of Horatio Viscount Nelson*, Revd. J. Stanier Clarke and J. McArthur, London 1809; 1840 edn., III, p. 145.)

Celebrations of the victory of Aboukir Bay ('Battle of the Nile') at Drury Lane, 1798. Rejoicing at such news was unbounded, with buildings commonly illuminated or decked with trophies. (Contemporary engraving)

Horatio, 1st Viscount Nelson (1758–1805); the jewelled cockade was bestowed by the Sultan of the Ottoman Empire. (Engraving by T. W. Harland after Lemuel Abbot)

The victory of Trafalgar was due in part to Nelson's innovative tactics – breaking the enemy line and bringing about a 'pell-mell' battle; though he was not the first to use such tactics, none perfected them like Nelson – and partly to the morale which his presence engendered. It is remarkable that this slight, mutilated figure should inspire such devotion among both his officers (his 'band of brothers') and his ordinary sailors, testimony of his demeanour and magnetic personality; he shared with Napoleon the capacity of instilling not only respect and admiration but unbounded affection in the eyes of the rank-and-file, though was free of Napoleon's more unpleasant traits of character, and thus overcame any criticisms of his unconventional life-style with the Hamiltons. The understanding of his tactics which this magnetism inculcated into his subordinates and the morale his presence engendered were major contributory factors to the excellence of the ships and crews which comprised his fleet. The admiration felt by the country at large – and the sorrow at his death – was boundless, and is reflected accurately in the closing paragraph of Clarke and McArthur's biography:

'. . . he acted on a superior principle: in every work . . . which he undertook, in the service of his king and country, he did it, in the language of the sacred historian, *with all his heart, and prospered*. The fame of Nelson will endure as long as the name of his country shall be pronounced, in new ages of the world, by future generations of men. Let posterity consecrate

his memory by emulating the perfection of his public character, and the disinterested zeal of his conduct; and should the time arrive, when on our native land we shall be called to protect the tomb of Nelson, and the liberties which he died to save, may his immortal spirit hover around us, and with the blessing of God's providence lead us to victory.'[1]

Note
1. 1840 edn, III, pp. 211–12.

References
There are many biographies of Nelson; one of the earliest is *The Life and Services of Horatio, Viscount Nelson, from his Lordship's Manuscripts*, J. Stanier Clarke and J. McArthur, London 1840 (orig. 1809), upon which Robert Southey's classic *Life of Nelson* was largely based. Excellent modern biographies include *Nelson*, C. Oman, London 1947, and *A Portrait of Lord Nelson*, O. Warner, London 1958. Nelson's correspondence is covered in *Despatches and Letters of Vice-Admiral Lord Viscount Nelson*, ed. Sir N. H. Nicolas, 1844–6.

A stone at Greenwich Hospital:

'In memory of THOMAS MAIN, Quartermaster's-Mate of H.M.S. Leviathan, Who died, aged, 39, of a wound which he received on the 21st of October, 1805, in the Memorable and Glorious Battle of TRAFALGAR. In this he shares but in common with many others and praise and glory of having died in the defence of his country; yet he further signalized himself by a display or fortitude which is not surpassed in the records of national intrepidity. The severity of his wound required the amputation of his left arm; he, nevertheless, hailed the triumph of British valour by exultingly singing the patriotic song of "Rule Britannia", even while the agonizing operation was performing.'

(*United Service Journal*, London 1839, III, p. 186.)

Ney, Michel (1769–1815)

Michel Ney is probably the most famous of Napoleon's marshals, and probably rightfully so. Born the son of a cooper of Saarlouis, of German descent, his rise from the ranks (he enlisted as a hussar in 1787) exemplifies the truth of Napoleon's statement that every French soldier carried a marshal's baton in his knapsack, if he had the aptitude and application. Commissioned in 1792, he was a *général de brigade* by August 1796 and *général de division* in March 1799; his service, which was distinguished, was in the northern and Rhine theatres. He was especially successful in Switzerland, and at Hohenlinden under Moreau, and in 1802 commanded the French armies in Switzerland. His original political beliefs (he had been an ardent republican) at this time changed completely, presumably due to Napoleon's personal magnetism (his wife, Aglaé Auguié, was supposedly chosen for him by Josephine); thereafter he was the most loyal of Napoleon's subordinates. Appointed a marshal in 1804, he commanded VI Corps and was greatly distinguished at Elchingen (from which action he took the title of his dukedom, 1808), at Eylau and Friedland. Service in the Peninsula was less successful, his relations with Massena

being hostile, but in 1812 he was appointed to command III Corps in the attack on Russia. This campaign made his name; Napoleon had styled him 'bravest of the brave' reputedly after Friedland, but in the horrors of the retreat from Moscow he more than fulfilled the title. Witnesses unanimously accord the success of the rearguard to Ney's personal heroism and leadership qualities; musket in hand, he defied the Russians almost single-handedly at times, and was reputedly the last Frenchman to quit Russian soil. The escape of the remnant of the *Grande Armée* quite literally might not have been possible without his untiring efforts; a title (Prince de la Moscowa) was never better deserved. In 1813–14, despite several wounds, Ney fought in almost every action, but was instrumental in persuading Napoleon to abdicate when the situation was obviously hopeless. Napoleon averred that the army would still obey him; Ney replied that they would obey their generals, which must have come to Napoleon as the *et tu, Brute?* of his life. Upon Napoleon's return Ney declared his loyalty to the king and vowed to bring back Napoleon a prisoner in an iron cage; in the event he defected to his old emperor and commanded at Quatre Bras, and was *de facto* battlefield commander at Waterloo, conceivably a reason for Napoleon's defeat. He was arrested after the battle and tried for treason; it was said that the king wished him to escape, as the baying for blood of the fanatic royalist element could only reflect ill upon the Bourbons, but Ney was tried, convicted, sentenced to death and shot on 7 December in the Luxembourg Gardens, to almost universal sorrow.

Michel Ney (1769–1815), in the dress uniform of a Marshal of France, wearing the cross and breast-star of the Légion d'honneur. (Engraving after Gérard)

'*Le Rougeaud*' (as Ney was called from his red hair) was not a great strategist, and has been criticized for his lethargy at Quatre Bras, but impetuosity at Busaco and especially Waterloo. Ideally, he was best employed as a corps commander with instructions to obey, when his courage and personal example could inspire his men (who admired him greatly) to an almost unequalled level. When given independent command, as he virtually had been at Waterloo, he was probably at the limit or even out of his depth. Nevertheless, his reckless bravery and tactical ability led Napoleon to greet him, when he appeared with the rearguard in 1812 (when everyone thought him dead) with the words: 'I would have given everything rather than lose you',[1] which is a fair reflection of his worth.

Note

1. *Memoirs of Baron Lejeune*, ed. Mrs. A. Bell, London 1897, II, p. 226.

References

Ney's own memoirs were never completed, but those of the period to Elchingen were published as *Mémoires du maréchal Ney*, Paris 1833. The best modern biographies are *Marshal Ney: The Romance and the Real*, R. Horricks, Tunbridge Wells 1982, and *Ney, le Brave des Braves*, Dr. F. G. Hourtoulle, Paris 1981.

Orange, Prince William of (1792–1849)

Driven from Holland with his father and family at the age of three by the French republican armies, the young Prince of Orange lived in exile until 1813. Educated at the military college in Berlin and at Oxford, he entered the British army and served as Wellington's ADC in the Peninsular War,

receiving a major-general's commission in 1813 at the age of 21. In 1815, as heir to his father's new throne (William I, King of the Netherlands), he commanded the Allied I Corps and was nominally Wellington's deputy, but his youth and lack of experience in command led to a number ghastly errors in the Waterloo campaign which sacrificed several units to no purpose; though his bravery was never in question, the Prince was prevented from causing any more damage by a wound at Waterloo. Married to the Tsar's sister, he became very popular in Holland and but for his father's intransigence might have brought about a peaceable settlement to the Belgian revolution of 1830 which would have enabled the House of Orange to maintain overlordship of Belgium. In the event, after a period of friction with his father during which the Prince lived in England, he commanded the Dutch forces in the 1831 invasion of Belgium, his last military service. Succeeding his father as King William II in 1840, though never an advocate of democracy, he supported electoral reforms and presided over the establishment of a constitutional rather than autocratic monarchy, and thus Holland was spared the spectre of revolution in the year of unrest in 1848. He died on 17 March 1849 much mourned by his nation.

References

The earliest biographies would seem to be *Leven van Koning Willem II*, J. J. Abbink, Amsterdam 1849, and *Het Leven van Willem den Tweede, Koning der Nederlanden*, J. Bosscha, Amsterdam 1852.

Oudinot, Nicolas Charles (1767–1847)

Although Ney was accorded the sobriquet 'bravest of the brave', none deserved it more than Nicolas Oudinot, for he was probably the most frequently wounded soldier of the age (at least 22 times). He conducted himself with such disregard for his personal safety that his servant took the unusual step of laying-out bandages and medical kit before every action, in the certain knowledge that Oudinot would be hit!

Coming from a lower middle-class family in Lorraine, Oudinot's chance of promotion in the royal army was almost nil, and he retired as a sergeant in 1787. The revolution was his salvation; elected lieutenant-colonel of the 3rd Meuse Volunteers in 1792, he had risen to the rank of *général de division* by April 1799 and was Massena's right hand in Switzerland in 1799–1800. In 1805 he commanded the élite 'combined grenadier' division, known to posterity as the *Grenadiers d'Oudinot*; he led his division at Friedland despite having broken a leg when his horse fell a month before; in 1809 he was wounded at Aspern-Essling and took command of Lannes' division at Wagram after the latter's death, where Oudinot almost had an ear shot off. In July 1809 he was elevated to the marshalate and ennobled as Duc de Reggio in April 1810. He was twice wounded in the Russian campaign but even as an invalid led his escort when ambushed by

Prince William of Orange (1792–1849), wearing Netherlands hussar uniform but with the breast-star of the British Order of the Bath uppermost on his pelisse. (Engraving after Joseph Oderaere)

Cossacks; he fought through the 1813–14 campaigns (wounded twice at Brienne and once at Arcis); and in 1815 remained loyal to the Bourbons, which guaranteed him a distinguished later career as commander of the Royal Guard, commander of a corps in the 1823 invasion of Spain, and finally as governor of the Invalides. His descendants formed a dynasty of distinguished soldiers. Oudinot made no pretence of being a great commander but was an ideal subordinate; as Massena reported, 'He has followed me in everything, and made a perfect second in command.'[1] In his almost 59 years' military service, Oudinot demonstrated that a braver man never lived; Napoleon once asked him, 'And yet there always comes a moment when the bravest man is afraid for at least once in his life.' 'Sire,' replied Oudinot, 'I have never had time for that.'[2]

Notes
1. *Memoirs*, p. 22.
2. ibid. p. 440.

Reference
Memoirs of Marshal Oudinot, Duc

de Reggio, ed. G. Stiegler, New York 1897, is basically the work of Oudinot's second wife; it appeared originally in French, Paris 1894.

Sir Thomas Picton (1758–1815) in the full-dress uniform of a lieutenant-general, with the aiguillette on the right shoulder which replaced epaulettes from 1811. (Engraving after M. A. Shee)

Nicolas Charles Oudinot (1767–1847) in the full-dress uniform of a Marshal of France. (Engraving by H. Wolf after R. Lefevre)

Picton, Sir Thomas (1758–1815)

Sir Thomas Picton was one of Wellington's most capable (and colourful) subordinates, a bluff and uncompromising Welshman. Commissioned in 1771, his promotion was slow despite a worthy record as a regimental officer. After living in retirement on his father's estate for twelve years he went to the West Indies as aide to Sir John Vaughan, took part in the captures of St. Lucia, St. Vincent and Trinidad under Abercromby, and was appointed governor of the latter island, being promoted to brigadier-general in 1801. He was arraigned for the use of torture in the interrogation of a mulatto woman suspected of theft, which charge (though basically unjust) blighted his career; the case dragged on from his return home in 1803 to a trial before Lord Ellenborough in 1806, the guilty verdict of which was overturned in 1808. As major-general he was appointed governor of Flushing during the Walcheren expedition (from which he was invalided home), and was given a divisional command in the Peninsular War at Wellington's request.

Though Wellington never reposed in him the confidence of an independent command, there was no better subordinate to execute a given task, and his 3rd Division became one of the finest in the army, its nickname 'The Fighting Division' being one which could equally have been applied to its commander. He was especially distinguished at Fuentes de Oñoro, Badajoz (where he was wounded at the escalade) and Vittoria; he received seven votes of thanks from the House of Commons but no peerage, probably a legacy of the Trinidad affair. Knighted and promoted to lieutenant-general in 1813, he commanded the 5th Division at Quatre Bras, concealing a severe wound to allow him to lead his troops at Waterloo, where he was killed by a shot through the head. A rough and undiplomatic warrior (he reputedly once threatened to hang a commissary if rations weren't delivered on time, though the story is also told of Craufurd), he was known for eccentricity of dress, wearing civilian clothes and round hat, as at Vittoria where Kincaid described him as swearing as roundly as if he were wearing two cocked ones; and at Busaco he wore his nightcap. Mercer described on the eve of Waterloo 'a man of no very prepossessing appearance came rambling amongst our guns . . . dressed in a shabby old grey greatcoat and rusty round hat. I took him at the time for some amateur from Brussels . . . and thinking many of his questions rather impertinent, was somewhat short in answering him. . . . How great was my astonishment on learning soon after that this was Sir Thomas Picton!'[1] His staff followed his lead in matters of uniform so that Picton and entourage were nicknamed 'the bear and ragged staff'!

Note

1. *Journal of the Waterloo Campaign*, C. Mercer, Edinburgh and London 1870, I, p. 284.

References

Myatt, F. *Peninsular General*, Newton Abbot 1980.
Robinson, H. B. *Memoirs and Correspondence of Lt. Gen. Sir Thomas Picton*, London 1836.

Poniatowski, Josef Anton (1763–1813)

Napoleon's Polish marshal came of princely stock, the Poniatowski family being of Italian origin (originally named Torelli, whose member Giuseppe married into the Lithuanian family of Poniator in the mid-seventeenth century). Stanislaus Poniatowski – an adopted son,

Josef Anton Poniatowski (1763–1813) in the staff uniform of the Duchy of Warsaw. (Engraving by C. State)

reputedly the natural son of the Prince Sapieha – served Charles XII of Sweden with great distinction, and later Augustus II and Augustus III of Poland. His son became king himself as Stanislaus II, whose brother Andrew (1735–73) became a *Feldzeugmeister* in the Austrian army. Andrew's son, Josef Anton, was born in Vienna and joined the Austrian army in which his father held such high rank; he was greatly distinguished in the Turkish war in 1788 and severely wounded at Sabac (25 April). With this experience he was recalled by his uncle Stanislaus II to serve as a general in the Polish army and performed with great skill in holding off immense Russian forces, in 1792 in the Ukraine and during Kościuszko's rebellion. After the fall of the republic – he was disgusted with the peace terms – he remained in exile or lived in Warsaw as a private citizen until after Jena he was offered command of the National Guard. From there he progressed to war minister of the Duchy of Warsaw, and commanded in the field against the Austrians in 1809, but his greatest fame was won as commander of V Corps of the *Grande Armée* in 1812, commanding Napoleon's right wing at Borodino and being wounded at the Berezina. Even after the disaster of 1812 he remained loyal, reforming a Polish army for Napoleon's service and acting with distinction in the Leipzig campaign, receiving his appointment as Marshal of France as a reward on 16 October 1813. Although wounded before Leipzig, he protected the French evacuation of the city with great courage, receiving four more wounds, and after the bridge over the Elster was blown prematurely he attempted to escape the Russians by swimming; he drowned in the attempt. One of the most heroic figures of the age, his remains were deposited in Cracow Cathedral alongside those of Kościuszko and Jan Sobieski; fitting company for Napoleon's only Polish marshal.

Reference

Askenazi, S. *Le Prince Joseph Poniatowski, Maréchal de France*, Paris 1921.

Scharnhorst, Gerhard Johann David von (1755–1813)

Scharnhorst never exercised an important, independent field command, but his significance far outstrips many of the better-known generals who did. Born in Hanover of farming stock, he educated himself and in 1778 was commissioned in the Hanoverian cavalry, transferring to the artillery in 1783. Appointed to the new artillery school, he made most of his living by writing military theory (two important books and a military journal). He served under the Duke of York in the Netherlands, writing a book on Menin (*Vertheidigung der Stadt Menin*, Hanover 1803), which is perhaps his best-known work, together with *Die Ursachen des Glücks der Franzosen im Revolutionskrieg*; after which he was transferred to the staff as a major. By now his reputation as a military theorist was so well-established that he received several offers of employment, which led in 1801 to his transferring to Prussian service as a lieutenant-colonel, with a patent of nobility and double his previous salary. Employed at the

War Academy in Berlin (where Clausewitz was a pupil), he was appointed chief of staff to the Duke of Brunswick, was slightly wounded at Auerstädt and, distinguished in the disastrous campaign, served with Blücher in the latter stages. After prisoner-exchange, he played a leading part with L'Estocq's corps serving with the Russians; for service at Eylau he received the coveted decoration *Pour le Mérite*.

Scharnhorst was promoted to major-general and appointed head of the reform commission to reconstruct the shattered Prussian army. His influence extended beyond mere organization and tactics: he recognized the necessity for a 'national' rather than semi-mercenary army, and the need to fight decisive battles as the only response to the situation created by the French Revolution, and as such is recognized as one of the founders of German nationalism. The patriotic fervour which characterized the Prussian armies of 1813–14, the enabling of commoners to aspire to commissions, and the foundation of the *Landwehr* and all it entailed, were all due to Scharnhorst; he might fairly be said to be the creator of the 1813 army and, in a much wider sphere, the champion of German nationhood. Forced into retirement by Napoleon, during which sojourn he wrote a book on firearms, he returned as Blücher's chief of staff in 1813 and was wounded in the foot at Lützen. It became infected and proved mortal; he died in June at Prague, where he had been sent to negotiate for Austria's entry into the war. It was singularly unfortunate that he did not live to see the success of his policy and organization, but his reputation is imperishable.

References

A leading biography is *Scharnhorst*, M. Lehmann, Leipzig 1886–8. Clausewitz himself wrote a memoir of his old tutor, *Über das Leben und de Charakter von Scharnhorst*, published in Leopold von Ranke's *Historisch-politischer Zeitschrift*, 1832.

Schwarzenberg, Karl Philipp, Prince zu (1771–1820)

This Austrian field marshal came from a most distinguished, aristocratic family, whose antecedents included the renowned general Adolf von Schwarzenberg (1547–1600) and Johann (1463–1528), jurist and friend of Luther. Karl Philipp fought against the Turks, but was especially distinguished in the Netherlands in 1793–4 (receiving the cross of the Order of Maria Theresa for his charge at le Cateau-Cambrésis); he served at Amberg and Würzburg, and commanded a division in 1800. At Hohenlinden he saved the Austrian right wing from defeat, and, commanding a division under Mack, was one of the band which cut itself free from the French encirclement at Ulm. Envoy to the Tsar in 1808, he returned for the Wagram campaign after which he was sent to Paris to negotiate Napoleon's marriage to Marie-Louise; it was his ball, given in honour of the event, which ended in a conflagration which killed many of the guests. Highly esteemed by Napoleon, he commanded the Austrian Reserve Corps in the attack on Russia, and as field marshal in 1813 was appointed overall commander of the Allied 'Grand Army of Bohemia'. He has been accused of timidity, but his task in 1813–14 was made immeasurably difficult by the conflict of opinion between the various allied nations (though he commanded at Leipzig, the three monarchs of the Allies were present to overshadow his actions); in fact he handled an impossible situation as well as could have been expected, though greatly exasperated by it all. Honoured highly after the war and appointed president of the *Hofkreigsrath*, he suffered partial paralysis after a stroke in 1817, and died of a second stroke whilst revisiting the scene of his victory at Leipzig.

Soult, Nicolas Jean de Dieu (1769–1851)

Nicolas Soult vies with Davoût and perhaps Massena for the title of the most capable of Napoleon's marshals. The son of a notary, his father's death while he was a boy caused him to enlist in the army in 1785. Commissioned in 1792, he was *général de brigade* in 1794 (after distinguished service at Fleurus), and *général de division* in 1799, moving from the Rhine to Switzerland where he served capably under Massena. Though he had served under Moreau (whose subordinates Napoleon generally disliked), he ingratiated himself sufficiently to be appointed one of the first marshals, and was especially distinguished at Austerlitz. Created Duke of Dalmatia in 1808, in Spain he enjoyed great success against the Spaniards (especially at Ocaña), but was defeated when he met Wellington, and considerably exacerbated the situation by his uneasy relations with other marshals, lack of co-ordination which played into the hands of his opponents. He refused even to obey King Joseph, and finally Joseph asked for him to be recalled.

Nicolas Jean de Dieu Soult (1769–1851), in the undress uniform of a Marshal of France.

Soult served at Lützen and Bautzen but the deteriorating situation in Spain led to his being sent back (much against his wife's will, who argued with Napoleon over the posting!) in overall command of the unified French armies. With these limited resources his defence of the Pyrenees and the South of France was an epic of great skill; though his raw troops were constantly defeated by Wellington's veterans, he performed prodigies and achieved vastly more than could ever have been expected. Though a general of great skill, it was said that 'he had character only in front of the enemy': politically he trod a careful path, declaring himself a royalist in 1814, rallied to Napoleon in 1815 (where his skills were squandered when he was appointed chief of staff instead of receiving a field command for which he was better fitted than those who were appointed), survived a brief exile after the second restoration and was re-appointed a Marshal of France in 1820. He served in a wide variety of diplomatic and the highest political offices, supported Louis Philippe and in 1848 again declared himself a republican. Whether he merited the title Marshal-General of France (previously held only by Turenne, Saxe and Villars) is doubtful, but his military skills were undoubtedly great, and despite his changes of political stance he did remain loyal to Napoleon.

Soult's reputation has suffered only through his ambition, fearsome reputation for avarice and plunder, and his unwillingness to co-operate with fellow-marshals or even obey orders from his superiors. Napoleon's faith in his skills would seem confirmed by the story that before Austerlitz his only instructions were 'act as you always do', and when ordered to advance Soult reputedly remarked 'this is not the proper time'. Napoleon's fury at being disobeyed turned to gratitude when Soult was proved right, and Napoleon declared 'Marshal, I account you the ablest tactician in my empire.'[1] An even great accolade is that delivered by his enemy William Napier: 'I take this opportunity to declare that respect which I believe every British officer who has had the honour to serve against him feels for his military talents. By those talents the French cause in Spain was long upheld, and after the battle of Salamanca, if his counsel had been followed by the intrusive monarch, the fate of the war might have been changed.'[2]

Notes
1. *Court and Camp of Bonaparte*, anon., London 1831, pp. 406–7.
2. *History of the War in the Peninsula*, London 1832, I, p. viii.

References
Soult's own papers were edited by his son Napoleon Hector, as *Mémoires de Maréchal-Général Soult*, Paris 1854; *Le Maréchal Soult*, A. de Grozelier, Castres 1851. The English biography is *Soult: Napoleon's Maligned Marshal*, Sir Peter Hayman, London 1990.

Uxbridge, Lord Henry William Paget, 2nd Earl of (1768–1854)

Henry William Paget was probably the most capable British cavalry general of his era. The eldest son of the 1st Earl of Uxbridge, he raised the 80th Foot from his father's Staffordshire estates in 1793, beginning his military career as their lieutenant-colonel. He served in the Netherlands in 1794 and 1799, entering the cavalry (16th Light Dragoons) in 1795, and as commander of the 7th Light Dragoons was so assiduous in his study of the arm that they became one of the best regiments in the service. Promoted to major-general in 1802 and lieutenant-general in 1808, he commanded Moore's cavalry in the Corunna campaign, winning great renown for his victories at Sahagun and Benevente. Despite his great talents and the obvious lack of a competent cavalry leader in British service, he was employed no more in the Peninsular War due to a family quarrel with Wellington (Paget having eloped with Wellington's sister-in-law, whom he married after his divorce from his first wife), spending these years as Member of Parliament for Milborne Port (1796–1810) and sitting in the House of Lords when he succeeded his father in 1812; and with a brief divisional command at Walcheren. In 1815 he was appointed to command the cavalry and horse artillery of the Anglo-Allied army and led them with some distinction in the Waterloo campaign, losing his leg when a grapeshot shattered his knee at the very end of the battle, which gave rise to a perhaps apocryphal but very famous exchange. Riding at Wellington's side (who supported him in the saddle after his injury), he supposedly looked down at the mangled knee and said, 'By God, Sir, I've lost my leg'; whereupon Wellington looked down and remarked, 'By God, Sir, so you have!' He was soon fitted with an artificial leg, and though his military service ended with Waterloo, he served two somewhat stormy periods as Lord-lieutenant of Ireland (being criticized for his leniency towards Roman Catholics), rose to field marshal in 1846 and served as master-general of the ordnance from 1846 to 1852. Shortly after Waterloo, in recognition of his services, he had been created 1st Marquess of Anglesey, by which title he is perhaps better known. He should not be confused with his brother, General Sir Edward Paget (1775–1849), one of Wellington's divisional commanders of considerable ability but no luck: he lost an arm at Oporto and was captured on the retreat from Burgos!

Reference
Anglesey, 7th Marquis of. *One-Leg: the Life and Letters of Henry William Paget*, London 1961.

Wellington, Arthur Wellesley, 1st Duke of (1769–1852)

The career of the man who was arguably Britain's greatest soldier began in Dublin, probably his place of birth, in 1765, as the fourth son of Garret Wesley, 1st Earl of Mornington (the family name later reverted to its older form, 'Wellesley'). His aristocratic background ensured him an education at Eton and at a French military academy, but though it brought influence there was little wealth associated with it, and as the impecunious dullard of the family, Arthur was consigned to the military, the only career for which he was thought fit. But his family's first impressions were wrong: he proved highly intelligent, with a penchant for hard work and no time for frivolity. Rising quickly by the system of 'purchase', he made the trip from ensign (7 March 1787) to lieutenant-colonel in command of the 33rd Foot (30

'A story is told of the Duke [of Wellington] that, on the morning of one of his great battles, whilst at breakfast with Lord Fitzroy Somerset, he appeared to be absorbed in reverie, but was at the same time eating his egg, and making strange wry faces; till at last, seemingly recovering himself, he exclaimed, "By-the-by, Fitzroy, is that egg of yours fresh? – for mine *was* quite rotten."

(*Wellington Anecdotes*, anon., London, n.d., p. 22.)

Arthur Wellesley, 1st Duke of Wellington (1769–1852), wearing the dress uniform of a Field Marshal; included among the decorations are the Peninsular Gold Cross, Order of the Golden Fleece and Swedish Order of the Sword (all around the neck), and the breast-stars of the Order of the Garter (top) and the Austrian Order of Maria Theresa (centre). (Engraving by W. Say after Thomas Phillips)

September 1793) in only six and a half years. He led the 33rd in the Netherlands in 1794–5 with distinction – where, he said, he learned 'how not to do it'! – and in 1797 went with his regiment to India. The subcontinent provided his real military education, and though his initial appointments owed much to his elder brother Richard, Marquess Wellesley (1760–1842) who was Governor-General, the remainder of his military service was dictated by his own immense talents.

His service in India made his reputation (though as a 'sepoy general' he had to a degree to re-establish it when he returned to Europe) and included a number of major triumphs, most notably against the Marathas at Assaye (23 September 1803) and Argaum (29 November 1803). Returning to England in 1805, he resumed his political career (he had been a Member of Parliament in Ireland as early as 1790) until being given a subsidiary command under Cathcart for the expedition to Denmark. His Indian reputation was confirmed by the action at Kjöge, and he was given command of the expedition to Portugal at the commencement of the Peninsular War. He won the battles of Roliça and Vimeiro, but was superseded in command by 'Betty' Burrard and 'Dowager' Dalrymple, who (under protest from Wellesley) concluded the shameful Convention of Cintra. All three were recalled to face an enquiry, from which Wellesley alone was vindicated; and following the death of Moore, he was sent back to the Peninsula in April 1809 in supreme command. From this moment his fame grew, but though in overall field command, with complete control over the army's movements, he had no 'unity of command' as enjoyed by Napoleon, for his responsibilities were immense. He led virtually the only army which Britain could deploy in Europe, and was totally dependent upon his own success to retain the support of his political masters at home, and throughout – even to 1815 – never had a free hand to appoint those officers he knew he required. That he was so successful with such limitations to his power, and few subordinates completely trustworthy with independent commands, is a testimony to his immense military skill. As a result, he probably tended to stifle any burgeoning talent among his subordinates by insisting on overseeing everything himself; he was his own chief of intelligence, chief of staff and operated with a staff so small that it might not have been sufficient for a French *corps d'armée*. Conversely, it ensured that the Peninsular army was the 'most complete

machine for its numbers now existing in Europe' as he described it; and while the inherent excellence of the British army and the careful reorganization of the Portuguese army by Beresford had much to do with this excellence, it was very much Wellesley's machine.

After Talavera Wellesley was created a Viscount, his title 'Wellington' being taken from the old family estates in Somerset, and in the following year he frustrated the French attempts to invade Portugal by his 'lines of Torres Vedras', the most effective fortification of the era, entirely his conception and to a considerable extent his design. Assuming the offensive in 1812, Wellington's army won a major victory at Salamanca, but was forced to retire after an injudicious attempt to take Burgos. In 1813, however, began the concerted drive of the French from Spain, smashing their main field army at Vittoria, piercing the Pyrenees and invading southern France before the 1814 armistice. By this time Wellington was a field marshal (appointed 21 June 1813), Generalissimo of the Spanish armies (12 August 1812) as well as Marshal-General of Portugal, and had risen through the British peerage to the exalted rank of Duke (3 May 1814), as well as receiving every major order of chivalry from the Allied sovereigns. His conduct in the 1815 campaign, when he blended successfully a heterogeneous army which included many unreliable or inexperienced units into a force which (with Blücher's assistance) comprehensively defeated Napoleon, established him as the leading general of his age, and one of the very greatest military commanders of all time.

Wellington has been criticized for being a 'defensive general', and certainly his early Peninsular battles were not characterized by the spirit of offence which he learned in India (immediate attacks being the recognized way for European armies to defeat immensely more numerous Indian opponents); but the defensive nature of the earlier Peninsular actions was largely forced upon him by circumstances, as was the classic defensive battle, Waterloo. His tactic of employing the 'reverse slope' to shield his forces from enemy reconnaissance and fire was the only effective

Sir Walter Scott's journal, 27 April 1828:
    'I heard the Duke [of Wellington] say to-day that the best troops would run now and then. He thought nothing of men running, he said, provided they came back again.'
    (*The Life of Wellington*, Sir Herbert Maxwell, London 1899, II, p. 139.)

counter to the French system of war, yet Wellington was the only commander to employ it (he implored the Prussians to shelter their troops at Ligny but they declined and were, as he predicted, severely mauled); yet in the offensive sphere, he proved himself a master of opportunity (as at Salamanca) and of manoeuvre (1813). He was, in effect, the most complete commander of his era, rivalled only by Napoleon himself, though being the opposite of the Emperor in every way save for personal courage, he was never defeated. His austere, aloof and even cold demeanour was partly an outward mask (he could be a most entertaining dinner host – though his meals were notoriously uncomplicated, even frugal – and was moved to tears by casualty-returns), which resulted in his being respected and trusted by his men but not revered in the way that Napoleon or Marlborough were worshipped by their followers. From the lowest ranks to the highest, however, Wellington's men knew that he would never risk one life unnecessarily, would do his utmost to ensure that they were adequately equipped and fed, and his presence with the army raised morale to such a degree that they had absolute faith in his defeating the French. This morale and trust in their commander was a major reason why the army that crossed the Pyrenees in the winter of 1813–14 was probably the finest ever fielded by Britain, at least until the British Expeditionary Force of a century later. Perhaps the most telling comment on the private soldier's opinion of 'Hooky' or 'Beaky' (their nickname for him, arising from his aquiline nose) was that given by Fusilier Horsefall of the 7th Fuzileers as he advanced into the storm of French fire at Albuera, in a position apparently without hope: 'Whore's ar Arthur? Aw wish he wor here.'[1]

After his active military career ended, Wellington fulfilled every office of state from Prime Minister to Commander-in-Chief with the same uncompromising attitude as he had commanded in battle, sacrificing everything for what he conceived to be the public good, at one period even his personal popularity, during which time a mob broke the windows of his London home, leading to the erection of iron shutters which gave him the nickname the 'Iron Duke'. Surviving to become the mentor of the young Queen Victoria, he transcended the ordinary status of public life to become a national symbol, and, quite simply, the greatest Britisher of his age. When he died peacefully at Walmer Castle, his residence as Lord Warden of the Cinque Ports, *The Times* described his career as simply 'one unclouded longest day'.

One of the most revealing remarks by this most remarkable and noble of men was that recorded by Lady Salisbury at Walmer in 1836, when she inquired when it was he realized that the victory of Waterloo 'had raised your name above every other'. Without a trace of false modesty, Wellington replied that he never even considered it, for 'That is a feeling of vanity; one's *first* thought is for the public service,' and continued, 'Perhaps there is no man now existing who would like to meet me on a field of battle; in that line I am superior. But when the war is over and the troops disbanded, what is your great general more than anybody else? I am necessarily inferior to every man in his own line, though I may excel him in others. I cannot saw and plane like a carpenter, or make shoes like a shoemaker, or understand cultivation like a farmer. Each of these, on his own ground, meets me on terms of superiority. I feel I am but a man.'[2] As he was styled at the time, he was indeed 'the Great Duke'.

Notes

1. *Rough Notes of Seven Campaigns*, J. S. Cooper, Carlisle 1869; 1914 edn, p. 68.
2. *The Life of Wellington*, Sir Herbert Maxwell, London 1899, II, pp. 92–3.

References

Wellington biographies are legion; the most modern are *Wellington: the Years of the Sword*, and *Wellington: Pillar of State*, Countess of Longford, London 1969 and 1972 respectively. *The Life of Wellington*, Sir Herbert Maxwell, London 1899, and *Wellington*, S. G. P. Ward, London 1963 are both excellent, and *Words on Wellington*, Sir William Fraser, Bt, London 1889, is a good collection of anecdotes. His military skills are analysed in *Wellington as Military Commander*, M. Glover, London 1968, and *Wellington Commander: the Iron Duke's Generalship*, ed. P. Griffith, Chichester 1985. Individual campaigns are covered in *Wellington in India*, *Wellington at Waterloo* and *Wellington in the Peninsula*, J. Weller, London 1972, 1967 and 1962 respectively. The immensity of the Duke's correspondence (most of it written in his own hand) can be judged from *Dispatches of Field Marshal the Duke of Wellington*, ed. J. Gurwood, London 1834–8, and *Supplementary Despatches and Memoranda of Field Marshal the Duke of Wellington*, ed. 2nd Duke of Wellington, London 1858–72.

Wrede, Carl Philipp, Prince von (1767-1838)

The outstanding Bavarian soldier of his time, Wrede was born at Heidelberg and was intended for a career in civil administration, but in 1799 raised a volunteer corps and was appointed its colonel. At Hohenlinden he commanded a Palatinate brigade with distinction, and after the Peace of Lunéville was appointed a lieutenant-general in the Bavarian army. He served with distinction at Pultusk, but the attitude of contempt shown by the French towards the Bavarians, and their accusations of looting against himself, turned him against the French alliance and in 1807 and 1809 only the tact of the king prevented an open split with his allies. Commanding in the bitter Tyrol campaign in 1809 (and being wounded at Wagram), Wrede was appointed a Count of the Empire by Napoleon, but his sympathies lay with the anti-French faction within Bavaria; though he served with great distinction in the 1812 campaign. By 1813 he was confirmedly anti-Napoleon, and after re-organizing the shattered Bavarian army he concluded the Peace of Reid with the Allies and after Leipzig took the Bavarian forces into the field against the French, a leading reason for the country's defection from Napoleon's camp. He was defeated at Hanau but led the Bavarians in the 1814 campaign. Created a prince of Bavaria in 1814, he became as leading figure in Bavarian politics and helped unseat Montgelas, whom he succeeded in 1817, and as commander-in-chief and head of the council of regency during the king's absence in 1835 remained a highly influential figure until his death in December 1838.

V
SOURCES

SOURCES

The number of volumes which have been written on the various aspects of the Napoleonic Wars runs into hundreds of thousands. Even while the Napoleonic Wars were still in progress what might be termed a 'Napoleonic book industry' was in operation, producing works of military instruction (drill-books and the like), personal accounts of events (many of which took the form of travelogues, a popular genre of the period) and volumes which may almost be regarded as reportage, expanding for the literary public on the accounts that had appeared recently in the popular press. The speed with which these accounts were produced could be very rapid; for example, the British public had an account of the 1812 Russian campaign (based on French official sources) within weeks of the events (e.g., 'War between France and Russia', in *Royal Military Chronicle*, 1812), and Robert Ker Porter published his account of the Corunna campaign within five months of the death of Moore (*Letters from Portugal and Spain*, London 1809, under the *nom-de-plume* of 'an Officer'). While works of this nature based on personal experience are of great value, the narrative accounts obviously suffer from the hasty production and the general unavailability of material emanating from more than one of the participating armies. Other contemporary works are of no more than 'curio' value and only of use in exemplifying attitudes prevalent in a part of society (e.g., *Bonaparte: an Heroic Ballad with a Sermon in its Belly*, anon., London 1803, which compares 'this raw-head and bloody-bon'd chief, Bonaparte' with the pickpocket Filch in *The Beggar's Opera*!).

After the end of the Napoleonic Wars the Napoleonic book-industry continued with an outpouring of history and memoirs, some making an honest attempt to present an accurate and balanced view, others suffering from national or personal bias, with many biographies tending to celebrate the deeds of their subjects without attempting any form of critical analysis. This period's most valuable works are probably those in which personal observations are recounted, when the participants were alive and not sufficiently removed from the period that memory had become totally fallible, and wished to record for posterity the events of the most memorable and exciting part of their lives.

Napoleonic books continued to be produced throughout the nineteenth century, though the publication of some works was undertaken for reasons far removed from those which might be appreciated immediately today. Many works were issued, and campaign-histories written, for the instruction of military officers then serving, and are angled towards providing practical lessons for use in the field rather than towards providing a detailed analysis of the actual events. When the Duc de Fezensac's account of the retreat from Moscow was published in Britain, its editor (W. T. Knowles, sometime Viscount Wallingford, himself a Peninsular veteran) wrote his lengthy introduction not so much as a work of history but because 'we may regard it, then, solely as a military professional question, and therefore worthy of a close investigation'.[1] Another instructed its readers that 'The numbers, as to which there is great discrepancy, are frequently only approximately accurate. The quotations are not always verbatim . . .'[2]

There is no space here to chart the progress of the writings on Napoleonic history; readers are recommended to the introduction by D. D. Horward to *Napoleonic Military History: A Bibliography* (London 1986), a work of immense value, not least in the essays by distinguished contributors which accompany each section of the bibliography. Notice should be taken, however, of the increase of interest in all aspects of the Napoleonic Wars within the last three or four decades. This has tended to include a shift of emphasis from the semi-academic or 'general interest' standpoint towards what might be termed the growth of 'military hobbies': the collecting of militaria, miniature military figures and wargaming. It is this increase of interest which has made possible the publication of a huge number of works covering one or other aspects of the Napoleonic period, including a great upsurge of interest in the military uniforms and equipment of the time (previously a much more specialized study which really only flourished in France and Germany), and in the mechanics of 'minor tactics'. The period from the late 1950s has equally seen the production of much 'academic' work and has encouraged research in contemporary archives, much of which has been published but due to its specialized nature has reached a much more restricted audience than those works of more general interest aimed at a wider readership. This period of increase of interest has produced scholars the equal of any of the great authorities of the past; the reader has only to consider David Chandler's monumental *The Campaigns of Napoleon* (London 1967) for the proof of this, probably the most valuable history and analysis of the subject ever produced.

The increasing interest over the last three decades has also resulted in the production of works which might be termed 'amateur' in that they are issued by very small publishing companies or by groups of enthusiasts (similar, in fact, to the privately-sponsored publication of a number of the earlier nineteenth-century works). Some of these are of little value, based upon third- or fourth-hand material, and including a few which contain the most elementary errors of fact. The majority, however, are all worth consideration as many of these enthusiasts have used original source-material not otherwise easily available to the general reader. A further result of the increase of interest is the fortunate modern proliferation of reprints of contemporary and later material, allowing the modern student easy access to works of great scarcity. A number of these reprints have been produced by publishers not specifically noted for the military content of their work, but others have undertaken a more comprehensive programme of reprinting, for example Ken Trotman Ltd. (Cambridge) which has an expanding selection of Napoleonic titles, Greenhill Books (London) which has a series entitled 'Napoleonic Library', and Worley Publications (Felling, Tyne & Wear) which has re-published a number of important French sources. J. Olmes' *Verlag 'Heere der Vergangeheit'* (Krefeld) has reproduced Malibran's *Guide des Artistes . . .* (Paris 1904), for example; AMS Press

(New York) has made available again Oman's classic *History of the Peninsular War*, and Editions D.A. (La Chapelle-en-Vercors) Leinhart & Humbert's *Les Uniformes de l'Armée Française depuis 1690 jusqu'à 1870* (Leipzig, 1897–1906). The range of reprints is not limited just to books; reprints of a limited number of Knötel's *Uniformenkunde* plates were reprinted by Olmes and a complete re-issue is planned by Friese and Lacina Editions (Hamburg), and similarly Lucien Rousselot's invaluable series *L'Armée Française* is again available. For commercial reasons many of these reprints are available only in small numbers, so that they should be considered as soon as they appear, for the original editions are in most cases prohibitively expensive even when they do appear for sale, which in many cases is very infrequently. Support of such reprints has the added advantage of providing incentive for publishers to re-issue additional titles.

A wide number of periodicals exist of interest to the Napoleonic student. Some of these are the journals of societies of varying degrees of sophistication, some of considerable age and great repute: the *Carnet de la Sabretache* (France, founded 1893), the British *Journal of the Society for Army Historical Research* and the US *Military Collector and Historian* are examples. Most such societies are concerned with military history in general but a few deal exclusively with the period under review, such as the Napoleonic Association. (For a comprehensive list, see Horward's *Bibliography* mentioned above.) More recent are a number of commercial magazines, made financially viable by the increasing interest in 'military hobbies', including some which maintain the highest standard of production and illustration, for example the British *Military Illustrated Past and Present*, the French *Uniformes* (ex-*Gazette des Uniformes*) and *Tradition*, a French publication bearing the same name as a previous British periodical; none of these should be overlooked by the Napoleonic enthusiast. Nor should other publications be disregarded: it is easy to be dismissive of wargamers as merely those who 'play with toy soldiers', but sceptics should realize that many wargamers have studied the period and its tactics to a very high degree. Doubters should refer to the periodical *Empires, Eagles and Lions*, the journal of the New Jersey Association of Wargamers (originally published in Cambridge, Ontario) which under the editorship of Jean Lochet and Thomas DeVoe has become an invaluable forum for discussion of Napoleonic history, especially 'minor tactics'.

Wargaming is one aspect of a comparatively new branch of 'military hobby', that of the construction of miniature military figures. While at the highest level these can attain the status of genuine works of art, the existence of so many modellers has facilitated the publication of many works concerning the uniforms and equipment of the Napoleonic period, for example in the Blandford Press 'Colour Series' of the 1970s and early 1980s, and the current 'Men-at-Arms' series of Osprey Publishing.

An even more modern manifestation of the growth of interest in the Napoleonic era is the creation of 'living history' or 're-enactment' groups, enthusiasts who dress in the costume of the period, learn the drill and give public exhibitions of 'bringing history to life'. Especially in the United States, but now increasingly in Europe, many of these bodies attain a high degree of authenticity in their dress and equipment so that they attain a greater significance than being simply the followers of a drum so distant as to be almost inaudible. Those members who study the period in depth can probably attain an understanding different from, if not necessarily better, than those whose province is merely the printed word, at least as far as the everyday life of the 'lowest common denominator' is concerned; though a complete transportation into the conditions and thought of the early nineteenth century is, of course, impossible.

Having thus surveyed briefly the aspects of source-material available to the student of Napoleonic history, a comment should be made upon the validity of some of these sources. At its most basic, some statements of 'fact' which appear even in modern works are incorrect, mistakes or based upon misapprehensions or faulty material, or statements which appeared accurate at the time of writing but which have since been called into question as a result of new research or further information. Fortunately few works are so patently absurd as the fascinating curio *Historic Doubts Relative to Napoleon Bonaparte* by 'Konx Ompax' (London 1819, 9th ed., London 1849) which propounds the startling theory – apparently written at a time when Napoleon was still in custody on St. Helena – that he *never* existed but was merely a combination of the deeds of many of his generals, a theory so bizarre that its inaccuracy is evident immediately. What is sometimes harder to detect is personal bias, though fortunately in many cases this is very obvious and the reader may take note accordingly. This is not to imply that judgements which appear to include personal or national bias are necessarily incorrect, though few modern historians would emulate Sir John Fortescue's robust and unequivocal style which makes his writing attractive to read as well as historically important; for example his description of the Prince of Orange as 'a meddlesome and mischievous encumbrance' whose father 'may well have thought that a crown adds an augmentation to the brain as well as an adornment to the brow',[3] or noting in his introduction to the 1928 edition of Coignet that the statements of that worthy and brave ordinary soldier were unusual in French memoirs in that 'They are free from boasting and self-glorification, and they say very little about glory or the superiority of France; all of which goes to show that the French soldier can be as simple, modest and straightforward as the English'![4]

Even today, the Napoleonic Wars arouse strong emotions. When the Peninsular army crossed the Pyrenees into France, the Duke of Wellington sent back his Spanish troops to prevent them looting French civilians ('I have not had thousands of officers and soldiers killed and wounded for the remainder to plunder the French.')[5] A modern Spanish author comments: 'The Duke's order seems innocent to me, to say the least; seeking kid glove treatment from men who were persecuted mercilessly like vermin for five years, shot instantly for being combatants, burn [sic] in their homes, retaliation taken against their families, with many of them held in France as hostages. The feeling of making them pay altogether was more than justified for them.'[6]

A further difficulty lies in the field of eye-witness accounts and contemporary writing, for in Wellington's analogy, a battle was like a ball in that a participant was only aware of what happened in his immediate vicinity. Nevertheless such events provoked much unwarranted speculation, or, as Wellington again expressed it, anyone who could write and who possessed a friend who could read would write an account of what he did not know and comment upon what he did not understand! A more charitable version of the same comment was that given by William Napier in the preface to the first volume of his *History of the War in the Peninsula*: '. . . two men observing the same object, will describe it diversely, following the point of view from which either beholds it. That which in the eyes of one is a fair prospect, to the other shall appear a barren waste, and yet neither may see it aright! Wherefore, truth being the legitimate object of history, I hold it better that she should be sought for by many than by few, lest, for want of seekers, amongst the mists of prejudice, and the false lights of interest, she be lost altogether.'[7] (Napier's own work is known for being perhaps unduly harsh on Beresford!)

'Contemporary' sources are of immense value, though a degree of circumspection is needed in evaluating even official documents. Napoleon's dispatches are notoriously inaccurate, though not quite so bad as his critics stated: William T. Knowles noted that 'We have known men that could not tell a lie. Napoleon could neither speak nor write truth . . . His life was one great lie from the day of his starting into notice';[8] but the fact that a common French expression was 'to lie like a bulletin' offers testimony to their veracity as seen at the time.

The manipulation of facts was not restricted to Napoleon; Wellington recalled that he received Beresford's first report of Albuera with dismay: 'He wrote me to the effect that he was delighted I was coming; that he could not stand the slaughter about him nor the vast responsibility. His letter was quite in a desponding tone. It was brought to me next day, I think, by General Arbuthnot when I was at dinner at Elvas, and I said directly, "This won't do; write me down a victory." The dispatch was altered accordingly.'[9]

Personal prejudices intrude perhaps more in the contemporary quotes about Napoleon than about any other figure or subject; for example: 'Between the dwarfish form of the man and his enormous arrogance, there is a disparity too preposterous for feeling to rid itself of; except by laughter. Yet how suddenly is this emotion checked, by the remembrance of the general destruction in which he endeavours to involve mankind. Is it not miserable to reflect that the paltry, the frothy, the despicable thing called vanity, raging in a being so impotent, should be the cause of such desolation?'[10] Other accounts are simply wrong; for example, 'Bonaparte is by no means popular – He is cold and

reserved – he knows not how to inspire affection,'[11] is patently ridiculous!

Contemporary press reports can be of great value, but bearing in mind Wellington's remark noted above regarding letters written by people on subjects they neither knew or understood, it should be borne in mind that many such accounts found their way into newspapers without alteration or any attempt to check the validity of their statements, usually printed under the heading of 'extract of a letter from . . .' Some reported stories were even completely false (a near-contemporary condemnation of this practice, and an explanation of how it could occur, is given in 'Penny-a-Liners', in *Chambers' Edinburgh Journal*, 1 February 1845, pp. 65–8). An example of the most glaring inaccuracy that may be encountered was presented to readers of *The News* (London) on 25 June 1815, perhaps the most garbled account of Waterloo ever written:

'Extract of a letter, dated Ostend, the 21st inst.:
"Accounts just received here state, that in the great battle of the 18th, Murat was killed by his brother-in-law Jerome Bonaparte, whether by accident, or intentionally, is not mentioned, and that Bonaparte himself was wounded; that the battle was twice lost, and twice regained by the coolness and bravery of the Duke of Wellington, who in making a charge at the head of the cavalry, had his sword shot out of his hand. We were only able to bring 50,000 men into the field. The Belgians behaved nobly . . ."'

With the exception of crediting Wellington with coolness and bravery, the whole of the above is totally inaccurate. Obviously it was not published with any intent to deceive, but having been written and received only a few days after the battle it was no doubt thought preferable to no news at all about this climactic event.

What follows is a list of some of the most valuable and accessible works for further reading, especially those that are not mentioned in the reference-lists for other sections. It does not pretend to be in any way comprehensive, and readers are again referred to Horward's invaluable *Bibliography* (noted above); for similar lists of titles concerning the War of 1812, see *War of 1812 Resource Guide* (J. C. Fredriksen, Los Angeles 1979), and for a bibliography of Peninsular War memoirs, see the appendix to *Wellington's Army* (Sir Charles Oman, London 1912). Every reader will form his or her own preferences, so the inclusion or omission of any particular title should not be taken as a comment upon its veracity.

Sir Charles Napier noted that only a soldier was truly fitted to write military history, in his comments on Scott's *Life of Napoleon*, stating that for a civilian to write on military affairs was akin to asking a shoemaker to produce a biography of a great surgeon: 'He might, perhaps, give a tolerable account of the gossip held in the patients' room by the servants, but he assuredly would give but a lame account of surgical operations.'[12] Perhaps with this in mind, Sir John Fortescue chose Bunbury's *Narratives* as being 'the best military history in our language',[13] and it is here recommended as an example of an account both informative and entertaining. There is an immense number of personal accounts of the Napoleonic Wars, so that the selection listed below is no more than a representative cross-section of the most accessible. Some of these – Marbot, Coignet, Kincaid, etc. – are deservedly accorded the status of 'classics', though especial mention must be made here of Blakeney's entertaining memoirs and Cooper's rare little work, all of which help to give a human face to the serious and often solid histories of the military operations.

'General' Histories

Alison, Sir Archibald. *History of Europe from the Commencement of the French Revolution to the Restoration of the Bourbons*, Edinburgh 1860 (still remains an interesting work, with informative statistical appendices).

Baines, E. *History of the Wars of the French Revolution*, London 1817 (an interesting contemporary view).

Bryant, Sir Arthur. *The Age of Elegance, 1812–22*, London 1950.

— *The Years of Endurance, 1793–1802*, London 1942.

— *The Years of Victory, 1802–12*, London 1944.

Bunbury, Sir Henry. *Narratives of Some Passages in the Great War with France 1799–1810*, London 1854; r/p with introduction by Hon. Sir John Fortescue, London 1927. (Concerns the 1799 campaign in north Holland, and the Mediterranean 1805–10.)

Chandler, D. G. *The Campaigns of Napoleon*, London 1967. (The leading and irreplaceable modern study.)

— *Dictionary of the Napoleonic Wars*, London 1979.

— (ed.) *Napoleon's Marshals*, London 1987.

Cust, Hon. Sir Edward. *Annals of the Wars of the Nineteenth Century*, London 1862, vol. I 1800–06, II 1807–09.

— *Annals of the Wars of the Eighteenth Century*, London 1862, succeeding vols. from the above: vol. III 1760–83, IV 1783-95, V 1796-99.

Dupuy, R. E., and Dupuy, T. M. *Encyclopedia of Military History*, London 1970 (invaluable in putting the Napoleonic Wars in historical context).

Esposito, V. J., and Elting, J. R. *Military History and Atlas of the Napoleonic Wars*, London 1964 (superb maps, covering all the campaigns in which Napoleon commanded).

Fitchett, W. H. *How England Saved Europe*, London 1899.

Fortescue, Hon. Sir John. *History of the British Army*, London 1899–1920.

Glover, M. *The Napoleonic Wars: An Illustrated History 1792–1815*, London 1979.

Griffith, P. (ed). *Wellington Commander: The Iron Duke's Generalship*, Chichester 1985.

Oman, Sir Charles. *Studies in the Napoleonic Wars*, London 1929 (r/p Elstree 1987).

Quennevat, J.-C. *Atlas de la Grande Armée*, Paris 1966 (excellent gazetteer).

The Revolutionary Wars

Goodspeed, D. J. *Bayonets at St. Cloud: the Story of the 18th Brumaire*, London 1965.

Heriot, A. *The French in Italy 1796–99*, London 1957.

Jonnès, M. *Adventures in the Revolution and under the Consulate*, London 1929 (r/p with introduction by M. Glover, London 1969).

Pakenham, T. *The Year of Liberty: the great Irish Rebellion of 1798*, London 1969.

Phipps, R. W. *The Armies of the First French Republic*, Oxford 1935–9.

Postgate, R. *1798: Story of a Year*, London 1969.

Rodger, A. B. *The War of the Second Coalition 1798–1801*, ed. C. Duffy, Oxford 1964.

Ross, M. *Banners of the King: the War of the Vendée*, London 1975.

Thiers, L. A. *A History of the French Revolution 1789–1800*, London 1895.

Tranié, J., and Carmigniani, J.-C. *Bonaparte: la Campagne d'Egypte*, Paris 1988.

— *La Patrie en Danger 1792–93: Les Campagnes de la Révolution*, Paris 1987.

1805–9

Bowden, S., and Tarbox, C. *Armies on the Danube 1809*, Arlington, Texas, 1980.

Duffy, C. *Austerlitz 1805*, London 1977.

Müller, W. *Relation of the Operations and Battles of the Austrian and French Armies in the Year 1809*, London 1810 (r/p Cambridge 1986).

Petre, F. L. *Napoleon and the Archduke Charles*, London 1909 (r/p with introduction by D. G. Chandler, London 1976). (The campaign of 1809.)

— *Napoleon's Campaign in Poland 1806-07*, London 1901 (r/p with introduction by D. G. Chandler, London 1972).

— *Napoleon's Conquest of Prussia 1806*, London 1907 (r/p with introduction by D. G. Chandler, London 1972).

Stutterheim, General. *A Detailed Account of the Battle of Austerlitz*, Cambridge 1985 (r/p).

Tranié, J., and Carmigniani, J. -C. *Napoléon et la Russie 1805–07*, Paris.

— *Napoléon et l'Autriche: la Campagne de 1809*, Paris 1979.

— *Napoléon et l'Allemagne: Prusse 1806*, Paris 1984.

Wilson, Sir Robert. *Brief Remarks on the Character and Composition of the Russian Army, and a Sketch of the Campaigns in Poland in the Years 1806–1807*, London 1810.

1812

Brett-James, A. *1812*, London 1966 (collection of first-hand accounts).

Duffy, C. *Borodino and the War of 1812*, London 1972.

Fezensac, Duc de. *A Journal of the Russian Campaign of 1812*, ed. W. Knollys, London 1852 (r/p Cambridge 1988).

Labaume, E. *Circumstantial Narrative of the Campaign in Russia*, London 1814.

Nafziger, G. F. *Napoleon's Invasion of Russia*, Novato, California 1988.

Palmer, A. *Napoleon in Russia*, London 1967.

Pivka, Otto von. *Armies of 1812*, Cambridge 1977.

Roeder, Captain F. *The Ordeal of Captain Roeder*, ed. H. Roeder, London 1960.

Ségur, P. *History of Napoleon's Expedition to Russia*, London 1825.

Uxkull, B. *Arms and the Woman: the Diaries of Baron Boris Uxkull*, ed. D. von Uexkull, London 1966.

Vossler, H. A. *With Napoleon in Russia*, London 1969.

Wilson, Sir Robert. *General Wilson's Journal 1812–14*, ed. A. Brett-James, London 1964.

— *Narrative of Events during the Invasion of Russia by Napoleon Bonaparte*, ed. Revd. H. Randolph, London 1860.

— *Private Diaries of Travels . . . with the European Armies in the Campaigns of 1812, 1813, 1814*, ed. Revd. H. Randolph, London 1861.

1813–14

Austin, T. *Old Stick-Leg: Extracts from the Diaries of Major Thomas Austin*, ed. H. H. Austin, London 1926 (1813–14 campaign in the Netherlands).

Brett-James, A. *Europe Against Napoleon*, London 1970 (first-hand accounts of the Leipzig campaign).

Delderfield, R. F. *Imperial Sunset: the Fall of Napoleon*, London 1969.

Petre, F. L. *Napoleon at Bay*, 1814, London 1914 (r/p with introduction by D. G. Chandler, London 1977).

Tranié, J., and Carmigniani, J. -C. *Napoléon 1813: la Campagne d'Allemagne*, Paris 1987.

Wilson, Sir Robert. *Private Diaries of Travels . . . with the European Armies in the Campaigns of 1812, 1813, 1814*, ed. Revd. H. Randolph, London 1861.

Peninsular War

Batty, R. *Campaign of the Left Wing of the Allied Army in the Western Pyrenees*, London 1823 (r/p London 1983).

Blakeney, R. *A Boy in the Peninsular War*, ed. J. Sturgis, London 1899.

D'Urban, Sir Benjamin. *The Peninsular Journal of Major-General Sir Benjamin D'Urban 1808–17*, ed. I. J. Rousseau, London 1930 (r/p as *The Peninsular Journal 1808–17*, London 1988).

Fletcher, I. *In Hell Before Daylight*. Tunbridge Wells 1984 (storm of Badajos).

Foy, Comte Maximilien. *Histoire de la Guerre de la Peninsule sous Napoléon*, Paris 1827; latest r/p as *History of the War in the Peninsula*, 1989.

Gleig, G. R. *The Subaltern*, Edinburgh 1872 (sometimes misclassified as fiction).

Glover, M. *Britannia Sickens: Sir Arthur Wellesley and the Convention of Cintra*, London 1970.

— *The Peninsular War 1807–14: a Concise Military History*, Newton Abbot 1974.

— *Wellington's Peninsular Victories*, London 1963.

Gordon, A. *A Cavalry Officer in the Corunna Campaign*, ed. H. C. Wylly, London 1913.

Grattan, W. *Adventures with the Connaught Rangers 1809–14*, London 1847, r/p ed. Sir Charles Oman 1902, r/p London 1989.

Green, W. *A brief outline of the Travels and Adventures of W. Green, Bugler, Rifle Brigade, during a period of ten years*, Coventry 1857; r/p as *Where Duty Calls Me*, ed. J. and D. Teague, West Wickham, Kent, 1975.

Harris, B. *The Recollections of Rifleman Harris*, ed. H. Curling, London 1848; r/p, ed. C. Hibbert, London 1970. (The author is sometimes referred to as 'John Harris', as in 1970 edn. v.; Curling identified him as Benjamin Harris, as in *United Services Journal* 1839, II, p. 399.)

Hawker, P. *Journal of a Regimental Officer during the Recent Campaign in Portugal and Spain*, London 1810 (published anonymously); r/p London 1981.

Hibbert, C. *Corunna*, London 1961.

Londonderry, Marquis of. *Narrative of the Peninsular War from 1808 to 1813*, London 1828.

Long, R. B. *Peninsular Cavalry General 1811–13*, ed. T. H. McGuffie, London 1951.

Myatt, F. *British Sieges of the Peninsular War*, Tunbridge Wells 1987.

Napier, W. F. P. *History of the War in the Peninsula*, London 1832–40 (the classic early history).

Oman, Sir Charles. *History of the War in the Peninsula*, Oxford 1902–30, r/p 1980 (the greatest and most indispensible history).

Rudorff, R. *War to the Death: the Sieges of Saragossa*, London 1974.

Sherer, M. *Recollections of the Peninsula*, London 1825 (published anonymously).

Simmons, G. *A British Rifle Man*, ed. W. Verner, London 1899.

Tranié, J., and Carmigniani, J. -C. *Napoléon et la Campagne d'Espagne*, Paris 1978.

Verner, W. *History and Campaigns of the Rifle Brigade, 1809–13*, London 1919 (the best 'Peninsular' regimental history).

Warre, W. *Letters from the Peninsular 1808–12*, ed. Revd. E. Warre, London 1909 (Portuguese staff).

Weller, J. *Wellington in the Peninsula*, London 1962.

Wood, G. *The Subaltern Officer*, London 1825 (r/p Cambridge 1986).

The War of 1812

Caffrey, K. *The Lion and the Unicorn: the Anglo-American War 1812–15*, London 1978.

Fredriksen, J. C. *War of 1812 Resource Guide*, Los Angeles 1979.

Gleig, G. R. *The Campaigns of the British Army at Washington and New Orleans*, London 1827 (r/p with introduction by R. Reilly, Wakefield 1972).

Lossing, B. J. *The Pictorial Field Book of the War of 1812*, New York 1869 (r/p New York 1970).

Padfield, P. *Broke and the Shannon*, London 1968.

Waterloo Campaign

Batty, R. *An Historical Sketch of the Campaign of 1815*, London 1820 (r/p London 1981).

Brett-James, A. *The Hundred Days*, London 1964 (collection of first-hand accounts).

Cotton, E. *A Voice from Waterloo*, 9th enlarged edn., Brussels 1900.

De Lancey, Lady. *A Week at Waterloo in 1815,* ed. B. R. Ward, London 1906.

Gourgaud, G. *The Campaign of MDCCCXV,* London 1818 (r/p London 1982).

Houssaye, H. *1815,* Paris 1893.

Howarth, D. *A Near Run Thing,* London 1968.

Kelly, C. *The Memorable Battle of Waterloo,* London 1817.

Lachouque, H. *Waterloo 1815,* Paris 1972.

Mercer, C. *Journal of the Waterloo Campaign,* Edinburgh 1870.

Müffling, F. C. F. von. *History of the Campaign of 1815,* ed. Sir J. Sinclair, Bt., London 1816 (r/p with introduction by Major-General B. P. Hughes, Wakefield 1970).

Naylor, J. *Waterloo,* London 1960.

Siborne, H. T. (ed.). *The Waterloo Letters,* London 1891 (r/p 1983).

Siborne, W. *The Waterloo Campaign,* London 1844.

Weller, J. *Wellington at Waterloo,* London 1967.

Wood, Sir Evelyn. *Cavalry in the Waterloo Campaign,* London 1895.

Naval Campaigns

Howarth, D. *Trafalgar: the Nelson Touch,* London 1969.

James, W. *The Naval History of Great Britain from the Declaration of War by the French Republic in 1793 to the Accession of George IV,* London 1837.

Lloyd, C. *St. Vincent and Camperdown,* London 1963.

Mahan, A.T. *The Influence of Sea Power in the French Revolution and Empire 1793–1812,* London 1892.

Masefield, J. *Sea Life in Nelson's Time,* 1905; r/p with introduction by C. C. Lloyd, London 1971.

Padfield, P. *Broke and the* Shannon, London 1968.

Pivka, Otto von. *Navies of the Napoleonic Era,* Newton Abbot 1980.

Pope, D. *The Great Gamble: Nelson at Copenhagen,* London 1972.

— *Life in Nelson's Navy,* London 1981.

Warner, O. *Nelson and the Age of Fighting Sail,* London 1963.

— *The Glorious First of June,* London 1961.

— *Trafalgar,* London 1959.

Prisoners of War

Abell, F. *Prisoners of War in Britain 1756 to 1815,* Oxford 1914.

Blayney, A. T. *Narrative of a Forced Journey through Spain and France as a Prisoner of War,* London 1814.

Elton, Mrs. O. *Locks, Bolts and Bars: Stories of Prisoners in the French Wars,* London 1945.

Fraser, E. *Napoleon the Gaoler,* London 1914.

Hewson, M. *Escape from the French,* ed. A. Brett-James, London 1981.

Law, E. B. *With Napoleon at Waterloo,* ed. McK. MacBride, London 1911 (includes *A British Prisoner in France: his Sufferings and Adventures,* D. Nicol).

MacDougall, I. *The Prisoners at Penicuik,* Dalkeith 1989.

Walker, T. J. *The Depot for Prisoners of War at Norman Cross,* London 1913.

Memoirs (excluding those concerned with a single campaign only)

Anon. ('T.S.') *Journal of a Soldier of the 71st or Glasgow Regiment, Highland Light Infantry, from 1806 to 1815,* Edinburgh 1819 (r/p as *A Soldier of the Seventy-First,* ed. C. Hibbert, London 1975).

Barrès, J.-B. *Memoirs of a Napoleonic Officer,* ed. M. Barrès, London 1925.

Bourgogne, A. J. B. F. *Memoirs of Sergt. Bourgogne 1812–13,* ed. P. Cottin and M. Henault, London 1899 (r/p with introduction by D. G. Chandler, London 1979).

Coignet, J.-R. *The Note-books of Capt. Coignet,* with introduction by Hon. Sir John Fortescue, London 1928.

Cooper, J. S. *Rough Notes of Seven Campaigns in Portugal, Spain, France and America,* Carlisle 1869.

Costello, E. *Memoirs of Edward Costello,* London 1857 (r/p as *The Peninsular and Waterloo Campaigns: Edward Costello,* ed. A. Brett-James, London 1967).

François, C. *From Valmy to Waterloo,* ed. R. B. Douglas, London 1906.

Gonneville, A. de. *Recollections of Colonel de Gonneville,* ed. C. M. Yonge, London 1875.

Kincaid, Sir John. *Adventures in the Rifle Brigade,* London 1830 (r/p in Maclaren's combined edn., London 1908, with *Random Shots from a Rifleman,* London 1835).

Leach, J. *Rough Sketches in the Life of an Old Soldier,* London 1831 (r/p London 1986).

Low, E. B. *With Napoleon at Waterloo,* ed. McK. MacBride, London 1911 (also includes accounts of Egypt and the Peninsula).

Marbot, General Baron. *The Memoirs of Baron de Marbot,* trans. A. J. Butler, London 1913.

Morris, T. *Recollections,* 1845, r/p as *The Napoleonic Wars: Thomas Morris,* ed. J. Selby, London 1967.

Neville, J. F. *Leisure Moments in the Camp and in the Guard-Room,* York 1812 (published under *nom-de-plume* 'A Veteran British Officer').

Parquin, C. *Napoleon's Army*: Charles Parquin, ed. B. T. Jones, London 1969.

Surtees, W. *Twenty-Five Years in the Rifle Brigade,* London 1833 (r/p with introduction by L. V. Archer, London 1973).

Tomkinson, W. *The Diary of a Cavalry Officer in the Peninsula and Waterloo Campaign,* ed. J. Tomkinson, London 1895.

Wheeler, W. *The Letters of Private Wheeler 1809–28,* ed. B. H. Liddell Hart, London 1951.

Notes

1. *Journal of the Russian Campaign,* London 1852, p. v.

2. *The Spanish Campaign of Sir John Moore,* J. H. Anderson, London 1905, written specifically for the military Promotion Examination of November 1905.

3. *History of the British Army,* vol. X, London 1920; an extract of which has been re-issued as *The Campaign of Waterloo,* Elstree 1987.

4. *The Note-books of Captain Coignet,* London 1928, p. vii.

5. *Dispatches of Field-Marshal the Duke of Wellington,* ed. J. Gurwood, London 1834–39, X, p. 287.

6. 'La Batalla de Vitoria, 21 de Junio de 1813', E. Larreina Escudero, in *La Batalla de*

Vitoria: 175 Años Despues,
Vitoria 1988.
7. London 1832, p. vii.
8. *Journal of the Russian Campaign
of 1812,* Duc de Fezensac;
extract from editor's
introduction to 1852 edn.,
London, p. viii.
9. *The Wellington Memorial,* A. J.
Griffiths, London 1897 pp.
307–8.

10. *Travels from Hamburgh through
Westphalia and the Netherlands to
Paris,* Thomas Holcroft,
London 1804.
11. *Bonaparte, and the French People
under his Consulate,* anon.
('Translated from the
German'), London 1804.
12. Fezensac, op. cit.; Knollys'
introduction, pp. vii, civ.
13. 1927 edn., p. xii.

LITERATURE AND FICTION OF THE NAPOLEONIC WARS

It could be said that the Napoleonic era produced only a limited amount of great literature, at least as a direct result of the wars; and there were few major 'soldier-authors' whose work has genuine literary merit rather than historical or autobiographical worth, William Napier perhaps being one exception, as some have regarded passages of his *History of the War in the Peninsula* as outstanding literature as well as history. Few great literary personalities actually served in the Napoleonic Wars; there was, for example, no major figure like the poet Ewald von Kleist (1715–59) who served in Frederick the Great's army and was mortally wounded at Kunersdorf. There were, however, a few exceptions.

Bernd H. W. von Kleist (1777–1811), the poet, dramatist and novelist, served in the Prussian army from 1792 to 1799, and was imprisoned by the French for six months as a spy. His work contains many analogies to patriotic indignation at his country's enemies, perhaps most markedly in *Die Hermannschlacht* (1809); his bitterness was probably responsible in part for his successful suicide-pact with his paramour! Friedrich M. von Klinger (1752–1831), born at Frankfurt-am-Main, rose to the rank of lieutenant-general in Russian service; he is probably best remembered for coining the phrase '*Sturm und Drang*' the title of a work of 1776. The Hanoverian Karl W. F. von Schlegel (1772–1829) served in 1809 as court secretary to Archduke Charles's headquarters; and similarly, Russia's great fabulist, Ivan A. Kriloff (1768–1844), himself the son of a distinguished officer, served as secretary to Prince Sergei Galitzin during the latter's tenure as military governor of Livonia. Samuel Taylor Coleridge (1772–1834) served a brief period in the 15th Light Dragoons under the pseudonym of Silas Tomkyn Comberbache, and like the majority of the British literary world, his original sympathies with the French Revolution turned to hostility. ('Bliss was it in that dawn to be alive/But to be young was very heaven!': William Wordsworth, *The Prelude*). William Cobbett (1766–1835) had a successful military career, rising to the rank of sergeant-major, but left the army at his own instigation in 1791, and his radical sentiments governed his writing from the beginning of the wars; he produced his own anti-government newspaper, *Cobbett's Weekly Political Register,* and eventually received two years' gaol over his outspoken criticism of the flogging of five members of the Cambridgeshire Local Militia.

In the Napoleonic age, France produced very few figures of the highest literary calibre, probably excluding only André de Chenier, Chateaubriand and Madame de Staël. The poet André de Chenier (1762–94) had served in the army, but was antagonistic towards the Convention and was guillotined for no good reason; his brother, the lesser poet and dramatist Marie-Joseph (1764–1811) was more in sympathy with the revolution, and voted for the death of Louis XVI, but his relationship with the later regime was somewhat awkward. François, Vicomte de Chateaubriand (1768–1848) was hardly in Napoleon's best favour; he gave great offence to the Emperor in 1807 in an article which included allusions to Nero, and in 1811 he was forbidden to deliver an address to the Academy on account of its hostile attitude towards Napoleon. Alphonse M. L. de Larmartine (1790–1869) was one of few major literary figures to serve in the the army, but as his family was royalist he only joined the *Garde du Corps* at the first Restoration, and went to safety in Switzerland during the Hundred Days! One of the best-remembered authors of the period, Claude J. Rouget de Lisle (1760–1836) was an engineer officer, but despite his hugely successful and influential *Marseillaise* (originally titled *Chant de guerre de l'armée du Rhin)* was suspected of being only a moderate republican and was cashiered and imprisoned for a time; his fame rests upon the one work, and that probably a result of its effect rather than its literary merit. Of the other literary giants of the period, Johann W. von Goethe (1749–1832), probably the greatest of all German authors (born at Frankfurt-am-Main) had no real sympathy with the 'war of liberation' or the German nationalist movement, and actually admired Napoleon. Goethe's friend Johann C. F. von Schiller (1759–1805), the other great German figure, died before such events could concern him.

A number of authors produced works occasioned by the events of their time: the German dramatist F. F. von Kotzebue (1761–1819), for example, produced satirical pieces against Napoleon (though his reactionary sentiments resulted in his murder in Mannheim). The greatest Russian poet of the age, Vasili Zhukovskiy (1783–1852), built much of his fame on Russian translations of foreign works – perhaps most notably Gray's *Elegy* – but his *The Poet in the Camp of the Russian Warriors* was hugely popular in 1812.

Given the importance of the events of the Napoleonic Wars, it is not surprising that the period has served as a background for innumerable works of fiction, of varying literary merit. These can be divided into two basic categories: those which feature the Napoleonic Wars as the central theme of the work, and those in which the period is subsidiary to the interplay of characters, who just happen to be set against a Napoleonic-era background. Both cases provide considerable interest.

The greatest novel which uses the Napoleonic Wars as its setting is Leo Tolstoy's *War and Peace,* which exemplifies what is perhaps the most successful style of Napoleonic novel, in which fictional characters are integrated into actual events; this is especially true in those cases where the author undertook research into the background, or who was himself a historian familiar with the subject in ways other than the work necessary to produce the single story in question. Occasionally this can lead to confusion if it becomes difficult to distinguish fact from fiction. Gleig's autobiographical account of his Peninsular War service, *The Subaltern*, for example, has in the past sometimes been confused with fiction; whereas *Stories from Waterloo* (W. H. Maxwell, London 1856) gives the impression from its title that it is an assemblage of Waterloo anecdotes, while in fact it blends fictional characters with conventional accounts of various actions.

Even works of total fiction, if produced by a writer who had lived through the period, are useful for presenting a view of the attitudes or events of the period, for example Jane Austen's *Northanger Abbey*, which features a light dragoon officer, Captain Frederick Tilney. (Two of the novelist's brothers, in fact, enjoyed distinguished naval careers at this time.) Sir Walter Scott's *The Antiquary* offers another example, in its valuable portrayal of attitudes to the threat of French invasion and support for the local volunteer forces, doubtless founded upon Scott's own enthusiasm for the volunteers: he was said to have acquired much of the inspiration for *Marmion* while exercising with his Edinburgh Light Dragoons, of which he was quartermaster and secretary; Lord Cockburn's *Memorials* includes an account of how Scott would practise enthusiastically with his sabre, slashing at a turnip mounted on a pole to represent a Frenchman, saying to himself all the while, 'Cut them down, the villains, cut them down!' Representative of other important works of literature include the stories of Erckmann-Chatrian (the *non-de-plume* of the joint authors Emile Erckmann and Louis G. C. A. Chatrian), whose *Histoire d'un conscrit de 1813* (1864) and *Waterloo* (1865) contain vivid battle-descriptions, even though both authors were born after the Napoleonic Wars. Other works are founded upon actual military experience: for example, Alfred de Vigny's important *Servitude et grandeur militaires* (1835), semi-novel, semi-commentary, though de Vigny's own military service began only in 1814 with the reconstituted *Maison du Roi* of the restored monarchy. (An excellent modern English translation of this work is *The Military Condition*, trans. M. Barnett, intro. J. Cruikshank, Oxford 1964.)

Some works of fiction transcend this category and become historical references in their own right, so closely are they based upon actual characters or events. Chief among these is Charles Lever's splendid *Charles O'Malley, the Irish Dragoon* (1841), in which can clearly be recognized real characters who appear in Grattan's account of his Peninsular services with the 88th Foot (Connaught Rangers). So much of Lever's material presumably came from anecdotes told by ex-Rangers that the eccentric surgeon well-known throughout the army, Maurice Quill, appears in *Charles O'Malley* without even a token change of name. Some works of literature are not fiction at all, but are accounts of actual events. For example, Thomas Hardy's story *The Melancholy Hussar of the German Legion* is a true story, of the York Hussars Matthaus Tina and Christoph Bless, who were shot for

desertion, Hardy's story being based upon the account given him by Tina's English girlfriend; Hardy's *A Tradition of Eighteen Hundred and Four* (which includes the most unlikely event of Napoleon making a personal reconnaissance of the landing-beaches for an invasion of southern England) is apparently based upon one of the many folk-tales accumulated by Hardy. Several of Hardy's novels refer to this period of rural life, and among the best references is the scene of the drilling of the local volunteers before church in *The Trumpet-Major*, again benefiting from stories heard by Hardy, so that this hilarious account is probably a very true reflection of events which occurred in countless British parishes during the time of the invasion-threat.

Some works of fiction are of very little merit, either literary or historical, though it is unwise to dismiss any without consideration. Even in the genre of juvenile fiction produced in the Victorian period may be encountered works which maintain some level of historic accuracy in the background material (including even battle-plans) which while intended to provide both interest and moral example for their youthful readership make some attempt to incorporate accounts of campaigns which are basically historically accurate. Most famous of such authors was probably G. A. Henty, and while to modern eyes statements such as 'Terence in time quite ceased to feel the loss of his leg, and was able to join in all field sports,'[1] may seem unusual, the phrasing is actually of a style which might have been employed by genuine veterans of the Napoleonic conflicts.

Many modern authors have produced works of fiction based on Napoleonic subjects, some of which enjoy a high level of accuracy; by no means are the authors concerned necessarily known as 'military' writers (e.g., Sir Arthur Conan Doyle's *Brigadier Gerard* stories, Georgette Heyer's *The Spanish Bride* and *An Infamous Army*, R. F. Delderfield's *Seven Men of Gascony*, etc.). Others are famous for producing series of novels, for example C. S. Forester's *Hornblower* stories (his Peninsular novel *The Gun* should not be overlooked), while more modern series include Dudley Pope's *Ramage* stories (by an author equally renowned for works of scholarship on the naval aspects of the Napoleonic Wars), Alexander Kent's *Bolitho* series, Patrick O'Brian's *Jack Aubrey* series, and Bernard Cornwell's *Sharpe* series, for example. These finest examples of Napoleonic fiction not only entertain but can be informative, and present such information in a manner less intimidating than that of some histories.

Much poetry was produced relative to, or describing events of, the Napoleonic Wars, some of which is universally famous, such as the Waterloo section of Byron's *Childe Harolde's Pilgrimage* ('There was a sound of revelry by night . . .'), or Felicia Heman's *Casabianca* ('The boy stood on the burning deck'); others of merit are now less well-known, such as Thomas Campbell's *Hohenlinden* ('Few, few shall part where many meet;/The snow shall be their winding-sheet') or *The Battle of the Baltic* (Copenhagen). It is likely that the proximity of the Napoleonic Wars cast a shadow longer than that covering just the poetry about the war itself; Robert Southey's *The Battle of Blenheim*, for example, may reflect the poet's thoughts on the effusion of blood of the Napoleonic conflicts rather than the farther-off Marlburian period which forms the poem's subject ('But what good came of it at last? ... Why that I cannot tell, said he/But 'twas a famous victory').

A great deal of the poetry of the time is totally devoid of literary merit:

'Ranked always with the foremost of the brave,
Our sires of old a bright example gave,
In battle frequent, from the pow'rful bow,
Their fatal arrows laid the foemen low.
In modern discipline the sword should be
As dreadful to a Briton's enemy:
And this our gallant countrymen proved true,
On the ensanguin'd plains of Waterloo . . .'[2]

Yet despite this, it can reflect different attitudes and provide a guide to contemporary thought, such as the 1805 verses concerning the fate of Napoleon should he encounter the Gateshead Volunteers:

'Like an anchor shank, smash! how they'll clatter 'im,
And turn 'im, and skelp 'im, and batter 'im,
His banes sall by pring,
Like a fryin pan ring
When he meets wi' the Bonny Geatsiders.'[3]

Rather typical of the level of popular verses is the following, which perhaps takes its inspiration from *To Lucasta, Going to the Wars* by Richard Lovelace (1618–58) ('I could not love thee, Dear, so much/Loved I not honour more.'):

'Yes! I must go; and tho' I grieve
To think that Love to War must yield,
Yet, Mary, wish me not to stay!
My Country calls me to the field . . .
I could not live a thing despis'd:
Depriv'd of Honour – farewell, Life!
Sweet Mary, if I know thee well,
Thou wouldst not be a Coward's Wife.
Cease then, thine anguish; let not thus
Thine eyes with fruitless tears run o'er!
Thy sighs almost unman my Soul:
I pray thee, weep no more!'[4]

Others express similar sentiments with a higher level of literary skill, for example Scott's stirring *War Song of the Edinburgh Light Dragoons* ('To horse! To horse! the standard flies . . .'), and even more effectively Robert Burns' *Dumfries Volunteers* (in which corps Burns himself served), alias *Does Haughty Gaul Invasion Threat?*, probably the best poetic expression of patriotism towards crown and *people* penned during the period ('Be Britain still to Britain true/Amang ourselves united:/For never but by British hands/Maun British wrangs be righted!'). Certain verses had a considerable effect during the period: it is interesting to note that Wolfe's reputed recitation before the Battle of Quebec of Thomas Gray's matchless *Elegy written in a country churchyard* has parallels in the Napoleonic Wars: it was recorded that

Burns' *Bannockburn* (or *Bruce's Address*) ('Scots, wha hae wi' Wallace bled/Scots, wham Bruce has aften led . . .') was recited before the French attacks at Waterloo, with the line 'See approach proud Edward's power' altered appropriately to 'Napoleon's power'. Much of this contemporary material, even if of very little literary merit, can help the reader approach a step closer to the attitudes of two centuries ago.

Notes

1. *Under Wellington's Command*, G. A.Henty, London 1899, p. 383.
2. *Cowdroy's Manchester Gazette*, 18 May 1816; see *The Earl of Chester's Regiment of Yeomanry Cavalry*, anon., Edinburgh 1898, p. 46; the verse gets even worse and ends, 'And while the nation shall enjoy sweet peace/May Stockport flourish and its trade increase'!).
3. *Rhymes of Northern Bards*, ed. J. Bell, Newcastle 1812, p. 30.
4. *Original Stanzas* by 'E.C.', *Morning Chronicle*, 27 July 1798.

ARTISTS OF THE NAPOLEONIC ERA

While most reference-works contain bibliographies of published sources, very few refer to the accuracy of contemporary or later artwork. Although it is generally true that all artwork executed during the Napoleonic Wars is worthy of consideration as a historical document, it should be realized that not all contemporary illustrations are necessarily accurate simply because they were done at the time; a common failing was for artists to depict the uniforms of their own nation with accuracy, but misunderstand or make errors in the portrayal of the troops of other nations, if for no other reason than the limited opportunities of seeing foreign troops at first hand. Conversely, while many later illustrations are from a viewpoint of authenticity wretched in the extreme, others are meticulous in detail and capture what (to modern eyes at least) would appear to be the genuine character of the Napoleonic Wars. A distinction should also be made between illustrations prepared specifically to depict the uniforms, and those in which uniform-detail is of secondary consideration to battle-scenes or overall design; many significant sources of the former category are poorly drawn or naïve, yet are of more relevance to the costume historian than many works of greater artistic merit.

In general, contemporary portraits should be regarded as accurate unless proven otherwise, as it was generally required of the artist to reproduce accurately the sitter's uniform. With coloured prints, however, it is important to note that there was no colour-printing as such during the Napoleonic era, and that all coloured prints were produced in black-and-white and subsequently hand-coloured. Thus, while most copied accurately the colouring which would have been indicated by the artist and/or publisher, errors can occur by the negligence of the colourist, which should be taken into account. Even those series of 'uniform' prints normally regarded as accurate depictions can suffer from the financial strictures of the period: for example, in order to enable one print to serve for two uniforms, the colourist might be instructed to obscure certain details of an engraving by a heavy layer of opaque watercolour, a process open to error: hence may be found, for example, Martinet prints of the French 'Red' (Dutch) Lancers of the Imperial Guard with the Maltese cross on the cockade still visible, though this was worn only by the 1st (Polish) Lancers of the Guard, whose uniform was that originally depicted on the print.

The artists listed here include many of those whose work will be encountered by the Napoleonic enthusiast, but the list is not comprehensive for reasons of space; any exclusion should not be taken as a comment upon the validity of an artist's work.

Adam, Albrecht (1786–1862)
Bavarian painter, engraver and lithographer; participated in the 1812 Russian campaign as an officer of the Topographical Bureau of the Italian Army, from which his most significant military work comes; published *Voyage de Willenberg en Prusse jusqu'à Moscou en 1812*, Munich 1828. Excellent and accurate artist; much of his work is reproduced in *Les Vrais Soldats de Napoléon*, J. C. Quennevat, Paris 1968.

Adam, Victor (1801–66)
French painter and lithographer, who was not an eye-witness to the campaigns of the Empire (he graduated from Beaux-Arts in 1819) but who published albums of military subjects from the Napoleonic period to the mid-nineteenth century.

Atkinson, John Augustus (1775–c.1833)
British painter and aquatinter. Nephew of the artist James Walker, with whom he worked in Russia for the book *Picturesque Representation of the Russians* (London, 1803–4), and followed it with *Picturesque Representation of the Naval, Military and Miscellaneous Costumes of Great Britain* (London 1807). His print of Waterloo was based on a trip with A. W. Devis in 1815; collaborated on Orme's *Historic Naval and Military Anecdotes*. His work gives a fine 'atmosphere' of the time but is more sketchy than a meticulous record of uniforms in the minutiae of which he evidently had little interest; for example, he shows perhaps five lace loops on the breast of a jacket to create the impression, instead of the correct ten. Nevertheless, his work is of great value in conveying the 'character' of the soldiers.

Von Bartsch, Adam (1757–1821)
Bartsch worked as an engraver in Vienna and is also known as a publisher; he collaborated with von Kobell in producing splendid military scenes.

Bellangé, Joseph Louis Hippolyte (1800–66), known as Hippolyte
French painter and lithographer, pupil of Gros. His early reputation was founded on depictions of Napoleonic subjects, and his most famous publication was *Uniformes de l'Armée française depuis 1815* (c.1831). Though not working contemporaneously with the Napoleonic Wars, his work is

generally accurate and is sometimes superbly if theatrically composed, for example his famous print of the last stand of the Old Guard at Waterloo.

Berka, Johann (1758–1815)
Bohemian engraver, working in Prague; illustrated *L'Armée française (Prague, c.1810)* which is interesting from a costume angle, if not of the highest artistic quality.

British Military Library
The *British Military Library or Journal* was a publication of 1799–1801 which included a series of fine uniform-studies, published by J. Carpenter, London, some of the earliest illustrations executed for the express purpose of illustrating military costume; they are generally very accurate though the same basic engraving may be found coloured for different regimental identities.

Bucquoy, Eugène Louis (1879–1958)
French army officer, author, artist and publisher responsible for the immense and valuable series of uniform-cards *Les Uniformes du Premier Empire*, begun in 1911; founder and editor of the periodical *Le Passepoile*. Artistically his own work was not distinguished but he employed such splendid artists as P. Benigni, H. Boisselier, Victor Huen and Maurice Toussaint, etc.; the standard of accuracy is generally meticulous and the whole production of great artistic merit. A recent series of books incorporating many of the Bucquoy cards forms an invaluable reference which every enthusiast should possess.

Butler, Lady Elizabeth (1846–1933)
Elizabeth Southernden Thompson, who married General Sir William Butler in 1877, is perhaps the best-known and certainly among the most talented of British 'military' artists of the Victorian period. Her fame was established as early as 1874 with her painting *The Roll Call* (depicting the 3/Grenadier Guards in the Crimea), which created a sensation at the Royal Academy. Her subsequent work was equally successful, and unlike many 'military' artists she was regarded as an artist first and a military illustrator second. Characteristics of her work are the sympathetic treatment of the hardships and sufferings of the ordinary soldiers, and the great pains she took to ensure accuracy, interviewing and sketching survivors of some of the battles she depicted. Her Napoleonic scenes (which form a minority of her work) includes one truly great painting (*Quatre Bras*), and one of the most powerful depictions of a cavalry charge ever painted (*Scotland For Ever*: the 2nd Dragoons at Waterloo), as well as a considerable number of less well-known works. While executed with supreme talent, these are not without queries on authenticity: *Quatre Bras*, for example (apparently inspired by a visit to the field, accompanied by a veteran of the action) shows the British 28th wearing the 'Belgic' shako, whereas it is almost certain that they retained the old 'stovepipe' cap; and *Scotland For Ever* depicts the Scots Greys with a guidon, not carried on campaign. Nevertheless, Lady

'Vive l'Empéreur!' A charge of French hussars, as portrayed by Edouard Détaille, which though not contemporary with the period portrays the spirit of the era. (Print after Détaille)

Butler's work establishes her as among the likes of Détaille in the very first rank of battle-painters. Her career is covered superbly in *Lady Butler, Battle Artist* (J. Spencer-Smith and P. Underwood, 1987), written to accompany the major exhibition of her work mounted by the National Army Museum, London.

Charlet, Nicolas-Toussaint (1792–1845)
French painter, engraver and lithographer. Though his work mostly post-dates the Napoleonic era, he was a diehard Bonapartist who had experienced the realities of Napoleonic warfare in his participation in the defence of the Clichy Gate at Paris in 1814; studied under Gros. Though he won repute for his caricatures, his most important military works were *Costumes militaires*(1817), *La vieille armée française, Costumes de l'ex-Garde, Costumes militaires françaises* (1818), etc. All his work tends to glorify Napoleon and especially the Imperial Guard, but is most distinctive, often 'atmospheric' and of a high artistic quality.

David, Jacques-Louis (1748–1825)
The most influential French painter of his generation and the leading neo-classicist. Distantly related to Boucher, but forsook Boucher's rococo in favour of more austere neo-classicism; his *Oath of the Horatii* is the most significant neo-classicist picture and highly topical at the time of its exhibition (1785) for its extolling of republican values. David embraced the revolution wholeheartedly, became a Deputy and voted for the execution of Louis XVI. Briefly imprisoned after the fall of Robespierre, he became an ardent Bonapartist after meeting Napoleon and became the emperor's propagandist, completing great canvases such as *Napoleon crossing the Alps* and the *Coronation*. After Napoleon's fall he fled to Switzerland, then settled in Brussels in 1816, where he died, and was buried with great ceremony. From the stern neo-classical style of his earlier pictures, his later work shows the beginnings of the influence of romanticism; his portraits in particular are supremely executed.

Dayes, Edward (1763–1804)
Born and working in London, Dayes was not primarily a 'military' artist but a watercolour painter of landscapes and miniatures, and mezzotint engraver, of great talent. He is renowned chiefly for a memorable series of uniform-plates of the British Army which were issued in 1792 (with other watercolours intended to increase the series but which were never reproduced); they are not only among the most reliable but have very considerable artistic merit. Dayes committed suicide in 1804.

Détaille, Edouard (1845–1912)
French historical painter, pupil of Meissonier, who served in the *Gardes Mobiles* in the Franco-Prussian War. One of the great battle-painters of history, renowned chiefly for his scenes of the 1870–1 war, but equally adept at evocative pictures of the Napoleonic era, accurately rendered and most evocative of the essence of the Napoleonic legend. Among his most effective paintings are *Vive l'Empéreur* (a charge of French hussars), and *Haut les têtes! La mitraille n'est pas de la merde* (the *Grenadiers à Cheval* of the Imperial Guard at Eylau). A splendid, illustrated review of the artist and his work is *Edouard Détaille: l'héroïsme d'un siècle*, J. Humbert, Paris 1979.

Dighton, Denis (1792-1827)
British painter, son of Robert Dighton, who painted many military pictures in his capacity as Military Painter to the Prince Regent; a fine draughtsman whose work (especially the Peninsular War material) is full of character and generally authentic, if less trustworthy in the field of French uniforms. Some of his battle-scenes in particular are very fine, and especially effective in capturing the character and appearance of the British troops; in 1811–12 he held a commission in the 90th Foot. His Peninsular portraits of Spanish and Portuguese subjects are full of character if perhaps edging towards national stereotyping. He made drawings at Waterloo in 1815, and accompanied the court when George IV visited Scotland in 1822, making many drawings of the events and personalities, but loss of royal favour appears to have affected his mind; he retired to Saint-Servan, Brittany, and died there. Many of his pictures are still in the Royal Collection; they exhibit remarkable skill in the handling of watercolour which compensates for slight errors of proportion.

Dighton, Robert (1752–1814)
Father of Denis Dighton, Robert was exhibiting professionally at the age of 17, and established his living as a miniaturist, watercolourist and writer on artistic technique. Though not primarily a 'military' artist, he made many caricatures-cum-character-studies of great charm from 1801–4, at Brighton and London, and some more finished and quite spectacular watercolour portraits such as one of his son, Robert Dighton Jnr., in the uniform of the Prince of Wales's Volunteers. These are minute records of regimental uniform; the caricatures are in many cases no less accurate but distort proportions to emphasize the character of the subject, and are especially valuable for the information they convey about the uniform of auxiliary units not recorded as fully elsewhere. His son, Robert Dighton Jnr. (1786–1865) produced military caricatures like his father and some superbly finished portraits; but he was a serving officer rather than a professional artist, serving in the Peninsula (wounded at Bayonne, 1/38th Foot) and in India. The work of all three Dightons can be found well represented in *Military Drawings and Paintings in the Royal Collection*, A. E. Haswell Miller and N. P. Dawnay, London 1966–70.

Von Faber Du Faur, Christian G. (1780–1857)
Württemberg artillery officer and military painter who survived the retreat from Moscow and published impressive scenes of the horrors of the campaign in a series of 100 lithographs (Stuttgart 1831–43). An excellent draughtsman, his work is a prime source for the 1812 campaign; a lieutenant of artillery at the time, he eventually attained the rank of general in Württemberg service. Some of his 1812 material is reproduced in *Les Vrais Soldats de Napoléon*, J.-C. Quennevat, Paris 1968.

Feyerabend, Franz (1755–1800)
Feyerabend worked at Basel as an artist and engraver, and produced a series of prints from life of members of the Swiss Confederation units (1792–7), a valuable record of uniform-details.

Finart, Noël-Dieudonné (1797–1852)
Finart was a French watercolourist whose military work appeared as early as 1814 in a series of engraved costume-prints, mostly showing the occupation forces in France; but though prolific, he showed little interest in an accurate rendition of uniform-details, and thus his work is as suspect as many of the hastily produced military prints issued in Paris during the Occupation.

Von Geissler, Heinrich-Christian (1782–1839)
Painter and watercolourist born and working in Leipzig, who made a number of important 'eye-witness' illustrations of the French troops passing through the city and in battle, 1803–13.

Gérard, Baron François-Paschal-Simon (1770–1837)
French historical and portrait painter; born in Rome, and one of the most famous of David's pupils. Served on a Revolutionary Tribunal (as a way of avoiding military service, a position gained by David's influence), but played no active part in its terrible duties as he claimed to be ill continuously! His *Belisarius* (1795) established his reputation, and thereafter he rivalled David as court painter to the empire; his *Austerlitz* is particularly impressive, as are many of his portraits. Enjoyed great animosity with David latterly, when Gérard espoused the Bourbon cause to secure his position as court painter; his barony was awarded by Louis XVIII in 1819. He ran a huge studio to enable the production of such a large number of portraits, which are generally lacking the depth of David's.

Géricault, Jean-Louis-André-Théodore (1791–1824)
French historical painter, better-known for equine subjects than military; nevertheless his portrait of Lieutenant Dieudonné of the *Chasseurs à Cheval* of the Imperial Guard (exhibited 1812) is one of the most popular images of the Napoleonic era. A pupil of Carle Vernet and influenced greatly by Gros, he is perhaps best-remembered for *The Raft of the Medusa*. During the first restoration he served in the royalist *Mousquetaires* and accompanied the king to Belgium during the Hundred Days. He was killed in a riding accident in England.

Goddard and Booth
T. Goddard (Pall Mall) and J. Booth (Portland Place) were British print-publishers best-known for their 16-part work (each of six plates) *The Military Costume of Europe* (1812; issued in two volumes, London 1822). The subjects of the 96 plates cover British and foreign armies, with a reasonable degree of accuracy, though in minor details errors and omissions are evident. It remains, nevertheless, one of the leading series of uniform-illustrations published during the period, and its coverage of British subjects is second only to Hamilton Smith's work of the same era.

de Goya y Lucientes, Francisco (1746–1828)
Arguably the greatest Spanish artist, certainly since Velasquez, Goya produced a considerable body of work despite an eccentric lifestyle involving brawls, stabbings, the attempted abduction of a nun, banishment from the Spanish court on account of his liaisons, the production of twenty children and increasing insanity. Painter to the Spanish court, his most famous military works are those chronicling the popular uprising in Madrid and its brutal suppression, the portraits of Peninsular War personalities (including the masterly Wellington, and that of Ferdinand VII which makes him appear an idiot), and the devastatingly horrific etchings *The Disasters of War* (1810–13), which perhaps owe much to Callot's *Misères et Malheures de Guerre* of the Thirty Years War. His portraits are excellent, but the scenes are impressions rather than photographic representations, conveying atmosphere rather than intricate details of costume and equipment.

Gros, Antoine Jean, Baron (1771–1835)
French historical painter, a pupil of David and introduced to Napoleon by Josephine. A leading battle-painter, he was a member of the committee which selected the works of art to be looted from Italy and taken to France. David's closest friend, he assumed the leadership of the neo-classical movement after David's death, but unlike David changed from Bonapartist to royalist; his barony was awarded by Charles X. His later classicist pictures were not well received, which rejection (combined with an unhappy marriage) led him to drown himself.

Hamilton Smith, Charles (1776–1859)
The leading British uniform-artist of his day, who rose to the rank of major in the British army (60th, 18th, 6th and 15th Foot). He was of Flemish birth (his family name was Smet) and almost certainly was employed as a British intelligence agent, especially during his tour of north America; he left the army in 1851, having been appointed a Knight of Hanover in 1834. Though his artistic interests were wide, his most famous production was *Costume of the Army of the British Empire*, London 1812–14, aquatinted by I. C. Stadler, depicting the uniform of the British army according to the 1812 regulations; it forms one of the most valuable records of military costume of the period, plates of which appear in countless modern books as virtually the 'standard work' on the subject.

Heath, William (*c.*1785 or 1795–1840)
British illustrator, best-known for his many vivid battle-scenes mostly of Peninsular subjects, published in *Martial Achievements of Great Britain* (Jenkins, London 1814, 51 plates), *Campaigns of Wellington* (1818), *The Wars of Wellington* (1818) and in collaboration with others in Orme's *Historic Military and Naval Anecdotes*; he also produced several series of military costume-prints in the post-Napoleonic era. Also a portraitist, he was a prolific caricaturist (under the famous pseudonym 'Paul Pry'). His battle-scenes are impressive,

sometimes frenetic, though the minutiae of costume-detail (especially those of foreign troops) is not exact.

Hess, Peter (1792–1871)
Bavarian battle-painter and engraver who served in the 1813–14 campaigns with the Bavarian army. Commissioned by the Tsar to paint battle-pictures of the 1812 campaign.

Hoffman, Nicolaus (1740–1823)
Hessian artist, miniaturist and engraver working in Paris 1775–1808, painting French military and court uniforms which he engraved in outline and hand-coloured personally for important clients; later published them tinted by professional colourists. His studies of French republican and Empire troops frequently have a jewel-like quality and are precise records of uniform-detail, but the poses and general demeanour of his subjects are very much those of the *ancien régime* under which he first worked.

Hollitzer, Carl
Austrian military painter whose work spanned the nineteenth and twentieth centuries and who captured the essence of his subject despite at times being almost Impressionistic in its freedom, ranging from precise uniform-studies to action scenes where 'impression' and movement take precedence. His genius can be appreciated from the reproductions of his work in *Napoléon et l'Autriche*, J. Tranié and J. C. Carmigniani, Paris 1979.

Huen, Victor (1874–1939)
French military illustrator and engraver, one of the most distinguished of Bucquoy's collaborators. Illustrated a number of significant uniform and military history books; his style is clear and the details excellently rendered.

'Job' (Jacques Onfroy de Bréville) (1858–1931)
French painter and principally book-illustrator whose colourful tableaux introduced generations of French children to historical art, yet were far more than merely adjuncts to the text of the books in question: 'Job' researched his subject thoroughly to ensure great accuracy of costume and topographical detail, and his love for the Napoleonic era sustained the 'Napoleonic myth' in such works as *La Cantinière* (the Napoleonic volume of a three-part work on French history), *Grand Napoléon des petits enfants* (1893), *Bonaparte* (1910), *Napoléon* (1920) and *Tenues des Troupes de France*. 'Job' was described as the Détaille of book-illustration, and his carefully researched uniform-studies are meticulous in their exactitude.

Kay, John
Kay was a miniature-painter in Edinburgh who produced a large number of semi-caricature engravings depicting personalities of the city, including a large number of military subjects, collected as *Edinburgh Portraits* (Edinburgh, 1837–8); many are dated and range from 1784 to 1816. Though naïve in style and less than completely precise in detail, they

'To the right about – face!'; a typically humorous cartoon by John Kay, depicting Sergeant-Major Gould of the Royal Edinburgh Volunteers; it is especially interesting to compare this depiction of that worthy man with the conventional portrait shown on p. 212.

include much interesting uniform-material. His son, W. Kay, also produced work of a similar nature.

Kininger, Vincenz Georg (1767–1851)
Austrian painter and engraver best-known for his plates of Austrian uniforms, published by Mansfeld in the late 1790s. Meticulous uniform-studies, they form a splendid pictorial gallery of reference for the Austrian army in the period.

Klein, Johann Adam (1792–1875)
Bavarian artist and engraver, trained in Vienna. Not primarily a 'military' artist, he was an eye-witness to the troops of the 1813–14 campaigns and painted many military uniforms, often for his own amusement, admitting a fascination with the colour and style of military costume. His battle-scenes are comparatively few; the bulk of his work

depicts soldiers in natural settings, frequently working or off-duty. Uniform-detail is exact and the skill considerable; collections have been published as *Osterreichische Soldatentypen 1814–15*, and *Bayerische Soldatentypen 1815*, Hamburg 1985.

Knötel, Richard (1857–1914)
German historical painter, arguably the greatest of all historians of military costume. His monumental series of plates *Uniformenkunde* (1890–1914) covers all armies and periods, the result of immense research and frequently utilizing rare contemporary sources. Knötel's uniform-studies are meticulous, but his skill was far more than merely as a portrayer of mannikins, as his historic scenes bear testimony, in such works as *Der Alte Fritz in 50 Bildern für Jung und Alt*, Berlin 1895, and *Die Königin Luise in 50 Bildern für Jung und Alt*, Berlin 1896, in collaboration with the similarly talented C. Röchling. His son, Herbert Knötel, continued his work after his death and revised his *Handbuch der Uniformenkunde*, Leipzig 1896; their painting can be distinguished easily by Herbert's signature 'Knötel d.J.': *Knötel der Junge*.

Von Kobell, Wilhelm (1766–1855)
The son of another distinguished artist, Ferdinand von Kobell, Wilhelm was a Bavarian landscape and military artist, known for several series of splendid uniform- and battle-paintings, many aquatinted by Bartsch. His work has the feel of eye-witness observation, and apart from great artistic merit conveys both the 'character' of the subject and a precise record of the uniform.

Lami, Eugène Louis (1800–90)
French painter and lithographer whose best-known military work is the collaboration with Horace Vernet in the production of *Collection des Uniformes 1791–1814*. Not eye-witness illustrations, they are authentic without involving the depth of research of such as Knötel.

Langendyk, Dirk (1748–1805)
A native of Rotterdam (where he died), Langendyk was a painter and engraver of talent, though by the time of the period in question, when he was working with his son, his work lacks imagination and is a very stereotyped vision of military scenes. However, the battle-scenes concerning the Anglo-Russian expedition to north Holland in 1799 may have been done from life – Langendyk conceivably was present at the British landing – and thus are valuable records of the uniforms. His son, Jan Anthony Langendyk (1780–1818) served in the Dutch navy and produced a considerable number of military paintings (there are more than 550 in the Royal Collection at Windsor), often almost indistinguishable from those of his father, but not generally reliable, and many apparently copied from military costume-prints.

Lawrence, Sir Thomas (1769–1830)
One of the greatest British portraitists, appointed Painter to the King upon the death of Sir Joshua Reynolds in 1792;

professional portraitist at the age of ten. Undeniably a master, his vast outpouring of work resulted in some pictures having a superficial quality, lacking the depth of his best work; yet his reputation was as immense as his income (though he was usually in debt); a considerable part of his fame rests with the commission from George IV to paint all the great personalities of the war against Napoleon. The finest collection of his work is still in the Waterloo Chamber at Windsor. He also formed one of the very finest collections of Old Master drawings ever assembled, a portion of which was bought for the Ashmolean, Oxford. His portraits of Wellington, that showing the Duke holding the Sword of State, and the half-length later used to decorate the British £5 note, are undisputedly among the finest of all portrayals of characters of the Napoleonic Wars.

Lecomte, Hippolyte (1781-1857)

French painter and lithographer who produced an immense series of plates of French costume in 1820–30. His best-known military work is in the form of battle-paintings of considerable merit.

Lejeune, Louis-François, General Baron (1775–1848)

Lejeune is unique in the list of great battle-painters, in that he was not only the leading artist of his genre in Napoleonic France, but a leading and very gallant soldier, A.D.C. or chief of staff to Berthier, Davoût and Oudinot. An engineer officer, rising to the rank of general, Lejeune served in many campaigns, surviving capture by guerrillas in Spain, injuries and the retreat from Moscow. He designed French military uniforms, and his artistic talent was diverse: he worked with the Austrian engraver Mansfeld and was the first to introduce lithography to France, having learned the technique from its inventor Senefelder while on duty with the army. Highly popular in his time, his battle-scenes are incredibly detailed and meticulous in execution, portraying uniforms with few errors. His method he described in his autobiography, which also casts light upon the short-cutting and implied negligence which afflicted the work of other artists of the time: 'Not depending as so many did on my art work for my daily bread, I was never afraid of giving too much time to details. One day, when I was making an excuse to David for having been so long over a painting, he reassured me by saying, "What is done quickly is quickly seen, and would not bear the test of careful examination."'[1] Lejeune's paintings, indeed, repay the most exhaustive examination.

Note
1. *Memoirs of Baron Lejeune*, ed.
   Mrs. A. Bell, London 1897, II,
   p.29.

De Loutherbourg, Philippe Jacques (1740-1812)

De Loutherbourg was born in Strasbourg, but moved to Paris to become a popular painter of landscapes and battle-scenes, Court Painter to Louis XV. He then settled in London, where he remained until his death, becoming a Royal Academician and scenery designer to the Theatre Royal, Drury Lane. He painted a number of dramatic battle-scenes, or scenes of military reviews, which are full of 'atmosphere' and based upon meticulous research into the details of military costume and equipment; for the costume-historian his preparatory sketches are probably as valuable as the finished works. His best-known paintings are *The Duke of York at the Siege of Valenciennes* (1793) and *The Review at Warley* (1780), and prints of Egypt and Maida.

Mansfeld, Sebastian (1751–1816)

Austrian painter and engraver, born in Prague. He painted historical work and portraits, but is probably better-known

Engineer of the Imperial Guard: a contemporary depiction of the uniform shown on p. 178, a print by Martinet with the common exaggeration of making the plume appear far too large.

as an engraver in a series of most accurate costume-prints illustrating Austrian uniforms; see the entry for Kininger.

Martinet, Pierre

French military painter, engraver and publisher, a pupil of Swebach, famous for his publication of uniform-studies in such collections as *Galerie des Enfants de Mars* (*c.*1812–13: uniforms of the Imperial Guard), *Troupes Françaises* and *Troupes Etrangères*. The Martinet series is a prime source of uniform-detail, though not without error nor of the highest artistic quality; plumes of impossible height are a common feature, and prone to variations by the colourist; yet it remains a very important documentation on the appearance of Napoleon's troops. Martinet continued to publish and illustrate after the Napoleonic period, and his company thrived through the Second Empire after his death *c.*1845.

Meissonier, Jean-Louis Ernest (1815–91)

Arguably the greatest of French historical painters, Meissonier's scope was wide but his Napoleonic scenes are the most famous, meticulous in detail and capturing the spirit of the troops of the First Empire in a manner never excelled. His large narrative canvases are well-known, painted on the very grandest scale as Théophile Gautier observed, but his uniform-sketches are equally superb, based on research and the study of extant relics. His most famous image of the Napoleonic era is *1814, la campagne de France*, showing Napoleon ploughing through snow at the head of an exhausted staff, which has been reproduced countless times under the impression that it represents the retreat from Moscow. His work is well covered in *Meissonier: trois siècles d'histoire*, P. Guilloux, Paris 1980.

Opitz, (or Opiz), Georg Emanuel (1775–1841)

German painter and miniaturist born in Prague; witnessed the arrival of the Allied armies in France in 1813–14. His main military work is in the form of uniform-illustrations, including *Russlands und Deutschlands Befreiungskriege*, engraved by Volz, Leipzig 1816–19. His work is generally accurate and based upon personal observation.

Orme, Edward

Orme was a London publisher who produced a number of series of prints depicting Napoleonic actions, using such artists as Atkinson, Dighton and Scharf, engraved by T. Sutherland, M. Dubourg and others: *Orme's Historic, Military, and Naval Anecdotes of Personal Valour, Bravery, and particular incidents . . . in the last long-contested war* (1819), *Battle of Waterloo* (1815), and *Campaigns in Spain and Portugal* (1809–14) are the most famous.

Von Ottenfeld, Rudolf

Austrian military artist best-known for his splendid plates and textual illustrations in *Die Oesterreichische Armee* (Vienna, 1895) in collaboration with Oscar Teuber, still the 'standard work' on Austrian military costume and graced by Ottenfeld's both accurate and artistically supremely competent work.

Pils, Grenadier (1785–1867)

One of the most remarkable artists of the Napoleonic era: an Alsatian who joined the 51st *Demi-Brigade* at the age of 16 as a musician, and who became Marshal Oudinot's valet, whom he served with great loyalty under the most trying of conditions, accompanying the Marshal into places of the greatest danger, forever ready to bind up the injuries of this most-wounded French commander. 'As he had a great natural talent for drawing, he liked to plant himself in a corner of the battle-field, take from his pocket a note-book and pencil, and calmly sketch the scene of the action and the action itself with ingenuous awkwardness but striking precision,' as Oudinot's memoirs state. The same work decries his book (*Journal du grenadier Pils*) as 'of no literary value, but sincere and refreshing in their very simplicity' and describes his drawings as 'daubs'.[1] He attempted to study under Horace Vernet but was unsuccessful; yet though the drawings are 'sketchy' in the extreme, hastily-done and lacking precision, to modern eyes more attuned to freer drawing, they have great vigour and are exciting in being perhaps the most immediate eye-witness sketches of the period, especially significant when they depict Napoleon and his generals, Pils having a unique opportunity to observe the great men at first hand. His son, Isadore Pils, who became a competent painter (his most famous work was *Rouget de l'Isle for the first time declaiming the Marseillaise*) remarked that 'My father was more of a painter than I,' and to a modern view the elder Pils was indeed more of an artist than many who in his time had a high repute.

Note

1. *Memoirs of Marshal Oudinot*, ed.   de Mattos, New York 1897,
   G. Stiegler, trans. A. Teixeira   pp. 28–30.

Porter, Sir Robert Ker (1777–1842)

British author, painter and diplomat, trained under Benjamin West and something of a *Wunderkind*: his immense (40-yard) painting *Storming of Seringapatam* was executed at the age of 15. A widely-travelled man, he had a long association with Russia, being appointed historical artist to the Tsar in 1804, married a Russian princess and died in St. Petersburg. He was knighted by Sweden and by George IV in 1826; served as British consul to Venezuela, and published accounts of his various travels. He accompanied Moore to the Peninsula, was present at Corunna and published *Letters from Portugal and Spain written during the March of the British Troops under Sir John Moore* (under the *nom-de-plume* 'An Officer'), London 1809, upon his return, and illustrated by his own pictures; and in 1813 *A Narrative of the Campaign in Russia During the Year 1812*, based on his experiences in Russia during that year.

Pyne, W. H.

British artist and engraver who published military uniform-plates as part of his *Costume of Great Britain* (London 1804), and more famously his scenes of everyday military life in *Pyne's Microcosm, or, a Picturesque Delineation of the Arts, Agriculture, Manufactures, etc., of Great Britain* (1806, though individual plates are dated 1802 and were probably drawn earlier), which have the air of accurate eye-witness observations of camp life.

Raffet, Auguste (1804–60)
French historical painter, engraver and lithographer; originally a porcelain-decorator. Produced a number of works on military costume, but his greatest fame rests in his scenes of Napoleon and his troops, unashamedly admiring. In 1859 he illustrated Fieffé's *Napoléon et la Garde Impériale*, and his *Voyage en Crimée* (a trip to the Crimea and the Balkans in 1837) is especially fine. The picture which perhaps best encapsulates his military work is *The Awakening*, in which to the sound of a drum the dead of Napoleon's battles rise again, grasp their weapons and prepare to follow their emperor; sentimental but typical of the Napoleonic 'legend'.

Robertson, A.
British artist responsible for a fine series of accurate uniform-studies of British volunteer regiments, 1806–7, mostly published by John Wallis of London, who also issued a series of plates on the same subject (1801–5), which are among the finest of the period.

Rowlandson, Thomas (1756–1827)
British painter and caricaturist, who began his artistic career with classical painting but who turned to caricature and engraving after his inherited fortune had been dissipated by gambling. His greatest fame is as a caricaturist (his great creation was Dr. Syntax) though his military work was considerable, most notably the magnificent *Loyal Volunteers of London and Environs* (London, 1798–9) in the production of which he received assistance from most of the corps portrayed, presumably ensuring accuracy. His military and caricature work overlaps in such works as *The Military Adventures of Johnny Newcome* (1815) in which the vicissitudes of a subaltern's life are illustrated humorously.

St. Clair, Thomas Staunton (1785–1847)
British infantry officer (1st Foot and 21st Portuguese, later commander of the 5th *Caçadores*) who was an artist of very considerable talent. He wrote *A Residence in the West Indies and America, With a Narrative of the Expedition to Walcheren* (London 1834), but is best known for his *Series of Views of the principal occurrence of the Campaign in Spain and Portugal*, Peninsular War scenes drawn from his own experience, engraved by C. Turner and among the most accurate views of the period.

Sauerweid, Alexander Ivanovich (1783–1844)
Russian painter and aquatinter who worked in Dresden until 1814, who produced battle-paintings for the Tsar in St. Petersburg from that year, but who is perhaps better known

for his albums of uniform-studies, on the Saxon and Westphalian armies (1810), the Polish (1813) and the Russian (1814); also produced uniform-illustrations of British troops, of great detail but apparently many derived from prints such as those of Hamilton Smith, and thus not of the greatest reliability.

Schadow, Gottfried (1764–1850)
Prussian painter and engraver, Director of the Berlin Academy in 1815, who produced military illustrations probably based upon eye-witness observation.

Scharf, Georg (1788–1860)
Bavarian painter and lithographer, who was employed by the Royal Geological Society in London, and who went to Paris with the British army in 1815. He collaborated on Orme's *Historic Military and Naval Anecdotes* (London 1818), and obviously benefited from personal observation of his subject.

Scott, Edmund
British artist responsible for a splendid series of accurate uniform-prints, depicting Foot Guards and Militia, in *Manual Exercise and Costumes*, London 1797; very accurate and decorative.

Seele, Johann Baptist (1775–1814)
German painter born in Mörsburg; became Court Painter and Director of the grand-ducal art gallery in Stuttgart in 1804. In the late 1790s he produced fine illustrations of Austrian troops in campaign uniforms, which have the stamp of eye-witness documents of great value to uniform-historians; and with the engraver L. Ebner produced fine uniform-prints of the Württemberg army, *Königliche Württembergische Garde du Corps, Infanterie, Chevauleger . . .*, Stuttgart 1813.

Suhr, Christoph and Cornelius
Christoph Suhr (1771–1842) was a German genre painter (later professor at the Berlin Academy) who produced a series of uniform-illustrations of troops stationed in or passing through Hamburg, 1808–15, which were produced as prints by his brother Cornelius (1751–1857) and reprinted (Paris 1899, Leipzig 1902) under the title *Manuscrit du Bourgeois de Hambourg*. These eye-witness sketches are among the most valuable documents of the period (the coverage of La Romana's Spaniards is especially significant) and though they have a slightly naïve feeling, are of great significance as records of the actual appearance of troops on active service. Ironically, Suhr is better-known by the sobriquet, not of his making, of *Bourgeois de Hambourg*.

Swebach-Desfontaines, Jacques-François Joseph
(known as 'Swebach') (1769–1823)
Military painter and engraver, chief porcelain-decorator for the Sèvres factory 1802–13, who produced a number of

significant battle-scenes, though some of the prints produced from his originals do not, perhaps, do him justice.

Vernet, Antoine Charles Horace (known as 'Carle Vernet') (1758–1836)

French historical painter and lithographer, a member of a distinguished artistic family which includes Claude Joseph, a well-known landscape-painter of the Claudian style. Carle is perhaps best known as a painter of horses and as a caricaturist, but his military work was extensive, including battle-scenes and series of uniform-studies, such as a most meticulous and superbly executed series of paintings illustrative of the so-called 'Bardin' uniform of the French army of 1812. His reputation as a battle-painter was such that he was awarded the *Légion d'honneur*. He also produced prints of troops involved in the occupation of France, especially Cossacks and the Royal Guard, e.g., the series *Collection de chevaux de tous pays montés*.

Vernet, Emile Jean Horace (known as 'Horace Vernet') (1789–1863).

Perhaps ideally for an artist, Horace Vernet was born in the Louvre, the son of Carle Vernet; despite the guillotining of his aunt (Carle's sister), he became a fervent admirer of Napoleon, served in the National Guard, and remained a Bonapartist even after the restoration. He collaborated with his father in *Recueil de chevaux de tout genre*, but is best known for his series of military uniform studies (e.g., *Collection des uniformes de 1791–1814*, in collaboration with Eugène Lami, and for his masterpiece *Barrière de Clichy* which was refused by the Salon of 1822 for political reasons. Louis-Philippe commissioned his major work, the painting of many battle-scenes at Versailles, and he was also official painter of the Second Empire.

Weiland, C.-F.

Weiland was an officer of the Württemberg army, later in Prussian service, who was a competent uniform-artist; he is best known for *Darstellung der K.K. Französischen Armee und ihrer Allirten*, Weimar 1807, a huge collection of uniform-studies of meticulous detail if slightly naïve in style.

Wolff, Ulrich Ludwig (usually known as Ludwig) (1776–1832)

Wolff was a leading Prussian historical painter, member of the Berlin Academy, known for splendid plates of military costume, most notably the collection *Abbildung der neuen Königl. Preuss. Armee Uniformen* (1812–15) which are often referred to as 'Wolff & Jügel', the latter being one of the aquatinters who collaborated in the production of the series. The Wolff plates are meticulous in detail and of the highest artistic merit.

Zix, Benjamin (1772–1811)

A native of Strasbourg, Zix produced a number of eye-witness paintings of the campaigns of 1792–1809 which are of great value in depicting the campaign appearance of the troops.

Modern Prints and Artists

The modern interest in military uniforms has produced a number of artists and series of prints as meticulous and carefully researched as any of those in the past. Among those recommended unreservedly are the great work by Lucien Rousselot, *L'Armée Française*; the work of Eugène Leliepvre; the *Le Plumet* series by 'Rigo' (Albert Rigondaud); and *Soldats et Uniformes du Premier Empire* by Jack Girbal (continued briefly by P. Courcelle), published by Dr. Hourtoulle, whose name the plates often bear; all these are concerned primarily with French or allied armies. Other armies are covered by the series *Ceux qui Bravaient l'Aigle* by P. Courcelle (exclusively the opponents of the French); *Heere der Vergangenheit*, published by J. Olmes (various artists, many armies and periods); *The Thin Red Line* by D. S. V. and B. K. Fosten (British regular army, not exclusively Napoleonic); and *Military Uniforms in America*, published by the *Military Collector and Historian* (Journal of the Company of Military Historians, Washington D.C.) (including all nations whose troops served in north America, not exclusively of the Napoleonic era). There are in addition many other, often smaller, series of high-quality plates in existence.

VI
MISCELLANEA

MISCELLANEA

THE REPUBLICAN CALENDAR

The Gregorian calendar was used throughout western Europe in the Napoleonic era, except for Russia, which used the Julian until 1917; it was twelve days behind the Gregorian. From 1792 to 1805 France used the 'Republican Calendar' by which months were re-named and years began with *An I* (Year One), dating from the proclamation of the republic. All months were of thirty days, with five extra days (six in leap years) being added to the twelfth month. Years ran from September to August:

Vendémiaire	22 September–21 October
Brumaire	22 August–20 November
Frimaire	21 November–20 December
Nivôse	21 December–19 January
Pluviôse	20 January–18 February
Ventôse	19 February–20 March
Germinal	21 March–19 April
Floréal	20 April–19 May
Prairial	20 May–18 June
Messidor	19 June–18 July
Thermidor	19 July–17 August
Fructidor	18 August–21 September

Years were numbered thus:

I	1792–3	VI	1797–8	XI	1802–3
II	1793–4	VII	1798–9	XII	1803–4
III	1794–5	VIII	1799–1800	XIII	1804–5
IV	1795–6	IX	1800–1	XIV	1805
V	1796–7	X	1801–2		

The Gregorian calendar was reinstated in 1806.

THE MUSLIM CALENDAR

The Christian calendar was not used in the Ottoman Empire, the records of which are rendered in the Muslim calendar, reckoned to begin at the Hegira (the flight of Mohammed from Mecca to Medina, AD 622). To calculate the year of the Hegira (AH), there being only 354 days in the Muslim year, 622 is subtracted from the date of the Christian year, multiplied by 11 and divided by 354, and the resulting calculation added to the first deduction. Thus AD 1798 can be rendered as 1212 AH ($1798-622 = 1176$; $\times 11 \div 354 = 36$; $1176 + 36 = 1212$).

COLOURS

The colours of Napoleonic uniforms were often described in terminology which is not immediately comprehensible today. Some of those encountered are described below; reference should be made to *The Methuen Handbook of Colour*, A. Kornerup and J. H. Wanscher, London 1963–7 (originally published as *Farver I Farver*, Copenhagen 1961) in which a number of exact shades can be found, but it should be noted that despite contemporary terminology, it was frequently impossible to ensure uniformity of dye, and in any case colours faded radically when exposed to sunlight and weather.

Amaranth (French): a medium violet shade.

Aurore (French): pinkish-orange.

Blue: French *bleu nationale* was a deep indigo.

Buff: an undefined colour which could range from off-white through flesh-colour to light tan; originally the colour of unstained 'buff-leather'.

Carmine: crimson.

Cendré or ash-grey: pale grey with a slight yellowish cast.

Chamois (French): ochre or brownish-yellow, but sometimes a true yellow.

Coffee (e.g., Russian): darkish brown.

Common colour (British): greenish-grey.

Cornflower-blue: a slightly greyish medium-blue.

Crab-red, crayfish or lobster (Austrian): a shade slightly darker than scarlet.

Drab: a medium greyish-brown, sometimes produced by a mixed weave of medium blue and brown threads; exact shade undefined.

Ecru (French): beige.

Full green (British): medium-deep green.

Garter-blue (British): a royal-blue shade, lighter than the British 'dark blue'.

Gosling-green (British): an indeterminate brownish-green.

Grey: Austrian grey used as a facing-colour was virtually indistinguishable from the off-white shade used for the coats of the rank-and-file.

Lie-de-vin (French): lit. 'wine dregs', a brownish-maroon.

Pale red (Austrian): a mauvish shade.

Parrot-green (Austrian): a medium-dark mossy green.

Pea-green (British): greyish-green.

Philemot-yellow (British): orig. *feuille mort*, lit. 'dead-leaf': a brownish yellow. (In British service, probably yellower than Methuen ref. 6D7).

Pike-grey (Austrian): a light grey.

Pompadour (Austrian): deep red.

Pompadour (British): purple.

Ponceau (French): poppy-red or coquelicot: a bright orange-red.

Popinjay-green (British): bright green.

Raspberry (Russian): a darkish, slightly brownish red.

Red: British 'red-coats' were scarlet for officers and a much duller shade for the rank-and-file, often described as 'brick-red', a brownish shade probably akin to the 'Venice-red' of the late seventeenth and early eighteenth centuries.

Rifle-green: very deep green, almost black.

Sap-green: a very pale, light green.

Snuff: dark brown.

Steel-grey (Austrian): greyish-green.

Straw-yellow: a pale yellowish shade which could vary to almost off-white.

Tobacco: very deep brown.

White: Austrian 'white' uniforms were usually a pale grey shade for the rank-and-file, and only pure white for officers.

Yolk: a vivid yellow with a brownish cast.

EXPENSES OF THE NAPOLEONIC WARS

It is impossible to equate the monetary cost of the Napoleonic Wars with modern governmental expenses in any way except as a percentage of gross annual expenditure; comparative values of the pound or franc would not be satisfactory. In the following sample annual budgets, it will be observed that military expenditure formed a vastly greater percentage of the whole than would be possible in modern times, for most of the domestic expenditure now undertaken by central government (welfare or poor-relief, maintenance of roads, etc.) was then financed at local level.

Income and Expenditure of Great Britain, 1810

Income

Customs	£13,816,218
Excise	25,350,990
Stamps	5,546,082
Taxes	21,503,420
Post office	1,471,746
Crown lands	110,273
Lottery	471,250
Loans	15,790,826
Others	1,387,095

Expenditure

Interest on national debt	21,773,227
Sinking fund	11,660,601
Interest on exchequer bills	1,815,105
Civil list	1,533,140
Civil government of Scotland	118,186
Miscellaneous	775,399
Loans to allied nations	2,050,082
Navy	20,058,412
Army and ordnance	23,188,631

(Note: *actual* expenditure rose by a further four million to £89,000,000.)

Income and Expenditure of France, 1812 (in Francs)

Income

Total receipts: 780,959,847 francs.

Expenditure

Public debt and pensions	142,046,343
Civil list	28,000,000
Administration of justice	25,683,246
Foreign expenses	8,364,295
Internal finances	81,907,971
Imperial treasury	8,367,889
Army	483,507,781
Navy	149,022,182
Religious expenses	16,627,824
Police	1,631,341
Miscellaneous	8,500,000

(Expenditure on army and navy alone exceeded 66 per cent of the gross national expenditure; this proportion would be even greater when pensions, police, etc., are included, as much of these expenses originated with the war).

THE MARSHALS

Pierre François Charles AUGEREAU (1757–1816), Duc de Castiglione; appointed 19 May 1804.

Jean-Baptiste Jules BERNADOTTE (1763–1844), Prince de Ponte-Corvo, later King Charles XIV of Sweden; appointed 19 May 1804.

Louis-Alexandre BERTHIER (1753–1815), Prince de Neuchâtel et Wagram; appointed 19 May 1804. Killed by accident or suicide at Bamberg.

Jean Baptiste BESSIERES (1763–1813), Duc d'Istrie; appointed 19 May 1804. Killed in action at Rippach.

Guillaume Marie Anne BRUNE (1763–1815); appointed 19 May 1804. Murdered by a royalist mob at Avignon.

Louis Nicolas DAVOUT (1770–1823), Prince d'Eckmühl, Duc d'Auerstädt; appointed 19 May 1804.

Laurent GOUVION ST. CYR (1764–1830), later Marquis de St. Cyr; appointed 27 August 1812.

Emmanuel, Marquis de GROUCHY (1766–1847); appointed 3 June 1815.

Jean Baptiste JOURDAN (1762–1833); appointed 19 May 1804.

François Etienne Christophe KELLERMANN (1735–1820), Duc de Valmy; appointed 19 May 1804.

Jean LANNES (1769–1809), Duc de Montebello; appointed 19 May 1804. Died of wounds received at Essling.

François Joseph LEFEBVRE (1755–1820), Duc de Danzig; appointed

19 May 1804.

Jacques Etienne Joseph Alexandre MACDONALD (1765–1840), Duc de Tarente; appointed 12 July 1809.

Auguste Frédéric Louis Viesse de MARMONT (1774–1852), Duc de Raguse; appointed 12 July 1809.

André MASSENA (1758–1817), Prince d'Essling, Duc de Rivoli; appointed 19 May 1804.

Bon Adrien Jannot de MONCEY (1754–1842), Duc de Conegliano; appointed 19 May 1804.

Adolphe Edouard Casimir Joseph MORTIER (1768–1835), Duc de Trévise; appointed 19 May 1804.

Murdered by the assassin Fieschi.

Joachim MURAT (1767–1815), King of Naples, Grand Duke of Berg; appointed 19 May 1804. Executed by firing-squad.

Michel NEY (1769–1815), Prince de la Moskowa, Duc d'Elchingen; appointed 19 May 1804. Executed by firing-squad.

Nicolas Charles OUDINOT (1767–1847), Duc de Reggio; appointed 12 July 1809.

Catherine Dominique PERIGNON (1754–1818), later Marquis de Pérignon; appointed 19 May 1804.

Josef Anton, Prince PONIATOWSKI (1763–1813); appointed 16 October

1813. Drowned in the Elster.

Jean Mathieu Philibert SERURIER (1742–1819); appointed 19 May 1804.

Nicolas Jean de Dieu SOULT (1769–1851), Duc de Dalmatie; appointed 19 May 1804.

Louis Gabriel SUCHET (1770–1826), Duc d'Albufera; appointed 1 July 1811.

Claude VICTOR (or VICTOR-PERRIN) (1764–1841), Duc de Bellune; appointed 13 July 1807.

Reference
The best modern work on the Marshalate is *Napoleon's Marshals*, ed. D. G. Chandler, London 1987.

SHIPS OF WAR

Warships were classified by the 'rating', calculated from the number of guns carried. This distinction was not so simple, however; carronades were not generally counted as part of the armament which dictated the rate, though ships with nothing but carronades were 'rated' by them, such as the British 56-gunner H.M.S *Glatton*, experimentally armed exclusively with carronades, counted as a 4th-rater; she fought at Copenhagen under Captain William Bligh of *Bounty* fame. Rating was normally calculated by the number of 'piercings' (i.e., gunports) rather than the actual number of guns mounted; thus a ship-of-the-line pierced for 60 guns but serving *en flûte* (i.e., with most guns removed) still was classified as a 4th-rater. Similarly, it is misleading to regard all ships of one 'rating' as approximately equal; the most

obvious exceptions are the US frigates of the War of 1812, which were as manoeuvrable as an ordinary frigate but with a firepower equating to that of a 4th-rate ship-of-the-line at least. The following table of 'rating' statistics published in 1802 refers principally to British vessels but may be taken as representative of the whole; anything of 100 guns or more was regarded as a '1st-rater', there being no higher category to accommodate such leviathans as the Spanish 130-gun *Santissima Trinidad*. Note that the 1st-rater described below was classified as a 100-gunner, though actually mounted 104 guns plus 8 carronades; the 42pdr gun is still listed even though by this time it had been replaced by the equally efficient but more manageable 32pdr.

Rate	Guns	42pdr	32	24	18	12	9	6	32*	24*	18*	12*	Crew	Marines
1st	100	28	–	28	–	30	–	18	2	6	–	–	875	104
2nd	98	–	28	–	30	40	–	–	2	–	6	–	750	102
3rd	80	–	26	–	26	–	24	4	2	–	6	–	650	84
	74	–	28	–	28	–	18	–	2	–	6	–	650	78
	70	–	28	–	28	–	14	–	2	–	6	–	650	74
	64	–	–	26	26	–	12	–	–	2	6	–	650	67
4th	60	–	–	24	–	26	–	10	–	–	–	–	650	63
	50	–	–	22	–	22	–	6	–	6	–	6	420	52
5th	44	–	–	–	20	22	–	6	–	–	–	–	300	45
	36	–	–	–	26	2	8	–	8	–	–	–	300	37
	32	–	–	–	–	26	–	6	–	6	–	–	300	33
6th	28	–	–	–	–	–	24	4	–	6	–	–	200	29
	24	–	–	–	–	–	22	2	–	2	6	–	200	25
	20	–	–	–	–	–	20	–	–	–	–	8	200	21
Sloops	18	–	–	–	–	–	–	18	–	–	–	8	125	19

*Carronades.

(Marines were normally calculated at one per gun plus officers.)

MEASUREMENTS

Distance

No constant system of measurement existed in Europe during the Napoleonic Wars, the local variations probably being responsible for the miscalculation of certain noted events. The most celebrated was the march of the British Light Brigade to Talavera, '62 miles in 26 hours', an erroneous figure probably arising from the confusion of the different 'leagues' used in Spain (as below); the actual distance marched was apparently 42 miles in 26 hours, and four or five miles beyond Talavera in addition. Similarly, Sir Charles Vaughan mis-calculated his great ride from the Tudela to Corunna via Salamanca and Madrid as 188 leagues in nine days, or 790 English miles; actually it was 595 miles. English measurement at the period was generally like that in use prior to the adoption of metric measures:

4 inches: 1 hand	40 poles: 1 furlong
3 hands: 1 foot	8 furlongs: 1 mile
3 feet: 1 yard	3 miles: 1 league
5½ yards: 1 pole or perch	

In France, prior to the adoption of metric measurement, the *toise* was used for military purposes, and also by other nations when calculating the dimensions of fortification, etc.:

12 points: 1 line	12 inches: 1 foot
12 lines: 1 inch	6 feet: 1 toise

In Germany and Holland the Rhineland rood was commonly used, divided into 12 feet; or into tenths or 'decimal feet', a Rhineland pace = two decimal feet or 2/10th of a rood. The following were the measurements of 'feet' in use, expressed as a percentage of an English foot:

English	1.000	Naples	0.861
Amsterdam	0.942	Nuremberg	1.006
Antwerp	0.946	Paris	1.068
Boulogne	1.204	Prague	1.026
Bavaria	0.954	Rhineland	1.033
Bremen	0.964	Strasbourg	0.920
Cologne	0.954	Toledo	0.899
Copenhagen	0.965	Turin	1.062
Danzig	0.944	Venice	1.153
Frankfurt	0.948	Vienna	1.053
Louvaine	0.958	(The above are approximate
Madrid	1.001	measurements; the Paris
Mantua	1.569	foot was actually 1.067977
Middleburg	0.991	of an English foot.)

The 'pace' was normally calculated as 2½ feet, but in the following list of the various 'miles' in use, each is expressed in 'geometric paces', one of which equalled 5 French feet, 7.6719 Rhineland feet or 6.1012 English feet:

English mile:	868	Italian mile:	1,000
Danish mile:	4,071	Russian *verst*:	575
Dutch mile:	3,158	Spanish league:	2,286
French league:	2,400	Swedish mile:	5,761
German mile:	4,000	Swiss mile:	4,512

As generally stated: by calculation 865.4 paces.

The 'Spanish league' above is that which was normally accepted, but in fact no less than four different measurements were in use during the Peninsular War, expressed below in the Spanish measurement of *varas* (a unit of approximately 33 English inches) and English miles:

Legales castellanas (Castilian leagues): 5,000 *varas*: 2.63 English miles.

Legales, una hora de camino (maritime leagues, or 'one hour's journey'): 6,626 *varas*: 3.49 English miles.

Legales géograficas (*del camino real*) ('Geographical' leagues, or 'on the king's highway': 7,572 *varas*: 4.00 English miles.

Legales de España: 8,000 *varas*: 4.21 English miles.

Examples of how errors occurred by misunderstanding these are included in the Talavera appendix to *History and Campaigns of the Rifle Brigade*, W. Verner, London 1919, vol. II.

Volume

The standard English units of volume were:

1,728 cubic inches: 1 cubic foot
27 cubic feet: 1 cubic yard
251 cubic inches: 1 gallon, wine measure
281 cubic inches: 1 gallon, beer measure
168.6 cubic inches: 1 gallon, dry measure

Dry measure was reckoned as:

8 pints: 1 gallon	2 cooms: 1 quarter
2 gallons: 1 peck	5 quarters: 1 wey
4 pecks: 1 bushel	2 weys: 1 last
4 bushels: 1 coom	

Prior to the adoption of the metric system, French weights were reckoned as follows; the system styled *Poids de Marc* or *de Paris*:

72 grains: 1 gros	8 ounces: 1 marc
8 gros: 1 ounce	2 marcs: 1 pound

The following were the measurements of 'pound' in use, expressed as a percentage of an English pound or 16 ounces or 256 drams:

English	1.00	Venice	1.51
Paris	1.08	Prague	1.06
Amsterdam	0.93	Copenhagen	0.94
Rhineland	0.96	Nuremberg	0.94
Antwerp	0.98	Vienna	0.83
Louvaine	0.98	Madrid	0.99
Middleburg	0.98	Toledo	1.00
Strasbourg	0.93	Boulogne	1.27
Bremen	0.94	Florence	1.23
Cologne	0.97	Genoa	1.42
Frankfurt	0.93	Mantua	1.43
Leipzig	1.17	Danzig	1.19
Hamburg	0.95		

The introduction of the metric system in France included two units which are not immediately recognizable today: the *are*, a unit of 100 square metres equivalent to two square perches in the old system; and the *stere*, a unit of one cubic metre of firewood, equivalent to 1 *demi-voie* of one-quarter of a cord in the old system.

ARTILLERY EQUIPMENT

To illustrate the immense quantity of supplies required by an army, the following is the list of stores required for field service for a *single* 6pdr gun in British service, 1802:

Ammunition, etc.: 120 rounds ball, 30 rounds case-shot, 120 flannel cartridges containing 2¼lb, 30 flannel cartridges containing 2lb powder, 12 empty cartridges, 178 fuze-tubes, 18 portfires, 28lb slow-match, 2 portfire sticks, 3 copper powder-measures (4, 2 and 1 oz.).

Vehicles and teams, etc.: 1 gun-carriage, 1 limber, 1 gun-tarpaulin, 1 limber-tarpaulin, 1 pair draught-chains, 1 wagon with painted canvas cover, 1 wadmiltilt, 1 linch-pin, 2 body-clouts, 1 linch-clout, 32 sixpenny clout-nails.

Other items: 1 lead apron, 2 sponges, 1 wad-hook, 2 handspikes, 1 tampion, 3 straps for attaching sidearms to carriage, 1 linstock, 2 drag-ropes, 3 padlocks and keys, 2 common spikes (for rendering gun inoperable), 1 spring-spike (which could only be removed by boring-out the vent-hole), 2 vent-punches, 1 budge barrel, 6 couples for traces, 1 spare sponge-head, 1 spare rammer-head, 1 claw hammer, 1 set priming-irons, 1 powder horn, 1 water-bucket, 1 felling-axe, 1 pickaxe, 1 bill, 2 spades, 1 skein tarred marline, 1 skein twine, 1 skein Hambro' line, 1lb packthread, 1 firkin grease, 2 grease-boxes, 1lb tallow, 1 dark lanthorn, 1 lifting-jack, 1 tanned hide, 1 set of men's harness (12 to a set), 1 set of chain harness (6 to a set), 1 set traces (4 to a set), 10 hemp halters, 1 wantie, 5 short whips, 10 nose-bags, 2 corn-sacks, 2 sets forage-cords, 1 ladle-stave, 2 tube-boxes, 1 cutting-knife, 1 pair scissors, ½oz. worsted thread, 1 needle, 2 cartridge-boxes, 2 thumb-stalls.

Chemical Compositions, etc.

Gunpowder: figures expressed as a percentage

	Saltpetre	Sulphur	Charcoal
Britain	75	10	15
France	75	9.5	15.5
Sweden	75	9	16
Poland	80	8	12
Italy	76	12	12
Russia	70	11.5	18.5

Slow Match

'The slow match used by the English is made by contract: one yard of it will burn about 8 hours. The French slow match is usually made by soaking light twisted white-rope for 3 days in a strong lye. It burns about 3 feet in 6 hours. Slow match was made at Gibraltar, during the last siege, in the following manner: eight ounces of saltpetre were put into a gallon of water, and just made to boil over a slow fire; strong blue paper was then wetted with the liquor, and hung to dry. When dry, each sheet was rolled up tight, and the outward edge pasted down, to prevent its opening; half a sheet, thus prepared, will burn 3 hours.

'Quick Match Compositions:

Worsted Match		*Cotton Match*	
Worsted	10oz.	Cotton	1lb 12oz.
Mealed powder	10lb	Saltpetre	1lb 8oz.
Spirits of wine	3 pints	Mealed powder	10lb
Water	3 pints	Spirits of wine	2 quarts
Isinglass	½-pint	Water	3 pints

'Note: The French have lately made their slow match by soaking the rope in a solution of sugar of lead and rain water: in the proportion of ¾ of an ounce of sugar of lead to one pint of water: and this they esteem as preferable to the old sort.'

(Adye, pp. 177-8).

ARTILLERY TABLES

The following tables of statistics are extracted from *The Bombardier and Pocket Gunner*, R. W. Adye, London 1802, where comprehensive specifications concerning the ordnance of most European nations can be found.

Calibres of guns, expressed in English inches

Weight	British	French	Spanish	Dutch	Russian	Portuguese
48pdr	–	–	–	–	–	7.49
42pdr	7.018	–	–	–	–	–
36pdr	–	6.90	6.84	–	6.86	6.80
32pdr	6.41	–	–	6.40	–	–
30pdr	–	–	–	–	6.47	–
24pdr	5.823	6.03	6.03	5.92	6.00	5.93
18pdr	5.292	–	5.52	5.45	5.45	5.40
16pdr	–	5.26	–	–	–	–
12pdr	4.623	4.78	4.8	4.76	4.76	4.70
9pdr	4.20	–	4.2	–	–	4.30
8pdr	–	4.18	–	4.13	4.17	–
6pdr	3.668	–	–	3.78	3.78	3.75
4pdr	3.204	3.315	–	–	–	–

The above proves that shot of the same ostensible 'weight' would not necessarily fit a gun of a different nation; Dutch or Russian 18pdr shot would not, for example, fit a British 18pdr. Part of the difference results from the differing weights of 'pound' throughout Europe; for example, an Austrian 12pdr calculated on the 'Vienna pound' (0.83 of a British pound) had a very much lighter shot than a French 12pdr calculated on the 'Paris pound' (1.08 of a British pound), the respective weights expressed in British measure being 9.96lb:12.96lb, hence the superiority of ordnance using a heavier 'pound' against guns of the same 'nature' but calculated on a lighter 'pound'.

Dimensions and Weights of Ordnance expressed in
British measure

	length	weight
British brass guns		
Medium new 12pdr	6ft 6in	2,016lb
Light new 12pdr	5ft	1,344
Desaguliers' medium 6pdr	7ft	1,368
Belford's 6pdr	5ft	637
Light 6pdr	4ft 6in	578
Desaguliers' 3pdr	6ft	672
Light 3pdr	3ft 6in	307
French brass guns		
12pdr	6ft 6in	1,952.6lb
8pdr	5ft 8in	1,291.7
4pdr	4ft 6in	637.2
British iron guns		
32pdr	10ft	6,160lb
24pdr	9ft 6in	5,544
18pdr	9ft 6in	4,704
12pdr	9ft 6in	3,808
12pdr	7ft 6in	3,276
9pdr	7ft 6in	2,744
6pdr	6ft	1,848
French iron guns		
36pdr	9ft 8in	8,260lb
24pdr	9ft 1½in	5,712
16pdr	8ft 4in	4,872
12pdr	8ft 2in	2,324
8pdr	6ft	1,792

Ranges with French Brass Guns, in French measurement

Nature	Elevation (Deg. Min.)	Range (toises)
12pdr		
(4lb charge)	− 58	300
	1 03	350
	1 39	400
	1 49	450
	1 56	480
8pdr (2½lb charge)	− 58	300
	1 24	350
	1 51	400
	2 08	450
	2 24	480
4pdr (1½lb) charge	− 58	250
	1 20	300
	1 40	350
	2 00	400
	2 20	450
	2 40	480

Range of Brass Guns, 1793

Nature	Charge	Point-blank	1°	2°	3°	4°	5°
		Distance to 'first graze' of shot at elevations: (in yards)					
Heavy 24pdr	8lb	473	781	1,032	1,405	1,585	1,710
Medium 24pdr	8lb	488	757	1,103	1,425	1,557	1,745
Light 24pdr	3lb	162	364	606	722		1,390
Medium 12pdr	4lb		705	973	1,189		
Light 12pdr	3lb		601	816	1,063		
Desaguliers' 6pdr	2lb		646	966	1,325		
6-foot 6pdr	2lb		683	948	1,327		
Medium 6pdr	2lb		775	1,003	1,444		
Reduced 6pdr	2lb		642	976	1,150		
5-foot 6pdr	24oz.		587	825	950		
4ft 6in 6pdr	24oz.		628	804	991		
Desaguliers' 3pdr	1lb		679	883	918		

Range of 'Sea Service' Iron Guns, 1796
Statistics the same for 32-, 24- and 18pdrs

Elevation	Proportion of powder to weight of shot	Type of projectile	Range (yards)	Elevation	Proportion of powder to weight of shot	Type of projectile	Range (yards)
2°	one-third	single roundshot to first graze	1,200	7°	one-quarter	single shot	2,020
2°	one-quarter	single roundshot to first graze	1,000	2°	one quarter	one roundshot and one grapeshot together	600
2°	one-quarter	double shot	500				
4°	one-third	single shot	1,600	4°	one-quarter	grapeshot	1,000
4°	one-quarter	single shot	1,500	2°	one-quarter	bar-shot	800
7°	one-third	single shot	2,150				

Ranges with a Heavy 5½in Howitzer, 1793

Elevation	To first graze (yards) 2lb charge	To first graze (yards) 3lb charge
Elevation	To first graze (yards) 2lb charge	To first graze (yards) 3lb charge
Elevation	To first graze (yards) 2lb charge	To first graze (yards) 3lb charge
1°	453	479
2°	595	722
3°	666	921
4°	847	1,000
5°	957	1,325
6°	1,173	1,530
7°	1,449	1,577
8°	1,355	1,721
9°	1,585	1,801
10°	1,853	1,791
11°	1,793	1,013
12°	1,686	

Maximum range calculated from 1,400–1,900 yards with 2lb charge, and 1,400–2,000 yards with 3lb)

Ranges with a Light 5½in Howitzer, 1798

Elevation	Ranges to 'first graze' (yards)			
point-blank	4oz. charge	8oz. charge	12oz. charge	16oz. charge
	-	96	140	159
1°	66	143	334	325
2°	85	184	351	490
3°	100	258	506	668
4°	110	307	500	728
5°	115	376	509	918
6°	168	408	581	823
7°	194	529	872	975
8°	226	630	975	1,044
9°	282	645	911	1,049
10°	279	642	1,021	1,104
11°	260	797	1,177	1,173
12°	315	715	–	–

(Maximum range calculated as between 400–600 yards with 4oz. charge, 700–1,000 with 8oz., 1,000–1,350 with 12oz., 1,100–1,400 with 16oz.)

Ranges with Carronades, 1798 (yards)

Nature	point-blank	1°	2°	3°	4°	5°
68pdr (charge 88oz.)	450	650	890	1,000	1,100	1,280
42pdr (charge 56oz.)	400	600	860	980	1,020	1,170
32pdr (charge 42oz.)	330	560	830	900	970	1,087
24pdr (charge 32oz.)	300	500	780	870	920	1,050
18pdr (charge 24oz.)	270	470	730	800	870	1,000
12pdr (charge 16oz.)	230	400	690	740	810	870

Ranges With Land Service Mortars, 1798, at 45° elevation

13in iron		10in iron		8in iron		5½in brass	
charge (oz.)	range (yds.)	charge (oz.)	range (yds.)	charge (oz.)	range (yds.)	charge (oz.)	range (yds.)
14	245	8	235	5	225	2	255
24	523	16	638	8	474	3	470
32	697	20	873	10	664	4	725
48	1,132	24	1,028	12	801	5	935
64	1,490	32	1,357	16	1,115	6	1,175
80	1,824	38	1,571	20	1,380		
96	2,095	44	1,825	22	1,530		
112	2,510	48	1,916	24	1,660		
128	2,706	64	2,485	25	1,720		
		72	2,536				

Ranges of French Mortars, at 45° elevation (charges in French measure)

12in		10in		8in	
charge (oz.)	range (yds.)	charge (oz.)	range (yds.)	charge (oz.)	range (yds.)
16	388	16	618	5	316
24	632	24	964	10	794
32	862	32	1,280	15	1,112
40	954	40	1,428	20	1,280
48	1,292	48	1,432		
56	1,390	58.25	1,920		

(The above 10in mortar is that classified as 'short range'; the 'long-range' 10in mortar had a range at 45° elevation varying from 450 yards with 16oz. charge to 2,304 yards with 98.5oz. charge.

Recoil of Fieldguns Set Upon Elm Planks

Nature	charge	recoil at 1°30' elevation	recoil with case-shot
Medium 12pdr	64oz.	12 feet	8½ feet
Heavy 6pdr	32oz.	7 feet	7½ feet
Light 6pdr	24oz.	12 feet	10 feet
Heavy 3pdr	16oz.	7 feet	3½ feet

VII
GLOSSARY

The purpose of this glossary is to explain contemporary military terms which might not be comprehensible with the use of a modern dictionary. Foreign terms are identified by the letters (F) French, (G) German, (R) Russian, (Sp) Spanish, (Sw) Swedish, (Pol) Polish and (Port) Portuguese; though it should be noted that many French terms, especially concerned with fortifications, were used by most nations. Note also that considerable differences exist between modern German and contemporary Austrian in the spelling of many words, e.g., 'Kasket' and 'Casquet' respectively.

abatis: barricade of felled trees.

adjoint (F): assistant adjutant-general.

adjutant: junior administrative officer or (French) warrant officer.

adjutant-chef (F): senior adjutant.

adjutant-commandant (F): adjutant-general after 1800.

adjutant-general: staff colonel often serving as corps or divisional chief of staff.

adjutant-major (F): staff officer, usually with rank of major.

adjutant-sous-officer (F): senior warrant officer.

advance-rods: bars attached to a gun-carriage at right-angles to the barrel to enable it to be pushed forward by the crew.

affût (F): gun-carriage.

affût de bord (F): naval gun-carriage.

affût de place (F): carriage for a garrison-gun.

aide-de-camp: junior staff officer attached to a marshal or general.

aiguillette: braided cord shoulder-knot.

amalgame (F): tactical amalgamation of regular and volunteer units.

amorce (F): priming-powder, of finer grade than ordinary gunpowder.

ammunition: colloquial description for any item of issue equipment, e.g., 'ammunition boot', 'ammunition loaf', etc.

ammuzette: large-calibre musket or 'wall-piece'.

anmarschbommer (Sw): *see* advance-rods.

appointé (F): soldier receiving the pay of a higher rank in recognition of lengthy or valiant service.

apron: lead sheet in two sizes: 'large' 12in × 10in, weighing 8¼lb; 'small' 6in × 4½in, weighing 1¾lb.

arme blanche (orig. F): (i) cavalry sabre; (ii) cavalry in general.

Armed Association: British local volunteer corps.

artillerie à cheval (F): horse artillery.

artillerie à pied (F): foot artillery.

artillerie volante (F): horse artillery, all gunners mounted.

aspirant (F): cadet.

Association: *see* Armed Association.

ataman (R): senior Cossack officer.

atirador (Port): Caçadore sharpshooter.

Auditor (G): legal officer.

August Allowances: British system whereby volunteer corps were paid for 20 days' training per year, in return for which they had to agree to serve in any part of the country in event of invasion.

avant-train (F): artillery limber.

ball (as in 'ball-ammunition'): musket-ball or musket-cartridge.

bancal (F): slightly curved cavalry sabre.

banquette: firing-step behind a parapet.

barbette: a cannon fired *en barbette* over a parapet without using an embrasure.

Bardin regulations: French uniform-regulations of 1812, named from the officer responsible for their issue.

Bärentatzen (G): lit. 'bear's paw': fringed lace loop worn on cuff of 'Hungarian' regiments of Austrian army.

barrelled sash: hussar girdle with lace binding or 'barrels'.

bar-shot: two half-roundshot connected by a bar, to act like chain-shot.

basane (F): leather reinforcing on riding-overalls.

bashkir: Russian asiatic light cavalry.

bastion: (i) a four-sided fortification; (ii) a lace loop on a uniform following the same shape.

bât: pack or pack-saddle; orig. French but also used in English; anything concerning provisions, baggage, etc.; hence 'batman'.

batardeau: coffer-dam to retain water in a fortress-ditch.

battalion company: 'centre' company of an infantry battalion.

battalion guns: light fieldpieces attached to infantry unit.

batterie (F): (i) *see* battery; (ii) *see* frizzen.

battering-train: siege-train.

battery: orig. a gun-emplacement; later used to describe a 6- or 8-gun artillery company.

battery fascine: fascine 8 to 12 feet long, 10 to 12 inches thick.

bavin: brushwood faggot.

Belemite: colloq. a malingerer; originated from the hospital at Belem near Lisbon.

belly-box: cartridge-box worn on the front of the waist-belt (archaic).

Bengal lights: carcass composed of saltpetre, sulphur and red orpiment.

black hole: guard-house.

blacking-ball: blackening agent for equipment.

black strap: British naval colloquialism for wine, as issued in Mediterranean.

blancs (F): nickname for the regular (ex-Royal) troops in the early Revolutionary Wars, from the retention of the white uniform.

bleus (F): nickname for the newly-raised units in the early Revolutionary Wars, from their blue uniforms. (Earlier *bleus* had been (i) supporters of the Gribeauval system of artillery, from the colour of the artillery-carriages; and (ii) naval officers originally trained in merchant service.)

boisseau (F): bushel (unit of measurement); colloquialism for a shako.

bomb: mortar-shell; applied loosely to all explosive projectiles.

bombardier: (i) junior N.C.O of artillery; (ii) artillery technician (German).

bombe (F): (i) bomb; (ii) skull of a helmet.

bonnet: triangular fortification in front of a ravelin.

bonnet à poil (F): (i) fur grenadier cap; (ii) colloquialism for Old Guard.

bonnet de police (F): undress cap.

bouget (orig. F): *see* budge barrel.

boulet à l'ange (F): lit. 'angel-shot': chain-shot.

boulet rouge (F): lit. 'red shot': hot-shot.

boute-feux (F): portfire.

bouton de canon (F): see cascabel.

brancardier (F): stretcher-bearer.

brandebourg (F): lace loop on a uniform.

Brandenburg (cuff)(G): cuff with rectangular flap bearing three buttons.

brassard: cloth arm-band.

breaking ground: commencing a siege.

breastplate: small badge worn on the shoulder-belt.

breastwork: parapet for protection of troops.

bricole: (i) rope or strap used for dragging a fieldpiece manually; (ii) a cannon fired *en bricole* when the shot struck a sloping revetment.

brigade: (i) tactical formation of two or more battalions or cavalry regiments; (ii) British artillery company.

brigadier (F): cavalry corporal.

brigadier: brigade-commander.

brigade-major: brigade staff officer.

briquet (F): infantry sabre.

brodequin (F): originally a short boot; by this period a colloquialism for the ordinary infantry boot.

brosseur (F): officer's servant.

Brown Bess: nickname of British musket, probably originating from 'brown' (colour) and 'buss' (anglicization of German *buchse*, gun). 'To hug Brown Bess': to enlist or serve as a soldier.

brown George: British army-issue loaf.

budge barrel: powder barrel, usually with rope hoops so as not to strike sparks from metal bands.

buffleterie (F): leather belts.

Burgergarde (G): local town-guard troops (also *Burgerwehr*).

busby: fur hussar cap (not in common use at this period).

Busche (G): large plume (lit. 'bush').

butcher's bill: colloquialism for casualty-returns.

butin (F): colloquialism for personal kit, orig. 'booty'.

cabinet (F): Napoleon's personal HQ staff.

Caçadore (Port): Portuguese light infantry/rifleman (lit. 'hunter').

cadenettes (F): tresses of plaited hair hanging from the temples, as worn by French hussars.

cadis (F): fabric like flannel.

cadre: officers and NCOs around which a unit would be formed and trained.

cahouk (F): mameluke head-dress.

caillou (F): lit. 'pebble': musket-flint.

caisson: ammunition-wagon (orig. French).

camp colour: battalion marker-flag.

canister: artillery projectile of lead balls in a tin container; case-shot.

canonnier (F): gunner.

cantinière (F): sutleress.

cap: generic term for any military head-dress.

caporal (F): corporal.

caponnière: (i) covered communication-trench from an enceinte to a detached work; (ii) casemated fortification projecting across a ditch for delivering flanking-fire.

capsquare: metal plate securing the trunnions of a cannon-barrel to the carriage.

captain-lieutenant: commissioned rank, orig. the actual commander of the company nominally led by the battalion-commander.

captain-general: Spanish commanding general (of a province, etc.).

carabinier (F): (i) French heavy cavalry; (ii) grenadier of a French light infantry regiment.

carbine: short cavalry musket.

carcass (or carcase): incendiary or illumination-shell; applied loosely to any illumination-device, e.g., tar-barrel.

carnets (F): notebooks kept by Napoleon to record details of units.

carriage: wooden framework supporting a cannon-barrel.

carronade: large-calibre, short-range cannon, principally naval, named from original place of manufacture, Carron Ironworks.

cartouche (F): (i) cartridge; (ii) cartridge-pouch.

cascabel: knob at 'sealed' end of a cannon-barrel.

casemate: chamber in a fortress-wall.

case-shot: canister.

Casquet (G): Austrian squat cap, like a peakless shako.

cavalier: raised battery, usually inside a bastion.

cazador (Sp): as 'chasseur'.

cazador a caballo (Sp): chasseur à cheval.

ceinturon-baudrier (F): waist-belt which could also be used as a shoulder-belt.

centenier (F): 2nd lieutenant in *infirmier* companies.

centre company: 'battalion company' (from their position in the centre of the battalion when arrayed in line).

chain-shot: two roundshot connected by chain, acting like a flail to destroy ships' rigging.

chapeau chinois (F): 'jingling johnny' (lit. 'chinese hat').

charivari (F): cavalry overalls strapped under the foot, often with leather reinforcing.

Charleville: general term for French infantry musket, from place of original manufacture.

charoual (or *serouel*)(F): mameluke-style baggy trousers.

chase: segment of a cannon-barrel between chase-girdle and muzzle.

chasse-marée (F): fast-sailing small privateer used by French in the English Channel.

chasseurs (F): light troops in general; more particularly, 'battalion' company of light infantry regiments (lit. 'hunters').

chasseurs à cheval (F): light cavalry.

chasseurs à pied (F): light infantry.

chat (F): item of artillery 'sidearms': a 'reliever' for clearing a cannon-barrel (lit. 'cat').

chef de bataillon (F): French battalion-commander, but a rank rather than an appointment.

chef de brigade (F): brigade-major.

chef de musique (F): bandmaster.

chef de peloton (F): platoon-leader.

chef d'escadron (F): cavalry squadron-commander.

chemin des rondes (F): sentry-walk around top of a revetment.

cheval-de-frise: barricade made of beams or planks studded with spikes or blades.

chevau-léger (F): light cavalry.

chevauxleger (G): light cavalry.

cheveux flottants (F): long, undressed hair popular with soldiers of the Revolutionary Wars, as a political reaction to the powdered coiffures of the *ancien régime*.

Chinese light: illumination-shell composed of nitre, sulphur, antimony and orpiment.

chock: quoin.

chosen man: British lance-corporal (archaic).

chouan (F): Breton royalist insurgent; *chouannerie*, a peasant rising; *chouanner*, to carry on a guerrilla war.

citadel: four- or five-sided strongpoint in a fortress.

clash pans: cymbals.

clinometer: instrument for measuring the gradient upon which a cannon stood.

clique (F): colloquialism for *tête de colonne*, q.v.

club: hair-dressing of a short queue, sometimes folded back upon itself.

clubbed muskets: carried over the shoulder with the butt to the rear, a popular method of marching at ease.

cockade: rosette of national colours worn on head-dress.

Coehorn (Coehoorn): mortar, named from its designer.

coffret (F): ammunition-chest.

cohort (F): National Guard unit (orig. Roman).

coin (F): quoin.

colback (or colpack): French hussar busby.

colour: infantry flag.

coloured clothes: non-uniform or civilian dress.

colour-sergeant: British senior NCO rank instituted 1813.

commissaire ordinaire (F): assistant-commissary.

commissaire ordonnateur (F): chief commissary.

common colour: the greenish-grey shade which British artillery carriages were painted.

company: basic tactical unit of infantry or cavalry, or 'battery' of artillery.

company colour: marker-flag or *fanion*.

company sergeant: British artillery colour-sergeant.

comrade: one of a pair of light infantrymen.

conducteur (F): artillery- or wagon-driver.

conductor: artillery- or wagon-driver.

cordon: (i) rounded coping-stone atop a revetment; (ii) chain of sentry-posts.

cornet: cavalry 2nd lieutenant.

corps: (i) largest tactical unit, properly *corps d'armée*, comprising two or more divisions; (ii) generic name for any military unit from company-strength to brigade.

corps d'observation (F): force detached from main army, protecting lines of communication, reconnoitering enemy, etc.

Corséhut (G): Austrian spelling of Korsehut, 'Corsican hat'.

Corsican hat: 'round hat' with upturned brim.

Cossack: generic term for Caucasian irregular cavalry in Russian army; from Turkish *quzzaq* = freebooter.

counterscarp: slope or retaining-wall on outer side of ditch.

countersign: password, usually one given in answer to a challenge.

couvre-bassinet (F): pan-cover on a musket-lock.

couvre-platine (F): protective cover for musket-lock.

covered way (or covert-way): infantry fire-step along a ditch.

crapaud: British nickname for French soldiers.

crapaux (F): metal bed of a mortar.

cravat: (i) streamer atop a standard-pole; (ii) pompom encircling sword-blade and hilt to prevent ingress of water into the scabbard.

crochet: miniature parallel trench.

croppy: British nickname for Irish rebel; 'croppyism', support for United Irishmen.

crownwork: fortification comprising two small bastions with two long bastions at either side.

cuirass: (i) breast- and back-plate; (ii) breastwork (fortification).

cuirassier: armoured heavy cavalryman

cuir jaune (F): tan or buff leather (lit. 'yellow leather').

cul de singe (F): colloquailism for cloth rear patch on a grenadier cap; lit. 'monkey's backside'.

Czaikisten (also *Tschaikisten*) (G): Hungarian pontoon corps.

czapka (Pol.; also *shapska*, *tchapka*, etc.): square-topped cap worn by lancers.

dead ground: a hollow or fold in terrain which would conceal troops or shield them from enemy fire.

Death or Glory men: nickname for Brunswick Corps (from their skull and crossed bones badge).

Degen (G): straight-bladed infantry sword; in British slang, any sword (e.g., 'a rum degen' = a good-looking sword).

demi-brigade (F): unit comprising originally one regular and two volunteer or conscript battalions; later applied to any provisional corps.

demi-lune: ravelin.

département: French internal administrative region.

Desagulier: (i) light fieldpiece named after its designer; (ii) Desagulier's Instrument: device for finding imperfections in the bore of a cannon-barrel.

detachment (as in 'battalion of detachments'): composite unit formed of many small contingents.

devil carriage: four-wheeled wagon for transporting heavy ordance.

dispart: half the difference between the diameter of a gun-barrel at the base-ring and the swell of the muzzle; usually 1/56th of the length.

division: (i) formation of two or more brigades; (ii) two companies of a battalion acting in concert; (iii) two fieldpieces with attendant vehicles.

doigtier (F): thumbstall used by the ventsman of an artillery crew.

dolman: braided, tail-less hussar jacket.

dolphin: lifting-handles on a cannon-barrel.

draft: system of breaking-up a unit, transferring its personnel to other regiments.

dragoon: 'medium' cavalry; orig. mounted infantry.

dumpling: short-barrelled pistol.

eagle: French Napoleonic standard; the sculpted head, not the flag.

eclaireur (F): cavalry scout.

ecoute (F): small mine-gallery.

Ehrentroddel (G): sword-knot carried by veterans of the 1806–7 campaign, lit. 'honour-knot'.

Eighteen Manoeuvres: the drill instituted by Dundas' British manual.

embrasure: opening of a parapet to allow guns to fire through.

émigré (F): royalist refugee serving in the army of another nation.

enceinte: fortress-wall or perimeter.

enfants-perdus (F): forlorn hope (lit. 'lost children').

enfilade: fire from a flank, raking the length of a formation.

en flûte: ship-of-the-line with most guns removed was described as *en flûte*.

ensign: infantry 2nd lieutenant.

envelope: continuous enceinte.

epaulement: breastwork.

épaulière: shoulder-strap of a cuirass.

Ersatz (G): replacement.

epinglette (F): priming-wire or pricker used to pierce a cartridge.

esplanade: open space between a citadel and the nearest buildings.

espontoon: *see* spontoon.

état-major (F): staff.

evolution: drill-movements.

expanding shot: naval ammunition of two half-balls linked by expanding bars, to act like a flail to destroy ships' rigging.

expense magazine: small magazine placed near a battery.

facings: (i) coloured distinctions on a uniform (collar, cuffs, lapels, etc.; (ii) drill-movements.

Fahne (G): infantry colour.

Fahnenträger (G): infantry colour-bearer.

Fahnrich (G): aspirant officer serving in the ranks, or ensign.

family: personal staff of a general officer (colloquialism).

fanfare (F): military band.

fanion (F): marker- or company-flag.

fantaisie (F): non-regulation uniform.

fantassin (F): infantryman.

farrier: cavalry pioneer or craftsman attending a unit's horses.

Faschinenmesser (G): straight-bladed, heavy sword carried by infantry; lit. 'fascine-cutter'.

fascine: bundle of brushwood used in fortification.

fausse-braye: lower outer rampart, usually earthen.

Faustriemen (G): cavalry sword-knot.

fauteuil (fanteuil) (F): nickname for Austrian grenadier cap, from its shape; lit. 'armchair'.

Feldbinde (G): waist-sash.

Feldmütze (G): undress- or field-cap.

Feld-Postillion (G): courier.

Feldwebel (G): sergeant-major.

fellahin: Egyptian peasant infantry.

felloe (or felly): curved wooden segment forming part of the outer ring of a wheel.

fencible: British home-defence unit enlisted under similar terms to regular army, but not liable for overseas service without their consent.

fermelet (F): mameluke waistcoat.

Feuerwerker (G): artillery NCO or technician.

fire ball: illumination-shell comprising rosin, sulphur, alum powder, starch, saltpetre, mealed powder and linseed oil.

firelock: flintlock musket.

fireworker: artillery technician.

fixed ammunition: artillery projectile with wooden 'sabot' affixed.

flamme (F): (i) lance-pennon; (ii) busby-bag (lit. 'flame').

flank company: élite company of a line battalion, either grenadiers or light infantry, named from their position on the flanks when the battalion was arrayed in line.

flanqueurs (F): light infantry.

flèche: arrow-shaped earthwork.

Fliegendes Lazarett (G): mobile field-hospital.

Flügel-Adjutant (G): ADC.

Flügelhorn (G): hunting-horn used by light infantry.

Flügelmütze (G): mirliton.

fly: rapidly moving wagon for transporting infantry.

flying artillery: mobile horse artillery.

foot: infantry (archaic).

forlorn hope: advance storming-party, especially in attack on a breach; prob. from Dutch 'lost party'; also referred to simply as a 'forlorn'.

fourgon (F): heavy transport-waggon.

Fourier (G): quartermaster.

fourrier (F): quartermaster-sergeant or corporal.

fraises: *see* storm-poles.

Freikorps (G): independent units; Austrian, 'Frei-Corps'.

Freiwilligenjäger (G): rifle companies of middle-class volunteers serving as NCO and officer-training units.

frizzen: part of a musket-lock from which the flint struck sparks.

fugelman: trained soldier who stood in front of a company during drill, from whom the others took their time.

Fuhrwesen (G): military train or transport-service.

furashka (R): undress-cap.

furniture: metal fittings on a musket.

furriel (Port.): quartermaster-corporal.

fusil: in English, a light musket; in French, any musket.

fusil dépareillé (F): musket made from spare parts of different patterns.

fusil d'honneur (F): presentation musket awarded for outstanding service.

fusilier: in French, 'centre' company of line infantry; in German, light infantry; in English, orig. one armed with a fusil (archaic); by this period, a member of the 7th, 21st or 23rd Regiments of Foot (also 'fuzileer').

gabion: earth-filled wicker basket used in fortification.

gabion farci: gabion rolled in front of a sapper to shield him from enemy fire; also 'sap roller'.

gaiter-trousers: one-piece legwear of breeches and gaiters combined; also 'mosquito trousers'.

Gala (G): 'gala uniform' = parade-dress.

gallery: large mine-tunnel.

galloper: light fieldpiece with shafts for a draught-horse instead of a limber.

gamelle (F): mess-tin.

garde du corps: French term used in German armies to describe heavy bodyguard cavalry.

gardes d'honneur (F): light cavalry; also the escort-units of individual towns.

garland: wooden framework used to keep roundshot in a neat pile.

Gefreiter (G): corporal.

gendarme (F): orig. used to describe any armed man; by this period used to describe troops employed in provost or security duties.

général de brigade, de division (F): French ranks of general officers, not appointments, i.e., *générals de brigade* did not necessarily command a brigade, nor were brigades necessarily commanded by them.

giberne (F): cartridge-box.

glacis: slope descending from a fortification.

glaive (F): guardless short sword carried by foot artillery, modelled on the Roman *gladius*.

Goddam: French nickname for British troops, derived from the British use of that expression; dates from Hundred Years War.

gorget: decorative metal crescent worn around the neck as a symbol of commissioned rank, a relic of the armoured neck-protection worn by officers to the 17th century.

Grand-Quartier-Général (F): general headquarters.

grand rounds: main inspection of sentries, usually conducted once per night.

grasshoppers: French nickname for British riflemen (from the green uniform).

graze: point at which a cannon-ball pitched (e.g., '1st graze': initial point of impact from where it ricocheted).

grenadier: élite infantry, orig. from their being armed with hand-grenades.

grenadiers à cheval (F): 'horse grenadiers': French Imperial Guard heavy cavalry.

Grenzers (G): Austrian border-troops.

grog: mixture of rum and water (named from Admiral Vernon, who introduced it, alias 'Old Grog', from his wearing grogram fabric).

grognard (F): lit. 'grumbler': nickname of Old Guard infantry.

gros bonnets (F): lit. 'big hats': colloquialism for staff officers.

grosse-bottes (F): lit. 'big boots': nickname for Imperial Guard Grenadiers à Cheval.

gros-talons (F): lit. 'big heels': alternative for 'Grosse-bottes'.

guard (F & G, 'Garde'): orig. royal bodyguard corps; use of term implied élite status.

guérite: sentry-box sited on fortress-rampart; loosely applied to sentry-boxes in general.

guerrilla (Sp): irregular patriot-fighter; lit. 'little war'.

guides (F): light cavalry, orig. escorts.

guidon: swallow-tailed cavalry standard.

gun-metal: usually refers to 'brass' guns, generally 8 to 10 parts tin to 100 parts copper.

habit (F): uniform-coat.

habit-veste (F): uniform-jacket.

halberd: polearm with axe-head, used by colour-escorts in some armies.

half-brigade: in French, *see* 'demi-brigade'; in English, a half-battery of artillery.

half-moon: *see* demi-lune.

half-pay: an officer on half-pay was one who still held his commission but had no employment.

handicraft: craftsman who practised his trade in a regiment, e.g., tailor, shoemaker, etc.

Handlanger (G): artillery labourer.

handspike: lever used to traverse a cannon.

Handwerker (G): artillery artificer.

hat company: 'battalion company', i.e., those wearing hats, not the fur caps of the grenadiers or small caps of the light infantry.

Hauptlazarett (G): base-hospital.

Hauptmann (G): captain.

hausse-col (F): gorget.

haversack: fabric bag used for carrying provisions, &c. (orig. from 'haver' = oats).

helmet-cap: term usually applied to a fur-crested 'round hat' made to resemble a 'Tarleton'.

hemmema (Sw): Swedish Baltic vessel of frigate-size.

Hessian boots: boots of below-knee length, often decorated with lace; one variety termed 'hussar boots'.

hetman (R): Cossack general.

Hirschfänger (G): wide-bladed, machete-like infantry sword.

hornwork: fortification consisting of a bastion front and two branches at the sides.

horse: cavalry (archaic).

hot shot: roundshot heated red-hot before firing, to act as incendiary, mostly used by shore-batteries against ships.

housings: horse-furniture.

howitzer: short-barrelled cannon designed for high-angle fire.

hussar (F *hussard*, G *Husar*): light cavalry, styled on Hungarian light horse.

hussar boot: *see* Hessian boot.

infirmier (F): medical orderly.

infirmier-brancardier (F): stretcher-bearer.

Inhaber (G): regimental 'proprietor' or colonel-in-chief, a ceremonial/administrative rank including the right to appoint company-officers.

Insurrectio (G): Hungarian and Croatian militia.

Interimsrock (G): officer's undress coat.

Instrument, The: *see* Desagulier.

intendant (F): commissary.

Invalides (F): military hospital founded by Louis XIV.

invalids: soldiers unfit for active service, used as static garrison-troops.

Jäger (G): rifle corps or light infantry, lit. 'huntsman'.

Jäger zu fuss (G): light infantry.

Jäger zu Pferd (G): light cavalry or mounted rifleman.

Jaggers: nickname of British 5/60th Foot, anglicization of '*Jägers*', from their predominantly German composition.

Jingling Johnny: percussion musical instrument consisting of bells suspended from an ornamental pole.

Johnny Newcombe: British colloquialism for an inexperienced soldier.

Jonathan: nickname for Americans.

July Allowances: British system whereby post-1803 volunteer corps were paid for 85 days' training per annum, in return for a requirement to serve anywhere within their military district.

junta forces (S): units raised under authority of Spanish local provisional governments during Peninsular War.

kalmuk (also *calmuk*, *kalmuck*, etc.) (R): Asiatic light cavalry.

Kasket (G): head-dress, usually applied to leather cap or helmet, excluding shakos.

Kinski (F): the '*habit à la Kinski*' was a single-breasted coatee worn from *c*.1810.

kiwer (R): lit. 'shako', but usually applied to the Russian 1812-pattern scuttle-shaped cap.

KK (G): abbreviation usually applied to Austrian organizations, '*kaiserlich und königlich*', i.e., signifying the Austrian emperor's position as Emperor of Austria and King of Hungary.

knapsack: infantry pack.

Kollet (G): short-tailed jacket.

konfederatka (Pol): squat, early version of czapka.

Korséhut (G): *see* Corsican hat.

Krankenträger (G): stretcher-bearer.

Krümper (G): Prussian reservist trained in 1808-12 period.

kurtka (Pol): lancer-jacket.

laboratory: room in a fortress or tent in camp where powder was made-up into cartridges; lit. a place for work.

lance à feu (F): quill or tube of powder inserted in cannon-vent to ignite the charge.

Landsturm (G): third-line home-defence militia or *levée en masse*.

Landregiment (G): militia.

Landwehr (G): militia.

langridge: coarse grapeshot.

leg bail: to pay by leg bail = to abscond without payment (archaic).

legion: orig. a self-contained unit of more than one 'arm' (e.g., infantry and cavalry), but term often used imprecisely.

Leib (G): lit. 'life'; used to indicate bodyguard or lifeguard status.

lentille (F): flat woollen disc worn on a shako instead of a pompom.

levée en masse (orig. F): mass-conscription; in Britain, styled levy en masse.

liberation band: white brassard instituted 2 February 1814 to identify Allied troops, following confusion caused by so many different uniforms within the Allied army.

licorne: *see* unicorn.

Light Bobs: British nickname for light infantry.

limber: two-wheeled carriage connecting fieldpiece to team.

limber-box: ammunition-chest carried on the limber.

line: term used to describe ordinary infantry, cavalry, etc.; orig. 'infantry of the line-of-battle'.

Liniengeschütze (G): 'battalion guns'.

linstock: pike to hold slow-match; orig. 'linkstock'.

litewka (G): thigh-length frock-coat.

lobster: colloquialism for British soldier (from the red coat).

Local Militia: British part-time home-defence force formed 1808.

loophole: small aperture broken through a wall or palisade to allow defenders to fire through.

lumière (F): vent of a cannon.

lunette: (i) triangular fortification on or beyond a glacis; (ii) small fortification sited to one end of a ravelin.

magazine: (i) storage-dump for munitions; (ii) container for cartridges carried by the soldier in addition to the usual cartridge-box.

Maison (F): Napoleon's household.

mameluke: Egyptian cavalry, inc. those incorporated into the French Imperial Guard; from Turkish *mamlūk*, a slave.

mantlet: wooden screen, often wheeled, protecting diggers at the head of a sap.

marmite (F): cooking-pot.

maréchal de camp (F): major-general.

maréchal des logis (F): cavalry quarter-master NCO.

maréchal-ferrant (F): cavalry farrier or shoeing-smith.

Marie-Louises (F): nickname for young conscripts of 1813–14, named after Napoleon's young empress.

marines: troops raised for service aboard ship.

martello: circular defensive tower erected mainly on southern coast of England; corruption of name of the tower at Mortella Point, Corsica.

marquis: large tent, now 'marquee'.

Mass: Austrian infantry formation, a tighly-packed column.

masse de manoeuvre (F): wing of an army to execute enveloping attack.

masse de rupture (F): force used to make a breakthrough of the enemy's line.

masse primaire (F): main part of army engaged in main battle.

masse secondaire (F): secondary part of army engaged in subsidiary action.

match: impregnated burning-cord for igniting cannon, etc.

match-case: metal cylinder worn on grenadier's cross-belt orig. to hold burning match for igniting grenades; by this period, purely decorative.

merlon: solid parapet between two embrasures.

militia: second-line, home-defence force.

mine: (i) subterranean gallery in which an explosive charge was placed, to bring down the wall of a fortification; (ii) any buried explosive charge.

mirliton: cylindrical head-dress with flying 'wing', popular with hussars.

mosquito trousers: *see* gaiter-trousers.

Mother Shipton: tall British 'round hat' named after famous Yorkshire witch.

mousquet à chevalet (F): *see* wall-piece.

muff cap: colloquialism for busby.

music: regimental band.

Musketier (G): 'centre' company of line infantry.

musketoon: light musket.

muzzle droop: distortion of cannon-barrel caused by barrel overheating.

National Guard: home-defence units (French, *Garde Nationale*).

nature: weight or classification of artillery piece.

nid d'hirondelles (F): *see* swallow's nest.

necessaries: items of personal kit.

Normal (G): title given to units formed of selected personnel.

Oberjäger (G): Jäger NCO.

Oberleutnant (G): 1st lieutenant.

Oberrock (G): frock-coat.

Oberst (G): colonel.

Oberstleutnant (G): lieutenant-colonel.

obusier (F): howitzer.

Old Trousers: British nickname for French drum-beat '*Pas de charge*'; hence 'here comes Old Trousers' = 'the French are charging'.

opolchenie (R): militia.

ordenanca (Port): militia.

ordre mixte (F): formation of attack including units arrayed both in line and column.

outpost: outlying picquet; scouting in general.

ouvriers (F): artisans, labour units.

paletot (F): tail-less jacket as worn by the Seamen of the Imperial Guard in undress.

palisade: fence of pointed stakes.

Pallasch (G): heavy, straight-bladed cavalry sabre.

panache (F): large feather plumes in a head-dress.

pantalon de route (F): overall-trousers.

parados: rearward parapet.

parallel: siege-trench running parallel to enemy fortification.

parapet: wall or earthern bank on forward edge of a fortification, protecting those behind.

park: artillery reserve.

parole: (i) system of releasing prisoners upon their guarantee of good behaviour; (ii) password.

Paroli (G): Austrian collar-patch.

partida (S): guerrilla band regulated from 2 December 1808 at 100 infantry or 50 cavalry, but this rule generally ignored.

partisan: guerrilla.

partizan: broad-bladed half-pike.

pavillon (F): naval ensign (ship's flag).

pelisse: (i) furred over-jacket of hussars; (ii) braided frock-coat.

peloton (F): platoon.

pennon: lance-flag.

petard: explosive device for blowing-in a door; almost redundant by this period.

Petit Quartier-Général (F): lit. 'little HQ.': staff which accompanied Napoleon in the field.

petlitzi (R): lace loops of 'Guard' style.

pickers: wire needles used for clearing musket touch-hole.

piece: any cannon (orig. 'fieldpiece').

pigtail: colloquialism for plug of tobacco.

picquet: infantry outpost or sentinel.

pioneer: artificer.

place of arms: enlargement of a covered way of a fortress where troops could be assembled for sorties.

plastron: coloured panel on breast of a jacket.

pojama (Sw): Swedish Baltic oar-powered gunboat.

pokalem (F): squat, pie-shaped undress cap.

polacca: Mediterranean lateen-rigged, three-masted vessel.

pomatum: hair-dressing.

pontoon: mobile bridge of boats.

Porte or 'Sublime Porte': Ottoman Empire.

porte-aigle (F): 'Eagle'-bearer, correctly '*Premier Porte-Aigle*'; escorts' style '2me' and '3me' *porte-aigle*'.

porte-drapeau (F): colour-bearer.

porte-étendard (F): cavalry standard-bearer.

Portepeefahnrich (G): cadet officer.

portfire: holder for slow-match.

post: outpost, sentinel.

praam (also pram): coastal barge, especially of Dutch origin, as used in Napoleon's invasion-fleet.

prepared ammunition: ball and propellant in a cartridge.

present: 'present fire' = 'take aim'.

prima plana (G): Austrian senior NCOs.

prize-money: cash payment made to seamen after the capture of an enemy vessel.

prog: British colloquialism for provisions/food.

prolonge: rope attaching cannon to team to obviate repeated unlimbering.

provisional regiment: composite unit formed from detachments.

pupilles (F): cadets.

queue: (i) pigtail-hairstyle; (ii) tobacco-plug shaped like a queue.

quick-match: quick-burning match.

qui vive? (F): challenge issued by sentries: 'who goes there?'

quoin: wooden block used for elevating a cannon-barrel.

rampart: earthern or masonry wall forming main part of a fortress-defence.

rangers: orig. used to describe light troops.

raquettes (F): 'flounders' or plaited cords on end of cap-lines.

Raupenhelm (G): crested helmet.

ravelin: triangular detached formation in front of a fortress-wall.

Rechnungsführer (G): administrative officer (lit. 'chief accountant').

recruiting regiment: one formed to be split up immediately and the men drafted to other regiments.

redan: V-shaped fortification.

redingote (or *redincote*) (F): greatcoat or overcoat, a corruption of English 'riding-coat'. *Redingote grise* ('grey overcoat'): nickname for Napoleon, from his customary grey coat.

redoubt: detached fortification, or a redan placed in a bastion.

réfracteur (F): evader of conscription.

reinforces: strengthening-bands on a cannon-barrel.

retrenchment: interior defences of a fortress.

reversed colours: system by which musicians wore uniforms of the regimental facing-colour.

revetment: retaining-wall of a fortification.

rifles: infantry armed with rifled muskets.

Rittmeister (G): cavalry captain.

roller: neck-cloth.

Roquelor (G): style of caped overcoat.

Rotte (G): basic three-man unit for cavalry manoeuvre.

rouleau (F): cylindrical shako.

round hat: squat top-hat with wide or upturned brim.

rounds: inspection of sentries.

ruban de queue (F): lit. 'queue-ribbon'; French slang for a long, fatiguing march.

running ball: musket-charge without wadding.

sabot: wooden 'shoe' on 'fixed ammunition'.

sabre: (i) cavalry sword; (ii) cavalryman.

sabre-briquet (or '*briquet*') (F): short infantry sword; orig. a derisory term bestowed by cavalry, from verb *bricoler*, to rake a fire.

sabretache: decorated leather wallet suspended from sword-belt.

sans-culottes (F): (i) French revolutionary troops, so called from their wearing trousers, not breeches; (ii) French nickname for kilted Scottish troops.

sap: narrow siege-trench.

sapeur (F): pioneer or engineer; not necessarily a 'sapper' in the original sense.

sap-faggot: eight-inch thick fascine, three feet long.

sap roller: see 'gabion farci'.

sapper: orig. one who dug saps; later, generic term for engineer.

saucissons: long, thin fascines (lit. 'sausages').

scarp: outer slope of a rampart.

Scharawaden (G): thigh-length hussar stockings.

Schirmütze (G): peaked cloth cap.

Schützen (G): riflemen.

sea fencibles: British home-defence naval volunteers based in sea-ports.

searcher: tool for detecting cracks in the inside of a cannon-barrel.

sentinel: sentry; also archaic term for private soldier.

serpent: twisted, woodwind musical instrument.

settee: single-decked Mediterranean ship with long prow and lateen sails.

shabraque: horse-cloth.

shako (also chako): peaked, cylindrical head-dress.

shell: (i) explosive projectile; (ii) shell-jacket.

shell-jacket: sleeveless over-jacket.

sidearms: artillery tools, handspikes, rammers, etc.

shinel (R): greatcoat.

shingle-kicking: colloquialism for coastal blockade/beach service.

shoulder-knot: epaulette or fringed shoulder-strap (archaic).

shoulder-scale: epaulette constructed of overlapping metal plates.

silex (F): musket-flint.

skilly: thin, watery soup.

sling-cart: 2-wheeled vehicle for transporting heavy ordnance or mortar.

slops (slop-clothing): undress uniform, especially naval.

slow-match: slow-burning match.

sod wad: turf packing for an artillery round.

sotnia (R): Cossack squadron.

sous-centenier (F): sergeant-major of an *infirmier* company.

sous-lieutenant (F): 2nd lieutenant.

sous-pied (F): boot-strap of a gaiter; nickname for the Grenadiers of the Imperial Guard.

spherical case: shrapnel.

spadroon: light, straight-bladed sword.

spatterdash: long gaiters.

spencer (F): short-tailed jacket.

spiking: method of rendering a cannon useless by blocking the vent with a metal spike, hammered in.

spontoon: short or half-pike.

spring-spike: artillery spike which expanded when inserted in the vent, which could be removed only by boring-out.

squadron: cavalry regimental sub-unit, usually of two companies or troops.

Stamm-regiment (G): regular regiment acting as depot or cadre for reserve regiment.

standard: rectangular cavalry flag.

Standartenträger (G): cavalry standard-bearer.

Stegen (G): leather reinforcing-chevron on side of shako.

steel: frizzen.

stirabout: stew or stock-pot.

stock: leather or fabric strap worn around the neck.

storm-poles: palisade planted on a scarp, projecting horizontally or slightly downwards.

stovepipe: cylindrical shako.

subdivision: British artillery unit of one gun, crew and wagon.

substitute: militiaman paid to serve in place of one selected by ballot.

suffocating pot: sulphur/nitre composition used when ignited to fumigate or cause distress to the enemy.

sugar-loaf: any tall, cylindrical head-dress.

supreveste: cloth over-jacket cut to resemble a cuirass, worn by German bodyguard units.

surtout (F): single-breasted coatee.

swallow's-nest: large 'wing' enveloping top of shoulder.

sweeps: (i) (nautical) oars; (ii) nickname of British 95th Rifles (from dark uniform).

tambour: (i) (F) drum; (ii) (F) drummer; (iii) small, palisaded fortification.

Tarleton: fur-crested leather helmet, named after General Banastre Tarleton.

tartan: lateen-rigged coaster, propelled by oars.

Tartar: Russian Asiatic light cavalry.

tenaille: small fortification in a ditch in front of a wall.

tenaillon: small fortification on one side of a ravelin.

tenue de Corvée (F): fatigue- or working-dress.

tenue de route (F): marching-order.

tenue de ville (F): walking-out-dress (also '*tenue de sortie*').

terreplein: wide upper part of a rampart.

tête de colonne (F): lit. 'head of column': colour-party, musicians, pioneers, etc.

time-beater: percussion musician.

timonier (F): wheel-horse.

tin helmet: lightweight tropical cavalry helmet.

tirailleur (F): sharpshooter.

toise (F): old French unit of measurement, 6.395 English feet, used for measuring fortifications.

tompion: plug for muzzle of a cannon.

tondu (F): '*le Tondu*': 'the shaven one'; nickname for Napoleon.

toug: mameluke standard: horsehair tail upon a pole.

Tow Rows: British nickname for grenadiers (from the refrain of the song *British Grenadiers*).

train: troops responsible for driving transport, artillery, etc., also their vehicles.

train d'artillerie (F): artillery drivers and transport.

train des equipages (F): 'equipment train' or transport-corps for other than artillery.

trench fascine: fascine from four to six feet long, four to nine inches thick.

trésorier (F): paymaster.

triangle: framework of spontoons to which a prisoner was tied for flogging.

trique-balle (F): 'devil carriage', q.v.

troop: cavalry unit approximating to an infantry company.

trou de loup: 'wolf pit', q.v.

trucks: small, solid artillery-carriage wheels.

trunnions: lugs projecting from a cannon-barrel, fitting on to the carriage.

Truppentrain (G): train detachments assigned to line units.

turban: ornamental cloth strip around a helmet.

Turkish bells: 'Jingling Johnny', q.v.

Turkish music: musical instruments of oriental origin, 'Jingling Johnny', cymbals, tambourine, kettle-drum, etc.

turnback: turned-back section of coat-tail.

Uberrock (G): see *Oberrock*.

Uhlan (G): lancer; orig. Turkish *oghlan*, = 'child'.

unicorn: Russian howitzer (also 'licorne').

unlaced: an 'unlaced' regiment was one in which the officers' uniforms had no metallic lace loops.

Unterleutnant (G): 2nd lieutenant.

Unteroffizier (G): NCO.

Valenciennes composition: incendiary mixture of saltpetre, sulphur, antimony and pitch, so called from its first use at the siege of that place.

Vandyke: zigzag lace edging.

vedette: cavalry scout.

vélites (F): trainees; orig. Roman light troops.

vent: touch-hole in a cannon-barrel.

ventsman: member of a gun-crew who placed his thumb over the vent during loading.

veterans: old or semi-invalid soldiers normally fit only for garrison duty.

vivandière (F): sutleress.

voisko (R): Cossack tribal regiment.

volée (F): muzzle of a cannon-barrel.

volley-gun: multi-barrelled firearm, all chambers igniting at once.

voltigeur (F): light infantry of line regiments; lit. 'vaulter'.

volunteers: (i) part-time home-defence troops; (ii) aspirant officers serving in the ranks in the hope of gaining a commission.

Wachtmeister (G): artillery or cavalry sergeant-major.

wad-cutter: implement for cutting 'sod wads' for use as packing for artillery rounds.

wad-hook: screw-ended shaft to extract unfired cartridges from a cannon.

wadmiltilt: waterproof tarpaulin made of woollen material, retaining the natural oils of the sheep.

Waldhorn (G): hunting-horn.

wall-piece: large-calibre musket mounted on a fortress-wall.

wantie: waggon-rope.

watch-coat: greatcoat, so termed from originally being supplied only to sentries going on watch.

waterdeck: waterproof, painted canvas saddle-cover.

water fascine: fascine six feet long, one to two feet thick, weighted with stones to make it sink into wet or marshy ground.

watering cap: cylindrical shako, usually with folding peak, worn by cavalry in undress.

white cockade corps: French emigrant units in foreign pay but retaining allegiance to French monarchy, signified by their white cockades.

white light: see 'Chinese light'.

White Terror: nickname of Royalist reprisals against Napoleon's supporters after the restoration of the monarchy.

windage: difference between bore and size of shot; the greater the windage, the greater the inaccuracy.

wing: (i) shell-like epaulette; (ii) half an infantry battalion, or more loosely any element of a battalion

larger in size than a company.

whiskers: (i) any facial hair, moustaches, etc.; (ii) colloquialism for grenadiers, who sometimes wore moustaches.

wolf-pit: cone-shaped pit, usually 6 feet deep and 4 to 5 feet wide at the top, used as anti-personnel trap. Often styled by its French name, *trou de loup*.

wolf-teeth: zigzag cloth or lace edging.

worm: corkscrew-device for extricating unfired charge from a barrel.

Würst-Wagen (G): artillery caisson with padded seat on top for transportation of crew; lit. 'sausage-wagon' from its appearance.

xebec (also 'schebeck'): lateen-rigged Mediterranean schooner, also propelled by oars.

yalek: mameluke jacket.

yeomanry: British volunteer cavalry; also applied to Irish volunteer corps, both cavalry and infantry.

zigzags: approach-trenches in siege-works.

Zimmermann (G): pioneer.

Zug: (G): platoon.

Zugführer (G): file-leader.

INDEX